LATIN DICTIONARY

TEACH YOURSELF BOOKS

LATIN DICTIONARY

Alastair Wilson

B.A.

TEACH YOURSELF BOOKS
Hodder and Stoughton

First Edition 1965
Fifth Impression 1980

Copyright © 1965
Hodder and Stoughton

This volume is published in the U.S.A. by David McKay Company Inc., 750 Third Avenue, New York, N.Y. 10017

ISBN 0 340 26166 8

Printed in Great Britain for
Hodder and Stoughton Paperbacks, a division of Hodder and
Stoughton Ltd, Mill Road, Dunton Green, Sevenoaks, Kent
(Editorial Office, 47 Bedford Square, London WC1 3DP)
by Richard Clay (The Chaucer Press), Ltd., Bungay, Suffolk

CONTENTS

1. INTRODUCTION AND ADVICE ON LEARNING VOCABULARY 1-2

2. ABBREVIATIONS USED 3-4

3. LATIN-ENGLISH 5-130

4. PROPER NAMES (LATIN-ENGLISH) . . . 131-147

5. ENGLISH-LATIN 149-291

6. PROPER NAMES (ENGLISH-LATIN) . . . 293

7. CONCISE GRAMMAR:

Alphabet and Pronunciation . . . 294

Nouns and Declensions 294-297

Adjectives and Declensions—Comparison of Adjectives 297-299

Verbs. Tables of Regular Verbs . . . 300-307

    Tables of Irregular Verbs . . . 307-310

    Deponent Verbs 310

    Impersonal Verbs 311

    Defective Verbs 312

Pronouns—Personal, Reflexive, Demonstrative, Emphatic, Relative, List of other Pronouns 313-314

Prepositions 314

Conjunctions 315

Adverbs—Comparison of Adverbs . . 316

Numerals—Cardinal, Ordinal, Distributive, Reflexive 316-318

Roman Calendar—Dating . . . 318-319

Money, Weights, Measures . . . 319

Time, Place, Space 320

INTRODUCTION

THE chief benefit that a knowledge of Latin confers is the ability to read the works of the Roman authors, particularly those of the Golden and Silver Ages of Latin Literature, i.e. 60 B.C.–A.D. 100. This Dictionary has been compiled with this in mind, and also with an eye to the "non-specialist". To this end, the equivalents in the Latin–English section of the Dictionary have been presented in as simple and "modern" a form as possible, while at the same time the most important distinctions in meaning which each Latin word bears have been indicated. The vocabulary has been based on that commonly used by the authors of the period mentioned above, and a person who is acquainted with Latin grammar and the common forms of the Latin language should be able, with a little help from this Dictionary, to read them without much difficulty. For those not so acquainted, for those whose memory may have dimmed with the passage of time, and for those who have never been fully conversant with a highly inflected language like Latin, a Concise Latin Grammar has been provided. This contains, in tabulated form and with simple explanations, all the basic regular and irregular word-forms needed for translation from the commoner Latin authors.

In the English–Latin section, the Latin equivalent given is that which represents the best *general* meaning of the English, and which is used in that sense by a Classical author. Occasionally, however, where no exact Latin equivalent for an English word exists, it has been necessary to give a short circumlocution: in this case the phrase given is always translated into English, e.g. **disinterested**, neutri favens (**favouring neither side**). Where several different meanings are borne by the same word, or where ambiguity may occur, care has been taken to differentiate between the various meanings, e.g. **order**, *nn*, (**arrangement**), ordo, *m*; (**in —**), *adj*, dispŏsĭtus; (**command, direction**), iussum, *n*; (**class, rank**), ordo, *m*; (**in — to**), ut.

Where fuller information is required about any of the words given in the Dictionary, reference should be made to the following standard works upon the subject: A Latin Dictionary by Charlton T. Lewis and Charles Short and Smaller English–Latin Dictionary by Dr. William Smith.

ADVICE ON LEARNING VOCABULARY

If you are gifted with a good memory, you will find it particularly easy to learn Latin vocabulary, especially if you try to link in your mind new Latin words and any English derivatives of them which you can think of, e.g. **mare**—sea—marine; **nauta**—ship—nautical. A high proportion of Latin words have quite common English derivatives. If you do this, not only will your interest in both languages grow, but you will begin to form an impression of the debt which our language owes to that of the Romans.

If on the other hand, you are one of those who find it "difficult to make words stick" in schoolboy phraseology, then here is a piece of simple advice —not to be despised because of its simplicity—which might help you to retain words in your memory. To learn a new word it is not only essential to find out and to understand its meaning, but also to see it working in relationship to other words, and to "meet" it as many times as possible immediately after first acquaintance. It is therefore advisable to *re-read* the piece in which you originally met the word two or three times after you have learned it, and to make an effort to find the same word again within a day or two of first meeting it, otherwise you may find, on ultimately seeing it again, that it has "gone". Above all, try to maintain your interest in learning new vocabulary, for without such interest no learning of real or lasting nature can take place.

ABBREVIATIONS USED

( ) Brackets are used to indicate alternative forms.

a, um, see adj.
abl. ablative case; see page 295.
acc. accusative case; see page 295.
acis⎫ genitive singular ending of nouns indicating that they belong to the
atis⎭ third declension.
adj. adjective, **a, um era, erum** after an adjective indicates that it belongs
to the First Class, "e" that it belongs to the Second Class; see page 297.
adv. adverb. The adverb ending is often given, e.g. **e, iter, nter, um, o,** and
should be attached to the *stem* of the adjective, e.g. **abditus** (*adj*);
abdite (*adv*). See page 316.
ae. genitive singular ending of a noun, indicating that it belongs to the first
declension.
arum, genitive plural ending, indicating that the noun belongs to the first
declension.
auxil. auxiliary verb.
c. common gender.
c. comp. comparative adjective or adverb, see pages 299–316.
conj. conjunction; see p. 315.
cris, cre. nominative feminine and neuter endings, indicating that an adjective belongs to the Second Class; see page 298.
cl. clause.
dat. dative case; see page 295; also some verbs take a dative case after them.
defect. a defective verb, i.e. it has not all its parts; see page 312.
demonst. demonstrative pronoun.
dep, see v. dep.
e, see adj.
ei. genitive singular ending of noun, indicating that it belongs to the fifth
declension.
enis⎫ genitive singular endings of nouns indicating that they belong to the
etis⎭ third declension.
exclam. exclamation.
f. feminine gender.
f.pl. feminine plural.
fut. future.
i, ii. genitive singular ending of noun, indicating that it belongs to the second
declension.
icis⎫ genitive singular endings of nouns indicating that they belong to the
inis⎭ third declension.
impers. impersonal verb; see page 311.
indecl. indeclinable.
inf. infinitive.
interj. interjective.
interr. interrogative.
irreg. irregular verb; see pages 307–310.
is. genitive singular of noun, indicating that it belongs to the third
declension.
iter, see adv.

itis. genitive singular ending of noun, indicating that it belongs to the third declension.

ium. genitive plural ending of noun, indicating that it belongs to the third declension.

m. masculine gender.

m.pl. masculine plural.

n. neuter gender.

nn. noun.

nter, see adv.

ntis. genitive singular ending of some nouns and adjectives of the third declension.

num. numeral.

n.pl. neuter plural.

onis}
oris } genitive singular noun ending, indicating that the noun belongs to the third declension.

orum. genitive plural ending, indicating that a noun belongs to the second declension.

partic. participle.

pass. a passive verb, conjugated in the passive voice only.

perf. perfect.

pers. personal.

phr. phrase.

pl. plural.

poss. possessive.

prep. preposition; see page 314: the case taken by the preposition is usually indicated.

pres. present.

pron. pronoun; see pages 312–314.

pron. adj. pronominal adjective; a pronoun which declines and agrees like an adjective.

reflex. reflexive.

rel. relative.

semi-dep. semi-deponent; verbs which are deponent in some of their tenses.

sup(erl). superlative adjective or adverb.

tis }
tris } genitive singular ending of some nouns and adjs. of the third declension.

um. genitive plural ending of noun, indicating that it belongs to the third declension.

ūs. genitive singular ending of noun, indicating that it belongs to the fourth declension.

v. vb. verb. The conjugation to which a verb belongs is indicated by the figure 1, 2, 3, or 4; see page 299. In the case of 3rd conjugation verbs, and other verbs whose Perfect stem and Supine are not regular, these are given with the verb, e.g. **aboleo, evi, itum.** If none of these parts are given, it may be assumed that the verb is regularly conjugated; if some, but not all parts are given, it may be assumed that the ones not given are not in regular use.

v. dep. verb deponent; see page 310.

v.i. verb intransitive, i.e. a verb which does not have a direct object.

v. impers. verb impersonal; see page 311.

v.i.t. a verb which can be used intransitively or transitively. The separate uses are indicated by the use of the semi-colon, e.g. **abhorreo,** *v.i.t.* 2, to shrink back (intransitive); to disagree with (transitive).

voc. vocative case, see page 295.

v.t. verb transitive, i.e. a verb which has a direct object.

LATIN – ENGLISH

For List of Abbreviations used, turn to pages 3, 4

A

ā, ăb, *prep. with abl*, by (agent); from (place, time); in, at (position); since

ăbăcus, i, *m*, sideboard, counting or gaming board, slab

ăbăliĕno, *v.t.* 1, to estrange, make a legal transfer

ăbăvus, i, *m*, great-great-grandfather, ancestor

abdĭcătĭo, ōnis, *f*, renunciation of office

abdico, *v.t.* 1, to resign

abdīco, xi, ctum, *v.t.* 3, to refuse assent

abdĭtus, a, um, *adj, adv,* ē, hidden, secret

abdo, dĭdi, dĭtum, *v.t.* 3, to conceal

abdōmĕn, ĭnis, *n*, belly

abdūco, xi, ctum, *v.t.* 3, to lead away

ăbĕo, *v.i.* 4, to go away

ăberro, *v.i.* 1, to go astray

ăbhinc, *adv*, ago

ăbhorrĕo, *v.i.t.* 2, to shrink back; disagree with

ăbi, see ăbĕo

ăbĭcio, iēci, iectum, *v.t.* 3, to throw away

abiectus, a, um, *adj, adv,* ē, downcast

ăbiēgnus, a um, *adj*, made of fir

ăbiēs, ĕtis, *f*, fir

ăbigo, ĕre, ēgi, actum, *v.t.* 3, to drive away

ăbĭtĭo, ōnis, *f*, departure

ăbĭtus, ūs, *m*, departure

abiūdico, *v.t.* 1, to deprive by legal sentence

abiungo, nxi, nctum, *v.t.* 3, to unyoke

abiūro, *v.t.* 1, to deny on oath

ablātus, a, um, *adj*. from suffero, taken away

ablēgătĭo, ōnis, *f*, banishment

ablēgo, *v.t.* 1, to send away

ablŭo, ŭi, ūtum, *v.t.* 3, to wash away

ablūtĭo, ōnis, *f*, ablution, washing

abnĕgo, *v.i.* 1, to refuse

abnormis, e, *adj*, irregular

abnŭo, ŭi, ūtum, *v.i.t.* 3, to refuse

ăbŏlĕo, ēvi, ĭtum, *v.t.* 2, to destroy

ăbŏlesco, ēvi, *v.i.* 3, to decay

ăbŏlĭtĭo, ōnis, *f*, abolition

ăbolla, ae, *f*, cloak

ăbōmĭnor, *v.t.* 1, *dep.* to wish away (being ominous)

ăbŏrīgĭnes, um, *m.pl*, natives

ăbortĭo, ōnis, *f*, miscarriage

ăbortus, ūs, *m*, abortion

abrādo, si, sum, *v.t.* 3, to scrape off

abrĭpio, ŭi, reptum, *v.t.* 3, to drag away

abrōdo, si, sum, *v.t.* 3, to gnaw away

abrŏgătĭo, ōnis, *f*, repeal

abrŏgo, *v.t.* 1, to repeal

abrumpo, rūpi, ruptum, *v.t.* 3, to break off

abruptus, a, um, *adj*, steep

abscēdo, cessi, cessum, *v.i.* 3, to go away

abscīdo, cīdi, scīsum, *v.t.* 3, to cut off

abscindo, scĭdi, scissum, *v.t.* 3, to tear away

abscīsus, a, um, *adj, adv,* ē, steep

abscondĭtus, a, um, *adj, adv,* ē, hidden

abscondo, dĭ, dĭtum, *v.t.* 3, to conceal

absens, entis, *adj*, absent

absentia, ae, *f*, absence

absĭlĭo, *v.i.* 4, to jump away

absĭmĭlis, e, *adj*, unlike

absinthĭum, ii, *n*, absinth

absisto, stĭti, *v.i.* 3, to stand aloof

absŏlūtĭo, ōnis, *f*, acquittal

absŏlūtus, a, um, *adj, adv,* ē, complete

absolvo, vi, sŏlūtum, *v.t.* 3, to unfasten, acquit

absŏnus, a, um, *adj, adv,* ē, discordant

absorbĕo, bŭi, ptum, *v.t.* 2, to swallow up

absquĕ, *prep. with abl*, without

abstēmĭus, a, um, *adj*, sober

abstergĕo, rsi, rsum, *v.t.* 2, to wipe off

absterrĕo, *v.t.* 2, to frighten away

abstĭnens, ntis, *adj, adv,* nter, temperate

abstĭnentĭa, ae, *f*, self-restraint

abstĭnĕo, ŭi, tentum, *v.i.t.* 2, to abstain from; restrain

abstrăho, xi, ctum, *v.t.* 3, to drag away

abstrūdo, si, sum, *v.t.* 3, to push away

abstrūsus, a, um, *adj, adv,* ē, hidden

absum, esse, abfui (afui), *v.i. irreg,* to be absent

absūmo, mpsi, mptum, *v.t.* 3, to take away, use up

absurdus, a, um, *adj, adv,* ē, stupid, tuneless

ăbundans, ntis, *adj, adv,* nter, plentiful

ăbundantia, ae, *f,* plenty

ăbundo, *v.i.* 1, to overflow

ăbūtor, i, usus sum, *v.* 3, *dep. with abl,* to use up, abuse

ăc, *conj,* and

ăcācia, ae, *f,* acacia

ăcădēmia, ae, *f,* academy

accēdo, cessi, cessum, *v.i.* 3, to approach

accělēro, *v.i.t.* 1, to hurry; quicken

accendo, ndi, nsum, *v.t.* 3, to set on fire

accensěo, ŭi, nsum, *v.t.* 2, to add to

accensus, i, *m,* attendant

accentus, ūs, *m,* accentuation

acceptio, ōnis, *f,* acceptance

acceptum, i, *n,* receipt

acceptus, a, um, *adj,* agreeable

accessio, ōnis, *f,* approach, increase

accessus, ūs, *m,* approach

accīdo, cīdi, cīsum, *v.t.* 3, to cut

accĭdo, cĭdi, *v.i.* 3, to fall upon, happen

accingo, nxi, nctum, *v.t.* 3, to equip, put on

accĭo, *v.t.* 4, to summon

accĭpio, cēpi, ceptum, *v.t.* 3, to receive

accĭpiter, tris, *m,* hawk

accītus,ūs, *m,* summons

acclāmātio, ōnis, *f,* shout

acclāmo, *v.t.* 1, to shout at

acclīnis, e, *adj,* leaning on

acclīno, *v.t.* 1, to lean

acclīvis, e, *adj,* uphill

acclīvitas, ātis, *f,* ascent

accŏla, ae, *c,* neighbour

accŏlo, cŏlui, cultum, *v.t.* 3, to live near

accommŏdātus, a, um, *adj, adv,* ē, suitable

accommŏdātio, ōnis, *f,* compliance

accommŏdo, *v.t.* 1, to adapt

accommŏdus, a, um, *adj,* suitable

accresco, crēvi, crētum, *v.i.* 3, to grow

accrētio, ōnis, *f,* increase

accŭbĭtio, ōnis, *f,* reclining

accŭbo, *v.i.* 1, to lie near, recline at table

accumbo, cŭbŭi, cŭbitum, *v.i.* 3, to lie near, recline at table

accŭmŭlo, *v.t.* 1, to heap up

accŭro, *v.t.* 1, to take care of

accŭrātus, a, um, *adj, adv,* ē, prepared carefully, precise

accurro, curri, cursum, *v.i.* 3, to run to

accūsātio, ōnis, *f,* accusation

accūsātor, ōris, *m,* accuser

accūso, *v.t.* 1, to accuse

ăcer, cris, e, *adj, adv,* iter, keen

ăcer, ěris, *n,* maple tree

ăcerbĭtas, ātis, *f,* bitterness

ăcerbo, *v.t.* 1, to embitter

ăcerbus, a, um, *adj,* bitter, keen

ăcernus, a, um, *adj,* made of maple

ăcerra, ae, *f,* incense-box

ăcervo, *v.t.* 1, to heap up

ăcervus, i, *m,* heap

ăcētāria, ōrum, *n.pl,* salad

ăcētum, i, *n,* vinegar

ăcidus, a, um, *adj, adv,* ē, sour

ăcies, ēi, *f,* edge, pupil of eye, battle-line, keenness

ăcĭnăces, is, *m,* scimitar

ăcĭnus, i, *m* (um, i, *n*), berry

ăcĭpenser, ěris, *m,* sturgeon

aclys, ȳdis, *f,* small javelin

ăcŏnītum, i, *n,* aconite

acquiesco, ēvi, ētum, *v.i.* 3, to rest, aquiesce

acquīro, sīvi, sītum, *v.t.* 3, to procure

ăcrĭmōnia, ae, *f,* sharpness

ācrĭter, *adv,* keenly

acta, ōrum, *n.pl,* acts, records

actio, ōnis, *f,* act, legal action

actor, ōris, *m,* driver, plaintiff, performer

actŭārius, a, um, *adj,* swift

actŭārius, i, *m,* notary

actum, i, *n,* deed

actus, a, um, see ăgo

actus, ūs, *m,* impulse, act (of drama)

ăcŭlěātus, a, um, *adj,* prickly

ăcŭlěus, i, *m,* sting

ăcūměn, ĭnis, *n,* point, sting

ăcŭo, ŭi, ūtum, *v.t.* 3, to sharpen

ăcus, ūs, *f,* needle, pin

ăcūtus, a, um, *adj, adv,* ē, sharp

ad, *prep. with acc,* to, towards, near (place), about (time), for (purpose)

ădaequo, *v.i.t.* 1, to be equal; to make equal

ădămas, ntis, *m,* steel, diamond

ădămo, *v.t.* 1, to love deeply

ădăpěrio, ŭi, rtum, *v.t.* 4, to open fully

ădaugěo, xi, ctum, *v.t.* 2, to increase

addīco, xi, ctum, *v.t.* 3, to assent, award

addictio, ōnis, *f,* adjudication

addictus, a, um, *adj,* dedicated

addo, dĭdi, dĭtum, *v.t.* 3, to add to

addŭbĭto, *v.i.t.* 1, to doubt

addūco, xi, ctum, *v.t.* 3, to lead to, influence

ădemptio, ōnis, *f,* seizure

ădĕo, v.i. 4, to approach, attack
ădĕo, adv, so much, so long
ădeps, ĭpis, c, fat
ădeptĭo, ōnis, f, attainment
ădēquĭto, v.i. 1, to gallop up
ădhaerĕo, si, sum, v.i. 2, to cling to
ădhaeresco, si, sum, v.i. 3, to cling to
ădhĭbĕo, v.t. 2, to apply, invite
ădhortātĭo, ōnis, f, encouragement
ădhortor, v.t. 1, dep, to encourage
ădhuc, adv, still
ădiăcĕo, v.i. 2, to adjoin
ădĭcĭo, iēci, iectum, v.t. 3, to throw to, add to
ădīgo, ēgi, actum, v.t. 3, to drive to, compel
ădīmo, ēmi, emptum, v.t. 3, to take away
ădĭpiscor, eptus, v.t. 3, dep, to obtain
ădĭtus, ūs, m, approach
ădĭūdĭco, v.t. 1, to assign
ădĭūmentum, i, n, assistance
ădiunctĭo, ōnis, f, union
ădiungo, xi, ctum, v.t. 3, to join to
ădiūro, v.t. 1, to swear, confirm
ădiūtor, ōris, m, helper
ădiŭvo, iūvi, iūtum, v.t. 1, to help
admātūro, v.t. 1, to precipitate
admētĭor, mensus, v.t. 4, dep, to measure out
admĭnĭcŭlum, i, n, prop
admĭnister, tri, m, servant
admĭnistrātĭo, ōnis, f, aid, management, arrangement
admĭnistro, v.t. 1, to assist, manage
admĭrābĭlis, e, adj, adv, iter, wonderful
admĭrātĭo, ōnis, f, admiration
admĭror, v.t. 1, dep, to wonder at
admiscĕo, scŭi, xtum, v.t. 2, to mix with
admissārĭus, ii, m, stallion
admissĭo, ōnis, f, reception
admissum, i, n, fault
admitto, mīsi, ssum, v.t. 3, to let in, let go, incur, commit
admixtĭo, ōnis, f, mixture
admŏdum, adv, up to the limit, very much, nearly
admŏnĕo, v.t. 2, to remind
admŏnĭtĭo, ōnis, f, warning
admŏnĭtus, ūs, m, suggestion
admordĕo, di, sum, v.t. 2, to bite at
admōtĭo, ōnis, f, application
admŏvĕo, mōvi, mōtum, v.t. 2, to conduct, assault
admurmŭrātĭo, ōnis, f, murmur
admurmŭro, v.i. 1, to murmur at
adn- see ann-
ădŏlĕo, ŭi, ultum, v.i. 3, to grow up
ădŏlescens, ntis, adj, young

ădŏlescens, ntis, c, young person
ădŏlescentĭa, ae, f, youth
ădŏlescentŭlus, i, m, very young man
ădŏlesco, ēvi, ultum, v.i.3, to grow up
ădŏpĕrĭo, ŭi, rtum, v.t. 4, to cover up
ădoptātĭo, ōnis, f, adoption
ădoptĭo, ōnis, f, adoption
ădoptīvus, a, um, adj, adoptive
ădopto, v.t. 1, to choose, adopt
ădor, ōris, n, grain
ădōrātĭo, ōnis, f, adoration
ădōrĕa, ae, f, reward for bravery
ădōrĭor, ortus, v.t. 4, dep, to attack, undertake
ădorno, v.t. 1, to equip, decorate
ădōro, v.t. 1, to worship, entreat
ădrādo, si, sum, v.t. 3, to shave
adsum, esse, adfui, v.i, irreg, to be near
ads . . . see ass . . .
ădūlātĭo, ōnis, f, flattery
ădūlātor, ōris, m, flatterer
ădūlor, v.t. 1, dep, to flatter
ădulter, ĕri, m, adulterer
ădultĕra, ae, f, adulteress
ădultĕrātĭo, ōnis, f, adulteration
ădultĕrīnus, a, um, adj, false
ădultĕrĭum, ii, n, adultery
ădultĕro, v.i.t. 1, to commit adultery; to falsify, pollute
ădultus, a, um, adj, grown up
ădumbrātĭo, ōnis, f, sketch
ădumbro, v.t. 1, to sketch
ăduncus, a, um, adj, hooked
ădurgĕo, v.t. 2, to press
ădūro, ssi, stum, v.t. 3, to scorch
ădusque, prep. with acc, right up to
ădusta, ōrum, n.pl, burns
ădustus, a, um, adj, burnt
advĕho, xi, ctum, v.t. 3, to carry to
advĕna, ae, c, stranger
advĕnĭo, vēni, ventum, v.t. 4, to reach
advento, v.t. 1, to approach
adventus, ūs, m, arrival
adversārĭus, ii, m, opponent
adversārĭus, a, um, adj, opposite, opposing
adversor, v. 1, dep. with dat, to oppose
adversus, a, um, adj, opposite; (of winds) contrary
adversus, prep. with acc, opposite
adversum, adv, opposite
adverto, ti, sum, v.t. 3, to direct towards
advespērascit, avit, v. impers, evening approaches
advĭgĭlo, v.i. 1, to keep watch
advŏcātĭo, ōnis, f, summons, legal assistance
advŏcātus, i, m, legal adviser
advŏco, v.t. 1, to call, summon help

For List of Abbreviations used, turn to pages 3, 4

advŏlo, v.i. 1, to fly towards
advolvo, vi, ūtum, v.t. 3, to roll, grovel before
ădўtum, i, n, sanctuary
aedēs, is, f, temple, house
aedĭcŭla, ae, f, shrine, niche
aedĭfĭcātor, ōris, m, builder
aedĭfĭcĭum, ii, n, building
aedĭfĭcātĭo, ōnis, f, constructing
aedĭfĭco, v.t. 1, to build
aedĭlĭcĭus, a, um, adj, of an aedile
aedĭlis, is, m, aedile—Roman magistrate
aedĭlĭtas, ātis, f, aedileship
aedĭtŭus, i, m, verger
aeger, ra, rum, adj, ill, sad
aegis, ĭdis, f, shield
aegrē, adv, with difficulty, scarcely, amiss, with displeasure
aegresco, v.i. 3, to fall ill
aegrĭtūdo, ĭnis, f, illness, grief
aegrōtātĭo, ōnis, f, sickness
aegrōto, v.i. 1, to be ill
aegrōtus, a, um, adj, ill
aemŭlātĭo, ōnis, f, rivalry
aemŭlor, v.t. 1, dep, to rival, envy
aemŭlus, a, um, adj, rivalling
aēnĕus, a, um, adj, of bronze
aenigma, ătis, n, riddle
aequābĭlis, e, adj, adv, ĭter, similar, uniform
aequābĭlĭtas, ātis, f, equality
aequaevus, a, um, adj, of equal age
aequālis, e, adj, adv, ĭter, level, contemporary
aequālĭtas, ātis, f, uniformity
aequē, adv, equally, justly
aequĭlĭbrĭum, ii, n, horizontal position
aequĭnoctĭum, i, n, equinox
aequĭpăro, v.i.t. 1, to equal; compare
aequĭtas, ātis, f, equality, fairness, calmness
aequo, v.i.t. 1, to equalize; match, raze
aequor, ōris, n, even surface, sea
aequum, i, n, plain, justice
aequus, a, um, adj, flat, friendly, equal, reasonable
āēr, ris, m, air
aerārĭa, ae, f, mine
aerārĭum, i, n, treasury
aerārĭus, a, um, adj, of bronze, of the treasury
aerātus, a, um, adj, bronze-covered
aerĕus, a, um, adj, of bronze
aerĭpes, ĕdis, adj, bronze-footed
āĕrĭus, a, um, adj, lofty
aerūgo, ĭnis, f, rust, envy
aerumna, ae, f, suffering

aerumnōsus, a, um, adj, wretched
aes, aeris, n, copper, money
aescŭlētum, i, n, oak-forest
aescŭlĕus, a, um, adj, oaken
aescŭlus, i, f, oak
aestas, ātis, f, summer
aestĭfer, ĕra, ĕrum, adj, hot, sultry
aestĭmābĭlis, e, adj, valuable
aestĭmātĭo, ōnis, f, valuation
aestĭmātor, ōris, m, valuer
aestĭmo, v.t. 1, to value, assess
aestīva, ōrum, n.pl, summer-camp
aestīvus, a, um, adj, adv, ē, summer-like
aestŭārĭum, ii, n, creek, air-hole
aestŭo, v.i. 1, to seethe, glow
aestŭōsus, a, um, adj, adv, ē, sweltering
aestus, ūs, m, heat, tide, rage, excitement
aetas, ātis, f, age, life-time
aetātŭla, ae, f, tender age
aeternĭtas, ātis, f, eternity
aeternus, a, um, adj, adv, um, everlasting
aether, ĕris, m, upper air, heaven
aethĕrĭus, a, um, adj, celestial
Aethĭops, ōpis, m, Aethiopian, negro
aethra, ae, f, upper air
aevum, i, n, lifetime, generation
affābĭlis, e, adj, adv, ĭter, courteous
affātim, adv, enough
affātus, partic. from affor
affectātĭo, ōnis, f, pretension, whim
affectātus, a, um, adj, far-fetched
affectĭo, ōnis, f, disposition, whim
affecto, v.t. 1, to strive after
affectus, ūs, m, mood, sympathy
afférro, afferre, attŭli, allātum, v.t, irreg, to bring to, announce, help, produce, confer
affĭcĭo, affēci, ctum, v.t. 3, to influence, seize
affīgo, xi, xum, v.t. 3, to fasten to
affingo, nxi, ictum, v.t. 3, to add to, fabricate
affīnis, e, adj, neighbouring, related
affīnĭtas, ātis, f, kinship
affirmātē, adv, explicitly
affirmātĭo, ōnis, f, assertion
affirmo, v.t. 1, to assert
affixus, a, um, adj, fastened to
afflātus, ūs, m, breath, blast
afflicto, v.t. 1, to trouble, shatter
afflictus, a, um, adj, damaged, prostrate
afflīgo, xi, ctum, v.t. 3, to dash to the ground, damage

afflo, v.t. 1, to breathe on, inspire

affluens, ntis, adj, adv, nter, rich in

affluo, xi, xum, v.i. 3, to flow towards, flock in

affor, v.t. 1, dep, to speak to, accost

affulgeo, ulsi, v.i. 2, to shine on

affundo, ūdi, ūsum, v.t. 3, to pour on, in

Āfricus (ventus), S.W. wind

āfui, see absum

ăgāso, ōnis, m, groom

ăgĕ!, come on!

ăgellus, i, m, small field

ăgens, ntis, adj, powerful

ăger, gri, m, field, territory

agger, ĕris, m, mound, rampart

aggĕro, ssi, stum, v.t. 3, to convey

aggĕro, v.t. 1, to heap up

agglŏmĕro, v.t. 1, to add to

aggrăvo, v.t. 1, to make heavier or worse

aggrĕdĭor, grĕssus, v.t. 3, dep, to approach, attack, undertake

aggrĕgo, v.t. 1, to adhere, join

aggressus, see aggrĕdĭor

ăgilis, e, adj, adv, ĭter, active

ăgĭlitas, ātis, f, activity

ăgĭtātĭo, ōnis, f, quick movement, contemplation

ăgĭtātor, ōris, m, charioteer

ăgĭtātus, a, um, adj, driven, dogged

ăgĭto, v.t. 1, to drive, shake, swing, torment, mock, consider

agmen, ĭnis, n, marching column

agna, ae, f, ewe lamb

agnātus, a, um, adj, related (male line)

agnĭtĭo, ōnis, f, recognition

agnōmen, ĭnis, n, surname, additional name

agnosco, nōvi, ĭtum, v.t. 3, to recognize, acknowledge

agnus, i, m, lamb

ăgo, ēgi, actum, v.t. 3, to drive, steal, bring, do, negotiate, pass (time), act, lead (life)

ăgrārius, a, um, adj, agrarian

ăgrārii, ōrum, m.pl, land reformers

ăgrestis, is, m, peasant

ăgrestis, e, adj, rural, coarse

agricŏla, ae, m, farmer, countryman

agricultūra, ae, f, agriculture

āio (parts only), to assert

āla, ae, f, wing, armpit, porch

ălăcer, cris, e, adj, adv, ĭter, brisk, vigorous

ălăcrĭtas, ātis, f, briskness

ălăpa, ae, f, slap

ălauda, ae, f, lark

albārium, ii, n, whitewash

albātus, a, um, adj, clothed in white

albĕo, v.i. 2, to be white

albesco, v.i. 3, to become white

album, i, n, whiteness, register

albus, a, um, adj, white

alces, is, f, elk

alcēdo, inis, f, kingfisher

alcўon, ŏnis, f, kingfisher

alcўōnēus, a, um, adj, halcyon

ālĕa, ae, f, gambling, a game with dice, chance, hazard

ālĕātor, ōris, m, gambler

ālĕs, ĭtis, adj, winged

ālĕs, ĭtis, c, bird

alga, ae, f, sea-weed

algĕo, si, v.i. 2, to feel cold

algĭdus, a, um, adj, cold

algor, ōris, m, coldness

ălĭā, adv, in a different way

ălĭās . . . ălĭās, adv, at one time . . . at another time, otherwise

ălĭbi, adv, elsewhere

ălĭcŭbi, adv, somewhere

ălĭcunde, adv, from somewhere

ălĭēnātĭo, ōnis, f, transfer, aversion, delirium

ălĭēnātus, a, um, adj, alienated

ălĭēnĭgĕna, ae, m, foreigner

ălĭēno, v.t. 1, to transfer, estrange

ălĭēnus, a, um, adj, someone else's, strange, hostile, unsuitable

ălĭēnus, i, m, stranger

ălĭēnum, i, n, stranger's property

āliger, ĕra, ĕrum, adj, winged

ălĭi, see ălĭus

ălĭmentum, i, n, nourishment

ălĭmōnĭum, ii, n, nourishment

ălĭō, adv, to another place

ălĭōquĭ(n), adv, in other respects

ălĭpēs, ĕdis, adj, wing-footed

ălĭquā, adv, somehow

ălĭquamdĭu, adv, for some time

ălĭquando, adv, at some time

ălĭquantus, a, um, adj, adv, ō, um, somewhat, some

ălĭqui, qua, quod, pron, adj, some, any

ălĭquis, quid, pron, someone, something

ălĭquō, adv, to some place

ălĭquot, adj, several

ălĭquŏtĭes, adv, at different times

ălĭter, adv, otherwise

ălĭunde, adv, from elsewhere

ălĭus, a, ud, pron, adj, other, different

allābor, psus, v. 3, dep, to glide, flow towards

allapsus, ūs, m, stealthy approach

allātro, v.t. 1, to bark at

allecto, v.t. 1, to entice

allēgo, v.t. 1, to commission

allēgo, ēgi, ectum, v.t. 3, to elect

allēgŏria, ae, f, allegory
allĕvātio, ōnis, f, raising up
allēvo, v.t. 1, to lift up, relieve
allĭcĭo, exi, ectum, v.t. 3, to attract
allīdo, si, sum, v.t. 3, to strike
alligo, v.t. 1, to bind, fasten
allĭno, ēvi, itum, v.t. 3, to bedaub
allĭum, i, n, garlic
allŏcūtĭo, ōnis, f, address
allŏquĭum, ii, n, exhortation
allŏquor, lŏcūtus, v.t. 3, dep, to speak to, exhort, console
allūdo, si, sum, v.i.t. 3, to play, joke; sport with
allŭo, ŭi, v.t. 3, to wash against, bathe
allŭvĭes, ēi, f, pool
allūvĭo, ōnis, f, inundation
almus, a, um, adj, nourishing, kind
alnus, i, f, alder
ălo, ŭi, altum, v.t. 3, to nourish, cherish, encourage
alŏē, ēs, f, aloe
alpīnus, a, um, adj, Alpine
alsĭus, a, um, adj, cold, chilly
alsus, a, um, adj, cold, chilly
altāre, altāris, n, high altar
altāria, ium, n.pl, high altar
alter, ĕra, ĕrum, adj, one or the other of two, second
altercātĭo, ōnis, f, dispute
altercor, v.i. 1, dep, to quarrel
alterno, v.i.t. 1, to hesitate; alternate
alternus, a, um, adj, alternate
altĕrŭter, ra, rum, adj, one or the other, either
altĭlis, e, adj, fattened, rich
altĭsŏnus, a, um, adj, high sounding
altĭtūdo, inis, f, height, depth
altor, ōris, m, foster-father
altrix, īcis, f, foster-mother
altum, i, n, the deep (sea)
altus, a, um, adj, high, deep, great
ălūcĭnor, v.i. 1, dep, to wander in the mind
ălumna, ae, f, foster-child
ălumnus, i, m, foster-child
ălūta, ae, f, soft leather
alvĕārĭum, ii, n, beehive
alvĕus, i, m, salver, channel, canoe
alvus, i, f, belly, stomach
ămābĭlis, e, adj, adv, ĭter, lovable, amiable
ămando, v.t. 1, to remove
ămans, ntis, adj, fond
ămans, ntis, m, lover
ămārĭtĭes, ēi, f, bitterness
ămārus, a, um, adj, bitter
ămātor, ōris, m, lover
ămātōrĭum, ii, n, love-philtre
ămātōrĭus, a, um, adj, amatory

ambactus, i, m, vassal
ambāges, is, f, roundabout way
ambĭgo, v.i. 3, to waver, go about
ambĭgŭĭtas, ātis, f, double sense
ambĭgŭum, i, n, uncertainty
ambĭgŭus, a, um, adj, adv, ē, doubtful, changeable
ambĭo, v.i.t. 4, to go round; solicit
ambĭtĭo, ōnis, f, canvassing
ambĭtĭōsus, a, um, adj, adv, ē, embracing, fawning
ambĭtus, ūs, m, going round, circuit, bribery
ambō, ae, ō, adj, both
ambrŏsĭa, ae, f, food of the gods
ambrŏsĭus, a, um, adj, immortal
ambŭlātĭo, ōnis, f, walk
ambŭlātor, ōris, m, walker
ambŭlo, v.i. 1, to walk, lounge
ambūro, ssi, stum, v.t. 3, to singe
ambustum, i, n, burn
amellus, i, m, star-wort
āmens, ntis, adj, out of one's mind
āmentĭa, ae, f, madness
āmentum, i, n, strap
āmĕs, itis, m, pole, shaft
ămĕthystus, i, f, amethyst
ămīca, ae, f, mistress
ămĭcĭo, ŭi, ctum, v.t. 4, to wrap
ămĭcĭtĭa, ae, f, friendship
ămictus, ūs, m, cloak
ămĭcŭlum, i, n, cloak
ămīcus, i, m, friend
ămīcus, a, um, adj, adv, ē, friendly
āmissĭo, ōnis, f, loss
ămīta, ae, f, paternal aunt
āmitto, misi, missum, v.t. 3, to let go, dismiss, lose
amnis, is, m, river
ămo, v.t. 1, to love, like
ămoenĭtas, ātis, f, pleasantness
ămoenus, a, um, adj, adv, ē, charming
āmōlĭor, v.t. 4, dep, to remove, refute
ămor, ōris, m, love, desire
ămŏvĕo, mōvi, tum, v.t. 2, to remove
amphĭthĕātrum, i, n, amphitheatre
amphŏra, ae, f, two-handled jar
amplector, xus, v.t. 3, dep, to embrace
amplexus, ūs, m, embrace
amplĭfĭcātĭo, ōnis, f, enlargement
amplĭfĭco, v.t. 1, to enlarge
amplĭo, v.t. 1, to enlarge
amplĭtūdo, inis, f, width, size
amplĭus, comp. adv, more
amplus, a, um, adj, adv, ē, ĭter, spacious, great, glorious
ampulla, ae, f, bottle
ampŭtātĭo, ōnis, f, pruning
ampŭto, v.t. 1, to cut away
ămurca, ae, f, dregs of oil

ămȳlum, i, *n,* starch

ăn, *conj,* or: also used to introduce a question

ănăphŏrä, ae, *f,* recurrence

ănăs, ătis, *f,* duck

ănătĭcŭla, ae, *f,* duckling

anceps, cĭpĭtĭs, *adj,* two-headed, doubtful

ancīle, is, *n,* oval shield

ancilla, ae, *f,* maidservant

ancŏra, ae, *f,* anchor

ancŏrāle, is, *n,* cable

ānellus, i, *m,* small ring

anfractus, ūs, *m,* circuitous route, digression

angīna, ae, *f,* quinsy

angĭportus, ūs, *m,* alley

ango, xi, ctum, *v.t.* 3, to strangle, torment

angor, ōris, *m,* strangling, distress

anguilla, ae, *f,* eel

anguīnĕus, a, um, *adj,* snaky

anguĭpēs, ēdĭs, *adj,* snake-footed

anguis, is, *c,* snake

angŭlātus, a, um, *adj,* angular

angŭlāris, e, *adj,* angular

angŭlus, i, *m,* corner

angustĭae, ārum, *f.pl,* defile, straits, difficulties

angustus, a, um, *adj, adv,* **ē,** narrow, difficult

ānhēlĭtus, ūs, *m,* panting, vapour

ānhēlo, *v.i.t.* 1, to pant; exhale

ānhēlus, a, um, *adj,* panting

ănĭcŭla, ae, *f,* little old woman

ānīlis, e, *adj, adv,* iter, old womanish

ănĭma, ae, *f,* breeze, breath, life, soul

ănĭmadversĭo, ōnis, *f,* attention, reproof

ănĭmadverto, ti, sum, *v.t.* 3, to pay attention to, notice, punish

ănĭmăl, ālis, *n,* animal

ănĭmālis, e, *adj, adv,* iter of air, living

ănĭmans, ntis, *adj,* living

ănĭmātus, a, um, *adj,* disposed, courageous

ănĭmo, *v.i.t.* 1, to have life; revive, give life to

ănĭmōsus, a, um, *adj, adv,* **ē,** bold

ănĭmōsus, a, um, *adj,* gusty, living, spirited

ănĭmus, i, *m,* soul, mind, memory, opinion, anger, purpose, courage, attitude

annāles, ium, *m.pl,* chronicles

annālis, e, *adj,* annual

annĕ—introduces a question

annecto, xŭi, xum, *v.t.* 3, to fasten to, add

annītor, nīsus (nixus), *v.i.* 3, *dep,* to lean against, exert oneself

ănnĭversārĭus, a, um, *adj,* anniversary

anno, *v.i.* 1, to swim to

annon, *conj,* or not

annōna, ae, *f,* annual produce, grain price

annōsus, a, um, *adj,* old

annōtātĭo, ōnis, *f,* annotation, note

annōto, *v.t.* 1, to note down

annŭa, ōrum, *n.pl,* annuity

annŭmĕro, *v.t.* 1, to pay, include

annŭo, ŭi, ūtum, *v.i.* 3, to nod, assent

annus, i, *m,* year

annŭus, a, um, *adj,* annual, yearly

ănōmālĭa, ae, *f,* anomaly

anquīro, sīvi, sītum, *v.t.* 3, to search for

ansa, ae, *f,* handle, opportunity

anser, ĕris, *m,* goose

antĕ, *prep. with acc,* before, in front of

antĕ (antĕā), *adv,* before

antĕcēdo, ssi, ssum, *v.i.t.* 3, to distinguish oneself; precede

antĕcello, *v.i.t.* 3, to be outstanding; surpass

antĕcessĭo, ōnis, *f,* antecedent

antĕcursor, ōris, *m,* advanced guard

antĕ-ĕo, *v.i.* 4, to go before, excel

antĕfĕro, ferre, tŭli, lātum, *v.t., irreg,* to carry in front, prefer

antĕgrĕdĭor, gressus, *v.t.* 3, *dep,* to go in front

antĕhāc, *adv,* previously

antĕlūcānus, a, um, *adj,* before daybreak

antĕmĕrīdĭānus, a, um, *adj,* before midday

antĕmitto, mīsi, missum, *v.t.* 3, to send on

antenna, ae, *f,* sail-yard

antĕpōno, pŏsŭi, ĭtum, *v.t.* 3, to place in front

antĕquam, *conj,* before

antēris, ĭdis, *f,* buttress (*pl.*)

antes, ĭum, *m.pl,* ranks

antĕsignānus, i, *m,* in front of the standard, selected soldier

antesto, ĕti, *v.i.* 1, to stand before, excel

antestor, *v.* 1, *dep,* to call a witness

antĕverto, ti, sum, *v.t.* 3, to precede, anticipate

anthrōpŏphăgus, i, *m,* cannibal

antīcus, a, um, *adj,* foremost

antĭcĭpo, *v.t.* 1, to anticipate

antĭdŏtum, i, *n,* remedy

antĭpŏdes, um, *m.pl,* antipodes

antīquĭtas, ātis, *f,* age, olden times

antīqui, ōrum, *m.pl,* old writers

For List of Abbreviations used, turn to pages 3, 4

antīquus, a, um, *adj, adv,* ē, old

antistēs, ĭtis, *m, f,* high priest

antistĭta, ae, *f,* high priestess

antlĭa, ae, *f,* pump

antrum, i, *n,* cave

ānŭlus, i, *m,* ring

ānus, ūs, *f,* old woman

anxĭĕtas, ātis, *f,* anxiety

anxĭus, a, um, *adj, adv,* ē, troubled

ăpăgĕ!, *interj,* begone!

ăper, pri, *m,* wild boar

ăpērĭo, rŭi, rtum, *v.t.* 4, to open, explain

ăpertus, a, um, *adj, adv,* ē, open, frank

ăpex, ĭcis, *m,* summit, crown

ăpis, is, *f,* bee

ăpiscor, aptus, *v.t.* 3, *dep,* to reach for, acquire

ăpĭum, ii, *n,* parsley

ăplustre, is, *n,* stern

ăpo, — aptum, *v.t.* 3, to fasten

ăpŏcha, ae, *f,* receipt

ăpŏthēca, ae, *f,* store-place

appărātĭo, ōnis, *f,* preparation

appărātus, a, um, *adj, adv,* ē, ready, elaborate

appărātus, ūs, *m,* preparation, apparatus, pomp

appārĕo, *v.i.* 2, to appear

appārĭtĭo, ōnis, *f,* service

appārĭtor, ōris, *m,* public servant

appăro, *v.t.* 1, to prepare

appellātĭo, ōnis, *f,* calling, appeal, title

appellātor, ōris, *m,* appellant

appellātus, a, um, *adj,* called

appello, ŭli, ulsum, *v.t.* 3, to drive towards, land

appello, *v.t.* 1, to speak to, appeal to, name

appendix, ĭcis, *f,* supplement

appendo, ndi, nsum, *v.t.* 3, to weigh

appĕtens, ntis, *adj, adv,* nter, eager for

appĕtentĭa, ae, *f,* desire

appĕtĭtĭo, ōnis, *f,* desire

appĕtītus, ūs, *m,* attack, passion

appĕto, ii, ītum, *v.i.t.* 3, to approach; strive after

applĭcātĭo, ōnis, *f,* inclination

applĭco, *v.t.* 1, to affix, attach, steer

appōno, pŏsŭi, sĭtum, *v.t.* 3, to put near, apply, add

apporto, *v.t.* 1, to conduct

appŏsĭtus, *adj, adv,* ē, bordering, suitable

apprĕhendo, di, sum, *v.t.* 3, to seize, understand

apprīmus, a, um, *adj, adv,* ē, very first

apprŏbātĭo, ōnis, *f,* sanction

apprŏbo, *v.t.* 1, to approve, make satisfactory

apprŏpĕro, *v.i.t.* 1, to hurry; speed up

apprŏpinquātĭo, ōnis, *f,* approach

apprŏpinquo, *v.i.* 1, to approach

appulsus, ūs, *m,* landing, approach

ăprīcātĭo, ōnis, *f,* sunning

ăprīcor, *v.i.* 1, *dep,* to sun oneself

ăprīcus, a, um, *adj,* sunny

Ăprīlis (mensis), April

aptātus, a, um, *adj,* suitable

apto, *v.t.* 1, to adjust

aptus, a, um, *adj, adv,* ē, suitable

ăpŭd, *with acc,* at the house of, in the works of, amongst, near

ăqua, ae, *f,* water, rain; *pl.* spa

ăquaeductus, ūs, *m,* aqueduct

ăquālis, is, *c,* wash-basin

ăquārĭus, ii, *m,* water-bearer, a Sign of the Zodiac

ăquātĭcus, a, um, *adj,* watery

ăquātĭlis, e, *adj,* aquatic

ăquātĭo, ōnis, *f,* water-fetching

ăquātor, ōris, *m,* water-carrier

ăquĭla, ae, *f,* eagle, standard

ăquĭlĭfer, ĕri, *m,* standard-bearer

ăquĭlīnus, a, um, *adj,* aquiline

ăquĭlo, ōnis, *m,* north wind, north

ăquĭlōnāris, e, *adj,* northern

ăquor, *v.i.* 1, *dep,* to fetch water

ăquōsus, a, um, *adj,* moist, rainy

āra, ae, *f,* altar

ărānĕa, ae, *f,* spider, web

ărānĕus, i, *m,* spider, web

ārātĭo, ōnis, *f,* cultivation

ārātor, ōris, *m,* ploughman

ārātrum, i, *n,* plough

arbĭter, tri, *m,* witness, umpire

arbĭtrātus, ūs, *m,* free-will

arbĭtrĭum, ii, *n,* verdict, power, inclination

arbĭtror, *v.i.* 1, *dep,* to think, decide

arbor, ōris, *f,* tree

arbŏrĕus, a, um, *adj,* tree-like

arbustum, i, *n,* plantation

arbŭtum, i, *n,* wild strawberry

arbŭtus, i, *f,* wild strawberry tree

arca, ae, *f,* box, dungeon

arcānus, a, um, *adj, adv,* ō, secret

arcĕo, *v.t.* 2, to confine, keep off

arcessītus, a, um, *adj,* sent for, far-fetched

arcesso, sīvi, sītum, *v.t.* 3, to send for

architector, *v.t.* 1, *dep,* to design

architectūra, ae, *f,* architecture

architectus, i, *m,* architect

arcĭtĕnens, ntis, *adj,* armed with bow
arctŏs, i, *f,* Bear, North Pole
arctūrus, i, *m,* chief star in constellation Boötes
arcŭla, ae, *f,* small box
arcŭo, *v.t.* 1, to bend
arcus, ūs, *m,* rainbow, arch
ardĕa, ae, *f,* heron
ardens, ntis, *adj, adv,* **nter,** burning, eager
ardĕo, arsi, sum, *v.i.* 2, to burn, be eager
ardesco, arsi, *v.i.* 3, to catch fire
ardor, ōris, *m,* blaze, desire
ardŭus, a, um, *adj,* high, difficult
ārēa, ae, *f,* open space, threshing-floor
ārēna, ae, *f,* sand, arena
ārēnātum, i, *n,* mortar, plaster
ārēnōsus, a, um, *adj,* sandy
ārens, ntis, *adj,* parched
ārĕo, *v.i.* 2, to be dry
āresco, ŭi, *v.i.* 3, to dry up
argentāria, ae, *f,* bank, silver-mine
argentārius, ii, *m,* banker, broker
argentātus, a, um, *adj,* silver-plated
argentĕus, a, um, *adj,* silver
argentum, i, *n,* silver, money
argilla, ae, *f,* white clay
argūmentātio, ōnis, *f,* proof
argūmentor, *v.i.* 1, *dep,* to prove
argūmentum, i, *n,* proof, content, artistic aim
argŭo, ŭi, ūtum, *v.t.* 3, to prove, accuse, convict
argūtiae, ārum, *f.pl,* liveliness
argūtus, a, um, *adj, adv,* **ē,** clear, witty, rattling
ārĭdĭtas, ātis, *f,* dryness
ārĭdum, i, *n,* dry land
ārĭdus, a, um, *adj,* dry
ārĭēs, tis, *m,* ram, battering-ram
ārista, ae, *f,* ear of corn
ārĭthmētĭca, ōrum, *n.pl,* arithmetic
arma, ōrum, *n.pl,* armour, shield, weapons, army, equipment
armāmenta, ōrum, *n.pl,* gear, tackle
armāmentārĭum, ii, *n,* arsenal
armāmentum, i, *n,* ship's tackle
armārĭum, ii, *n,* cupboard
armātūra, ae, *f,* equipment, (light-)armed troops
armātus, a, um, *adj,* equipped
armentārĭus, ii, *m,* herdsman
armentum, i, *n,* plough-animal, herd
armĭfer, ĕra, ĕrum, *adj,* warlike, armoured
armĭger, ĕra, ĕrum, *adj,* warlike, armoured
armilla, ae, *f,* bracelet
armĭpŏtens, ntis, *adj,* valiant

armĭsŏnus, a, um, *adj,* with clashing armour
armo, *v.t.* 1, to arm, equip
armus, i, *m,* shoulder, side
āro, *v.t.* 1, to plough
arquātus, a, um, *adj,* bent
arrectus, a, um, *adj,* steep
arrēpo, psi, ptum, *v.i.* 3, to creep towards
arrha, ae, *f,* money given as a pledge
arrĭdĕo, si, sum, *v.i.* 2, to laugh at, favour
arrĭgo, rexi, rectum, *v.t.* 3, to erect, excite
arrĭpĭo, ŭi, reptum, *v.t.* 3, to seize, indict
arrŏgans, ntis, *pres. partic, adj, adv,* **nter,** haughty
arrŏgantĭa, ae, *f,* haughtiness
arrŏgo, *v.t.* 1, to claim, confer
ars, tis, *f,* art, skill, theory, habit, stratagem
artē, *adv,* closely
arthrītĭcus, a, um, *adj,* arthritic
artĭcŭlātim, *adv,* piece by piece
artĭcŭlo, *v.t.* 1, to articulate
artĭcŭlus, i, *m,* joint, movement
artĭfex, fĭcis, *m,* artist, author
artĭfĭcĭōsus, a, um, *adj, adv,* **ē,** skilful
artĭfĭcĭum, ii, *n,* trade, skill; (*pl*) intrigue
arto, *v.t.* 1, to compress
artus, ūs, *m,* limb
artus, a, um, *adj, adv,* **ē,** confined
ārun, ārus . . see **hārun, hārus** . .
arvīna, ae, *f,* grease
arvum, i, *n,* cultivated land
arvus, a, um, *adj,* ploughed
arx, cis, *f,* citadel
as, assis, *m,* pound weight, coin
ascendo, ndi, nsum, *v.i.t.* 3, to climb
ascensus, ūs, *m,* ascent
ascĭa, ae, *f,* adze
ascĭo, *v.t.* 4, to receive
ascisco, īvi, ītum, *v.t.* 3, to admit
ascītus, ūs, *m,* reception
ascrībo, psi, ptum, *v.t.* 3, to insert, enrol, attribute
ascrīptīvus, a, um, *adj,* supernumerary
ascrīptus, a, um, *adj,* appointed
āsella, ae, *f,* small ass
āsellus, i, *m,* small ass
āsĭnus, i, *m,* ass, simpleton
aspectābĭlis, e, *adj,* visible
aspecto, *v.t.* 1, to look at eagerly
aspectus, ūs, *m,* look, sight
asper, ĕra, ĕrum, *adj, adv,* **ē,** rough, bitter, austere, adverse
aspĕrĭtas, ātis, *f,* roughness
aspĕrum, i, *n,* rough ground

aspergo, si, sum, *v.t.* 3, to scatter, sprinkle, defile

aspergo, inis, *f*, sprinkling, spray

aspĕritas, ātis, *f*, roughness

aspernātio, ōnis, *f*, disdain

aspernor, *v.t.* 1, *dep*, to despise

aspĕro, *v.t.* 1, to roughen, rouse

aspersio, ōnis, *f*, sprinkling

aspĭcio, exi, ectum, *v.t.* 3, to look at

aspīrātio, ōnis, *f*, exhalation

aspīro, *v.i.t.* 1, to aspire to; breathe on

aspis, idis, *f*, adder

asporto, *v.t.* 1, to carry away

assĕcla, ae, *c*, attendant

assectātio, ōnis, *f*, attendance

assectātor, ōris, *m*, follower

assector, *v.t.* 1, *dep*, to wait upon

assensio, ōnis, *f*, approval

assensus, ūs, *m*, approval

assentātio, ōnis, *f*, flattery

assentātor, ōris, *m*, flatterer

assentior, sus, *v.* 4, *dep. with dat*, to agree with

assentor, *v.* 1, *dep. with dat*, to flatter

assĕquor, sĕcūtus, *v.t.* 3, *dep*, to pursue, overtake, comprehend

asser, ĕris, *m*, stake

assĕro, rŭi, sertum, *v.t.* 3, to claim, set free

assertor, ōris, *m*, protector

asservo, *v.t.* 1, to keep, guard

assessor, ōris, *m*, assessor

assĕvērātio, ōnis, *f*, assertion

assĕvĕro, *v.t.* 1, to assert

assĭdĕo, sēdi, sessum, *v.i.* 2, to sit by, wait upon, blockade, resemble

assĭdŭĭtas, ātis, *f*, constant presence

assĭdŭus, a, um, *adj, adv*, ē, constantly present

assignātio, ōnis, *f*, allotment

assigno, *v.t.* 1, to distribute

assĭlio, ŭi, sultum, *v.i.* 4, to spring upon

assĭmĭlis, e, *adj, adv*, ĭter, like

assĭmŭlo, *v.i.t.* 1, to resemble; imitate

assĭmŭlātus, a, um, *adj*, similar

assisto, astĭti, *v.i.* 3, to stand near, aid

assŏlĕo, *v.i.* 2, to be in the habit of doing

assŭĕfăcĭo, fēci, factum, *v.t.* 3, to make someone used to

assŭesco, ēvi, ētum, *v.i.t.* 3, to become used to; familiarise

assŭētūdo, ĭnis, *f*, habit

assŭētus, a, um, *adj*, customary

assulto, *v.t.* 1, to jump on, attack

assultus, ūs, *m*, attack

assūmo, mpsi, mptum, *v.t.* 3, to take up, adopt

assŭo, *v.t.* 3, to sew on

assurgo, surrexi, rectum, *v.i.* 3, to rise, stand up

assūla, ae, *f*, splinter, chip

assus, a, um, *adj*, roasted; assa, ōrum, *n.pl*, turkish bath

ast, see at

astĭpŭlātor, ōris, *m*, assistant

astĭpŭlor, *v.* 1, *dep. with dat.* to bargain with

asto, stĭti, *v.i.* 1, to stand near

astrĕpo, *v.i.t.* 3, to make a noise; applaud

astringo, nxi, ctum, *v.t.* 3, to bind, fasten, cool, limit

astrictus, a, um, *adj, adv*, ē, tight, concise

astrŏlŏgĭa, ae, *f*, astronomy

astrŏlŏgus, i, *m*, astronomer

astrum, i, *n*, star, constellation

astrŭo, xi, ctum, *v.t.* 3, to build near, add

astŭpĕo, *v.i.* 2, to be astonished

astus, ūs, *m*, dexterity, craft

astūtĭa, ae, *f*, dexterity, slyness

astūtus, a, um, *adj, adv*, ē, shrewd, sly

ăsȳlum, i, *n*, place of refuge

at, *conj*, but, on the other hand

ătāvĭa, ae, *f*, ancestor

ătāvus, i, *m*, ancestor

āter, tra, trum, *adj*, black, deadly

ăthĕŏs, i, *m*, atheist

athlēta, ae, *c*, wrestler, athlete

ătŏmus, i, *f*, atom

atque, *conj*, and, and also

atqui, *conj*, but, nevertheless

ātrāmentum, i, *n*, ink, varnish

ātrātus, a, um, *adj*, in mourning

ātriensis, is, *m*, house-steward

ātrĭŏlum, i, *n*, ante-room

ātrĭum, ii, *n*, hall, forecourt

ătrōcĭtas, ātis, *f*, harshness, cruelty

ātrox, ōcis, *adj, adv*, ĭter, horrible, fierce, stern

attactus, ūs, *m*, touch

attāmen, *adv*, but nevertheless

attendo, di, tum, *v.t.* 3, to stretch out, give attention to

attentĭo, ōnis, *f*, attention

attento, *v.t.* 1, to try, attack

attentus, a, um, *adj, adv*, ē, engrossed, frugal

attĕnŭo, *v.t.* 1, to impair, reduce

attĕro, trĭvi, trītum, *v.t.* 3, to rub away, exhaust

attĭnĕo, ŭi, tentum, *v.i.t.* 2, to stretch, concern; retain

attingo, tĭgi, tactum, *v.t.* 3, to touch, reach, attack

attollo, *v.t.* 3, to raise

attondĕo, di, sum, *v.t.* 2, to shear

attŏnĭtus, a, um, *adj*, *adv*, ē, astonished

attŏno, ŭi, ĭtum, *v.t.* 1, to stun

attorquĕo, *v.t.* 2, to hurl

attrăho, xi, ctum, *v.t.* 3, to drag towards, attract

attrecto, *v.t.* 1, to handle

attrĭbŭo, ŭi, ūtum, *v.t.* 3, to assign

attrĭbūtum, i, *n*, predicate

attrītus, ūs, *m*, rubbing against

auceps, ŭpis, *c*, bird-catcher, eavesdropper

auctĭo, ōnis, *f*, auction, increase

auctĭōnor, *v.i.* 1, *dep*, to hold an auction

auctor, ōris, *c*, creator, master, witness, supporter, author

auctōritas, ātis, *f*, influence, power

auctumnālis, e, *adj*, autumnal

auctumnus, a, um, *adj*, autumnal

auctumnus, i, *m*, autumn

auctus, a, um, *adj*, enlarged

auctus, ūs, *m*, increase

aucŭpĭum, ĭi, *n*, bird-catching

aucŭpor, *v.i.t.* 1, *dep*, to go bird-catching; pursue, watch for

audācĭa, ae, *f*, boldness, insolence

audax, ācis, *adj*, *adv*, cter, bold, rash

audens, ntis, *adj*, *adv*, nter, bold

audentĭa, ae, *f*, boldness

audĕo, ausus, *v.i.t.* 2 (*semi-dep.*), to dare

audĭentĭa, ae, *f*, hearing, audience

audĭo, *v.t.* 4, to hear, understand, obey

audītĭo, ōnis, *f*, a hearing, report

audītor, ōris, *m*, hearer, pupil

audītus, ūs, *m*, sense of hearing

aufĕro, ferre, abstŭli, ablātum, *v.t.* *irreg*, to take away, rob, obtain

aufŭgĭo, fūgi, ĭtum, *v.i.* 3, to run away

augĕo, xi, ctum, *v.i.t.* 2, to grow; enlarge

augesco, *v.i.* 3, to grow

augur, ŭris, *c*, diviner, prophet

augŭrālis, e, *adj*, prophetic

augŭrātus, ūs, *m*, office of augur

augŭrĭum, ĭi, *n*, omen, augury

augŭrĭus, a, um, *adj*, augural

augŭror, *v.t.* 1, *dep*, to prophesy, suppose

augustus, a, um, *adj*, *adv*, ē, venerable

aula, ae, *f*, palace, court

aulaeum, i, *n*, curtain

aulĭcus, i, *m*, courtier

aura, ae, *f*, air, soft breeze, sky, publicity, gleam

aurārĭa, ae, *f*, gold mine

aurātus, a, um, *adj*, gilded

aurĕus, i, *m*, gold piece

aurĭcŏmus, a, um, *adj*, golden-haired

aurĭcŭla, ae, *f*, ear

aurĭfer, ĕra, ĕrum, *adj*, gold-producing

aurĭfex, fĭcis, *m*, goldsmith

aurīga, ae, *c*, charioteer

aurĭger, ĕra, ĕrum, *adj*, bearing gold

auris, is, *f*, ear

aurītus, a, um, *adj*, long-eared

aurōra, ae, *f*, dawn

aurum, i, *n*, gold

auscvlto, *v.i.t.* 1, to listen

auspex, ĭcis, *c*, diviner

auspĭcātō, *adv*, after taking the auspices

auspĭcĭum, ĭi, *n*, divination

auspĭcor, *v.i.t.* 1, *dep*, to take the auspices, begin

auster, tri, *m*, south wind

austērus, a, um, *adj*, *adv*, ē, harsh, severe

austrālis, e, *adj*, southern

austrīnus, a, um, *adj*, southern

ausum, i, *n*, bold attempt

aut, *conj*, or, aut . . . aut, either . . . or

autem, *conj*, but

autumnālis, *adj*, autumnal

autumnus, a, um, *adj*, autumnal

autŭmo, *v.i.* 1, to assert

auxĭlĭa, ōrum, *n.pl*, auxiliary troops

auxĭlĭāris, e, *adj*, helping

auxĭlĭāres, ĭum, *m.pl*, auxiliary troops

auxĭlĭor, *v.* 1, *dep*. *with dat.* to help

auxĭlĭum ĭi, *n*, help

ăvārĭtĭa, ae, *f*, greediness

ăvārus, a, um, *adj*, *adv*, ē, greedy

ăve! (*pl*, ăvete), hail! farewell!

ăvĕho, vexi, ctum, *v.t.* 3, to carry away

ăvello, velli, vulsum, *v.t.* 3, to tear away

ăvēna, ae, *f*, oats, shepherd's pipe

ăvēnācĕus, a, um, *adj*, oaten

ăvĕo, *v.t.* 2, to long for

ăvĕo, *v.i.* 2, to be well

āversor, *v.t.* 1, *dep*, to turn away from, avoid

āversor, ōris, *m*, embezzler

āversus, a, um, *adj*, backwards, hostile

āverto, ti, sum, *v.t.* 3, to push aside, steal, estrange

ăvĭa, ae, *f*, grandmother

ăvĭārĭum, ĭi, *n*, bird-haunts

ăvĭdĭtas, ātis, *f*, eagerness, desire

ăvĭdus, a, um, *adj*, *adv*, ē, greedy

ăvis, is, *f*, bird

ăvītus, a, um, *adj*, ancestral

āvĭum, ĭi, *n*, pathless place

āvĭus, a, um, *adj*, pathless

āvŏcātĭo, ōnis, *f*, calling away, distraction

For List of Abbreviations used, turn to pages 3, 4

āvŏco, *v.t.* 1, to call away

āvŏlo, *v.i.* 1, to fly away

ăvuncŭlus, i, *m*, uncle

ăvus, i, *m*, grandfather

axis, is, *m*, axle, chariot, region

B

băca, ae, *f*, berry

băcātus, a, um, *adj*, pearl-set

baccar, ăris, *n*, fox-glove

baccha, ae, *f*, bacchanal

bacchānālĭa, ĭum, *n.pl*, orgies of Bacchus

bacchātĭo, ōnis, *f*, orgy

bacchor, *v.i.* 1, *dep*, to rave

băcĭfer, ĕra, ĕrum, *adj*, berry-bearing

băcillum, i, *n*, stick

băcŭlum, i, *n*, stick, sceptre

băiŭlo, *v.t.* 1, to carry a load

băiŭlus, i, *m*, porter

bālaena, ae, *f*, whale

bālănus, i, *f*, acorn

bălātro, ōnis, *m*, comedian

bālātus, ūs, *m*, bleating

balbus, a, um, *adj, adv*, ē, stammering

balbūtĭo, *v.i.t.* 4, to stammer

ballista, ae, *f*, artillery engine

balnĕae, ārum, *f.pl*, baths

balnĕātor, ōris, *m*, bath-keeper

balnĕum, i, *n*, bath

bālo, *v.i.* 1, to bleat

balsāmum, i, *n*, balm

baltĕus, i, *m*, belt, sword-belt

bārăthrum, i, *n*, abyss

barba, ae, *f*, beard

barbărĭa, ae, *f*, foreign country, rudeness

barbărus, i, *m*, foreigner, stranger

barbărus, a, um, *adj, adv*, ē, foreign, rude, savage

barbātus, a, um, *adj*, bearded

barbĭtos, *m*, *f*, (*pl*, a), lute, lyre

bardus, a, um, *adj*, stupid

bāro, ōnis, *m*, blockhead

barrus, i, *m*, elephant

băsĭlĭca, ae, *f*, town-hall

băsĭlĭcus, a, um, *adj*, royal

bāsĭo, *v.t.* 1, to kiss

bāsis, is, *f*, pedestal, base

bāsĭum, ii, *n*, kiss

battŭo, ŭi, *v.i.t.* 3, to fence; beat

bĕātĭtas, ātis, *f*, happiness

bĕātĭtūdo, ĭnis, *f*, happiness

bĕātus, a, um, *adj, adv*, ē, happy, fortunate

bellans, see bello

bellārĭa, ōrum, *n.pl*, dessert

bellātor, ōris, *m*, warrior

bellātrix, īcis, *f*, female-warrior

bellē, *adv*, prettily

bellĭcōsus, a, um, *adj*, warlike

bellĭcum, i, *n*, signal for march or attack

bellĭcus, a, um, *adj*, military

bellĭger, ĕra, ĕrum, *adj*, warlike

bellĭgĕro, *v.t.* 1, to wage war

bellis, ĭdis, *f*, daisy

bello, *v.i.* 1 (bellor, *v.* 1, *dep*), to make war

bellum, i, *n*, war

bellus, a, um, *adj*, pretty

bēlŭa, ae, *f*, beast

bĕnĕ, *adv*, well, very

bĕnēdīco, xi, ctum, *v.i.t.* 3, to praise

bĕnēdictĭo, ōnis, *f*, blessing

bĕnĕfăcĭo, fēci, factum, *v.t.* 3, to do well, oblige

bĕnĕfactum, i, *n*, good deed

bĕnĕfĭcentĭa, ae, *f*, kind treatment

bĕnēfĭcĭārĭi, ōrum, *m.pl*, privileged soldiers (excused fatigues)

bĕnĕfĭcĭum, ii, *n*, a kindness

bĕnĕfĭcus, a, um, *adj*, obliging

bĕnĕvŏlentĭa, ae, *f*, good will

bĕnĕvŏlus, a, um, *adj, adv*, ē, well-disposed

bĕnignē, *adv*, thank you; no thank you; courteously

bĕnignus, a, um, *adj*, kind, fruitful

bĕnignĭtas, ātis, *f*, kindness

bĕo, *v.t.* 1, to bless, enrich

bes, bessis, *m*, eight ounces

bestĭa, ae, *f*, wild beast

bestĭārĭus, ii, *m*, wild-beast fighter

bestĭŏla, ae, *f*, small animal

bēta, ae, *f*, beet

bētŭla, ae, *f*, birch

biblĭa, ōrum, *n.pl*, the Bible

biblĭŏpōla, ae, *m*, bookseller

biblĭŏthēca, ae, *f*, library

biblĭŏthēcārĭus, ii, *m*, librarian

bĭbo, bĭbi, ĭtum, *v.t.* 3, to drink

bĭbŭlus, a, um, *adj*, given to drink, porous

bĭceps, cĭpĭtis, *adj*, two-headed

bĭcŏlŏr, ōris, *adj*, two-coloured

bĭcornis, e, *adj*, two-horned

bĭdens, ntis, *adj*, two-pronged

bĭdens, ntis, *m*, hoe

bĭdŭum, ii, *n*, space of two days

biennĭum, ii, *n*, space of two years

bĭfărĭam, *adv*, in two ways

bĭfer, ĕra, ĕrum, *adj*, blooming or fruiting twice a year

bĭfĭdus, a, um, *adj*, cut in two

bǐfŏris, e, *adj*, with double opening

bǐformis, e, *adj*, two-shaped

bǐfrons, ntis, *adj*, two-headed

bǐfurcus, a, um, *adj*, two-pronged

bīgae, ārum, *f.pl*, pair of horses, two-horsed chariot

bǐgātus, a, um, *adj*, stamped with a two-horsed chariot (of coins)

bĭiŭgus, a, um, *adj*, yoked two together

bǐlǐbris, e, *adj*, weighing two pounds

bǐlinguis, e, *adj*, bilingual

bǐliōsus, a, um, *adj*, bilious

bīlis, is, *f*, bile

bǐmāris, e, *adj*, lying between two seas

bǐmārǐtus, i, *m*, bigamist

bǐmembris, e, *adj*, half-man, half-beast

bǐmestris, e, *adj*, two months old

bīmus, a, um, *adj*, two years old

bīni, ae, a, *adj*, two each, a pair

bǐpartio, *v.t.* 4, to bisect

bǐpartīto, *adv*, in two ways

bǐpĕdālis, e, *adj*, measuring two feet

bǐpennǐfer, ĕra, ĕrum, *adj*, carrying a double-edged axe

bǐpennis, e, *adj*, double-edged

bǐpēs, ēdis, *adj*, two-legged

bǐrēmis, e, *adj*, two-oared

bǐrēmis, is, *f*, a galley with two banks of oars

bis, *adv*, twice

bisextilis, e, *adj* (of years) leap

bisulcus, a, um, *adj*, cloven

bǐtūmen, ĭnis, *n*, bitumen

bǐvǐum, ii, *n*, cross-road

bǐvius, a, um, *adj*, going in two directions

blaesus, a, um, *adj*, stammering

blandīmentum, i, *n*, flattery

blandǐor, *v*. 4, *dep. with dat*, to flatter

blandǐtia, ae, *f*, flattery

blandus, a, um, *adj*, *adv*, ē, smooth-tongued, enticing

blasphēmo, *v.t.* 1, to revile

blătĕro, *v.t.* 1, to babble

blătĕro, ōnis, *m*, gabbler

blatta, ae, *f*, cockroach, moth

bŏārius, a, um, *adj*, of cattle

bŏlētus, i, *m*, mushroom

bombyx, ȳcis, *m*, silk, silk-worm

bŏnǐtas, ātis, *f*, excellence

bŏna, ōrum, *n.pl*, goods, property

bŏnum, i, *n*, goodness, profit

bŏnus, a, um, *adj*, good

bŏrĕas, ae, *m*, north wind

bŏrĕus, a, um, *adj*, northern

bōs, bŏvis, *c*, ox; *pl*, cattle

bŏvārius, see boārius

brācae, ārum, *f.pl*, trousers

brācātus, a, um, *adj*, wearing trousers, foreign

bracchium, ii, *n*, fore-arm, branch, dike

bractĕa, ae, *f*, thin metal plate

branchiae, ārum, *f.pl*, fish-gills

brassica, ae, *f*, cabbage

brĕvī, *adv*, in a short time, in a few words

brĕviārium, ii, *n*, summary

brĕvis, e, *adj*, *adv*, ǐter, short, brief

brĕvǐtas, ātis, *f*, conciseness, shortness

brūma, ae, *f*, shortest day, winter

brūmālis, e, *adj*, wintry

brūtus, a, um, *adj*, unwieldy, dull

būbo, ōnis, *m*, owl

būbulcus, i, *m*, ploughman

būbŭlus, a, um, *adj*, of cattle

bucca, ae, *f*, the cheek

buccŭla, ae, *f*, small mouth, helmet

būcǐna, ae, *f*, trumpet

būcŭla, ae, *f*, heifer

būfo, ōnis, *m*, toad

bulbus, i, *m*, bulb

bulla, ae, *f*, bubble, knob, amulet

bullo, *v.i.* 1, to bubble

būmastus, i, *f*, grape which grows in large bunches

būris, is, *m*, plough-beam

bustum, i, *n*, funeral pyre, grave

būtȳrum, i, *n*, butter

buxǐfer, ĕra, ĕrum, *adj*, growing box-trees

buxum, i, *n*, box-wood

buxus, i, *f*, box-tree

byssus, i, *f*, cotton

C

căballus, i, *m*, pack-horse

căcăbus, i, *m*, saucepan

căchinnātio, ōnis, *f*, guffaw

căchinno, *v.i.* 1, to laugh aloud

căchinnus, i, *m*, laughter, jeering

căcūmen, ĭnis, *n*, extremity, peak

căcūmǐno, *v.t.* 1, to make into a point

cădāver, ĕris, *n*, corpse

cădo, cĕcǐdi, cāsum, *v.i.* 3, to fall, wane, occur, decay

cādūcĕātor, ōris, *m*, herald

cādūcĕum, i, *n* (us, i, *m*), herald's staff, Mercury's wand

cādūcǐfer, ĕra, ĕrum, *adj*, carrying a herald's staff (Mercury)

cădūcus, a, um, *adj*, falling, doomed

cădus, i, *m*, large jar (for liquids)

caecǐtas, ātis, *f*, blindness

caeco, *v.t.* 1, to blind

caecus, a, um, *adj*, blind, hidden

caedēs, is, *f*, slaughter

caedo, cĕcĭdi, caesum, *v.t.* 3, to cut, strike, slaughter

caelātor, ōris, *m*, engraver

caelātūra, ae, *f*, carving

caelebs, lĭbis, *adj*, unmarried

caelĕs, ĭtis, *adj*, heavenly

caelĭtes, um, *pl*, gods

caelestĭa, ĭum, *n.pl.*, the heavenly bodies

caelestis, e, *adj*, heavenly

caelestis, is, *m*, god

caelĭbātus, ūs, *m*, celibacy

caelĭcŏla, ae, *m. f*, inhabitant of heaven

caelĭfer, ĕra, ĕrum, *adj*, supporting the heavens (Atlas)

caelo, *v.t.* 1, to engrave

caelum, ĭ, *n*, heaven, climate

caelum, ĭ, *n*, chisel

caementum, ĭ, *n*, quarry-stone

caenum, ĭ, *n*, dirt

caepa, ae, *f* (e, is, *n*), onion

caerimōnĭa, ae, *f*, religious ceremony, awe

caerŭlĕus(lus), a, um, *adj*, dark blue

caesărĭēs, ĕi, *f*, the hair

caesim, *adv*, by cutting

caesĭus, a, um, *adj*, green or grey-eyed

caespĕs, ĭtis, *m*, a turf

caestus, ūs, *m*, boxing-glove

caetra, ae, *f*, native shield

călămister, tri, *m*, curling-iron; *pl*, flourishes

călămĭtas, ātis, *f*, disaster

călămĭtōsus, a, um, *adj*, *adv*, ē, destructive, unhappy

călămus, ĭ, *m*, cane, reed-pen

călăthus, ĭ, *m*, basket

calcăr, āris, *n*, spur, stimulus

calcĕāmentum, ĭ, *n*, shoe

calcĕo, *v.t.* 1, to shoe

calcĕus, ĭ, *m*, shoe

calcĭtrātus, ūs, *m*, kicking

calcĭtro, *v.i.* 1, to kick, resist

calco, *v.t.* 1, to tread on, oppress

calcŭlātor, ōris, *m*, accountant

calcŭlus, ĭ, *m*, pebble, calculation, vote, piece (chess, draughts)

călĕfăcĭo, fēci, factum, *v.t.* 3, to heat, excite

călĕo, *v.i.* 2, to be warm, roused

călesco, *v.i.* 3, to become warm

călĭdus, a, um, *adj*, warm, hot, hot-headed

călĭga, ae, *f*, leather boot

călĭgātus, a, um, *adj*, wearing soldier's boots

călĭgĭnōsus, a, um, *adj*, obscure

cālīgo, ĭnis, *f*, mist, gloom

cālīgo, *v.i.* 1, to steam, be dark

călix, ĭcis, *m*, cup

calyx, see calix

callĕo, *v.i.t.* 2, to be callous, insensible; to know by experience

callĭdĭtas, ātis, *f*, skill, cunning

callĭdus, a, um, *adj*, *adv*, ē, skilful, sly

callis, is, *m*, footpath

callum, ĭ, *n*, hard or thick skin

cālo, ōnis, *m*, soldier's servant, menial

călor, ōris, *m*, heat, ardour

caltha, ae, *f*, marigold

călumnĭa, ae, *f*, trickery, libel

călumnĭātor, ōris, *m*, slanderer

călumnĭor, *v.t.* 1, *dep*, to blame or accuse unjustly

calva, ae, *f*, scalp

calvārĭa, ae, *f*, skull

calvĭtĭum, ĭ, *n*, baldness

calvus, a, um, *adj*, bald

calx, cis, *f*, heel

calx, cis, *f*, limestone, chalk

cămēlŏpardālis, is, *f*, giraffe

cămēlus, ĭ, *m*, camel

cămēna, ae, *f*, muse

cămĕra, ae, *f*, vault

cămīnus, ĭ, *m*, forge, furnace

campester, tris, e, *adj*, on level ground

campestre, is, *n*, wrestling trunks

campus, ĭ, *m*, plain, open country, opportunity, scope

cămŭr, ŭra, ŭrum, *adj*, curved inwards

cănālis, is, *m*, pipe, groove

cancelli, ōrum, *m.pl*, railings

cancer, cri, *m*, crab

candēla, ae, *f*, candle

candēlābrum, ĭ, *n*, candlestick

candens, ntis, *adj*, shining white, glowing hot

candĕo, *v.i.* 2, to shine, glow

candesco, ŭi, *v.i.* 3, to glisten

candĭdātus, ĭ, *m*, candidate

candĭdus, a, um, *adj*, *adv*, e, dazzling white, beautiful, honest

candor, ōris, *m*, whiteness, beauty, honesty

cānens, ntis, *adj*, grey, white

cānĕo, *v.i.* 2, to be white, grey

cānesco, *v.i.* 3, to grow white

cănīcŭla, ae, *f*, small dog, Dog-star

cănīnus, a, um, *adj*, dog-like

cănis, is, *c*, dog, Dog-star

cănistrum, ĭ, *n*, open basket

cānĭtĭes, (no *genitive*) *f*, grey hair, old age

canna, ae, *f*, reed, flute

cannăbis, is, *f*, hemp

căno, cěcĭni, cantum, *v.i.t.* 3, to sing, play; prophesy
cănor, ōris, *m*, tune
cănōrus, a, um, *adj*, melodious
cantērius, see canthērius
cantātor, ōris, *m*, singer
canthăris, ĭdis, *f*, beetle
canthărus, i, *m*, tankard
canthērius, ii, *m*, mule, rafter
cantĭcum, i, *n*, song
cantilēna, ae, *f*, hackneyed song
canto, *v.i.t.* 1, to sing, act; predict
cantor, ōris, *m*, singer, actor
cantus, ūs, *m*, music, prophecy, singing
cānus, a, um, *adj*, white, old
căpācĭtas, ātis, *f*, capacity
căpax, ācis, *adj*, roomy, capable
căpella, ae, *f*, she-goat
căper, pri, *m*, goat
căpesso, ĭvi, ĭtum, *v.t.* 3, to seize, undertake, reach for
căpillāmentum, i, *n*, wig
căpillāre, is, *n*, hair-oil
căpillātus, a, um, *adj*, hairy
căpillus, i, *m*, the hair
căpĭo, cēpi, captum, *v.t.* 3, to take, capture, tempt, choose, obtain, undertake, hold, grasp
căpistrum, i, *n*, halter
căpĭtālis, e, *adj*, of life and death, criminal, dangerous
capra, ae, *f*, she-goat
căprĕa, ae, *f*, wild she-goat, roe
căprĕŏlus, i, *m*, roebuck, prop
căprĭcornus, i. *m*, capricorn
căprĭfĭcus, i, *f*, wild fig-tree
căprĭgĕnus, a, um, *adj*, goat-born
căprīnus, a, um, *adj*, of a goat
capsa, ae, *f*, box, satchel
captātor, ōris, *m*, fortune-hunter
captĭo, ōnis, *f*, fraud, quibble
captīvĭtas, ātis, *f*, captivity
captīvus, a, um, *adj* (i, *m*), prisoner
capto, *v.t.* 1, to chase, entice
captus, ūs, *m*, grasp, capacity
captus, a, um, *adj*, taken, disabled
căpŭlus, i, *m*, tomb, handle
căpŭt, ĭtis, *n*, head, person, chief, origin, summit, status, paragraph, chapter
carbāsĕus, a, um, *adj*, made of flax, linen
carbāsus, i, *f*, flax, linen
carbo, ōnis, *m*, charcoal, coal
carbuncŭlus, i, *m*, ruby, carbuncle
carcer, ĕris, *m*, prison, jail-bird
carchēsĭum, ii, *n*, goblet, mast-head
cardĭăcus, a, um, *adj*, dyspeptic
cardo, ĭnis, *m*, hinge, crisis

cardŭus, i, *m*, thistle
cărĕo, *v.i.* 2 (*with abl.*), to lack
cărex, ĭcis, *f*, reed-grass
căries, (*no genitive*) *f*, decay
cārĭca, ae, *f*, dried fig
cărīna, ae, *f*, hull, keel, boat
cărĭōsus, a, um, *adj*, decayed
cārĭtas, ātis, *f*, costliness, affection
carmen, ĭnis, *n*, song, poem
carnārĭum, ii, *n*, larder
carnĭfex, ĭcis, *m*, executioner
carnĭfĭcĭna, ae, *f*, execution, torment
carnĭfĭco, *v.t.* 1, to execute
carnĭvŏrus, a, um, *adj*, carnivorous
carnōsus, a, um, *adj*, fleshy
cāro, carnis, *f*, flesh, meat
carpentum, i, *n*, chariot
carpo, psi, ptum, *v.t.* 3, to pluck, graze, slander, weaken, pass over
carptim, *adv*, separately
carrus, i, *m*, two-wheeled cart
cartĭlāgo, ĭnis, *f*, cartilage
cārus, a, um, *adj*, *adv*, ē, dear
căsa, ae, *f*, cottage, hut
cāsĕus, i, *m*, cheese
căsĭa, ae, *f*, cinnamon (tree)
casses, ĭum, *m.pl*, hunting-net, spider's web
cassis, ĭdis, *f*, helmet
cassĭda, ae, *f*, helmet
cassus, a, um, *adj*, empty, vain
castănĕa, ae, *f*, chestnut
castē, *adv*, purely
castellum, i, *n*, stronghold
castīgātĭo, ōnis, *f*, punishment
castīgātor, ōris, *m*, critic
castīgo, *v.t.* 1, to correct, punish
castĭmōnĭa, ae, *f*, purity
castĭtas, ātis, *f*, chastity
castor, ōris, *m*, beaver
castra, ōrum, *n.pl*, camp
castrensis, e, *adj*, of the camp, military
castro, *v.t.* 1, to castrate
castrum, i, *n*, fort
castus, a, um, *adj*, pure, virtuous
cāsū, *adv*, accidentally
cāsus, ūs, *m*, fall, chance, mishap
cătăpulta, ae, *f*, catapult
cătăracta, ae, *f*, waterfall, portcullis
cătellus, i, *m* (a, ae, *f*), puppy
cătēna, ae, *f*, chain, fetter
cătēnātus, a, um, *adj*, chained
căterva, ae, *f*, crowd, company
cătervātim, *adv*, by companies
căthēdra, ae, *f*, chair
cătillus, i, *m*, dish
cătīnus, i, *m*, bowl, dish
cătŭlus, i, *m*, puppy, young animal
cătus, a, um, *adj*, *adv*, ē, intelligent, sly

For List of Abbreviations used, turn to pages 3, 4

cauda, ae, *f*, tail

caudex, icis, *m*, tree-trunk, ledger

caulae, ārum, *f.pl*, hole, enclosure

caulis, is, *m*, stem, cabbage

caupo, ōnis, *m*, retailer, innkeeper

caupōna, ae, *f*, shop, inn

caupōnor, *v.t.* 1, *dep*, to trade

causa, ae, *f*, reason, cause, motive; *abl.* causā for the sake of

causidĭcus, i, *m*, counsel

causor, *v.i.t.* 1, *dep*, to make excuses; plead

cautē, *adv*, cautiously

cautēs, is, *f*, crag, rock

cautio, ōnis, *f*, precaution

cautus, a, um, *adj*, safe, cautious

căvĕa, ae, *f*, den, coop

căvĕo, căvi, cautum, *v.i.t.* 2, to be on one's guard; stipulate

căverna, ae, *f*, cave, ship's hold

căvillātio, ōnis, *f*, jeering

căvillor, *v.i.t.* 1, *dep*, to jeer; taunt, quibble

căvo, *v.t.* 1, to hollow out

căvum, i, *n* (us, i, *m*), hole

căvus, a, um, *adj*, hollow

cēdo, cessi, cessum, *v.i.t.* 3, to move, yield, happen; befall

cēdo, *imperative*, here! say! give!

cĕdrus, i, *f*, cedar (wood, tree, oil)

cĕlĕbĕr, ĕbris, ĕbre, *adj*, much frequented, crowded, famous

cĕlĕbrātio, ōnis, *f*, crowd, festival,

cĕlĕbrātus, a, um, *adj*, popular, usual, well-known

cĕlĕbritas, ātis, *f*, crowd, fame

cĕlĕbro, *v.t.* 1, to frequent, use, celebrate, praise, proclaim, solemnize

cĕlĕr, ĕris, ĕre, *adj*, *adv*, ĭter, swift, lively, rash

cĕlĕritas, ātis, *f*, speed

cĕlĕro, *v.i.t.* 1, to hurry; quicken

cella, ae, *f*, store-room

cellārius, i, *m*, butler

cēlo, *v.t.* 1, to conceal

cēlox, ōcis, *f*, yacht

celsus, a, um, *adj*, high, eminent

cēna, ae, *f*, dinner

cēnācŭlum, i, *n*, attic, refectory

cēnātio, ōnis, *f*, dining-room

cēnātus, a, um, *adj*, having dined

cēno, *v.i.t.* 1, to dine; eat

censĕo, ŭi, censum, *v.t.* 2, to assess, give an opinion

censor, ōris, *m*, censor

censōrius, a, um, *adj*, censorial

censūra, ae, *f*, censorship

census, ūs, *m*, census, wealth

centaurēum, i, *n*, herb (century)

centaurus, i, *m*, a Centaur

centēni, ae, a, *adj*, a hundred each

centēsimus, a, um, *adj*, hundredth

centiens (centies), *adv*, a hundred times

centimănus, a, um, *adj*, hundred-handed

cento, ōnis, *m*, patchwork

centum, a hundred

centumgĕminus, a, um, *adj*, a hundredfold

centumpondium, ii, *n*, weight of a hundred pounds

centŭplex, plĭcis, *adj*, hundredfold

centŭria, ae, *f*, division, century

centŭriātim, *adv*, by hundreds

centŭrio, ōnis, *m*, centurion

centŭrio, *v.t.* 1, to divide into centuries

cēnŭla, ae, *f*, small dinner

cēra, ae, *f*, wax, writing-tablet

cĕrăsus, i, *f*, cherry (tree)

cerdo, ōnis, *m*, handicraftsman

cĕrēbrōsus, a, um, *adj*, hot-headed

cĕrēbrum, i, *n*, brain, understanding

cērĕus, a, um, *adj*, of wax

cērĕus, i, *m*, wax taper

cerevisia, ae, *f*, beer

cērintha, ae, *f*, wax-flower

cerno, crēvi, crētum, *v.t.* 3, to perceive, decide

cernŭus, a, um, *adj*, headfirst

cēro, *v.t.* 1, to smear with wax

cerrītus, a, um, *adj*, frantic, crazy

certāmen, ĭnis, *n*, struggle

certātim, *adv*, eagerly

certātio, ōnis, *f*, contest

certē, *adv*, undoubtedly

certiōrem făcĭo, to inform

certō, *adv*, certainly

certo, *v.i.t.* 1, to struggle; contest

certus, a, um, *adj*, certain, fixed

cērussa, ae, *f*, white lead

cerva, ae, *f*, doe

cervĭcal, ālis, *n*, pillow

cervīnus, a, um, *adj*, of a deer

cervisia, see cerevisia

cervix, ĭcis, *f*, neck

cervus, i, *m*, deer

cessātio, ōnis, *f*, loitering

cessātor, ōris, *m*, idler

cessātrix, ĭcis, *f*, idler

cesso, *v.i.t.* 1, to loiter, cease; fail

cētārium, ii, *n*, fish-pond

cētārius, ii, *m*, fishmonger

cētĕrōqui, *adv*, in other respects

cētĕrum, *adv.* otherwise, but yet

cētĕrus, a, um, *adj, adv,* um, the rest, remainder

cētus, i, *m,* sea-monster, whale

ceu, *adv.* as, just as

chălybs, ўbis, *m,* steel

charta, ae, *f,* writing paper

chĕlўdrus, i, *m,* water-snake

chĕrăgra, ae, *f,* gout in the hand

chīrŏgrăphum, i, *n,* handwriting

chīrurgia, ae, *f,* surgery

chīrurgus, i, *m,* surgeon

chlămys, ўdis, *f,* military cloak

chorda, ae, *f,* string of a musical instrument

chŏrēa, ae, *f,* dance

chŏrus, i, *m,* dance, chorus, group

Christus, i, *m,* Christ

Christiānus, a, um, *adj,* Christian

cībāria, ōrum, *n.pl,* food

cībārius, a, um, *adj,* of food

cībōrium, ii, *n,* drinking-cup

cībus, i, *m,* food

cĭcāda, ae, *f,* grasshopper

cĭcātrix, īcis, *f,* scar

cĭcer, ĕris, *n,* chick pea

cĭcĭnus, a, um, *adj,* of the cici tree

cĭcōnia, ae, *f,* stork

cĭcur, ūris, *adj,* tame

cĭcūta, ae, *f,* hemlock

cĭĕo, cĭvi, cĭtum, *v.t.* 2, to rouse, move, summon

cĭlĭcium, ii, *n,* coarse cloth

cīmex, īcis, *m,* bug

cĭncinnātus, a, um, *adj,* with ringlets

cincinnus, i, *m,* lock of hair

cinctus, ūs, *m,* girdle

cĭnĕrĕus, a, um, *adj,* ash-coloured

cingo, nxi, nctum, *v.t.* 3, to enclose, encircle, fasten on, crown, besiege

cingŭla, ae, *f,* (um, i, *n*), girdle

cĭnis, ĕris, *m,* ashes, death

cippus, i, *m,* stake

circā, *adv. and prep. with acc,* round about

circenses, ĭum, *m.pl,* The Games

circĭnus, i, *m,* pair of compasses

circĭter, *adv. and prep. with acc,* round about, near

circĭtor, ōris, *m,* patrol

circŭĭtĭo, ōnis, *f,* patrolling

circŭĭtus, ūs, *m,* circuit

circŭlor, *v.i.* 1, *dep,* to form a group

circŭlus, i, *m,* circle, orbit

circum, *adv. and prep. with acc,* around, near

circŭmăgo, ēgi, actum, *v.t.* 3, to wheel, drive round, pass (time)

circumcīdo, cīdi, cīsum, *v.t.* 3, to cut around, reduce

circumcīsus, a, um, *adj,* cut off

circumclūdo, si, sum, *v.t.* 3, to shut in, surround

circumdătus, a, um, *adj,* surrounded

circumdo, dĕdi, dătum, *v.t.* 1, to put around, shut in, surround

circumdūco, xi, ctum, *v.t.* 3, to lead around

circŭmĕo, circŭĭtum, *v.i.t.* 4, to go around; surround, canvass

circumfĕro, ferre, tŭli, lātum, *v.t., irreg,* to carry or pass around

circumflecto, xi, xum, *v.t.* 3, to bend, turn round

circumflŭo, xi, ctum, *v.i.t.* 3, to flow round; overflow with

circumfŏrānĕus, a, um, *adj,* movable

circumfundo, fūdi, fūsum, *v.t.* 3, to pour around, envelop, hem in

circumgrĕdĭor, gressus, *v.i.t.* 3, *dep,* to go around

circumicio, iēci, ctum, *v.t.* 3, to throw or set round

circumiectus, a, um, *adj,* surrounding

circumlĭgo, *v.t.* 1, to tie round

circumlĭno,—ĭtum, *v.t.* 3, to besmear

circummitto, mīsi, missum, *v.t.* 3, to send around

circummūnĭo, *v.t.* 4, to fortify round

circumplector, xus, *v.t.* 3, *dep,* to embrace, surround

circumplĭco, *v.t.* 1, to wind round

circumrōdo, di, *v.t.* 3, to nibble round

circumscrībo, psi, ptum, *v.t.* 3, to draw a line round, restrict, deceive

circumscriptio, ōnis, *f,* circle, outline

circumsĕdĕo, sēdi, sessum, *v.t.* 2, to surround, blockade

circumsisto, stĕti, *v.i.t.* 3, to stand around; surround

circumsŏno, *v.i.t.* 1, to resound; fill with sound

circumspecto, *v.i.t.* 1, to look round; survey carefully

circumspectus, a, um, *adj.* guarded, considered

circumspectus, ūs, *m,* contemplation, spying

circumspĭcĭo, spexi, ctum, *v.i.t.* 3, to look around, take care; survey, search for

circumsto, stĕti, *v.i.t.* 1, to stand around; surround, besiege

circumtextus, a, um, *adj,* woven round

circumtŏno, ŭi, *v.t.* 1, to thunder around

circumvādo, si, *v.t.* 3, to envelop

circumvallo, *v.t.* 1, to surround with a wall, blockade

circumvector, v. 1, dep, to ride around

circumvehor, vectus, v.i.t. 3, dep, to ride around

circumvĕnĭo, vēni, ventum, v.t. 4, to surround

circumvŏlĭto, v.i.t. 1, to flit; fly around

circumvŏlo, v.t. 1, to fly around

circumvolvo—vŏlūtum, v.t. 3, to roll around

circus, i, m, circle, ring

cīris, is, f, sea-bird

cirrus, i, m, curl

cis, prep, with acc, on this side of, within

cisium, ii, n, two-wheeled vehicle

cista, ae, f, box, chest

cisterna, ae, f, cistern

citātus, a, um, adj, urged on, quick

citĕrior, comp. adj, on this side

cithăra, ae, f, guitar, lute

cithărista, ae, m, guitar-player

cithăroedus, i, m, a singing guitar-player

cĭto, adv, soon, quickly

cĭto, v.t. 1, to incite, call

cĭtrā, adv. and prep. with acc, on this side (of)

cĭtrĕus, a, um, adj, of citrus-wood, of the citrus tree

cĭtrō, adv. (with ultro), to and fro, backwards and forwards

cĭtrus, i, f, citrus-tree

cĭtus, a, um, adj, swift, quick

cīvĭcus, a, um, adj, of a citizen, civic, civil

cīvīlis, e, adj, adv, ĭter, of a citizen, civic, civil

cīvis, is, c, citizen

cīvĭtas, ātis, f, citizenship, the state, the citizens

clādes, is, f, disaster, massacre

clam, adv. and prep. with acc, secretly; unknown to

clāmĭto, v.i.t. 1, to call out

clāmo, v.i.t. 1, to shout; declare

clāmor, ōris, m, shout, applause

clāmōsus, a, um, adj, noisy, bawling

clandestīnus, a, um, adj, adv, o, secret, hidden, furtive

clangor, ōris, m, noise, clash

clārĕo, v.i. 2, to shine, be famous

clāresco, clārŭi, v.i. 3, to become clear or famous

clārĭtas, ātis, f, brightness, renown

clārĭtūdo, ĭnis, f, renown

clārus, a, um, adj, adv, e, clear, bright, plain, famous

classiārii, ōrum, m. pl, marines

classĭcum, i, n, battle-signal

classis, is, f, fleet, class or muster of citizens

claudĕo, v.i. 2 (no perf), to limp, be lame

claudĭco, v.i. 1, to limp, be lame

claudĭcātĭo, ōnis, f, limping

claudo, si, sum, v.t. 3, to shut, cut off, enclose, blockade

claudus, a, um, adj, lame

claustra, ōrum, n. pl, lock, bolt, barricade

clausŭla, ae, f, conclusion, end

clausum, i, n, enclosed space

clāva, ae, f, club, cudgel

clāvĭger, ĕra, ĕrum, adj, club-armed

clāvĭger, ĕri, m, key-bearer

clāvis, is, f, key

clāvŭlus, i, m, small nail

clāvus, i, m, nail, tiller, stripe

clēmens, ntis, adj, adv, nter, gentle, mild, merciful

clēmentĭa, ae, f, mildness, mercy

clēpo, psi, ptum, v.t. 3, to steal

clepsȳdra, ae, f, water-clock

cliens, ntis, c, retainer, follower

clientēla, ae, f, patronage, train of dependants

clĭpĕus, i, m, Roman round shield

clĭtellae, ārum, f. pl, saddle-bags

clīvōsus, a, um, adj, hilly

clīvus, i, m, slope, hill

clŏāca, ae, f, sewer, drain

clūnis, is, m, f, buttock, haunch

cŏăcervo, v.t. 1, to pile together

cŏactor, ōris, m, money-collector

cŏactum, i, n, a thick covering

cŏactus, a, um, adj, adv, e, forced

cŏaequo, v.t. 1, to level, equalize

cŏagmento, v.t. 1, to join together

cŏagŭlo, v.t. 1, to coagulate

cŏālesco, ălŭi, ălĭtum, v.i. 3, to grow together, combine

cŏargŭo, ŭi, v.t. 3, to convict, refute, demonstrate

cŏarto, v.t. 1, to compress

coccĭnĕus, a, um, adj, scarlet

coccum, i, n, scarlet colour

cochlĕa, ae, f, snail, spiral

cōclĕa, ae, f, snail, spiral

cŏclĕar, āris, n, spoon

coctĭlis, e, adj, baked, burned

cŏcus, i, m, cook

cōdex, ĭcis, m, tree-trunk, ledger

cōdĭcilli, ōrum, m. pl, note-book

cŏēmo, ēmi, emptum, v.t. 3, to buy up

coenum, i, n, dirt

cŏēo, v.i. 4, to assemble, unite, encounter, conspire

(coepĭo) coepi, coeptum, v.i.t. 3, defect, to begin

coeptum, i, n, attempt

coeptus, ūs, m, undertaking

cŏercĕo, v.t. 2, to confine, curb

cŏercĭtĭo, ōnis, f, coercion, restraint

coetus, ūs, m, meeting, crowd

cōgĭtātĭo, ōnis, f, thought, reflection, purpose

cōgĭtātum, i, n, idea, thought

cōgĭtātus, a, um, adj, thought out

cōgĭto, v.t. 1, to consider, think, be disposed towards, plan

cognātĭo, ōnis, f, blood relationship, family

cognātus, a, um, adj, related by birth; (as a noun) blood-relative

cognĭtĭo, ōnis, f, study, knowledge, recognition, idea, trial

cognĭtor, ōris, m, legal representative

cognĭtus, a, um, adj, known, approved

cognōmen, ĭnis, n, surname

cognōmĭnis, e, adj, of the same name

cognōsco, gnōvi, gnĭtum, v.t. 3, to learn, understand, inquire

cōgo, cŏēgi, cŏactum, v.t. 3, to collect, compel, restrict

cŏhaerens, see cohaerĕo

cŏhaerĕo, si, sum, v.i. 2, to cling together, agree with

cŏhēres, ēdis, c, fellow-heir

cŏhĭbĕo, v.t. 2, to hold together, confine, restrain

cŏhŏnesto, v.t. 1, to honour

cŏhorresco, horrŭi, v.i. 3, to shudder

cŏhors, tis, f, company of soldiers ($\frac{1}{10}$ of a legion); enclosure

cŏhortālis, e, adj, of the poultry-farm

cŏhortātĭo, ōnis, f, encouragement

cŏhortor, v.t. 1, dep, to encourage

cŏĭtĭo, ōnis, f, meeting, conspiracy

cŏĭtus, ūs, m, meeting, crowd, sexual intercourse

cōlăphus, i, m, blow, cuff

collăbĕfacto, v.t. 1, to dislodge

collăbĕfīo, fĭeri, factus, v. irreg, to be overthrown, disabled

collābor, psus, v.i. 3, dep, to fall, faint, decay

collăcrĭmo, v.i.t. 1, to weep; deplore

collactĕus, i, m, (a, ae, f.) foster-brother (sister)

collātĭo, ōnis, f, collection, encounter, comparison

collaudo, v.t. 1, to praise highly

collēga, ae, m, partner, colleague

collēgĭum, ii, n, organization, body of officials

collĭbet, v. impers, 2, it is agreeable

collīdo, si, sum, v.t. 3, to beat or strike together

collĭgo, lēgi, ctum, v.t. 3, to collect, compress, consider

collĭgo, v.t. 1, to tie together

collĭno, lēvi, lĭtum, v.t. 3, to besmear, defile

collīnus, a, um, adj, hilly

collis, is, m, hill, high ground

collŏcātĭo, ōnis, f, setting up, giving in marriage

collŏco, v.t. 1, to arrange, give in marriage, invest, employ

collŏquĭum, ii, n, conversation

collŏquor, cūtus, v.i. 3, dep, to hold a conversation, discuss

collūcĕo, v.i, 2, to shine

collūdo, si, sum, v.i. 3, to play with, be in collusion with

collum, i, n, neck, throat

collumna, see columna

collŭo, lŭi, lūtum, v.t. 3, to rinse

collūsĭo, ōnis, f, collusion

collūsor, ōris, m. playmate

collustro, v.t. 1, to illumine

collŭvĭo, ōnis, f, heap of rubbish

collŭvies, —, f, heap of rubbish

cōlo, ŭi, cultum, v.t. 3, to cultivate improve, worship, study

cōlo, v.t. 1, to filter

cōlŏcāsĭa, ae, f, marsh-lily

cōlon, i, n, colon

cōlōna, ae, f, farmer's wife

cŏlōnĭa, ae, f, Roman outpost, colonial settlement, farm

cŏlōnus, i, m, farmer, colonist

cŏlŏr, ōris, m, colour, dye, beauty

cŏlōrātus, a, um, adj, coloured

cŏlōro, v.t. 1, to colour, dye

cŏlossus, i, m, gigantic statue

cŏlŭber, bri, m (bra, ae, f), snake

cōlum, i, n, strainer, colander

cŏlumba, ae, f. (us, i, m), dove

cŏlumbārĭum, ii, n, dove-cot

cŏlumbīnus, a, um, adj, of a dove, dove-coloured

cŏlŭmella, ae, f, small pillar

cŏlŭmen, ĭnis, n, summit, prop

cŏlumna, ae, f, pillar, post

cŏlurnus, a, um, adj, of hazel

cŏlus, ūs, f, distaff

cōma, ae, f, hair, crest, foliage

cōmans, ntis, adj, hairy

cōmātus, a, um, adj, long-haired

combĭbo, bĭbi, v.t. 3, to drink up

combūro, ussi, ustum, v.t. 3, to burn, consume completely

cŏmĕdo, ēdi, ēsum, v.t. 3, to eat up, waste

cōmes, ĭtis, c, companion, attendant

cōmētes, ae, m, comet

cōmĭcus, a, um, adj, adv, ē, comic

For List of Abbreviations used, turn to pages 3, 4

cŏmĭcus, ĭ, *m*, comedian

cŏmis, e, *adj, adv*, ĭter, courteous, obliging

cōmissātĭo, ōnis, *f*, drinking-party

cōmissātor, ōris, *m*, reveller

cōmissor, *v.i.* 1, *dep*, to have a party

cōmĭtas, ātis, *f*, affability

cŏmĭtātus, a, um, *adj*, accompanied

cŏmĭtātus, ūs, *m*, escort, retinue

cŏmĭtĭa, ōrum, *n.pl*, Roman assembly for electing magistrates

cŏmĭtĭālis, e, *adj*, of the elections; (with morbus) epilepsy

cŏmĭtĭum, ĭi, *n*, assembly place for voting

cŏmĭtor, *v.t.* 1, *dep*, to accompany

commācŭlo, *v.t.* 1, to stain

commĕātus, ūs, *m*, expedition, leave of absence, convoy, supplies

commĕmŏrātĭo, ōnis, *f*, mention

commĕmŏro, *v.t.* 1, to remember, relate

commendātīcĭus, a, um, *adj*, commendatory

commendātĭo, ōnis, *f*, recommendation

commendo, *v.t.* 1, to entrust, recommend

commentārĭus, ĭi, *m* (ĭum, ĭi, *n*), notebook, record

commentātĭo, ōnis, *f*, careful study

commentīcĭus, a, um, *adj*, thought-out, imaginary, false

commentor, *v.i.t.* 1, *dep*, to study

commentor, ōris, *m*, inventor

commentum, ĭ, *n*, fabrication

commĕo, *v.i.* 1, to come and go, frequent

commercĭum, ĭi, *n*, commerce, trade, a relationship with

commĕrĕo, *v.t.* 2, to deserve fully, be guilty of

commigro, *v.t.* 1, to migrate

commīlĭtĭum, ĭi, *n*, comradeship

commīlĭto, ōnis, *m*, comrade

commĭnātĭo, ōnis, *f*, threats

commĭnīscor, mentus, *v.t.* 3, *dep*, to devise, invent

commĭnor, *v.t.* 1, *dep*, to threaten

commĭnŭo, ŭi, ūtum, *v.t.* 3, to crush, lessen, weaken

commĭnus, *adv*, at close quarters

commiscĕo, scŭi, xtum, *v.t.* 2, to mix together

commĭsĕror, *v.t.* 1, *dep*, to pity

commissĭo, ōnis, *f*, opening of the games, prepared speech

commissum, ĭ, *n*, offence, secret

commissūra, ae, *f*, knot, joint

committo, mīsi, ssum, *v.t.* 3, to connect, engage in, begin, entrust, do something wrong, bring together in combat

commŏdātum, ĭ, *n*, loan

commŏdē, *adv*, appropriately, just in time

commŏdĭtas, ātis, *f*, benefit

commŏdo, *v.t.* 1, to adjust, lend, be kind to, oblige

commŏdum, ĭ, *n*, convenient time or opportunity, advantage

commŏdus, a, um, *adj*, suitable, obliging, advantageous

commŏnĕfăcĭo, fēci, factum, *v.t.* 3, to remind, impress upon

commŏnĕo, *v.t.* 2, to impress upon

commonstro, *v.t.* 1, to point out

commŏrātĭo, ōnis, *f*, delay

commŏror, *v.i.t.* 1, *dep*, to wait, stay

commŏtĭo, ōnis, *f*, commotion, excitement

commŏtus, a, um, *adj*, aroused

commŏvĕo, mōvi, mōtum, *v.t.* 2, to shake, move, arouse, disturb

commūnĭcātĭo, ōnis, *f*, communication

commūnĭco, *v.t.* 1, to share with another, consult, unite, partake

commūnĭo, *v.t.* 4, to fortify strongly

commūnĭo, ōnis, *f*, partnership

commūnē, is, *n*, community, state

commūnis, e, *adj, adv*, ĭter, common, general

commūnĭtas, ātis, *f*, fellowship

commūtābĭlis, e, *adj*, changeable

commūtātĭo, ōnis, *f*, change

commūto, *v.t.* 1, to change, exchange

cōmo, mpsi, mptum, *v.t.* 3, to arrange comb, braid, adorn

cōmoedĭa, ae, *f*, comedy

cōmoedus, a, um, *adj*, comic

cōmoedus, ĭ, *m*, comic actor

compactum, ĭ, *n*, agreement

compactus, a, um, *adj*, thick-set

compāges, is, *f*, joint, structure

compār, ăris, *adj*, equal, like

compār, ăris, *m*, companion

compărātĭo, ōnis, *f*, comparison, preparation

compărātīvus, a, um, *adj*, comparative

compărĕo, *v.i.* 2, to be evident

compăro, *v.t.* 1, to pair off, compare, make ready, provide

compello, pŭli, pulsum, *v.t.* 3, to collect, compel

compello, *v.t.* 1, to address, rebuke

compendiārius, a, um, *adj*, short

compendium, ii, *n*, gain, saving, abbreviation

compensātio, ōnis, *f*, compensation

compenso, *v.t.* 1, to make things balance, compensate

compĕrendīno, *v.t.* 1, to remand

compĕrio, pĕri, pertum, *v.t.* 4, to ascertain

compertus, a, um, *adj*, proved

compēs, ēdis, *f*, chain, shackle for the feet

compesco, scŭi, *v.t.* 3, to restrain

compĕtitor, ōris, *m*, rival

compĕto, īvi, ītum, *v.i.* 3, to correspond, coincide

compĭlo, *v.t.* 1, to plunder

compingo, pēgi, pactum, *v.t.* 3, to construct, fasten together

compĭtum, i, *n*, cross-road

complāno, *v.t.* 1, to level

complector, xus, *v.t.* 3, *dep*, to embrace, value, enclose, understand

complēmentum, i, *n*, complement

complĕo, ēvi, ētum, *v.t.* 2, to fill up, supply

complexio, ōnis, *f*, combination

complexus, ūs, *m*, embrace, love

complĭco, *v.t.* 1, to fold up

complōrātio, ōnis, *f*, lamentation

complōrātus, ūs, *m*, lamentation

complōro, *v.t.* 1, to lament

complūres, a, *pl. adj*, several

compōno, pŏsŭi, pŏsĭtum, *v.t.* 3, to put together, unite, build, arrange, compare, put to sleep, adjust, pretend, agree upon

comporto, *v.t.* 1, to bring together

compōs, ŏtis, *adj, with genit. or abl*, having control of

compōsĭtio, ōnis, *f*, arranging

compōsĭtus, a, um, *adj, adv,* ē, well-arranged, suitable: ex compōsĭto, by previous agreement

comprĕhendo, di, sum, *v.t.* 3, to seize, perceive, recount, understand

comprĕhensio, ōnis, *f*, arrest

comprĭmo, pressi, pressum, *v.t.* 3, to press together, restrain

comprŏbo, *v.t.* 1, to approve, prove

comptus, a, um, *m, adj*, dressed-up

compulsus, a, um, *adj*, collected, driven

compungo, nxi, nctum, *v.t.* 3, to prick, sting

compŭto, *v.t.* 1, to calculate

cōnāmen, ĭnis, *n*, effort

cōnāta, ōrum, *n.pl*, undertaking

cōnātum, i, *n*, attempt

cōnātus, ūs, *m*, effort, enterprise

concăvus, a, um, *adj*, hollow, arched

concēdo, cessi, ssum, *v.i.t.* 3, to go away, yield; permit

concĕlĕbro, *v.t.* 1, to frequent, celebrate, notify

concentus, ūs, *m*, harmony

conceptio, ōnis, *f*, comprehension, conception

conceptus, ūs, *m*, gathering

concertātio, ōnis, *f*, dispute

concerto, *v.t.* 1, to dispute

concessio, ōnis, *f*, permission

concessu (*abl*), by permission

concessus, a, um, *adj*, yielded, confirmed

concha, ae, *f*, shell-fish, oyster-shell, Triton's trumpet

conchўlium, ii, *n*, shell-fish

concĭdo, cĭdi, *v.i.* 3, to collapse

concīdo, cīdi, cīsum, *v.t.* 3, to cut up, kill, annihilate

concĭĕo, īvi, ītum, *v.t.* 2, to bring together

conciliābŭlum, i, *n*, assembly-place

conciliātio, ōnis, *f*, union

conciliātor, ōris, *m*, promoter

concĭlio, *v.t.* 1, to unite, win over, bring about

concĭlium, ii, *n*, meeting, assembly

concinnĭtas, ātis, *f*, elegance

concinnus, a, um, *adj, adv,* ē, well-adjusted, graceful

concĭno, nŭi, *v.i.t.* 3, to harmonize; celebrate

concĭpio, cēpi, ceptum, *v.t.* 3, to take hold of, become pregnant, understand, formulate, designate

concīsus, a, um, *adj, adv,* ē, cut short

concĭtātio, ōnis, *f*, quick motion

concĭtātus, a, um, *adj, adv,* ē, swift, roused

concĭto, *v.t.* 1, to stir up, rouse

conclāmo, *v.i.t.* 1, to shout out; call upon

conclāve, is, *n*, room

conclūdo, si, sum, *v.t.* 3, to enclose, include, conclude

concoctio, ōnis, *f*, digestion

concŏlor, ōris, *adj*, similar in colour

concŏquo, xi, ctum, *v.t.* 3, to boil together, digest, put up with

concordia, ae, *f*, agreement

concordo, *v.i.* 1, to agree

concors, cordis, *adj, adv,* ĭter, of the same mind

concrēdo, dĭdi, dĭtum, *v.t.* 3, to entrust

concrĕmo, *v.t.* 1, to burn up

concrĕpo, ŭi, ĭtum, *v.i.t.* 3, to creak, crack; 2 rattle, clash

concresco, crēvi, tum, *v.i.* 3, to grow together, harden

concrētus, a, um, *adj*, hardened

concŭbīna, ae, *f*, concubine

concŭbĭus, a, um, *adj*, (with **nox**) at dead of night

conculco, *v.t.* 1, to trample on

concŭpisco, cŭpīvi, ītum, *v.t.* 3, to long for, strive after

concurro, curri, cursum, *v.i.* 3, to rush together, assemble, join battle

concursātio, ōnis, *f*, running together

concursĭo, ōnis, *f*, running together

concurso, *v.i.t.* 1, to run, travel about, skirmish; frequent

concursus, ūs, *m*, rush, collision

concŭtĭo, cussi, ssum, *v.t.* 3, to shake, disturb, terrify, examine

condemno, *v.t.* 1, to convict

condenso, *v.t.* 1, to condense

condensus, a, um, *adj*, thick

condĭcĭo, ōnis, *f*, agreement, proposition, terms, alliance, rank, situation

condĭmentum, i, *n*, seasoning

condĭo, *v.t.* 4, to pickle

condiscĭpŭlus, i, *m*, school-friend

condisco, dĭdĭci, *v.t.* 3, to learn carefully

condĭtor, ōris, *m*, builder, author, founder

condĭtus, a, um, *adj*, fashioned, composed

condītus . a, um, *adj*, savoury

condo, dĭdi, dĭtum, *v.t.* 3, to construct, found, store up, hide, thrust in

condŏlesco, lŭi, *v.i.* 3, to suffer pain

condōno, *v.t.* 1, to present, give up, surrender, pardon

condūco, xi, ctum, *v.i.t.* 3, to be useful; collect, connect, hire

conductĭo, ōnis, *f*, hiring

conductor, ōris, *m*, tenant, contractor

conductum, i, *n*, tenement

conductus, a, um, *adj*, hired

cōnecto, xŭi, xum, *v.t.* 3, to tie together, involve

cōnfarrēātĭo, ōnis, *f*, marriage

cōnfectĭo, ōnis, *f*, arrangement, completion

cōnfectus, a, um, *adj*, completed, exhausted

cōnfercĭo, (*no perf.***) fertum,** *v.t.* 4, to cram, stuff together

cōnfěro, ferre, tŭli, collātum, *v.t, irreg*, to bring together, contribute, confer, talk about, engage, fight, compare, condense, convey, postpone; (*reflex.*) to betake oneself, go

cōnfertus, a, um, *adj, adv,* e, crowded

cōnfessĭo, ōnis, *f*, confession

cōnfessus, a, um, *adj*, admitted

cōnfestim, *adv*, immediately

cōnficĭo, fēci, fectum, *v.t.* 3, to complete, produce, exhaust, kill

cōnfīdens, ntis, *adj, adv,* nter, bold, impudent

cōnfīdentĭa, ae, *f*, boldness

cōnfīdo, fīsus sum, *v.i.* 3, *semi-dep*, to feel confident; *with dat*, to trust

cōnfīgo, xi, xum, *v.t.* 3, to nail, fasten together, transfix

cōnfingo, nxi, ctum, *v.t.* 3; to fashion, invent

cōnfīnis, e, *adj*, adjoining

cōnfīnĭum, ĭi, *n*, border

cōnfirmātĭo, ōnis, *f*, encouragement, confirming

cōnfirmātus, a, um, *adj*, resolute

cōnfirmo, *v.t.* 1, to strengthen, encourage, prove

cōnfīsus, a, um, *adj*, trusting

cōnfĭtĕor, fessus, *v.t.* 2, *dep*, to acknowledge, own

cōnflăgro, *v.i.* 1, to burn

cōnflicto, *v.t.* 1, to strike or dash together, ruin, harass

cōnflīgo, xi, ctum, *v.i.t.* 3, to fight, struggle; strike or dash together

cōnflo, *v.t.* 1, to kindle, cause

cōnflŭens, ntis, *m*, confluence of rivers

cōnflŭo, xi, *v.i.* 3, to flow together, unite, come in crowds

cōnfŏdĭo, fŏdi, fossum, *v.t.* 3, to dig thoroughly, stab, pierce

cōnformātĭo, ōnis, *f*, shaping

cōnformo, *v.t.* 1, to form, fashion

cōnfrăgōsus, a, um, *adj*, broken

cōnfringo, frēgi, fractum, *v.t.* 3, to smash up

cōnfŭgĭo, fūgi, *v.i.* 3, to run away for help, take refuge

cōnfundo, fūdi, sum, *v.t.* 3, to pour together, confuse

cōnfūsĭo, ōnis, *f*, blending, disorder

cōnfūsus, a, um, *adj, adv,* ē, disorderly

cōnfūto, *v.t.* 1, to repress, silence

congĕlo, *v.i.t.* 1, to freeze; thicken

congĕmĭno, *v.t.* 1, to redouble

congĕmo, ŭi, *v.i.t.* 3, to sigh; mourn

congĕrĭes, ēi, *f*, heap

congĕro, ssi, stum, *v.t.* 3, to bring together, accumulate

congestus, ūs, *m*, heap

congĭārĭum, ĭi, *n*, gratuity

congĭus, ĭi, *m*, 6-pint measure

conglŏbo, *v.t.* 1, to gather, press into a ball

conglūtino, v.t. 1, to glue or cement together, unite

congrēdior, gressus, v.i. 3, dep, to meet, encounter

congrēgātio, ōnis, f, assembly

congrēgo, v.t. 1, to collect into a flock, unite

congressus, ūs, m, meeting, combat

congrūens, ntis, adj, adv, nter, appropriate, proper, consistent

congrūentia, ae, f, agreement

congrŭo, ŭi, v.i. 3, to meet, coincide

cōnicio, iēci, iectum, v.t. 3, to hurl, infer, drive

coniecto, v.t. 1, to hurl, foretell

coniectūra, ae, f, inference

coniectus, ūs, m, throwing, heap

coniectus, a, um, adj, thrown together

cōnifer, ĕra, ĕrum, adj, cone-bearing

cōnitor, nisus (nixus), v.i. 3, dep, to strive, struggle towards

cōnīvĕo, nīvi, v.i. 2, to wink, blink

coniŭgium, ii, n, union, marriage

coniunctio, ōnis, f, uniting, junction

coniunctus, a, um, adj, adv. e, near, connected, allied

coniungo, nxi, nctum, v.t. 3, to join together, marry

coniunx, iŭgis, m, f, husband, wife

coniŭrātio, ōnis, f, conspiracy

coniŭrātus, i, m, conspirator

coniŭro, v.i. 1, to conspire, band together

conl . . . see coll . . .

connecto, . . . see cōnecto

connīvĕo, see cōnīvĕo

connūbium, ii, n, marriage

cōnōpĕum, i, n, gauze-net

cōnor, v.t. 1, dep, to try, undertake

conquĕror, questus, v.i.t. 3, dep, to complain (of)

conquiesco, quiēvi, quiētum, v.i. 3, to rest, pause

conquiro, quīsīvi, sītum, v.t. 3, to search for

conquīsītio, ōnis, f, search

conquīsītus, a, um, adj, sought after

cōnsălūto, v.t. 1, to greet

cōnsānesco, ŭi, v.i. 3, to heal

consanguĭnĕus, a, um, adj, related by blood

consanguĭnĭtas, ātis, f, blood-relationship

conscendo, di, sum, v.i.t. 3, to embark; mount

conscientia, ae, f, joint knowledge, moral sense

conscindo, ĭdi, issum, v.t. 3, to tear in pieces

conscisco, scīvi, ītum, v.t. 3, to make a joint resolution, decree, inflict

conscius, a, um, adj, sharing knowledge of, (with sibi) conscious of

conscius, i, m, accomplice

conscrībo, psi, ptum, v.t. 3, to enroll, enlist, compose

conscriptus, i, m, senator

consĕco, cŭi, ctum, v.t. 1, to cut up

consecrātio, ōnis, f, consecration

consecro, v.t. 1; to dedicate, doom

consector, v.t. 1, dep, to pursue eagerly, imitate

consĕnesco, nŭi, v.i. 3, to grow old or weak

consensĭo, ōnis, f, agreement, plot

consensus, ūs, m, agreement, plot

consentānĕus, a, um, adj, suited

consentĭo, sensi, sum, v.i.t. 4, to agree, conspire, resolve; plot

consĕquens, ntis, adj, according to reason, fit

consĕquor, secŭtus, v.t. 3, dep, to follow, pursue, overtake, attain, obtain

consĕro, sēvi, sĭtum (sătum), v.t. 3, to plant, sow

consĕro, rŭi, rtum, v.t. 3, to fasten together

consertus, a, um, adj, adv, ē, joined, close, serried

conservātio, ōnis, f, maintenance

conservo, v.t. 1, to maintain, keep safe

conservus, i, m, fellow-slave

consessus, ūs, m, assembly

consĭdĕrātus, a, um, adj, adv, e, well-considered, cautious, discreet

consĭdĕrātio, ōnis, f, consideration

consīdĕro, v.t. 1, to examine, contemplate

consīdo, sēdi, sessum, v.i. 3, to sit down, take up position, subside

consigno, v.t. 1, to seal, certify

consiliārius, ii, m, adviser

consilior, v.i. 1, dep, to consult

consilium, ii, n, plan, deliberation, policy, advice, assembly, wisdom

consĭmĭlis, e, adj, quite like

consisto, stĭti, stĭtum, v.i. 3, to stand, halt, take up position, endure, exist, settle

consōbrīnus, i, m (a, ae, f), cousin

consŏcĭātus, a, um, adj, united

consŏcĭo, v.t. 1, to share, unite

consōlātĭo, ōnis, f, comfort

consōlātor, ōris, m, comforter

consōlor, v.t. 1, dep, to comfort

consŏnans, ntis (with littera), consonant

For List of Abbreviations used, turn to pages 3, 4

consŏno, ŭi, *v.i.* 1, to resound, harmonize, agree

consŏnus, a, um, *adj, adv,* ē, fit, harmonious

consōpĭo, *v.t.* 4, to put to sleep

consors, rtis, *adj,* partner

consortĭo, ōnis, *f,* association

conspectus, ūs, *m,* look, sight, view, presence

conspectus, a, um, *adj,* distinguished, visible

conspergo, si, sum, *v.t.* 3, to sprinkle

conspĭcĭo, spexi, ctum, *v.t.* 3, to look at, understand

conspĭcor, *v.t.* 1, *dep,* to catch sight of

conspĭcŭus, a, um, *adj,* visible, striking

conspīrātĭo, ōnis, *f,* agreement, plot

conspīro, *v.i.* 1, to agree, plot

consponsor, ōris, *m,* joint surety

conspŭo, —, ŭtum, *v.t.* 3, to spit on, cover

constans, ntis, *adj, adv,* nter, firm, resolute, consistent

constantĭa, ae, *f,* firmness, consistency

constat, *v. impers,* it is agreed

consternātĭo, ōnis, *f,* dismay

consterno, strāvi, strātum, *v.t.* 3, to cover over

consterno, *v.t.* 1, to alarm, provoke

constĭtŭo, ŭi, ŭtum, *v.t.* 3, to put, place, draw up, halt, establish, arrange, determine, decide

constĭtūtĭo, ōnis, *f,* arrangement, establishment

constĭtūtum, i, *n,* agreement

constĭtūtus, a, um, *adj,* arranged

consto, stĭti, stātum, *v.i.* 1, to agree with, endure, be established, exist, consist of, cost

constrātus, a, um, *adj,* covered

constringo, nxi, ctum, *v.t.* 3, to tie up, restrain

constrŭo, xi, ctum, *v.t.* 3, to heap up, build

constŭpro, *v.t.* 1, to ravish

consŭēfăcĭo, fēci, factum, *v.t.* 3, to accustom

consŭesco, sŭēvi, sŭētum, *v.i.t.* 3, to be accustomed; train

consŭētūdo, ĭnis, *f,* habit, custom, intimacy

consŭētus, a, um, *adj,* customary

consŭl, ŭlis, *m,* consul (highest Roman magistrate)

consŭlāris, e, *adj,* of a consul

consŭlātus, ūs, *m,* consulship

consŭlo, ŭi, sultum, *v.i.t.* 3, to consider, consult; *with dat.* promote the interests of

consulto, *v.i.t.* 1, to deliberate; consult

consultor, ōris, *m,* adviser, client

consultum, i, *n,* decision, decree

consultus, a, um, *adj, adv,* e, o, well-considered

consummātĭo, ōnis, *f,* summing-up, completion

consūmo, mpsi, mptum, *v.t.* 3, to use, eat up, consume, waste, destroy

consumptĭo, ōnis, *f,* wasting, use

consurgo, surrexi, surrectum, *v.i.* 3, to stand up, rise

contăbŭlātĭo, ōnis, *f,* flooring

contăbŭlo, *v.t.* 1, to board over

contactus, ūs, *m,* touch, contact, contagion

contāgĭo, ōnis, *f,* touch, contact, contagion

contāmĭnātus, a, um, *adj,* impure

contāmĭno, *v.t.* 1, to blend, stain

contĕgo, xi, ctum, *v.t.* 3, to cover up, hide

contemnendus, a, um, *adj,* contemptible

contemno, mpsi, mptum, *v.t.* 3, to despise

contemplātĭo, ōnis, *f,* observation

contemplor, *v.t.* 1, *dep,* to observe

contemptor, ōris, *m,* despiser

contemptus, ūs, *m,* contempt

contemptus, a, um, *adj,* despicable

contendo, di, tum, *v.i.t.* 3, to strive, march, fight, stretch; compare, make a bid for

contentĭo, ōnis, *f,* struggle, effort, contrast, dispute

contentus, a, um, *adj,* strained

contentus, a, um, *adj,* satisfied

contermĭnus, a, um, *adj,* bordering on

contĕro, trīvi, trītum, *v.t.* 3, to grind, wear away, waste

conterrĕo, *v.t.* 2, to frighten

contestor, *v.t.* 1, *dep,* to call to witness

contexo, ŭi, xtum, *v.i.t.* 3, to weave together; build, compose

contextus, ūs, *m,* connection

contĭcesco, tĭcŭi, *v.i.* 3, to be silent, cease

contignātĭo, ōnis, *f,* wooden floor

contĭgŭus, a, um, *adj,* adjoining

contĭnens, ntis, *f,* continent

contĭnens, ntis, *adj, adv,* nter, moderate, adjacent, unbroken

contĭnentĭa, ae, *f,* self-restraint

contĭnĕo, ŭi, tentum, *v.t.* 2, to keep together, contain, enclose, restrain

contingo, tĭgi, tactum, *v.i.t.* 3, to happen; touch, border on, reach

contĭnŭātĭo, ōnis, *f*, succession

contĭnŭō, *adv*, immediately

contĭnŭo, *v.t.* 1, to connect, to do one thing after another

contĭnŭus, a, um, *adj*, unbroken

contĭō, ōnis, *f*, meeting, speech

contĭōnātor, ōris, *m*, demagogue

contĭōnor, *v.* 1, *dep*, to expound

contorquĕo, torsi, tortum, *v.t.* 2, to twist, brandish, hurl

contortĭo, ōnis, *f*, twisting, intricacy

contortus, a, um, *adj*, *adv*, ē, energetic, complicated

contrā, *adv*, *prep. with acc*, opposite, facing, contrary to

contractĭo, ōnis, *f*, contraction

contractus, a, um, *adj*, compressed

contrādīco, xi, ctum, *v.t.* 3, to reply

contrādictĭo, ōnis, *f*, reply

contrăho, xi, ctum, *v.t.* 3, to bring together, shorten, produce, check

contrārĭum, ii, *n*, the contrary

contrārĭus, a, um, *adj*, *adv*, ē, opposite, injurious

contrecto, *v.t.* 1, to handle, feel

contrĕmisco, mŭi, *v.i.t.* 3, to quake; tremble at

contrĭbŭo, ŭi, ūtum, *v.t.* 3, to incorporate, unite

contristo, *v.t.* 1, to sadden, cloud

contrītus, a, um, *adj*, worn out

controversĭa, ae, *f*, dispute

controversus, a, um, *adj*, questionable

contrūcĭdo, *v.t.* 1, to slash

contŭbernālis, is, *c*, messmate

contŭbernĭum, ii, *n*, companionship

contŭĕor, *v.t.* 2, *dep*, to survey

contŭmācĭa, ae, *f*, obstinacy

contŭmax, ācis, *adj*, *adv*, ĭter, stubborn, insolent

contŭmēlĭa, ae, *f*, insult

contŭmēlĭōsus, a, um, *adj*, abusive

contŭmŭlo, *v.t.* 1, to bury

contundo, tŭdi, tūsum, *v.t.* 3, to grind, crush, subdue

conturbo, *v.t.* 1, to confuse

contus, i, *m*, pole

contūsum, i, *n*, bruise

cōnūbĭum, ĭi, *n*, marriage

cōnus, i, *m*, cone, helmet-tip

convălesco, lŭi, *v.i.* 3, to regain strength or health

convallis, is, *f*, valley

convecto, *v.t.* 1, to collect

convĕho, xi, ctum, *v.t.* 3, to bring together

convello, velli, vulsum, *v.t.* 3, to tear up

convĕnĭens, ntis, *adj*, *adv*, nter, consistent, appropriate

convĕnĭentĭa, ae, *f*, consistency, symmetry

convĕnĭo, vēni, ventum, *v.i.t.* 4, to assemble, agree with; meet

convĕnit, *impers*, it is agreed, it is right, it suits

conventum, i, *n*, agreement

conventus, ūs, *m*, meeting, assizes

conversĭo, ōnis, *f*, revolution

conversus, a, um, *adj*, reversed, turned, transposed

converto, ti, sum, *v.i.t.* 3, to turn; change, alter

convexus, a, um, *adj*, arched

convīcĭum, ii, *n*, outcry, squabbling, abuse

convictor, ōris, *m*, close friend

convictus, ūs, *m*, intimacy

convinco, vīci, victum, *v.t.* 3, to conquer, prove

convīva, ae, *c*, guest

convīvĭum, ii, *n*, dinner-party

convīvor, *v.i.* 1, *dep*, to banquet

convŏco, *v.t.* 1, to call together

convŏlo, *v.i.* 1, to flock together

convolvo, volvi, vŏlūtum, *v.t.* 3, to roll up, interweave

convulsĭo, ōnis, *f*, convulsion

convulsus, a, um, *adj*, torn-up

cŏŏpĕrĭo, rŭi, rtum, *v.t.* 4, to cover up, overwhelm

cŏŏptātĭo, ōnis, *f*, election

cŏŏpto, *v.t.* 1, to nominate, elect

cŏŏrĭor, ortus, *v.i.* 4, *dep*, to arise, break out

cōphĭnus, i, *m*, wicker basket

cōpĭa, ae, *f*, abundance, power, supply, opportunity; (*pl*) forces

cōpĭōsus, a, um, *adj*, *adv*, ē, wellsupplied, eloquent

cōpŭla, ae, *f*, thong, grappling-iron

cōpŭlo, *v.t.* 1, to link, join

cŏquo, xi, ctum, *v.t.* 3, to cook, burn, ripen, devise, harass

cŏquus, i, *m*, cook

cŏr, cordis, *n*, heart, mind

cŏrālĭum, ii, *n*, coral

cōram, *adv. and prep. with abl*, in the presence of, openly

corbis, is, *c*, basket

corbīta, ae, *f*, merchant ship

cordātus, a, um, *adj*, shrewd

cŏrĭārĭus, ii, *m*, tanner

cŏrĭum, ii, *n*, skin, hide, leather, layer, stratum

cornĕus, a, um, *adj*, horny

cornĕus, a, um, *adj*, of cornel-wood

cornĭcen, ĭnis, *m*, horn-player

cornĭcŭla, ae, *f*, jackdaw

cornĭcŭlum, ĭ, *n*, little horn, feeler

cornĭger, ĕra, ĕrum, *adj*, horned

cornĭpēs, ĕdis, *adj*, hoofed

cornix, ĭcis, *f*, crow

cornū, ūs, *n*, horn, hoof, beak, tributary, promontory, knob, wing of army, bow, trumpet, drinking horn

cornum, ĭ, *n*, cornel-cherry

cornus, ĭ, *f*, cornel-cherry tree, cornelwood javelin

cŏrōna, ae, *f*, garland, wreath, crown, ring, circle, crowd

cŏrōno, *v.t.* 1, to crown, encircle

corpŏrĕus, a, um, *adj*, physical

corpŭlentus, a, um, *adj*, corpulent

corpus, ōris, *n*, body

correctĭo, ōnis, *f*, improvement

corrector, ōris, *m*, reformer

correpo, psi, *v.i.* 3, to creep

corrigia, ae, *f*, shoe-lace

corrigo, rexi, ctum, *v.t.* 3, to put right, improve

corripĭo, pŭi, reptum, *v.t.* 3, to snatch, plunder, attack, shorten

corrōbŏro, *v.t.* 1, to strengthen

corrūgo, *v.t.* 1, to wrinkle

corrumpo, rūpi, ptum, *v.t.* 3, to destroy, corrupt, spoil

corrŭo, ŭi, *v.i.t.* 3, to collapse; overthrow

corruptēla, ae, *f*, corruption

corruptor, ōris, *m*, corruptor, seducer

corruptus, a, um, *adj*, *adv*, ē, spoiled, damaged, tainted

cortex, ĭcis, *m*, bark, rind

cortĭna, ae, *f*, kettle, cauldron

cŏrusco, *v.i.t.* 1, to glitter; shake

cŏruscus, a, um, *adj*, glittering, vibrating

corvus, ĭ, *m*, raven

cŏrўlus, ĭ, *f*, hazel shrub

cŏrymbus, ĭ, *m*, cluster of fruit or flowers

cŏrўtŏs, ĭ, *m*, quiver

cōs, cōtis, *f*, flintstone

costa, ae, *f*, rib, wall

cōthurnus, ĭ, *m*, hunting-boot, buskin (worn by tragic actors)

cottĭdĭānus, a, um, *adj*, *adv*, ō, daily, usual

cottĭdĭē, *adv*, daily

cŏturnix, ĭcis, *f*, quail

coxendix, ĭcis, *f*, hip

crabro, ōnis, *m*, hornet

crambē, es, *f*, cabbage, kale

crāpŭla, ae, *f*, intoxication

crās, *adv*, tomorrow

crassĭtūdo, ĭnis, *f*, thickness

crassus, a, um, *adj*, *adv*, ē, thick, fat, solid

crastĭnus, a, um, *adj*, of tomorrow

crātēr, ēris, *m*, mixing-bowl, basin

crātēra, ae, *f*, mixing-bowl, basin

crātĭcŭla, ae, *f*, gridiron

crātis, is, *f*, wicker-work, hurdle

crĕatĭo, ōnis, *f*, appointing

crĕator, ōris, *m*, founder, creator

crĕatrix, ĭcis, *f*, mother

crēber, bra, brum, *adj*, *adv*, o, thick, numerous, repeated

crēbresco, brŭi, *v.i.* 3, to become frequent, gain strength

crēdens, ntis, *c*, believer

crēdĭbĭlis, e, *adj*, *adv*, ĭter, credible, probable

crēdĭtor, ōris, *m*, creditor

crēdo, dĭdi, dĭtum, *v.t.* 3, to lend, entrust, trust, believe in (*with dat*); suppose

crēdŭlĭtas, ātis, *f*, credulity

crēdŭlus, a, um, *adj*, ready to believe

crĕmo, *v.t.* 1, to burn

crĕo, *v.t.* 1, to produce, appoint

crĕpĭda, ae, *f*, sandal

crĕpĭdo, ĭnis, *f*, pedestal, dike

crĕpĭtācŭlum, ĭ, *n*, rattle

crĕpĭto, *v.i.* 1, to rattle, rustle

crĕpĭtus, ūs, *m*, rattling, clashing, cracking

crĕpo, ŭi, ĭtum, *v.i.t.* 1, to rattle, creak, jingle; prattle about

crĕpundia, ōrum, *n.pl*, child's rattle

crĕpuscŭlum, ĭ, *n*, twilight, dusk

cresco, crēvi, crētum, *v.i.* 3, to arise, grow, appear, thrive

crēta, ae, *f*, chalk

crētus, a, um, *adj*, arisen, born of

crībro, *v.t.* 1, to sift

crībrum, ĭ, *n*, sieve

crimen, ĭnis, *n*, accusation, offence

crĭmĭnātĭo, ōnis, *f*, accusation, calumny

crĭmĭnor, *v.t.* 1, *dep*, to accuse

crĭmĭnōsus, a, um, *adj*, *adv*, ē, slanderous, culpable

crīnālis, e, *adj*, of the hair

crīnis, is, *m*, the hair

crīnītus, a, um, *adj*, long-haired

crispo, *v.i.t.* 1, to curl; brandish

crispus, a, um, *adj*, curled, quivering

crista, ae, *f*, crest, plume

cristātus, a, um, *adj*, crested

crĭtĭcus, ĭ, *m*, critic

crŏcĕus, a, um, *adj*, of saffron or yellow

crŏcĭo, *v.i.* 4, to croak

crŏcŏdīlus, ĭ, *m*, crocodile

crŏcus, i, m (um, i, n), crocus

crŭciātus, ūs, m, torture, pain

crŭcio, v.t. 1, to torture

crūdēlis, e, adj, adv, iter, cruel

crūdēlitas, ātis, f, cruelty

crūdesco, dŭi, v.i. 3, to get worse

crūditas, ātis, f, indigestion

crūdus, a, um, adj, raw, fresh, unripe, cruel

crŭento, v.t. 1, to stain with blood

crŭentus, a, um, adj, blood-stained, blood-thirsty

crŭmēna, ae, f, small purse

crŭor, ōris, m, blood (from a wound), murder

crūs, ūris, n, leg, shin

crusta, ae, f, crust, bark, mosaic

crustūlārius, ii, m, confectioner

crustūlum, i, n, confectionery

crustum, i, n, confectionery

crux, ŭcis, f, cross

crypta, ae, f, cloister, vault

crystallum, i, n, crystal

cŭbicŭlārius, ii, m, chamber-servant

cŭbicŭlum, i, n, bedroom

cŭbicus, a, um, adj, cubic

cŭbile, is, n, bed, lair

cŭbĭtal, ālis, n, cushion

cŭbĭtum, i, n, elbow

cŭbĭtus, i, m, elbow

cŭbĭtum, see cŭbo

cŭbo, ŭi, ĭtum, v.i. 1, to lie down, sleep, lie ill, slant

cŭcullus, i, m, hood

cŭcŭlus, i, m, cuckoo

cŭcŭmis, ēris, m, cucumber

cŭcurbita, ae, f, cup

cūdo, v.t. 3, to beat, strike, stamp

cŭius, a, um, interr. adj, whose?

cŭius, genit, of qui, quis

culcita, ae, f, mattress, cushion

cŭlex, icis, m, gnat, mosquito

cŭlīna, ae, f, kitchen, food

cullěus, i, m, leather bag

culmen, ĭnis, n, summit, roof

culmus, i, m, stem, stalk

culpa, ae, f, blame, fault, weakness

culpābĭlis, e, adj, culpable

culpandus, a, um, adj, culpable

culpo, v.t. 1, to blame

culter, tri, m, knife, ploughshare

cultor, ōris, m, cultivator, supporter, inhabitant

cultrix, icis, f, female inhabitant

cultūra, ae, f, cultivation, care

cultus, a, um, adj, cultivated, elegant

cultus, ūs, m, farming, education, culture-pattern, reverence, dress

cŭlullus, i, m, drinking-cup

cum, conj, when, whenever, since, al-

though, cum ... tum, both ... and, not only ... but also

cum, prep. with abl, with, together with; it is attached to the abl. case of personal prons, e.g. mecum, with me

cumba, ae, f, small boat

cŭmĕra, ae, f, box, chest

cŭmĭnum, i, n, cumin (plant)

cumquě, adv, however, whenever

cŭmŭlātus, a, um, adj, adv, ē, full, increased

cŭmŭlo, v.t. 1, to heap up, complete

cŭmŭlus, i, m, heap, "last straw"

cūnābŭla, ōrum, n.pl, cradle

cūnae, ārum, f. pl, cradle

cunctans, ntis, adj, adv, nter, loitering, sluggish

cunctātio, ōnis, f, delay, doubt

cunctātor, ōris, m, loiterer, cautious person

cunctor, v.i. 1, dep, to hesitate, delay

cunctus, a, um, adj, all together

cŭnĕātim, adv, wedge-shaped

cŭnĕo, v.t. 1, to fasten with wedges

cŭnĕus, i, m, wedge, wedge-shaped block of theatre-seats or troopformation

cūnĭcŭlum, i, n, tunnel, mine

cūnĭcŭlus, i, m, rabbit

cūpa, ae, f, barrel, cask

cūpēdia, ōrum, n.pl, delicacies

cŭpĭdē, adv, eagerly

cŭpĭdĭtas, ātis, f, desire, longing

cŭpĭdo, ĭnis, f, lust, greed

cŭpĭdus, a, um, adj, eager, longing for, greedy, passionate

cŭpiens, ntis, adj, adv, nter, eager or longing for

cŭpĭo, ivi, ĭtum, v.t. 3, to desire

cŭpressus, i, f, cypress tree

cūr, adv, why

cūra, ae, f, care, attention, management, anxiety

cūrātio, ōnis, f, administration, cure

cūrātor, ōris, m, manager

cūrātus, a, um, adj, urgent

curcŭlio, ōnis, m, weevil

cūria, ae, f, senate-house, city-ward

cūriālis, e, adj, of the same ward

cūriōsus, a, um, adj, adv, e, careful, inquisitive

cūro, v.t. 1, to take care of; with acc. and gerundive, to see to it that ... to arrange, command

currĭcŭlum, i, n, race-course, chariot, racing, career

curro, cŭcurri, cursum, v.i. 3, to run

currus, ūs, m, chariot

cursim, adv, swiftly

For List of Abbreviations used, turn to pages 3, 4

curso, *v.i.* 1, to run to and fro

cursor, ōris, *m*, runner, courier

cursus, ūs, *m*, running, journey, speed, direction

curtus, a, um, *adj*, shortened, humble

cŭrūlis, e, *adj*, of a chariot; **sella cŭrūlis**, ivory chair of office used by high magistrates

curvāmen, ĭnis, *n*, curve

curvo, *v.t.* 1, to bend

curvus, a, um, *adj*, bent, stooping

cuspis, ĭdis, *f*, point, lance, spit, sting

custōdĭa, ae, *f*, watch, guard, imprisonment, guard-room

custōdĭo, *v.t.* 4, to guard, watch, keep, preserve

custos, ōdis, *c*, guardian, goaler

cŭtis, is, *f*, skin, surface

cўăthus, i, *m*, small ladle

cўcnēus, a, um, *adj*, of a swan

cўcnus, i, *m*, swan

cўlindrus, i, *m*, roller, cylinder

cymba, ae, *f*, small boat

cymbălum, i, *n*, cymbal, bell

cymbĭum, ii, *n*, bowl, basin

Cўnĭcus, i, *m*, a Cynic philosopher

cўpărissus, i, *f*, cypress tree

D

dactўlus, i, *m*, dactyl (metrical foot consisting of 1 long and 2 short syllables)

daedălus, a, um, *adj*, skilful

daemŏnĭum, ii, *n*, demon

damma (dāma), ae, *f*, deer

damnātĭo, ōnis, *f*, condemnation

damnātōrĭus, a, um, *adj*, condemnatory

damnātus, a, um, *adj*, guilty

damno, *v.t.* 1, to condemn

damnōsus, a, um, *adj*, *adv*, e, destructive

damnum, i, *n*, damage, loss, fine

daps, dăpis, *f*, formal banquet

dătĭo, ōnis, *f*, distribution

dător, ōris, *m*, giver

dē, *prep. with abl*, from, down from, about, concerning, on account of

dĕa, ae, *f*, goddess

dĕalbo, *v.t.* 1, to whitewash

dĕambŭlo, *v.i.* 1, to take a walk

dĕarmo, *v.t.* 1, to disarm

dēbacchor, *v.i.* 1, *dep*, to rage

dēbellātor, ōris, *m*, conqueror

dēbello, *v.t.* 1, to finish a war; subdue

dēbĕo, *v.i.t.* 2, to be indebted; owe, (one) ought

dēbĭlis, e, *adj*, disabled, weak

dēbĭlĭtas, ātis, *f*, weakness

dēbĭlĭtātĭo, ōnis, *f*, maiming, enervating

dēbĭlĭto, *v.t.* 1, to cripple, weaken

dēbĭtor, ōris, *m*, debtor

dēbĭtum, i, *n*, debt

dēbĭtus, a, um, *adj*, owed

dēcanto, *v.i.* 1, to sing repeatedly

dēcēdo, ssi, ssum, *v.i.* 3, to go away, cease, yield, resign

dĕcem, *indecl. adj*, ten

December (mensis), December

dĕcempĕda, ae, *f*, measuring rod (ten feet long)

dĕcempĕdātor, ōris, *m*, surveyor

dĕcemvirālis, e, *adj*, of the decemviri

dĕcemvirātus, ūs, *m*, the rank of decemvir

dĕcemviri, ōrum, *m.pl*, commission of ten (early rulers of Rome)

dĕcens, ntis, *adj*, *adv*, nter, proper, graceful

dĕcentĭa, ae, *f*, comeliness

dēceptus, a, um, *adj*, deceived

dēcerno, crēvi, crētum, *v.i.t.* 3, to decide, resolve; fight

dēcerpo, psi, ptum, *v.t.* 3, to pluck, gather

dēcertātĭo, ōnis, *f*, struggle

dēcerto, *v.i.t.* 1, to fight it out; struggle for

dēcessĭo, ōnis, *f*, departure

dēcessus, ūs, *m*, departure

dĕcet, cŭit, *v.* 2, *impers*, it is becoming or proper

dēcĭdo, cĭdi, *v.i.* 3, to fall down, die, perish

dēcīdo, cĭdi, cīsum, *v.t.* 3, to cut off, settle

dĕcĭēs (dĕcĭens), *adv*, ten times

dĕcĭma, ae, *f*, tenth part, tithe

dĕcĭmānus, a, um, *adj*, of tithes, of the tenth legion; **porta dĕcĭmāna**, main camp-gate

dĕcĭmo, *v.t.* 1, to punish every tenth man, decimate

dĕcĭmus, a, um, *adj*, tenth

dēcĭpĭo, cēpi, ptum, *v.t.* 3, to deceive

dēcĭsĭo, ōnis, *f*, decision

dēclāmātĭo, ōnis, *f*, practice in public speaking

dēclāmātor, ōris, *m*, speech-expert

dēclāmātōrĭus, a, um, *adj*, rhetorical

dēclāmo, *v.i.* 1, to practise speaking

dēclāro, *v.t.* 1, to make clear

dēclīnātĭo, ōnis, *f*, avoidance, bending

dēclīno, *v.i.t.* 1, to turn aside

dēclīve, is, *n*, slope

dēclīvis, e, *adj*, sloping downwards

dēclīvitas, ātis, *f*, slope

dēcoctor, ōris, *m*, bankrupt

dēcoctus, a, um, *adj*, boiled, refined

dēcŏlor, ōris, *adj*, discoloured

dēcŏlōro, *v.t.* 1, to discolour

dēcŏquo, xi, ctum, *v.t.* 3, to boil down, go bankrupt

dĕcor, ōris, *m*, elegance

dĕcŏro, *v.t.* 1, to adorn

dĕcōrum, i, *n*, decency

dĕcōrus, a, um, *adj*, *adv*, ē, becoming, proper, elegant

dēcrĕpitus, a, um, *adj*, decrepit

dēcresco, crēvi, tum, *v.i.* 3, to diminish, wane

dēcrētum, i, *n*, decree, decision

dĕcŭma, dĕcŭmānus, see decim . . .

dēcumbo, cŭbŭi, *v.i.* 3, to lie down, lie ill

dĕcŭria, ae, *f*, section of ten

dĕcŭrio, *v.t.* 1, to divide into sections

dĕcŭrio, ōnis, *m*, the head of ten, superintendent

dēcurro, cŭcurri, cursum, *v.i.* 3, to run down, complete a course, manoeuvre, have recourse to

dēcursus, ūs, *m*, descent, course, manoeuvre, attack

dĕcus, ōris, *n*, ornament, splendour

dēcussātio, ōnis, *f*, intersection

dēcŭtio, cussi, ssum, *v.t.* 3, to shake off, beat off

dēdĕcet, cŭit, *v.* 2, *impers*, it is unbecoming

dēdĕcŏro, *v.t.* 1, to disgrace

dēdĕcus, ōris, *n*, disgrace, shame

dēdĭcātio, ōnis, *f*, dedication

dēdĭco, *v.t.* 1, to dedicate

dēdignor, *v.t.* 1, *dep*, to disdain

dēdisco, dĭdĭci, *v.t.* 3, to forget

dēdĭtĭcius, ii, *m*, prisoner-of-war

dēdĭtio, ōnis, *f*, surrender

dēdĭtus, a, um, *adj*, addicted to

dēdo, dēdĭdi, dĭtum, *v.t.* 3, to give up, surrender, devote

dēdŏcĕo, *v.t.* 2, to teach one not to . . .

dēdŏlĕo, *v.i.* 2, to stop grieving

dēdūco, xi, ctum, *v.t.* 3, to bring, lead down, withdraw, conduct, escort, mislead, subtract, launch

dēductio, ōnis, *f*, diversion, transplanting, inference

dēductus, a, um, *adj*, fine-spun

dēerro, *v.i.* 1, to go astray

dēfătīgātio, ōnis, *f*, exhaustion

dēfătīgo, *v.t.* 1, to exhaust

dēfectio, ōnis, *f*, rebellion, failure, eclipse

dēfectus, ūs, *m*, rebellion, failure, eclipse

dēfectus, a, um, *adj*, worn out

dēfendo, di, sum, *v.t.* 3, to repel, defend, support

dēfensio, ōnis, *f*, defence

dēfensor, ōris, *m*, protector

dēfĕro, ferre, tŭli, lātum, *v.t. irreg*, to bring down or away, convey, refer, announce, indict, offer

dēfervesco, fervi, *v.i.* 3, to cool down

dēfessus, a, um, *adj*, weary

dēfĕtiscor, fessus, *v.i.* 3, *dep*, to grow tired

dēficio, fēci, fectum, *v.i.t.* 3, to fail, disappear, revolt; desert

dēfigo, xi, xum, *v.t.* 3, to fasten down, astound

dēfingo, nxi, *v.t.* 3, to shape

dēfinio, *v.t.* 4, to mark off, restrict, define

dēfinitio, ōnis, *f*, definition

dēfinitus, a, um, *adj*, *adv*, ē, precise

dēfixus, a, um, *adj*, fixed

dēflăgrātio, ōnis, *f*, destruction by fire

dēflăgro, *v.i.* 1, to burn out

dēflecto, xi, xum, *v.i.t.* 3, to swerve; divert

dēflĕo, ēvi, ētum, *v.t.* 2, to deplore

dēflōresco, rŭi, *v.i.* 3, to wither

dēflŭo, xi, xum, *v.i.* 3, to flow down, vanish

dēfŏdio, fōdi, ssum, *v.t.* 3, to dig deep, bury

dēfŏre, *fut. infinitive* (dēsum)

dēformis, e, *adj*, deformed, ugly

dēformĭtas, ātis, *f*, ugliness

dēformo, *v.t.* 1, to shape

dēformo, *v.t.* 1, to disfigure

dēfossus, a, um, *adj*, buried

dēfraudo, *v.t.* 1, to cheat

dēfrico, cŭi, ctum, *v.t.* 1, to rub hard

dēfringo, frēgi, fractum, *v.t.* 3, to break up, break off

dēfrŭtum, i, *n*, syrup

dēfŭgio, fūgi, *v.i.t.* 3, to escape; avoid

dēfunctus, a, um, *adj*, having finished, deceased

dēfundo, fūdi, fūsum, *v.t.* 3, to pour out

dēfungor, functus, *v.* 3, *dep. with abl*, to bring to an end

dēgĕner, ĕris, *adj*, unworthy of one's birth, ignoble

dēgĕnĕro, *v.i.t.* 1, to deteriorate; impair

dēgo, dēgi, *v.i.t.* 3, to live; spend

dēgrandinat, *v. impers*, it is hailing, ceasing to hail

dēgrăvo, *v.t.* 1, to weigh down

dēgrĕdĭor, gressus, *v.i.* 3, *dep*, to step down, dismount

dēgusto, *v.t.* 1, to taste, graze

dēhinc, *adv*, from here, hence, next, afterwards

dēhisco, hīvi, *v.i.* 3, to split open, gape

dēhŏnesto, *v.t.* 1, to disgrace

dēhortor, *v.t.* 1, *dep*, to dissuade

dēĭcĭo, lēci, iectum, *v.t.* 3, to throw down, drive out, lower

dēiectus, a, um, *adj*, downcast

dēiectus, ūs, *m*, descent, felling

dēin, *adv*, from there, after that, afterwards

dēindĕ, *adv*, from there, after that, afterwards

dēinceps, *adv*, in succession

dēlābor, lapsus, *v.i.* 3, *dep*, to fall, sink, glide down

dēlasso, *v.t.* 1, to tire out

dēlātĭo, ōnis, *f*, accusation

dēlātor, ōris, *m*, informer

dēlectābĭlis, e, *adj*, delightful

dēlectātĭo, ōnis, *f*, delight, pleasure

dēlecto, *v.t.* 1, to allure, charm

dēlectus, a, um, *adj*, chosen

dēlectus, ūs, *m*, choice, selection, levy

dēlectum hăbēre, to hold a levy

dēlēgo, *v.t.* 1, to dispatch, assign, attribute

dēlēnimentum, i, *n*, allurement

dēlēnĭo, *v.t.* 4, to soothe, charm

dēlĕo, lēvi, lētum, *v.t.* 2, to destroy, finish

dēlībērātĭo, ōnis, *f*, careful thought

dēlībērātus, a, um, *adj*, settled

dēlībĕro, *v.t.* 1, to consider, consult, resolve

dēlībo, *v.t.* 1, to taste, pluck, detract from

dēlībūtus, a, um, *adj*, smeared

dēlĭcātus, a, um, *adj, adv*, e, charming, luxurious

dēlĭcĭae, ārum, *f. pl*, pleasure, luxury, sweetheart, pet

dēlictum, i, *n*, crime, offence

dēlĭgo, lēgi, lectum, *v.t.* 3, to pick, choose, gather

dēlĭgo, *v.t.* 1, to tie down

dēlinquo, līqui, lictum, *v.i.* 3, to fail, offend

dēlīrātĭo, ōnis, *f*, silliness

dēlīrium, ii, *n*, delirium

dēlīro, *v.i.* 1, to be out of one's mind

dēlīrus, a, um, *adj*, crazy

dēlĭtesco, tŭi, *v.i.* 3, to lurk

delphīnus, i, *m*, dolphin

dēlūbrum, i, *n*, sanctuary

dēlūdo, si, sum, *v.t.* 3, to mock

dēmando, *v.t.* 1, to entrust

dēmens, ntis, *adj, adv*, nter, out of one's mind

dēmensum, i, *n*, ration

dēmentia, ae, *f*, insanity

dēmĕrĕo, *v.t.* 2, to deserve, oblige

dēmergo, si, sum, *v.t.* 3, to immerse, sink

dēmētĭor, mensus, *v.t.* 4, *dep*, to measure off

dēmēto, messŭi, ssum, *v.t.* 3, to mow, reap, gather

dēmigro, *v.i.* 1, to emigrate

dēminŭo, ŭi, ūtum, *v.t.* 3, to lessen, infringe

dēminūtĭo, ōnis, *f*, decrease

dēmīror, *v.t.* 1, *dep*, to wonder

dēmissĭo, ōnis, *f*, abasement

dēmissus, a, um, *adj, adv*, ē, low-lying, drooping, downcast, shy

dēmitto, mīsi, ssum, *v.t.* 3, to send down, lower, descend, enter upon, lose heart

dēmo, mpsi, mptum, *v.t.* 3, to take away, remove

dēmōlĭor, *v.t.* 4, *dep*, to pull down, destroy

dēmonstrātĭo, ōnis, *f*, indication

dēmonstro, *v.t.* 1, to point out

dēmŏrĭor, mortŭus, *v.i.* 3, *dep*, to die

dēmŏror, *v.i.t.* 1, *dep*, to loiter; restrain

dēmŏvĕo, mōvi, mōtum, *v.t.* 2, to remove, put aside

dēmum, *adv*, at last, not until then, only

dēmūto, *v.i.t.* 1, to change

dēnārius, ii, *m*, small Roman silver coin

dēnāto, *v.i.* 1, to swim down

dēnĕgo, *v.t.* 1, to deny completely

dēni, ae, a, *adj*, ten each, ten

dēnĭque, *adv*, and then, at last, in short

dēnōmĭno, *v.t.* 1, to name

dēnormo, *v.t.* 1, to disfigure

dēnŏto, *v.t.* 1, to mark out, point out

dens, ntis, *m*, tooth, prong

denso, *v.t.* 1, to thicken, close up

densus, a, um, *adj*, thick, frequent

dentālĭa, ĭum, *n.pl*, plough-beam

dentātus, a, um, *adj*, with teeth

dentifrĭcium, ii, *n*, tooth-powder

dentĭo, *v.i.* 4, to teethe

dentītĭo, ōnis, *f*, teething

dentiscalpium, ii, *n*, toothpick

dēnūbo, psi, ptum, *v.i.* 3, to marry

dēnūdo, *v.t.* 1, to lay bare

dēnuntĭātĭo, ōnis, *f*, declaration

dēnuntĭo, *v.t.* 1, to announce, command, warn

dēnŭŏ, *adv*, anew, again

dĕorsum, *adv*, downwards

dēpāciscor, see dēpĕciscor

dēpasco, pāvi, pastum, *v.t.* 3, to feed on, consume

dēpĕciscor, pectus (pactus), *v.t.* 3, *dep*, to bargain for

dēpĕcūlor, *v.t.* 1, *dep*, to plunder

dēpello, pŭli, pulsum, *v.t.* 3, to drive away, dissuade

dēpendĕo, *v.i.* 2, to hang down, depend on

dēpendo, di, sum, *v.t.* 3, to spend, pay

dēperdo, dĭdi, dĭtum, *v.t.* 3, to destroy, lose

dēpĕrĕo, *v.i.* 4, to perish completely, die with love for

dēpingo, pinxi, pictum, *v.t.* 3, to paint, portray, sketch

dēplōro, *v.i.t.* 1, to lament; deplore

dēpōno, pŏsŭi, pŏsitum, *v.t.* 3, to put aside, entrust, bet, get rid of

dēpŏpŭlātio, ōnis, *f*, pillaging

dēpŏpŭlor, *v.t.* 1, *dep*, to plunder

dēporto, *v.t.* 1, to carry down, carry away, banish, earn

dēposco, pŏposci, *v.t.* 3, to demand, challenge

dēpŏsĭtum, i, *n*, deposit, trust

dēprāvātio, ōnis, *f*, corruption

dēprāvo, *v.t.* 1, to pervert, corrupt

dēprĕcātio, ōnis, *f*, pleading, intercession

dēprĕcātor, ōris, *m*, pleader

dēprĕcor, *v.t.* 1, *dep*, to avert by prayer, beseech, plead for

dēprĕhendo, di, sum, *v.t.* 3, to catch, overtake, discover

dēpressus, a, um, *adj*, low-lying

dēprimo, pressi, pressum, *v.t.* 3, to press down, sink, suppress

dēproelior, *v.i.* 1, *dep*, to battle fiercely

dēprōmo, mpsi, mptum, *v.t.* 3, to fetch out

dēprŏpĕro, *v.i.t.* 1, to hasten; prepare hastily

dēpugno, *v.i.* 1, to fight it out

dēpulsio, ōnis, *f*, warding off

dēpŭto, *v.t.* 1, to prune

dērēlinquo, līqui, lictum, *v.t.* 3, to abandon completely

dērīdĕo, si, sum, *v.t.* 2, to mock

dērigesco, gŭi, *v.i.* 3, to stiffen

dērĭpio, rĭpŭi, reptum, *v.t.* 3, to tear off, pull down

dērīsor, ōris, *m*, scoffer

dērīvātio, ōnis, *f*, turning off

dērīvo, *v.t.* 1, to divert water

dērŏgo, *v.t.* 1, to remove, restrict

dērōsus, a, um, *adj*, nibbled

dēruptus, a, um, *adj*, broken, steep

dēsaevio, *v.i.* 4, to rage

dēscendo, di, sum, *v.i.* 3, to go down, come down, go into battle, penetrate, resort to

dēscensus, ūs, *m*, descent

dēscisco, īvi, ītum, *v.i.* 3, to revolt, desert, degenerate

dēscrībo, psi, ptum, *v.t.* 3, to transcribe, describe, define, arrange

dēscripta, ōrum, *n.pl*, records

dēscriptio, ōnis, *f*, sketch, description, arrangement

dēsĕco, cŭi, ctum, *v.t.* 1, to cut off

dēsĕro, rŭi, rtum, *v.t.* 3, to abandon

dēserta, ōrum, *n.pl*, desert

dēsertor, ōris, *m*, deserter

dēsertus, a, um, *adj*, abandoned

dēservio, *v.i.* 4, to serve wholeheartedly

dēses, ĭdis, *adj*, indolent

dēsĭdĕo, sēdi, *v.i.* 2, to sit idle

dēsīdĕrium, ii, *n*, longing, grief, request

dēsīdĕro, *v.t.* 1, to miss, crave for

dēsĭdia, ae, *f*, idleness

dēsĭdĭōsus, a, um, *adj*, lazy

dēsīdo, sēdi, *v.i.* 3, to sink down

dēsignātio, ōnis, *f*, description, arrangement

dēsignātor, ōris, *m*, master of ceremonies, undertaker

dēsignātus, a, um, *adj*, elect

dēsigno, *v.t.* 1, to mark out, indicate, appoint

dēsĭlio, silŭi, sultum, *v.i.* 4, to jump down

dēsĭno, sĭi, ĭtum, *v.i.t.* 3, to cease; put an end to

dēsĭpio, *v.i.* 3, to be foolish

dēsisto, stĭti, stĭtum, *v.i.* 3, to leave off, halt

dēsōlātus, a, um, *adj*, forsaken

dēsōlo, *v.t.* 1, to abandon

dēspecto, *v.t.* 1, to look down on

dēspectus, ūs, *m*, view down on

dēspectus, a, um, *adj*, despicable

dēspērātio, ōnis, *f*, hopelessness

dēspērātus, a, um, *adj*, past hope

dēspēro, *v.i.t.* 1, to despair; give up as lost

dēspĭcio, exi, ctum, *v.i.t.* 3, to look down; despise

dēspŏlio, *v.t.* 1, to plunder

dēspondĕo, di, nsum, *v.t.* 2, to promise (in marriage)

dēspūmo, *v.t.* 1, to skim off

dēspŭo, *v.i.t.* 3, to spit; reject

dēstillo, *v.i.* 3, to trickle, drip

dēstĭnātio, ōnis, *f*, purpose

For List of Abbreviations used, turn to pages 3, 4

dēstǐnātum, ǐ, *n*, aim, intention

dēstǐnātus, a, um, *adj*, fixed

dēstǐno, *v.t.* 1, to secure, intend

dēstǐtǔo, ǔǐ, ǔtum, *v.t.* 3, to place, desert

dēstǐtūtus, a, um, *adj*, abandoned

dēstringo, nxǐ, ctum, *v.t.* 3, to strip off, unsheath, graze

dēstrǔo, xǐ, ctum, *v.t.* 3, to demolish

dēsǔesco, sǔēvǐ, sǔētum, *v.i.t.* 3, to become unused; cease to use

dēsǔētus, a, um, *adj*, disused

dēsultor, ōris, *m*, acrobat on horseback

dēsum, dēesse, dēfǔǐ, *v.i*, to be lacking, fail, lack

dēsūmo, mpsǐ, mptum, *v.t.* 3, to select

dēsǔpěr, *adv*, from above

dēsurgo, *v.i.* 3, to rise from

dētěgo, xǐ, ctum, *v.t.* 3, to expose

dētentus, a, um, *adj*, kept back

dētergěo, sǐ, sum, *v.t.* 2, to wipe clean

dētěrior, ius, *adj*, lower, worse

dētěrius, *adv*, worse, less

dētermǐno, *v.t.* 1, to fix limits

dētěro, trǐvǐ, trǐtum, *v.t.* 3, to rub or wear away, impair

dēterrěo, *v.t.* 2, to discourage

dētestābǐlis, e, *adj*, detestable

dētestātǐo, ōnis, *f*, cursing

dētestor, *v.t.* 1, *dep*, to curse, loathe, ward off

dētexo, xǔǐ, xtum, *v.t.* 3, to weave, finish

dētǐněo, tǐnǔǐ, tentum, *v.t.* 2, to keep back, delay, lengthen

dētǒno, ǔǐ, *v.i.* 1, to thunder, cease thundering

dētorquěo, sǐ, tum, *v.t.* 2, to turn aside, distort

dētrǎho, xǐ, ctum, *v.t.* 3, to pull down, remove, deprecate

dētrecto, *v.t.* 1, to reject, detract from

dētrǐmentum, ǐ, *n*, loss, damage, defeat

dētrūdo, sǐ, sum, *v.t.* 3, to push down, dislodge

dētrunco, *v.t.* 1, to lop off

dēturbo, *v.t.* 1, to throw down

dēǔro, ussǐ, ustum, *v.t.* 3, to burn

děus, ǐ, *m*, god

dēvasto, *v.t.* 1, to devastate

dēvěho, xǐ, ctum, *v.t.* 3, to carry down, carry away

dēvěnǐo, věnǐ, ventum, *v.i.* 4, to come down, arrive at

dēversor, *vi.* 1, *dep*, to lodge

dēversor, ōris, *m*, lodger

dēversōrǐum, ǐǐ, *n*, inn

dēverto, tǐ, sum, *v.i.t.* 3, to lodge, stay; turn aside

dēvexus, a, um, *adj*, sloping down

dēvia, ōrum, *n.pl*, lonely places

dēvincǐo, nxǐ, nctum, *v.t.* 4, to tie up, endear

dēvinco, vǐcǐ, ctum, *v.t.* 3, to conquer completely

dēvinctus, see dēvincǐo

dēvǐto, *v.t.* 1, to avoid

dēvǐus, a, um, *adj*, out-of-the-way

dēvǒco, *v.t.* 1, to call away

dēvǒlo, *v.i.* 1, to fly down

dēvolvo, volvǐ, vǒlūtum, *v.t.* 3, to roll down

dēvǒro, *v.t.* 1, to gulp down

dēvōtǐo, ōnis, *f*, consecration

dēvōtus, a, um, *adj*, devoted

dēvǒvěo, vōvǐ, vōtum, *v.t.* 2, to dedicate, doom, devote

dexter, těra, těrum (tra, trum), *adj*, on the right, skilful, suitable

dextěra (dextra), ae, *f*, right hand

dextěritas, ātis, *f*, dexterity

dextrorsum, *adv*, to the right

dǐ, *pl.* of děus

dǐādēma, ătis, *n*, crown, diadem

dǐāgōnālis, e, *adj*, diagonal

dǐālecticus, a, um, *adj*, of debate

dǐālǒgus, ǐ, *m*, conversation

dǐārǐa, ōrum, *n.pl*, rations

dǐca, ae, *f*, lawsuit

dǐcācǐtas, ātis, *f*, wit

dǐcax, ācis, *adj*, witty

dǐcǐo, ōnis, *f*, dominion, power

dǐco, *v.t.* 1, to dedicate, devote

dǐco, xǐ, ctum, *v.t.* 3, to say, tell, appoint

dicta, see dictum

dictāta, ōrum, *n.pl*, written exercises

dictātǐo, ōnis, *f*, dictation

dictātor, ōris, *m*, dictator (Roman magistrate appointed in emergencies)

dictātūra, ae, *f*, dictatorship

dictǐo, ōnis, *f*, speaking, style

dictǐto, *v.t.* 1, to repeat, dictate, compose

dicto, *v.t.* 1, to declare, dictate

dictum, ǐ, *n*, saying, proverb, order

dictus, a, um, *adj*, said, told

dīdo, dīdǐdǐ, dīdǐtum, *v.t.* 3, to distribute

dīdūco, xǐ, ctum, *v.t.* 3, to divide, scatter

dǐēs, dǐēǐ, *m*, *f*, day

diffěro, differre, distǔlǐ, dīlātum, *v.i.t.*, *irreg*, to differ; scatter, publish, defer

differtus, a, um, *adj,* crowded

diffíbŭlo, *v.t.* 1, to unbuckle

difficilis, e, *adj, adv,* **ē, iter,** difficult, surly

difficultas, ātis, *f,* difficulty, obstinacy

diffidens, ntis, *adj,* distrustful

diffidentia, ae, *f,* mistrust, despair

diffído, físus sum, *v.i.* 3, *semi-dep. with dative,* to mistrust, despair

diffindo, fídi, físum, *v.t.* 3, to split, divide

diffingo, *v.t.* 3, to re-shape

diffítĕor, *v.t.* 2, *dep,* to deny

difflŭo, *v.i.* 3, to flow away

diffŭgio, fŭgi, *v.i.* 3, to disperse

diffundo, fŭdi, fŭsum, *v.t.* 3, to pour out, scatter

diffŭsus, a, um, *adj, adv,* **ē,** spread out, wide

dĭgĕro, gessi, gestum, *v.t.* 3, to separate, arrange, interpret

dĭgesta, ōrum, *n.pl,* digest of writings

dĭgitus, i, *m,* finger, toe, inch

dĭglădior, *v.i.* 1, *dep,* to fight fiercely

dignātio, ōnis, *f,* reputation

dignitas, ātis, *f,* worthiness, rank, authority

dignor, *v.t.* 1, *dep,* to consider someone worthy

dignus, a, um, *adj, adv,* **ē,** *with abl,* worthy, suitable

dĭgrĕdior, gressus, *v.i.* 3, *dep,* to go away

dĭgressio, ōnis, *f,* digression

dĭgressus, ūs, *m,* departure

dĭiūdico, *v.t.* 1, to decide

diiun . . . see **disiun . . .**

dīlābor, lapsus, *v.i.* 3, *dep,* to dissolve, scatter, perish

dīlăcĕro, *v.t.* 1, to tear apart, or to pieces

dīlănio, *v.t.* 1, to tear apart, or to pieces

dīlātio, ōnis, *f,* delay

dīlāto, *v.t.* 1, to enlarge

dīlātor, ōris, *m,* delayer

dīlātus, a, um, *adj,* scattered

dilectus, a, um, *adj,* beloved

dīligens, ntis, *adj, adv,* **nter,** scrupulous, thrifty

dīligentia, ae, *f,* care, economy

dīligo, lexi, lectum, *v.t.* 3, to value highly

dīlūcesco, luxi, *v.i.* 3, to grow light, dawn

dīlūcĭdus, a, um, *adj,* clear

dīlūcŭlum, i, *n,* dawn

dīlŭo, ŭi, ŭtum, *v.t.* 3, to wash away, dilute, drench, weaken

dīlūtum, i, *n,* solution

dīlŭvies, ēi, *f* (. . . **ium, ii,** *n*), flood, destruction

dīmētior, mensus, *v.t.* 4, *dep,* to measure out

dīmicātio, ōnis, *f,* struggle

dīmico, *v.i.* 1, to struggle

dīmĭdiātus, a, um, *adj,* halved

dīmĭdium, ii, *n,* a half

dīmĭdius, a, um, *adj,* half

dīmissio, ōnis, *f,* sending out

dīmitto, mĭsi, missum, *v.t.* 3, to send away, break up, disband, throw away, give up

dīmŏvĕo, mŏvi, mōtum, *v.t.* 2, to divide, part, remove

dīnŭmĕro, *v.t.* 1, to count up

dĭplōma, ātis, *n,* official letter of recommendation

dīra, ōrum, *n.pl,* curses

dīrectus, a, um, *adj, adv,* **ē,** straight, level

dīreptio, ōnis, *f,* plundering

dīreptor, ōris, *m,* plunderer

dīrĭgo, rexi, ctum, *v.t.* 3, to put in a straight line, arrange

dīrĭmo, ēmi, emptum, *v.t.* 3, to part, divide, interrupt

dīrĭpio, ŭi, reptum, *v.t.* 3, to tear apart, plunder

dīrumpo, rŭpi, ptum, *v.t.* 3, to break in pieces, sever

dīrŭo, ŭi, ŭtum, *v.t.* 3, to destroy

dīrus, a, um, *adj,* fearful, ill-omened

discēdo, cessi, cessum, *v.i.* 3, to depart, abandon, gape, deviate

disceptātio, ōnis, *f,* discussion

discepto, *v.t.* 1, to debate

discerno, crēvi, tum, *v.t.* 3, to separate, distinguish between

discerpo, psi, ptum, *v.t.* 3, to tear in pieces

discessus, ūs, *m,* departure

discidium, ii, *n,* separation

discinctus, a, um, *adj,* casually-dressed, slovenly

discindo, cĭdi, cissum, *v.t.* 3, to cut to pieces, divide

discingo, nxi, nctum, *v.t.* 3, to take off or undo (clothing)

disciplīna, ae, *f,* teaching, knowledge, system, tactics

discĭpŭlus, i, *m,* pupil

disclŭdo, si, sum, *v.t.* 3, to keep apart, separate

disco, dĭdici, *v.t.* 3, to learn

discŏlor, ōris, *adj,* of different colours

discordia, ae, *f,* disagreement

discordo, *v.i.* 1, to differ

discors, dis, *adj,* disagreeing

discrĕpantia, ae, *f,* discrepancy

discrĕpo, ŭi, v.i. 1, to differ

discrībo, scripsi, ptum, v.t. 3, to distribute

discrīmen, ĭnis, n, division, distinction, crisis, danger

discrīmĭno, v.t. 1, to divide

discrŭcĭo, v.t. 1, to torture

discumbo, cŭbŭi, cŭbĭtum, v.i. 3, to recline at table

discurro, curri, cursum, v.i. 3, to run about

discursus, ūs, m, bustle, activity

discus, i, m, discus, quoit

discŭtĭo, cussi, ssum, v.t. 3, to shatter, disperse

dīsertus, a, um, adj, adv, ē, fluent, clear

dīsĭcĭo, ĭēci, ctum, v.t. 3, to scatter, destroy

disiunctus, a, um, adj, adv, ē, distant, abrupt

disiungo, nxi, nctum, v.t. 3, to separate, unyoke

dispar, ăris, adj, unlike, unequal

dispăro, v.t. 1, to divide

dispello, pŭli, pulsum, v.t. 3, to drive away, scatter

dispendĭum, ii, n, expense, cost

dispenso, v.t. 1, to pay out, distribute, manage

disperdo, dĭdi, dĭtum, v.t. 3, to spoil, ruin

dispĕrĕo, v.i. 4, to perish

dispergo, si, sum, v.t. 3, to scatter about

dispertĭo, v.t. 4, to distribute

dispĭcĭo, spexi, ctum, v.i.t. 3, to look around; discern, reflect on

displĭcĕo, v.i. 2, to displease

dispōno, pŏsŭi, pŏsĭtum, v.t. 3, to arrange, dispose

dispŏsĭtus, a, um, adj, arranged

dispungo, xi, ctum, v.t. 3, to check

dispŭtātĭo, ōnis, f, debate, dispute

dispŭtātor, ōris, m, debater

dispŭto, v.i.t. 1, to theorise; examine, discuss

dissēmĭno, v.t. 1, to spread about

dissensĭo, ōnis, f, disagreement

dissentĭo, si, sum, v.i. 4, to disagree, differ

dissĕrēnat, v. impers. 1, to be clear

dissĕro, rŭi, rtum, v.t. 3, to discuss, argue

dissĭdĕo, ēdi, essum, v.i. 2, to differ, disagree

dissĭlĭo, ŭi, v.i. 4, to leap apart, split

dissĭmĭlis, e, adj, adv, ĭter, unlike, different

dissĭmĭlĭtūdo, ĭnis, f, unlikeness

dissĭmŭlātus, a, um, adj, disguised

dissĭmŭlo, v.t. 1, to disguise, hide

dissĭpātĭo, ōnis, f, scattering, destruction

dissĭpo, v.t. 1, to scatter, rout

dissŏcĭābĭlis, e, adj, dividing

dissŏcĭo, v.t. 1, to estrange

dissŏlūtĭo, ōnis, f, break-up, destruction

dissŏlūtus, a, um, adj, loose

dissolvo, solvi, sŏlūtum, v.t. 3, to unloose, separate, pay, annul, destroy

dissŏnus, a, um, adj, discordant

dissuādĕo, si, sum, v.t. 2, to advise against

dissulto, v.i. 1, to burst apart

distans, ntis, adj, distant

distendo, di, tum, v.t. 3, to stretch out, distend, torture

distentus, a, um, adj, full

distentus, a, um, adj, busy

distinctĭo, ōnis, f, difference

distinctus, a, um, adj, adv, ē, separate, clear, adorned

distĭnĕo, tĭnŭi, tentum, v.t. 2, to keep apart, perplex, hinder

distinguo, nxi, nctum, v.t. 3, to separate, discriminate, adorn

disto, v.i. 1, to be distant, differ

distorquĕo, rsi, rtum, v.t. 2, to twist, distort, torture

distortĭo, ōnis, f, distortion

distortus, a, um, adj, deformed

distractĭo, ōnis, f, division

distractus, a, um, adj, bewildered

distrăho, xi, ctum, v.t. 3, to pull apart, divide, distract, perplex

distrĭbŭo, ŭi, ūtum, v.t. 3, to distribute

distrĭbūtē, adv, methodically

distrĭbūtĭo, ōnis, f, distribution

districtus, a, um, adj, busy, strict

distringo, nxi, ctum, v.t. 3, to stretch tight, distract the attention

disturbo, v.t. 1, to disturb, demolish, frustrate

dīto, v.t. 1, to enrich

dĭū, adv, a long time

dĭurnus, a, um, adj, daily

dĭurna, ōrum, n.pl, records

dĭūtĭnus, a, um, adj, long-lasting

dĭūtĭus, comp. adv, longer

dĭūturnĭtas, ātis, f, long duration

dĭūturnus, a, um, adj, adv, ē, long-lasting

dīva, ae, f, goddess

dīvello, velli, vulsum, v.t. 3, to tear to pieces, destroy

dīvendo, (no perfect), itum, v.t. 3, to retail

dīverbĕro, v.t. 1, to cut

dīversĭtas, ātis, f, disagreement

dīversus, a, um, adj, adv, ē, opposite, contrary, hostile, separate, different

dīverto, ti, sum, v.i. 3, to diverge

dīves, ĭtis, adj, rich

dīvido, vīsi, sum, v.t. 3, to separate, distribute, destroy

dīvidŭus, a, um, adj, divisible

dīvīnĭtas, ātis, f, divinity

dīvīnĭtus, adv, providentially

dīvīno, v.t. 1, to prophesy

dīvīnus, a, um, adj, adv, ē, divine, prophetic, superhuman

dīvīnus, i, m, prophet

dīvīsĭo, ōnis, f, division

dīvīsor, ōris, m, distributor of bribes to electors

dīvĭtiae, ārum, f.pl. wealth

dīvortĭum, ii, n, separation

dīvulgo, v.t. 1, to make known

dīvum, i, n, sky

dīvus, a, um, adj, divine

dīvus, i, m (a, ae, f), god, (goddess)

do, dĕdi, dătum, v.t. 1, to give

dŏcĕo, ŭi, doctum, v.t. 2, to teach, inform

dŏcĭlis, e, adj, easily taught

doctor, ōris, m, teacher

doctrīna, ae, f, teaching, education, learning

doctus, a, um, adj, adv, ē, learned, skilled

dŏcŭmentum, i, n, lesson, example

dōdrans, ntis, m, three quarters

dogma, ătis, n, doctrine, dogma

dŏlābra, ae, f, pick-axe

dŏlĕo, v.i.t. 2, to suffer pain; grieve, deplore

dōlĭum, ii, n, large jar

dŏlo, v.t. 1, to chop, beat

dŏlor, ōris, m, pain, sorrow

dŏlōsus, a, um, adj, deceitful

dŏlus, i, m, fraud, trick

dŏmābĭlis, e, adj, tamable

dŏmestĭcus, a, um, adj, of the home

dŏmestĭci, ōrum, m. pl, family, servants, escort

dŏmi, adv, at home

dŏmĭcĭlĭum, ii, n, dwelling place

dŏmĭna, ae, f, mistress, lady

dŏmĭnans, ntis, adj, ruling

dŏmĭnātĭo, ōnis, f, absolute rule

dŏmĭnātus, ūs, m, absolute rule

dŏmĭnĭum, ii, n, banquet, property-ownership

dŏmĭnor, v.i. 1, dep, to reign

dŏmĭnus, i, m, master, owner

dŏmĭto, v.t. 1, to tame

dŏmĭtor, ōris, m, tamer

dŏmĭtus, a, um, adj, tamed

dŏmo, ŭi, ĭtum, v.t. 1, to tame, conquer

dŏmus, ūs, f, house, home

dōnārĭum, ii, n, altar, sanctuary

dōnātĭo, ōnis, f, donation

dōnātus, a, um, adj, presented

dōnĕc, conj, while, until

dōno, v.t. 1, to present, remit

dōnum, i, n, gift, present

dorcas, ădis, m, gazelle

dormĭo, v.i. 4, to sleep

dormĭto, v.i. 1, to fall asleep

dorsum, i, n, the back, ridge, ledge

dōs, dōtis, f, dowry

dōtālis, e, adj, of a dowry

dōtātus, a, um, adj, endowed

dōto, v.t. 1, to endow

drachma, ae, f, small Greek silver coin

drāco, ōnis, m, water-snake

drŏmas, ădis, m, dromedary

drўas, ădis, f, wood-nymph

dŭbĭē, adv, doubtfully

dŭbĭtātĭo, ōnis, f, doubt, uncertainty

dŭbĭto, v.i.t. 1, to hesitate; doubt

dŭbĭum, ii, n, doubt

dŭbĭus, a, um, adj, doubtful, dangerous

dŭcēni, ae, a, adj, two hundred each

dŭcenti, ae, a, adj, two hundred

dūco, xi, ctum, v.t. 3, to lead, marry, construct, receive, prolong, consider

ductĭlis, e, adj, moveable, malleable

ductor, ōris, m, leader

ductus, ūs, m, bringing, leadership

dūdum, adv, some time ago, formerly

dulcē, adv, sweetly

dulcēdo, ĭnis, f, sweetness, charm

dulcĭtūdo, ĭnis, f, sweetness, charm

dulcis, e, adj, adv, ĭter, sweet, pleasant, dear

dum, conj, while, until, provided that

dūmētum, i, n, thicket

dummŏdo, adv, as long as

dūmōsus, a, um, adj, bushy

dūmus, i, m, bramble

dumtaxat, adv, in so far as, merely, at least

dŭŏ, ae, ŏ, adj, two

dŭŏdĕcies, adv, twelve times

dŭŏdĕcim, adj, twelve

dŭŏdĕcĭmus, a, um, adj, twelfth

dŭŏdēni, ae, a, adj, twelve each

dŭŏdēvīcensĭmus, a, um, adj, eighteenth

dŭŏdēvīgintī, adj, eighteen

dŭŏvĭri, ōrum, m.pl, board or commission of two men

dŭplex, ĭcis, adj, adv, ĭter, double, deceitful

For List of Abbreviations used, turn to pages 3, 4

dŭplĭco, *v.t.* 1, to double

dŭplus, a um, *adj*, double

dūra, ōrum, *n.pl*, hardship

dūrābĭlis, e, *adj*, durable

dūrātus, a, um, *adj*, hardened

dūrē, *adv*, roughly

dūresco, rŭi, *v.i.* 3, to harden

dūrĭtĭa, ae, *f*, hardness, strictness, austerity

dūro, *v.i.t.* 1, to be hard, endure; harden

dūrus, a, um, *adj*, *adv*, ē, ĭter, hard, rough, harsh, stern

dux, dŭcis, *m*, leader, commander

dўnastes, ae, *m*, chieftain

dўsentĕrĭa, ae, *f*, dysentery

dyspnoea, ae, *f*, asthma

E

ē, *prep. with abl*, out of, from, since

ĕa, see is

ĕādem, see idem

ĕātĕnus, *adv*, so far

ĕbĕnus, i, *f*, ebony (tree)

ĕbĭbo, bi, bĭtum, *v.t.* 3, to drink up, absorb, squander

ēblandĭor, *v. t.* 4, *dep*, to obtain by flattery

ēbrĭĕtas, ātis, *f*, drunkenness

ēbrĭōsus, a, um, *adj*, addicted to drink

ēbrĭus, a, um, *adj*, drunk

ēbullĭo, *v.t.* 4, to boast about

ēbŭlum, i, *n*, dwarf-elder

ĕbŭr, ŏris, *n*, ivory

ĕburnĕus, a, um, *adj*, of ivory

ecce, *demonstrative adv*, see!

ĕchīnus, i, *m*, hedgehog, sea-urchin, rinsing bowl

ēchō, ūs, *f*, echo

ecquando, *interr. adv*, at any time?

ecqui, ae, od, *interr. pron, adj*, any? anyone?

ecquis, id, *interr. pron*, anyone? anything?

ĕdācĭtas, ātis, *f*, gluttony

ĕdax, ācis, *adj*, greedy

ēdentŭlus, a, um, *adj*, toothless

ēdīco, xi, ctum, *v.t.* 3, to publish, declare

ēdictum, i, *n*, proclamation

ēdisco, dĭdĭci, *v.t.* 3, to learn by heart, study

ēdissĕro, rŭi, rtum, *v.t.* 3, to explain in full

ēdĭtĭo, ōnis, *f*, bringing out, publishing

ēdĭtus, a, um, *adj*, high, raised, brought out

ĕdo, ēdi, ēsum, *v.t.* 3, to eat

ēdo, dĭdi, dĭtum, *v.t.* 3, to produce, bring out, declare, cause, erect

ēdŏcĕo, cŭi, ctum, *v.t.* 2, to teach thoroughly

ēdŏmo, ŭi, ĭtum, *v.t.* 1, to subdue

ēdŭcātĭo, ōnis, *f*, bringing up, education

ēdŭco, xi, ctum, *v.t.* 3, to lead or bring out, summon, educate, erect

ēdŭco, *v.t.* 1, to bring up (child)

ĕdūlis, e, *adj*, eatable

effātus, a, um, *adj*, established

effectĭo, ōnis, *f*, doing, performing

effectus, a, um, *adj*, completed

effectus, ūs, *m*, accomplishment

effēmĭnātus, a, um, *adj*, effeminate

effĕrātus, a, um, *adj*, wild

effĕro, efferre, extŭli, ēlātum, *v.t. irreg*, to bring out, bury, declare, raise; *in passive or with* se, to be haughty

effĕro, *v.t.* 1, to brutalize

effĕrus, a, um, *adj*, savage

effervesco, ferbŭi, *v.i.* 3, to boil up, rage

effervo, *v.i.* 3, to boil over

effētus, a, um, *adj*, exhausted

efficax, ācis, *adj*, efficient

efficĭens, ntis, *adj*, *adv*, nter, efficient

efficĭo, fēci, fectum, *v.t.* 3, to bring about, complete, produce

effictus, a, um, *adj*, fashioned

effigĭes, ēi, *f*, portrait, copy

effingo, nxi, ctum, *v.t.* 3, to shape, fashion, portray

efflāgĭto, *v.t.* 1, to request urgently

efflo, *v.t.* 1, to breathe out

efflōresco, rŭi, *v.i.* 3, to bloom

efflŭo, xi, *v.i.* 3, to flow out, vanish

effŏdĭo, fōdi, fossum, *v.t.* 3, to dig out, dig up

effor, *v. t.* 1, *dep*, to speak out

effrēnātus, a, um, *adj*, unruly

effrēnus, a, um, *adj*, unrestrained

effringo, frēgi, fractum, *v.t.* 3, to break open, smash

effŭgĭo, fūgi, *v.i.t.* 3, to escape; flee from, avoid

effŭgĭum, ii, *n*, escape

effulgĕo, si, *v.i.* 2, to gleam

effundo, fūdi, fūsum, *v.t.* 3, to pour out, let loose, squander; *in pass. or with reflexive*, to rush out

effūsĭo, ōnis, *f*, outpouring, profusion

effūsus, a, um, *adj*, *adv*, ē, poured out, spread out, wide, loosened

effūtĭo, *v.t.* 4, to blurt out

ēgĕlidus, a, um, *adj*, cool

ĕgens, ntis, *adj*, in want of

ĕgēnus, a, um, *adj*, in want of

ĕgĕo, *v.i.* 2, *with abl*, to be in need of

ĕgĕro, ssi, stum, *v.t.* 3, to bring out

ĕgestas, ātis, *f*, poverty

ĕgō, *pers. pron*, I

ĕgŏmet, *pron*, I myself

ĕgrĕdior, gressus, *v.i.t.* 3, *dep*, to go or come out; leave, exceed

ĕgrĕgius, a, um, *adj*, *adv*, ē, distinguished

ēgressus, ūs, *m*, departure, passage

ēheu! alas!

ēiă! hey! I say!

ēiăcŭlor, *v. t.* 1, *dep*, to shoot out

ēicio, ēci, iectum, *v.t.* 3, to drive out, expel, wreck; *with reflexive*, to rush out

ēiecto, *v.t.* 1, to vomit

ēiūro, *v.t.* 1, to reject on oath, abandon

ēius, *genit. of* is, ea, id

ēiusmŏdi, in such a manner

ēlābor, lapsus, *v.i.* 3, *dep*, to slip away, escape

ēlābōrātus, a, um, *adj*, elaborate

ēlābŏro, *v.i.t.* 1, to make an effort; take pains with

ēlanguesco, gŭi, *v.i.* 3, to grow feeble

ēlātio, ōnis, *f*, lifting up, passion

ēlātro, *v.t.* 1, to bark loudly

ēlātus, a, um, *adj*, raised, lofty

ēlectio, ōnis, *f*, selection

ēlectrum, i, *n*, amber

ēlectus, a, um, *adj*, selected

ēlĕgans, ntis, *adj*, *adv*, nter, refined, tasteful

ēlĕgantia, ae, *f*, refinement

ēlĕgi, ōrum, *m. pl*, elegy

ēlĕgia, ae, *f*, elegy

ēlĕmentum, i, *n*, element, first principle; *pl*, rudiments

ēlĕphantus, i, *m*, elephant, ivory

ēlĕvo, *v.t.* 1, to lift up, weaken, disparage

ēlicio, cŭi, cĭtum, *v.t.* 3, to lure out, call out

ēlīdo, si, sum, *v.t.* 3, to knock or force out, shatter

ēligo, lēgi, ctum, *v.t.* 3, to choose

ēlinguis, e, *adj*, speechless

ēlixus, a, um, *adj*, boiled

ellychnium, ii, *n*, lampwick

ēlŏco, *v.t.* 1, to let (a farm)

ēlŏcūtio, ōnis, *f*, expression, elocution

ēlŏgium, ii, *n*, saying, inscription

ēlŏquens, ntis, *adj*, eloquent

ēlŏquentia, ae, *f*, eloquence

ēlŏquor, ēlŏcūtus, *v. t.* 3, *dep*, to speak out, declare

ēlūcĕo, xi, *v.i.* 2, to shine out

ēluctor, *v.i.t.* 1, *dep*, to struggle out; struggle out of

ēlūdo, si, sum, *v.t.* 3, to evade, cheat, frustrate

ēlūgĕo, xi, *v.t.* 2, to mourn for

ēlŭo, ŭi, ūtum, *v.t.* 3, to wash off, clean

ēlūtus, a, um, *adj*, insipid

ēlŭvies, *no genit*, *f*, inundation

ēlŭvio, ōnis, *f*, inundation

ēmancĭpo, *v.t.* 1, to set free, transfer, sell

ēmāno, *v.i.* 1, to flow out, arise from

embŏlium ii, *n*, interlude

ēmendātio, ōnis, *f*, correction

ēmendātor, ōris, *m*, corrector

ēmendātus, a, um, *adj*, faultless

ēmendo, *v.t.* 1, to correct

ēmentior, *v. t.* 4, *dep*, to assert falsely

ēmercor, *v. t.* 1, *dep*, to purchase

ēmĕrĕo, *v.t.* 2 (ēmĕrĕor, *v.t.* 2, *dep*), to deserve, earn, complete one's military service

ēmergo, si, sum, *v.i.* 3, to come out, escape

ēmĕrĭtus, a, um, *adj*, worn out

ēmētior, mensus, *v.t.* 4, *dep*, to measure out, travel over

ēmĭco, ŭi, ātum, *v.ï.* 1, to spring out, appear

ēmĭgro, *v.i.* 1, to depart

ēmĭnens, ntis, *adj*, projecting, distinguished

ēmĭnentia, ae, *f*, prominence

ēmĭnĕo, *v.i.* 2, to stand out, excel

ēmĭnus, *adv*, from or at a distance

ēmissārium, ii, *n*, drain, vent

ēmissārius, ii, *m*, spy

ēmissio, ōnis, *f*, sending out, hurling (of missiles)

ēmitto, mīsi, ssum, *v.t.* 3, to send out, produce, publish; *with* manū, to set free

ēmo, ēmi, emptum, *v.t.* 3, to buy

ēmŏdŭlor, *v. t.* 1, *dep*, to sing

ēmollio, *v.t.* 4, to soften

ēmŏlūmentum, i, *n*, effort, profit

ēmŏrĭor, mortuus, *v.i.* 3, *dep*, to die

ēmŏvĕo, mōvi, tum, *v.t.* 2, to remove, shake

empĭrĭcus, a, um, *adj*, empirical

emplastrum, i, *n*, plaster

empŏrium, ii, *n*, market

emptio, ōnis, *f*, purchase

emptor, ōris, *m*, buyer

ēmunctus, a, um, *adj*, clean, shrewd

ēmungo, nxi, nctum, *v.t.* 3, to wipe the nose

ēmūnio, *v.t.* 4, to fortify

ēn! see! come!

ēnarro, v.t. 1, to expound

ēnascor, nātus, v. i. 3, dep, to spring up, be born

ēnăto, v.i. 1, to swim away

ēnectus, a, um, adj, killed

ēnĕco, ŭi, ctum, v.t. 1, to kill, exhaust

ēnervo, v.t. 1, to weaken

ēnim, conj, for, indeed

ēnimvēro, conj, certainly

ēnīsus, a, um, adj, strenuous

ēnitĕo, v.i. 2, to shine out

ēnitesco, tŭi, v.i. 3, to shine out

ēnītor, nīsus (nixus), v. i. t. 3, dep, to struggle upwards, climb, strive; give birth to, ascend

ēnixus, a, um, adj, adv, ē, strenuous, earnest

ēno, v.i. 1, to swim out or away

ēnōdātĭo, ōnis, f, explanation

ēnōdis, e, adj, smooth, clear

ēnōdo, v.t. 1, to elucidate

ēnormis, e, adj, enormous, shapeless

ēnormitas, ātis, f, shapelessness

ēnōto, v.t. 1, to note down

ensiger, ēra, ērum, adj, carrying a sword

ensis, is, m, sword

ēnūclĕātus, a, um, adj, adv, ē, pure, clear, simple

ēnŭmĕrātĭo, ōnis, f, counting, recapitulation

ēnŭmĕro, v.t. 1, to count, relate

ēnuntĭo, v.t. 1, to disclose, declare

ĕo, īre, īvi (ii), ĭtum, v.i. irreg, to go; with pedibus, to vote for

ĕō, adv, to that place, to such an extent, so long, besides

eo . . . quo, (with comparatives) the more . . . the more

ĕōdem, adv, to the same place, to the same point or purpose

ĕōus, i, m, (a, um, adj), east

ĕphēbus, i, m, a youth

ĕphippĭum, ii, n, saddle

ĕphŏrus, i, m, Spartan magistrate

ĕpicus, a, um, adj, epic

ĕpiscŏpus, i, m, bishop

ĕpigramma, ătis, n, inscription

ĕpistŏla, ae, f, letter

ĕpistŏmĭum, ii, n, valve

ĕpitŏmē (ĕpitŏma), ēs, f, abridgement

ĕpŏs, n, epic poem

ēpōto, pōtum, v.t. 1, to drink up

ēpŭlae, ārum, f. pl, food, banquet

ēpŭlor, v.i.t. 1, dep, to banquet; eat

ĕqua, ae, f, mare

ĕquāria, ae, f, stud of horses

ĕques, ĭtis, m, horseman, Knight

ĕquester, tris, tre, adj, of a horseman, of cavalry

ĕquidem, adv, indeed, of course, for my part

ĕquīnus, a, um, adj, of horses

ĕquitātĭo, ōnis, f, riding on horseback

ĕquitātus, ūs, m, cavalry

ĕquito, v.i. 1, to ride

ĕquŭlēus, i, m, colt, the rack

ĕquus, i, m, horse

ēra, ae, f, lady of the house

ērādīco, v.t. 1, to root out

ērādo, si, sum, v.t. 3, to scrape out, abolish

ērectus, a, um, adj, upright, noble, haughty, resolute

ērēpo, psi, v.i.t. 3, to creep out; creep over

ergā, prep. with acc, towards

ergastŭlum, i, n, detention centre

ergō, adv, therefore; prep. following genit, on account of

ērigo, rexi, rectum, v.t. 3, to raise up, encourage

ĕrīlis, e, adj, of the master, or mistress

ēripĭo, rĭpŭi, reptum, v.t. 3, to snatch, take away; with reflexive, to escape

ērŏgatĭo, ōnis, f, paying out

ērŏgo, v.t. 1, to pay out, squander

errābundus, a, um, adj, wandering

errātĭcus, a, um, adj, rambling

errātum, i, n, mistake

erro, v.i. 1, to stray, err

erro, ōnis, m, wanderer

error, ōris, m, straying, mistake

ērŭbesco, bŭi, v.i. 3, to blush, feel ashamed

ērūca, ae, f, caterpillar

ēructo, v.t. 1, to belch, emit

ērŭdĭo, v.t. 4, to polish, instruct

ērŭdītĭo, ōnis, f, learning

ērŭdītus, a, um, adj, adv, ē, learned, skilled

ērumpo, rūpi, ptum, v.i.t. 3, to break out; burst

ērŭo, ŭi, ŭtum, v.t. 3, to throw out, dig out, destroy, rescue

ēruptĭo, ōnis, f, break-out

ĕrus, i, m, master of the house

ervum, i, n, wild pea

esca, ae, f, food, bait

ēscendo, di, sum, v.i. 3, to climb

ēscensĭo, ōnis, f, ascent

escŭlentus, a, um, adj, eatable

esse, see sum

essĕdārĭus, i, m, chariot-fighter

essĕdum, i, n, war-chariot

ēsŭriens, ntis, adj, hungry

ēsŭrio, *v.i.t.* 4, to be hungry; long for

ĕt, *conj*, and, as

ĕtĕnim, *conj*, and indeed

ĕtĭam, *conj*, also, even, still

ĕtĭamnum, ĕtĭamnunc, *adv*, even then, till now

etsi, *conj*, although, even if

eu!, well done!

eurĭpus, i, *m*, canal

eurōus, a, um, *adj*, eastern

eurus, i, *m*, east wind

ēvādo, si, sum, *v.i.t.* 3, to go out, escape; leave behind

ēvăgor, *v.i.t.* 1, *dep.* to stray; overstep

ēvălesco, lŭi, *v.i.* 3, to grow strong, to be able

ēvānesco, nŭi, *v.i.* 3, to vanish

ēvānidus, a, um, *adj*, vanishing

ēvasto, *v.t.* 1, to devastate

ēvĕho, xi, ctum, *v.t.* 3, to carry out; *in passive*, to ride or move out

ēvello, velli, vulsum, *v.t.* 3, to tear out, eradicate

ēvĕnio, vēni, ventum, *v.i.* 4, to come out, turn out, result

ēventum, i, *n*, occurrence, result, fortune

ēventus, ūs, *m*, occurrence, result, fortune

ēverbĕro, *v.t.* 1, to strike hard

ēverro, verri, versum, *v.t.* 3, to sweep out

ēversio, ōnis, *f*, destruction

ēversor, ōris, *m*, destroyer

ēversus, a, um, *adj*, overthrown

ēverto, ti, sum, *v.t.* 3, to overthrow, ruin

ēvĭdens, ntis, *adj*, apparent

ēvĭgilo, *v.i.t.* 1, to wake up; keep awake, keep watch through

ēvincio, nxi, nctum, *v.t.* 4, to bind round

ēvinco, vici, ctum, *v.t.* 3, to conquer completely, succeed

ēviscĕro, *v.t.* 1, to tear apart

ēvito, *v.t.* 1, to avoid

ēvŏcāti, ōrum, *m. pl*, reservists

ēvŏco, *v.t.* 1, to call out

ēvŏlo, *v.i.* 1, to fly away

ēvolvo, vi, vŏlūtum, *v.t.* 3, to unroll (and read a book), disclose

ēvŏmo, ŭi, ĭtum, *v.t.* 3, to spit out, vomit

ēvulsio, ōnis, *f*, pulling out

ex(ē), *prep. with abl*, out of, from, after, since, on account of, according to, made of

exăcerbo, *v.t.* 1, to irritate

exactio, ōnis, *f*, debt or tax collecting, expelling

exactor, ōris, *m*, expeller, superintendent, tax-collector

exactus, a, um, *adj*, accurate

exăcŭo, ŭi, ūtum, *v.t.* 3, to sharpen, stimulate

exadversum (. . . us), *adv. and prep.* with *acc*, opposite

exaedĭfĭco, *v.t.* 1, to construct

exaequo, *v.t.* 1, to place equal

exaestŭo, *v.i.* 1, to seethe

exaggĕro, *v.t.* 1, to heap up

exăgĭto, *v.t.* 1, to disturb

exalbesco, bŭi, *v.i.* 3, to turn pale

exāmen, ĭnis, *n*, crowd, swarm

exāmĭno, *v.t.* 1, to weigh, test

exănĭmātĭo, ōnis, *f*, terror

exănĭmātus, a, um, *adj*, out of breath

exănĭmis, e, *adj*, lifeless

exănĭmus, a, um, *adj*, lifeless

exănĭmo, *v.t.* 1, to deprive of breath, kill, terrify

exardesco, arsi, sum, *v.i.* 3, to be inflamed

exāresco, rŭi, *v.i.* 3, to dry up

exăro, *v.t.* 1, to plough, write

exaspĕro, *v.t.* 1, to roughen, provoke

exauctōro, *v.t.* 1, to discharge honourably or dishonourably from army

exaudĭo, *v.t.* 4, to hear, grant

excandesco, dŭi, *v.i.* 3, to glow

excēdo, ssi, ssum, *v.i.t.* 3, to depart, die; leave, exceed

excellens, ntis, *adj, adv*, nter, distinguished, excellent

excello, cellŭi, lsum, *v.i.* 3, to be eminent, excel

excelsus, a, um, *adj*, distinguished

exceptio, ōnis, *f*, restriction

excepto, *v.t.* 1, to catch

excerno, crēvi, crētum, *v.t.* 3, to separate

excerpo, psi, ptum, *v.t.* 3, to select

excessus, ūs, *m*, departure

excidium, ii, *n*, destruction

excido, cidi, *v.i.* 3, to fall from, escape, disappear, slip the memory, fail in

excīdo, cīdi, cīsum, *v.t.* 3, to cut down, destroy

excio, *v.t.* 4, to call or bring out.

excĭpio, cēpi, ceptum, *v.t.* 3, to take out, make an exception, receive, capture, follow after, overhear, intercept

excitātus, a, um, *adj*, roused, vigorous

excito, *v.t.* 1, to rouse up, excite

exclāmātĭo, ōnis, *f*, exclamation

exclāmo, *v.i.t.* 1, to call out

exclūdo, si, sum, *v.t.* 3, to shut out, drive out, remove, hinder, hatch

exclūsio, ōnis, *f*, exclusion

For List of Abbreviations used, turn to pages 3, 4

excōgĭto, *v.t.* 1, to think out

excŏlo, cŏlŭi, cultum, *v.t.* 3, to cultivate, improve, refine

excŏquo, xi, ctum, *v.t.* 3, to boil away, purify

excors, dis, *adj,* stupid

excresco, crēvi, crētum, *v.i.* 3, to grow up

excrētus, a, um, *adj,* full grown

excrētus, a, um, *adj,* separated

excrŭcĭo, *v.t.* 1, to torture

excŭbĭae, ārum, *f. pl,* watch, guard

excŭbĭtor. ōris, *m,* watchman

excŭbo, ŭi, ĭtum, *v.i.* 1, to sleep out of doors, keep watch

excŭdo, di, sum, *v.t.* 3, to hammer out

exculco, *v.t.* 1, to trample down

excurro, cŭcurri, cursum, *v.i.* 3, to run out, make a sortie, extend

excursĭo, ōnis, *f,* attack, invasion, sally

excursus, ūs, *m,* attack, invasion, sally

excūsābĭlis, e, *adj,* excusable

excūsātĭo, ōnis, *f,* excuse

excūso, *v.t.* 1, to excuse, plead in excuse

excŭtĭo, cussi, cussum, *v.t.* 3, to shake off, get rid of, hurl, examine

exĕdo, ēdi, ēsum, *v.t.* 3, to eat up

exemplar, āris, *n,* copy, model

exemplum, i, *n,* copy, model, precedent, warning, example

exemptus, a, um, *adj,* removed

exĕo, *v.i.t.* 4, to depart, run out (time); die; cross, avoid

exercĕo, *v.t.* 2, to keep busy, train, exercise, pester

exercĭtātĭo, ōnis, *f,* practice

exercĭtātus, a, um, *adj,* trained

exercĭtor, ōris, *m,* trainer

exercĭtus, ūs, *m,* army

exercĭtus, a, um, *adj,* trained, harrassed

exhālātĭo, ōnis, *f,* exhalation

exhālo, *v.t.* 1, to breathe out

exhaurĭo, si, stum, *v.t.* 4, to draw out, exhaust, empty

exhaustus, a, um, *adj,* drained, worn out

exhērēdo, *v.t.* 1, to disinherit

exhĭbĕo, *v.t.* 2, to present, display, procure, cause

exhĭbĭtus, a, um, *adj,* produced

exhĭlăro, *v.t.* 1, to delight

exhorresco, rŭi, *v.i.t.* 3, to tremble; shrink from, dread

exhortor, *v. t.* 1, *dep,* to encourage

exiens, see exeo

exĭgo, ēgi, actum, *v.t.* 3, to drive out, enforce, demand, complete, examine, estimate, spend (time)

exigŭĭtas, ātis, *f,* small size

exigŭus, a, um, *adj, adv,* ē, small, short

exilis, e, *adj, adv,* ĭter, small, thin, feeble, insignificant

exilĭum, ii, *n,* exile

exĭmĭus, a, um, *adj, adv,* ē, unusual, distinguished

exĭmo, ēmi, emptum, *v.t.* 3, to take away, free, waste

exĭnānĭo, *v.t.* 4, to empty

exinde (exin), *adv,* from there, then, next, accordingly

existĭmātĭo, ōnis, *f,* opinion, reputation, character

existĭmātor, ōris, *m,* critic

existĭmo, *v.t.* 1, to estimate, think

exitĭābĭlis, e, *adj,* fatal, deadly

exitĭālis, e, *adj,* fatal, deadly

exitĭōsus, a, um, *adj,* destructive

exitĭum, ii, *n,* destruction

exitus, ūs, *m,* departure, outlet, conclusion, result, death

exŏlesco, ŏlēvi, lētum, *v.i.* 3, to grow up, disappear

exŏnĕro, *v.t.* 1, to unload

exoptātus, a, um, *adj,* longed for

exopto, *v.t.* 1, to long for

exōrābĭlis, e, *adj,* easily persuaded

exordĭor, orsus, *v. t.* 4, *dep,* to begin, weave

exordĭum, ii, *n,* beginning, introduction

exŏrĭor, ortus, *v. i.* 4, *dep,* to spring up, arise, appear

exornātĭo, ōnis, *f,* decoration

exorno, *v.t.* 1, to equip, adorn

exōro, *v.t.* 1, to prevail upon

exorsus, a, um, *adj,* begun

exortus, ūs, *m,* rising

exōsus, a, um, *adj,* hating, detested

expăvesco, pāvi, *v.i.t.* 3, to be afraid; dread

expect, see exspect

expēdĭo, *v.t.* 4, to set free, prepare, arrange, explain; *impers,* it is expedient

expēdĭtĭo, ōnis, *f,* campaign

expēdĭtē, *adv,* promptly

expēdĭtus, a, um, *adj,* ready

expēdĭtus, i, *m,* soldier in light-marching-order

expello, pŭli, pulsum, *v.t.* 3, to drive away

expendo, di, sum, *v.t.* 3, to pay out, consider, pay the penalty

expergēfăcĭo, fēci, factum, *v.t.* 3, to arouse

expergiscor, perrectus, *v.i.* 3, *dep.* to awake

expĕrĭens, ntis, *adj,* enterprising

expĕrĭentĭa, ae, *f,* experiment, practice

expĕrīmentum, i, *n,* proof, experience

expĕrĭor, pertus, *v. t.* 4, *dep,* to prove, test, try; *perf,* know from experience

expers, rtis, *adj,* devoid of

expertus, a, um, *adj,* proved

expĕto, īvi (ĭi), ītum, *v.t.* 3, to long for, aim at, reach

expĭātĭo, ōnis, *f,* atonement

expĭlo, *v.t.* 1, to plunder

expīlātĭo, ōnis, *f,* plundering

expingo, nxi, ctum, *v.t.* 3, to paint

expĭo, *v.t.* 1, to atone for

expiscor, *v. t.* 1, *dep,* to search out

explānātĭo, ōnis, *f,* explanation

explāno, *v.t.* 1, to explain

explĕo, ēvi, ētum, *v.t.* 2, to fill up, fulfil, finish

explētĭo, ōnis, *f,* satisfying

explētus, a, um, *adj,* full, complete

explĭcātĭo, ōnis, *f,* unfolding, explanation

explĭcātus, a, um, *adj,* spread-out, plain

explĭco, *v.t.* 1, (or . . . ŭi . . . ĭtum) to unfold, spread out, deploy, arrange, explain

explōdo, si, sum, *v.t.* 3, to hiss off the stage, disapprove

explōrātor, ōris, *m,* spy, scout

explōrātus, a, um, *adj, adv,* ē, established, certain

explōro, *v.t.* 1, to search out, spy, test

expŏlĭo, *v.t.* 4, to polish

expōno, pŏsŭi, pŏsĭtum, *v.t.* 3, to expose, put on shore, explain

exporto, *v.t.* 1, to carry away

exposco, pŏposci, *v.t.* 3, to implore, require

expŏsĭtĭo, ōnis, *f,* elucidation

expŏsĭtus, a, um, *adj,* accessible

expostŭlātĭo, ōnis, *f,* complaint

expostŭlo, *v.t.* 1, to demand, upbraid, complain

expressus, a, um, *adj,* clear

exprĭmo, pressi, pressum, *v.t.* 3, to press out, model, extort

exprŏbrātĭo, ōnis, *f,* reproach

exprŏbro, *v.t.* 1, to reproach

exprōmo, mpsi, mptum, *v.t.* 3, to fetch out, display, explain

expugnātĭo, ōnis, *f,* capture by assault

expugno, *v.t.* 1, to storm, capture

expurgo, *v.t.* 1, to purify, justify

exquīro, sīvi, sītum, *v.t.* 3, to search out

exquīsĭtus, a, um, *adj, adv,* ē, choice, excellent

exsanguis, e, *adj,* bloodless, weak

exsătĭo, *v.t.* 1, to satisfy

exsătūro, *v.t.* 1, to satiate

exscensĭo, ōnis, *f,* landing

exscindo, ĭdi, issum, *v.t.* 3, to destroy completely

exscrībo, psi, ptum, *v.t.* 3, to write out, copy

exsĕco, cŭi, ctum, *v.t.* 1, to cut out, cut off

exsēcrābĭlis, e, *adj,* accursed

exsēcrātĭo, ōnis, *f,* curse

exsēcrātus, a, um, *adj,* accursed

exsēcror, *v. i.t.* 1, *dep,* to take an oath; curse,

exsĕcūtĭo, ōnis, *f,* execution

exsĕquĭae, ārum, *f. pl,* funeral

exsĕquor, sĕcūtus, *v.t.* 3, *dep,* to pursue, follow, carry out, describe, avenge

exsĕro, rŭi, rtum, *v.t.* 3, to put out, uncover, protrude

exserto, *v.t.* 1, to stretch out

exsicco, *v.t.* 1, to dry up

exsĭlĭo, ĭlŭi, *v.i.* 4, to leap out, jump up

exsĭlĭum, ii, *n,* exile

exsisto, stĭti, stĭtum, *v.i.* 3, to come out, appear, arise, exist

exsolvo, solvi, sŏlūtum, *v.t.* 3, to unloose, free, discharge

exsomnis, e, *adj,* sleepless

exsorbĕo, *v.t.* 2, to suck up

exsors, rtis, *adj,* specially chosen, deprived of

exspătĭor, *v.i.* 1, *dep,* to digress, launch out

exspectātĭo, ōnis, *f,* expectation

exspectātus, a, um, *adj,* desired

exspecto, *v.t.* 1, to look out for, wait for, hope for

exspergo (spargo), *no perfect,* **spersus** *v.t.* 3, to scatter

exspīrātĭo, ōnis, *f,* breathing out

exspīro, *v.i.t.* 1, to rush out, expire, cease; breathe out

exspŏlĭo, *v.t.* 1, to plunder

exstĭmŭlo, *v.t.* 1, to goad on

exstinctor, ōris, *m,* destroyer

exstinctus, a, um, *adj,* destroyed, extinct

exstinguo, nxi, nctum, *v.t.* 3, to quench, kill, destroy

exstirpo, *v.t.* 1, to uproot

exsto, *v.i.* 1, to project, be conspicuous, exist

exstructĭo, ōnis, *f*, structure

exstrŭo, xi, ctum, *v.t.* 3, to heap up, build up

exsūdo, *v.t.* 1, to toil or sweat at

exsul (exul), ŭlis, *c*, an exile

exsŭlo (exulo), *v.i.* 1, to live in exile

exsultans, ntis, *adj*, boastful

exsultātĭo, ōnis, *f*, rapture

exsultim, *adv*, friskingly

exsulto, *v.i.* 1, to jump about, run riot, boast

exsŭpĕrābĭlis, e, *adj*, surmountable

exsŭpĕro, *v.i.t.* 1, to get the upper hand; pass over, exceed

exsurdo, *v.t.* 1, to deafen, dull

exsurgo, surrexi, *v.i.* 3, to rise, stand up

exsuscĭto, *v.t.* 1, to awaken

exta, ōrum, *n.pl*, the inwards

extemplō, *adv*, immediately

extendo, di, tum, *v.t.* 3, to stretch out, enlarge, prolong

extentus, a, um, *adj*, extensive

extĕnŭātĭo, ōnis, *f*, attenuation

extĕnŭo, *v.t.* 1, to diminish, weaken

exter (extĕrus), ĕra, ĕrum, *adj*, external, strange, foreign

extergĕo, si, sum, *v.t.* 2, to plunder

extĕrĭor, us, *comp. adj*, outer

extermĭno, *v.t.* 1, to expel

externus, a, um, *adj*, external, foreign

extĕro, trĭvi, trītum, *v.t.* 3, to rub off, wear away

exterrĕo, *v.t.* 2, to frighten

extĭmesco, mŭi, *v.i.t.* 2, to be afraid; to dread

extollo, sustŭli, *v.t.* 3, to raise

extorquĕo, si, sum, *v.t.* 2, to wrench away from, extort

extorris, e, *adj*, exiled

extrā, *adv. and prep. with acc.* outside, beyond, except

extrăho, xi, ctum, *v.t.* 3, to drag out, release, prolong

extrānĕus, i, *m*, stranger

extrāordĭnārĭus, a, um, *adj*, extraordinary

extrēma, ōrum, *n.pl*, last resort

extrēmĭtas, ātis, *f*, extremity

extrēmum, i, *n*, the end

extrēmum, *adv*, for the last time, finally

extrēmus, a, um, *adj*, furthest, the end of, or extremity of

extrīco, *v.t.* 1, to disentangle

extrinsĕcus, *adv*, from, or on, the outside

extrūdo, si, sum, *v.t.* 3, to push out

extundo, tūdi, tūsum, *v.t.* 3, to force out, hammer out

exturbo, *v.t.* 1, to drive away

exūbĕro, *v.i.* 1, to be abundant

exul, see exsul

exulcĕro, *v.t.* 1, to aggravate

exŭlŭlo, *v.i.* 1, to howl

exundo, *v.i.* 1, to overflow

exŭo, ŭi, ūtum, *v.t.* 3, to strip, deprive of, discard

exūro, ussi, ustum, *v.t.* 3, to burn up, consume

exustĭo, ōnis, *f*, conflagration

exŭvĭae, ārum, *f. pl*, stripped-off clothing or equipment

F

fāba, ae, *f*, bean

fābella, ae, *f*, short story

fāber, bri, *m*, smith, carpenter

fābrĭca, ae, *f*, workshop, a trade, a skilled work

fābrĭcātĭo, ōnis, *f*, structure

fābrĭcātor, ōris, *m*, maker

fābrĭcor, *v.t.* 1, *dep* (fabrico, *v.t.* 1), to construct, form

fābrīlis, e, *adj*, of a craftsman

fābŭla, ae, *f*, story, play

fābŭlor, *v.t.* 1, *dep*; to talk, chat

fābŭlōsus, a, um, *adj*, legendary

fācesso, cessi, ītum, *v.i.t.* 3, to depart; perform, cause

fācētĭae, ārum, *f. pl*, witticisms

fācētus, a, um, *adj, adv*, ē, courteous, elegant, witty

fācĭes, ēi, *f*, face, shape, appearance

fācĭlĕ, *adv*, easily

fācĭlis, e, *adj*, easy, quick, good-natured

fācĭlĭtas, ātis, *f*, ease, affability

fācĭnus, ŏris, *n*, deed, crime

fācĭo, fēci, factum, *v.i.t.* 3, to do, act, to side with (cum, ab), or against (contra), to be useful; to make, do, produce, assert, pretend, practise (trade)

factĭo, ōnis, *f*, faction, party

factĭōsus, a, um, *adj*, mutinous

factĭto, *v.t.* 1, to keep doing

factum, i, *n*, deed

făcultas, ātis, *f*, power, opportunity, supply

fācundĭa, ae, *f*, eloquence

fācundus, a, um, *adj, adv*, ē, eloquent

faecŭla, ae, *f*, wine-dregs

faenĕrātĭo, ōnis, *f*, money-lending

faenĕrātor, ōris, *m*, money-lender

faenĕrātōrĭus, a, um, *adj*, usurious

faenĕror, v.t. 1, dep (faenĕro, v.t. 1), to lend on interest

faenīlia, ĭum, n. pl, hay-loft

faenum, i, n, hay

faenus, ōris, n, interest, profit

faex, cis, f, dregs, sediment

fāginĕus (nus), a, um, adj, of beech

fāgus, i, f, beech-tree

fālārica, ae, f, burning missile

falcātus, a, um, adj, armed with scythes, curved

falcĭfer, ĕra, ĕrum, adj, holding a sickle

falco, ōnis, m, falcon

fallācia, ae, f, trick, deceit

fallax, ācis, adj, adv, ĭter, deceitful, fallacious

fallo, fĕfelli, falsum, v.t. 3, to deceive, betray, escape the notice of, appear

falsum, i, n, falsehood

falsus, a, um, adj, adv, ē, or o, false, counterfeit, deceptive

falx, cis, f, scythe, hook

fāma, ae, f, rumour, public opinion, reputation, fame

fāmes, is, f, hunger, famine

fāmilia, ae, f, domestic servants, family property, crowd or set

fāmiliāris, e, adj, adv, ĭter, domestic, intimate

fāmiliāris, is, m, friend

fāmiliāritas, ātis, f, friendship

fāmōsus, a, um, adj, notorious

fāmŭla, ae, f, maid-servant

fāmŭlātus, ūs, m, servitude

fāmŭlor, v.i. 1, dep, to serve, wait on

fāmŭlus, i, m, servant

fānāticus, a, um, adj, inspired, frantic

fandus, a, um, adj, lawful

fānum, i, n, temple, shrine

fār, farris, n, grain, corn

farcimen, ĭnis, n, sausage

farcĭo, rsi, rtum, v.t. 4, to cram

fārina, ae, f, flour

farrāgo, ĭnis, f, hotchpotch

fartor, ōris, m, poultry-farmer

fartum, i, n, stuffing

fartūra, ae, f, cramming, padding

fās, n (indeclinable), divine law, right

fascēs, ĭum, m. pl, bundle of rods and axes; symbol of magistrates' power of scourging and beheading

fascia, ae, f, band, head-band

fascĭcŭlus, i, m, small bundle

fascĭnātio, ōnis, f, bewitching

fascĭno, v.t. 1, to charm, enchant

fascĭnum, i, n, lucky charm

fascĭōla, ae, f, small bandage

fascis, is, m, bundle, pack

fassus, a, um, participle, having acknowledged

fasti, ōrum, m. pl, working days, calendar

fastīdio, v.i.t. 4, to be disgusted; to loathe

fastīdiōsus, a, um, adj, adv, ē, scornful, squeamish, disagreeable

fastīdium, ii, n, loathing, scorn

fastīgātus, a, um, adj, adv, ē, sloping

fastīgium, ii, n, gable, top, bottom, slope

fastīgo, v.t. 1, to make jointed

fastus, a, um (diēs), court-day

fastus, ūs, m, arrogance

fātālis, e, adj, adv, ĭter, destined, deadly

fātĕor, fassus, v.t. 2, dep, to admit confess

fātĭdicus, a, um, adj, prophetic

fātĭfer, ĕra, ĕrum, adj, deadly

fātĭgātio, ōnis, f, exhaustion

fātĭgātus, a, um, adj, exhausted

fātĭgo, v.t. 1, to weary, harass, torment

fātisco, v.i. 3, to fall apart

fātŭĭtas, ātis, f, foolishness

fātum, i, n, destiny, calamity, prophetic saying

fātŭus, a, um, adj, foolish

faucēs, ĭum, f. pl, throat, narrow passage

faustus, a, um, adj, adv, ē, fortunate

fautor, ōris, m, supporter

fautrix, īcis, f, patroness

fāvĕo, fāvi, fautum, v.i. 2, with dat; to favour, befriend

fāvilla, ae, f, embers

fāvor, ōris, m, good-will, applause

fāvōrābilis, e, adj, popular

fāvus, i, m, honey-comb

fax, fācis, f, torch, stimulus

febrĭcŭlōsus, a, um, adj, feverish

fēbris, is, f, fever

Fēbruārius (mensis), February

fēbrŭum, i, n, atonement

fēcundĭtas, ātis, f, fertility

fēcundo, v.t. 1, to fertilize

fēcundus, a, um, adj, fertile, abundant

fel, fellis, n, gall-bladder, poison, bitterness

fēles, is, f, cat

fēlīcĭtas, ātis, f, happiness

fēlix, īcis, adj, adv, ĭter, happy, fortunate, abundant

fēmina, ae, f, woman

fēmĭnĕus, a, um, adj, feminine

fĕmur, ōris (ĭnis), n, thigh

fēn. . see faen

For List of Abbr viations used, turn to pages 3, 4

fĕnestra, ae, *f*, window

fĕra, ae, *f*, wild animal

fērālis, e, *adj*, of the dead

fērax, ācis, *adj*, fertile

fercŭlum, i, *n*, barrow, dish

fĕrē, *adv*, almost, nearly, usually

fĕrentārius, ii, *m*, light-armed soldier

fĕrētrum, i, *n*, bier

fēriae, ārum, *f. pl*, holidays

fēriātus, a, um, *adj*, on holiday

fĕrīnus, a, um, *adj*, of wild animals

fĕrio, *v.t.* 4, to strike, kill; with foedus, to make a treaty

fĕritas, ātis, *f*, wildness

fermē, *adv*, almost, usually

fermentum, i, *n*, yeast, beer

fĕro, ferre, tŭli, lātum, *v.t. irreg*, to bear, bring, move, produce, plunder, offer, tolerate, show, assert; fertur, ferunt, it is said

fĕrōcia, ae, *f*, high spirits, ferocity

fĕrōcitas, ātis, *f*, high spirits, ferocity

fĕrōciter, *adv*, bravely, fiercely

fĕrox, ōcis, *adj*, brave, fierce

ferrāmentum, i, *n*, iron tool

ferrātus, a, um, *adj*, iron-clad

ferrĕus, a, um, *adj*, made of iron

ferrūginĕus, a, um, *adj*, rusty, dark red

ferrūgo, ĭnis, *f*, rust, dark red

ferrum, i, *n*, iron, sword

ferrūmen, ĭnis, *n*, cement, glue, solder

ferrūmĭno, *v.t.* 1, to cement, solder

fertĭlis, e, *adj*, fertile

fertĭlĭtas, ātis, *f*, fertility

fĕrŭla, ae, *f*, stalk, rod

fĕrus, a, um, *adj*, wild, cruel

fĕrus, i, *m*, wild animal

fervēfăcio, fēci, factum, *v.t.* 3, to heat, melt

fervens, ntis, *adj*, *adv*, nter, burning, boiling, hot

fervĕo, bŭi, *v.i.* 2, to boil, burn, rage, swarm

fervĭdus, a, um, *adj*, burning, impetuous

fervor, ōris, *m*, heat, passion

fessus, a, um, *adj*, tired

festīnans, ntis, *adj*, *adv*, nter, in haste

festīnātio, ōnis, *f*, haste

festīno, *v.i.t.* 1, to hurry

festīnus, a, um, *adj*, quick

festīvĭtas, ātis, *f*, humour

festīvus, a, um, *adj*, *adv*, ē, witty, lively, cheerful

festum, i, *n*, holiday, banquet

festus, a, um, *adj*, festive, gay

fētĕo, *v.i.* 2, to stink

fētiāles, ĭum, *m*, *pl*, college of priests concerned with war-ceremonies

fētĭdus, a, um, *adj*, stinking

fētor, ōris, *m*, stench

fētūra, ae, *f*, bearing of young, young brood

fētus, ūs, *m*, bearing of young, young brood

fētus, a, um, *adj*, pregnant, fruitful, newly delivered

fībra, ae, *f*, fibre, nerve

fībŭla, ae, *f*, brooch, pin

fībŭlo, *v.t.* 1, to fasten

fictĭlis, e, *adj*, made of clay

fictĭle, is (ia, ĭum), *n*, earthen pottery

fictor, ōris, *m*, designer

fictus, a, um, *adj*, imagined

ficus, i, or, ūs, *f*, fig-tree

fĭdēlis, e, *adj*, *adv*, ĭter, faithful, true, sure

fĭdēlĭtas, ātis, *f*, faithfulness

fīdens, ntis, *adj*, *adv*, nter, self-confident

fīdentia, ae, *f*, confidence

fĭdes, ĕi, *f*, trust, faith, confidence, honesty, promise

fĭdes, ĭum, *f. pl*, lute, guitar

fĭdĭcen, ĭnis, *m*, lute-player

fīdo, fīsus sum, *v.* 3, *semi-dep. with dat*; to trust

fīdūcia, ae, *f*, confidence

fīdus, a, um, *adj*, trustworthy

fĭĕri, see fio

fīgo, xi, xum, *v.t.* 3, to fix, fasten, transfix

fĭgŭlāris, e, *adj*, of a potter

fĭgŭlus, i, *m*, potter

fĭgūra, ae, *f*, shape, phantom, atom, nature

fĭgūrātus, a, um, *adj*, shaped

fĭgūro, *v.t.* 1, to shape

fīlia, ae, *f*, daughter

fīliŏla, ae, *f*, little daughter

fīliŏlus, i, *m*, little son

fīlius, i, *m*, son

fĭlix, ĭcis, *f*, hair, fern

fīlum, i, *n*, thread, texture

fimbriae, ārum, *f. pl*, threads, fringe

fĭmus, i, *m*, manure

findo, fĭdi, ssum, *v.t.* 3, to split

fīnes, ĭum, *m. pl*, territory

fingo, nxi, ctum, *v.t.* 3, to shape, adorn, imagine, devise

fīnio, *v.t.* 4, to enclose, limit, prescribe, end, die

fīnis, is, *m*, boundary, limit, end

fīnĭtĭmus, a, um, *adj*, adjoining

fīnĭtĭmi, ōrum, *m. pl*, neighbours

finĭtor, ōris, *m*, surveyor

fīo, fĭĕri, factus sum, *v*, *irreg*, to become, happen

firmāmen, ĭnis, *n*, prop, support

firmāmentum, ĭ, *n*, prop, support

firmĭtas, ātis, *f*, strength, firmness

firmĭtūdo, ĭnis, *f*, strength, firmness

firmo, *v.t.* 1, to strengthen, encourage, promise

firmus, a, um, *adj*, *adv*, ē, ĭter, strong, stable, constant, true

fiscella, ae, *f*, small basket, muzzle

fiscĭna, ae, *f*, small basket

fiscus, ĭ, *m*, purse, imperial treasury

fissĭlis, e, *adj*, breakable

fissum, ĭ, *n*, cleft, chink

fissūra, ae, *f*, split, chink

fistūca, ae, *f*, rammer

fistŭla, ae, *f*, pipe, tube

fistŭlātor, ōris, *m*, piper

fīsus, a, um, *adj*, trusting, relying on

flābellum, ĭ, *n*, small fan

flābra, ōrum, *n. pl*, gusts

flaccĭdus, a, um, *adj*, flabby

flăgello, *v.t.* 1, to whip

flăgellum, ĭ, *n*, whip, thong

flăgĭtātio, ōnis, *f*, demand

flăgĭtiōsus, a, um, *adj*, *adv*, e, disgraceful

flăgĭtĭum, ĭi, *n*, disgraceful conduct, shame

flăgĭto, *v.t.* 1, to demand

flăgrans, ntis, *adj*, burning

flăgro, *v.i.* 1, to blaze, glow

flăgrum, ĭ, *n*, whip

flāmen, ĭnis, *m*, priest

flāmen, ĭnis, *n*, blast

flāmĭnĭum, ĭi, *n*, priesthood

flamma, ae, *f*, flame, blaze

flammĕum, ĭ, *n*, bridal-veil

flammĕus, a, um, *adj*, flaming

flammĭfer, ĕra, ĕrum, *adj*, flame-carrying

flammo, *v.i.t.* 1, to burn

flātus, ūs, *m*, blowing, bluster

flāvens, ntis, *adj*, yellow

flāvĕo, *v.i.* 2, to be golden, yellow

flāvesco, *v.i.* 3, to turn golden

flāvus, a, um, *adj*, golden, yellow

flēbĭlis, e, *adj*, *adv*, ĭter, lamentable, tearful

flecto, xi, xum, *v.i.t.* 3, to turn; bend, curve, wheel, persuade

flĕo, ēvi, tum, *v.i.t.* 2, to weep; mourn

flētus, ūs, *m*, weeping

flexĭbĭlis, e, *adj*, flexible

flexĭo, ōnis, *f*, curve

flexŭōsus, a, um, *adj*, crooked

flexus, ūs, *m*, bend, turning

flictus, ūs, *m*, collision

flō, *v.i.t.* 1, to blow

floccus, ĭ, *m*, lock of wool

flōrens, ntis, *adj*, shining, flourishing

flōrĕo, *v.i.* 2, to bloom, flourish

flōresco, *v.i.* 3, to come into flower, flourish

flōrĕus, a, um, *adj*, made of flowers

flōrĭdus, a, um, *adj*, blooming

flōs, ōris, *m*, flower, ornament

floscŭlus, ĭ, *m*, small flower

fluctŭo, *v.i.* 1, to ripple, undulate, hesitate

fluctŭōsus, a, um, *adj*, billowy

fluctus, ūs, *m*, wave

flŭens, ntis, *adj*, lax, fluent

flŭentum, ĭ, *n*, stream, flood

flŭĭdus, a, um, *adj*, flowing, slack

flŭĭto, *v.i.* 1, to flow, float

flūmen, ĭnis, *n*, river, flood

flūmĭnĕus, a, um, *adj*, of a river

flŭo, xi, xum, *v.i.* 3, to flow, wave, vanish

flŭvĭālis, e, *adj*, of a river

flŭvĭus, ĭi, *m*, river

fluxĭo, ōnis, *f*, flowing

fluxus, a, um, *adj*, fluid, slack

fŏcāle, is, *n*, neck-tie

fŏcŭlus, ĭ, *m*, brazier

fŏcus, ĭ, *m*, fire-place, home

fŏdĭco, *v.t.* 1, to dig, nudge, stab

fŏdĭo, fōdi, fossum, *v.i.t.* 3, to dig; dig up, prick, stab

foedĕrātus, a, um, *adj*, allied

foedĭtas, ātis, *f*, filthiness

foedo, *v.t.* 1, to disfigure, disgrace, stain

foedus, a, um, *adj*, *adv*, ē, filthy, shameful

foedus, ĕris, *n*, treaty, contract

foet . . . see fet . . .

fŏlĭum, ĭi, *n*, leaf

follĭcŭlus, ĭ, *m*, small bag

follis, is, *m*, pair of bellows

fōmentum, ĭ, *n*, poultice, comfort

fōmes, ĭtis, *m*, firewood

fons, ntis, *m*, fountain, origin

fontĭcŭlus, ĭ, *m*, small fountain

for, *v.i.t.* 1, *dep*, to speak; say, predict

fŏrāmen, ĭnis, *n*, hole

fŏrās, *adv*, out-of-doors

forceps, ĭpis, *m*, *f*, tongs, pincers

fŏrĕ = futurum esse see esse

fŏrem = essem,

fŏrensis, e, *adj*, concerning the courts of law

fŏres, um , *f. pl*, door, entrance

forfex, ĭcis, *f*, scissors (*usually in pl.*)

fŏrĭca, ae, *f*, public convenience

fŏrĭcŭlae, ārum, *f. pl,* shutters

fŏris, is, *f,* door, entrance

fŏris, *adv,* outside, from outside

forma, ae, *f,* form, shape, beauty

formica, ae, *f,* ant

formīdābĭlis, e, *adj,* fearful

formīdo, *v.i.t.* 1, to be afraid; fear

formīdo, ĭnis, *f,* fear, terror

formīdŭlōsus, a, um, *adj, adv,* ē, dreadful, fearful

formo, *v.t.* 1, to shape

formōsus, a, um, *adj,* beautiful

formŭla, ae, *f,* rule, principle, agreement, lawsuit

fornax, ācis, *f,* oven

fornix, ĭcis, *m,* arch, vault

fors, rtis, *f,* chance, luck

fors, *adv,* perhaps

forsan, *adv,* perhaps

forsĭtan, *adv,* perhaps

fortassē, *adv,* perhaps

fortē, *adv,* by chance

fortis, e, *adj, adv,* ĭter, strong, brave

fortĭtūdo, ĭnis, *f,* bravery

fortŭĭtō(ū), *adv,* by chance

fortŭĭtus, a, um, *adj,* accidental

fortūna, ae, *f,* luck, fate, fortune (good or bad), circumstances, property

fortūnātus, a, um, *adj, adv,* ē, lucky, happy

fortūno, *v.t.* 1, to enrich, bless

fŏrum, i, *n,* market-place, business

fŏrus, i, *m,* gangway, passage, row of seats

fossa, ae, *f,* ditch

fossĭo, ōnis, *f,* excavation

fossor, ōris, *m,* digger, miner

fŏvĕa, ae, *f,* pit, pitfall

fŏvĕo, fōvi, fōtum, *v.t.* 2, to warm, caress, love

fractūra, ae, *f,* fracture

fractus, a, um, *adj,* weak, feeble

frāga, ōrum, *n. pl,* strawberries

frăgĭlis, e, *adj,* brittle, frail

frăgĭlĭtas, ātis, *f,* frailty

fragmen, ĭnis, *n,* fracture, splinter

fragmentum, i, *n,* fragment

frăgor, ōris, *m,* crash

frăgōsus, a, um, *adj,* rugged, crashing

fragro, *v.i.* 1, to smell

frăgum, i, *n,* strawberry plant

frango, frēgi, fractum, *v.t.* 3, to break, crush, weaken

frāter, tris, *m,* brother

frāternĭtas, ātis, *f,* brotherhood

frāternus, a, um, *adj, adv,* ē, brotherly

frātrĭcīda, ae, *m,* a fratricide

fraudātĭo, ōnis, *f,* deceit

fraudātor, ōris, *m,* deceiver

fraudo, *v.t.* 1, to cheat, defraud

fraudŭlentus, a, um, *adj,* deceitful

fraus, dis, *f,* deceit, crime, mistake, injury

fraxĭnĕus, a, um, *adj,* of ash

fraxĭnus, i, *f,* ash-tree

frĕmĭtus, ūs, *m,* murmur, roar

frĕmo, ŭi, ĭtum, *v.i.t.* 3, to roar, murmur, howl; grumble at

frĕmor, ōris, *m,* murmuring

frendĕo, ŭi, frĕsum, *v.i.* 2, to gnash the teeth, crush

frēno, *v.t.* 1, to bridle, curb

frēnum, i, *n,* bridle, restraint

frĕquens, ntis, *adj, adv,* nter, usual, repeated, crowded

frĕquentātĭo, ōnis, *f,* frequency

frĕquentĭa, ae, *f,* crowd

frĕquento, *v.t.* 1, to frequent, repeat, crowd, celebrate

frĕtum, i, *n,* channel, strait

frētus, a, um, *adj. with abl,* relying on

frĭco, cŭi, ctum, *v.t.* 1, to rub

frictus, a, um, *adj,* rubbed, (frico); roasted (frigo)

frĭgĕo, *v.i.* 2, to be cold or languid, to be slighted

frĭgesco, frixi, *v.i.* 3, to grow cold, become languid

frĭgĭdus, a, um, *adj,* cold, stiff, feeble, spiritless

frĭgĭda, ae, *f,* cold water

frīgo, xi, ctum, *v.t.* 3, to roast

frīgus, ōris, *n,* cold, winter

fringilla, ae, *f,* small bird, robin, chaffinch

frondātor, ōris, *m,* pruner

frondĕo, *v.i.* 2, to be in leaf

frondesco, dŭi, *v.i.* 3, to come into leaf

frondĕus, a, um, *adj,* leafy

frondōsus, a, um, *adj,* leafy

frons, dis, *f,* foliage, leaf

frons, ntis, *f,* forehead, front, appearance

fructŭōsus, a, um, *adj,* fruitful, advantageous

fructus, ūs, *m,* enjoyment, fruit, profit

frūgālis, e, *adj, adv,* ĭter, thrifty, careful

frūgālĭtas, ātis, *f,* thrift, worth

frūges, um, *f. pl,* see frux

frūgi, *indecl. adj,* worthy, useful

frūgĭfer, a, ērum, *adj,* fertile

frūmentārĭus, a, um, *adj,* of corn

frūmentor, *v.i.* 1, *dep,* to fetch corn

frūmentum, i, *n,* corn

frŭor, fructus, *v.* 3, *dep. with abl,* to enjoy

frustrā, *adv*, in vain

frustrātio, **ōnis**, *f*, deception, frustration

frustror, *v.t.* 1, *dep*, to deceive

frustum, **i**, *n*, piece

frūtex, **icis**, *m*, bush

frūticētum, **i**, *n*, thicket

frūticōsus, **a**, **um**, *adj*, bushy

frux, **frūgis**, *f*, fruit, crops, value, result

fūcātus, **a**, **um**, *adj*, painted, counterfeit

fūco, *v.t.* 1, to paint, dye

fūcōsus, **a**, **um**, *adj*, coloured, spurious

fūcus, **i**, *m*, rouge, disguise

fūcus, **i**, *m*, drone

fūga, **ae**, *f*, flight, exile

fūgax, **ācis**, *adj*, runaway, swift

fūgiens, **ntis**, *adj*, fleeing

fūgio, **fūgi**, **fūgitum**, *v.i.t.* 3, to run away; flee from, avoid

fūgitīvus, **a**, **um**, *adj*, fugitive

fūgitīvus, **i**, *m*, runaway slave, deserter

fūgito, *v.t.* 1, to flee, avoid

fūgo, *v.t.* 1, to rout, chase

fulcio, **fulsi**, **fultum**, *v.t.* 4, to prop up, strengthen

fulcrum, **i**, *n*, foot (of couch)

fulgens, **ntis**, *adj*, shining

fulgeo, **lsi**, *v.i.* 2, to flash, shine

fulgidus, **a**, **um**, *adj*, flashing, shining

fulgor, **ōris**, *m*, lightning, gleam, splendour

fulgur, **ūris**, *n*, lightning

fulgūrat, *v*, *impers*, it lightens

fūlica, **ae**, *f*, moor-hen

fūligo, **inis**, *f*, soot

fūligīnōsus, **a**, **um**, *adj*, sooty

fulmen, **inis**, *n*, thunderbolt, lightning

fulmīnēus, **a**, **um**, *adj*, of lightning, destructive, brilliant

fulmino, *v.i.* 1, to thunder

fultūra, **ae**, *f*, prop, tonic

fulvus, **a**, **um**, *adj*, deep yellow

fūmēus, **a**, **um**, *adj*, smoky

fūmidus, **a**, **um**, *adj*, smoky

fūmifer, **ēra**, **ērum**, *adj*, smoking, steaming

fūmificus, **a**, **um**, *adj*, smoking, steaming

fūmigo, *v.t.* 1, to smoke out, fumigate

fūmo, *v.i.* 1, to smoke

fūmōsus, **a**, **um**, *adj*, smoky, smoke-dried

fūmus, **i**, *m*, smoke

fūnāle, **is**, *n*, cord, torch

functio, **ōnis**, *f*, performing

functus, **a**, **um**, *partic. adj*, *with abl*, having completed

funda, **ae**, *f*, sling, missile

fundāmen, **inis**, *n*, foundation

fundāmentum, **i**, *n*, foundation

funditor, **ōris**, *m*, slinger

funditus, *adv*, from the bottom, completely

fundo, **fūdi**, **fūsum**, *v.t.* 3, to pour out, spread out, scatter, overthrow, produce

fundo, *v.t.* 1, to found, fix

fundus, **i**, *m*, the bottom, a farm

fundus, **i**, *m*, guarantor

fūnēbris, **e**, *adj*, of a funeral

fūnērēus, **a**, **um**, *adj*, of a funeral

fūnēro, *v.t.* 1, to bury, kill

fūnesto, *v.t.* 1, to pollute

fūnestus, **a**, **um**, *adj*, fatal, sad

fungor, **functus**, *v.* 3, *dep*, *with abl*, to perform, complete

fungus, **i**, *m*, mushroom, fungus

fūnis, **is**, *m*, rope

fūnus, **ĕris**, *n*, funeral, death, ruin

fūr, **fūris**, *c*, thief, rogue

fūrax, **ācis**, *adj*, light-fingered

furca, **ae**, *f*, two-pronged fork or pole for punishment

furcifer, **ĕri**, *m*, gallows-bird

furcilla, **ae**, *f*, small fork

furcūla, **ae**, *f*, fork-shaped prop, ravine

fūrens, **ntis**, *adj*, raging

furfur, **ŭris**, *m*, bran

fūriae, **ārum**, *f. pl*, rage, frenzy, avenging Furies

fūriālis, **e**, *adj*, *adv*, **iter**, raging, wild

fūribundus, **a**, **um**, *adj*, raging

fūrio, *v.t.* 1, to enrage

fūriōsus, **a**, **um**, *adj*, raging

furnus, **i**, *m*, oven

fūro, **ŭi**, *v.i.* 3, to rage, be mad

fūror, *v.t.* 1, *dep*, to steal

fūror, **ōris**, *m*, rage, fury

furtim, *adv*, stealthily

furtīvus, **a**, **um**, *adj*, stolen, secret

furtum, **i**, *n*, theft, trick

furtō, *adv*, secretly

fūruncŭlus, **i**, *m*, pilferer, sore, boil

furvus, **a**, **um**, *adj*, gloomy, swarthy

fuscina, **ae**, *f*, trident

fusco, *v.t.* 1, to blacken, darken

fuscus, **a**, **um**, *adj*, dark, swarthy

fūsilis, **e**, *adj*, fluid, soft

fustis, **is**, *m*, cudgel, club

fūsus, **a**, **um**, *adj*, spread out, wide

fūsus, **i**, *m*, spindle

futtilis (fūtilis), **e**, *adj*, worthless

futtilitas (fūtilitas), **ātis**, *f*, worthlessness

fūtūra, **ōrum**, *n. pl*, the future

fūtūrum, **i**, *n*, the future

For List of Abbreviations used, turn to pages 3, 4

fŭtūrus, a, um, *adj*, future

G

gaesum, i, *n*, heavy Gallic javelin
galbĭnus, a, um, *adj*, greenish-yellow
gălĕa, ae, *f*, helmet
gălĕo, *v.t.* 1, to issue with helmets
gălērum, i, *n* (us, i, *m*), hat
galla, ae, *f*, oak-apple
gallīna, ae, *f*, hen
gallīnārĭum, ii, *n*, hen-house
gallus, i, *m*, cock
gānĕa, ae, *f*, eating-house
gānĕo, ōnis, *m*, glutton
gannĭo, *v.i.* 4, to bark, snarl
gannītus, ūs, *m*, chattering
garrĭo, *v.t.* 4, to chatter
garrŭlĭtas, ātis, *f*, chattering
garrŭlus, a, um, *adj*, talkative
gărum (garon), i, *n*, fish-sauce
gaudĕo, gāvīsus, *v.i.t.* 2, *semi-dep*, to
  rejoice
gaudĭum, ii, *n*, joy, delight
gausāpa, ae, *f*, rough cloth
gāvĭa, ae, *f*, sea-bird
gāza, ae, *f*, treasure (of Persia)
gĕlĭdus, a, um, *adj*, *adv*, ē, ice-cold,
  frosty
gĕlo, *v.i.t.* 1, to freeze
gĕlum, i (gĕlu, ūs), *n*, frost, cold
gĕmellus, a, um, *adj*, (us, i, *m*), twin
gĕmĭno, *v.t.* 1, to double, pair
gĕmĭnus, a, um, *adj*, twin
gĕmĭni, ōrum, *m. pl*, twins
gĕmĭtus, ūs, *m*, lamentation
gemma, ae, *f*, bud, jewel, goblet,
  signet-ring
gemmārĭus, ii, *m*, jeweller
gemmātus, a. um *adj*, set with jewels
gemmĕus, a, um, *adj*, set with jewels
gemmo, *v.i.* 1, to come into bud
gĕmo, ŭi, ĭtum, *v.i.t.* 3, to groan,
  creak; deplore
gĕna, ae, *f*, the cheek
gĕner, ĕri, *m*, son-in-law
gĕnērālis, e, *adj*, of a certain kind,
  general
gĕnērātim, *adv*, in classes, in general
gĕnērātor, ōris, *m*, breeder
gĕnĕro, *v.t.* 1, to create, produce, be
  born (passive)
gĕnĕrōsus, a, um, *adj*, *adv*, ē, of noble
  birth, generous
gĕnesta, ae, *f*, small shrub with yellow
  flowers, broom
gĕnĕtīvus, a, um, *adj*, inborn
gĕnĕtrix, īcis, *f*, mother

gĕnĭālis, e, *adj*, *adv*, ĭter, bridal,
  cheerful
gĕnĭtālis, e, *adj*, of birth, fruitful
gĕnĭtor, ōris, *m*, father
gĕnĭus, ii, *m*, guardian angel
gens, ntis, *f*, clan, race, descendant,
  nation
gentīlĭcĭus, a, um, *adj*, of the same
  clan
gentīlis, e, *adj*, of the same clan
gentīlis, is, *c*, relative
gĕnu, ūs, *n*, knee
gĕnŭīnus, a, um, *adj*, innate
gĕnŭīnus, a, um, *adj*, of the cheek
  or jaw
gĕnus, ĕris, *n*, birth, race, kind, type,
  descendant
gĕōgrăphĭa, ae, *f*, geography
gĕōmĕtres, ae, *m*, mathematician
gĕōmĕtrĭa, ae, *f*, geometry
germānĭtas, ātis, *f*, brotherhood
germānus, a, um, *adj*, own
germānus, i, *m* (a, ae, *f*), brother,
  (sister)
germen, ĭnis, *n*, bud, sprig
germĭno, *v.i.* 1, to bud
gĕro, gessi, stum, *v.t.* 3, to bear, wear,
  bring, produce, behave, display,
  carry on, honour
gerrae, ārum, *f.pl*, nonsense
gĕrŭlus, i, *m*, porter
gestāmen, ĭnis, *n*, load
gestātĭo, ōnis, *f*, riding, driving
gestĭo, *v.i.* 4, to be joyful, desire
  passionately
gesto, *v.t.* 1, to carry, wear, have
gestus, ūs, *m*, posture, gesture
gestus, a, um, *adj*, achieved, carried
gibber, ĕris, *m*, hump; *as adj*, hunchbacked
gibbus, i, *m*, hump; *as adj*, hunchbacked
gĭgantĕus, a, um, *adj*, of giants
gĭgās, ntis, *m*, giant
gigno, gĕnŭi, gĕnĭtum, *v.t.* 3, to give
  birth to; *(passive)* be born
gilvus, a, um, *adj*, pale yellow
gingīva, ae, *f*, gum
glăber, bra, brum, *adj*, bald
glăcĭālis, e, *adj*, frozen
glăcĭes, ēi, *f*, ice
glăcĭo, *v.t.* 1, to freeze
glădĭātor, ōris, *m*, gladiator
glădĭātōrĭus, a, um, *adj*, gladiatorial
glădĭus, ii, *m*, sword
glaeba (glēba), ae, *f*, clod
glans, ndis, *f*, acorn, bullet
glārĕa, ae, *f*, gravel

glaucus, a, um, *adj*, blue-grey

glēba, see glaeba

glis, glīris, *m*, dormouse

glisco,–*v.i.* 3, to swell, grow

glŏbōsus, a, um, *adj*, spherical

glŏbus, i, *m*, ball, crowd

glŏmĕro, *v.t.* 1, to gather into a heap, crowd together

glŏmus, ĕris, *n*, ball of thread

glōria, ae, *f*, glory, boasting

glōriātĭo, ōnis, *f*, boasting

glōrior, *v.i.t.*1, *dep*, to boast

glōriōsus, a, um, *adj*, *adv*, ē, famous, conceited

glossārĭum, ii, *n*, glossary

glūten, ĭnis, *n*, glue

glūtĭnātor, ōris, *m*, bookbinder

glūtĭno, *v.t.* 1, to glue

gluttĭo, *v.t.* 4, to gulp

gnārus, a, um, *adj. with genit*, acquainted with, expert in

gnātus, a, um, *adj*, born

gnāv ... see nāv ...

gossypĭum, ii, *n*, cotton

grăcĭlis, e, *adj*, slender

grăcĭlĭtas, ātis, *f*, slenderness

grăcŭlus, i, *m*, jackdaw

grădātim, *adv*, gradually

grădātĭo, ōnis, *f*, gradation, climax

grădĭor, gressus, *v.i.* 3, *dep*, to walk, go, move

grădus, ūs, *m*, pace, step, rank, position, station, stair, plait

graecor, *v.i.* 1, *dep*, to live like the Greeks

grallae, ārum, *f. pl*, stilts

grāmen, ĭnis, *n*, grass

grāmĭnĕus, a, um, *adj*, grassy

grammătĭca, ae, *f*, grammar

grammătĭcus, i, *m*, grammarian

grānārĭa, ōrum, *n. pl*, granary

grānātus, a, um, *adj*, with many seeds

grandaevus, a, um, *adj*, old

grandĭlŏquus, a, um, *adj*, boastful

grandĭnat, *v.* 1, *impers*, it is hailing

grandis, e, *adj*, full-grown, large, old, strong, noble

grando, ĭnis, *f*, hail, hail-storm

grānum, i, *n*, grain, seed

grānōsus, a, um, *adj*, seedy

grassātor, ōris, *m*, idler, footpad

grassor, *v.i.* 1, *dep*, to hang about, attack, rage

grātē, *adv*, gratefully, willingly

grātes, *f. pl*, thanks

grātĭa, ae, *f*, esteem, friendship, charm, beauty, kindness, favour, gratitude; *in abl*, for the sake of; grātĭīs (grātĭs), as a favour; *pl*, thanks

grātĭfĭcātĭo, ōnis, *f*, doing favours

grātĭfĭcor, *v.* 1, *dep*, to do as a favour, oblige

grātĭōsus, a, um, *adj*, popular

grātor, *v. i.t.* 1, *dep*, to congratulate

grātuītus, a, um, *adj*, voluntary

grātŭlātĭo, ōnis, *f*, rejoicing

grātŭlor, *v.i.t.* 1, *dep*, to congratulate

grātus, a, um, *adj*, pleasing, grateful

grăvāte, *adv*, unwillingly

grăvēdo, ĭnis, *f*, cold, catarrh

grăvĕŏlens, ntis, *adj*, stinking

grăvesco, *v.i.* 3, to grow heavy

grăvĭdus, a, um, *adj*, pregnant

grăvis, e, *adj*, *adv*, ĭter, heavy, loaded, low, pregnant, severe, unpleasant, serious, urgent, important

grăvĭtas, ātis, *f*, weight, heaviness, severity, dignity, urgency

grăvo, *v.t.* 1, to load, oppress

grăvor, *v.i.t.* 1, *dep*, to be irritated or reluctant; not to tolerate

grĕgālis, e, *adj*, of the herd, gregarious

grĕgārĭus, a, um, *adj*, common

grĕgātim, *adv*, in herds

grĕmĭum, ii, *n*, bosom, lap

gressus, ūs, *m*, step, way

grex, grĕgis, *m*, flock, herd

grūmus, i, *m*, hillock

grunnĭo, *v.i.* 4, to grunt

grunnītus, ūs, *m*, grunt

grus, grŭis, *m*, *f*, crane

grŷllus, i, *m*, grasshopper

gryps, gryphis, *m*, griffin

gŭbernācŭlum, i, *n*, rudder

gŭbernātĭo, ōnis, *f*, management

gŭbernātor, ōris, *m*, steersman

gŭberno, *v.t.* 1, to, steer, manage

gŭla, ae, *f*, throat, appetite

gŭlōsus, a, um, *adj*, gluttonous

gummi, *n*, (*indecl.*), gum

gurges, ĭtis, *m*, whirlpool, abyss

gustātĭo, ōnis, *f*, taste

gustātus, ūs, *m*, sense of taste

gusto, *v.t.* 1, to taste

gustus, ūs, *m*, tasting, snack

gutta, ae, *f*, drop, spot

guttur, ŭris, *n*, throat

gutus (guttus), i, *m*, flask

gymnăsĭum, ii, *m*, gymnasium

gymnĭcus, a, um, *adj*, gymnastic

gypsātus, a, um, *adj*, covered with lime

gypso, *v.t.* 1, to plaster

gypsum, i, *n*, white lime

gŷrus, i, *m*, circuit, ring

H

hăbēna, ae, *f*, thong, rein

hăbĕo, v.t. 2, to have, keep, be able, render, esteem, use, deal with, know; with in animo, to intend

hăbilis, e, adj, convenient, expert

hăbităbilis, e, adj, habitable

hăbĭtātĭo, ōnis, f, residence

hăbĭto, v.i.t. 1, to live; inhabit

hăbĭtus, ūs, m, condition, bearing, state, dress, shape

hāc, adv, by this way, here

hactĕnus, adv, up to this point

haec, see hic

haedus, i, m, young goat

haemorrhăgĭa, ae, f, haemorrhage

haerĕo, si, sum, v.i. 2, to hang, cling, hesitate

haesĭtans, ntis, adj, hesitant

haesĭtantĭa, ae, f, stammering

haesĭtātĭo, ōnis, f, embarrassment

haesĭto, v.i. 1, to hesitate

hālĭtus, ūs, m, breath, steam

hālo, v.i.t. 1, to breathe; exhale

hāma, ae, f, bucket

hāmātus, a, um, adj, hooked

hāmus, i, m, hook, fish-hook

hāra, ae, f, coop, pen, sty

hărēna, ae, f, sand, arena

hărēnārĭus, a, um, adj, of sand

hărēnōsus, a, um, adj, sandy

hărĭŏlor, v.i. 1, dep, to foretell

hărĭŏlus, i, m, prophet

harmŏnĭa, ae, f, harmony

harpăgo, ōnis, m, grappling-hook

hărundo, ĭnis, f, reed, fishing-rod, shaft, shepherd's pipe

hăruspex, ĭcis, m, clairvoyant

hasta, ae, f, spear, lance

hastāti, ōrum, m. pl, pike-men; front line of a Roman army

hastīle, is, n, spear-shaft

haud (haut), adv, not at all

haudquāquam, adv, by no means

haurĭo, si, stum, v.t. 4, to draw up, drink in, drain, exhaust

haustus, ūs, m, a drink, draught

hav . . . see av . . .

hĕbĕnus, i, f, ebony

hĕbĕo, v.i. 2, to be dull

hĕbes, ĕtis, adj, blunt, dull

hĕbesco, v.i. 3, to grow dull

hĕbĕto, v.t. 1, to blunt

hĕdĕra, ae, f, ivy

hei, interj, ah! alas!

hellŭo, ōnis, m, glutton

hellŭor, v. 1, dep, with abl, to squander

hem! (em!), interj, ah! indeed!

hēmĭcyclĭum, ii, n, semi-circle

hēmisphaerĭum, ii, n, hemisphere

hĕra, ae, f, lady of the house

herba, ae, f, grass, plant

herbārĭus, a, um, adj, of plants

herbĭdus, a, um, adj, grassy

herbōsus, a, um, adj, grassy

hercŭle (hercle)! by Hercules!

hĕrē, adv, yesterday

hērēdĭtārĭus, a, um, adj, inherited

hērēdĭtas, ātis, f, inheritance

hēres, ēdis, c, heir, heiress

hĕri, adv, yesterday

hĕrīlis, e, adj, of the master or mistress

hernĭa, ae, f, rupture

hērōĭcus, a, um, adj, heroic

hēros, ōis, m, demigod

hĕrus, i, m, master of the house

hespĕris, ĭdis, adj, western

hespĕrĭus, a, um, adj, western

hesternus, a, um, adj, yesterday's

heu!, interj, oh! alas!

heus!, interj, hallo there!

hexămĕter, tri, m, a verse metre consisting of six feet

hians, see hio

hĭātus, ūs, m, aperture

hīberna, ōrum, n.pl, winter-quarters

hībernācŭla, ōrum, n.pl, tents to spend winter in

hīberno, v.i. 1, to spend the winter

hībernus, a, um, adj, of winter

hibrĭda, ae, c, cross-breed

hīc, haec, hōc, pron, this

hīc, adv, here

hiĕmālis, e, adj, of winter

hiĕmo, v.i.t. 1, to spend the winter; freeze

hiems (hiemps), hiĕmis, f, winter, stormy weather

hilāris, e, adj, adv, ē, cheerful

hilărĭtas, ātis, f, gaiety

hilăro, v.t. 1, to cheer up

hillae, ārum, f. pl, sausage

hinc, adv, from here, hence

hinnĭo, v.i. 4, to neigh

hinnītus, ūs, m, neighing

hinnŭlĕus, i, m, young stag

hĭo, v.i. 1, to gape open

hippŏpŏtămus, i, m, hippopotamus

hircīnus, a, um, adj, of a goat

hircus, i, m, goat

hirsūtus, a, um, adj, shaggy

hirtus, a, um, adj, rough, shaggy

hirūdo, ĭnis, f, leech

hirundĭnīnus, a, um, adj, of swallows

hirundo, ĭnis, f, a swallow

hisco,– v.i.t. 3, to gape; whisper

hispĭdus, a, um, adj, rough, shaggy

histŏrĭa, ae, f, story, account

histŏrĭcus, a, um, adj, historical

histŏrĭcus, i, m, historian

histrĭo, ōnis, m, actor

hiulcus, a, um, adj, gaping; (of speech) badly connected

hoc, see hic

hŏdiē, *adv*, today

hŏdiernus, a, um, *adj*, of today

hŏlus, ĕris, *n*, vegetables

hŏluscŭlum, i, *n*, small vegetable

hŏmĭcīda, ae, *c*, murderer

hŏmĭcīdium, ii, *n*, homicide

hŏmo, ĭnis, *c*, human being

hŏmullus, i, *m*, puny man

hŏmuncŭlus, i, *m*, puny man

hŏnestas, ātis, *f*, honour, good name, integrity

hŏnesto, *v.t.* 1, to honour, adorn

hŏnestum, i, *n*, integrity

hŏnestus, a, um, *adj*, *adv*, ē, respectable, esteemed, eminent

hŏnor (hŏnos), ōris, *m*, esteem, public office, reward, charm

hŏnōrārius, a, um, *adj*, honorary

hŏnōrātus, a, um, *adj*, respected

hŏnōrĭfĭcus, a, um, *adj*, *adv*, ē, complimentary

hŏnōro, *v.t.* 1, to honour, respect, adorn

hŏnos, see hŏnor

hŏnus ... see ŏnus ...

hōra, ae, *f*, hour, time, season

hōrārium, ii, *n*, hour-glass

hordĕŏlus, i, *m*, sty (eye)

hordĕum, i, *n*, barley

hōrĭŏla, ae, *f*, fishing-boat

hornōtĭnus, a, um, *adj*, this year's

hornus, a, um, *adj*, this year's

hōrōlŏgium, ii, *n*, clock

horrendus, a, um, *adj*, terrible

horrĕo, *v.i.t.* 2, to bristle, tremble; dread

horresco, horrŭi, *v.i.* 3, to become ruffled or frightened

horrĕum, i, *n*, barn, warehouse

horrĭbĭlis, e, *adj*, terrible

horrĭdŭlus, a, um, *adj*, rough

horrĭdus, a, um, *adj*, *adv*, ē, rough, bristly, wild, uncouth

horrĭfer, ĕra, ĕrum, *adj*, dreadful

horrĭfĭco, *v.t.* 1, to ruffle, terrify

horrĭfĭcus, a, um, *adj*, terrible

horrĭsŏnus, a, um, *adj*, with fearful sounds

horror, ōris, *m*, bristling, trembling, chill, terror

hortāmen, ĭnis, *n*, encouragement

hortātĭo, ōnis, *f*, encouragement

hortātor, ōris, *m*, encourager

hortātus, ūs, *m*, encouragement

hortor, *v.t.* 1, *dep*, to encourage, urge, cheer on

hortŭlus, i, *m*, little garden

hortus, i, *m*, garden

hospēs, ĭtis, *m*, (hospĭta, ae, *f*), host(ess), guest, stranger

hospĭtālis, e, *adj*, hospitable

hospĭtĭum, ii, *n*, hospitality, friendship, lodgings

hostia, ae, *f*, sacrificial victim

hostĭcus, a, um, *adj*, of the enemy

hostīlis, e, *adj*, *adv*, iter, hostile

hostis, is, *c*, enemy, stranger

hūc, *adv*, to this place or point

hui!, *interj*, oh!

huius, *genitive of* hic

hūiuscĕmŏdi, hūiusmŏdi, *pron. adj*, (indecl.) of this sort

hūmāna, ōrum, *n.pl*, human affairs

hūmānē, *adv*, like a reasonable human being, courteously

hūmānĭtas, ātis, *f*, humanity, gentleness, refinement

hūmānĭter, *adv*, see hūmānē

hūmānus, a, um, *adj*, human, mortal, humane, gentle, kind

hūmecto, *v.t.* 1, to moisten

hūmĕo, *v.i.* 2, to be wet

hūmĕrus, i, *m*, shoulder, arm

hūmi, *adv*, on or to the ground

hūmĭdus, a, um, *adj*, damp, wet

hūmĭlis, e, *adj*, *adv*, iter, low, humble, abject

hūmĭlĭtas, ātis, *f*, lowness, insignificance, meanness

hūmo, *v.t.* 1, to bury

hūmor, ōris, *m*, liquid

hūmus, i, *f*, the ground, region

hyăcinthus(os), i, *m*, blue iris

hyaena, ae, *f*, hyena

hyălus, i, *m*, glass

hybrida, ae, *c*, cross-breed

hydra, ae, *f*, seven-headed watersnake

hydria, ae, *f*, jug

hydrops, ōpis, *m*, dropsy

hydrus, i, *m*, water-snake

hymen, mĕnis, *m*, marriage

hyperbŏlē, es, *f*, exaggeration, hyperbole

hystrix, ĭcis, *f*, porcupine

I

ĭambēus, a, um, *adj*, iambic

ĭambus, i, *m*, iambic foot (2 syllables, short followed by long)

ĭanthĭnus, a, um, *adj*, violet in colour

ĭāpyx, iapўgis, *m*, West-North-West wind

ĭaspis, ĭdis, *f*, jasper

ĭbī, *adv*, there, then

ĭbīdem, *adv*, in that same place, at that very moment

ībis, ĭdis, *f*, sacred bird, ibis

ĭcĭo (īco), ĭci, ictum, *v.t.* 3, to hit, strike (a bargain)

For List of Abbreviations used, turn to pages 3, 4

ictus, ūs, *m*, blow, stroke, shot

id, see is

idcirco, *adv*, for that reason

idem, ĕădem, idem, *pron*, the same

identidem, *adv*, repeatedly

ideo, *adv*, for that reason

idiōta, ae, *m*, layman

idōnĕus, a, um, *adj*, suitable, capable, sufficient

idus, ŭum, *f. pl*, the Ides, 13th or 15th day of the month

idyllium, ii, *n*, idyll

igitur, *adv*, therefore, then

ignārus, a, um, *adj*, unaware

ignāvia, ae, *f*, laziness, cowardice

ignāvus, a, um, *adj*, *adv*, ē, lazy, cowardly

ignesco, *v.i.* 3, to catch fire

ignĕus, a, um, *adj*, burning

igniculus, i, *m*, spark

ignifer, ĕra, ĕrum, *adj*, fiery

ignis, is, *m*, fire, glow

ignōbilis, e, *adj*, unknown, obscure

ignōbilitas, ātis, *f*, obscurity

ignōminia, ae, *f*, disgrace

ignōminiōsus, a, um, *adj*, shameful

ignōrans, ntis, *adj*, unaware

ignōrantia, ae, *f*, ignorance

ignōrātio, ōnis, *f*, ignorance

ignōro, *v.i.t.* 1, to be unaware (of)

ignosco, nōvi, nōtum, *v.t.* 3 (*with dat. of person*), to forgive

ignōtus, a, um, *adj*, unknown, of low birth

ii, see is

ilex, icis, *f*, evergreen oak

ilia, ium, *n.pl*, groin, flank

ilicet, *adv*, immediately

ilico, *adv*, immediately

ilignus, a, um, *adj*, of oak

illa, see ille

illăbĕfactus, a, um, *adj*, unbroken

illābor, psus, *v.i.* 3, *dep*, to slip, glide, fall

illac, *adv*, on that side

illăcessītus, a, um, *adj*, unprovoked

illăcrimābilis, e, *adj*, unlamented

illăcrĭmo, *v.i.* 1, to weep over

illaesus, a, um, *adj*, unhurt

illaetābilis, e, *adj*, gloomy

illăquĕo, *v.t.* 1, to ensnare

illātus, see infero

ille, a, ud, *pron*, *adj*, that, he, she, it

illĕcĕbra, ae, *f*, charm, allurement, bait

illĕcĕbrōsus, a, um, *adj*, alluring

illĕpidus, a, um, *adj*, ill-mannered, rude

illex, icis, *c*, decoy

illībātus, a, um, *adj*, unimpaired

illibĕrālis, e, *adj*, mean

illic, *adv*, there, over there

illicio, lexi, ctum, *v.t.* 3, to allure, entice

illicitus, a, um, *adj*, forbidden

illico, *adv*, there, immediately

illīdo, si, sum, *v.t.* 3, to strike, dash, beat

illigo, *v.t.* 1, to tie, fasten

illinc, *adv*, from there

illino, lēvi, litum, *v.t.* 3, to smear, spread

illittĕrātus, a, um, *adj*, illiterate

illius, *genitive of* ille

illō, *adv*, to that place

illōtus, a, um, *adj*, dirty

illūc, *adv*, to that place

illūcesco, luxi, *v.i.* 3, to grow light, dawn, shine

illud, see ille

illūdo, si, sum, *v.i.t.* 3, to play; mock, ridicule

illūmino, *v.t.* 1, to light up

illustris, e, *adj*, lighted up, distinct, distinguished

illustro, *v.t.* 1, to elucidate, make famous

illŭvies, ēi, *f*, dirt

imāgo, inis, *f*, statue, picture, copy, echo, conception

imbēcillitas, ātis, *f*, weakness

imbēcillus, a, um, *adj*, weak

imbellis, e, *adj*, unwarlike

imber, bris, *m*, rain, shower

inberbis, e, *adj*, beardless

imbĭbo, bibi, *v.t.* 3, to drink in

imbrex, icis, *f*, gutter, tile

imbrifer, ĕra, ĕrum, *adj*, rainy

imbŭo, ŭi, ūtum, *v.t.* 3, to soak, infect, instil, train

imitābilis, e, *adj*, easily imitated

imitātio, ōnis, *f*, imitation

imitātor, ōris, *m*, imitator

imitātrix, icis, *f*, imitator

imitor, *v.t.* 1, *dep*, to imitate

immădesco, dŭi, *v.i.* 3, to become wet

immānia, ium, *n.pl*, horrors

immanis, e, *adj*, *adv*, ē, iter, enormous, frightful, savage

immānitas, ātis, *f*, enormity, barbarism, vastness

immansuētus, a, um, *adj*, untamed

immātūrus, a, um, *adj*, untimely, immature

immĕdĭcābilis, e, *adj*, incurable

immĕmor, ōris, *adj*, heedless

immĕmŏrātus, a, um, *adj*, unmentioned

immensĭtas, ātis, *f,* immensity

immensum, i, *n,* immensity

immensus, a, um, *adj,* measureless, endless

immĕrens, ntis, *adj,* undeserving, innocent

immergo, si, sum, *v.t.* 3, to dip, plunge, immerse

immĕrĭtus, a, um, *adj,* undeserved

immētātus, a, um, *adj,* unmeasured

immĭgro, *v.i.* 1, to go into

immĭnĕo, *v.i.* 2, to overhang, overlook, threaten, strive for

immĭnŭo, ŭi, ūtum, *v.t.* 3, to reduce, weaken, destroy

immĭnūtĭo, ōnis, *f,* weakening

immĭnūtus, a, um, *adj,* unabated

immiscĕo, scŭi, xtum, *v.t.* 2, to mix in, blend, unite

immiserābĭlis, e, *adj,* unpitied

immisērĭcors, cordis, *adj,* merciless

immissĭo, ōnis, *f,* admission

immītis, e, *adj,* harsh, rough

immitto, mīsi, ssum, *v.t.* 3, to send in, let fly, incite, allow to grow wild

immo, *adv,* on the contrary

immōbĭlis, e, *adj,* immovable

immōbĭlĭtas, ātis, *f,* immobility

immŏdĕrātus, a, um, *adj, adv,* ē, excessive

immŏdĭcus, a, um, *adj,* excessive

immŏlātĭo, ōnis, *f,* sacrifice

immŏlo, *v.t.* 1, to sacrifice, kill

immŏrior, mortŭus, *v.i.* 3, *dep,* to die, die away

immortāles, ĭum, *m. pl,* the gods

immortālis, e, *adj,* immortal

immortālĭtas, ātis, *f,* immortality

immōtus, a, um, *adj,* unmoved

immūgĭo, *v.i.* 4, to roar, resound

immundus, a, um, *adj,* dirty

immūnis, e, *adj,* exempt, idle, devoid of

immūnĭtas, ātis, *f,* exemption

immūnītus, a, um, *adj,* unfortified

immurmŭro, *v.i.* 1, to murmur at

immūtābĭlis, e, *adj,* unchangeable

immūtātĭo, ōnis, *f,* interchange

immūto, *v.t.* 1, to change, alter

impācātus, a, um, *adj,* unsubdued

impar, ăris, *adj, adv,* ĭter, unequal, uneven

imparātus, a, um, *adj,* unprepared

impastus, a, um, *adj,* hungry

impătĭens, ntis, *adj,* impatient

impăvĭdus, a, um, *adj,* fearless

impeccābĭlis, e, *adj,* faultless

impēdīmenta, ōrum, *n.pl,* luggage

impĕdīmentum, i, *n,* obstacle

impēdĭo, *v.t.* 4, to hinder, entangle, hamper

impĕdītus, a, um, *adj,* difficult; (soldiers) in full marching-kit

impĕdītĭo, ōnis, *f,* obstruction

impello, pŭli, pulsum, *v.t.* 3, to strike upon, drive on, urge, overthrow

impendens, ntis, *adj,* overhanging

impendĕo, *v.i.t.* 2, to overhang; threaten

impendĭum, ii, *n,* cost, expense

impendo, di, sum, *v.t.* 3, to expend, devote

impĕnētrābĭlis, e, *adj,* impenetrable

impensa, ae, *f,* cost, expense

impensus, a, um, *adj, adv,* ē, large, strong, expensive

impĕrātor, ōris, *m,* general

impĕrātōrĭus, a, um, *adj,* of a general

impĕrātum, i, *n,* order

imperfectus, a, um, *adj,* incomplete

impĕrĭōsus, a, um, *adj,* powerful, mighty, tyrannical

impĕrītĭa, ae, *f,* inexperience

impĕrĭto, *v.i.t.* 1, to command

impĕrītus, a, um, *adj, with genit,* unskilled, or inexperienced in

impĕrĭum, ii, *n,* power, command, control, dominion

impermissus, a, um, *adj,* forbidden

impĕro, *v.t.* 1, *with dat. of person,* to command, impose on, demand, requisition, rule

impertĭo, *v.t.* 4, to share

impervĭus, a, um, *adj,* impervious

impĕtībĭlis, e, *adj,* intolerable

impĕtrābĭlis, e, *adj,* attainable

impĕtro, *v.t.* 1, to obtain, get

impĕtus, ūs, *m,* attack, impetuosity, impulse

impexus, a, um, *adj,* uncombed

impĭĕtas, ātis, *f,* lack of respect for duty, disloyalty

impĭger, gra, grum, *adj,* energetic

impingo, pēgi, pactum, *v.t.* 3, to thrust, drive, strike (something) against

impĭus, a, um, *adj,* undutiful, unpatriotic, disloyal, wicked

implācābĭlis, e, *adj,* implacable

implācātus, a, um, *adj,* unsatisfied

implācĭdus, a, um, *adj,* rough

implecto, xi, xum, *v.t.* 3, to plait, interweave

implĕo, ēvi, ētum, *v.t.* 2, to fill, complete, fulfil

implĭcātĭo, ōnis, *f,* entwining, complication

implĭcātus, a, um, *adj,* entangled, confused

implĭco, *v.t.* 1, to entangle, involve, grasp, unite

implōrātĭo, ōnis, *f,* entreaty

implōro, *v.t.* 1, to implore, beg for

implūmis, e, *adj*, unfledged, callow

implŭvĭum, ĭi, *n*, rain-tank in floor of atrium of Roman house

impŏlītus, a, um, *adj*, unpolished

impōno, pŏsŭi, pŏsĭtum, *v.t.* 3, to place in or on, impose, assign

importo, *v.t.* 1, to carry in, import, cause

importūnĭtas, ātis, *f*, insolence

importūnus, a, um, *adj*, *adv*, ē, inconvenient, unsuitable, troublesome, rude

impŏtens, ntis, *adj*, powerless, weak, violent, headstrong

impŏtentĭa, ae, *f*, violence

impransus, a, um, *adj*, fasting

imprĕcātĭo, ōnis, *f*, imprecation, curse

imprĕcor, *v.t.* 1, *dep*, to pray for something for someone

impressĭo, ōnis, *f*, imprint, onset

impressus, a, um, *adj*, stamped, printed

imprīmīs, *adv*, especially

imprimo, pressi, ssum, *v.t.* 3, to stamp, imprint, engrave

imprŏbĭtas, ātis, *f*, wickedness

imprŏbo, *v.t.* 1, to disapprove

imprŏbus, a, um, *adj*, *adv*, ē, bad, wicked, violent, enormous, shameless

imprōvĭdus, a, um, *adj*, not anticipating

imprōvīsus, a, um, *adj*, *adv*, o, unexpected

imprūdens, ntis, *adj*, *adv*, nter, unsuspecting, unaware

imprūdentĭa, ae, *f*, lack of foresight

impūbes, is, *adj*, youthful

impŭdens, ntis, *adj*, shameless

impŭdentĭa, ae, *f*, impudence

impŭdīcĭtĭa, ae, *f*, shameful behaviour

impŭdīcus, a, um, *adj*, shameless, lewd, disgusting

impugno, *v.t.* 1, to attack

impulsor, ōris, *m*, instigator

impulsus, ūs, *m*, pressure, impulse, suggestion

impūnĕ, *adv*, without punishment

impūnĭtas, ātis, *f*, impunity

impūnītus, a, um, *adj*, unpunished

impūrus, a, um, *adj*, filthy

impŭto, *v.t.* 1, to reckon, ascribe, impute

īmus, a, um, *adj*, lowest, last

in, *prep. with abl*, in, on, within, among; *with acc*, into, towards, till, against

ĭnaccessus, a, um, *adj*, inaccessible

ĭnaedĭfĭco, *v.t.* 1, to build on

ĭnaequābĭlis, e, *adj*, uneven, unlike

ĭnaequālis, e, *adj*, uneven, unlike

ĭnaequālĭtas, ātis, *f*, inequality

ĭnaestĭmābĭlis, e, *adj*, inestimable

ĭnāmābĭlis, e, *adj*, hateful

ĭnāmāresco, *v.i.* 3, to become bitter

ĭnambŭlo, *v.i.* 1, to walk up and down

ĭnāne, is, *n*, emptiness

ĭnānĭmus, a, um, *adj*, lifeless

ĭnānis, e, *adj*, *adv*, ĭter, empty, useless, vain

ĭnānĭtas, ātis, *f*, emptiness

ĭnārātus, a, um, *adj*, unploughed

ĭnardesco, arsi, *v.i.* 3, to catch fire, glow

ĭnassŭētus, a, um, *adj*, unaccustomed

ĭnaudax, ācis, *adj*, timid

ĭnaudĭo, *v.t.* 4, to hear

ĭnaudītus, a, um, *adj*, unheard of

ĭnaugŭro, *v.i.t.* 1, to divine omens; to consecrate, inaugurate

ĭnaurātus, a, um, *adj*, golden

ĭnauro, *v.t.* 1, to cover with gold

ĭnauspĭcātus, a, um, *adj*, without good omens

ĭnausus, a, um, *adj*, unattempted

incaedŭus, a, um, *adj*, uncut

incālesco, cālŭi, *v.i.* 3, to grow hot, glow

incallĭdus, a, um, *adj*, stupid

incandesco, dŭi, *v.i.* 3, to grow hot, glow

incānesco, nŭi, *v.i.* 3, to grow grey or white

incanto, *v.t.* 1, to chant, bewitch

incānus, a, um, *adj*, grey, white

incassum, *adv*, in vain

incastīgātus, a, um, *adj*, unpunished

incautus, a, um, *adj*, *adv*, ē, rash, careless, unexpected

incēdo, cessi, ssum, *v.i.* 3, to advance, appear, enter

incendĭārĭus, ĭi, *m*, an incendiary

incendĭum, ĭi, *n*, fire, heat

incendo, cendi, censum, *v.t.* 3, to burn, excite, irritate

incensus, a, um, *adj*, unregistered

incensus, a, um, *adj*, burning, excited

inceptĭo, ōnis, *f*, an attempt, undertaking

inceptum, ĭ, *n*, an attempt, undertaking

incertum, ĭ, *n*, uncertainty

incertus, a, um, *adj*, uncertain, hesitating, doubtful

incesso, cessīvi, *v.t.* 3 to attack, accuse

incessus, ūs, *m*, walk, pace, approach

incesto, *v.t.* 1, to pollute

incestum, ĭ, *n*, adultery, incest

incestus, a, um, *adj*, impure

incĭdo, cĭdi, cāsum, *v.i.* 3, to fall into or upon, meet, happen, occur

incĭdo, cĭdi, sum, *v.t.* 3, to cut into, carve, interrupt

incingo, nxi, nctum, *v.t.* 3, to encircle

incĭpio, cēpi, ceptum, *v.i.t.* 3, to begin; undertake

incīsĭo, ōnis, *f*, an incision

incitāmentum, i, *n*, incentive

incitātĭo, ōnis, *f*, instigation, energy

incīsūra, ae, *f*, cutting, incision

incitātus, a, um, *adj*, swift

incĭto, *v.t.* 1, to urge on, rouse, excite, inspire

incitus, a, um, *adj*, swift

inclāmo, *v.i.t.* 1, to cry out; call out, to rebuke, abuse

inclēmens, ntis, *adj*, *adv*, nter, harsh, severe

inclēmentĭa, ae, *f*, harshness

inclīnātĭo, ōnis, *f*, leaning, tendency

inclīno, *v.i.t.* 1, to sink, yield; bend, turn, change

inclīnātus, a, um, *adj*, bent, disposed

inclĭtus, a, um, *adj*, famous

inclūdo, si, sum, *v.t.* 3, to shut in, include, finish

inclūsĭo, ōnis, *f*, confinement

inclŭtus, a, um, *adj*, famous

incoctus, a, um, *adj*, uncooked

incognĭtus, a, um, *adj*, unknown

incŏhātus, a, um, *adj*, incomplete

incŏho, *v.i.t.* 1, to begin; undertake

incŏla, ae, *c*, inhabitant

incŏlo, lŭi, *v.i.t.* 3, to settle; inhabit

incŏlŭmis, e, *adj*, safe, sound

incŏlŭmĭtas, ātis, *f*, safety

incŏmĭtātus, a, um, *adj*, unaccompanied

incommŏdĭtas, ātis, *f*, unsuitability

incommŏdo, *v.i.* 1, to be annoying

incommŏdum, i, *n*, disadvantage

incommŏdus, a, um, *adj*, *adv*, ē, troublesome, unsuitable

incompertus, a, um, *adj*, unknown

incompŏsĭtus, a, um, *adj*, badly-arranged

incomptus, a, um, *adj*, unadorned

inconcessus, a, um, *adj*, illicit

inconcinnus, a, um, *adj*, awkward

incondĭtus, a, um, *adj*, irregular, confused, rude

inconsīdĕrātus, a, um, *adj*, *adv*, ē, thoughtless, inconsiderate

inconsōlābĭlis, e, *adj*, inconsolable

inconstans, ntis, *adj*, *adv*, nter, inconsistent, fickle

inconstantĭa, ae, *f*, inconstancy

inconsultus, a, um, *adj*, *adv*, ē, without advice, indiscreet

inconsumptus, a, um, *adj*, unconsumed

incontāmĭnātus, a, um, *adj*, uncontaminated

incontĭnens, ntis, *adj*, *adv*, nter, immoderate

incŏquo, xi, ctum, *v.t.* 3, to boil, dye

incorruptus, a, um, *adj*, unspoiled

incrēbresco, brŭi, *v.i.* 3, to increase, become prevalent

incrēdĭbĭlis, e, *adj*, *adv*, ĭter, incredible, unbelievable

incrēdŭlus, a, um, *adj*, unbelieving

incrēmentum, i, *n*, increase

incrēpĭto, *v.t.* 1, to rebuke

increpo, ŭi, ĭtum, *v.i.t.* 1, to rattle, clatter; blare out, rebuke, reprimand

incresco, ēvi, *v.i.* 3, to grow

incrŭentus, a, um, *adj*, bloodless

incrusto, *v.t.* 1, to coat over

incŭbo, ŭi, ĭtum, *v.i.* 1, to lie in or on, rest on, fall upon

inculco, *v.t.* 1, to trample on, cram in, force on, obtrude

incultus, a, um, *adj*, *adv*, ē, uncultivated, unpolished

incumbo, cŭbŭi, ĭtum, *v.i.* 3, to lean or lie on, overhang, fall upon, take pains over, influence

incūnābŭla, ōrum, *n.pl*, cradle, birthplace, origin, swaddling-clothes

incūrĭa, ae, *f*, neglect

incūrĭōsus, a, um, *adj*, *adv*, ē, indifferent

incurro, curri, cursum, *v.i.t.* 3, to run at, happen; attack

incursĭo, ōnis, *f*, raid, attack

incurso, *v.i.t.* 1, to run to; attack, strike

incursus, ūs, *m*, attack

incurvo, *v.t.* 1, to bend

incurvus, a, um, *adj*, bent

incūs, ūdis, *f*, anvil

incūso, *v.t.* 1, to accuse, blame

incustōdītus, a, um, *adj*, unguarded

incŭtĭo, cussi, cussum, *v.t.* 3, to strike upon, hurl, inflict

indāgātĭo, ōnis, *f*, investigation

indāgo, *v.t.* 1, to track down

indāgo, ĭnis, *f*, enclosing

indĕ, *adv*, from there, then

indēbĭtus, a, um, *adj*, not due

indēcor, ōris, *adj*, disgraceful

indēcŏro, *v.t.* 1, to disgrace

indēcŏrus, a, um, *adj*, *adv*, ē, unbecoming, unsightly, disgraceful

indēfensus, a, um, *adj*, undefended

indēfessus, a, um, *adj*, unwearied

indēlēbĭlis, e, *adj*, indestructible

indēlībātus, a, um, *adj*, untouched

For List of Abbreviations used, turn to pages 3, 4

indemnātus, a, um, *adj*, unsentenced

indēprensus, a, um, *adj*, unnoticed

index, īcis, *m, f*, forefinger, informer, sign, list

indicium, ii, *n*, information, evidence, proof, indication

indĭco, *v.t.* 1, to show, indicate, give evidence

indīco, xi, ctum, *v.t.* 3, to announce, appoint, impose

indictus, a, um, *adj*, unsaid

indĭdem, *adv*, from the same place

indiēs, *adv*, from day to day

indifferens, ntis, *adj*, indifferent

indigĕna, ae, *adj*, native

indigĕo, *v.i.* 2, to need, want

indigestus, a, um, *adj*, confused

indignans, ntis, *adj*, enraged

indignātĭo, ōnis, *f*, indignation

indignitas, ātis, *f*, shameful behaviour, unworthiness

indignor, *v.t.* 1, *dep*, to be indignant at, scorn

indignus, a, um, *adj, adv*, ē, unworthy, shameful, cruel

indĭgus, a, um, *adj*, needing

indīligens, ntis, *adj, adv*, nter, careless

indīligentia, ae, *f*, carelessness

indiscrētus, a, um, *adj*, unseparated

indisertus, a, um, *adj*, at a loss for words

indīvīdŭus, a, um, *adj*, indivisible

indo, dĭdi, dĭtum, *v.t.* 3, to put or place upon or into, attach

indŏcilis, e, *adj*, unteachable, untaught

indoctus, a, um, *adj*, untaught

indŏles, is, *f*, inborn abilities

indŏlesco, lŭi, *v.i.* 3, to be in pain, to be troubled

indŏmĭtus, a, um, *adj*, untamed

indormĭo, *v.i.* 4, to fall asleep over

indōtātus, a, um, *adj*, without a dowry, poor

indŭbĭto, *v.i.* 1, to distrust

indŭbius, a, um, *adj*, not doubtful

indūco, xi, ctum, *v.t.* 3, to lead in, conduct, exhibit, spread over, put on (clothes), induce, resolve, cancel

inductĭo, ōnis, *f*, introduction, exhibition, intention

indulgens, ntis, *adj, adv*, nter, kind, indulgent, fond

indulgentia, ae, *f*, indulgence

indulgĕo, si, tum, *v.i.t.* 2, *with dat*, to be kind to; permit, grant

indŭo, ŭi, ūtum, *v.t.* 3, to put on (garment), assume

indūro, *v.t.* 1, to harden

indūsĭum, ii, *n*, woman's petticoat

industria, ae, *f*, diligence; *with* de *or* ex, on purpose

industrius, a, um, *adj*, diligent

indūtiae, ārum, *f. pl*, truce

indūtus, a, um, *adj*, clothed

inēdĭa, ae, *f*, fasting

inēlĕgans, ntis, *adj, adv*, nter, unrefined

inēluctābĭlis, e, *adj*, unavoidable

inemptus, a, um, *adj*, unbought

inēnarrābĭlis, e, *adj*, indescribable

inĕo, *v.i.t.* 4, to begin; enter, calculate, estimate, contrive

ineptiae, ārum, *f. pl*, absurdities

ineptus, a, um, *adj, adv*, ē, improper, inept, foolish

inermis, e, *adj*, unarmed

iners, rtis, *adj*, unskilful, idle, sluggish

inertia, ae, *f*, ignorance, idleness

inērŭdītus, a, um, *adj*, illiterate

inēvītābĭlis, e, *adj*, unavoidable

inexcūsābĭlis, e, *adj*, inexcusable

inexercĭtātus, a, um, *adj*, untrained

inexhaustus, a, um, *adj*, inexhaustible

inexōrābĭlis, e, *adj*, inexorable

inexpectātus, a, um, *adj*, unexpected

inexpertus, a, um, *adj*, inexperienced, untried

inexpĭābĭlis, e, *adj*, irreconcilable

inexplēbĭlis, e, *adj*, insatiable

inexplētus, a, um, *adj*, unsatisfied

inexplĭcābĭlis, e, *adj*, inexplicable

inexplōrātus, a, um, *adj*, unexplored

inexpugnābĭlis, e, *adj*, impregnable

inexstinctus, a, um, *adj*, imperishable

inextrīcābĭlis, e, *adj*, inextricable

infābrē, *adv*, unskilfully

infăcētus, a, um, *adj*, coarse

infāmĭa, ae, *f*, disgrace

infāmis, e, *adj*, disreputable

infāmo, *v.t.* 1, to disgrace

infandus, a, um, *adj*, unutterable

infans, ntis, *adj*, speechless

infans, ntis, *c*, child, baby

infantĭa, ae, *f*, speechlessness, infancy

infătŭo, *v.t.* 1, to make a fool of

infaustus, a, um, *adj*, unfortunate

infector, ōris, *m*, dyer

infectus, a, um, *adj*, unfinished

infēcundus, a, um, *adj*, unfruitful

infēlix, īcis, *adj*, unhappy, unfortunate, barren

infensus, a, um, *adj*, enraged

infĕri, ōrum, *m. pl*, the dead

infĕriae, ārum, *f. pl*, sacrifices in honour of the dead

infĕrĭor, ĭus, *adv*, lower, later, younger, inferior

inferius, *adv,* lower

infernus, a, um, *adj,* lower, underground

inferi, ōrum, *m. pl,* inhabitants of the underworld, the dead

infero, inferre, intŭli, illātum, *v.t. irreg,* to bring to or against, attack, produce, inflict

inferus, a, um, *adj,* below, lower

infervesco, ferbŭi, *v.i.* 3, to boil

infesto, *v.t.* 1, to attack, molest

infestus, a, um, *adj, adv,* ē, dangerous, hostile, unsafe

inficio, fēci, fectum, *v.t.* 3, to stain, dye, taint, corrupt

infidēlis, e, *adj,* untrustworthy

infidēlitas, ātis, *f,* treachery

infidus, a, um, *adj,* treacherous

infigo, xi, xum, *v.t.* 3, to fix into, drive in, imprint

infimus, a, um, *adj,* lowest

infindo, fīdi, fissum, *v.t.* 3, to cut into

infinitas, ātis, *f,* endlessness

infinītus, a, um, *adj, adv,* ē, unlimited, endless

infirmātio, ōnis, *f,* weakening

infirmitas, ātis, *f,* weakness

infirmo, *v.t.* 1, to weaken, annul

infirmus, a, um, *adj, adv,* ē, weak

infit, *v, defect,* he (she, it) begins

infitias ĕo (ire, ii), to deny

infitiātio, ōnis, *f,* denial

infitiātor, ōris, *m,* bad debtor

infitior, *v.t.* 1, *dep,* to deny

inflammātio, ōnis, *f,* inflammation, setting on fire

inflammo, *v.t.* 1, to set on fire

inflātus, ūs, *m,* blast

inflātus, a, um, *adj,* puffed up, haughty, inflated

inflecto, xi, xum, *v.t.* 3, to bend

inflētus, a, um, *adj,* unmourned

inflexibilis, e, *adj,* inflexible

inflexio, ōnis, *f,* bending

inflīgo, xi, ctum, *v.t.* 3, to strike (something) against

inflo, *v.t.* 1, to blow into

influo, xi, xum, *v.i.* 3, to flow into, crowd in

infŏdio, fŏdi, fossum, *v.t.* 3, to dig in, bury

informātio, ōnis, *f,* outline

informis, e, *adj,* shapeless

informo, *v.t.* 1, to shape, sketch, educate

infortūnātus, a, um, *adj,* unfortunate

infrā, *adv, and prep. with acc,* below, under

infractio, ōnis, *f,* breaking

infractus, a, um, *adj,* broken, exhausted

infrēmo, ŭi, *v.i.* 3, to growl

infrendĕo, *v.i.* 2, to gnash the teeth, threaten

infrēnis, e (us, a, um), *adj,* unbridled

infrēno, *v.t.* 1, to bridle, curb

infrēquens, ntis, *adj,* rare, not well filled

infrēquentia, ae, *f,* scantiness

infringo, frēgi, fractum, *v.t.* 3, to break off, crush, weaken

infŭla, ae, *f,* head-band, ribbon

infundĭbŭlum, i, *n,* funnel

infundo, fūdi, fūsum, *v.t.* 3, to pour out, lay before, impart

infusco, *v.t.* 1, to darken, stain

infūsus, a, um, *adj,* streaming or falling over

ingĕmino, *v.i.t.* 1, to increase; repeat, redouble

ingĕmisco, mŭi, *v.i.* 3, to sigh

ingĕmo, ŭi, *v.i.t.* 3, to groan; lament, mourn

ingĕnĕro, *v.t.* 1, to produce

ingĕnĭōsus, a, um, *adj, adv,* ē, talented, adapted to

ingĕnium, ii, *n,* natural disposition, abilities, intelligence

ingens, ntis, *adj,* huge, famous

ingĕnŭĭtas, ātis, *f,* good birth, gentlemanly character

ingĕnŭus, a, um, *adj, adv,* ē, natural, in-born, free-born, frank, honourable

ingĕnŭus, i, *m* (a, ae, *f*), free-born man or woman

ingĕro, gessi, gestum, *v.t.* 3, to carry, throw or thrust into

ingigno, gĕnŭi, gĕnitum, *v.t.* 3, to implant, produce

inglōrius, a, um, *adj,* inglorious

inglŭvies, ēi, *f,* gizzard, maw

ingrātiis, *adv,* unwillingly

ingrātus, a, um, *adj, adv,* ē, unpleasant, ungrateful

ingrăvesco, *v.i.* 3, to become heavy or worse

ingrăvo, *v.t.* 1, to aggravate

ingrĕdior, gressus, *v.i.t.* 3, *dep,* to advance; enter, upon

ingressio, ōnis, *f,* entering, pace

ingressus, ūs, *m,* entrance, inroad, commencement

ingrŭo, ŭi, *v.i.* 3, to attack

inguen, ĭnis, *n,* groin, abdomen

ingurgito, *v.t.* 1, (*with* se) to gorge, addict one's self to

inhăbilis, e, *adj,* unwieldy, incapable

inhăbitābilis, e, *adj,* uninhabitable

inhaerĕo, si, sum, *v.i.* 2, to cling to, adhere to

ĭnhaerēsco, haesi, haesum, *v.i.* 3, to cling to, adhere to

ĭnhĭbĕo, *v.t.* 2, to restrain

ĭnhĭo, *v.i.* 1, to gape, gaze

ĭnhŏnestus, a, um, *adj,* shameful

ĭnhŏnōrātus, a, um, *adj,* unhonoured

ĭnhorrĕo, *v.i.* 2, to bristle, shiver

ĭnhorrēsco, *v.i.* 3, to bristle, shiver

ĭnhospĭtālis, e, *adj,* inhospitable

ĭnhospĭtus, a, um, *adj,* inhospitable

ĭnhūmānĭtas, ātis, *f,* barbarity, niggardliness

ĭnhūmānus, a, um, *adj, adv,* ē, **ĭter,** savage, uncivilized, rude

ĭnhŭmātus, a, um, *adj,* unburied

ĭnĭbi, *adv,* there

ĭnĭcĭo, iēci, iectum, *v.t.* 3, to throw into, seize, inspire

ĭnĭmīcĭtĭa, ae, *f,* enmity

ĭnĭmīco, *v.t.* 1, to make into enemies

ĭnĭmīcus, a, um, *adj, adv,* ē, unfriendly, hostile

ĭnĭmīcus, i, *m* **(a, ae,** *f*)**,** enemy

ĭnīquĭtas, ātis, *f,* unevenness, difficulty, injustice

ĭnīquus, a, um, *adj, adv,* ē, uneven, unfair, unfortunate, hostile, disadvantageous

ĭnĭtĭo, *v.t.* 1, to initiate

ĭnĭtĭō, *adv,* in the beginning

ĭnĭtĭum, ii, *n,* beginning, origin; (*in pl*) first principles, sacred rites

ĭnĭūcundus, a, um, *adj, adv,* ē, unpleasant

ĭnĭungo, nxi, nctum, *v.t.* 3, to join on to, inflict, impose

ĭnĭūrātus, a, um, *adj,* without taking an oath

ĭnĭūrĭa, ae, *f,* injury, wrong

ĭnĭūrĭōsus, a, um, *adj,* wrongful

ĭnĭussu, *adv,* without orders

ĭnĭussus, a, um, *adj,* of one's accord

ĭnĭustĭtĭa, ae, *f,* injustice

ĭnĭustus, a, um, *adj, adv,* ē, unjust, wrongful, harsh

innascor, nātus, *v.i.* 3, *dep,* to be born in, grow up in

innăto, *v.t.* 1, to swim, float in

innātus, a, um, *adj,* innate

innāvĭgābĭlis, e, *adj,* unnavigable

innecto, xŭi, xum, *v.t.* 3, to tie, fasten, attach, contrive

innītor, nixus (nīsus), *v.* 3, *dep, with dat. or abl,* to lean on

inno, *v.i.* 1, to swim, float in

innŏcens, ntis, *adj,* harmless, blameless

innŏcentĭa, ae, *f,* integrity

innŏcŭus, a, um, *adj,* harmless

innoxĭus, a, um, *adj,* harmless, innocent, unhurt

innūbus, a, um, *adj,* unmarried

innŭmĕrābĭlis, e, *adj,* countless

innŭmĕrus, a, um, *adj,* countless

innŭo, ŭi, ūtum, *v.i.* 3, to nod, hint

innuptus, a, um, *adj,* unmarried

ĭnobservātus, a, um, *adj,* unperceived

ĭnoffensus, a, um, *adj,* untouched, uninterrupted

ĭnŏlesco, lēvi, lĭtum, *v.i.* 3, to grow in, take root

ĭnŏpĭa, ae, *f,* lack, need

ĭnŏpīnans, ntis, *adj,* unaware

ĭnŏpīnātus, a, um, *adj, adv,* ē, ō, unexpected

ĭnŏpīnus, a, um, *adj,* unexpected

ĭnopportūnus, a, um, *adj,* unfitting, inopportune

ĭnops, ŏpis, *adj,* helpless, needy

ĭnordĭnātus, a, um, *adj,* in disorder

ĭnornātus, a, um, *adj,* unadorned

inquam, *v. irreg,* I say

inquĭes, ētis, *f,* restlessness

inquĭētus, a, um, *adj,* restless

inquĭlīnus, i, *m,* lodger

inquĭnātus, a, um, *adj,* filthy

inquĭno, *v.t.* 1, to stain, corrupt

inquīro, sīvi, sītum, *v.t.* 3, to search for, examine

inquīsītĭo, ōnis, *f,* legal investigation

insălūbris, e, *adj,* unhealthy

insălūtātus, a, um, *adj,* without saying goodbye

insānābĭlis, e, *adj,* incurable

insānĭa, ae, *f,* madness, folly

insānĭo, *v.i.* 4, to be insane, to rage

insānĭtas, ātis, *f,* disease

insānus, a, um, *adj, adv,* ē, insane, frantic, excessive

insătĭābĭlis, e, *adj,* insatiable

insciens, ntis, *adj,* unaware

inscĭentĭa, ae, *f,* ignorance, inexperience

inscĭtĭa, ae, *f,* ignorance, inexperience

inscĭtus, a, um, *adj, adv,* ē, ignorant, stupid

inscĭus, a, um, *adj,* unaware

inscrībo, psi, ptum, *v.t.* 3, to write on, attribute

inscrīptĭo, ōnis, *f,* title

insculpo, psi, ptum, *v.t.* 3, to engrave

insĕco, cŭi, ctum, *v.t.* 1, to cut up

insectātĭo, ōnis, *f,* pursuit

insectātor, ōris, *m,* pursuer

insector, *v.t.* 1, *dep,* to pursue, reproach

insectum, i, *n,* insect

insĕnesco, nŭi, *v.i.* 3, to grow old at

insĕpultus, a, um, *adj,* unburied

insĕquor, sĕcūtus, *v.i.t.* 3, *dep,* to follow; pursue, reproach

insĕro, sēvi, sĭtum, *v.t.* 3, to implant, ingraft

insĕro, rŭi, rtum, *v.t.* 3, to put in, introduce

inserto, *v.t.* 1, to insert

inservio, *v.t.* 4, to serve, be submissive to, attend to

insĭdĕo, sēdi, sessum, *v.i.t.* 2, to sit upon, be fixed; occupy, inhabit

insĭdiae, ārum, *f. pl*, ambush, plot; *with* ex *or* per, craftily

insĭdior, *v.* 1, *dep, with dat*, to lie in ambush

insĭdiōsus, a, um, *adj, adv*, ē, cunning, dangerous

insĭdo, sēdi, sessum, *v.i.t.* 3, to settle on or in; occupy

insigne, is, *n*, mark, sign, costume, signal, ornament

insignio, *v.t.* 4, to make distinguished

insignis, e, *adj*, conspicuous, famous, distinguished

insĭlio, ŭi, *v.i.* 4, to spring upon

insĭmŭlo, *v.t.* 1, to accuse

insincērus, a, um, *adj*, tainted

insĭnŭo, *v.i.t.* 1, to penetrate; insinuate

insĭpiens, ntis, *adj*, foolish

insĭpientia, ae, *f*, folly

insisto, stĭti, *v.i.t.* 3, to step, stand, begin, halt; devote oneself to

insĭtus, a, um, *adj*, inborn

insŏlens, ntis, *adj, adv*, nter, unusual, unaccustomed, haughty

insŏlentia, ae, *f*, strangeness, novelty, affectation, arrogance

insŏlĭtus, a, um, *adj*, unaccustomed, unusual

insomnia, ae, *f*, sleeplessness

insomnis, e, *adj*, sleepless

insomnĭum, ii, *n*, dream

insŏno, ŭi, *v.i.* 1, to resound

insons, ntis, *adj*, innocent, harmless

inspecto, *v.t.* 1, to look at

inspērans, ntis, *adj*, not hoping

inspērātus, a, um, *adj*, unhoped for, unexpected

inspergo, si, sum, *v.t.* 3, to sprinkle

inspĭcio, spexi, spectum, *v.t.* 3, to examine, consider

inspīro, *v.t.* 1, to breathe on, inspire

instābĭlis, e, *adj*, unsteady, changeable

instans, ntis, *adj*, present

instar, *n*, *indecl*, resemblance, appearance, value; *with genit*, as big as, like

instauro, *v.t.* 1, to renew

insterno, strāvi, strātum, *v.t.* 3, to spread or cover over

instīgo, *v.t.* 1, to incite

instillo, *v.t.* 1, to instil

instĭmŭlo, *v.t.* 1, to spur on

instinctus, ūs, *m*, impulse

instinctus, a, um, *adj*, incited

institor, ōris, *m*, commercial-traveller

instĭtŭo, ŭi, ūtum, *v.t.* 3, to set up, appoint, undertake, resolve, arrange, train

institūtio, ōnis, *f*, arrangement, custom, education

institūtum, i, *n*, purpose, plan, custom

insto, stĭti, stātum, *v.i.* 1, to stand over, harass, impend, urge on, pursue

instructus, a, um, *adj*, arranged, provided with

instrūmentum, i, *n*, tool, stores

instrŭo, xi, ctum, *v.t.* 3, to erect, arrange, provide, teach

insŭāvis, e, *adj*, unpleasant

insuesco, ēvi, ētum, *v.i.t.* 3, to become accustomed; to accustom

insuētus, a, um, *adj*, unaccustomed to, unusual

insŭla, ae, *f*, island, block of flats

insŭlānus, i, *m*, islander

insulsĭtas, ātis, *f*, silliness

insulsus, a, um, *adj, adv*, ē, tasteless, silly

insulto, *v.i.t.* 1, to jump, leap; to spring at, abuse

insum, inesse, infŭi, *v.i, irreg*, to be in, be contained in

insūmo, mpsi, mptum, *v.t.* 3, to employ, expend

insŭo, ŭi, ūtum, *v.t.* 3, to sew on

insŭper, *adv, and prep. with acc*, moreover, besides; above

insŭpĕrābĭlis, e, *adj*, insurmountable

insurgo, surrexi, rectum, *v.i.* 3, to arise, rise to

insŭsurro, *v.i.t.* 1, to whisper

intābesco, bŭi, *v.i.* 3, to waste away

intactus, a, um, *adj*, untouched, unattempted, chaste

intāmĭnātus, a, um, *adj*, pure

intectus, a, um, *adj*, uncovered

intĕger, gra, grum, *adj, adv*, ē, untouched, perfect, blameless, unspoiled, undecided

intĕgo, xi, ctum, *v.t.* 3, to cover

intĕgrĭtas, ātis, *f*, completeness, uprightness

intĕgro, *v.t.* 1, to renew, refresh

intĕgŭmentum, i, *n*, covering, disguise

intellĕgens, ntis, *adj*, understanding

intellĕgentia, ae, *f*, understanding

intellĕgo, xi, ctum, *v.t.* 3, to understand, perceive

intĕmĕrātus, a, um, *adj*, pure

intempĕrans, ntis, *adj*, extravagant

intempĕrantia, ae, *f*, extravagance

For List of Abbreviations used, turn to pages 3, 4

intempĕries, ĕi, *f*, inclement weather, violence

intempestīvus, a, um, *adj*, *adv*, ē, untimely, inconvenient

intempestus, a, um, *adj*, unseasonable, unhealthy; (with nox) the dead of night

intendo, di, tum (sum), *v.t.* 3, to stretch or spread out, aim, direct, threaten, concentrate, intend

intentātus, a, um, *adj*, untried

intentio, ōnis, *f*, tension, effort, application

intentus, a, um, *adj*, *adv*, ē, stretched, bent, intent

intĕpesco, pŭi, *v.i.* 3, to grow warm

inter, *adv*, *and prep. with acc*, among, between, during

intercēdo, cessi, ssum, *v.i.* 3, to go between, intervene, occur

intercessio, ōnis, *f*, veto, intervention

intercessor, ōris, *m*, mediator, surety, user of the veto

intercīdo, di, sum, *v.t.* 3, to cut up

intercĭdo, di, *v.i.* 3, to happen, fall down, perish

intercĭpio, cēpi, ceptum, *v.t.* 3, to intercept, seize, steal

interclūdo, si, sum, *v.t.* 3, to block, cut off, hinder, separate, blockade

intercurro, curri, cursum, *v.i.* 3, to run between, intercede

interdīco, dixi, dictum, *v.t.* 3, to prohibit, banish

interdictum, i, *n*, prohibition

interdiu, *adv*, in the daytime

interdum, *adv*, sometimes

intĕrĕā, *adv*, meanwhile

intĕrĕo, ĭi, ĭtum, *v.i.* 4, to perish, die, become lost

intĕrest, see intersum

interfector, ōris, *m*, murderer

interfĭcio, fēci, fēctum, *v.t.* 3, to kill, destroy

interflŭo, xi, *v.i.* 3, to flow between

interfūsus, a, um, *adj*, poured between, interposed, stained

intĕrim, *adv*, meanwhile

intĕrĭmo, ēmi, emptum, *v.t.* 3, to take away, destroy, kill

intĕrior, ius, *comp. adj*, inner

intĕrius, *adv*, inside

intĕrĭtus, ūs, *m*, annihilation

interiăcĕo, *v.i.* 2, to lie between

interĭcio, iēci, iectum, *v.t.* 3, to put or throw between

interiectus, a, um, *adj*, interposed

interlābor, lapsus, *v.i.* 3, *dep*, to glide or flow between

interlĕgo, lēgi, lectum, *v.t.* 3, to pluck, pick

interlūcĕo, luxi, *v.i.* 2, to shine out, appear

interlŭo, *v.t.* 3, to flow between

interminātus, a, um, *adj*, endless

intermiscĕo, scŭi, xtum, *v.t.* 2, to intermix

intermissio, ōnis, *f*, interruption, cessation

intermitto, mīsi, missum, *v.i.t.* 3, to cease; neglect, omit, stop, pause, interrupt

intermortŭus, a, um, *adj*, lifeless

internĕcīnus, a, um, *adj*, deadly, internecine

internĕcio, ōnis *f*, massacre

internecto, *v.t.* 3, to bind up

internosco, nōvi nōtum, *v.t.* 3, to distinguish between

internuntius, ii, *m*, negotiator

internus, a, um *adj*, internal

interpellātio, ōnis, *f*, interruption

interpello, *v.t.* 1, to interrupt

interpŏlo, *v.t.* 1, to furbish

interpōno, pŏsŭi, ĭtum, *v.t.* 3, to put between, introduce; with se, to interfere; with fidem, to pledge

interpŏsĭtio, ōnis, *f*, insertion

interprĕs, ĕtis, *c*, negotiator

interprĕtātio, ōnis, *f*, explanation

interprĕtor, *v.t.* 1, *dep*, to explain

interpunctio, ōnis, *f*, punctuation

interpungo, nxī, ctum, *v.t.* 3, to punctuate

interquĭesco, quĭēvi, quĭētum, *v.i.* 3, to rest for a while

interregnum, i, *n*, vacancy in the kingship or high office

interrex, rēgis, *m*, regent

interrĭtus, a, um, *adj*, fearless

interrŏgātor, ōris, *m*, questioner

interrŏgātum, i, *n*, question

interrŏgo, *v.t.* 1, to inquire

interrumpo, rūpi, ruptum, *v.t.* 3, to break up, interrupt

intersaepio, psi, ptum, *v.t.* 4, to hedge in, cut off

interscĭndo, scĭdi, scissum, *v.t.* 3, to tear down, divide

intersĕro, rŭi, rtum, *v.t.* 3, to interpose

intersum, esse, fŭi, *v.i*, *irreg*, to lie between, differ, take part in; interest. *v. impers*, it concerns, it is of importance

intertexo, xŭi, xtum, *v.t.* 3, to intertwine

intervallum, i, *n*, space, pause

intervĕnĭo, vēni, ventum, *v.i.* 4, to interrupt, happen, prevent

interventus, ūs, *m*, intervention

intervīso, si, sum, *v.t.* 3, to inspect, visit occasionally

intestābĭlis, e, *adj*, abominable

intestīna, ōrum, *n.* pl, intestines

intestīnus, a, um, *adj*, internal

intexo, xŭi, xtum, *v.t.* 3, to interlacé

intĭmus, a, um, *adj*, inmost

intŏlĕrābĭlis, e, *adj*, intolerable

intŏlĕrandus, a, um, *adj*, intolerable

intŏlĕrans, ntis, *adj*, *adv*, nter, impatient, intolerable

intŏno, ŭi, *v.i.* 1, to thunder

intonsus, a, um, *adj*, unshaven

intorquĕo, si, sum, *v.t.* 2, to twist, sprain, hurl

intrā, *adv*, *and prep. with acc*, on the inside, within

intractābĭlis, e, *adj*, unmanageable

intractātus, a, um, *adj*, untried

intrĕmo, ŭi, *v.i.* 3, to tremble

intrĕpĭdus, a, um, *adj*, fearless

intrō, *adv*, within, inside

intro, *v.i.t.* 1, to enter

intrōdūco, xi, ctum, *v.t.* 3, to lead in, introduce

intrōductĭo, ōnis, *f*, introduction

intrōĕo, *v.i.* 4, to enter

intrōfĕro, ferre, tŭli, lātum, *v.t*, *irreg*, to bring in

intrōgrĕdĭor, gressus, *v.i.* 3, *dep*, to enter

intrōĭtus, ūs *m*, entrance

intrōmitto, mī si, ssum, *v.t.* 3, to send in

introrsum (us), *adv*, within

intrōspĭcĭo, spexi, spectum, *v.t.* 3, to look into, examine

intŭĕor, *v.t.* 2, *dep*, to look at

intŭmesco, mŭi, *v.i.* 3, to swell

intus, *adv*, within, inside

intūtus, a, um, *adj*, unguarded

inultus, a, um, *adj*, unavenged

ĭnumbro, *v.t.* 1, to shade

ĭnundātĭo, ōnis, *f*, flooding

ĭnundo, *v.i.t.* 1, to overflow; flood

ĭnungo, nxi, unctum, *v.t.* 3, to anoint

ĭnurbānus, a, um, *adj*, rude

ĭnūro, ssi, stum, *v.t.* 3, to brand

ĭnūsĭtātus, a, um, *adj*, *adv*, ē, unusual, strange

ĭnūtĭlis, e, *adj*, useless

ĭnūtĭlĭtas, ātis, *f*, uselessness

ĭnvādo, si, sum, *v.i.t.* 3, to enter; attack, invade, seize

ĭnvălĭdus, a, um, *adj*, weak

ĭnvĕho, xi, ctum, *v.t.* 3, to carry, bring to; *passive or reflex*, to ride, drive, attack (with words)

invĕnĭo, vēni, ventum, *v.t.* 4, to find, meet with, devise

inventĭo, ōnis, *f*, invention

inventor, ōris, *m*, inventor

inventum, i, *n*, invention

invĕnustus, a, um, *adj*, unattractive

invĕrēcundus, a, um, *adj*, immodest

invergo, *v.t.* 3, to pour on

inversus, a, um, *adj*, inverted, perverted

inverto, ti, sum, *v.t.* 3, to turn upside down, exchange

invespĕrascit, *v. impers*, evening is approaching

investīgātĭo, ōnis, *f*, investigation

investīgo, *v.t.* 1, to search for

invĕtĕrasco, rāvi, *v.i.* 3, to grow old, become permanent

invĕtĕrātus, a, um, *adj*, old-established

invĕtĕro, *v.t.* 1, to endure

invĭcem, *adv*, alternately

invictus, a, um, *adj*, unconquered, invincible

invĭdĕo, vīdi, vīsum, *v.t.* 2, *with dat*; to envy, grudge

invĭdĭa, ae, *f*, envy, ill-will

invĭdĭōsus, a, um, *adj*, *adv*, ē, jealous, enviable

invĭdus, a, um, *adj*, envious

invĭgĭlo, *v.i.* 1, to be watchful

invĭŏlātus, a, um, *adj*, unharmed

invīso, si, sum, *v.t.* 3, to visit

invīsus, a, um, *adj*, hated

invīsus, a, um, *adj*, unseen

invītātĭo, ōnis, *f*, challenge, invitation

invīto, *v.t.* 1, to invite, challenge, tempt

invītus, a, um, *adj*, unwilling

invĭus, a, um, *adj*, pathless

invŏcātus, a, um, *adj*, uninvited

invŏco, *v.t.* 1, to appeal to

invŏlĭto, *v.i.* 1, to hover

invŏlo, *v.i.t.* 1, to fly at; attack

invŏlūcrum, i, *n*, wrapper

invŏlūtus, a, um, *adj*, intricate

involvo, volvi, vŏlūtum, *v.t.* 3, to roll on, wrap up, envelop

invulnĕrābĭlis, e, *adj*, invulnerable

ĭō, *interj*, oh! ah! ho!

ipse, a, um (*genit*, ipsius, *dat*, ipsi), *emphatic pron*, himself, herself, itself, precisely, just

īra, ae, *f*, anger

īrācundĭa, ae, *f*, rage, temper

īrācundus, a, um, *adj*, irritable

īrascor, īrātus, *v.* 3, *dep. with dat*, to be angry with

īrātus, a, um, *adj*, angry

īre, see ĕo

īris, ĭdis, *f*, iris

īrōnĭa, ae, *f*, irony

irpex, ĭcis, *m*, harrow
irrĕmĕābilis, e, *adj*, irretraceable
irrĕpĕrābilis, e, *adj*, irrecoverable
irrĕpertus, a, um, *adj*, undiscovered
irrēpo, psi, ptum, *v.i.* 3, to creep in, insinuate oneself
irrĕquiĕtus, a, um, *adj*, restless
irrētio, *v.t.* 4, to entangle
irrĕtortus, a, um, *adj*, not turned back
irrĕvŏcābilis, e, *adj*, irrevocable
irrīdĕo, si, sum, *v.i.t.* 2, to joke, jeer; mock, ridicule
irrĭgātio, ōnis, *f*, irrigation
irrĭgo, *v.t.* 1, to water, refresh
irrĭgŭus, a, um, *adj*, well-watered, moistening
irrīsio, ōnis, *f*, mockery
irrīsus, ūs, *m*, mockery
irrīsor, ōris, *m*, scoffer
irrītābilis, e, *adj*, irritable
irrītāmen, ĭnis, *n*, incentive
irrītāmentum, ĭ, *n*, incentive
irrīto, *v.t.* 1, to provoke
irrītus, a, um, *adj*, invalid, unsuccessful
irrŏgo, *v.t.* 1, to propose (against someone), inflict
irrŏro, *v.t.* 1, to bedew
irrumpo, rūpi, ptum, *v.i.t.* 3, to break in; attack, interrupt
irrŭo, ŭi, *v.i.* 3, to rush in, seize
irruptus, a, um, *adj*, unbroken
is, ĕa, id, *demonst. pron*, he, she, it, that
ischĭas, ădis, *f*, sciatica
iste, a, ud, *demonst. pron*, that
isthmus, ĭ, *m*, isthmus
istic, *adv*, there
istinc, *adv*, from there
istūc, *adv*, to that place
ită, *adv*, in such a way, so
ĭtăque, *conj*, and so, therefore
ĭtem, *adv*, likewise, also
iter, ĭtĭnĕris, *n*, route, journey, march
ĭtĕrātio, ōnis, *f*, repetition
ĭtĕro, *v.t.* 1, to repeat
ĭtĕrum, *adv*, again
ĭtĭdem, *adv*, in the same way
ĭtio, ōnis, *f*, travelling

J (consonantal i)

iăcĕo, *v.i.* 2, to lie (recumbent), lie sick
iăcio, iēci, iactum, *v.t.* 3, to throw, lay down
iactans, ntis, *pres. part, adj*, boastful
iactantia, ae, *f*, ostentation
iactātio, ōnis, *f*, tossing, bragging
iactātor, ōris, *m*, braggart
iacto, *v.t.* 1, to throw about, boast

iactūra, ae, *f*, throwing overboard, sacrifice
iactus, ūs, *m*, throw, shot
iăcŭlātor, ōris, *m*, thrower
iăcŭlātrix, īcis, *f*, huntress
iăcŭlor, *v.t.* 1, *dep*, to hurl
iăcŭlum, ĭ, *n*, javelin
iam, *adv*, already, now
iamdūdum, *adv*, a long time ago
iamprīdem, *adv*, for a long time now
iānĭtor, ōris, *m*, doorkeeper
iānŭa, ae, *f*, door, entrance
Iānŭārius (mensis), January
iĕcur, ōris, *n*, liver
iĕiūnĭtas, ātis, *f*, meagreness
iĕiūnĭum, ĭi, *n*, fast, hunger
iĕiūnus, a, um, *adj*, hungry, barren
ientācŭlum, ĭ, *n*, breakfast
iento, *v.i.* 1, to breakfast
iŏcātio, ōnis, *f*, joke
iŏcor, *v.t.* 1, *dep*, to joke
iŏcōsus, a, um, *adj*, humorous
iŏcŭlāris, e, *adj*, amusing
iŏcŭlātor, ōris, *m*, joker
iŏcus, ĭ, *m*, joke
iŭba, ae, *f*, mane, crest
iŭbar, ăris, *n*, radiance
iŭbĕo, iussi, iussum, *v.t.* 2, to order, tell
iūcundĭtas, ātis, *f*, pleasantness
iūcundus, a, um, *adj*, pleasant
iūdex, ĭcis, *m*, judge
iudicĭalis, e, *adj*, judicial
iudicatio ōnis, *f*, judgement
iūdĭcium, ĭi, *n*, trial, verdict, court discretion, judgement
iūdĭco, *v.t.* 1, to judge, decide
iŭgālis, e, *adj*, yoked together
iŭgāles, *m. pl*, chariot-horses
iŭgĕrum, ĭ, *n*, acre (approx.)
iŭgis, e, *adj*, perpetual
iūglans, dis, *f*, walnut
iŭgo, *v.t.* 1, to marry, connect
iŭgōsus, a, um, *adj*, mountainous
iŭgŭlo, *v.t.* 1, to cut the throat
iŭgum, ĭ, *n*, yoke, bench, mountain-ridge
Iūlius (mensis), July
iūmentum, ĭ, *n*, pack-animal
iuncĕus, a, um, *adj*, made of rushes
iuncōsus, a, um, *adj*, full of rushes
iunctio, ōnis, *f*, junction
iunctūra, ae, *f*, joint
iuncus, ĭ, *m*, bullrush
iungo, nxi, nctum, *v.t.* 3, to join
iūnior, *comp. adj*, from iŭvĕnis, younger
iūnĭpĕrus, ĭ, *f*, juniper tree
Iūnius (mensis), June
iūrātor, ōris, *m*, commissioner of oaths

iūrātus, a, um, *adj*, bound by oath

iurgium, ii, *n*, quarrel

iurgo, *v.i.t.* 1, to quarrel; upbraid

iūris consultus, i, *m*, lawyer

iūris dictio, ōnis, *f*, jurisdiction

iūro, *v.i.t.* 1, to take an oath; to swear by

iūs, iūris, *n*, law, legal status, right, authority

iūs, iūris, *n*, soup

iusiūrandum, i, *n*, oath

iussum, i, *n*, order

iusta, ōrum, *n.pl*, due ceremonies

iustē, *adv*, rightly

iustitia, ae, *f*, justice

iustitium, *n*, holiday for lawcourts, public mourning

iustum, i, *n*, fairness

iustus, a, um, *adj*, fair, lawful

iŭvĕnālis, e, *adj*, youthful

iŭvenca, ae, *f*, heifer

iŭvencus, i, *m*, bullock

iŭvĕnesco, nŭi, *v.i.* 3, to reach youth

iŭvĕnilis, e, *adj*, youthful

iŭvĕnis, is, *m*, *f*, young person; (*adj*) young

iŭvĕnor, *v.i.* 1, *dep*, to act youthfully

iŭventa, ae, *f*, the age of youth

iŭventas, ātis, *f*, the age of youth

iŭventus, ūtis, *f*, the age of youth

iŭvo, iūvi, iūtum, *v.t.* 1, to help, gratify; iŭvat (*impers. with acc*), it pleases, it is of use

iuxtā, *adv*, *and prep. with acc*, near

iuxtim, *adv*, *and prep. with acc*, next to

K

Kalendae, ārum, *f. pl*, the Kalends, the first day of the month

L

lăbĕfăcĭo, fēci, factum, *v.t.* 3, to shake, loosen, overthrow

lăbĕfacto, *v.t.* 1, to shake, destroy

lăbellum, i, *n*, a lip

lăbellum, i, *n*, tub, basin

lābes, is, *f*, sinking, downfall

lābes, is, *f*, spot, blemish

lābo, *v.i.* 1, to totter, waver

lābor, lapsus, *v.i.* 3, *dep*, to slip, slide, glide, pass away, be mistaken

lābor, ōris, *m*, work, toil, workmanship, distress

lăbōrĭōsus, a, um, *adj*, *adv*, ē, laborious, industrious

lăbōro, *v.i.t.* 1, to strive, be in trouble or difficulty; to make, prepare

lăbrum, i, *n*, lip

lābrum, i, *n*, tub, basin

lăbўrinthus, i, *m*, labyrinth

lac, lactis, *n*, milk

lăcer, ĕra, ĕrum, *adj*, mangled

lăcerna, ae, *f*, cloak

lăcĕrātĭo, ōnis, *f*, laceration

lăcĕro, *v.t.* 1, to tear, rend, censure, destroy

lăcerta, ae, *f* (us, i, *m*), lizard

lăcertōsus, a, um, *adj*, brawny

lăcertus, i, *m*, arm, strength

lăcertus, i, *m*, lizard, newt

lăcesso, īvi, ītum, *v.t.* 3, to provoke, attack, irritate, urge

lăcinia, ae, *f*, edge of garment

lăcrima, ae, *f*, tear

lăcrimābilis, e, *adj*, mournful

lăcrimo, *v.i.* 1, to weep

lăcrimōsus, a, um, *adj*, tearful

lactens, ntis, *f*, very young (unweaned) animal

lactĕus, a, um, *adj*, milky

lacto, *v.i.t.* 1, to have milk; suck

lactūca, ae, *f*, lettuce

lăcūna, ae, *f*, ditch, pond, gap

lăcūnar, āris, *n*, ceiling

lăcus, ūs, *m*, lake, tank, tub

laedo, si, sum, *v.t.* 3, to injure, offend

laena, ae, *f*, cloak

laetābilis, e, *adj*, joyful

laetifico, *v.t.* 1, to delight

laetitia, ae, *f*, joyfulness

laetor, *v.i.* 1, *dep*, to rejoice

laetus, a, um, *adj*, *adv*, ē, glad, cheerful, willing, pleased, prosperous, beautiful

laeva, ae, *f*, the left hand

laevus, a, um, *adj*, on the left side, unfortunate, foolish

lăgănum, i, *n*, a cake

lăgēna, ae, *f*, wine-jar

lăgōis, idis, *f*, grouse

lăgōpūs, ŏdis, *f*, grouse

lăguncŭla, ae, *f*, small bottle

lambo, bi, bĭtum, *v.t.* 3, to lick

lāmentābilis, e, *adj*, mournful

lāmentātio, ōnis, *f*, mourning

lāmentor, *v.i.t.* 1, *dep*, to weep; mourn

lāmenta, ōrum, *n.pl*, moaning

lāmia, ae, *f*, witch, vampire

lāmina, ae, *f*, thin metal plate

lampas, ădis, *f*, torch

lāna, ae, *f*, wool

lancĕa, ae, *f*, lance, spear

lānĕus, a, um, *adj*, woollen

languens, ntis, *adj*, faint, weak

languĕo, *v.i.* 2, to be faint or listless

languesco, gŭi, *v.i.* 3, to become faint or listless

languidus, a, um, *adj*, faint, weary, sluggish

For List of Abbreviations used, turn to pages 3, 4

languor, ōris, *m*, weakness, weariness, sluggishness

lănĭātus, ūs, *m*, laceration

lānĭcĭum, ii, *n*, wool

lănĭēna, ae, *f*, butcher's stall

lānĭfĭcus, a, um, *adj*, weaving

lānĭger, ĕra, ĕrum, *adj*, fleecy

lănĭo, *v.t.* 1, to mutilate

lănista, ae, *m*, fencing-master

lănĭus, ii, *m*, butcher

lanterna, ae, *f*, lamp, torch

lānūgo, ĭnis, *f*, down, hair

lanx, ncis, *f*, dish, plate

lăpăthus, i, *f*, sorrel

lăpĭcīda, ae, *m*, quarryman

lăpĭcīdĭnae, ārum, *f. pl*, stone-quarries

lăpĭdātĭo, ōnis, *f*, stoning

lăpĭdēus, a, um, *adj*, of stone

lăpĭdōsus, a, um, *adj*, stony

lăpillus, i, *m*, pebble, grain

lăpis, ĭdis, *m*, stone, milestone, jewel

lappa, ae, *f*, a bur

lapso, *v.i.* 1, to slip, stumble

lapsus, a, um, *adj*, fallen, sinking, ruined

lapsus, ūs, *m*, fall, slip, gliding

lăquĕar, āris, *n*, ceiling

lăquĕātus, a, um, *adj*, panelled

lăquĕus, i, *m*, noose, snare

lar, ăris, *m*, guardian deity of a house, home

largĭor, *v.t.* 4, *dep*, to lavish, give

largĭtas, ātis, *f*, abundance

largĭtĭo, ōnis, *f*, generous distribution, bribery

largītor, ōris, *m*, briber, generous giver

largus, a, um, *adj*, *adv*, ē, ĭter, abundant, lavish, large

lārīdum (lardum), i, *n*, lard

lārix, ĭcis, *f*, larch

larva, ae, *f*, ghost, mask

lascīvĭa, ae, *f*, playfulness

lascīvĭo, *v.i.* 4, to frolic

lascīvus, a, um, *adj*, playful, licentious

lassĭtūdo, ĭnis, *f*, weariness

lasso, *v.t.* 1, to tire, fatigue

lassus, a, um, *adj*, exhausted

lātē, *adv*, far and wide

lătĕbra, ae, *f*, hiding-place, subterfuge

lătĕbrōsus, a, um, *adj*, full of hiding-places, secret

lătens, ntis, *adj*, *adv*, nter, hidden, secret

lătĕo, *v.i.* 2, to lie hidden, keep out of sight

lăter, ĕris, *m*, brick, tile, ingot

lătērīcĭus, a, um, *adj*, made of bricks

lătex, ĭcis, *m*, liquid

lătĭbŭlum, i, *n*, hiding-place

Lătīnē, *adv*, in Latin

lătĭto, *v.i.* 1, to lie hidden

lātĭtūdo, ĭnis, *f*, breadth

lātor, ōris, *m*, proposer of a law

lātrātor, ōris, *m*, a barker

lātrātus, ūs, *m*, barking

lātrīna, ae, *f*, water-closet

lātro, *v.i.t.* 1, to bark; bark at

lătro, ōnis, *m*, robber

lătrōcĭnĭum, ii, *n*, robbery, fraud, robber-band

lătrōcĭnor, *v.i.* 1, *dep*, to practise highway robbery

lătruncŭlus, i, *m*, robber

lātus, a, um, *adj*, *adv*, ē, wide

lătus, ĕris, *n*, the side, flank, lungs

laudābĭlis, e, *adj*, praiseworthy

laudātĭo, ōnis, *f*, praises, eulogy

laudātor, ōris, *m*, praiser

laudātus, a, um, *adj*, praiseworthy

laudo, *v.t.* 1, to praise, name

laurĕa, ae, *f*, laurel (tree)

laurĕātus, a, um, *adj*, crowned with laurel (of victory)

laurĕus, a, um, *adj*, of laurel

laurus, i, *f*, laurel

laus, dis, *f*, praise, merit

lautē, *adv*, elegantly

lautĭtĭa, ae, *f*, elegance

lautŭmĭae, ārum, *f. pl*, stone-quarry

lautus, a, um, *adj*, elegant, splendid, noble

lăvātĭo, ōnis, *f*, ablution, washing

lăvo, lăvi, lautum, *v.i.t.* 1 or 3, to wash or wet

laxĭtas, ātis, *f*, spaciousness

laxo, *v.t.* 1, to enlarge, loosen, relax, relieve, weaken

laxus, a, um, *adj*, wide, loose

lĕa, ae, *f*, lioness

lĕaena, ae, *f*, lioness

lĕbes, ētis, *m*, copper basin

lectĭca, ae, *f*, sedan, litter

lectĭo, ōnis, *f*, selection, reading aloud

lector, ōris, *m*, reader

lectŭlus, i, *m*, sofa, couch

lectus, a, um, *adj*, chosen, excellent

lectus, i, *m*, bed, couch

lectus, ūs, *m*, reading

lēgātĭo, ōnis, *f*, delegation

lēgātum, i, *n*, legacy

lēgātus, i, *m*, ambassador, delegate, lieutenant-general

lēges, see lex

lēgĭfer, ĕra, ĕrum, *adj*, law-giving

lēgĭo, ōnis, *f*, Roman legion (4,000–6,000 soldiers)

lēgĭōnārĭus, a, um, *adj*, of a legion

lēgĭtĭmus, a, um, *adj*, legal, legitimate, proper, right

lēgo, *v.t.* 1, to send with a commission, appoint as a deputy, leave as a legacy

lēgo, lēgi, lectum, *v.t.* 3, to read, gather, select, steal, pass through, sail by, survey

lēgūmen, ĭnis, *n*, pulse, beans

lembus, i, *m*, yacht, cutter

lēmŭres, um, *m. pl*, ghosts, spirits

lēna, ae, *f*, bawd

lēnīmen, ĭnis, *n*, alleviation, palliative

lēnīmentum, i, *n*, alleviation, palliative

lēnĭo, *v.t.* 4, to soften, soothe

lēnis, e, *adj, adv*, ĭter, soft, smooth, gentle, calm

lēnĭtas, ātis, *f*, gentleness

lēno, ōnis, *m*, pimp, seducer

lēnōcĭnĭum, ĭi, *n*, pandering, ornamentation

lēnōcĭnor, *v.1, dep, with dat*, to flatter, promote

lens, ntis, *f*, lentil

lentesco, *v.i.* 3, to become soft or sticky

lentīgo, ĭnis, *f*, freckle

lentĭtūdo, ĭnis, *f*, apathy, sluggishness

lento, *v.t.* 1, to bend

lentus, a, um, *adj, adv*, ē, slow, flexible, sticky, tedious, calm (of character)

lēnuncŭlus, i, *m*, boat

lĕo, lōnis, *m*, lion

lĕpĭdus, a, um, *adj, adv*, ē, charming, elegant, pleasant

lĕpor (lĕpos), ōris, *m*, charm, pleasantness, wit

lĕpōrārĭum, ĭi, *n*, warren

leprae, ārum, *f. pl*, leprosy

lĕprōsus, a, um, *adj*, leprous

lĕpus, ŏris, *m*, a hare

lĕpuscŭlus, i, *m*, leveret

lētālis, e, *adj*, fatal

lēthargĭcus, a, um, *adj*, lethargic

lēthargus, i, *m*, stupor

lētĭfer, ĕra, ĕrum, *adj*, deadly

lētum, i, *n*, death

lĕvāmen, ĭnis, *n*, consolation, comfort

lĕvāmentum, i, *n*, consolation, comfort

lĕvātĭo, ōnis, *f*, raising

lĕvis, e, *adj, adv*, ĭter, light, mild, light-armed, agile, trivial, unreliable

lēvis, e, *adj*, smooth, soft

lĕvĭtas, ātis, *f*, inconstancy

lēvĭtas, ātis, *f*, smoothness

lĕvo, *v.t.* 1, to raise, relieve, take away, support, soothe, release

lēvo, *v.t.* 1, to smooth

lex, lēgis, *f*, law, condition

lībāmen, ĭnis, *n*, drink-offering

lībāmentum, i, *n*, drink-offering

lībella, ae, *f*, small coin

lībellus, i, *m*, small book, pamphlet, diary

lībens, ntis, *adj, adv*, nter, with pleasure, willing

līber, ĕra, ĕrum, *adj, adv*, ē, free, frank

1. līber, ĕri, *m*, wine

2. līber, ĕri, *m*, child

līber, bri, *m*, book, tree-bark

lībĕrālis, e, *adj, adv*, ĭter, honourable, generous

lībĕrālĭtas, ātis, *f*, generosity

lībĕrātĭo, ōnis, *f*, release

lībĕrātor, ōris, *m*, liberator

lībĕri, ōrum, *m. pl*, children

lībĕro, *v.t.* 1, to release, free from slavery, acquit

lībertas, ātis, *f*, freedom

lībertīnus, i, *m*, freedman

lībertīnus, a, um, *adj*, of a freedman

lībertus, i, *m*, a freedman

lĭbet, lĭbŭit, lĭbitum est, *v.* 2, *impers*, it is agreeable

lĭbīdĭnōsus, a, um, *adj*, lecherous

lĭbīdo, ĭnis, *f*, desire, passion, whim

lībo, *v.t.* 1, to taste, touch, pour out an offering of wine

lībra, ae, *f*, Roman pound (12 oz.), pair of scales

lībrāmentum, i, *n*, a weight

lībrārĭus, i, *m*, secretary

lībrārĭus, a, um, *adj*, of books

lībrātus, a, um, *adj*, balanced

lībrīlis, e, *adj*, weighing a pound

lībro, *v.t.* 1, to balance, hurl

lībum, i, *n*, pancake

līburna, ae, *f*, fast sailing-ship

lĭcenter, *adv*, without restraint

lĭcentĭa, ae, *f*, freedom, licence

lĭcĕo, *v.i.* 2, to be for sale, be valued at

lĭcĕor, *v.t.* 2, *dep*, to bid (for)

lĭcet, cŭit, cĭtum est, *v.* 2, *impers*, it is allowed, one may

lĭcet, *conj*, although

lĭcĭtus, a, um, *adj*, permitted

lĭcĭtātĭo, ōnis, *f*, bidding

lĭcĭum, ĭi, *n*, a thread

lictor, ōris, *m*, official attendant of high magistrates

lĭēn, ēnis, *m*, spleen

lĭgāmen, ĭnis, *n*, bandage

lĭgāmentum, i, *n*, ligament

lignārĭus, ĭi, *m*, carpenter, joiner

lignātĭo, ōnis, *f*, wood-gathering

lignātor, ōris, *m*, wood-cutter

lignĕus, a, um, *adj*, wooden

lignor, *v.i.* 1, *dep*, to collect wood

lignum, i, *n*, wood
ligo, *v.t.* 1, to tie, bind
ligo, ōnis, *m*, hoe
ligŭla, ae, *f*, small tongue (of land); tongue of a shoe
ligŭrio, *v.t.* 4, to lick, desire
ligustrum, i, *n*, a plant, privet
lilĭum, ii, *n*, lily
lima, ae, *f*, file
limax, ācis, *f*, slug
limbus, i, *m*, border, edge
limen, ĭnis, *n*, door-step, door, lintel
limĕs, ĭtis, *m*, boundary, track
limo, *v.t.* 1, to file, polish, finish
limōsus, a, um, *adj*, slimy, muddy
limpĭdus, a, um, *adj*, clear, bright
limus, a, um, *adj*, aslant
limus, i, *m*, slime, mud
limus, i, *m*, apron
lināmentum, i, *n*, linen, lint
linĕa, ae, *f*, thread, string, line, end, goal
linĕāmentum, i, *n*, line, feature
linĕus, a, um, *adj*, linen
lingo, nxi, *v.t.* 3, to lick
lingua, ae, *f*, tongue, speech, language
liniger, ĕra, ĕrum, *adj*, clothed in linen
lino, lēvi, lĭtum, *v.t.* 3, to daub, smear over
linquo, līqui, *v.t.* 3, to leave
lintĕo, ōnis, *m*, linen-weaver
linter, tris, *f*, boat, tray
lintĕum, i, *n*, linen
lintĕus, a, um, *adj*, of linen
linum, i, *n*, flax, linen, thread, rope, net
lippĭtūdo, ĭnis, *f*, inflammation of the eyes
lippus, a, um, *adj*, blear-eyed
liquĕfăcio, fēci, factum, *v.t.* 3, to melt, dissolve
liquĕfactus, a, um, *adj*, molten
liquens, ntis, *adj*, liquid
liquĕo, līqui, *v.i.* 2, to be clear
liquesco, licŭi, *v.i.* 3, to melt
liquĭdus, a, um, *adj*, liquid, flowing, clear
liquo, *v.t.* 1, to melt, filter
liquor, *v.i.* 3, *dep*, to melt, flow
liquor, ōris, *m*, a liquid
lis, tis, *f*, dispute, lawsuit
litigĭōsus, a, um, *adj*, quarrelsome
litĭgo, *v.i.* 1, to quarrel
lito, *v.i.t.* 1, to make a sacrifice with favourable omens; appease
lītŏrĕus, a, um, *adj*, of the sea-shore
littĕra, ae, *f*, a letter of the alphabet
littĕrae, ārum, *f. pl*, a letter, document, literature, learning
littĕrātus, a, um, *adj*, educated

littĕrŭla, ae, *f*, small letter, moderate literary knowledge
litūra, ae, *f*, smear, erasure
litus, ōris, *n*, sea-shore
litŭus, i, *m*, augur's staff, trumpet
livens, ntis, *adj*, bluish
livĕo, *v.i.* 2, to be black and blue
livĭdus, a, um, *adj*, bluish, black and blue, envious
livor, ōris, *m*, leaden colour, envy, malice
lixa, ae, *m*, camp-follower
lŏca, ōrum, *n.pl*, a region
lŏcātĭo, ōnis, *f*, placing, arrangement, lease
lŏco, *v.t.* 1, to place, arrange, give in marriage, lease, contract for
lŏcŭlāmentum, i, *n*, box
lŏcŭlus, i, *m*, satchel, purse
lŏcŭplēs, ētis, *adj*, wealthy
lŏcŭplēto, *v.t.* 1, to enrich
lŏcus, i, *m*, place, position, topic, subject, cause, reason
lŏcusta, ae, *f*, locust
lŏcūtĭo, ōnis, *f*, speaking, pronunciation, phrase
lōdix, ĭcis, *f*, blanket
lŏgĭca, ōrum, *n.pl*, logic
lŏgĭcus, a, um, *adj*, logical
lōlīgo, ĭnis, *f*, cuttle-fish
lōlĭum, ii, *n*, darnel
longaevus, a, um, *adj*, ancient
longē, *adv*, far off, greatly
longinquĭtas, ātis, *f*, duration, distance
longinquus, a, um, *adj*, distant, strange, prolonged
longĭtūdo, ĭnis, *f*, length
longŭrĭus, ii, *m*, long pole
longus, a, um, *adj*, long, tall, vast, distant, tedious
lŏquācĭtas, ātis, *f*, talkativeness
lŏquax, ācis, *adj*, *adv*, ĭter, talkative, babbling
lŏquēla, ae, *f*, speech, discourse
lŏquor, lŏcūtus, *v.i.t.* 3, *dep*, to speak; tell, mention, declare
lōrīca, ae, *f*, breastplate
lōrĭpēs, pēdis, *adj*, bandy-legged
lōrum, i, *n*, strap, whip
lōtos (lōtus), i, *f*, lotus-tree
lŭbens, lŭbet, see libens, libet
lūbrĭcus, a, um, *adj*, slippery, dangerous, deceitful
lŭcellum, i, *n*, slight profit
lūcĕo, xi, *v.i.* 2, to shine
lūcet, *v. impers.*, day breaks
lŭcerna, ae, *f*, lamp
lūcesco, *v.i.* 3, to dawn
lūcĭdus, a, um, *adj*, bright, clear
lūcĭfer, ĕra, ĕrum, *adj*, light-bringing;
lūcĭfer ĕri, *m*, morning-star

lūcĭfŭgus, a, um, *adj*, retiring
lŭcrātīvus, a, um, *adj*, profitable
lŭcror, *v.t.* 1, *dep*, to gain, win
lŭcrum, i, *n*, profit, advantage
luctāmen, ĭnis, *n*, wrestling, struggle
luctātĭo, ōnis, *f*, wrestling, struggle
luctātor, ōris, *m*, wrestler
luctĭfĭcus, a, um, *adj*, woeful
luctor, *v.i.* 1, *dep*, to struggle
luctŭōsus, a, um, *adj*, sorrowful
luctus, ūs, *m*, grief, mourning (clothes)
lūcŭbrātĭo, ōnis, *f*, night-work
lūcŭlentus, a, um, *adj*, bright
lūcus, i, *m*, wood, grove
lūdĭbrĭum, ii, *n*, mockery, jest, laughing-stock
lūdĭbundus, a, um, *adj*, playful
lūdĭcer, ĭcra, ĭcrum, *adj*, sportive, theatrical
ludĭcrum, i, *n*, public show or games, a play
lūdĭfĭcātĭo, ōnis, *f*, mocking
lūdĭfĭcor, *v.i.t.* 1, *dep* (lūdĭfĭco, *v.t.* 1), to mock, deceive
lūdĭmăgister, tri, *m*, schoolmaster
lūdĭus, ii, *m*, pantomine-actor
lūdo, si, sum, *v.i.t.* 3, to play, frolic; mock, deceive
lūdus, i, *m*, a play, game, public games, school, joke
lŭes, is, *f*, an epidemic
lūgĕo, xi, ctum, *v.i.t.* 2, to mourn
lūgŭbris, e, *adj*, lamentable, disastrous
lumbus, i, *m*, loin
lūmen, ĭnis, *n*, light, lamp, gleam, life, eye, glory
lūna, ae, *f*, moon
lūnāris, e, *adj*, lunar
lūnātus, a, um, *adj*, crescent-shaped
lūno, *v.t.* 1, to bend into a crescent-shape
lŭo, lŭi, *v.t.* 3, to pay a debt or penalty, undergo, atone for
lŭpāta, ōrum, *n.pl*, horse-bit
lŭpātus, a, um, *adj*, jagged
lŭpīnus, a, um, *adj*, of the wolf
lŭpīnus, i, *m*, lupin (plant)
lŭpus, i, *m*, wolf, pike (fish), a jagged bit, hook
lūrĭdus, a, um, *adj*, lurid, sallow
luscinia, ae, *f*, nightingale
lūsor, ōris, *m*, player, mocker
lustrālis, e, *adj*, expiatory
lustrātĭo, ōnis, *f*, purification by sacrifice
lustro, *v.t.* 1, to purify by sacrifice, wander over, review
lustrum, i, *n*, den, wood
lustrum, i, *n*, purificatory sacrifice, period of five years

lūsus, ūs, *m*, play, sport, game
lūtĕŏlus, a, um, *adj*, yellow
lūtĕus, a, um, *adj*, golden-yellow
lūtĕus, a, um, *adj*, muddy, worthless
lūtra, ae, *f*, otter
lŭtŭlentus, a, um, *adj*, filthy
lūtum, i, *n*, yellow
lŭtum, i, *n*, mud, clay
lux, lūcis, *f*, light, dawn, day, life, brightness, glory
luxŭria, ae, *f*, luxuriance, extravagance
luxŭrĭo, *v.i.* 1 (luxŭrĭor, *v.* 1, *dep*), to be overgrown, to have in excess, run riot
luxŭrĭōsus, a, um, *adj*, luxuriant, excessive
luxus, ūs, *m*, extravagance, pomp
lychnūcus, i, *m*, lamp-stand
lychnus, i, *m*, light, lamp
lympha, ae, *f*, water
lymphātus, a, um, *adj*, frenzied
lyncēus, a, um, *adj*, sharp-eyed
lynx, cis, *c*, lynx
lўra, ae, *f*, lute, poetry, song
lўrĭcus, a, um, *adj*, of the lute, lyric

M

măcellum, i, *n*, food-market
măcer, cra, crum, *adj*, lean, thin
măcĕria, ae, *f*, wall
măcĕro, *v.t.* 1, to soften, weaken, torment
māchĭna, ae, *f*, engine, machine, battering-ram, trick, plan
māchĭnālis, e, *adj*, mechanical
māchĭnātĭo, ōnis, *f*, contrivance, machine, trick
māchĭnātor, ōris, *m*, engineer, inventor
māchĭnor, *v.t.* 1, *dep*, to design, plot
măcĭes, ēi, *f*, thinness, poverty
macte or macti (*voc. of* mactus), good luck! well done!
macto, *v.t.* 1, to sacrifice a victim, reward, honour, destroy
mactus, a, um, *adj*, worshipped
măcŭla, ae, *f*, spot, stain, fault, mesh
măcŭlo, *v.t.* 1, to stain, disgrace
măcŭlōsus, a, um, *adj*, spotted, dishonoured
mădĕfăcĭo, fēci, factum, *v.t.* 3, to soak, drench
mădens, ntis, *adj*, moist, drunk
mădĕo, *v.i.* 2, to be moist, to drip, to be boiled, softened
mădesco, dŭi, *v.i.* 3, to become wet
mādĭdus, a, um, *adj*, soaked
maena, ae, *f*, small salted fish

For List of Abbreviations used, turn to pages 3, 4

maeniānum, i, *n*, balcony
maerens, ntis, *adj*, mourning
maerĕo, *v.i.t.* 2, to mourn; bewail
maeror, ōris, *m*, grief, mourning
maestĭtia, ae, *f*, sadness
maestus, a, um, *adj*, sad
māga, ae, *f*, witch
māgālĭa, ĭum, *n.pl*, huts
māgĭcus, a, um, *adj*, magic
māgis, *comp. adv* (magnus), more,
   rather
māgister, tri, *m*, master, leader,
   director, teacher
māgistērĭum, ii, *n*, president's position
māgistra, ae, *f*, mistress
māgistrātus, ūs, *m*, magistracy, magistrate
magnănĭmĭtas, ātis, *f*, magnanimity
magnănĭmus, a, um, *adj*, great-
   hearted
magnes, ētis, *m*, magnet
magnētĭcus, a, um, *adj*, magnetic
magni, see magnus
magnĭfĭcentia, ae, *f*, nobleness, splendour, boasting
magnĭfĭcus, a, um, *adj, adv*, ē, noble,
   distinguished, sumptuous, bragging
magnĭlŏquentia, ae, *f*, high-sounding
   language
magnĭtūdo, ĭnis, *f*, size
magnŏpĕrē, *adv*, very much
magnus, a, um, *adj*, large, great;
   magni or magno, at a high price
māgus, i, *m*, magician
Māius (mensis), May
māiestas, ātis, *f*, greatness, grandeur,
   sovereignty, treason
māior, *comp. adj*, larger, greater;
   māiōres, um, *m. pl*, ancestors, the
   Senate; maior nātu, older
māla, ae, *f*, cheek-bone, jaw
mălăcia, ae, *f*, a calm at sea
mălagma, ătis, *n*, poultice
mălē, *adv*, badly, exceedingly; often
   reverses the meaning of an adj:
   male sānus, deranged
mălēdīcens, ntis, *adj*, abusive
mălēdīco, xi, ctum, *v.i.* 3, to abuse,
   slander
mălēdictĭo, ōnis, *f*, abuse
mălēdictum, i, *n*, abusive word
mălēdĭcus, a, um, *adj*, abusive
mălēfĭcĭum, ii, *n*, wrongdoing
mălēfĭcus, a, um, *adj*, evil-doing
mălēsuādus, a, um, *adj*, persuading
   towards wrong
mălēvŏlens, ntis, *adj*, spiteful
mălēvŏlentia, ae, *f*, malice
mălēvŏlus, a, um, *adj*, spiteful

mālignus, a, um, *adj*, malicious
mālĭtia, ae, *f*, malice
mālĭtiōsus, a, um, *adj*, wicked
mallĕus, i, *m*, hammer
mālo, malle, mālŭi, *v.t. irreg*, to prefer
mālŏbăthrum, i, *n*, a costly ointment
mālum, i, *n*, apple, fruit
mālum, i, *n*, evil, misfortune
mālus, a, um, *adj*, bad, harmful
mālus, i, *m*, mast
malva, ae, *f*, the mallow
mamma, ae, *f*, breast, teat
manceps, cĭpis, *m*, contractor
mancĭpĭum, ii, *n*, legal purchase, right
   of ownership, slave
mancĭpo, *v.t.* 1, to sell, transfer
mancus, a, um, *adj*, maimed
mandātum, i, *n*, order, commission
mandātus, ūs, *m*, order, commission
mando, *v.t.* 1, to order, commission,
   commit
mandūco, *v.t.* 1, to chew
māne, *indecl. n*, morning; *adv*, in the
   morning
mănĕo, nsi, nsum, *v.i.t.* 2, to stay,
   remain, continue; await
mānes, ĭum, *m. pl*, deified ghosts of
   the dead
mănĭcae, ārum, *f. pl*, glove, gauntlet,
   handcuff
mănĭfestus, a, um, *adj, adv*, ō, clear,
   apparent
mănĭpŭlāris, e, *adj*, belonging to a
   company (a soldier)
mănĭpŭlus, i, *m*, handful, bundle,
   company of soldiers
mannus, i, *m*, coach-horse, pony
māno, *v.i.t.* 1, to flow, trickle; pour out
mansĭo, ōnis, *f*, a stay, inn
mansŭēfăcĭo, fēci, factum, *v.t.* 3, to
   tame, civilize
mansŭesco, sŭēvi, sŭētum, *v.i.* 3, to
   grow tame or gentle
mansŭētus, a, um, *adj*, gentle
mansŭētūdo, ĭnis, *f*, gentleness
mansūrus, a, um, *adj*, lasting
mantēle, is, *n*, towel, cloth
mantĭca, ae, *f*, suit-case
mănŭbĭae, ārum, *f. pl*, money from
   the sale of booty
mănŭbrĭum, ii, *n*, handle
mănŭmissĭo, ōnis, *f*, the freeing of a
   slave
mănŭmitto, mīsi, missum, *v.t.* 3, to set
   free a slave
mănus, ūs, *f*, hand, bravery, combat,
   violence, grappling-iron, armed
   band
măpālĭa, ĭum, *n. pl*, African huts

MAP 73 MEN

mappa, ae, *f,* towel, napkin
marcĕo, *v.i.* 2, to be weak
marcesco, *v.i.* 3, to wither
marcidus, a, um, *adj,* decayed
măre, is, *n,* the sea
marga, ae, *f,* marl
margărĭta, ae, *f,* pearl
margo, ĭnis, *m, f,* edge, border
mărīnus, a, um, *adj,* of the sea
mărĭta, ae, *f,* wife
mărītālis, e, *adj,* matrimonial
mărĭtĭmus, a, um, *adj,* of the sea
mărītus, a, um, *adj,* matrimonial
mărītus, i, *m,* husband
marmor, ŏris, *n,* marble, statue; *in pl,* surface of the sea
marmŏrĕus, a, um, *adj,* of marble
martĭālis, e, *adj,* sacred to Mars
martĭus, a, um, *adj,* sacred to Mars
Martĭus (mensis), March
martyr, ўris, *c,* martyr
martўrĭum, ĭi, *n,* martyrdom
măs, măris, *adj,* male
mascŭlus, a, um, *adj,* male, bold
massa, ae, *f,* lump, mass
mătellĭo, ōnis, *m,* pot
măter, tris, *f,* mother
māterfămĭlĭas, mātrisfămĭlĭas, *f,* mistress of the house
mātĕrĭa, ae, *f,* timber, materials, topic, opportunity
matĕris, is, *f,* Celtic javelin
māternus, a, um, *adj,* maternal
mātertĕra, ae, *f,* maternal aunt
măthēmătĭca, ae, *f,* mathematics
măthēmătĭcus, a, um, *adj,* mathematical
mātrĭcīda, ae, *c,* murderer of his (her) mother
mātrĭmōnĭum, ĭi, *n,* marriage
mātrōna, ae, *f,* married woman
mātrōnālis, e, *adj,* of a married woman
mātūrē, *adv,* at the proper time, soon, quickly
mātūresco, rŭi, *v.i.* 3, to ripen
mātūritas, ātis, *f,* ripeness
mātūro, *v.i.t.* 1, to ripen, hurry; bring to maturity
mātūrus, a, um, *adj,* mature, ripe, early
mātūtīnus, a, um, *adj,* of the morning
maxilla, ae, *f,* jawbone, jaw
maxĭmē, *adv,* especially, very
maxĭmus, a, um, *sup. adj,* very large or great
māzŏnŏmus, i, *m,* dish
me, *acc. or abl.* of ego (1)
mĕātus, ūs, *m,* motion, course
mĕdĕor, *v.* 2, *dep. with dat,* to heal, remedy, amend
mĕdĭastĭnus, i, *m,* drudge

mĕdĭca, ae, *f,* a kind of clover
mĕdĭcābĭlis, e, *adj,* curable
mĕdĭcāmen, ĭnis, *n,* remedy, drug
mĕdĭcāmentum, i, *n,* remedy, drug
mĕdĭcāmentārĭus, a, um, *adj,* of drugs
mĕdĭcīna, ae, *f,* the art of medicine, remedy
mĕdĭco, *v.t.* 1, to heal, sprinkle, dye
mĕdĭcor, *v.t.* 1, *dep,* to heal
mĕdĭcus, a, um, *adj,* healing
mĕdĭcus, i, *m,* doctor, surgeon
mĕdimnum, i, *n,* bushel
mĕdĭŏcris, e, *adj, adv, ĭter,* ordinary, insignificant
mĕdĭŏcritas, ātis, *f,* a middle state, insignificance
mĕdĭtātĭo, ōnis, *f,* contemplation, preparation
mĕdĭtātus, a, um, *adj,* considered
mĕdĭterrānĕus, a, um, *adj,* inland
mĕdĭtor, *v.i.t.* 1, *dep,* to consider, muse; study, intend, practise
mĕdĭum, ĭi, *n,* middle, the public
mĕdĭus, a, um, *adj,* middle, neutral
mĕdĭus, i, *m,* mediator
mĕdulla, ae, *f,* kernel, marrow
mēĭo, *v.i.* 3, to urinate
mĕl, mellis, *n,* honey
mĕlanchŏlĭcus, a, um, *adj,* melancholic
mēles, is, *f,* badger
mēlĭmēla, ōrum, *n. pl,* honey apples
mēlĭor, us, *comp. adj,* better
mēlisphyllum, i, *n,* balm
**mēlĭus, comp. adv,* better
mellĭfer, ĕra, ĕrum, *adj,* honey-producing
**mellĭfĭco, v.t.* 1, to make honey
mellītus, a, um, *adj,* of honey
mēlo, ōnis, *m,* melon
mēlos, i, *n,* tune, song
membrāna, ae, *f,* skin, parchment
membrātim, *adv,* piece by piece
membrum, i, *n,* limb, division
**mĕmĭni, isse, v.i. defective,* to remember
mĕmor, ŏris, *adj,* remembering, mindful
mĕmŏrābĭlis, e, *adj,* memorable
mĕmŏrandus, a, um, *adj,* memorable
mĕmŏrātus, a, um, *adj,* renowned
mĕmŏrĭa, ae, *f,* memory, posterity, historical account, tradition
**mĕmŏro, v.t.* 1, to mention
menda, ae, *f,* defect
mendācĭum, ĭi, *n,* a lie
mendax, ācis, *adj,* lying, false
mendĭcĭtas, ātis, *f,* poverty
mendĭco, *v.i.* 1, to beg
mendĭcus, a, um, *adj,* needy
mendĭcus, i, *m,* beggar

mendōsus, a, um, *adj, adv,* ē, faulty, false

mendum, i, *n,* blunder, defect, mistake

mens, ntis, *f,* mind, intellect, understanding, intention, courage

mensa, ae, *f,* table, course; **sĕcunda mensa,** dessert

mensārius, ii, *m,* banker

mensis, is, *m,* month

mensor, ōris, *m,* valuer, surveyor

menstrŭus, a, um, *adj,* monthly

mensūra, ae, *f,* measurement, quantity

mensus, a, um, *adj,* measured off

menta, ae, *f,* mint

mentio, ōnis, *f,* recollection, mention

mentior, *v.i.t.* 4, *dep,* to lie, cheat; counterfeit, imitate

mentītus, a, um, *adj,* counterfeit

mentum, i, *n,* chin

mĕo, *v.i.* 1, to go

mĕrācus, a, um, *adj,* unmixed

mercātor, ōris, *m,* wholesaler

mercātūra, ae, *f,* trade

mercātus, ūs, *m,* trade, market

mercēdŭla, ae, *f,* small wages

mercēnārius, a, um, *adj,* hired

merces, ēdis, *f,* pay, wages, rent, interest, reward

merces (*pl*), see merx

mercor, *v.t.* 1, *dep,* to buy

mĕrens, ntis, *adj,* deserving

mĕrĕo, *v.t.* (mĕrĕor, *v. dep*) 2, to deserve, earn; with **stipendia,** to serve as a soldier

mĕrētrīcius, a, um, *adj,* of prostitutes

mĕrētrix, trīcis, *f,* prostitute

merges, ĭtis, *f,* sheaf

mergo, si, sum, *v.t.* 3, to immerse

mergus, i, *m,* sea-bird (diver)

mĕrīdiānus, a, um, *adj,* of midday

mĕrīdies, ēi, *m,* midday, south

mĕrĭtōrius, a, um, *adj,* bringing in money

mĕritum, i, *n,* reward, benefit, fault, blame

mĕritus, a, um, *adj, adv,* ō, deserved, deserving

mĕrops, ōpis, *m,* bee-eating bird

merso, *v.t.* 1, to immerse, drown

mĕrŭla, ae, *f,* blackbird

mĕrum, i, *n,* pure wine

mĕrus, a, um, *adj,* pure, only, genuine

merx, cis, *f,* goods, commodities

messis, is, *f,* harvest, crops

messor, ōris, *m,* harvester

mēta, ae, *f,* winning-post, end, cone

mĕtallicus, a, um, *adj,* metallic

mĕtallicus, i, *m,* miner

mĕtallum, i, *n,* mine, metal

mētātor, ōris, *m,* surveyor

mētior, mensus, *v.t.* 4, *dep,* to measure, distribute, traverse, estimate, value

mēto, ssŭi, ssum, *v.t.* 3, to mow, gather, cut down

mētor, *v.t.* 1, *dep,* to measure, mark out, traverse

mĕtricus, a, um, *adj,* metrical

mĕtŭendus, a, um, *adj,* formidable

mĕtŭo, ŭi, ūtum, *v.i.t.* 3, to be afraid; to fear

mĕtus, ūs, *m.* fear, awe

mĕus, a, um, *adj,* my, mine: **mĕi,** ōrum, *m. pl,* my relatives

mīca, ae, *f,* crumb

mīco, ŭi, *v.i.* 1, to tremble, sparkle

mīgrātio, ōnis, *f,* migration

mīgro, *v.i.* 1, to depart, change

mīles, ĭtis, *c,* soldier, army

mīlia, see mille

mīliārium, ii, *n,* mile-stone

mīlitāris, e, *adj,* military

mīlitāris, is, *m,* soldier

mīlitia, ae, *f,* military service, warfare

mīlito, *v.i.* 1, to serve as a soldier

mīlium, ii, *n,* millet

mille (*pl,* mīlia, with *genit.*), a thousand; **mille passus,** or **passuum, a mile**

millēsimus, a, um, *adj,* the thousandth

millĭes (milliens), *adv,* a thousand times

mīluīnus, a, um, *adj,* kite-like

mīluus, i, *m,* kite, gurnard

mīmĭcus, a, um, *adj,* farcical

mīmus, i, *m,* mime, mimic actor

mīna, ae, *f,* Greek silver coinage

mīnae, ārum, *f. pl,* threats

mĭnax, ācis, *adj, adv,* ĭter, threatening, projecting

mĭnĭmē, *sup. adv,* very little

mĭnĭmus, a, um, *sup. adj,* very small

mĭnister, tri, *m,* mĭnistra, ae, *f,* servant, assistant

mĭnistĕrium, ii, *n,* service, occupation

mĭnistrātor, ōris, *m,* servant

mĭnistro, *v.t.* 1, to wait upon, serve, manage

mĭnĭtor, *v.i.t.* 1, *dep,* to threaten

mĭnium, ii, *n,* red-lead

mĭnor, *v.i.t.* 1, *dep,* to threaten

mĭnor, us, *comp. adj,* smaller

mĭnŭo, ŭi, ūtum, *v.i.t.* 3, to ebb; to reduce, weaken, chop up

mĭnus, *comp. adv,* less

mĭnuscŭlus, a, um, *adj,* rather small

mĭnūtal, ālis, *n,* mincemeat

mĭnūtātim, *adv,* little by little

mĭnūtus, a, um, *adj, adv,* ē, small

mīrābilis, e, *adj, adv,* ĭter, wonderful, strange

mīrācŭlum, i, *n,* a wonder, marvel

mīrandus, a, um, *adj,* wonderful

mīrātio, ōnis, *f,* surprise

mīrātor, ōris, *m,* admirer

mīrīficus, a, um, *adj, adv, ē,* marvellous, extraordinary

mīror, *v.i.t.* 1, *dep,* to be amazed; to marvel at, admire

mīrus, a, um, *adj, adv, ē,* marvellous, extraordinary

miscĕo, scŭi, xtum, *v.t.* 2, to mix, unite, disturb

mīsellus, a, um, *adj,* wretched

mīser, ĕra, ĕrum, *adj, adv, ē,* wretched, pitiable, worthless

mīsĕrābilis, e, *adj, adv, īter,* pitiable, sad

mīsĕrandus, a, um, *adj,* pitiable

mīsĕrātio, ōnis, *f,* pity

mīsĕrĕor, *v.* 2, *dep, with gen,* to pity

mīsĕret (me, te, etc.**),** *v.* 2, *impers,* it distresses (me), I pity, am sorry for

mīsĕresco, *v.i.* 3, to feel pity

mīsĕria, ae, *f,* misfortune, wretchedness

mīsĕricordia, ae, *f,* pity

mīsĕricors, dis, *adj,* merciful

mīsĕror, *v.t.* 1, *dep,* to lament, pity

missĭle, is, *n,* missile, javelin

missĭlis, e, *adj,* that is thrown

missĭo, ōnis, *f,* throwing, discharge, release

missus, ūs, *m,* dispatching, throwing, shot

mītella, ae, *f,* turban, bandage

mītesco, *v.i.* 3, to grow mild or soft or ripe

mītĭgātĭo, ōnis, *f,* mitigation

mītigo, *v.t.* 1, to make soft or ripe, to tame, soothe

mītis, e, *adj,* mild, ripe, calm

mītra, ae, *f,* head-band

mitto, mīsi, missum, *v.t.* 3, to send, announce, cease, release, throw, escort

mītŭlus, i, *m,* sea-mussel

mixtūra, ae, *f,* mixture

mixtus, a, um, *adj,* mixed

mōbĭlis, e, *adj, adv, īter,* movable, agile, flexible, fickle

mōbĭlĭtas, ātis, *f,* speed, inconstancy

mŏdĕrāmen, ĭnis, *n,* rudder, management

mŏdĕrātĭo, ōnis, *f,* moderation, restraint

mŏdĕrātor, ōris, *m,* manager

mŏdĕrātus, a, um, *adj, adv, ē,* moderate

mŏdĕror, *v.t.* 1, *dep,* to restrain, govern

mŏdestĭa, ae, *f,* moderation, discretion, modesty

mŏdestus, a, um, *adj, adv, ē,* modest, gentle

mŏdĭcus, a, um, *adj, adv, ē,* modest, ordinary

mŏdĭfĭcātus, a, um, *adj,* measured

mŏdĭus, ii, *m,* peck, measure

mŏdŏ, *adv,* only, but, just, lately; non mŏdŏ, not only; mŏdŏ . . . mŏdŏ, at one time . . . at another time

mŏdŭlātor, ōris, *m,* musician

mŏdŭlor, *v.t.* 1, *dep,* to sing, play

mŏdŭlātus, a, um, *adj,* sung, played

mŏdŭlus, i, *m,* a small measure

mŏdus, i, *m,* measure, quantity, rhythm, limit, restriction, end, method, way

moechus, i, *m,* adulterer

moenĭa, ĭum, *n.pl,* ramparts

mŏla, ae, *f,* millstone, grain mixed with salt to be sprinkled on sacrificial animals

mŏlāris, is, *m,* millstone

mōles, is, *f,* mass, bulk, dam, pier, power, difficulty

mŏlestĭa, ae, *f,* trouble, affectation

mŏlestus, a, um, *adj, adv, ē,* troublesome, affected

mōlīmen, ĭnis, *n,* undertaking, attempt

mōlīmentum, i, *n,* undertaking, attempt

mōlĭor, *v.i.t.* 4, to strive, depart; to rouse, construct, attempt

mōlĭtor, ōris, *m,* miller

mōlĭtor, ōris, *m,* contriver

mollesco, *v.i.* 3, to grow soft

mollĭo, *v.t.* 4, to soften, restrain

mollis, a, *adj, adv, īter,* soft, supple, tender, effeminate

mollĭtĭa, ae, *f,* softness, weakness

mollĭtĭes, ĕi, *f,* softness, weakness

mollĭtūdo, ĭnis, *f,* softness, weakness

mŏlo, ŭi, ĭtum, *v.t.* 3, to grind

mōmentum, i, *n,* movement, motion, moment, instant, cause, influence, importance

mŏnăcha, ae, *f,* nun

mŏnastērĭum, ii, *n,* monastery

mŏnēdŭla, ae, *f,* jackdaw

mŏnĕo, *v.t.* 2, to warn, advise, remind, instruct, tell

mŏnēta, ae, *f,* the mint, coin

mŏnētālis, e, *adj,* of the mint

mŏnīle, is, *n,* necklace, collar

mŏnĭtĭo, ōnis, *f,* warning

mŏnĭtor, ōris, *m,* adviser, instructor

mŏnĭtum, i, *n,* advice

mŏnĭtus, ūs, *m,* warning, omen

For List of Abbreviations used, turn to pages 3, 4

mŏnŏcĕros, ōtis, *m*, unicorn

mŏnŏpōlĭum, ii, *n*, monopoly

mons, ntis, *m*, mountain

monstrātĭo, ōnis, *f*, showing, pointing out

monstrātor, ōris, *m*, teacher

monstro, *v.t.* 1, to show, tell

monstrum, i, *n*, omen, monster

monstrŭōsus, a, um, *adj*, strange, monstrous

montānus, a, um, *adj*, of a mountain, mountainous

montĭcŏla, ae, *c*, mountain-dweller

montīvăgus, a, um, *adj*, wandering in the mountains

montŭōsus, a, um, *adj*, mountainous

mŏnŭmentum, i, *n*, monument, memorial, written record

mŏra, ae, *f*, delay, hindrance

mōrālis, e, *adj*, moral

mōrātus, a, um, *adj*, mannered; mōrātus *partic.* from mŏror, having delayed

morbĭdus, a, um, *adj*, diseased

morbus, i, *m*, illness, disease

mordax, ācis, *adj*, biting, stinging

mordĕo, mŏmordi, morsum, *v.t.* 2, to bite, clasp, sting

mordĭcus, a, um, *adj*, by biting

mōres, see mos

mōrētum, i, *n*, salad

mōrĭbundus, a, um, *adj*, dying

mōrĭens, ntis, *adj*, dying

mŏrior, mortŭus, *v.i.* 3, *dep*, to die

mŏror, *v.i.t.* 1, *dep*, to delay

mōrōsĭtas, ātis, *f*, fretfulness

mōrōsus, a, um, *adj*, fretful, fastidious

mors, mortis, *f*, death

morsus, ūs, *m*, bite, pungency

mortālis, e, *adj*, mortal, human, temporary

mortālis, is, *c*, human being

mortālĭtas, ātis, *f*, mortality

mortārĭum, ii, *n*, a mortar

mortĭfer, ĕra, ĕrum, *adj*, fatal

mortŭus, a, um, *adj*, dead

mortŭus, i, *m*, a dead person

mōrum, i, *n*, blackberry

mōrus, i, *f*, blackberry-bush

mos, mōris, *m*, custom, manner, habit, fashion; *in pl*, character

mōtăcilla, ae, *f*, wagtail

mōtĭo, ōnis, *f*, motion

mōto, *v.t.* 1, to move about

mōtus, ūs, *m*, motion, movement, impulse, emotion, rebellion

mŏvĕo, mōvi, mōtum, *v.t.* 2, to move, stir, excite, cause

mox, *adv*, soon, immediately

mūcĭdus, a, um, *adj*, musty

mūcor, ōris, *m*, mouldiness

mūcōsus, a, um, *adj*, mucous

mūcro, ōnis, *m*, sword's point

mūgil, is, *m*, mullet

mūgĭnor, *v.i.* 1, *dep*, to hesitate

mūgĭo, *v.i.* 4, to low, bellow, groan, crash

mūgītus, ūs, *m*, bellowing, roaring

mūla, ae, *f*, she-mule

mulcĕo, si, sum, *v.t.* 2, to stroke, soothe

mulco, *v.t.* 1, to maltreat

mulctra, ae, *f*, milk-bucket

mulctrārĭum, ii, *n*, milk-bucket

mulgĕo, si, sum, *v.t.* 2, to milk

mūlĭĕbris, e, *adj, adv*, iter, female, effeminate

mūlĭer, ĕris, *f*, woman, wife

mūlĭercŭla, ae, *f*, girl

mūlĭo, ōnis, *m*, mule-driver

mullus, i, *m*, mullet

mulsum, i, *n*, honey-wine

multa, ae, *f*, penalty, fine

multātĭo, ōnis, *f*, penalty, fine

multi, see multus

multĭfārĭam, *adv*, on many sides

multĭplex, ĭcis, *adj*, with many windings, numerous, many

multĭplĭcātĭo, ōnis, *f*, multiplication

multĭplĭco, *v.t.* 1, to multiply

multĭtūdo, ĭnis, *f*, crowd, great number

multō, *adv*, a great deal

multo, *v.t.* 1, to punish

multum, *adv*, very much, greatly

multus, a, um, *adj*, much; *pl*. many

mūlus, i, *m*, mule

mundĭtĭa, ae, *f*, cleanliness, neatness

mundĭtĭes, ĕi, *f*, cleanliness, neatness

mundo, *v.t.* 1, to cleanse

mundus, a, um, *adj*, clean, elegant

mundus, i, *m*, world, universe, ornaments

mūnĕro, *v.t.* 1 (mūnĕror, *v.t.* 1, *dep.*), to reward, honour

mūnĭa, ōrum, *n.pl*, duties

mūnĭceps, cĭpis, *c*, citizen

mūnĭcĭpālis, e, *adj*, municipal

mūnĭcĭpĭum, ii, *n*, self-governing town

mūnĭfĭcentĭa, ae, *f*, generosity

mūnĭfĭcus, a, um, *adj, adv*, ē, generous

mūnīmen, ĭnis, *n*, rampart, protection

mūnīmentum, i, *n*, rampart, protection

mūnĭo, *v.t.* 4, to fortify, secure, make a way

mūnītĭo, ōnis, *f*, fortification

mūnĭtor, ōris, *m*, engineer

mūnītus, a, um, *adj*, fortified

mūnus, ĕris, *n*, service, duty, employment, post, tax, gift, public show

mūnuscŭlum, i, *n*, small present

mūrālis, e, *adj*, of a wall

mūrex, ĭcis, *m*, purple fish, purple dye, pointed rock

mūrĭa, ae, *f*, brine, pickle

murmur, ŭris, *n*, murmur, crash

murmŭro, *v.i.* 1, to murmur, roar

murra, ae, *f*, myrrh (tree)

murrĕus, a, um, *adj*, perfumed with myrrh

mūrus, i, *m*, wall, defence

mūs, mūris, *c*, mouse

mūsa, ae, *f*, goddess of the arts

musca, ae, *f*, a fly

muscĭpŭlum, i, *n*, mouse-trap

muscōsus, a, um, *adj*, mossy

muscŭlus, i, *m*, little mouse, mussel, muscle, military shed

muscus, i, *m*, moss

mūsēum, i, *n*, museum

mūsĭca, ae, *f*, music

mūsĭcus, a, um, *adj*, musical

mūsĭcus, i, *m*, musician

musso, *v.i.* 1, to mutter, be silent, be in doubt

mustēla, ae, *f*, weasel

mustum, i, *n*, new wine

mūtābĭlis, e, *adj*, changeable

mūtābĭlĭtas, ātis, *f*, changeableness

mūtātĭo, ōnis, *f*, alteration

mūtĭlo, *v.t.* 1, to cut off, maim

mūtĭlus, a, um, *adj*, maimed

mūto, *v.i.t.* 1, to alter, change

mūtŭlus, i, *m*, bracket

mūtŭō, *adv*, in turns

mūtŭor, *v.t.* 1, *dep*, to borrow

mūtus, a, um, *adj*, dumb, mute

mūtŭum, i, *n*, loan

mūtŭus, a, um, *adj*, borrowed, mutual

myrīca, ae, *f*; myrīce, es, *f*, a shrub, tamarisk

myrr . . . see murr . . .

myrtētum, i, *n*, myrtle-grove

myrtĕus, a, um, *adj*, of myrtle

myrtum, i, *n*, myrtle-berry

myrtus, i, *f*, myrtle-tree

mysta (es), ae, *f*, priest of Ceres' mysteries

mystērĭum, ii, *n*, secret rites

mystĭcus, a, um, *adj*, mystical

N

naevus, i, *m*, wart, mole

Nāĭăs, ădis, *f*, water-nymph

nam, *conj*, for

namque, *conj*, for indeed

nanciscor, nactus, *v.t.* 3, *dep*, to obtain, meet with, find

nānus, i, *m*, dwarf

nāpus, i, *m*, turnip

narcissus, i, *m*, narcissus

nardus, i, *f*, perfumed balm

nāris, is, *f*, nostril; *pl*, nose

narrātĭo, ōnis, *f*, narrative

narrātor, ōris, *m*, narrator

narro, *v.t.* 1, to tell, relate

narthēcĭum, ii, *n*, medicine-chest

nascor, nātus, *v.i.* 3, *dep*, to be born, rise, proceed

nasturtium, ii, *n*, cress

nāsus, i, *m*, nose

nāsūtus, a, um, *adj*, large-nosed

nāta, ae, *f*, daughter

nātālĭcĭus, a, um, *adj*, birthday

nātālis, e, *adj*, of birth

nātālis, is, *m*, birthday

nātantes, um, *f. pl*, fish

nātātĭo, ōnis, *f*, swimming

nātātor, ōris, *m*, swimmer

nātĭo, ōnis, *f*, race, nation

nătis, is, *f*, buttock

nātīvus, a, um, *adj*, created, inborn, natural

năto, *v.i.* 1, to swim, float, waver

nătrix, ĭcis, *f*, water-snake

nātūra, ae, *f*, nature

nātūrālis, e, *adj*, *adv*, ĭter, by birth, natural

nātus, ūs, *m*, birth

nātus, i, *m*, son

nātus, a, um, *adj*, born, aged

nauarchus, i, *m*, ship's master

naufrăgĭum, ii, *n*, shipwreck

naufrăgus, a, um, *adj*, shipwrecked

naumăchĭa, ae, *f*, mock sea-fight

nausĕa, ae, *f*, sea-sickness

nausĕābundus, a, um, *adj*, sea-sick

nausĕo, *v.i.* 1, to be sea-sick

nauta, ae, *m*, sailor

nautĭcus, a, um, *adj*, nautical

nāvālĭa, ium, *n.pl*, dockyard

nāvāle, is, *n*, dockyard

nāvālis, e, *adj*, naval

nāvĭcŭla, ae, *f*, boat

nāvĭcŭlārĭus, ii, *m*, ship-owner

nāvĭfrăgus, a, um, *adj*, ship-wrecking

nāvĭgābĭlis, e, *adj*, navigable

nāvĭgātĭo, ōnis, *f*, sailing

nāvĭger, ĕra, ĕrum, *adj*, navigable

nāvĭgĭa, ōrum, *n.pl*, ships, shipping

nāvĭgĭum, ii, *n*, ship, boat

nāvĭgo, *v.i.t.* 1, to sail; navigate

nāvis, is, *f*, ship; nāvis longa, warship

nāvĭta, ae, *m* (nauta), sailor

nāvĭter, *adv*, completely

nāvo, *v.t.* 1, to do vigorously

nāvus, a, um, *adj*, hard-working

nē, *conj*, lest; nē ... quidem, not even ...

-nē, attached to the first word of a sentence to form a question

nē, *interj*, indeed, truly

nēbŭla, ae, *f*, mist, fog, smoke

nēbŭlo, ōnis, *m*, rascal, wretch

nēbŭlōsus, a, um, *adj*, misty

nĕc, *adv*, not; *conj*, and not; nĕc ... nĕc, neither ... nor

necdum, *conj*, not yet

nĕcessārius, a, um, *adj*, *adv*, ō, unavoidable, necessary, related

nĕcessārius, ii, *m*, relative

nĕcesse, *indecl. adj*, unavoidable

nĕcessĭtas, ātis, *f*, necessity, compulsion, destiny

nĕcessĭtūdo, ĭnis, *f*, necessity, relationship

necnĕ, *adv*, or not

nec-non, and also

nĕco, *v.t.* 1, to kill

nĕcŏpīnans, ntis, *adj*, unaware

nĕcŏpīnātus, a, um, *adj*, *adv*, ō, unexpected

nĕcŏpīnus, a, um, *adj*, unexpected

nectar, ăris, *n*, the drink of the gods

nectărĕus, a, um, *adj*, of nectar

necto, xŭi, xum, *v.t.* 3, to tie, fasten together

nĕcŭbi, *adv*, so that nowhere

nēdum, *conj*, still less

nĕfandus, a, um, *adj*, abominable, heinous, wrong

nĕfārius, a, um, *adj*, heinous, wrong

nĕfas, *n*, *indecl*, wrong, sin

nĕfastus, a, um, *adj*, with dies, a day on which neither trials nor public meetings could be held, wicked, unlucky

nĕgātĭo, ōnis, *f*, denial

nĕgĭto, *v.t.* 1, to persist in denying

neglectus, a, um, *adj*, despised

neglĕgens (negligens), ntis, *adj*, careless, indifferent

neglĕgentia, ae, *f*, carelessness

neglĕgo, xi, ctum, *v.t.* 3, to neglect, slight, despise

nĕgo, *v.i.t.* 1, to say no (not); refuse

nĕgōtĭātĭo, ōnis, *f*, wholesale-business, banking

nĕgōtĭātor, ōris, *m*, wholesaler, banker

nĕgōtĭor, *v.i.* 1, *dep*, to carry on business, trade or banking

nĕgōtĭōsus, a, um, *adj*, busy

nĕgōtĭum, ii, *n*, business, occupation, difficulty

nēmo, ĭnis, *m*, *f*, nobody

nĕmŏrālis, e, *adj*, woody

nĕmŏrōsus, a, um, *adj*, woody

nempĕ, *conj*, certainly

nĕmus, ŏris, *n*, wood, grove

nēnĭa, ae, *f*, funeral hymn, sad song, popular song

nĕo, nēvi, nētum, *v.t.* 2, to spin

nēpa, ae, *f*, scorpion

nĕpos, ōtis, *m*, *f*, grandson (... daughter), descendant, spendthrift

neptis, is, *f*, grand-daughter

nēquam, *indecl. adj*, *adv*, nēquiter, worthless, bad

nēquāquam, *adv*, not at all

nēque, a, um, *adj*; *conj*, and not; nēque ... nēque, neither ... nor

nēquĕo, īvi (ii), ĭtum, *v.i.* 4, to be unable

nēquĭquam, *adv*, in vain

nēquĭtĭa, ae, *f*, worthlessness, idleness, extravagance

nervōsus, a, um, *adj*, *adv*, ē, sinewy, energetic

nervus, i, *m*, sinew, string of musical instrument or bow

nescĭo, *v.t.* 4, not to know, to be unable

nescĭus, a, um, *adj*, unaware

neu, *adv*, and so that ... not

neuter, tra, trum, *adj*, neither the one nor the other

neutĭquam, *adv*, not at all

neutrō, *adv*, neither way

nēve, *adv*, and so that ... not

nex, nĕcis, *f*, death, slaughter

nexilis, e, *adj*, tied together

nexum, i, *n*, slavery for debt, obligation

nexus, ūs, *m*, tying together

nī, *conj*, unless

nictātĭo, ōnis, *f*, winking

nicto, *v.i.* 1, to wink, blink

nīdor, ōris, *m*, steam, smell

nīdŭlus, i, *m*, little nest

nīdus, i, *m*, nest, home; *in pl*, nestlings

niger, gra, grum, *adj*, black, dark, ill-omened, funereal

nigrans, ntis, *adj*, black

nigresco, grŭi, *v.i.* 3, to grow dark

nihil (nīl), *n*, *indecl*, nothing

nihili, of no value

nihilŏmĭnus, *adj*, nevertheless

nihĭlum, i, *n*, nothing

nīl, *n*, *indecl*, nothing

nimbĭfer, ĕra, ĕrum, *adj*, stormy, rainy

nimbōsus, a, um, *adj*, stormy, rainy

nimbus, i, *m*, heavy rain, rain-cloud, cloud

nīmīrum, *adv*, without doubt

nimis, *adv*, too much

nĭmĭum, *adv*, too much

nĭmĭum, ii, *n*, excess

nĭmĭus, a, um, *adj*, excessive

ningit, *v.i.* 3, *impers*, it is snowing

nĭsĭ, *conj*, if not, unless

nīsus, ūs, *m*, pressure, effort, labour of childbirth

nĭtēdŭla, ae, *f*, dormouse

nĭtens, ntis, *adj*, bright, shining, sleek, beautiful

nĭtĕo, *v.i.* 2, to shine, to look handsome, thrive

nĭtesco, tŭi, *v.i.* 3, to shine

nĭtĭdus, a, um, *adj*, shining, sleek, handsome, refined

nītor, nīsus (nixus), *v.i.* 3, *dep*, to lean, press forward, fly, make an effort, argue

nĭtor, ōris, *m*, brightness, splendour, beauty, elegance

nĭtrum, i, *n*, soda

nĭvālis, e, *adj*, snowy, cold

nĭvĕus, a, um, *adj*, snowy, white

nĭvōsus, a, um, *adj*, snowy

nix, nĭvis, *f*, snow

nixor, *v.i.* 1, *dep*, to strive

nixus, ūs, *m*, pressure, effort, labour of childbirth

no, *v.i.* 1, to swim

nōbĭlis, e, *adj*, famous, noble

nōbĭlĭtas, ātis, *f*, fame, noble birth

nōbĭlĭto, *v.t.* 1, to make famous

nōbis, *dat. or abl. of* nos

nŏcens, ntis, *adj*, wicked, bad, harmful, injurious

nŏcĕo, *v.i.* 2, *with dat*, to harm

nocte, *adv*, at night

noctĭlūca, ae, *f*, moon

noctĭvăgus, a, um, *adj*, wandering at night

noctu, *adv*, at night

noctŭa, ae, *f*, night owl

nocturnus, a, um, *adj*, nocturnal

nōdo, *v.t.* 1, to tie in a knot

nōdōsus, a, um, *adj*, knotty, difficult

nōdus, i, *m*, knot, knob, band, obligation, difficulty

nōli, nōlĭte, *imper*, do not . . .

nōlo, nolle, nōlŭi, *v*, *irreg*, to be unwilling

nōmen, ĭnis, *n*, name, debt, fame, repute, excuse, reason

nōmenclātor, ōris, *m*, slave who reminded his master of the names of the people he met

nōmĭnātim, *adj*, by name

nōmĭnātĭo, ōnis, *f*, nomination

nōmĭnātus, a, um, *adj*, renowned

nōmĭno, *v.t.* 1, to name, make famous

nŏmisma, ātis, *n*, a coin

nōn, *adv*, not

nōnae, ārum, *f. pl*, the Nones; 5th or 7th day of the month

nōnāgēni, ae, *adj*, ninety each

nōnāgēsĭmus, a, um, *adj*, ninetieth

nōnāgies, *adv*, ninety times

nōnāgintā, *indecl. adj*, ninety

nondum, *adj*, not yet

nongenti, ae, a, *adj*, nine hundred

nonnĕ, *adv*, used to introduce a question expecting the answer "yes"

nonnēmo, ĭnis, *m*, someone

nonnĭhil, *n*, something

nonnisi, *adv*, only

nonnullus, a, um, *adj*, several

nonnumquam, *adv*, sometimes

nōnus, a, um, *adj*, ninth

norma, ae, *f*, rule, pattern, standard

nōs, *pron, pl. of* ĕgŏ, we, us

noscĭto, *v.t.* 1, to know, observe

nosco, nōvi, nōtum, *v.t.* 3, to get to know, know, recognise, acknowledge

noster, tra, trum, *adj*, our, ours

nostras, ātis, *adj*, of our country

nŏta, ae, *f*, mark, sign, brand

nŏtābĭlis, e, *adj*, noteworthy

nŏtātĭo, ōnis, *f*, branding, observation

nōthus, a, um, *adj*, illegitimate, counterfeit

nōtĭo, ōnis, *f*, investigation

nōtĭtĭa, ae, *f*, fame, knowledge

nŏto, *v.t.* 1, to mark, write, indicate, brand, reprimand

nōtus, a, um, *adj*, well-known

nŏtus, i, *m*, the south wind

nŏvācŭla, ae, *f*, razor

nŏvālis, is, *f*, fallow land

nŏvellus, a, um, *adj*, young, new

nŏvem, *indecl. adj*, nine

Nŏvember (mensis), November

nŏvendĭālis, e, *adj*, lasting nine days

nŏvēnus, a, um, *adj*, nine each

nŏverca, ae, *f*, stepmother

nŏvĭcĭus, a, um, *adj*, new

nŏviens, *adv*, nine times

nŏvies, *adv*, nine times

nŏvissĭmus, a, um, *adj*, last; in *m. pl*, or nŏvissĭmum agmen, rear ranks

nŏvĭtas, ātis, *f*, novelty, unusualness

nŏvo, *v.t.* 1, to renew, refresh, change

nŏvus, a, um, *adj*, new, recent, fresh; nŏvus hŏmo an upstart; nŏvae res, revolution

nox, noctis, *f*, night

noxa, ae, *f*, injury, harm, fault, crime

noxĭa, ae, *f*, injury, harm, fault, crime

noxĭus, a, um, *adj*, harmful, guilty

nūbes, is, *f*, cloud

nūbĭfer, ĕra, ĕrum, *adj*, cloud-capped, cloud-bringing

For List of Abbreviations used, turn to pages 3, 4

nūbĭla, ōrum, *n.pl*, the clouds
nūbĭlis, e, *adj*, marriageable
nūbĭlus, a, um, *adj*, overcast
nūbo, psi, ptum, *v.i.t.* 3, *with dat*,
  to marry
nŭclĕus, i, *m*, nut, kernel
nŭdĭus, with a number (tertĭus)
  (three) days ago
nūdo, *v.t.* 1, to strip, expose
nūdus, a, um, *adj*, naked, destitute
  of, poor, simple
nūgae, ārum, *f. pl*, jokes, nonsense,
  trifles
nūgātor, ōris, *m*, silly person
nūgātōrĭus, a, um, *adj*, trifling
nūgor, *v.i.* 1, *dep*, to play the fool
nullus, a, um, *adj*, none, no
nullus, ius, *m*, no-one
num, *adv*, used to introduce a question
  expecting answer "no"; whether
nūmen, ĭnis, *n*, divine will, divine
  power, divinity
nŭmĕrābĭlis, e, *adj*, able to be
  counted
nŭmĕrātor, ōris, *m*, counter
nŭmĕrātum, i, *n*, ready money
nŭmĕro, *v.t.* 1, to count, pay out,
  number
nŭmĕrō, *adv*, in number, just
nŭmĕrōsus, a, um, *adj, adv*, ē,
  numerous, rhythmic
nŭmĕrus, i, *m*, number, band (of
  soldiers), class, category, sequence,
  rhythm, poetic-metre
nummārĭus, a, um, *adj*, of money
nummātus, a, um, *adj*, rich
nummus, i, *m*, money, a Roman
  silver coin, farthing
numquam, *adv*, never
numquid, *interr. adv*, is there anything . . .?
nunc, *adv*, now, at present
nuncia, nuncius . . . see nunt . . .
nuncŭpo, *v.t.* 1, to call, name
nundĭnae, ārum, *f. pl*, ninth day,
  market-day
nundĭnātĭo, ōnis, *f*, trading
nundĭnor, *v.i.t.* 1, *dep*, to trade; buy,
  sell
nunquam, *adv*, never
nuntĭātĭo, ōnis, *f*, announcement
nuntĭo, *v.t.* 1, to announce, tell
nuntĭus, i, *m*, messenger, message
nūper, *adv*, lately, recently
nupta, ae, *f*, wife, bride
nuptĭae, ārum, *f. pl*, marriage
nuptĭālis, e, *adj*, of marriage
nuptus, a, um, *adj*, married

nŭrus, ūs, *f*, daughter-in-law, young
  wife
nusquam, *adv*, nowhere
nūto, *v.i.* 1, to nod, waver
nūtrīcĭus, a, um, *adj*, foster-father
nūtrīco, *v.t.* 1, to nurse, rear
nūtrīcula, ae, *f*, nurse
nūtrīmen, ĭnis, *n*, nourishment
nūtrīmentum, i, *n*, nourishment
nūtrĭo, *v.t.* 4, to feed, bring up, support
nūtrix, īcis, *f*, nurse
nūtus, ūs, *m*, nod, command
nux, nŭcis, *f*, nut
nympha, ae, *f*, bride, nymph (demi-
  goddess inhabiting woods, trees,
  fountains, etc.)

O

ŏb, *prep. with acc*, on account of, in
  front of
ŏbaerātus, a, um, *adj*, involved in
  debt
ŏbambŭlo, *v.i.* 1, to walk about
obdo, dĭdi, dĭtum, *v.t.* 3, to shut,
  place, expose
obdormĭo, *v.i.* 4, to fall asleep
obdormisco, *v.i.* 3, to fall asleep
obdūco, xi, ctum, *v.t.* 3, to lead forward, bring forward, cover over,
  swallow
obdūresco, rŭi, *v.i.* 3, to become
  hardened
obdūro, *v.i.* 1, to persist
ŏbēdĭens, ntis, *adj*, obedient
ŏbēdĭentĭa, ae, *f*, obedience
ŏbēdĭo, *v.i.* 4, to obey, be subject to
ŏbēliscus, i, *m*, obelisk
ŏbĕo, *v.i.t.* 4, to go to meet, die, set
  (constellations); to go to, reach,
  travel over, visit, undertake, perform
ŏbĕquito, *v.i.* 1, to ride towards
ŏbēsitas, ātis, *f*, fatness
ŏbēsus, a, um, *adj*, fat, dull
ōbex, ĭcis, *m, f*, bolt, barrier
obiăcĕo, *v.i.* 2, to lie opposite
ŏbĭcĭo, iēci, iectum, *v.t.* 3, to throw
  forward, expose, oppose, taunt,
  reproach
obiectātĭo, ōnis, *f*, reproach
obiecto, *v.t.* 1, to place against,
  expose, reproach, accuse
obiectus, ūs, *m*, opposing, putting in
  the way
obiectus, a, um, *adj*, lying opposite
ōbĭtus, ūs, *m*, setting, downfall
obiurgātĭo, ōnis, *f*, rebuke

obiurgātor, ōris, *m*, blamer
obiurgātōrius, a, um, *adj*, reproachful
obiurgo, *v.t.* 1, to blame, rebuke
oblectāmen, inis, *n*, pleasure, delight
oblectāmentum, i, *n*, pleasure, delight
oblecto, *v.t.* 1, to amuse, please
obligātio, ōnis, *f*, obligation
obligo, *v.t.* 1, to bind, put under obligation, render liable
oblīmo, *v.t.* 1, to cover with mud, squander
oblino, lēvi, litum, *v.t.* 3, to besmear, defile
obliquo, *v.t.* 1, to bend aside
obliquus, a, um, *adj*, *adv*, ē, slanting, sideways
oblīvio, ōnis, *f*, oblivion
oblīviōsus, a, um, *adj*, forgetful, producing forgetfulness
oblīviscor, oblītus, *v.* 3, *dep*, *with genit*, to forget
oblīvium, ii, *n*, oblivion
oblŏquor, lŏcūtus, *v.i.* 3, *dep*, to contradict, accompany a song
obluctor, *v.i.* 1, *dep*, to struggle against
obmūtesco, tŭi, *v.i.* 3, to become speechless
obnitor, xus, *v.i.* 3, *dep*, to push or struggle against
obnixus, a, um, *adj*, resolute
obnoxius, a, um, *adj*, liable to, submissive, indebted
obnūbo, psi, ptum, *v.t.* 3, to veil
obnuntiātio, ōnis, *f*, announcement of bad omens
obnuntio, *v.t.* 1, to announce bad omens
ŏboediens, oboedīo, see obēd . . .
ŏbŏrior, ortus, *v.i.* 4, *dep*, to arise, appear
obrēpo, psi, ptum, *v.t.* 3, to creep up to, surprise
obrigesco, gŭi, *v.i.* 3, to stiffen
obrŏgo, *v.t.* 1, to invalidate
obrŭo, ŭi, ŭtum, *v.t.* 3, to overwhelm, bury, hide
obsaepio, psi, ptum, *v.t.* 4, to fence in
obscēnitas, ātis, *f*, obscenity, foulness
obscēnus, a, um, *adj*, ominous, filthy, obscene
obscūritas, ātis, *f*, uncertainty, lowness
obscūro, *v.t.* 1, to darken, hide
obscūrus, a, um, *adj*, *adv*, ē, dark, shady, indistinct, ignoble, humble, reserved
obsĕcrātio, ōnis, *f*, appeal
obsĕcro, *v.t.* 1, to implore
obsĕcundo, *v.t.* 1, to humour, obey

obsēp . . . see obsaep . . .
obsĕquens, ntis, *adj*, amenable
obsĕquium, ii, *n*, compliance, obedience
obsĕquor, sĕcūtus, *v.* 3, *dep*, *with dat.* to comply with, submit to, humour
obsĕro, *v.t.* 1, to fasten
obsĕro, sēvi, situm, *v.t.* 3, to sow, plant
observans, ntis, *adj*, attentive
observantia, ae, *f*, attention, respect
observātio, ōnis, *f*, care, observation
observo, *v.t.* 1, to watch, take note of, respect, comply with
obses, idis, *m, f*, hostage
obsessio, ōnis, *f*, blockade
obsessor, ōris, *m*, besieger
obsīdĕo, sēdi, sessum, *v.t.* 2, to besiege, hem in, frequent
obsidio, ōnis, *f*, siege
obsido, *v.t.* 3, to besiege
obsignātor, ōris, *m*, witness
obsigno, *v.t.* 1, to seal up
obsisto, stiti, stitum, *v.i.* 3, to resist, oppose
obsitus, a, um, *adj*, covered over
obsŏlesco, lēvi, lētum, *v.i.* 3, to wear out, decay
obsŏlētus, a, um, *adj*, worn out, low, mean
obsōnium, ii, *n*, eatables
obsōnātor, ōris, *m*, caterer
obsōno, *v.t.* 1, (obsōnor, *v.*1, *dep*), to cater
obsorbĕo, *v.t.* 2, to swallow
obstĕtrix, īcis, *f*, midwife
obstinātio, ōnis, *f*, firmness, obstinacy
obstinātus, a, um, *adj*, *adv*, ē, determined, resolute, stubborn
obstīpesco, pŭi, *v.i.* 3, to be amazed
obstīpus, a, um, *adj*, bent
obsto, stiti, ātum, *v.i.* 1, *with dat*, to obstruct, withstand
obstrĕpo, ŭi, ĭtum, *v.i.* 3 to roar at, resound
obstringo, nxi, ctum, *v.t.* 3, to tie up, put under obligation
obstrŭo, xi, ctum, *v.t.* 3, to build up, barricade, impede
obstŭpĕfăcio, fēci, factum, *v.t.* 3, to astonish
obstŭpesco, pŭi, *v.i.* 3, to be stupified, amazed
obsum, obesse, obfŭi, *v.i.*, *irreg*, to hinder, injure
obsŭo, ŭi, ŭtum, *v.t.* 3, to sew up
obsurdesco, dŭi, *v.i.* 3, to grow deaf
obtĕgo, xi, ctum, *v.t.* 3, to cover up

obtempĕro, v.t. 1, with dat, to comply with

obtendo, di, tum, v.t. 3, to spread before, hide

obtentus, ūs, m, outspreading

obtĕro, trīvi, trītum, v.t. 3, to crush to pieces

obtestātio, ōnis, f, appeal

obtestor, v.t. 1, dep, to call as a witness, implore

obtexo, xŭi, v.t. 3, to cover

obticesco, tĭcŭi, v.i. 3, to be struck dumb

obtĭnĕo, nŭi, tentum, v.i.t. 2, to prevail, continue; keep, hold, gain, obtain

obtingo, tĭgi, v.i. 3, to befall

obtorpesco, pŭi, v.i. 3, to become stiff

obtorquĕo, si, tum, v.t. 2, to twist, wrench

obtrectātio, ōnis, f, disparagement

obtrectātor, ōris, m, slanderer

obtrecto, v.i.t. 1, to disparage

obtrunco, v.t. 1, to trim, kill

obtundo, tŭdi, tūsum, v.t. 3, to blunt, weaken, deafen, annoy

obtūrācŭlum, i, n, stopper

obtūrāmentum, i, n, stopper

obturbo, v.t. 1, to disturb

obtūro, v.t. 1, to close

obtūsus, a, um, adj, blunt, dull

obtūtus, ūs, m, gaze, stare

ŏbumbro, v.t. 1, to overshadow

ŏbuncus, a, um, adj, hooked

ŏbustus, a, um, adj, hardened in fire

obvĕnio, vēni, ventum, v.i. 4, to meet, befall one, happen

obversor, v.i. 1, dep, to move to and fro, hover

obversus, a, um, adj, directed towards

obverto, ti, sum, v.t. 3, to turn towards

obvĭam, adv, with verbs of motion; towards, against

obvĭus, a, um, adj, in the way, so as to meet, courteous, exposed

obvolvo, volvi, vŏlūtum, v.t. 3, to wrap round, cover

occaeco, v.t. 1, to blind, hide

occāsio, ōnis, f, opportunity

occāsus, ūs, m, setting (of sun, etc.) downfall, ruin

occĭdens, ntis, m, the west

occĭdentālis, e, adj, west

occĭdio, ōnis, f, massacre

occĭdo, cĭdi, cĭsum, v.t. 3, to strike down, crush, kill

occĭdo, cĭdi, cāsum, v.i. 3, to fall, perish, set (of sun, etc.)

occĭdŭus, a, um, adj, setting, western

occīsio, ōnis, f, slaughter

occlūdo, si, sum, v.t. 3, to close

occo, v.t. 1, to harrow

occŭbo, v.i. 1, to lie down, rest

occŭlo, lŭi, ltum, v.t. 3, to hide

occultātio, ōnis, f, concealment

occulto, v.t. 1, to hide

occultus, a, um, adj, adv, ē, hidden, secret

occumbo, cŭbŭi, cŭbĭtum, v.i. 3, to die

occŭpātio, ōnis, f, employment

occŭpātus, a, um, adj, busy

occŭpo, v.t. 1, to seize, occupy, attack, anticipate, fill

occurro, curri, cursum, v.i. 3, to meet

occursātio, ōnis, f, greeting

occurso, v.i. 1, to meet, attack

occursus, ūs, m, meeting

ŏcĕānus, i, m, ocean

ŏcellus, i, m, small eye, darling

ōchra, ae, f, ochre

ōcior, ĭus, comp. adj, swifter

ōcius, adv, more quickly

ŏcrĕa, ae, f, leg-shield, greave

octāvus, a, um, adj, eighth

octiens (octies), adv, eight times

octingenti, ae, a, pl. adj, eight hundred

octō, indecl. adj, eight

Octōber (mensis), October

octōgēsĭmus, a, um, adj, eightieth

octōginta, indecl. adj, eighty

octōgōnum, i, n, octagon

octōni, ae, a, pl. adj, eight each

octōphŏron, i, m, sedan carried by eight men

ŏcŭlārius, a, um, adj, of the eyes

ŏcŭlus, i, m, eye, bud

ōdi, ōdisse, v.t. defect, to hate

ŏdiōsus, a, um, adj, adv, ē, hateful, troublesome

ŏdium, ii, n, hatred

ŏdor, ōris, m, odour, smell

ŏdōrātio, ōnis, f, smell

ŏdōrātus, ūs, m, smelling

ŏdōrātus, a, um, adj, scented

ŏdōrĭfer, ĕra, ērum, adj, fragrant

ŏdōro, v.t. 1, to perfume

ŏdōror, v.t. 1, dep, to smell out, investigate

ŏdōrus, a, um, adj, fragrant

oestrus, i, m, gad-fly

offa, ae, f, morsel

offendo, di, sum, v.i.t. 3, to make a mistake; strike against, meet with, find, offend

offensa, ae, f, hatred, crime

offensio, ōnis, f, stumbling, dislike, displeasure

offensus, a, um, adj, offensive, offended

offĕro, offerre, obtŭli, oblātum, *v.t, irreg,* to offer, show, cause, bring

officīna, ae, *f,* workshop

officio, fēci, fectum, *v.i.* 3, to obstruct, hinder

officiōsus, a, um, *adj, adv,* ē, obliging, courteous

officium, ii, *n,* kindness, duty, employment, office

offirmātus, a, um, *adj,* firm

offulgĕo, si, *v.i.* 2, to shine on, appear

offundo, fūdi, fūsum, *v.t.* 3, to pour out, spread over

ōhē, *interj,* ho there!

ŏlĕa, ae, *f,* olive

ŏlĕācĕus, a, um, *adj,* oily

ŏlĕārius, a, um, *adj,* of oil; (.. ĭ, *m*), oil-seller

ŏlĕaster, stri, *m,* wild olive-tree

ŏlens, ntis, *adj,* fragrant, rank

ŏlĕo, ūi, *v.i.t.* 2, to smell of

ŏlĕum, i, *n,* olive-oil

olfăcio, fēci, factum, *v.t.* 3, to smell

ŏlidus, a, um, *adj,* stinking

ōlim, *adv,* once upon a time, once, sometime in the future

ŏlitor, ōris, *m,* market-gardener

ŏlīva, ae, *f,* olive tree, olive branch

ŏlīvētum, i, *n,* olive-grove

ŏlīvifer, ĕra, ĕrum, *adj,* olive-growing

ŏlīvum, i, *n,* oil

olla, ae, *f,* pot, jar

ŏlor, ōris, *m,* swan

ŏlōrīnus, a, um, *adj,* of swans

ŏlus, ĕris, *n,* vegetables

ŏmāsum, i, *n,* tripe

ōmen, ĭnis, *n,* omen, sign

ōminor, *v.t.* 1, *dep,* to forbode

ōmitto, mīsi, missum, *v.t.* 3, to put aside, give up, leave out

omnigĕnus, a, um, *adj,* of all kinds

omnīno, *adv,* altogether, entirely

omnipārens, ntis, *adj,* all-producing

omnipŏtens, ntis, *adj,* almighty

omnes, ium, *c, pl,* all men

omnia, ium, *n.pl,* all things

omnis, e, *adj,* all, every

omnivăgus, a, um, *adj,* wandering everywhere

ŏnăger (grus), i, *m,* wild ass

ŏnĕrāria, ae, *f,* merchant ship

ŏnĕrārius, a, um, *adj,* of, or for, freight

ŏnĕro, *v.t.* 1, to load, oppress

ŏnĕrōsus, a, um, *adj,* burdensome

ŏnus, ĕris, *n,* load, burden

ŏnustus, a, um, *adj,* loaded, full

ŏnyx, ychis, *m, f,* yellow marble

ŏpāco, *v.t.* 1, to cover, shade

ŏpācus, a, um, *adj,* shady

ŏpālus, i, *m.,* opal

ŏpem (*no nomin.***),** *f,* power, wealth, help

ŏpĕra, ae, *f,* exertion, effort; *in pl,* workmen

ŏpĕram do, to give careful attention to

ŏpĕrārius, a, um, *adj,* of labour

ŏpĕrārius, ii, *m,* labourer

ŏpercŭlum, i, *n,* lid, cover

ŏpĕrimentum, i, *n,* lid, cover

ŏpĕrio, ŭi, ŏpertum, *v.t.* 4, to cover, hide

ŏpĕror, *v.i.* 1, *dep,* to work, labour, perform a sacrifice

ŏpĕrōsus, a, um, *adj, adv,* ē, painstaking, busy, troublesome

ŏpertus, a, um, *adj,* hidden

ŏpes, um, *f. pl,* wealth, resources

ŏpifer, ĕra, ĕrum, *adj,* helping

ŏpifex, icis, *c,* craftsman

ŏpimus, a, um, *adj,* fat, rich, fertile; spolia ŏpima, arms won by a general in single combat with opposing general

ŏpīnābilis, e, *adj,* imaginary

ŏpīnātio, ōnis, *f,* supposition

ŏpīnātus, a, um, *adj,* imagined

ŏpīnio, ōnis, *f,* supposition, belief, reputation, rumour

ŏpīnor, *v.i.t.* 1, *dep,* to suppose

ŏpīpărē, *adv,* sumptuously

ŏpitŭlor, *v.i.* 1, *dep,* to help

ŏpium, ii, *n,* opium

ŏportet, *v.* 2, *impers, with acc. of person,* it is necessary

oppĕrior, pertus, *v.i.t.* 4, *dep,* to wait; wait for

oppĕto, īvi, ītum, *v.t.* 3, to encounter (especially death)

oppidāni, ōrum, *m. pl,* townspeople

oppidānus, a, um, *adj,* provincial

oppidŭlum, i, *n,* small town

oppidum, i, *n,* town

oppignĕro, *v.t.* 1, to pledge

oppilo, *v.t.* 1, to shut, stop

opplĕo, ēvi, ētum, *v.t.* 2, to fill up

oppōno, pŏsŭi, situm, *v.t.* 3, to place opposite, oppose, offer, expose, object

opportūnĭtas, ātis, *f,* convenience, advantage

opportūnus, a, um, *adj, adv,* ē, suitable, convenient

oppŏsitio, ōnis, *f,* opposition

oppŏsitus, a, um, *adj,* opposite

opprimo, pressi, ssum, *v.t.* 3, to suppress, close, surprise, hide

opprŏbrium, i, *n,* scandal, taunt

oppugnātio, ōnis, *f,* attack, siege

For List of Abbreviations used, turn to pages 3, 4

oppugnātor, ōris, *m*, attacker

oppugno, *v.t.* 1, to attack

ops, ŏpis, *f*, power, aid

optābilis, e, *adj*, desirable

optātio, ōnis, *f*, wish

optātum, i, *n*, wish

optātus, a, um, *adj, adv*, ō, desired, pleasant

optĭmas, ātis, *adj*, aristocratic

optĭmātes, um, *c, pl*, the aristocratic party

optĭmus, a, um, *adj, adv*, ē, best

optĭo, ōnis, *f*, choice

optĭo, ōnis, *m*, assistant

opto, *v.t.* 1, to choose, desire

ŏpŭlens, ntis, *adj*, rich

ŏpŭlentia, ae, *f*, wealth

ŏpŭlentus, a, um, *adj*, rich

ŏpus, ĕris, *n*, work, task; **ŏpus est**, there is need (a necessity)

ŏpuscŭlum, i, *n*, a small work

ōra, ae, *f*, border, sea-coast, region

ōrācŭlum, i, *n*, oracle

ōrātĭo, ōnis, *f*, speech, language, eloquence

ōrātĭuncŭla, ae, *f*, brief speech

ōrātor, ōris, *m*, speaker, orator, ambassador

ōrātōrĭus, a, um, *adj*, oratorical

orbĭcŭlātus, a, um, *adj*, circular

orbis, is, *m*, circle; **orbis terrarum**, the world

orbĭta, ae, *f*, track, rut

orbĭtas, ātis, *f*, bereavement

orbo, *v.t.* 1, to bereave, deprive

orbus, a, um, *adj*, bereaved, destitute

orca, ae, *f*, large tub

orchas, ādis, *f*, olive

orchēstra, ae, *f*, a place at the front of the theatre

orchis, is, *f*, orchid

Orcus, i, *m*, death, the Lower World

ordĭnārĭus, a, um, *adj*, regular, usual, orderly

ordĭnātim, *adv*, in proper order

ordĭnātus, a, um, *adj*, orderly, regulated

ordĭne, *adv*, in order

ordĭno, *v.t.* 1, to arrange

ordĭor, orsus, *v.i.t.* 4, *dep*, to begin, undertake

ordo, ĭnis, *m*, row, rank, band or company of soldiers, series, class of society

Ŏrēas, ādis, *f*, mountain-nymph

orgĭa, ōrum, *n.pl*, revels in honour of Bacchus

ōrĭchalcum, i, *n*, copper ore

ōrĭens, ntis, *m*, the east

ōrīgo, ĭnis, *f*, beginning, origin, family, ancestor

ōrĭor, ortus, *v.i.* 4, *dep*, to arise, appear, originate

ōrĭundus, a, um, *adj*, descended or sprung from

ornāmentum, i, *n*, equipment, decoration

ornātus, a, um, *adj, adv*, ē, equipped, decorated

ornātus, ūs, *m*, equipment, dress, ornament

orno, *v.t.* 1, to equip, adorn, praise

ornus, i, *f*, mountain-ash

ōro, *v.t.* 1, to plead, beg, pray

orsa, ōrum, *n.pl*, undertaking, speech

orsus, ūs, *m*, undertaking

ortus, ūs, *m*, rising (of sun, etc.), beginning, source

ōrȳsa, ae, *f*, rice

ōs, ōris, *n*, mouth, face, opening

ŏs, ossis, *n*, bone

oscen, ĭnis, *m*, singing bird from whose notes omens were taken

oscillātĭo, ōnis, *f*, swinging

oscillum, i, *n*, small mask

oscĭtātĭo, ōnis, *f*, yawning

oscĭto, *v.i.* 1, to gape, yawn

oscŭlor, *v.i.t.* 1, *dep*, to kiss

oscŭlum, i, *n*, mouth, kiss

ossĕus, a, um, *adj*, made of bone

ossĭfrăgus, i, *m*, sea-eagle

ostendo, di, sum, *v.t.* 3, to show, make known

ostentātĭo, ōnis, *f*, display

ostento, *v.t.* 1, to show, display

ostentum, i, *n*, prodigy

ostĭārĭum, ii, *n*, door-tax

ostĭātim, *adv*, from door to door

ostĭum, ii, *n*, door, entrance

ostrĕa, ae, *f*, oyster

ostrĕārĭum, ii, *n*, oyster-bed

ostrum, i, *n*, purple, purple coverings or dress

ōtĭor, *v.i.* 1, *dep*, to be on holiday

ōtĭōsus, a, um, *adj, adv*, ē, at leisure, unemployed, quiet

ōtĭum, ii, *n*, leisure, peace

ŏvans, ntis, *adj*, triumphant

ŏvātus, a, um, *adj*, oval

ŏvillus, a, um, *adj*, of sheep

ŏvīlis, e, *adj*, of sheep

ŏvīle, is, *n*, sheepfold

ŏvis, is, *f*, sheep

ŏvo, *v.i.* 1, to exult

ōvum, i, *n*, egg

P

păbo, ōnis, *m*, wheelbarrow
păbŭlātio, ōnis, *f*, collection of fodder
păbŭlātor, ōris, *m*, forager
păbŭlor, *v.i.* 1, *dep*, to look for fodder
păbŭlum, i, *n*, food, fodder
păcālis, e, *adj*, peaceful
păcātus, a, um, *adj*, peaceful
păcĭfer, ĕra, ĕrum, *adj*, peace-bringing
păcĭfĭcātĭo, ōnis, *f*, pacification
păcĭfĭco, *v.t.* 1, to make peace
păcĭfĭcus, a, um, *adj*, peaceable
păcĭscor, pactus, *v.i.t.* 3, *dep*, to make a bargain; barter
păco, *v.t.* 1, to subdue, pacify
pactio, ōnis, *f*, an agreement
pactum, i, *n*, an agreement
pactus, a, um, *adj*, agreed
paean, ānis, *m*, hymn to Apollo
paedăgōgus, i, *m*, slave who took children to school, and looked after them at home
paedor, ōris, *m*, filth
paelex, ĭcis, *f*, concubine
paene, *adv*, almost, nearly
paeninsŭla, ae, *f*, peninsula
paenĭtens, ntis, *adj*, repentant
paenĭtentĭa, ae, *f*, penitence
paenitet, *v.* 2, *impers, with acc. of person*, it grieves
paenŭla, ae, *f*, cloak
paenultĭmus, a, um, *adj*, penultimate
paetus, a, um, *adj*, with a slight cast in the eye
păgānus, a, um, *adj*, rural
păgānus, i, *m*, country-dweller
păgĭna, ae, *f*, page, leaf, book
păgus, i, *m*, village, district
păla, ae, *f*, spade
pălaestra, ae, *f*, wrestling ground or school, wrestling, rhetorical exercise
pălam, *adv*, openly; *prep. with abl*, in the presence of
pălātĭum, ii, *n*, palace
pălātum, i, *n*, palate
pălĕa, ae, *f*, chaff
pălĭūrus, i, *m*, Christ's thorn (plant)
palla, ae, *f*, stole, robe
pallens, ntis, *adj*, pale
pallĕo, *v.i.* 2, to be pale
pallesco, pallŭi, *v.i.* 3, to turn pale
pallĭātus, a, um, *adj*, cloaked like Greeks
pallĭdus, a, um, *adj*, pale
pallĭŏlum, i, *n*, hood

pallĭum, ii, *n*, coverlet, cloak
pallor, ōris, *m*, paleness
palma, ae, *f*, palm, hand, oar-blade, palm-tree, broom, palm-wreath, prize, glory
palmāris, e, *adj*, excellent, worthy of the palm
palmātus, a, um, *adj*, marked with the hand, decorated with palm
palmĕs, ĭtis, *m*, wine-shoot
palmētum, i, *n*, palm-grove
palmĭfer, ĕra, ĕrum, *adj*, palm-bearing
palmōsus, a, um, *adj*, with many palm trees
palmŭla, ae, *f*, oar-blade
palmus, i, *m*, palm of hand, span
pālor, *v.i.* 1, *dep*, to wander
palpĕbra, ae, *f*, eyelid
palpĭtātĭo, ōnis, *f*, palpitation
palpĭto, *v.i.* 1, to throb, pant
palpo, *v.t.* 1, to stroke, caress
pălŭdāmentum, i, *n*, military cloak, general's cloak
pălŭdātus, a, um, *adj*, dressed in general's cloak
pălŭdōsus, a, um, *adj*, marshy
pălumbes, is, *m, f*, wood-pigeon
pālus, i, *m*, stake
pălus, ūdis, *f*, marsh
păluster, tris, tre, *adj*, marshy
pampĭnĕus, a, um, *adj*, full of vine-leaves
pampĭnus, i, *m, f*, vine-shoot, vine-leaf
pănăcĕa, ae, *f*, a herb which healed all diseases
panchrestus, a, um, *adj*, good for anything
pando, di, nsum, *v.t.* 3, to unfold, open out, spread out, publish
pandus, a, um, *adj*, curved
pango, pĕpĭgi, pactum, *v.t.* 3, to fasten, settle, agree upon
pānis, is, *m*, bread
pannōsus, a, um, *adj*, tattered
pannus, i, *m*, garment, rags
panthēra, ae, *f*, panther
pantŏmīmus, i, *m*, ballet-dancer
păpāver, ĕris, *n*, poppy
păpĭlĭo, ōnis, *m*, butterfly
păpilla, ae, *f*, breast, nipple
păpŭla, ae, *f*, pimple
păpȳrĭfer, ĕra, ĕrum, *adj*, papyrus-producing
păpȳrus, i, *m, f*, paper
pār, păris, *adj*, equal, suitable
pār, păris, *m*, companion
părābĭlis, e, *adj*, easily-procured
părăbŏla, ae, *f*, parable, comparison

părallēlus, a, um, *adj*, parallel

părălўsis, is, *f*, paralysis, palsy

părăsītus, i, *m*, parasite

părātus, a, um, *adj*, prepared

părātus, ūs, *m*, preparation

parco, pĕperci, parsum, *v.i.* 3, *with dat*, to spare, desist

parcus, a, um, *adj*, *adv*, ē, thrifty, sparing, scanty

părens, ntis, *adj*, obedient

părens, ntis, *m*, *f*, parent, ancestor, founder

părentālĭa, ĭum, *n.pl*, festival in honour of dead relations

părentālis, e, *adj*, parental

părento, *v.t.* 1, to honour dead relatives, avenge a relative's death by killing

părĕo, *v.i.* 2, *with dat*, to obey, to appear

părĭes, ĕtis, *m*, wall

părĭĕtinae, ārum, *f.pl*, ruins

părīlis, e, *adj*, equal

părĭo, pĕpĕri, partum, *v.t.* 3, to bring forth, produce, acquire

părĭter, *adv*, equally, at the same time

parma, ae, *f*, small round shield

parmŭla, ae, *f*, small round shield

păro, *v.t.* 1, to prepare, intend, obtain

părŏchus, i, *m*, caterer

păroecĭa, ae, *f*, parish

parra, ae, *f*, owl

parrīcīda, ae, *c*, murderer of a parent or relative, assassin

parricīdĭum, ii, *n*, murder of a parent or relative, treason

pars, partis, *f*, part, party, faction, part in a play; *in pl*, duty, office; in utramque partem, on both sides; pro parte, to the best of one's ability

parsimōnĭa, ae, *f*, thrift

particeps, cĭpis, *adj*, *with genit*, sharing; (*as noun*) sharer

partĭcĭpo, *v.t.* 1, to give a share of

partĭcŭla, ae, *f*, small part

partim, *adv*, partly

partĭo, *v.t.* 4, to share, divide

partĭor, *v.t.* 4, *dep*, to share, divide

partītĭo, ōnis, *f*, division

partītus, a, um, *adj*, divided

partūrĭo, *v.i.t.* 4, to be pregnant or in labour; produce

pārtus, ūs, *m*, birth, confinement, offspring

părum, *adv*, too little

părumper, *adv*, for a short time

parvĭtas, ātis, *f*, smallness

parvŭlus, a, um, *adj*, slight

parvus, a, um, *adj*, small, petty, short; parvi, of little value

pasco, pāvi, pastum, *v.i.t.* 3, to feed; pasture, nourish

pascor, pastus, *v.i.* 3, *dep*, to graze, feast

pascŭum, i, *n*, pasture

pascŭus, a, um, *adj*, for grazing

passer, ĕris, *m*, sparrow, turbot

passim, *adv*, in all directions

passum, i, *n*, raisin-wine

passus, a, um, *adj*, spread out, dried

passus, a, um, *partic. adj*, having suffered

passus, ūs, *m*, step, pace

pastillus, i, *m*, lozenge to dispel bad breath

pastor, ōris, *m*, shepherd

pastōrālis, e, *adj*, of shepherds, pastoral

pastōrĭcĭus, a, um, *adj*, of shepherds, pastoral

pastōrĭus, a, um, *adj*, of shepherds, pastoral

pastus, ūs, *m*, pasture, food

pătĕfăcĭo, fēci, factum, *v.t.* 3, to throw open, disclose

pătĕfactĭo, ōnis, *f*, opening up

pătella, ae, *f*, plate

pătens, ntis, *adj*, open

pătĕo, *v.i.* 2, to be open, to extend, to be evident

păter, tris, *m*, father; *in pl.* fore-fathers, senators

pătĕra, ae, *f*, saucer, bowl

păterfămĭlĭas, patrisfămĭlĭas, *m*, master of the house

păternus, a, um, *adj*, of a father

pătesco, pătŭi, *v.i.* 3, to be opened, to extend, be evident

pătĭbilis, e, *adj*, endurable

pătĭbŭlum, i, *n*, fork-shaped yoke or gibbet

pătĭens, ntis, *adj*, *adv*, nter, suffering, patient, hard

pătĭentĭa, ae, *f*, endurance

pătĭna, ae, *f*, pan, dish

pătĭor, passus, *v.t.* 3, *dep*, to suffer, bear, allow

pătrĭa, ae, *f*, fatherland

pătrĭarcha, ae, *m*, patriarch

pătrĭcĭus, a, um, *adj*, noble

pătrĭcĭus, i, *m*, member of the Roman nobility

pătrĭmōnĭum, ii, *n*, inherited estate

pătrītus, a, um, *adj*, of one's father or ancestor

pătrĭus, a, um, *adj*, of a father, hereditary, established, native

pătro, *v.t.* 1, to perform, finish

pătrōcĭnĭum, ii, *n*, defence

pătrōna, ae, *f*, patroness

pătrōnus, i, *m*, protector, patron, counsel

pătruēlis, is, *c*, cousin

pătrŭus, i, *m*, uncle

pătrŭus, a, um, *adj*, of an uncle

pătŭlus, a, um, *adj*, open, wide

pauci, ae, a, *pl. adj*, few

paucĭtas, ātis, *f*, small number

paucŭlus, a, um, *adj*, very few

paucus, a, um, *adj*, few, little

paulātim, *adv*, gradually

paulisper, *adv*, for a short time

paulō, *adv*, a little, somewhat

paulŭlum, *adv*, a little, somewhat

paulum, *adv*, a little, somewhat

pauper, ĕris, *adj*, poor, meagre

pauper, ĕris, *c*, a poor man

paupĕries, ēi, *f*, poverty

paupertas, ātis, *f*, poverty

paupĕro, *v.t.* 1, to impoverish

pausa, ae, *f*, stop, end

păvēfăcio, fēci, factum, *v.t.* 3, to alarm

păvĕo, păvi, *v.i.t.* 2, to be afraid; dread

păvesco, *v.i.* 3, to become alarmed

păvĭdus, a, um, *adj*, terrified

păvīmentum, i, *n*, pavement

păvĭo, *v.t.* 4, to beat, strike

păvĭto, *v.i.t.* 1, to tremble (at)

păvo, ōnis, *m*, peacock

păvor, ōris, *m*, anxiety, dread

pax, pācis, *f*, peace, grace, favour, tranquillity; *in abl*, by permission

peccans, ntis, *c*, offender

peccātor, ōris, *m*, sinner

peccātum, i, *n*, fault, mistake

pecco, *v.i.t.* 1, to make a mistake; to miss

pecten, ĭnis, *m*, comb, reed, rake, a plectrum to strike the strings of the lyre

pecto, pexi, xum, *v.t.* 3, to comb

pectōrālis, e, *adj*, pectoral

pectus, ōris, *n*, breast, heart, soul, mind

pĕcŭārius, a, um, *adj*, of cattle

pĕcŭārius, ii, *m*, cattle-breeder

pĕcūlātor, ōris, *m*, embezzler

pĕcūlātus, ūs, *m*, embezzlement

pĕcūliāris, e, *adj*, one's own, special

pĕcūlium, ii, *n*, property, savings

pĕcūnĭa, ae, *f*, money

pĕcūniārius, a, um, *adj*, pecuniary

pĕcūniōsus, a, um, *adj*, rich

pĕcus, ŏris, *n*, cattle, herd

pĕcus, ŭdis, *f*, an animal, beast

pĕdālis, e, *adj*, a foot in length or thickness

pĕdes, ĭtis, *m*, infantryman

pĕdes, see pes

pĕdester, tris, tre, *adj*, on foot, prosaic, plain

pĕdĕtemptim, *adv*, gradually

pĕdĭca, ae, *f*, shackle, snare

pĕdĭcŭlōsus, a, um, *adj*, lousy

pĕdĭcŭlus, i, *m*, louse

pĕdĭsĕquus, i, *m*, footman

pĕdĭtātus, ūs, *m*, infantry

pĕdum, i, *n*, shepherd's crook

pēiĕro, *v.i.* 1, to swear falsely

pēior, *comp. adj*, worse

pēius, *comp. adv*, worse

pĕlăgus, i, *n*, open sea

pellax, ācis, *adj*, seductive

pellex, ĭcis, *f*, concubine

pellicio, lexi, lectum, *v.t.* 3, to allure, coax

pellicŭla, ae, *f*, small skin

pellis, is, *f*, skin, leather, tent

pellītus, a, um, *adj*, clothed in skins

pello, pĕpŭli, pulsum, *v.t.* 3, to strike, push, drive out, rout, affect, impress

pellūcĕo, xi, *v.i.* 2, to shine through, be transparent

pellūcĭdus, a, um, *adj*, transparent

pēlōris, ĭdis, *f*, mussel

pelta, ae, *f*, small shield

pelvis, is, *f*, basin

pēnārius, a, um, *adj*, for provisions

pēnātes, ĭum, *m. pl*, guardian deities of the home, home

pendĕo, pĕpendi, *v.i.* 2, to hang, float, loiter, depend upon, be interrupted, be in suspense

pendo, pĕpendi, pensum, *v.t.* 3, to weigh or pay out, ponder

pendŭlus, a, um, *adj*, hanging, uncertain

pĕnēs, *prep. with acc*, in the power of

pĕnētrābilis, e, *adj*, penetrable, penetrating

pĕnētrālĭa, ĭum, *n. pl*, inner places or rooms

pĕnētrālis, e, *adj*, inner

pĕnētro, *v.i.t.* 1, to enter; penetrate

pēnicillum, i, *n*, painter's brush, pencil

pēnĭcŭlāmentum, i, *n*, train of a dress

pēnĭcŭlus, i, *m*, brush

pēnis, is, *m*, tail, penis

pēnĭtus, *adv*, inwardly, deep within, entirely

penna, ae, *f*, feather, wing

pennātus, a, um, *adj*, winged

penniger, ĕra, ĕrum, *adj*, winged

pensilis, e, *adj*, hanging

pensio, ōnis, *f*, payment

pensĭto, *v.t.* 1, to pay, weigh, ponder

For List of Abbreviations used, turn to pages 3, 4

penso, *v.t.* 1, to weigh out, repay, consider

pensum, i, *n*, a task

pēnūria, ae, *f*, need, want

pēnus, ūs (*or* i), *m, f*, store of food

pēpo, ŏnis, *m*, pumpkin

per, *prep. with acc*, through, during, by means of, on account of

per . . . in compound words usually adds intensity: very. . . .

pěractĭo, ōnis, *f*, completion

pěrăgo, ēgi, actum, *v.t.* 3, to complete, relate, transfix

pěrăgro, *v.t.* 1, to travel over

pěrambŭlo, *v.t.* 1, to go through

pěrăro, *v.t.* 1, to plough through

perbrěvis, e, *adj*, very short

perca, ae, *f*, perch (fish)

percělěbro, *v.t.* 1, to say frequently

percello, cŭli, culsum, *v.t.* 3, to upset, destroy, dishearten

percensěo, *v.t.* 2, to reckon up

perceptĭo, ōnis, *f*, perception

percĭpĭo, cēpi, ceptum, *v.t.* 3, to gather, perceive, understand

percontātĭo, ōnis, *f*, inquiry

percontor, *v.i.t.* 1, *dep*, to investigate

percŏquo, xi, ctum, *v.t.* 3, to boil, cook, heat

percrēbesco, bŭi, *v.i.* 3, to become prevalent

percrěpo, ŭi, ĭtum, *v.i.* 1, to resound, ring

perculsus, a, um, *adj*, upset

percurro, curri, cursum, *v.i.t.* 3, to run; pass over, mention

percussĭo, ōnis, *f*, beating

percussor, ōris, *m*, assassin

percŭtĭo, cussi, cussum, *v.t.* 3, to thrust through, kill, strike, astound

perdisco, dĭdĭci, *v.t.* 3, to learn thoroughly

perditor, ōris, *m*, destroyer

perdĭtus, a, um, *adj, adv*, ē, ruined, desperate, corrupt

perdix, ĭcis, *c*, partridge

perdo, dĭdi, dĭtum, *v.t.* 3, to destroy, waste, lose

perdŏcěo, *v.t.* 2, to teach thoroughly

perdŏmo, ŭi, ĭtum, *v.t.* 1, to subdue completely

perdūco, xi, ctum, *v.t.* 3, to conduct, bedaub, prolong, induce

perductor, ōris, *m*, pimp

perdŭellĭo, ōnis, *f*, treason

perdŭellis, is, *m*, public enemy

pěrědo, ēdi, sum, *v.t.* 3, to eat up

pěrēgrē, *adv*, abroad

pěrēgrīnātĭo, ōnis, *f*, travel abroad

pěrēgrīnātor, ōris, *m*, traveller

pěrēgrīnor, *v.i.* 1, *dep*, to live or travel abroad

pěrēgrīnus, a, um, *adj*, foreign

pěrēgrīnus, i, *m*, foreigner

pěrendĭě, *adv*, on the day after tomorrow

pěrennis, e, *adj*, everlasting

pěrenno, *v.i.* 1, to last, endure

pěrěo, ii, ĭtum, *v.i.* 4, *irreg*, to pass away, disappear, die, to be ruined or wasted

pěrěquito, *v.i.* 1, to ride about

pěrerro, *v.t.* 1, to wander through

perfectĭo, ōnis, *f*, completion

perfectus, a, um, *adj, adv*, ē, complete, perfect

perfěro, ferre, tŭli, lātum, *v.t.* *irreg*, to bring or bear through, convey, announce, complete, suffer

perfĭcĭo, fēci, fectum, *v.t.* 3, to complete, finish

perfĭdĭa, ae, *f*, treachery

perfĭdĭōsus, a, um, *adj*, treacherous

perfĭdus, a, um, *adj*, treacherous

perflo, *v.t.* 1, to blow through

perflŭo, xi, *v.i.* 3, to flow through

perfŏdĭo, fōdi, fossum, *v.t.* 3, to dig through

perfŏro, *v.t.* 1, to bore through

perfrĭco, cŭi, cātum, *v.t.* 1, to rub all over, put on a bold front

perfringo, frēgi, fractum, *v.t.* 3, to shatter, infringe

perfrŭor, fructus, *v.* 3, *dep, with abl*, to enjoy thoroughly

perfŭga, ae, *m*, deserter

perfŭgĭo, fūgi, *v.i.* 3, to flee for refuge, desert

perfŭgĭum, ii, *n*, shelter

perfundo, fūdi, fūsum, *v.t.* 3, to pour over, besprinkle

perfungor, functus, *v.* 3, *dep, with abl*, to fulfil, discharge

perfŭro, —*v.i.* 3, to rage

pergo, perrexi, perrectum, *v.i.t.* 3, to proceed, go; continue

pěrhĭběo, ŭi, ĭtum, *v.t.* 2, to extend, assert, name

pěrhorresco, rŭi, *v.i.t.* 3, to tremble; shudder at

pěrĭclĭtor, *v.i.t.* 1, *dep*, to try, be in danger; test, endanger

pěrĭcŭlōsus, a, um, *adj, adv*, ē, dangerous

pěrĭcŭlum, i, *n*, danger, proof, attempt

pĕrĭmo, ēmi, emptum, *v.t.* 3, to annihilate, prevent

pĕrinde, *adv*, just as, equally

pĕrĭŏdus, i, *f*, complete sentence

pĕrītĭa, ae, *f*, experience, skill

pĕrītus, a, um, *adj*, *adv*, ē, *with genit*,
skilled, expert

perĭūrĭum, ii, *n*, perjury

perĭūro, see pēiēro

perĭūrus, a, um, *adj*, perjured, lying

perlābor, lapsus, *v.i.* 3, *dep*, to glide
through

perlectĭo, ōnis, *f*, reading through

perlēgo, lēgi, lectum, *v.t.* 3, to survey,
examine, read through

perlūcĕo, xi, *v.i.* 2, to shine through,
be transparent

perlŭo, ŭi, ūtum, *v.t.* 3, to wash

perlūcĭdus, a, um, *adj*, transparent

perlustro, *v.t.* 1, to wander through

permănĕo, nsi, nsum, *v.i.* 2 to last,
continue

permāno, *v.i.* 1, to flow through, penetrate

permansĭo, ōnis, *f*, persisting

permĕo, *v.t.* 1, to cross, penetrate

permētĭor, mensus, *v.t.* 4, *dep*, to measure out, travel over

permiscĕo, scŭi, xtum, *v.t.* 2, to mix
together

permissĭo, ōnis, *f*, permission, surrender

permissū, *abl*, by permission

permitto, mīsi, missum, *v.t.* 3, to let
loose, commit, entrust; allow (*with
dat*)

permōtĭo, ōnis, *f*, excitement

permŏvĕo, mōvi, mōtum, *v.t.* 2, to stir
up, rouse

permulcĕo, mulsi, mulsum, *v.t.* 2, to
stroke, charm, flatter

permultus, a, um, *adj*, *adv*, ō, or um,
very much

permūtātĭo, ōnis, *f*, exchange

permūto, *v.t.* 1, to change

perna, ae, *f*, leg of pork

pernĕgo, *v.t.* 1, to deny flatly

pernĭcĭes, ēi, *f*, disaster

pernĭcĭōsus, a, um, *adj*, *adv*, ē, destructive

pernīcĭtas, ātis, *f*, agility

pernix, īcis, *adj*, agile

pernocto, *v.i.* 1, to stay all night

pernox, ctis, *adj*, night-long

pēro, ōnis, *m*, rawhide boot

pērōsus, a, um, *adj*, detesting, detested

pĕrōro, *v.t.* 1, to wind up a speech

perpendĭcŭlum, i, *n*, plumb-line

perpendo, pendi, pensum, *v.t.* 3, to
ponder, consider

perpĕram, *adv*, untruly

perpĕtĭor, pessus, *v.i.t.* 3, *dep*, to suffer;
endure

perpĕtŭĭtas, ātis, *f*, continuity

perpĕtŭus, a, um, *adv*, ō, perpetual,
entire, continuous

perplexus, a, um, *adj*, intricate

perpŏlĭo, *v.t.* 4, to perfect

perprĭmo, pressi, ssum, *v.t.* 3, to press
hard

perpurgo, *v.t.* 1, to clean up

perquam, *adv*, very much

perquīro, sīvi, sītum, *v.t.* 3, to make a
careful search for

perrārō, *adv*, very rarely

perrumpo, rūpi, ruptum, *v.i.t.* 3, to
break through

perscrībo, psi, ptum, *v.t.* 3, to write in
full

perscrīptĭo, ōnis, *f*, written entry or
note

perscrūtor, *v.t.* 1, *dep*, to examine

persĕco, cui, ctum, *v.t.* 1, to cut up

persentĭo, si, sum, *v.t.* 4, to perceive
plainly, feel deeply

persĕquor, sĕcūtus, *v.t.* 3, *dep*, to pursue, overtake, revenge

persĕvērantĭa, ae, *f*, constancy

persĕvēro, *v.i.t.* 1, to persevere; persist
in

persīdo, sēdi, sessum, *v.i.* 3, to penetrate

persisto, stĭti, *v.i.* 3, to persist

persolvo, solvi, sŏlūtum, *v.t.* 3, to pay
out, give

persōna, ae, *f*, mask, character, part,
person

persōnātus, a, um, *adj*, fictitious

persŏno, ŭi, ĭtum, *v.i.t.* 1, to resound;
fill with sound

perspectus, a, um, *adj*, well-known

perspĭcācĭtas, ātis, *f*, perspicacity

perspĭcax, ācis, *adj*, astute

perspĭcĭo, spexi, spectum, *v.t.* 3, to
look at, examine, perceive

perspĭcŭĭtas, ātis, *f*, clearness, per-
spicuity

perspĭcŭus, a, um, *adĵ*, *adv*, ē, clear,
evident

persto, stĭti, stātum, *v.i.* 1, to endure,
continue, persist

perstringo, nxi, ctum, *v.t.* 3, to graze,
blunt, stun, blame, allude to,
slight

persŭādĕo, si, sum, *v.t.* 2, *with dat*, to
persuade

persŭāsĭo, ōnis, *f*, conviction

persŭāsus, a, um, *adj*, settled

persuāsum hăbēre, to be convinced

pertento, v.t. 1, to consider

pertĕrĕbro, v.t. 1, to bore through

perterrĕo, v.t. 2, to frighten thoroughly

pertica, ae, f, pole, rod

pertĭmesco, mŭi, v.i.t. 3, to be very afraid; to fear greatly

pertĭnācĭa, ae, f, obstinacy

pertĭnax, ācis, adj, firm, constant, stubborn

pertĭnĕo, v.i. 2, to extend, pertain, concern, be applicable

pertracto, v.t. 1, to touch

pertundo, tŭdi, tūsum, v.t. 3, to make a hole through

perturbātĭo, ōnis, f, confusion

perturbātus, a, um, adj, disturbed

perturbo, v.t. 1, to disturb

pĕrungo, nxi, nctum, v.t. 3, to besmear

pĕrūro, ssi, stum, v.t. 3, to burn up, rub sore, nip

pervādo, si, sum, v.i. 3, to spread through, pervade

pervăgātus, a, um, adj, well-known

pervăgor, v.i.t. 1, dep, to wander through; pervade

pervĕho, xi, ctum, v.t. 3, to carry through

pervello, velli, v.t. 3, to pull, disparage

pervĕnĭo, vēni, ventum, v.i. 4, to reach, arrive at

perversĭtas, ātis, f, obstinacy

perversus, a, um, adj, askew, perverse

perverto, ti, sum, v.t. 3, to overturn, destroy, corrupt

pervestĭgo, v.t. 1, to investigate

pervĭcācĭa, ae, f, obstinacy

pervĭcax, ācis, adj, adv, ĭter, stubborn, wilful

pervĭdĕo, vīdi, vīsum, v.t. 2, to view, survey

pervĭgil, is, adj, ever-watchful

pervĭgĭlātĭo, ōnis, f, vigil

pervĭgĭlo, v.i. 1, to remain awake all night

pervinco, vīci, victum, v.t. 3, to gain victory over

pervĭus, a, um, adj, able to be crossed or passed

pervŏlĭto, v.i. 1, to flit about

pervŏlo, v.i. 1, to fly about or through or to

pervŏlo, velle, vŏlŭi, v.i, irreg, to wish greatly

pervulgo, v.t. 1, to spread about

pēs, pĕdis, m, foot; rope attached to a sail, sheet

pessĭmē, adv, very badly

pessĭmus, a, um, adj, very bad

pessŭlus, i, m, latch

pessum, adv, to the ground; pessum ire, to go to ruin

pestĭfer, ĕra, ĕrum, adj, destructive, harmful

pestĭlens, ntis, adj, unhealthy

pestĭlentĭa, ae, f, infectious disease

pestis, is, f, disease, ruin

pĕtăsātus, a, um, adj, dressed for a journey

pĕtăsus, i, m, travelling-hat

pĕtītĭo, ōnis, f, blow, candidature for office

pĕtītor, ōris, m, candidate, plaintiff

pĕto, īvi, ītum, v.t. 3, to make for, seek, aim at, request

pĕtōrĭtum, i, n, four-wheeled carriage

pĕtŭlans, ntis, adj, impudent

pĕtŭlantĭa, ae, f, impudence

pexus, a, um, adj, new

phălanx, ngis, f, military formation

phălĕrae, ārum, f. pl, military decoration

phărĕtra, ae, f, quiver

phărĕtrātus, a, um, adj, wearing a quiver

pharmăcŏpōla, ae, m, quack

phărus, i, f, lighthouse

phăsēlus, i, m, f, kidney-bean, light boat, yacht

phengītes, ae, m, selenite, mica

phĭlŏlŏgĭa, ae, f, love of learning

phĭlŏlŏgus, i, m, man of learning

phĭlŏmēla, ae, f, nightingale

phĭlŏsŏphĭa, ae, f, philosophy

phĭlŏsŏphor, v.i. 1, dep, to study philosophy

phĭlŏsŏphus, i, m, philosopher

phĭlyra, ae, f, bark of the linden-tree

phĭmus, i, m, dice-box

phōca, ae, f, seal, sea-dog

phoenix, īcis, m, bird which was said to live 500 years

phthĭsis, is, f, phthisis

phylarchus, i, m, chief, prince

physĭca, ōrum, n. pl, physics

physĭcus, i, m, naturalist

physĭŏlŏgĭa, ae, f, physiology

pĭācŭlārĭs, e, adj, expiatory

pĭācŭlum, i, n, sacrificial offering of atonement, victim, sin, crime

pīca, ae, f, magpie

pĭcĕa, ae, f, pitch-pine

pĭcĕus, a, um, adj, pitch-black

pictor, ōris, m, painter

pictūra, ae, f, painting, picture

pictūrātus, a, um, adj, embroidered

pictus, a, um, adj, painted, decorated

pīcus, i, m, woodpecker

pĭĕtas, ātis, f, sense of duty, loyalty, mercy

piger, gra, grum, *adj*, lazy, sluggish

piget (me, te), *v. 2, impers*, it annoys or displeases (me, you)

pigmentum, i, *n*, paint, pigment

pignĕro, *v.t.* 1, to pledge, pawn

pignĕror, *v.t.* 1, *dep*, to take possession of

pignus, ŏris (ĕris), *n*, security, mortgage, pledge, bet

pigrĭtia, ae, *f*, laziness, indolence

pigrĭties, ĕi, *f*, laziness, indolence

pīla, ae, *f*, pillar, pier

pĭla, ae, *f*, ball

pīlātus, a, um, *adj*, armed with javelins

pīlentum, i, *n*, carriage

pillĕātus, a, um, *adj*, wearing a felt cap, *see below*

pillĕus, i, *m* (pillĕum, i, *n*), felt cap, worn by Romans at festivals, and by freed slaves

pĭlōsus, a, um, *adj*, hairy

pĭlŭla, ae, *f*, pill

pīlum, i, *n*, the heavy javelin of the Roman infantry

pĭlus, i, *m*, a hair, the hair

pīlus, i, *m* (with prīmus), senior centurion, senior division of trĭārĭimen who fought in the 3rd rank

pīnētum, i, *n*, a wood of pines

pīnĕus, a, um, *adj*, of pinewood

pingo, nxi, ctum, *v.t.* 3, to paint, decorate

pinguesco, *v.i.* 3, to grow fat or fertile

pingue, is, *n*, fat

pinguis, e, *adj*, rich, fertile, plump, dull, stupid

pinguitūdo, ĭnis, *f*, plumpness, richness

pīnĭfer, ĕra, ĕrum, *adj*, pine-bearing

pīnĭger, ĕra, ĕrum, *adj*, pine-bearing

pinna, ae, *f*, feather, wing

pinnātus, a, um, *adj*, winged

pinnĭger, ĕra, ĕrum, *adj*, winged

pīnus, ūs (or i,) *f*, pine tree

pĭo, *v.t.* 1, to appease, atone for

pīpātus, ūs, *m*, chirping

pĭper, ĕris, *n*, pepper

pīpĭlo, *v.i.* 1, to chirp

pīpĭo, *v.i.* 4, to chirp

pīrāta, ae, *m*, pirate

pīrātĭcus, a, um, *adj*, of pirates

pĭrum, i, *n*, pear

pĭrus, i, *f*, pear-tree

piscātor, ōris, *m*, fisherman

piscātōrius, a, um, *adj*, of fishing or fishermen

piscātus, ūs, *m*, fishing

piscīna, ae, *f*, fish-pond

piscis, is, *m*, a fish

piscor, *v.i.* 1, *dep*, to fish

piscōsus, a, um, *adj*, full of fish

pistor, ōris, *m*, miller, baker

pistrīnum, i, *n*, mill

pistris, is (pistrix, ĭcis), *f*, sea-monster

pīsum, i, *n*, pea

pītūīta, ae, *f*, phlegm

pii, ōrum, *m. pl*, the departed

pius, a, um, *adj, adv*, ē, dutiful, loyal, kind, affectionate

pix, pĭcis, *f*, pitch

plācābilis, e, *adj*, easily pacified, mild

plācātus, a, um, *adj, adv*, ē, calmed, still

plăcens, ntis, *adj*, pleasing

plăcenta, ae, *f*, cake

plăcĕo, *v.i.* 2, *with dat*, to please, to be welcome

plăcĭdus, a, um, *adj, adv*, ē, quiet, calm, peaceful

plăcĭtus, a, um, *adj*, agreeable

plāco, *v.t.* 1, to reconcile, soothe

plāga, ae, *f*, wound, blow

plăga, ae, *f*, region

plăga, ae, *f*, hunting-net

plăgĭārĭus, ii, *m*, oppressor

plăgōsus, a, um, *adj*, fond of flogging

plăgŭla, ae, *f*, curtain

planctus, ūs, *m*, lamentation

plango, nxi, nctum, *v.t.* 3, to beat, strike, lament

plangor, ōris, *m*, lamentation

plānĭties, ĕi, *f*, plain

planta, ae, *f*, shoot, twig

plantārĭa, ium, *n. pl*, young trees

plantārĭum, ii, *n*, plantation

plānum, i, *n*, plain

plānus, a, um, *adj, adv*, ē, flat, level, clear

plānus, i, *m*, imposter, cheat

plătănus, i, *f*, plane-tree

plătĕa, ae, *f*, street

plaudo, si, sum, *v.i.t.* 3, to applaud; strike, beat

plausĭbilis, e, *adj*, acceptable

plaustrum, i, *n*, cart, waggon

plausus, ūs, *m*, applause

plēbēcŭla, ae, *f*, the mob

plēbēius, a, um, *adj*, vulgar

plēbĭcŏla, ae, *c*, demagogue

plebs (plēbes), is, *f*, the common people

plecto, *v.t.* 3, to punish

plectrum, i, *n*, quill with which to strike a stringed instrument

plēnĭtūdo, ĭnis, *f*, fulness

plēnus, a, um, *adj, adv*, ē, full, laden, complete, plentiful

For List of Abbreviations used, turn to pages 3, 4

plērīque, aeque, āque, *adj*, most, very many

plērumque, *adv*, for the most part

pleurītis, ĭdis, *f*, pleurisy

plico, *v.t.* 1, to fold up

plinthus, i, *m*, *f*, plinth

plōrātus, ūs, *m*, weeping

plōro, *v.i.t.* 1, to weep; bewail

plostellum, i, *n*, small cart

plŭit, *v. impers*, it rains

plūma, ae, *f*, feather, down

plumbĕus, a, um, *adj*, made of lead, heavy

plumbum, i, *n*, lead, bullet

plūmĕus, a, um, *adj*, downy, soft

plūrālis, e, *adj*, plural

plūres, es, a, *comp. adj*, more

plūrĭmum, *adv*, very much

plūrĭmus, a, um, *adj*, very much

plūs, plūris, *n*, more

plūs, *adv*, more

pluscŭlum, i, *n*, somewhat more

plŭtĕus, i, *m*, shed, parapet, shelf

plŭvia, ae, *f*, rain

plŭviālis, e, *adj*, rainy

plŭvius, a, um, *adj*, rainy

pōcŭlum, i, *n*, cup, beaker

pŏdăgra, ae, *f*, gout

pŏdia, ae, *f*, sail-rope

pŏdium, ii, *n*, height, balcony

pŏēma, ătis, *n*, poem

poena, ae, *f*, punishment, penalty

poenālis, e, *adj*, penal

pŏēsis, is, *f*, poetry

pŏēta, ae, *m*, poet

pŏētĭcus, a, um, *adj*, poetical

poi!, *interj*, indeed!

pŏlĭo, *v.t.* 4, to polish, improve

pŏlītĭcus, a, um, *adj*, political

pŏlītus, a, um, *adj*, *adv*, ē, polished, refined

pollens, ntis, *adj*, powerful

pollĕo, *v.i.* 2, to be powerful, to prevail

pollex, ĭcis, *m*, thumb

pollĭcĕor, *v.i.t.* 2, *dep*, to promise

pollĭcĭtātĭo, ōnis, *f*, promise

pollĭcĭtum, i, *n*, promise

pollinctor, ōris, *m*, undertaker

pollŭo, ŭi, ūtum, *v.t.* 3, to pollute, contaminate

pŏlus, i, *m*, pole, north-pole

pŏlўpus, i, *m*, polypus

pōmārĭum, ii, *n*, orchard

pōmārĭus, ii, *m*, fruiterer

pōmērĭdĭānus, a, um, *adj*, in the afternoon

pōmĭfer, ĕra, ĕrum, *adj*, fruit-bearing

pōmoerĭum, ii, *n*, open space inside and outside city walls

pompa, ae, *f*, procession, retinue, pomp

pōmum, i, *n*, fruit

pōmus, i, *f*, fruit-tree

pondĕro, *v.t.* 1, to consider

pondĕrōsus, a, um, *adj*, ponderous

pondo, *adv*, by weight

pondus, ĕris, *n*, weight, mass, influence, authority

pōne, *adv. and prep. with acc*, behind, after

pōno, pŏsŭi, pŏsĭtum, *v.t.* 3, to put, place, set, plant, wager, invest, spend, lay aside, appoint, calm, allege, propose

pons, ntis, *m*, bridge

pontĭcŭlus, i, *m*, drawbridge

pontĭfex, ĭcis, *m*, high-priest

pontĭfĭcĭus, a, um, *adj*, of a high-priest

pontus, i, *m*, the sea

pŏpa, ae, *m*, priest's assistant

pŏpīna, ae, *f*, restaurant

pŏplĕs, ĭtis, *m*, knee

pŏpŭlāris, e, *adj*, *adv*, ĭter, of the people, popular, democratic

pŏpŭlāris, c, fellow-countryman

pŏpŭlāres, ium, *m*. *pl*, the people's party

pŏpŭlātĭo, ōnis, *f*, devastation

pŏpŭlātor, ōris, *m*, plunderer

pŏpŭlĕus, a, um, *adj*, of poplars

pŏpŭlo, *v.t.* 1, to plunder, devastate

pŏpŭlor, *v.t.* 1, *dep*, to plunder, devastate

pŏpŭlus, i, *m*, the people

pōpŭlus, i, *f*, poplar tree

porcīna, ae, *f*, pork

porcŭlus, i, *m*, young pig; (with mārīnus), porpoise

porcus, i, *m*, pig

porrectĭo, ōnis, *f*, extension

porrectus, a, um, *adj*, extended

porrĭcĭo, ēci, ctum, *v.t.* 3, to offer to the gods

porrĭgo, rexi, rectum, *v.t.* 3, to stretch out, offer

porrĭgo, ĭnis, *f*, dandruff

porro, *adv*, forwards, next, moreover

porrum, i, *n*, leek

porta, ae, *f*, gate, door

portendo, di, tum, *v.t.* 3, to foretell

portentum, i, *n*, omen, monster

portĭcus, ūs, *f*, colonnade

portĭo, *in phrase*, pro portĭōne, in proportion

portĭtor, ōris, *m*, customs-officer

portĭtor, ōris, *m*, boatman

porto, *v.t.* 1, to carry, bring

portōrĭum, ii, *n*, customs-duty

portŭōsus, a, um, *adj*, with many harbours

portus, ūs, *m*, harbour, refuge

posco, pŏposci, *v.t.* 3, to demand

pŏsĭtĭo, ōnis, *f*, placing, situation

pŏsĭtus, a, um, *adj*, situated

pŏsĭtus, ūs, *m*, arrangement, disposition

possessĭo, ōnis, *f*, seizure, occupation

possessor, ōris, *m*, possessor

possĭdĕo, sēdi, sessum, *v.t.* 2, to be master of, possess

possĭdo, sēdi, sessum, *v.t.* 3, to take possession of, occupy

possum, posse, pŏtŭi, *v.i, irreg*, to be able, to have power

post, *adv. and prep. with acc*, behind, backwards, after

postĕā, *adv*, afterwards

postĕāquam, *conj.* after

postĕri, ōrum, *m. pl*, posterity

postĕrior, ĭus, *comp. adj*, next, worse

postĕritas, ātis, *f*, posterity

postĕrius, *adv*, later

postĕrus, a, um, *adj*, next

postgĕnĭti, ōrum, *m. pl*, posterity

posthăbĕo, *v.t.* 2, to postpone, neglect

posthāc, *adv*, in future

postīcum, i, *n*, back door

postis, is, *m*, door-post

postmōdo, *adv*, afterwards

postpōno, pŏsŭi, pŏsĭtum, *v.t.* 3, to postpone, neglect

postquam, *conj*, after, when

postrēmo, *adv*, at last

postrēmus, a, um, *adj*, the last

postrīdĭē, *adv*, on the next day

postŭlāta, ōrum, *n. pl*, demand, request

postŭlātĭo, ōnis, *f*, demands, requests

postŭlo, *v.t.* 1, to demand, prosecute, accuse

postŭmus, a, um, *adj*, last-born, posthumous

pŏtātĭo, ōnis, *f*, drinking

pŏtātor, ōris, *m*, drinker

pŏtens, ntis, *adj*, powerful, master of (*with genit*)

pŏtentātus, ūs, *m*, power, rule

pŏtentĭa, ae, *f*, power, authority

pŏtestas, ātis, *f*, power, dominion, control, value, force, ability, permission, opportunity

pŏtĭo, ōnis, *f*, a drink

pŏtĭor, *v.* 4, *dep, with abl*, to obtain, hold, possess

pŏtĭor, ĭus, *comp. adj*, preferable

pŏtis, e, *adj*, possible

pŏtĭus, *adv*, preferably

pōto, *v.i.t.* 1, to drink

pōtor, ōris, *m*, drinker

pōtus, a, um, *adj*, intoxicated, drained

pōtus, ūs, *m*, a drink

prae, *adv. and prep. with abl*, before, in comparison with

prae se ferre (gĕrere), to reveal

praeăcŭo, ŭi, ūtum, *v.t.* 3, to sharpen

praeăcūtus, a, um, *adj*, pointed

praebĕo, *v.t.* 2, to offer, give, show

praecăvĕo, cāvi, cautum, *v.i.t.* 2, to be on one's guard; prevent

praecēdo, cessi, cessum, *v.i.t.* 3, to lead the way; precede

praecellens, ntis, *adj*, excellent

praecelsus, a, um, *adj*, very high

praeceps, cĭpĭtis, *adj*, headlong

praeceps, cĭpĭtis, *n*, precipice, danger

praeceptor, ōris, *m*, teacher

praeceptum, i, *n*, rule, maxim, order, command

praecerpo, psi, ptum, *v.t.* 3, to gather before time

praecīdo, cīdi, cīsum, *v.t.* 3, to cut off, cut short

praecingo, nxi, nctum, *v.t.* 3, to encircle, gird

praecĭno, nŭi, centum, *v.i.t.* 3, to sing before; predict

praecĭpĭo, cēpi, ceptum, *v.t.* 3, to receive in advance, anticipate, advise, teach

praecĭpĭto, *v.i.t.* 1, to rush down; throw headlong

praecĭpŭus, a, um, *adj, adv*, ē, particular, especial, excellent

praeclārus, a, um, *adj, adv*, ē, splendid, excellent

praeclūdo, si, sum, *v.t.* 3, to close

praeco, ōnis, *m*, herald

praecōnĭum, ii, *n*, office of herald, proclamation

praecōnĭus, a, um, *adj*, of a herald

praecordĭa, ōrum, *n.pl*, midriff, heart

praecox, ŏcis, *adj*, premature

praecurro, cŭcurri, cursum, *v.i.t.* 3, to run in front; excel

praecursor, ōris, *m*, scout, spy

praecŭtĭo, cussi, cussum, *v.t.* 3, to brandish in front

praeda, ae, *f*, plunder, prey

praedātor, ōris, *m*, plunderer

praedātōrĭus, a, um, *adj*, predatory

praedĭātor, ōris, *m*, estate agent

praedĭcātĭo, ōnis, *f*, proclamation, commendation

praedīco, v.t. 1, to proclaim, declare, praise

praedīco, xi, ctum, v.t. 3, to predict, advise, command

praedictio, ōnis, f, prediction

praedictum, i, n, prediction

praedisco, v.t. 3, to learn beforehand

praedĭtus, a, um, adj, provided with

praedĭum, ii, n, farm, estate

praedīvĕs, ĭtis, adj, very rich

praedo, ōnis, m, robber

praedor, v.i.t. 1, dep, to plunder

praedūco, xi, ctum, v.t. 3, to make or put in front

praedulcis, e, adj, very sweet

praedūrus, a, um, adj, very hard

praeĕo, ii, ĭtum, v.i.t. 4, to lead the way; recite, dictate

praefātĭo, ōnis, f, preface

praefectūra, ae, f, superintendence

praefectus, i, m, director, commander, governor

praefĕro, ferre, tŭli, lātum, v.t, irreg, to carry in front, offer, prefer, show

praefīcĭo, fēci, fectum, v.t. 3, to put in command

praefīdens, ntis, adj, over-confident

praefīgo, xi, xum, v.t. 3, to fix in front

praefīnio, v.t. 3, to fix, appoint

praefīŭo, v.i. 3, to flow past

praefŏdĭo, fōdi, v.t. 3, to dig in front

praefor, fātus, v.i.t. 1, dep, to say in advance

praefringo, frēgi, fractum, v.t. 3, to break off

praefulgĕo, si, v.i. 2, to glitter

praegestio, v.i. 4, to desire greatly

praegnans, ntis, adj, pregnant

praegrăvis, e, adj, very heavy

praegrĕdĭor, gressus, v.i.t. 3, dep, to go in advance

praeiūdĭcātus, a, um, adj, preconceived

praeiūdĭcĭum, ii, n, precedent (at law)

praeiūdĭco, v.t. 1, to pre-judge

praelābor, lapsus, v.i.t. 3. dep, to glide or flow along or past

praelambo, v.t. 3, to taste in advance

praelūcĕo, xi, v.i. 2, to carry a light in front

praemandāta, ōrum, n. pl, warrant of arrest

praemĕdĭtātĭo, ōnis, f, premeditation

praemĕdĭtor, v.t. 1, dep, to premeditate

praemitto, mīsi, missum, v.t. 3, to send in advance

praemĭum, ii, n, booty, reward

praemŏnĕo, v.t. 2, to forewarn

praemūnĭo, v.t. 4, to fortify

praenāto, v.i. 1, to flow past

praenĭtĕo, v.i. 2, to outshine

praenōmen, ĭnis, n, first (Christian) name

praenosco, v.t. 3, to learn in advance

praenuntio, v.t. 1, to predict

praenuntĭus, a, um, adj, foreboding

praenuntĭus, i, m, foreteller

praeoccŭpo, v.t. 1, to seize in advance

praeopto, v.t. 1, to prefer

praepărātĭo, ōnis, f, preparation

praepăro, v.t. 1, to prepare

praepĕdĭo, v.t. 4, to bind, obstruct

praependĕo, v.i. 2, to hang down in front

praepes, ĕtis, adj, swift

praepes, ĕtis, c, bird

praepinguis, e, adj, very fat

praepōno, pŏsŭi, pŏsĭtum, v.t. 3, to put first, put in command, prefer

praepŏsĭtĭo, ōnis, f, preference

praepŏsĭtus, i, m, chief, head

praepostĕrus, a, um, adj, preposterous

praepŏtens, ntis, adj, very powerful

praeprŏpĕrus, a, um, adj, sudden, precipitate

praerĭpĭo, rĭpŭi, reptum, v.t. 3, to snatch away

praerōdo, rōsum, v.t. 3, to nibble

praerŏgātīva, ae, f, the Roman tribe to which the first vote was allotted

praerumpo, rūpi, ruptum, v.t. 3, to break off

praeruptus, a, um, adj, steep

praes, dis, m, security, bail

praesaepe, is, n, stable, pen

praesaepio, psi, ptum, v.t. 4, to barricade

praesāgĭo, v.t. 4, to have a presentiment or premonition

praesāgĭum, ii, n, a foreboding

praesāgus, a, um, adj, foretelling

praescisco, v.t. 3, to learn in advance

praescĭus, a, um, adj, knowing in advance

praescrībo, psi, ptum, v.t. 3, to order, appoint, prescribe

praescriptĭo, ōnis, f, excuse, order, law

praescriptum, i, n, order, law

praesens, ntis, adj, present, prompt, powerful, resolute, helping

praesensĭo, ōnis, f, foreboding

praesentia, ae, f, presence

praesentia, ĭum, n. pl, present circumstances

praesentĭo, si, sum, v.t. 4, to have a premonition

praesēpe, see praesaepe

praesertim, adv, especially

praeses, ĭdis, *adj*, guarding

praeses, ĭdis, *c*, guardian, chief

praesĭdĕo, sēdi, *v.i.t.* 2, to guard, direct, superintend

praesĭdĭum, ii, *n*, garrison, fortification, camp

praesignis, e, *adj*, excellent, distinguished

praestābĭlis, e, *adj*, excellent, distinguished

praestans, ntis, *adj*, excellent, distinguished

praestantĭa, ae, *f*, excellence

praestat, *v.* 1, *impers*, it is preferable

praestīgĭae, ārum, *f. pl*, juggling-tricks

praestĭtŭo, ŭi, ūtum, *v.t.* 3, to appoint in advance

praesto, *adv*, ready, present

praesto, stĭti, stĭtum, *v.i.t.* 1, to be superior; surpass, vouch for, perform, fulfil, show, give, offer

praestringo, nxi, ctum, *v.t.* 3, to tie up, graze, blunt

praestrŭo, xi, ctum, *v.t.* 3, to build or block up

praesum praeesse, praefŭi, *v.i, irreg, with dat*, to be in command of

praesūmo, mpsi, mptum, *v.t.* 3, to anticipate, imagine in advance

praetendo, di, tum, *v.t.* 3, to hold out, pretend

praetento, *v.t.* 1, to examine in advance

praeter, *adv, and prep. with acc*, past, beyond, beside, except, unless

praetĕrĕā, *adv*, besides, henceforth

praetĕrĕo, ĭi, ĭtum, *v.i.t.* 4, to pass by; go past, omit, neglect

praeterflŭo, xi, ctum, *v.i.* 3, to flow past

praetergrĕdĭor, gressus, *v.i.t.* 3, *dep*, to pass beyond

praetĕrĭtus, a, um, *adj*, past, gone

praeterlābor, lapsus, *v.i.t.* 3, *dep*, to glide or flow past

praetermissĭo, ōnis, *f*, omission

praetermitto, mīsi, missum, *v.t.* 3, to let pass, omit, neglect

praeterquam, *adv*, besides, except

praetervĕhor, vectus, *v.i.t.* 3, *dep*, to sail, ride or drive past

praetervŏlo, *v.i.t.* 1, to escape; fly past

praetexo, xŭi, xtum, *v.t.* 3, to edge, border, pretend

praetexta, ae, *f*, purple-edged toga worn by Roman magistrates and children

praetexta, ae, *f*, a tragedy

praetextātus, a, um, *adj*, wearing the toga praetexta

praetextus, a, um, *adj*, wearing the toga praetexta

praetor, ōris, *m*, chief, head, Roman magistrate concerned with administration of justice

praetōrĭum, ii, *n*, general's tent, governor's residence

praetōrĭus, a, um, *adj*, of the praetor or general

praetūra, ae, *f*, praetorship

praeūro, ussi, ustum, *v.t.* 3, to burn at the end

praeustus, a, um, *adj*, burnt, frost-bitten

praevălĕo, *v.i.* 2, to be superior

praevălĭdus, a, um, *adj*, very strong

praevĕhor, ctus, *v.i.t.* 3, *dep*, to ride, fly or flow in front

praevĕnĭo, vēni, ventum, *v.i.t.* 4, to come before; outstrip

praeverto, ti, *v.t.* 3, to outstrip, anticipate, prevent

praevertor, sus, *v.i.t.* 3, *dep*, to concentrate one's attention (on)

praevĭdĕo, vīdi, vīsum, *v.t.* 2, to anticipate, see in advance

praevius, a, um, *adj*, leading the way

prandĕo, di, sum, *v.i.t.* 2, to breakfast, lunch, (on)

prandĭum, ii, *n*, breakfast, luncheon

pransus, a, um, *adj*, having breakfasted

prātensis, e, *adj*, growing in meadows

prātŭlum, i, *n*, small meadow

prātum, i, *n*, meadow

prāvĭtas, ātis, *f*, deformity, depravity

prāvus, a, um, *adj, adv*, ē, wrong, bad, deformed

prĕcārĭus, a, um, *adj, adv*, ō, obtained by prayer

prĕcātĭo, ōnis, *f*, prayer

prĕcĭae, ārum, *f. pl*, grape-vine

prĕcor, *v.i.t.* 1, *dep*, to pray, beg

prĕhendo, di, sum, *v.t.* 3, to seize, detain, take by surprise

prĕhenso, *v.t.* 1, to grasp, detain

prēlum, i, *n*, wine-press

prĕmo, ssi, ssum, *v.t.* 3, to press, grasp, cover, close, pursue closely, load, overwhelm, plant, prune, check, repress

prendo, see prĕhendo

prensus, a, um, *adj*, grasped

presso, *v.t.* 1, to press

pressus, ūs, *m*, pressure

pressus, a, um, *adj*, subdued, compact

prĕtĭōsus, a, um, *adj, adv*, ē, valuable, costly

For List of Abbreviations used, turn to pages 3, 4

prĕtĭum, ii, *n*, price, value, money, wages, reward

prex, prĕcis, *f*, prayer, request

prīdem, *adv*, long ago

prīdĭē, *adv*, on the day before

prīmaevus, a, um, *adj*, youthful

prīmārĭus, a, um, *adj*, of the first rank, chief

prīmĭgĕnus, a, um, *adj*, primitive

prīmĭpĭlus, *see* pilus

prīmĭtĭae, ārum, *f. pl*, first-fruits

prīmō, *adv*, at first

prīmordĭa, ōrum, *n. pl*, origin

prīmōris, e, *adj*, first, front end

prīmōres, um, *m. pl*, nobles

prīmum, *adv*, at first; cum prīmum, as soon as; quam prīmum, as soon as possible

prīmus, a, um, *adj*, first, chief

princeps, cĭpis, *adj*, first, chief

princeps, cĭpis, *m*, chief, originator

princĭpālis, e, *adj*, original, primitive, principal

princĭpālis, is, *m*, overseer

princĭpātus, ūs, *m*, the first place, command, rule

princĭpĭo, *adv*, in the beginning

princĭpĭum, ii, *n*, origin; *in pl*, principles, elements

prĭor, ĭus, *comp. adj*, previous, former

prĭōres, um, *m. pl*, ancestors

priscus, a, um, *adj*, ancient

prisma, ătis, *n*, prism

pristĭnus, a, um, *adj*, primitive

prĭus, *comp. adv*, previously

prĭusquam, *conj*, before

prīvātim, *adv*, privately

prīvātĭo, ōnis, *f*, taking-away

prīvātus, a, um, *adj*, private

prīvātus, i, *m*, private citizen

prīvigna, ae, *f*, step-daughter

prīvignus, i, *m*, step-son

prīvilēgĭum, ii, *n*, bill or law concerned with an individual

prīvo, *v.t.* 1, to deprive, release

prīvus, a, um, *adj*, one's own

prō, *prep. with abl*, before, in front of, on behalf of, instead of, just as, on account of, according to, in relation to

prō! (prōh!), *interj*, Ah! Alas!

prōăvus, i, *m*, great-grandfather

prŏbābilis, e, *adj*, *adv*, ĭter, likely, pleasing

prŏbābilitas, ātis, *f*, probability

prŏbātĭo, ōnis, *f*, trial, proving

prŏbātus, a, um, *adj*, tried, good

prŏbĭtas, ātis, *f*, honesty

prŏbo, *v.t.* 1, to try, test, approve of, recommend, prove

prōboscis, idis, *f*, elephant's trunk

prŏbrōsus, a, um, *adj*, shameful

prŏbrum, i, *n*, disgraceful deed, lechery, disgrace, abuse

prŏbus, a, um, *adj*, *adv*, ē, good, honest, virtuous

prŏcācitas, ātis, *f*, impudence

prŏcax, ācis, *adj*, impudent

prōcēdo, cessi, cessum, *v.i.* 3, to go forward, advance, turn out, prosper

prŏcella, ae, *f*, storm, violence

prŏcellōsus, a, um, *adj*, tempestuous

prŏcer, ēris, *m*, chief, prince

prōcērĭtas, ātis, *f*, height

prōcērus, a, um, *adj*, tall

prōcessus, ūs, *m*, advance

prōcĭdo, di, *v.i.* 3, to fall flat

prōcinctus, ūs, *m*, readiness for battle

prōclāmo, *v.t.* 1, to cry out

prōclīno, *v.t.* 1, to bend forwards

prōclive, is, *n*, slope, descent

prōclīvis, e, *adj*, sloping downhill, liable, willing

prōconsul, is, *m*, provincial governor

prōcrastino, *v.t.* 1, to defer

prōcrēātĭo, ōnis, *f*, procreation

prōcrēātor, ōris, *m*, creator

prōcrĕo, *v.t.* 1, to produce

prōcŭbo, *v.i.* 1, to lie stretched-out

prōcūdo, di, sum, *v.t.* 3, to forge

prōcul, *adv*, in the distance

prōculco, *v.t.* 1, to trample on

prōcumbo, cŭbŭi, cŭbĭtum, *v.i.* 3, to lean or fall forwards, sink

prōcūrātĭo, ōnis, *f*, administration

prōcūrātor, ōris, *m*, manager, agent

prōcūro, *v.t.* 1, to look after

prōcurro, curri, cursum, *v.i.* 3, to run forward, project

prŏcus, i, *m*, suitor

prōdĕo, ii, ĭtum, *v.i.* 3, to come forward, appear

prōdesse, *see* prōsum

prōdigĭōsus, a, um, *adj*, strange, marvellous

prōdigĭum, ii, *n*, omen, monster

prōdigus, a, um, *adj*, wasteful

prōdĭtĭo, ōnis, *f*, treachery

prōdĭtor, ōris, *m*, traitor

prōdo, dĭdi, dĭtum, *v.t.* 3, to bring out, relate, betray, bequeath

prōdūco, xi, ctum, *v.t.* 3, to lead forward, prolong, produce, promote

prōductus, a, um, *adj*, *adv*, ē, prolonged

proelĭor, *v.i.* 1, *dep*, to join battle

proelĭum, ii, *n,* battle

prōfāno, *v.t.* 1, to desecrate

prōfānus, a, um, *adj,* wicked, common

prŏfectio, ōnis, *f,* departure

prŏfectō, *adv,* certainly

prŏfectus, ūs, *m,* advance

prŏfectus, a, um, *adj,* having advanced

prōfĕro, ferre, tŭli, lātum, *v.t, irreg,* to bring out, extend, defer, reveal, mention; with **gradum,** to proceed; with **signa,** to march forward

prŏfessor, ōris, *m,* teacher, professor

prŏfessio, ōnis, *f,* declaration

prŏfessus, a, um, *adj,* avowed

prŏfestus, a, um, *adj,* working (days)

prŏfĭcio, fēci, fectum, *v.i.t.* 3, to progress; perform, help

prŏfĭciscor, prŏfectus, *v.i.* 3, *dep,* to set out, originate

prŏfĭtĕor, fessus, *v.i.* 2, *dep,* to declare, acknowledge, promise

prōfĭgātus, a, um, *adj,* wretched, dissolute

prōfĭigo, *v.t.* 1, to overthrow

prōflo, *v.t.* 1, to blow out

prōflŭo, xi, xum, *v.i.* 3, to flow out, proceed

prōflŭens, ntis, *adj,* fluent

prōflŭvium, ii, *n,* flowing out

prōfor, *v.t.* 1, *dep,* to speak, say

prŏfŭgio, fūgi, *v.i.t.* 3, to escape; flee from

prŏfŭgus, a, um, *adj,* fugitive

prŏfŭgus, i, *m,* fugitive, exile

prŏfundo, fūdi, fūsum, *v.t.* 3, to pour out, utter, squander

prŏfundum, i, *n,* the deep, the sea, an abyss

prŏfundus, a, um, *adj,* deep

prŏfūsio, ōnis, *f,* outpouring, prodigal use

prŏfūsus, a, um, *adj,* extravagant

prōgĕnĕro, *v.t.* 1, to beget

prōgĕnies, ēi, *f,* family, offspring

prōgigno, gĕnŭi, gĕnĭtum, *v.t.* 3, to produce

prōgnātus, a, um, *adj,* born

prōgnātus, i, *m,* descendant

prōgrĕdior, gressus, *v.i.* 3, *dep,* to advance, proceed

prōgressio, ōnis, *f,* growth

prōgressus, ūs, *m,* advance

proh!, see **prō!**

prōhĭbĕo, *v.t.* 2, to prevent, prohibit, defend

prōĭectus, a, um, *adj,* projecting

prōĭcio, iēci, iectum, *v.t.* 3, to throw forward, extend, expel, yield, disdain

prŏin or **prŏinde,** *adv,* in the same way, equally, accordingly, therefore

prōlābor, lapsus, *v.i.* 3, *dep,* to slip or slide forward, fall

prōlātio, ōnis, *f,* postponement, mentioning

prōlāto, *v.t.* 1, to postpone

prōles, is, *f,* offspring, child

prōlētārius, ii, *m,* citizen of lowest class

prōlixus, a, um, *adj, adv,* ē, stretched out, fortunate

prōlŏgus, i, *m,* prologue

prōlūdo, si, sum, *v.i.* 3, to practise in advance

prōlŭo, lŭi, lūtum, *v.t.* 3, to wash away, moisten

prōlūsio, ōnis, *f,* prelude

prōlŭvies, ēi, *f,* overflow

prōmĕrĕo, *v.t.* 2, to deserve, merit

prōmĕrĕor, *v.t.* 2, *dep,* to deserve, merit

prōmĭnens, ntis, *adj,* prominent

prōmĭnĕo, *v.i.* 2, to project

prōmiscŭus, a, um, *adj,* common, indiscriminate

prōmissio, ōnis, *f,* promise

prōmissum, i, *n,* promise

prōmissus, a, um, *adj,* hanging

prōmitto, mīsi, missum, *v.t.* 3, to promise, assure

prōmo, mpsi, mptum, *v.t.* 3, to bring out, produce, tell

prōmontūrium, ii, *n,* headland

prōmŏvĕo, mōvi, mōtum, *v.t.* 2, to move forward, extend

promptus, a, um, *adj,* ready, quick

promptus, ūs, *m,* only in phrase; **in promptu,** in public; **in promptu esse,** to be at hand

prōmulgo, *v.t.* 1, to publish

prōmus, i, *m,* butler

prōmūtŭus, a, um, *adj,* loaned

prōnĕpos, ōtis, *m,* great-grandson

prōnōmen, ĭnis, *n,* pronoun

prōnŭba, ae, *f,* bridesmaid

prōnuntiātio, ōnis, *f,* proclamation

prōnuntio, *v.t.* 1, to announce

prōnus, a, um, *adj,* leaning or bending forward, disposed; setting, sinking (of stars, etc.)

prŏoemĭum, ii, *n,* preface

prōpāgātio, ōnis, *f,* extension

prōpāgo, *v.t.* 1, to generate, extend

prōpāgo, ĭnis, *f,* shoot (of plant), offspring, child

prōpālam, *adv,* openly

prōpātŭlus, a, um, *adj,* uncovered

prŏpe, *adv. and prep. with acc,* near, nearly

prōpĕdiem, *adv,* soon

prŏpello, pŭli, pulsum, *v.t.* 3, to push or drive forward

prŏpĕmŏdum, *adv*, almost

prŏpendĕo, di, sum, *v.i.* 2, to be inclined or disposed

prŏpensus, a, um, *adj*, inclined, disposed

prŏpĕro, *v.i.t.* 1, to hurry

prŏpĕrus, a, um, *adj, adv*, ē, quick, hurrying

prŏpexus, a, um, *adj*, combed forward

prŏpino, *v.t.* 1, to drink a toast

prŏpinquĭtas, ātis, *f*, nearness, relationship

prŏpinquo, *v.i.t.* 1, to approach; hasten

prŏpinquus, a, um, *adj*, near

prŏpinquus, i, *m*, relative

prŏpĭor, ius, *comp. adj*, nearer

prŏpĭtius, a, um, *adj*, kind, favourable

prŏpĭus, *comp. adv*, nearer

prŏpōno, pŏsŭi, pŏsĭtum, *v.t.* 3, to put forward, state, display, offer

prŏpŏsĭtio, ōnis, *f*, representation, theme

prŏpŏsĭtum, i, *n*, plan, purpose

prŏprĭĕtas, ātis, *f*, peculiarity

prŏprĭus, a, um, *adj, adv*, ē, special, particular, its (his, her) own

propter, *prep. with acc*, on account of, near; *adv*, nearby

proptĕrĕā, *adv*, for that reason

prŏpugnācŭlum, i, *n*, rampart

prŏpugnātĭo, ōnis, *f*, defence

prŏpugnātor, ōris, *m*, defender

prŏpugno, *v.i.t.* 1, to make sorties; defend

prŏpulso, *v.t.* 1, to ward off

prōra, ae, *f*, prow, ship

prōrepo, psi, ptum, *v.i.* 3, to creep out, crawl forward

prōripio, pŭi, reptum, *v.t.* 3, to drag forward; with se, to rush

prōrŏgātio, ōnis, *f*, prolonging

prōrŏgo, *v.t.* 1, to prolong, defer

prorsus (prorsum), *adv*, certainly, utterly

prōrumpo, rūpi, ruptum, *v.i.t.* 3, to rush forward; send forward

prōrŭo, rŭi, rŭtum, *v.i.t.* 3, to rush forward; overthrow

proscaenium, ii, *n*, stage

prōscindo, scĭdi, scissum, *v.t.* 3, to tear up, plough

prōscrĭbo, psi, ptum, *v.t.* 3, to publish, confiscate, outlaw

prōscriptĭo, ōnis, *f*, confiscation, outlawing

prōscriptus, i, *m*, outlaw

prōsēmĭno, *v.t.* 1, to sow

prōsĕquor, sĕcūtus, *v.t.* 3, *dep*, to accompany, follow, pursue, bestow, proceed with

prōsĭlĭo, ŭi, *v.i.* 4, to leap up

prospecto, *v.t.* 1, to look at, expect, await

prospectus, ūs, *m*, view, sight

prospĕrus, a, um, *adj, adv*, ē, favourable, fortunate

prospĕrĭtas, ātis, *f*, prosperity

prospĕro, *v.t.* 1, to make (something) successful

prospĭcio, spexi, spectum, *v.i.t.* 3, to look out; discern, overlook, foresee

prosterno, strāvi, strātum, *v.t.* 3, to overthrow, prostrate

prōsūbigo, *v.t.* 3, to dig up

prōsum, prōdesse, prōfŭi, *v.i, irreg. with dat*, to be useful

prōtectum, i, *n*, eaves

prōtĕgo, xi, ctum, *v.t.* 3, to cover, protect

prōtēlum, i, *n*, team of oxen

prōtendo, di, sum (tum), *v.t.* 3, to stretch out, extend

prōtĕro, trĭvi, trītum, *v.t.* 3, to trample down, crush, destroy

prōterrĕo, *v.t.* 2, to terrify

prōtervĭtas, ātis, *f*, impudence

prōtervus, a, um, *adj, adv*, ē, forward, impudent, violent

prōtĭnus, *adv*, straightforwards, continuously, immediately

prōtrăho, xi, ctum, *v.t.* 3, to drag forward, reveal

prōtrūdo, si, sum, *v.t.* 3, to push out

prōturbo, *v.t.* 1, to repel

prout, *adv*, just as

prōvectus, a, um, *adj*, advanced (of time)

prōvĕho, xi, ctum, *v.t.* 3, to carry forward, advance, promote

prōvĕnĭo, vēni, ventum, *v.i.* 4, to be born, thrive, occur, turn out (well or badly)

prōventus, ūs, *m*, produce, result

prōverbĭum, ii, *n*, proverb

prōvĭdens, ntis, *adj*, prudent

prōvĭdentĭa, ae, *f*, foresight

prōvĭdĕo, vīdi, vīsum, *v.i.t.* 2, to make preparations; foresee, provide for

prōvĭdus, a, um, *adj*, prudent

prōvincĭa, ae, *f*, province, duty, sphere of duty

prōvincĭālis, e, *adj*, provincial

prōvŏcātĭo, ōnis, *f*, appeal

prōvŏco, *v.i.t.* 1, to appeal; call out, challenge, rouse

prōvŏlo, *v.i.* 1, to fly out

prŏvolvo, volvi, vŏlūtum, v.t. 3, to roll forward

proximē, adv, nearest, next

proximĭtas, ātis, f, proximity

proximus, a, um, adj, nearest, next, previous

prūdens, ntis, adj, adv, nter, experienced, wise, sensible

prūdentĭa, ae, f, experience, skill, discretion

prūīna, ae, f, frost, snow

prūīnōsus, a, um, adj, frosty

prūna, ae, f, burning coal

prūnum, i, n, plum

prūnus, i, f, plum-tree

prūrĭo, v.i. 4, to itch

prūrītus, ūs, m, itching

psallo, i, v.i. 3, to play on an instrument

psalmus, i, m, a psalm

psittācus, i, m, parrot

ptĭsāna, ae, f, pearl-barley

pūbens, ntis, adj, flourishing

pūbertas, ātis, f, puberty, manhood

pūbes (pūber), ĕris, adj, adult

pūbes, is, f, young men

pūbesco, bŭi, v.i. 3, to grow up, ripen

pūblĭcānus, i, m, tax-collector

pūblĭcātĭo, ōnis, f, confiscation

pūblĭco, v.t. 1, to confiscate

pūblĭcum, i, n, a public place

pūblĭcus, a, um, adj, adv, ē, of the state, public, general

pŭdendus, a, um, adj, disgraceful

pŭdens, ntis, adj, adv, nter, modest

pŭdet, v. 2, impers, it brings shame

pŭdībundus, a, um, adj, modest

pŭdīcĭtĭa, ae, f, modesty, virtue

pŭdīcus, a, um, adj, modest, pure

pŭdor, ōris, m, a sense of decency, shyness

pŭella, ae, f, girl, sweetheart, young wife

pŭellāris, e, adj, girlish

pŭer, ĕri, m, boy

pŭerīlis, e, adj, youthful

pŭerĭtĭa (pŭertĭa), ae, f, childhood, youth

pūgil, ilis, m, boxer

pūgillāres, ium, m. pl, writing-tablets

pūgĭo, ōnis, m, dagger

pugna, ae, f, fight, battle

pugnātor, ōris, m, fighter

pugnax, ācis, adj, warlike, quarrelsome

pugno, v.i. 1, to fight, disagree, struggle

pugnus, i, m, fist

pulcher, chra, chrum, adj, adv, ē, beautiful, handsome, glorious

pulchrĭtūdo, ĭnis, f, beauty

pūlex, ĭcis, m, flea

pullārĭus, ii, m, chicken-keeper

pullŭlo, v.i. 1, to sprout

pullus, i. m, young animal, chicken

pullus, a, um, adj, dark, black

pulmentārĭum, ii, n, sauce

pulmentum, i, n, sauce

pulmo, ōnis, m, lung

pulpĭtum, i, n, platform

puls, pultis, f, porridge

pulsātĭo, ōnis, f, beating

pulso, v.t. 1, to beat, push, touch, disturb

pulsus, ūs, m, push, blow, beating

pulvĕrĕus, a, um, adj, dusty

pulvĕrŭlentus, a, um, adj, dusty

pulvīnar, āris, n, couch

pulvīnus, i, m, cushion

pulvis, ĕris, m, dust

pūmex, ĭcis, m, pumice-stone

pūmilĭo, ōnis, m, dwarf

punctim, adv, with the point

punctum, i, n, point, vote, moment

pungo, pŭpŭgi, punctum, v.t. 3, to prick, sting, vex, annoy

pūnĭcĕus, a, um, adj, red

pūnĭo, v.t. (pūnĭor, v.t.dep.) 4, to punish

pūpa, ae, f, doll

pūpilla, ae, f, orphan, ward

pūpillus, i, m, orphan, ward

puppis, is, f, ship's stern

pūpŭla, ae, f, pupil of the eye

purgāmen, ĭnis, n, refuse, filth

purgāmentum, i, n, refuse, filth

purgātĭo, ōnis, f, cleansing

purgo, v.t. 1, to clean, purify, excuse, justify, atone for

purpŭra, ae, f, purple, purple clothes

purpŭrĕus, a, um, adj, purple, clothed in purple, brilliant

pūrum, i, n, clear sky

pūrus, a, um, adj, adv, ē, pure, clean, plain

pūs, pūris, n, pus

pūsillus, a, um, adj, little, petty

pūsĭo, ōnis, m, urchin

pustŭla, ae, f, pimple

pŭtāmen, ĭnis, f, peel, shell

pŭtĕal, ālis, n, fence of a well

pŭtĕo, v.i. 2, to stink

pūter (pūtris), tris, tre, adj, decaying, rotten

pūtesco, pūtŭi, v.i. 3, to rot

pŭtĕus, i, m, well, pit

pūtĭdus, a, um, adj, rotten, disgusting

pŭto, v.t. 1, to think, prune

pŭtresco, v.i. 3, to decay

pŭtrĭdus, a, um, adj, rotten

pyra, ae, f, funeral pyre

For List of Abbreviations used, turn to pages 3, 4

pȳrămis, ĭdis, *f*, pyramid
pȳrum, i, *n*, pear
pȳrus, i, *f*, pear-tree
pȳthon, ŏnis, *m*, python
pyxis, ĭdis, *f*, box

Q

quā, *adv*, where, in which direction, how; **qua ... qua**, partly ... partly
quācumque, *adv*, wheresoever
quădra, ae, *f*, square, dining-table
quădrāgēni, ae, a, *adj*, forty each
quădrāgēsimus, a, um, *adj*, fortieth
quădrāgĭes, *adv*, forty times
quădrāgĭnta, *adj*, forty
quădrans, ntis, *m*, a quarter
quădrātum, i, *n*, square
quădrātus, a, um, *adj*, square
quădrĭdŭum, ii, *n*, period of four days
quădrĭfāriam, *adv*, into four parts
quădrĭfīdus, a, um, *adj*, split into four
quădrīgae, ārum, *f. pl*, four-horse team or chariot
quădrĭiŭgis, e, *adj*, yoked in a four-horse team
quădrĭiŭgus, a, um, *adj*, yoked in a four-horse team
quădrĭlătĕrus, a, um, *adj*, quadrilateral
quădrīmus, a, um, *adj*, four years old
quădringēnārius, a, um, *adj*, of four hundred each
quădringenti, ae, a, *adj*, four hundred
quădringentĭes, *adv*, four hundred times
quădro, *v.i.t.* 1, to be square, agree; make square, complete
quădrum, i, *n*, square
quădrŭpēdans, ntis, *adj*, galloping
quădrŭpēs, ēdis, *adj*, galloping, going on four feet
quădrŭplex, ĭcis, *adj*, quadruple
quădrŭplum, i, *n*, fourfold amount
quaero, sīvi, sītum, *v.t.* 3, to search for, acquire, inquire
quaesītio, ōnis, *f*, investigation
quaesītor, ōris, *m*, investigator
quaesītum, i, *n*, question
quaesītus, a, um, *adj*, far-fetched
quaeso, īvi, *v.t.* 3, to beseech, seek
quaestio, ōnis, *f*, investigation, trial, case, question, problem
quaestor, ōris, *m*, Roman magistrate in charge of public revenues
quaestōrius, a, um, *adj*, of a quaestor

quaestŭōsus, a, um, *adj*, profitable
quaestūra, ae, *f*, quaestorship
quaestus, ūs, *m*, gain, profit, employment
quālis, e, *adj*, of what kind
quāliscumque, quālēcumque, *adj*, of whatever kind
quālĭtas, ātis, *f*, state, condition
quālum, i, *n*, basket, hamper
quam, *adv*, how; *with comparatives*, than
quamdĭu, *adv*, as long as, until
quamlĭbet, *adv*, as much as you wish
quāmobrem, *adv*, why, wherefore
quamprīmum, *adv*, as soon as possible
quamquam, *conj*, although
quamvīs, *conj*, although; *adv*, very
quando, *adv*, when?, some time; *conj*, since, because
quandōcumque, *adv*, whenever
quandōque, *adv*, whenever, at some time or other
quandōquĭdem, *adv*, since
quanti? at what price?
quantō, *adv*, by as much as
quantŏpĕrĕ, *adv*, how much
quantŭlus, a, um, *adj*, how small
quantŭluscumque, *adj*, however small
quantum, *adv*, as much as
quantus, a, um, *adj*, how great
quantuscumque, *adj*, however big
quantusvis, quantāvis, quantumvis, *adj*, as big as you like
quāpropter, *adv*, wherefore
quārē, *adv*, wherefore, why
quartānus, a, um, *adj*, occurring on the fourth day
quartum, *adv*, for the fourth time
quartō, *adv*, for the fourth time
quartus, a, um, *adj*, fourth
quăsi, *adv*, as if, just as
quāsillum, i, *n*, small basket
quassātio, ōnis, *f*, shaking
quasso, *v.t.* 1, to shake, shatter
quātĕnus, *adv*, to what extent, how long, since
quăter, *adv*, four times
quăterni, ae, a, *pl. adj*, four each
quătio (*no perf.*), quassum, *v.t.* 3, to shake, shatter, excite
quattŭor, *indecl. adj*, four
quattŭordĕcim, *adj*, fourteen
quĕ *conj*, and
quĕmadmŏdum, *adv*, how
quĕo, ĭi, ĭtum, *v.i.* 4, to be able
quercētum, i, *n*, oak-forest
quercus, ūs, *f*, oak-tree
quĕrēla, ae, *f*, complaint

quĕrĭbundus, a, um, *adj*, complaining
quĕrĭmōnĭa, ae, *f*, complaint
quernus, a, um, *adj*, of oak
quĕror, questus, *v.i.t.* 3, *dep*, to complain
quĕrŭlus, a, um, *adj*, full of complaints, cooing, chirping
questus, ūs, *m*, complaint
quī, quae, quod, *rel. pron*, who, which, what
quī, *adv*, how, wherewith
quĭā, *conj*, because
quicquid, *pron*, whatever
quīcumque, quaecumque, quodcumque, *pron*, whoever, whatever
quid, *interr. pron*, what? why?
quīdam, quaedam, quoddam, *pron*, a certain somebody or something
quĭdem, *adv*, indeed; ne . . . quidem, not even . . .
quĭdnī, why not?
quĭes, ētis, *f*, rest, quiet
quĭescens, ntis, *adj*, quiescent
quĭesco, ēvi, ētum, *v.i.* 3, to rest, keep quiet, sleep
quĭētus, a, um, *adj*, calm
quīlĭbet, quaelĭbet, quodlĭbet, *pron*, anyone or anything you like
quīn, *conj*, that not, but that, indeed, why not
quīnam, quaenam, quodnam, *pron*, who, what, which
quincunx, ncis, *m*, five-twelfths, trees planted in oblique lines
quindĕcĭes, *adv*, fifteen times
quindĕcim, *indecl. adj*, fifteen
quingēni, ae, a, *pl. adj*, five hundred each
quingenti, ae, a, *pl. adj*, five hundred
quingentĭes, *adv*, five hundred times
quīni, ae, a, *pl. adj*, five each
quinquāgēni, ae, a, *pl. adj*, fifty each
quinquāgēsĭmus, a, um, *adj*, fiftieth
quinquāginta, *indecl. adj*, fifty
quinquātrĭa, ōrum, *n.pl*, festival of Minerva (19th–23rd March)
quinquĕ, *indecl. adj*, five
quinquennālis, e, *adj*, quinquennial
quinquennis, e, *adj*, every fifth year
quinquennĭum, ii, *n*, period of five years
quinquĕrēmis, *adj*, ship with five banks of oars
quinquĭens, *adv*, five times
Quintīlis (mensis), July
quintus, a, um, *adj*, fifth
quippe, *adv*, certainly; *conj*, in as much as
quis, quid, *interr pron*, who? which? what? *indef. pron*, anyone, anything

quisnam, quaenam, quidnam, *interr. pron*, who? which?
quispĭam, quaepĭam, quodpĭam, *indef. pron*, anybody, anything
quisquam, quaequam, quicquam, *indef. pron*, anyone, anything
quisque, quaeque, quodque, *indef. pron*, each, every, everybody, everything
quisquĭlĭae, ārum, *f. pl*, rubbish
quisquis, quaeque, quodquod, *indef. pron*, whoever, whatever
quīvis, quaevis, quodvis, *indef. pron*, anyone or anything you please
quō, *adv. and conj*, wherefore, where to, whither, so that
quŏad, *adv*, as long as, until, as far as
quŏcircā, *conj*, wherefore
quŏcumque, *adv*, to whatever place
quod, *conj*, because
quod, *neuter of* qui
quŏdammŏdo, in a certain manner
quōmĭnus, *conj*, that . . . not
quōmŏdŏ, *adv*, how
quondam, *adv*, once, at times
quŏnĭam, *adv*, since, because
quŏquam, *adv*, to any place
quŏque, *conj*, also, too
quōquō, *adv*, to whatever place
quorsum (quorsus), *adv*, to what place, to what purpose
quŏt, *indecl. adj*, how many
quŏtannis, *adv*, every year
quŏtīdĭānus, a, um, *adj*, daily
quŏtīdĭe, *adv*, daily
quŏtĭes (quŏtĭens), *adv*, how often
quŏtĭescumquĕ, *adv*, however often
quotquŏt, *adv*, however many
quŏtus, a, um, *adj*, how many
quŏusquĕ, *adv*, how long
quum, see cum

R

rābĭdus, a, um, *adj*, raving, mad
rābĭes (em, e), *f*, madness, anger
rābĭōsus, a, um, *adj*, raging
rābŭla, ae, *f*, argumentative lawyer
rācēmĭfer, ĕra, ĕrum, *adj*, clustering
rācēmus, i, *m*, bunch, cluster
rādīcĭtus, *adv*, by the roots
rādĭans, ntis, *adj*, shining
rādĭātĭo, ōnis, *f*, shining
rādĭo, *v.i.* 1, to shine
rādĭus, ii, *m*, rod, spoke, radius, shuttle, ray
rādix, īcis, *f*, root, radish, source
rādo, si, sum, *v.t.* 3, to scrape, shave
raeda, ae, *f*, carriage

raedārius, i, *m*, coachman

raia, ae, *f*, ray (fish)

rāmālia, ium, *n.pl*, brushwood

rāmōsus, a, um, *adj*, branching

rāmus, i, *m*, branch

rāna, ae, *f*, frog

rancidus, a, um, *adj*, rancid

rānuncŭlus, i, *m*, tadpole

răpācitas, ātis, *f*, rapacity

răpax, ācis, *adj*, grasping

rāphănus, i, *m*, radish

răpĭdus, a, um, *adj*, *adv*, ē, swift, violent, tearing

răpĭna, ae, *f*, robbery, plunder

răpĭo, ŭi, raptum, *v.t.* 3, to seize, snatch, drag away

raptim, *adv*, hurriedly

raptio, ōnis, *f*, abduction

rapto, *v.t.* 1, to snatch, drag away, plunder

raptor, ōris, *m*, robber

raptum, i, *n*, plunder

raptus, ūs, *m*, robbery, rape

răpŭlum, i, *n*, turnip

rāpum, i, *n*, turnip

rāresco, *v.i.* 3, to grow thin, open out

rāritas, ātis, *f*, looseness, rarity, infrequency

rārus, a, um, *adj*, *adv*, ē, ō, loose, loose in texture, thin, scattered, straggling, few, remarkable, rare

rāsilis, e, *adj*, polished

rastellus, i, *m*, hoe, rake

rastrum, i, *n*, rake, hoe

rātio, ōnis, *f*, account, calculation, business affairs, relationship, concern for, consideration, conduct, plan, reason, motive, reckoning, order, law, theory, system, way, manner

rātiōcinor, *v.i.t.* 1, *dep*, to calculate

rātiōnalis, e, *adj*, rational, theoretical

rātis, is, *f*, raft

rātus, a, um, *adj*, established; (*partic.*) having thought; pro rātā, proportionally

raucus, a, um, *adj*, hoarse

rāvus, a, um, *adj*, grey, tawny

rē, rēvērā (*adv.*), really

rēapse, *adv*, (re ipsa), in fact

rēbellio, ōnis, *f*, revolt

rēbellis, e, *adj*, rebellious

rēbello, *v.i.* 1, to rebel, rebuff

rēbŏo, *v.i.* 1, to re-echo

rēcalcĭtro, *v.i.* 1, to kick back

rēcalfăcio, fēci, *v.t.* 3, to warm

rēcandesco, dŭi, *v.i.* 3, to grow white or hot

rēcanto, (*no perf*) *v.t.* 1, to retract

rēcēdo, cessi, cessum, *v.i.* 3, to retreat, withdraw

rēcens, ntis, *adj*, fresh, new

rēcens, *adv*, newly, recently

rēcensĕo, ŭi, ĭtum, *v.t.* 2, to count, reckon, survey, review

rēcensio, ōnis, *f*, review

receptācŭlum, i, *n*, shelter

rēcepto, *v.t.* 1, to recover

rēceptor, ōris, *m*, receiver

rēceptus, ūs, *m*, retreat

rēcessus, ūs, *m*, retreat, recess

rēcĭdīvus, a, um, *adj*, recurring

rēcĭdo, cĭdi, cāsum, *v.i.* 3, to fall back, recoil, return

rēcīdo, cĭdi, cīsum, *v.t.* 3, to cut down, cut off, cut short

rēcingo, (*no perf*,) cinctum, *v.t.* 3, to loosen

rēcĭno, *v.i.* 3, to re-echo

rēcĭpĕro (rēcŭp-), *v.t.* 1, to regain

rēcĭpio, cēpi, ceptum, *v.t.* 3, to take back, regain, receive, give an assurance; with sē, to retreat, recover oneself

rēcĭprŏco, *v.i.t.* 1, to move backwards

rēcĭprŏcus, a, um, *adj*, receding

rēcĭtātio, ōnis, *f*, reading aloud

rēcĭtātor, ōris, *m*, reader

rēcĭto, *v.t.* 1, to read aloud

rēclāmātio, ōnis, *f*, remonstrance

rēclāmo, *v.i.t.* 1, to resound; contradict loudly, remonstrate

rēclīno, *v.t.* 1, to lean back

rēclūdo, si, sum, *v.t.* 3, to reveal

rēcognĭtio, ōnis, *f*, review

rēcognosco, gnōvi, gnĭtum, *v.t.* 3, to recollect, investigate

rēcŏlo, cŏlŭi, cultum, *v.t.* 3, to cultivate again, renew

rēconcĭliātio, ōnis, *f*, re-establishment, reconciliation

rēconcĭlio, *v.t.* 1, to restore, reconcile

rēcondĭtus, a, um, *adj*, hidden

rēcondo, dĭdi, dĭtum, *v.t.* 3, to put away, hide

rēcŏquo, xi, ctum, *v.t.* 3, to cook again, forge again

rēcordātio, ōnis, *f*, recollection

rēcordor, *v.i.t.* 1, *dep*, to think over, remember

rēcrĕātio, ōnis, *f*, recovery

rēcrĕo, *v.t.* 1, to revive, reproduce

rēcresco, crēvi, crētum, *v.i.* 3, to grow again

rectā, *adv*, straightforwards

rector, ōris, *m*, master, leader, helmsman

rectum, i, *n*, virtue

rectus, a, um, *adj*, *adv*, ē, straight, upright, correct

rĕcŭbans, ntis, *adj*, recumbent

rĕcŭbo, *v.i.* 1, to lie back

rĕcumbo, cŭbŭi, *v.i.* 3, to lie down

rĕcŭpĕrātĭo, ōnis, *f*, recovery

rĕcŭpĕro, *v.t.* 1, to recover, regain

rĕcurro, curri, *v.i.* 3, to run back, return

rĕcurso, *v.i.* 1, to return

rĕcursus, ūs, *m*, return, retreat

rĕcurvo, *v.t.* 1, to bend back

rĕcurvus, a, um, *adj*, bent

rĕcūsātĭo, ōnis, *f*, refusal

rĕcūso, *v.t.* 1, to refuse

rĕcussus, a, um, *adj*, roused

rĕdargŭo, ŭi, *v.t.* 3, to contradict

reddo, dĭdi, dĭtum, *v.t.* 3, to give back, deliver, pay, produce, render, translate, recite, repeat, resemble

rĕdemptĭo, ōnis, *f*, buying back

rĕdemptor, ōris, *m*, contractor

rĕdĕo, ii, ĭtum, *v.i.* 4, to go back, return, be reduced to

rĕdĭgo, ēgi, actum, *v.t.* 3, to bring back, restore, collect, reduce to

rĕdĭmīcŭlum, i, *n*, necklace

rĕdĭmĭo, *v.t.* 4, to encircle

rĕdĭmo, ēmi, emptum, *v.t.* 3, to re-purchase, ransom, release, hire, obtain

rĕdintĕgro, *v.t.* 1, to restore

rĕdĭtus, ūs, *m*, return

rĕdŏlĕo, *v.i.t.* 2, to smell; smell of

rĕdōno, *v.t.* 1, to restore

rĕdūco, xi, ctum, *v.t.* 3, to bring back, restore

rĕductus, a, um, *adj*, remote

rĕdundantĭa, ae, *f*, redundancy

rĕdundo, *v.i.* 1, to overflow, abound in

rĕdux, dŭcis, *adj*, brought back

rĕfello, felli, *v.t.* 3, to refute

rĕfercĭo, si, tum, *v.t.* 4, to cram

rĕfĕro, ferre, rettŭli, rĕlātum, *v.t.* *irreg*, to bring back, restore, repay, report, reply, propose, record, reckon, refer, resemble; with pe-dem, to retreat

rĕfert, *v*, *impers*, it is of importance, it matters

rĕfertus, a, um, *adj*, filled

rĕfĭcĭo, fēci, fectum, *v.t.* 3, to re-make, repair, refresh

rĕfīgo, xi, xum, *v.t.* 3, to unfix

rĕfingo, *v.t.* 3, to renew

rĕflecto, xi, xum, *v.i.t.* 3, to turn back; bend back

rĕflo, *v.i.* 1, to blow back

rĕflŭo, *v.i.* 3, to flow back

rĕformīdo, (*no perf*,) *v.t.* 1, to dread, avoid

rĕfrāgor, *v.i.* 1, *dep*, to resist

rĕfrēno, *v.t.* 1, to curb, check

rĕfrĭco, ŭi, *v.t.* 1, to scratch open

rĕfrĭgĕro, *v.t.* 1, to cool

rĕfrĭgesco, frixi, *v.i.* 3, to grow cool, grow stale

rĕfringo, frēgi, fractum, *v.t.* 3, to break open, break off

rĕfŭgĭo, fūgi, *v.i.t.* 3, to run away, escape; flee from, avoid

rĕfulgĕo, si, *v.i.* 2, to shine

rĕfundo, fūdi, fūsum, *v.t.* 3, to pour out, cause to overflow

rĕfūtandus, *gerundive*, see rĕfūto

rĕfūto, *v.t.* 1, to repress, refute

rēgālis, e, *adj*, royal, splendid

rēgĭa, ae, *f*, palace, court

rēgĭfĭcus, a, um, *adj*, royal

rēgigno, *v.t.* 3, to reproduce

rēgĭmen, ĭnis, *n*, guidance

rēgīna, ae, *f*, queen

rēgĭo, ōnis, *f*, district, region, direction, boundary; ē rēgĭōne, in a straight line

rēgĭus, a, um, *adj*, *adv*, ē, royal, magnificent

regnātor, ōris, *m*, ruler

regno, *v.i.t.* 1, to reign; rule

regnum, i, *n*, kingdom, sovereignty, dominion

rĕgo, xi, ctum, *v.t.* 3, to rule, guide, direct

rĕgrĕdĭor, gressus, *v.i.* 3, *dep*, to re-turn, retreat

rĕgressus, ūs, *m*, return, retreat

rēgŭla, ae, *f*, wooden-ruler, model, pattern

rēgŭlus, i, *m*, prince

rēĭcĭo, iēci, iectum, *v.t.* 3, to throw back, repel, reject, postpone

rēiectĭo, ōnis, *f*, rejection

rēlābor, lapsus, *v.i.* 3, *dep*, to slide or sink back

rēlanguesco, gŭi, *v.i.* 3, to grow faint, relax

rēlātĭo, ōnis, *f*, proposition

rēlaxo, *v.t.* 1, to loosen, ease

rēlēgātĭo, ōnis, *f*, banishment

rēlēgo, *v.t.* 1, to send away, ban-ish

rĕlĕgo, lēgi, lectum, *v.t.* 3, to gather together, travel over again, read over again

rĕlĕvo, *v.t.* 1, to lift up, lighten, com-fort, refresh

rĕlictĭo, ōnis, *f*, abandonment

rĕlictus, a, um, *adj*, left

rĕlĭgĭo, ōnis, *f*, piety, religion,

For List of Abbreviations used, turn to pages 3, 4

religious scruple, good faith, conscientiousness, sanctity

rĕlĭgĭōsus, a, um, *adj*, devout, scrupulous, precise, sacred

rĕlĭgo, *v.t.* 1, to bind, fasten

rĕlĭno, lēvi, *v.t.* 3, to unseal

rĕlinquo, rĕlīqui, lictum, *v.t.* 3, to leave, leave behind, abandon, surrender

rĕlĭquĭae, ārum, *f. pl*, remains

rĕlĭquum, i, *n*, remainder

rĕlĭquus, a, um, *adj*, remaining

rĕlūcĕo, xi, *v.i.* 2, to shine

rĕluctor, *v.i.* 1, *dep*, to resist

rĕmănĕo, nsi, *v.i.* 2, to stay behind, endure

rĕmĕdĭum, ii, *n*, cure, relief

rĕmĕo, *v.i.* 1, to return

rĕmētĭor, mensus, *v.t.* 4, *dep*, to remeasure

rēmex, ĭgis, *m*, oarsman

rēmĭgĭum, ii, *n*, rowing, oars, rowers

rēmĭgo, *v.i.* 1, to row

rēmĭgro, *v.i.* 1, to return

rĕmĭniscor, *v.* 3, *dep*, *with genit*, to remember

rĕmiscĕo, *no perf*, mixtum, *v.t.* 2, to mix up

rĕmissĭo, ōnis, *f*, relaxation

rĕmissus, a, um, *adj*, *adv*, ē, loose, gentle, cheerful

rĕmitto, mĭsi, missum, *v.i.t.* 3, to decrease; send back, send out, yield, loosen; slacken, grant, surrender, give up; *with infin*, to cease

rĕmollesco, *v.i.* 3, to grow soft

rĕmordĕo, *no perf*, morsum, *v.t.* 2, to torment

rĕmŏror, *v.i.t.* 1, *dep*, to loiter; obstruct

rĕmōtus, a, um, *adj*, distant

rĕmŏvĕo, mōvi, mōtum, *v.t.* 2, to remove, withdraw, set aside

rĕmūgĭo, *v.i.* 4, to resound

rĕmulcum, i, *n*, tow-rope

rĕmūnĕrātĭo, ōnis, *f*, reward

rĕmūnĕror, *v.t.* 1, *dep*, to reward

rĕmurmŭro, *v.i.t.* 1, to murmur back

rēmus, i, *m*, oar

rēnascor, nātus, *v.i.* 3, *dep*, to be born again, spring up again

rēnes, um, *m. pl*, kidneys

rēnĭdĕo, *v.i.* 2, to glisten

rĕnŏvātĭo, ōnis, *f*, renewal

rĕnŏvo, *v.t.* 1, to renew, restore, refresh, repeat

rēnuntĭātĭo, ōnis, *f*, announcement

rēnuntĭo, *v.t.* 1, to report, announce, refuse, renounce

rĕnŭo, ŭi, *v.i.t.* 3, to refuse

rĕor, rātus, *v.t.* 2, *dep*, to suppose, think, believe

rĕpāgŭla, ōrum, *n.pl*, bolts, bars

rĕpărābĭlis, e, *adj*, able to be repaired

rĕpăro, *v.t.* 1, to recover, repair, restore, refresh

rĕpello, pŭli, pulsum, *v.t.* 3, to drive back, reject

rĕpendo, di, sum, *v.t.* 3, to weigh out in return, repay

rĕpens, ntis, *adj*, *adv*, ē, sudden

rĕpentīnus, a, um, *adj*, *adv*, ō, sudden, unexpected

rĕpercussus, ūs, *m*, reflection

rĕpercŭtĭo, cussi, cussum, *v.t.* 3, to drive back, reflect

rĕpĕrĭo, repperi, rĕpertum, *v.t.* 4, to find, discover

rĕpertor, ōris, *m*, discoverer

rĕpĕto, ii, ītum, *v.t.* 3, to attack again, re-visit, fetch back, resume, recollect, demand back

rĕpĕtundae, ārum, *f.pl*, (*with* res), extortion

rĕplĕo, ēvi, ētum, *v.t.* 2, to fill up, complete

rĕplētus, a, um, *adj*, full

rēpo, psi, ptum, *v.i.* 3, to creep

rĕpōno, pŏsŭi, pŏsĭtum, *v.t.* 3, to replace, preserve, put away

rĕporto, *v.t.* 1, to bring back, carry back, obtain

rĕposco, *v.t.* 3, to demand back

rĕpraesentātĭo, ōnis, *f*, representation

rĕpraesento, *v.t.* 1, to display, do immediately

rĕprĕhendo, di, sum, *v.t.* 3, to blame, rebuke, convict

rĕprĕhensĭo, ōnis, *f*, blame

rĕprĭmo, pressi, ssum, *v.t.* 3, to keep back, check, restrain

rĕpŭdĭātĭo, ōnis, *f*, refusal, renunciation

rĕpŭdĭo, *v.t.* 1, to divorce, reject, scorn

rĕpugnans, ntis, *adj*, contradictory, irreconcilable

rĕpugnantĭa, ae, *f*, opposition, inconsistency

rĕpugno, *v.i.* 1, to resist, disagree with

rĕpulsa, ae, *f*, refusal, rejection

rĕpurgo, *v.t.* 1, to clean

rĕpŭto, *v.t.* 1, to ponder, reckon

rĕquĭes, ētis, *f*, rest, relaxation

rĕquiesco, ēvi, ētum, *v.i.* 3, to rest

rĕquiro, sīvi, sītum, *v.t.* 3, to search for, enquire, need, notice to be missing

rēs, rĕi, *f*, thing, matter, affair, reality, fact, property, profit, advantage, business, affair, lawsuit; rēs nŏvae, rērum nŏvārum, *f. pl*, revolution, respublĭca, rĕipublĭcae, *f*, the State, statesmanship

rēscindo, scĭdi, ssum, *v.t.* 3, to cut down, break down, abolish

rēscisco, īvi, ītum, *v.t.* 3, to learn, ascertain

rēscrībo, psi, ptum, *v.t.* 3, to write back, reply, repay

rĕsĕco, ŭi, ctum, *v.t.* 1, to cut off, curtail

rĕsĕro, *v.t.* 1, to unlock, open

rĕservo, *v.t.* 1, to save up, keep

rĕsēs, ĭdis, *adj*, inactive

rĕsĭdĕo, sēdi, *v.i.* 2, to remain, linger, sit

rĕsĭdo, sēdi, *v.i.* 3, to settle

rĕsĭdŭus, a, um, *adj*, remaining

rĕsigno, *v.t.* 1, to unseal, open

rĕsĭlio, ŭi, *v.i.* 4, to recoil

rēsīna, ae, *f*, resin

rĕsĭpĭo, *v.t.* 3, to taste of

rĕsĭpisco, īvi, *v.i.* 3, to revive

rĕsisto, stĭti, *v.i.* 3, to stop, remain; *with dat*, to resist

rĕsolvo, solvi, sŏlūtum, *v.t.* 3, to untie, release, open, relax, annul, abolish

rĕsŏno, *v.i.t.* 1, to resound; re-echo with

rĕsŏnus, a, um, *adj*, resounding

rĕsorbĕo, *v.t.* 2, to re-swallow

respecto, *v.t.* 1, to look at, respect

respectus, ūs, *m*, looking back, retreat, refuge, respect

rēspergo, si, sum, *v.t.* 3, to besprinkle

rēspĭcio, spexi, spectum, *v.i.t.* 3, to look back, give attention; look at, regard, respect

rēspīrātio, ōnis, *f*, breathing

rēspīro, *v.i.t.* 1, to revive; breathe out, breathe

rēsplendĕo, *v.i.* 2, to shine

rēspondĕo, di, sum, *v.t.* 2, to reply, give advice, agree, correspond, answer one's hopes

rēsponso, *v.t.* 1, to reply, resist

rēsponsum, i, *n*, answer

respublica, see rēs

rēspŭo, ŭi, *v.t.* 3, to spit out, expel, reject

rēstinguo, nxi, nctum, *v.t.* 3, to quench, extinguish

restis, is, *f*, rope

rēstĭtŭo, ŭi, ūtum, *v.t.* 3, to replace, rebuild, renew, give back, restore

rēstĭtūtio, ōnis, *f*, restoration

rēsto, stĭti, *v.i.* 1, to remain

rēstrictus, a, um, *adj*, bound

rēstringo, nxi, ctum, *v.t.* 3, to bind, restrain

rĕsulto, *no perf*, *v.i.* 1, to jump back, resound

rĕsūmo, mpsi, mptum, *v.t.* 3, to resume, take back, recover

rĕsŭpīnus, a, um, *adj*, lying on one's back

rĕsurgo, surrexi, surrectum, *v.i.* 3, to rise, re-appear

rĕsurrectio, ōnis, *f*, resurrection

rĕsuscito, *v.t.* 1, to revive

rĕtardo, *v.i.t.* 1, to delay

rēte, is, *n*, net, snare

rĕtĕgo, xi, ctum, *v.t.* 3, to uncover, reveal

rĕtendo, di, tum, *v.t.* 3, to slacken

rĕtento, *v.t.* 1, to keep back

rĕtento, *v.t.* 1, to try again

rĕtexo, ŭi, xtum, *v.t.* 3, to unravel, cancel

rĕtĭcĕo, *v.i.t.* 2, to be silent; conceal

rĕtĭcŭlātus, a, um, *adj*, net-like

rĕtĭcŭlum, i, *n*, small net

rĕtīnācŭlum, i, *n*, rope, cable

rĕtĭnens, ntis, *adj*, tenacious

rĕtĭnĕo, ŭi, tentum, *v.t.* 2, to hold back, restrain, maintain

rĕtorquĕo, si, tum, *v.t.* 2, to twist back, drive back

rĕtracto, *v.t.* 1, to handle or undertake again, reconsider, refuse

rĕtrăho, xi, ctum, *v.t.* 3, to draw back, call back, remove

rĕtrĭbŭo, ŭi, ūtum, *v.t.* 3, to repay

rĕtrō, *adv*, backwards, formerly, back, behind, on the other hand

rĕtrorsum(s), *adv*, backwards

rĕtundo, tŭdi, tūsum, *v.t.* 3, to blunt, dull, weaken

rĕtūsus, a, um, *adj*, blunt, dull

rĕus, i, *m* (rĕa, ae, *f*), defendant, criminal, culprit

rĕvălesco, lŭi, *v.i.* 3, to grow well again

rĕvĕho, xi, ctum, *v.t.* 3, to bring back; *in passive*, to return

rĕvello, velli, vulsum, *v.t.* 3, to pull out, tear away

rĕvĕnio, vēni, ventum, *v.i.* 4, to return

rĕvērā, *adv*, really

rĕvĕrens, ntis, *adj*, reverent

rĕvĕrentia, ae, *f*, respect

rĕvĕrĕor, *v.t.* 2, *dep*, to revere

rĕverto, ti, v.i. 3, to return

rĕvertor, versus, v.i. 3, dep, to return

rĕvincendus, gerundive, see revinco

rĕvincio, nxi, nctum, v.t. 4, to bind, fasten

rĕvinco, vīci, victum, v.t. 3, to conquer, convict

rĕviresco, rŭi, v.i. 3, to grow green again

rĕviso, v.i.t. 3, to revisit

rĕvīvisco, vixi, v.i. 3, to revive

rĕvŏcābĭlis, e, adj, able to be recalled

rĕvŏcāmen, inis, n, recall

rĕvŏcātĭo, ōnis, f, recalling

rĕvŏco, v.t. 1, to recall, restrain, refer

rĕvŏlo, v.i. 1, to fly back

rĕvolvo, volvi, vŏlūtum, v.t. 3, to unroll, repeat

rĕvŏmo, ŭi, v.t. 3, to vomit up

rex, rēgis, m, king

rhēda, ae, f, carriage

rhētor, ōris, m, teacher of oratory

rhētŏrica, ae, f, rhetoric

rhētŏricus, a, um, adj, rhetorical

rhīnŏcĕros, ōtis, m, rhinoceros

rhombus, i, m, magic circle, turbot

rhonchus, i, m, snore, sneer

rīca, ae, f, veil

rīcīnĭum, ii, n, small veil

rictus, ūs, m, gaping mouth

rīdĕo, si, sum, v.i.t. 2, to laugh, smile; laugh at, ridicule

rīdĭcŭlum, i, n, joke

rīdĭcŭlus, a, um, adj, adv, ē, amusing, absurd

rĭgĕo, v.i. 2, to be stiff

rĭgesco, gŭi, v.i. 3, to stiffen

rĭgĭdus, a, um, adj, stiff, stern

rĭgo, v.t. 1, to wet, water

rĭgor, ōris, m, stiffness, hardness, chilliness, severity

rĭgŭus, a, um, adj, irrigating

rīma, ae, f, crack, chink

rīmor, v.t. 1, dep, to tear up, explore, examine

rīmōsus, a, um, adj, leaky

rīpa, ae, f, river bank

rīsus, ūs, m, laughter

rītĕ, adv, rightly, properly

rītus, ūs, m, religious ceremony, custom, way; rītu, with genit, in the manner of

rīvālis, is, m, rival

rīvŭlus, i, m, brook

rīvus, i, m, brook, stream

rixa, ae, f, quarrel

rixor, v.i. 1, dep, to quarrel

rōbĭgĭnōsus, a, um, adj, rusty

rōbīgo, inis, f, rust, mould

rōbŏro, v.t. 1, to strengthen

rōbur, ōris, n, oak, strength, power, vigour, force

rōbustus, a, um, adj, oaken, firm, strong, robust

rōdo, si, sum, v.t. 3, to gnaw, corrode, slander

rŏgātĭo, ōnis, f, proposed law or bill, request

rŏgātor, ōris, m, polling-clerk

rŏgo, v.t. 1, to ask; with legem, to propose (law), beg

rŏgus, i, m, funeral pile

rōro, v.i.t. 1, to drop, drip, trickle; wet, besprinkle

rōs, rōris, m, dew, moisture

rōsa, ae, f, rose

rōsārĭum, ii, n, rose-garden

rōscĭdus, a, um, adj, dewy

rōsētum, i, n, rose-bed

rōsĕus, a, um, adj, of roses, rose-coloured

rostra, ōrum, n.pl, speaker's platform

rostrātus, a, um, adj, with beaks

rostrum, i, n, beak, snout

rŏta, ae, f, wheel, chariot

rŏto, v.i.t. 1, to revolve; swing round, whirl around

rŏtundĭtas, ātis, f, rotundity

rŏtundo, v.t. 1, to round off

rŏtundus, a, um, adj, round, polished

rŭbĕfăcio, fēci, factum, v.t. 3, to redden

rŭbens, ntis, adj, red

rŭbĕo, v.i. 2, to be red, blush

rŭber, bra, brum, adj, red

rŭbesco, bŭi, v.i. 3, to grow red

rŭbēta, ae, f, toad

rŭbēta, ōrum, n.pl, brambles

rŭbicundus, a, um, adj, red

rŭbĭgo . . . see rōbĭgo . . .

rŭbor, ōris, m, redness, blush, bashfulness

rŭbrīca, ae, f, red-chalk

rŭbus, i, m, bramble-bush

ructo, v.i.t. 1, to belch

ructor, v. 1, dep, to belch

ructus, ūs, m, belching

rŭdens, ntis, m, rope, rigging

rŭdīmentum, i, n, first try

rŭdis, e, adj, rough, raw, wild, awkward, inexperienced

rŭdis, is, f, stick, wooden sword

rŭdo, ivi, ītum, v.i. 3, to bellow

rŭdus, ĕris, n, broken stones, rubbish

rūfus, a, um, adj, red

rūga, ae, f, wrinkle

rūgo, v.i.t. 1, to wrinkle

rūgōsus, a, um, adj, shrivelled

rŭīna, ae, f, downfall, ruin
rŭīnōsus, a, um, adj, in ruins
rūmĭno, v.t. 1, to chew over
rūmor, ōris, m, rumour, general opinion, reputation
rumpo, rūpī, ruptum, v.t. 3, to break, burst, destroy, interrupt
runcĭna, ae, f, plane
runcĭno, v.t. 1, to plane
runco, v.t. 1, to weed
rŭo, ŭi, ŭtum, v.i.t. 3, to fall, rush, hurry; hurl down, throw up
rūpes, is, f, rock
rūrĭcŏla, ae, adj, rural
rursus (rursum), adv, again, on the contrary, backwards
rūs, rūris, n, countryside
rustĭcānus, a, um, adj, rustic
rustĭcĭtas, ātis, f, behaviour of country-people
rustĭcor, v.i. 1, dep, to live in the country
rustĭcus, a, um, adj, rural
rustĭcus, i, m, countryman
rūta, ae, f, bitter herb, rue
rŭtĭlo, v.i. 1, to be red
rŭtĭlus, a, um, adj, red

S

sabbăta, ōrum, n.pl, sabbath
săbīnum, i, n, Sabine wine
săbŭlum, i, n, gravel
săburra, ae, f, sand, ballast
sacchăron, i, n, sugar
saccŭlus, i, m, small bag
saccus, i, m, bag
săcellum, i, n, chapel
săcer, cra, crum, adj, sacred, venerable, accursed
săcerdos, dōtis, c, priest
săcerdōtālis, e, adj, priestly
săcerdōtium, ii, n, priesthood
săcra, ōrum, n.pl, worship, religion
săcrāmentum, i, n, oath
săcrārium, ii, n, sanctuary
săcrātus, a, um, adj, sacred
săcrĭfĭcĭum, ii, n, sacrifice
săcrĭfĭco, v.i.t. 1, to sacrifice
săcrĭfĭcus, a, um, adj, sacrificial
săcrĭlĕgus, a, um, adj, temple-robbing, sacrilegious
săcro, v.t. 1, to consecrate, condemn, doom
săcrōsanctus, a, um, adj, sacred, inviolable
săcrum, i, n, sacred thing, religious act, religion
saecŭlum, i, n, age, generation, century

saepe, adv, often
saepes, is, f, hedge, fence
saepīmentum, i, n, fencing
saepĭo, psi, ptum, v.t. 4, to fence in, surround
saeptum, i, n, fence, pen
saeta, ae, f, hair, bristle
saetĭger, ĕra, ĕrum, adj, bristly
saetōsus, a, um, adj, bristly
saevĭo, v.i. 4, to rage
saevĭtĭa, ae, f, savageness
saevus, a, um, adj, savage, violent, furious, cruel
săga, ae, f, fortune-teller
săgācĭtas, ātis, f, shrewdness
săgax, ācis, adj, adv, ĭter, keen, shrewd, acute
săgīno, v.t. 1, to fatten
săgitta, ae, f, arrow
săgittārĭus, ii, m, archer
săgŭlum, i, n, military cloak
săgum, i, n, military cloak
sal, sălis, m, salt, sea, wit, sarcasm
sălāco, ōnis, m, braggart
sălārĭum, ii, n, pension, salary (salt money)
sălax, ācis, adj, lecherous
sălĕbra, ae, f, roughness
sălĭāris, e, adj, splendid
sălictum, i, n, willow-grove
sălignus, a, um, adj, of willow
Sălii, ōrum, m. pl, priests of Mars
sălīnae, ārum, f. pl, salt-works
sălīnum, i, n, salt-cellar
sălĭo, ĭi, saltum, v.i. 4, to jump
sălīva, ae, f, saliva
sălix, ĭcis, f, willow-tree
salmo, ōnis, m, salmon
salsāmentum, i, n, brine
salsus, a, um, adj, adv, ē, salted, witty
saltātĭo, ōnis, f, dancing
saltātor, ōris, m, dancer
saltātrix, īcis, f, dancing-girl
saltātus, ūs, m, dancing
saltem, adv, at least
salto, v.i.t. 1, to dance
saltus, ūs, m, leap, bound
saltus, ūs, m, woodland, mountain-pass
sălūbris, e, adj, adv, ĭter, health-giving, beneficial
sălūbrĭtas, ātis, f, wholesomeness
sălum, i, n, sea
sălūs, ūtis, f, welfare, safety
sălūtāris, e, adj, adv, ĭter, beneficial, wholesome
sălūtātĭo, ōnis, f, greeting
sălūtātor, ōris, m, visitor
sălūtĭfer, ĕra, ĕrum, adj, healing

For List of Abbreviations used, turn to pages 3, 4

sălūto, *v.t.* 1, to greet

salvē, salvēte, salvēto, *v, imperative* how are you? welcome!

salvia, ae, *f,* sage (herb)

salvus, a, um, *adj,* safe, well; *with noun in abl,* e.g. salvā lege, without violating the law

sambūcus, i, *f,* elder-tree

sānābilis, e, *adj,* curable

sānātio, ōnis, *f,* cure

sancio, xi, ctum, *v.t.* 4, to appoint, establish, ratify

sanctificātio, ōnis, *f,* sanctification

sanctio, ōnis, *f,* establishing

sanctitas, ātis, *f,* sacredness, purity

sanctus, a, um, *adj, adv,* ē, sacred, inviolable, good

sandix, īcis, *f,* scarlet

sānē, *adv,* certainly, very

sanguinārius, a, um, *adj,* bloody, blood-thirsty

sanguineus, a, um, *adj,* bloody

sanguinōlentus, a, um, *adj,* bloody

sanguis, inis, *m,* blood, bloodshed, race, stock

sānies, em, e, *f,* bad blood

sānitas, ātis, *f,* health, good sense, discretion

sannio, ōnis, *m,* buffoon

sāno, *v.t.* 1, to cure, restore

sānus, a, um, *adj,* healthy, rational, discreet

sāpidus, a, um, *adj,* tasty

sāpiens, ntis, *adj, adv,* nter, wise, sensible

sāpiens, ntis, *m,* wise man

sāpientia, ae, *f,* discretion, philosophy

sāpio, īvi, *v.i.t.* 3, to be wise, discreet; to taste of, savour of

sāpo, ōnis, *m,* soap

sāpor, ōris, *m,* flavour, taste

sapphīrus, i, *f,* sapphire

sarcina, ae, *f,* pack, load

sarcio, si, tum, *v.t.* 4, to patch

sarcŏphăgus, i, *m,* sarcophagus

sarcŭlum, i, *n,* light hoe

sarda, ae, *f,* sardine

sarīsa, ae, *f,* Macedonian lance

sarmentum, i, *n,* brushwood

sarrācum, i, *n,* cart

sarrānus, a, um, *adj,* Tyrian

sarrio, *v.t.* 4, to hoe

sartāgo, inis, *f,* frying-pan

sartus, a, um, *adj,* repaired

sāta, ōrum, *n.pl,* crops

sătelles, itis, *c,* attendant; *in pl,* escort

sătias, ātis, *f,* abundance, disgust

sătiĕtas, ātis, *f,* abundance, disgust

sătio, *v.t.* 1, to satisfy, glut

sătio, ōnis, *f,* sowing

sătiricus, a, um, *adj,* satirical

sătis (săt), *adv, or indecl. adj,* enough

sătisdātio, ōnis, *f,* giving bail

sătisfăcio, fēci, factum, *v.t.* 3, to satisfy, make amends

sătisfactio, ōnis, *f,* excuse, reparation

sătius, *comp. adv,* better

sător, ōris, *m,* sower, creator

sătrāpes, is, *m,* viceroy, satrap

sătur, ŭra, ŭrum, *adj,* full, fertile

sătūra, ae, *f,* food made of various ingredients, satire

Săturnālia, ōrum, *n.pl,* festival in honour of Saturn (Dec. 17th)

sătŭro, *v.t.* 1, to fill, glut

sătus, ūs, *m,* planting

sătus, a, um, *adj,* sprung from

sătÿrus, i, *m,* forest-god

saucio, *v.t.* 1, to wound

saucius, a, um, *adj,* wounded

saxĕus, a, um, *adj,* rocky

saxĭficus, a, um, *adj,* petrifying

saxōsus, a, um, *adj,* rocky

saxum, i, *n,* rock

scăbellum, i, *n,* stool

scăber, bra, brum, *adj,* rough, scabby

scăbies, em, e, *f,* roughness, scab, itch

scăbo, scăbi, *v.t.* 3, to scratch

scaena, ae, *f,* stage, scene

scaenicus, a, um, *adj,* theatrical

scaenicus, i, *m,* actor

scāla, ae, *f,* ladder, stairs

scalmus, i, *m,* rowlock

scalpo, psi, ptum, *v.t.* 3, to carve

scalpellum, i, *n,* lancet

scalprum, i, *n,* chisel

scalptor, ōris, *m,* engraver

scalptūra, ae, *f,* engraving

scamnum, i, *n,* bench

scando, *v.i.t.* 3, to rise; climb

scăpha, ae, *f,* small boat

scăpŭlae, ārum, *f. pl,* shoulder-blades

scărăbaeus, i, *m,* beetle

scărus, i, *m,* sea-fish (scar)

scătĕbra, ae, *f,* spring water

scătĕo, *v.i.* 2, to bubble, swarm with

scaurus, a, um, *adj,* with swollen ankles

scĕlĕrātus, a, um, *adj,* wicked

scĕlĕro, *v.t.* 1, to contaminate

scĕlestus, a, um, *adj,* wicked

scĕlus, ĕris, *n,* crime, scoundrel

scēna, see scaena

scēnicus, see scaenicus

sceptrum, i, *n,* sceptre; *in pl,* dominion, authority

schĕda, ae, *f,* sheet of paper

schŏla, ae, *f,* lecture, school

sciens, ntis, *adj, adv,* nter, knowing, (*i.e.* purposely), expert in

scientĭa, ae, *f,* knowledge

scīlicet, *adv,* certainly, of course, namely

scilla, ae, *f,* sea-onion, prawn

scindo, scĭdi, scissum, *v.t.* 3, to split

scintilla, ae, *f,* spark

scintillans, ntis, *adj,* sparkling

scintillo, *v.i.* 1, to sparkle

scĭo, *v.t.* 4, to know, understand

scīpĭo, ōnis, *m,* staff

scirpĕus, a, um, *adj,* of rushes

sciscĭtor, *v.t.* 1, *dep,* to enquire

scisco, scīvi, scītum, *v.t.* 3, to approve, appoint, decree

scissūra, ae, *f,* tearing, rending

scītor, *v.t.* 1, *dep,* to inquire

scītum, i, *n,* decree, statute

scītus, a, um, *adj, adv,* ē, shrewd, sensible, witty

sciūrus, i, *m,* squirrel

scŏbīna, ae, *f,* rasp, file

scŏbis, is, *f,* sawdust

scomber, bri, *m,* mackerel

scōpae, ārum, *f.pl,* broom

scōpŭlōsus, a, um, *adj,* rocky

scŏpŭlus, i, *m,* rock, cliff

scŏpus, i, *m,* target

scorpĭo, ōnis, *m,* scorpion, missile-launcher

scortum, i, *n,* prostitute

scrība, ae, *m,* clerk

scrībo, psi, ptum, *v.t.* 3, to write, draw, compose, describe, enroll

scrīnĭum, ii, *n,* letter-case

scriptĭo, ōnis, *f,* writing

scriptor, ōris, *m,* secretary, author

scriptum, i, *n,* book, writing

scriptūra, ae, *f,* composition

scriptus, a, um, *adj,* written

scrōbis, is, *m,* ditch

scrūpēus, a, um, *adj,* rugged

scrūpŭlus, i, *m,* anxiety, embarrassment

scrūta, ōrum, *n.pl,* frippery

scrūtātĭo, ōnis, *f,* scrutiny

scrūtor, *v.t.* 1, *dep,* to examine

sculpo, psi, ptum, *v.t.* 3, to carve

sculpōnĕae, ārum, *f. pl,* clogs

sculptor, ōris, *m,* sculptor

sculptūra, ae, *f,* sculpture

scurra, ae, *m,* clown, dandy

scurrīlis, e, *adj,* jeering

scūtātus, a, um, *adj,* armed with oblong shields

scŭtella, ae, *f,* salver

scŭtĭca, ae, *f,* whip

scŭtŭla, ae, *f,* wooden roller

scūtum, i, *n,* oblong shield

scўphus, i, *m,* goblet

sē, *acc. or abl. of reflexive pron,* herself, itself etc.

sēbum, i, *n,* suet

sēcāle, is, *n,* rye

sēcēdo, cessi, cessum, *v.i.* 3, to go away, withdraw

sēcerno, crēvi, crētum, *v.t.* 3, to separate, part

sēcessĭo, ōnis, *f,* withdrawal

sēcessus, ūs, *m,* solitude

sēcĭus (sēquĭus), *comp. adv,* differently

sēclūdo, si, sum, *v.t.* 3, to separate, shut off

sēclūsus, a, um, *adj,* remote

sēco, ŭi, ctum, *v.t.* 1, to cut, wound, separate

sēcrētum, i, *n,* solitude

sēcrētus, a, um, *adj, adv,* ō, separate, remote, secret

secta, ae, *f,* way, method, sect

sectātor, ōris, *m,* follower

sectĭo, ōnis, *f,* sale by auction

sector, ōris, *m,* cutthroat, bidder at an auction

sector, *v.t.* 1, *dep,* to pursue

sectūra, ae, *f,* mine

sēcul . . . see saecul

sēcundārĭus, a, um, *adj,* secondary, second-rate

sēcundo, *v.t.* 1, to favour

sēcundum, *prep, with acc,* after, behind, by, next to, according to

sēcundus, a, um, *adj,* following, second, favourable

sēcūriger, ĕra, ĕrum, *adj,* armed with a battle-axe

sēcūris, is, *f,* axe, hatchet

sēcūritas, ātis, *f,* freedom from care

sēcūrus, a, um, *adj,* carefree, tranquil

sēcus, *adv,* differently

sĕd, *conj,* but

sēdātĭo, ōnis, *f,* a calming

sēdātus, a, um, *adj,* calm

sēdĕcim, *indecl. adj,* sixteen

sēdentārĭus, a, um, *adj,* sedentary

sēdĕo, sēdi, sessum, *v.i.* 2, to sit, remain, settle, be settled

sēdes, is, *f,* seat, residence, temple, bottom, foundation

sēdīle, is, *n,* seat

sēdītĭo, ōnis, *f,* mutiny

sēdītĭōsus, a, um, *adj, adv,* ē, mutinous, rebellious

sēdo, *v.t.* 1, to calm, check

sēdūco, xi, ctum, *v.t.* 3, to lead aside, separate

sēdŭlĭtas, ātis, *f*, zeal

sēdŭlō, *adv*, diligently, on purpose

sēdŭlus, a, um, *adj*, industrious

sēges, ĕtis, *f*, cornfield, crop

segmenta, ōrum, *n.pl*, trimmings

segmentum, i, *n*, piece

segnis, e, *adj*, *adv*, **ĭter** lazy

segnĭtia, ae, *f*, inactivity, slowness

segnĭties, em, e, *f*, inactivity, slowness

sēgrēgo, *v.t.* 1, to separate

sēiungo, nxi, nctum, *v.t.* 3, to separate, divide

sēlĭgo, lēgi, lectum, *v.t.* 3, to select

sella, ae, *f*, seat, chair

sēmĕl, *adv*, once

sēmen, ĭnis, *n*, seed, cutting, graft, offspring, instigator

sēmentis, is, *f*, sowing

sēmestris, e, *adj*, half-yearly

sēmēsus, a, um, *adj*, half-eaten

sēmĭănĭmis, e, *adj*, half-dead

sēmĭdĕus, a, um, *adj*, half-divine

sēmĭfer, ēra, ērum, *adj*, half-man, half-beast

sēmĭhŏmo, ĭnis, *m*, half-human

sēmĭhōra, ae, *f*, half-hour

sēmĭnārĭum, ii, *n*, nursery

sēmĭnātor, ōris, *m*, author

sēmĭnēcis, is, *adj*, half-dead

sēmĭno, *v.t.* 1, to produce

sēmĭplēnus, a, um, *adj*, half-full

sēmĭrūtus, a, um, *adj*, half-ruined

sēmis, issis, *m*, half a farthing

sēmĭsomnus, a, um, *adj*, half-asleep

sēmĭta, ae, *f*, footpath

sēmĭustus, a, um, *adj*, half-burned

sēmĭvir, vĭri, *m*, half-man; *as adj*, effeminate

sēmĭvīvus, a, um, *adj*, half-alive

sēmōtus, a, um, *adj*, remote

sēmŏvĕo, mōvi, mōtum, *v.t.* 2, to remove, separate

semper, *adv*, always

sempĭternus, a, um, *adj*, everlasting

sēmustŭlo, *v.t.* 1, to half burn

sēnātor, ōris, *m*, senator

sēnātōrĭus, a, um, *adj*, senatorial

sēnātus, ūs, *m*, the Senate

sēnecta, ae, *f*, old age

sēnectus, ūtis, *f*, old age

sēnesco, nŭi, *v.i.* 3, to grow old

sēnex, sēnis, *m*, old man

sēni, ae, a, *pl. adj*, six each

sēnŭlis, e, *adj*, old (of people)

sēnĭor, ōris, *c*, elderly person

sēnĭum, ii, *n*, old age, decay, trouble

sensĭlis, e, *adj*, sensitive

sensim, *adv*, slowly, gently

sensus, ūs, *m*, perception, disposition, good taste, sense, understanding, meaning

sent>entĭa, ae, *f*, opinion, decision, meaning, sentence, axiom; **ex mēā sententĭā**, to my liking

sententĭōsus, a, um, *adj*, sententious

sentīna, ae, *f*, bilge-water, dregs, ship's hold

sentĭo, sī, sum, *v.t.* 4, to feel, perceive, endure, suppose

sentis, is, *m*, thorn, bramble

sentus, a, um, *adj*, rough

sēorsum, *adv*, separately

sēpărātim, *adv*, separately

sēpărātĭo, ōnis, *f*, separation

sēpărātus, a, um, *adj*, separate

sēpăro, *v.t.* 1, to separate

sēpĕlĭo, līvi, pultum, *v.t.* 4, to bury, overwhelm

sēpĭa, ae, *f*, cuttle-fish

sēpĭo, see saepĭo

sēpōno, pōsŭi, pōsĭtum, *v.t.* 3, to put aside, select

septem, *indecl. adj*, seven

September (mensis), September

septemgēmĭnus, a, um, *adj*, seven-fold

septemplex, ĭcis, *adj*, seven-fold

septendĕcim, *indecl. adj*, seventeen

septēni, ae, a, *pl. adj*, seven each

septentrĭōnālis, e, *adj*, northern

septentrĭōnes, um, *m. pl*, the Great Bear, the North

septĭes, *adv*, seven times

septĭmus, a, um, *adj*, seventh

septingenti, ae, a, *pl. adj*, seven hundred

septŭāgēsĭmus, a, um, *adj*, seventieth

septŭāginta, *indecl. adj*, seventy

septum, see saeptum

sēpulcrum, i, *n*, grave, tomb

sēpultūra, ae, *f*, burial

sēquax, ācis, *adj*, pursuing

sēquens, ntis, *adj*, following

sēquester, tris, *m*, agent

sēquor, secūtus, *v.i.t.* 3, *dep*, to follow, attend, pursue

sēra, ae, *f*, bolt, bar

sērēnĭtas, ātis, *f*, fair weather

sērēno, *v.t.* 1, to brighten

sērēnum, i, *n*, fair weather

sērēnus, a, um, *adj*, clear, fair, cheerful, glad

sērĭa, ōrum, *n.pl*, serious matters

sērĭcus, a, um, *adj*, silken

sēries, em, e, *f*, row, series

sērĭus, a, um, *adj*, serious

sermo, ōnis, *m*, talk, conversation, common talk

sĕro, sēvi, sătum, *v.t.* 3, to sow, plant, cause

sĕro, ŭi, sertum, *v.t.* 3, to plait, join, connect, compose

sērŏ, *adv*, late

serpens, ntis, *f*, snake

serpo, psi, ptum, *v.i.* 3, to crawl

serpyllum, i, *n*, thyme

serra, ae, *f*, saw

serrŭla, ae, *f*, small saw

serta, ōrum, *n.pl*, garlands

sĕrum, i, *n*, whey

sērus, a, um, *adj*, late

serva, ae, *f*, maid-servant

servātor, ōris, *m*, saviour

servilis, e, *adj*, *adv*, ĭter, of a slave, servile

servio, *v.i.* 4, to be a servant, to be of use to

servĭtium, ii, *n*, slavery, slaves

servĭtus, ūtis, *f*, slavery, slaves

servo, *v.t.* 1, to save, protect, preserve, keep, keep watch

servus, a, um, *adj*, servile

servus, i, *m*, slave, servant

sescēni, ae, a, *pl. adj*, six hundred each

sescenti, ae, a, *pl. adj*, six hundred

sescenties, *adv*, six hundred times

sesquipĕdālis, e, *adj*, one foot and a half long

sessio, ōnis, *f*, sitting, session

sestertium, 1,000 sestertii

sestertius, ii, *m*, small silver coin (worth about 2¼d.)

sēt . . . see saet. . . .

seu, *conj*, whether, or

sēvēritas, ātis, *f*, sternness

sēvērus, a, um, *adj*, *adv*, ē, stern, serious, harsh, gloomy

sēvōco, *v.t.* 1, to call aside

sex, *indecl adj*, six

sexāgēnārius, i, *m*, sexagenarian

sexāgēni, ae, a, *pl. adj*, sixty each

sexāgēsimus, a, um, *adj*, sixtieth

sexāgies, *adv*, sixty times

sexāginta, *indecl. adj*, sixty

sexennium, ii, *n*, six years

sextans, ntis, *m*, a sixth part

sextārius, ii, *m*, a pint

Sextilis, (mensis), August

sextus, a, um, *adj*, sixth

sexus, ūs, *m*, sex

si, *conj*, if

sibi, *dat. of reflexive pron*, to himself, herself, itself, etc.

sībilo, *v.i.t.* 1, to hiss; hiss at

sībilus, i, *m*, hissing

sĭbylla, ae, *f*, prophetess

sīc, *adv*, so, in this way

sĭca, ae, *f*, dagger

sĭcārius, ii, *m*, assassin

siccitas, ātis, *f*, dryness, firmness

sicco, *v.t.* 1, to dry up, drain

siccum, i, *n*, dry land

siccus, a, um, *adj*, dry, firm, tough, thirsty, sober

sīcŭbi, *adv*, if anywhere

sīcut, (sīcŭti), *adv*, just as

sīdĕrĕus, a, um, *adj*, starry

sīdo, di, *v.i.* 3, to sit down, settle, sink

sīdus, ĕris, *n*, star, sky, constellation, season, weather

sigilla, ōrum, *n. pl*, little figures or images

sĭgillātus, a, um, *adj*, figured

signifer, ĕri, *m*, standard-bearer

significātio, ōnis, *f*, sign, mark

signĭfico, *v.t.* 1, to show, notify

significans, antis, *adj*, significant

signo, *v.t.* 1, to mark out, seal, indicate

signum, i, *n*, mark, sign, military standard, watchword, statue, constellation, symptom

silens, ntis, *adj*, still, quiet

silentium, ii, *n*, stillness, quietness

sĭlĕo, *v.i.t.* 2, to be silent; to keep quiet about

silesco, *v.i.* 3, to grow quiet

sĭlex, icis, *m*, flint-stone

sīlus, a, um, *adj*, snub-nosed

silva, ae, *f*, wood, forest, grove, abundance

silvestria, ium, *n. pl*, woodlands

silvestris, e, *adj*, woody, rural

silvĭcŏla, ae, *adj*, living in woods

sīmia, ae, *f*, ape

similis, e, *adj*, *adv*, ĭter, similar, like

sĭmĭlĭtūdo, ĭnis, *f*, resemblance

sīmius, ii, *m*, ape

simplex, icis, *adj*, *adv*, ĭter, unmixed, simple, frank

simplĭcĭtas, ātis, *f*, honesty

simul, *adv*, at once, together, at the same time, as soon as

sĭmŭlac, *conj*, as soon as

sĭmŭlatque, *conj*. as soon as

sĭmŭlācrum, i, *n*, portrait, statue, phantom

sĭmŭlātio, ōnis, *f*, pretence

sĭmŭlātor, ōris, *m*, pretender

sĭmŭlātus, a, um, *adj*, feigned

sĭmŭlo, *v.t.* 1, to imitate, pretend

sĭmultas, ātis, *f*, animosity

sīmus, a, um, *adj*, snub-nosed

sĭn, *conj*, but if

sināpi, is, *n*, mustard

sincēritas, ātis, *f*, cleanness, purity, entirety, sincerity

sincērus, a, um, *adj*, *adv*, ē, clean, pure, genuine, entire, sincere

For List of Abbreviations used, turn to pages 3, 4

sĭnĕ, *prep. with abl,* without

singillātim, *adv,* one by one

singŭlāris, e, *adj,* single, solitary, unique, remarkable

singŭlātim, see singillātim

singŭli, ae, a, *pl. adj,* one each

singultim, *adv,* with sobs

singultĭo, *v.i.* 4, to hiccup

singultŏ, (*no perf.*), *v.i.* 1, to sob

singultus, ūs, *m,* sobbing

sĭnister, tra, trum, *adj,* left, awkward, wrong, unlucky, lucky

sĭnistra, ae, *f,* left hand

sĭnistrorsus, *adv,* to the left

sĭnŏ, sĭvi, sĭtum, *v.t.* 3, to allow

sĭnum, i, *n,* drinking-cup

sĭnŭŏ, *v.t.* 1, to bend, curve

sĭnŭōsus, a, um, *adj,* curved

sĭnus, ūs, *m,* curve, fold, bosom, lap, hiding-place, bay

sīpho, ōnis, *m,* siphon, syringe

sĭquandŏ, *adv,* if ever

sĭquĭdem, *adv,* if indeed

sĭquis, *pron,* if any

sīrēn, ēnis, *f,* siren

sisto, stiti, stātum, *v.i.t.* 3, to stand still, resist, hold out; put, place, bring, check, establish

sīstrum, i, *n,* rattle

sĭtĭens, ntis, *adj, adv,* nter, thirsty

sĭtĭo, *v.i.t.* 4, to thirst; long for

sĭtis, is, *f,* thirst, drought

sĭtŭla, ae, *f,* bucket

sĭtus, a, um, *adj,* situated

sĭtus, ūs, *m,* position, site, rust, mould, inactivity

sīve, *conj,* whether, or

smăragdus, i, *c,* emerald

sŏbŏles, is, *f,* sprout, twig, offspring

sōbrĭĕtas, ātis, *f,* sobriety, temperance

sōbrīnus, i, *m,* cousin

sōbrĭus, a, um, *adj, adv,* ē, sober, moderate, sensible

soccus, i, *m,* slipper

sŏcer, ĕri, *m,* father-in-law

sŏcĭālis, e, *adj,* allied

sŏcĭĕtas, ātis, *f,* fellowship, partnership, alliance

sŏcĭo, *v.t.* 1, to unite

sŏcĭus, ii, *m,* companion, ally

sŏcĭus, a, um, *adj,* allied

sōcordĭa, ae, *f,* laziness, folly

sōcors, cordis, *adj,* lazy, careless, stupid

socrus, ūs, *f,* mother-in-law

sŏdālĭcĭum, ii, *n,* secret society

sŏdālis, is, *c,* companion

sŏdālĭtas, ātis, *f,* friendship

sōdes, if you wish

sōl, sōlis, *m,* sun, sunshine

sōlācĭum, ii, *n,* comfort, solace

sōlāmen, ĭnis, *n,* consolation

sōlārĭum, ii, *n,* sundial

sōlātĭum, see sōlācĭum

soldūrii, ōrum, *m. pl,* retainers of a chieftain

sōlĕa, ae, *f,* sandal, sole (fish)

sōlĕātus, a, um, *adj,* wearing sandals

sōlĕŏ, sōlĭtus, *v.i.* 2, *semi-dep,* to be accustomed

sōlĭdĭtas, ātis, *f,* solidity

sōlĭdo, *v.t.* 1, to strengthen

sōlĭdum, i, *n,* a solid, solidity

sōlĭdus, a, um, *adj,* compact, complete, genuine, real

sōlĭtārĭus, a, um, *adj,* alone

sōlĭtūdo, ĭnis, *f,* loneliness, desert

sōlĭtus, a, um, *adj,* usual

sōlĭum, ii, *n,* seat, throne

sollemnis, e, *adj,* established, appointed, usual, religious

sollemne, is, *n,* religious ceremony, sacrifice

sollers, tis, *adj,* skilled

sollertĭa, ae, *f,* skill, ingenuity

sollĭcĭtātĭo, ōnis, *f,* instigation

sollĭcĭto, *v.t.* 1, to stir up, molest, instigate

sollĭcĭtūdo, ĭnis, *f,* anxiety

sollĭcĭtus, a, um, *adj,* troubled

sōlor, *v.t.* 1, *dep,* to comfort, relieve

solstĭtĭālis, e, *adj,* of summer

solstĭtĭum, ii, *n,* summer-time

sōlum, i, *n,* bottom, base, floor, sole, soil, ground, country, place

sōlum, *adv,* only

sōlus, a, um, *adj,* alone, only, lonely, deserted

sōlūtĭo, ōnis, *f,* unloosing, payment, explanation

sōlūtus, a, um, *adj, adv,* ē, free, loose, independent

solvendum, see solvo

solvo, solvi, sōlūtum, *v.t.* 3, to set free, dissolve, release, open up, pay, perform, fulfil, acquit; with ancŏram, to sail

somnĭcŭlōsus, a, um, *adj,* drowzy

somnĭfer, ĕra, ĕrum, *adj,* sleep-bringing

somnĭfĭcus, a, um, *adj,* sleep-bringing

somnĭo, *v.t.* 1, to dream

somnĭum, ii, *n,* dream

somnus, i, *m,* sleep

sŏnĭpēs, pĕdis, *adj*, noisy-footed

sŏnĭtus, ūs, *m*, noise, sound

sŏno, ŭi, ĭtum, *v.i.t.* 1, to resound; call out, utter

sŏnor, ōris, *m*, noise, sound

sŏnōrus, a, um, *adj*, resounding

sons, ntis, *adj*, guilty

sŏnus, i, *m*, noise, sound

sŏphistes, ae, *m*, philosopher

sōpĭo, *v.t.* 4, to lull to sleep

sŏpor, ōris, *m*, sleep

sŏpōrĭfer, ĕra, ĕrum, *adj*, sleep-bringing

sŏpōro, *v.t.* 1, to heat, stupefy

sŏpōrus, a, um, *adj*, sleep-bringing

sorbĕo, *v.t.* 2, to suck in

sordĕo, *v.i.* 2, to be dirty, to be despised

sordes, is, *f*, dirt, mourning-dress, meanness

sordĭdātus, a, um, *adj*, shabbily dressed (in mourning)

sordĭdus, a, um, *adj*, *adv*, ē, dirty, despicable, mean

sŏror, ōris, *f*, sister

sŏrōrius, a, um, *adj*, of a sister

sors, tis, *f*, chance, lot, drawing of lots, prophesy, fortune, share, destiny

sortĭor, *v.i.t.* 4, *dep*, to draw lots; to appoint by lot, obtain by lot, choose

sortītĭo, ōnis, *f*, drawing of lots

sortītō, *adv*, by lot

sortītus, a, um, *adj*, drawn by lot

sospes, ĭtis, *adj*, safe, lucky

spādix, īcis, *adj*, nut-brown

spargo, si, sum, *v.t.* 3, to sprinkle, scatter, spread

spărus, i, *m*, hunting-spear

spasmus, i, *m*, spasm

spătĭor, *v.i.* 1, *dep*, to walk about

spătĭōsus, a, um, *adj*, spacious

spătĭum, ii, *n*, space, room, distance, walk, track, interval

spĕcĭes, ēi, *f*, sight, view, shape, appearance, pretence, display, beauty

spĕcĭmen, inis, *n*, mark, sign, pattern

spĕcĭōsus, a, um, *adj*, handsome, plausible

spectābĭlis, e, *adj*, visible, remarkable

spectācŭlum, i, *n*, show, spectacle

spectātĭo, ōnis, *f*, sight

spectātor, ōris, *m*, onlooker

spectātus, a, um, *adj*, tested, respected

specto, *v.t.* 1, to watch, face, examine, consider, refer

spectrum, i, *n*, image

spēcŭla, ae, *f*, look-out point

spĕcŭla, ae, *f*, slight hope

spĕcŭlātor, ōris, *m*, spy, scout

spĕcŭlor, *v.t.* 1, *dep*, to watch, observe, explore

spĕcŭlum, i, *n*, mirror

spĕcus, ūs, *m*, cave, pit

spēlunca, ae, *f*, cave, den

sperno, sprēvi, sprētum, *v.t.* 3, to despise, scorn

spēro, *v.t.* 1, to hope, expect

spes, spēi, *f*, hope

sphaera, ae, *f*, sphere

spīca, ae, *f*, ear (of corn)

spīcĕus, a, um, *adj*, made of ears of corn

spīcŭlum, i, *n*, point, dart

spīna, ae, *f*, thorn, spine, difficulties

spīnētum, i, *n*, thorn-hedge

spīnōsus, a, um, *adj*, thorny

spīnus, i, *f*, sloe-tree

spīra, ae, *f*, coil, twist

spīrābĭlis, e, *adj*, breathable

spīrācŭlum, i, *n*, air-hole

spīrāmentum, i, *n*, air-hole

spīrĭtus, ūs, *m*, breath, breeze, pride, arrogance, soul

spīro, *v.i.t.* 1, to breathe, blow, live; exhale

spisso, *v.t.* 1, to condense

spissus, a, um, *adj*, thick, dense

splendĕo, *v.i.* 2, to shine

splendesco, *v.i.* 3, to become bright

splendĭdus, a, um, *adj*, *adv*, ē, shining, magnificent, noble

splendor, ōris, *m*, brilliance, excellence

spŏlĭa, see spŏlĭum

spŏlĭātĭo, ōnis, *f*, plundering

spŏlĭo, *v.t.* 1, to plunder, rob

spŏlĭum, ii, *n*, skin (of an animal); *in pl*, booty, spoils

spondĕo, spŏpondi, sponsum, *v.t.* 2, to promise, pledge, betroth, warrant

spongia, ae, *f*, sponge

spongĭōsus, a, um, *adj*, spongy

sponsa, ae, *f*, bride

sponsālĭa, ium, *n. pl*, betrothal

sponsĭo, ōnis, *f*, promise, guarantee, security

sponsor, ōris, *m*, surety

sponsum, i, *n*, covenant

sponsus, a, um, *adj*, promised

sponsus, i, *m*, bridegroom

spontē, (*abl.*) *f*, *with* mēā, sŭā, *etc.*, voluntarily

sportella, ae, *f*, fruit-basket

sportŭla, ae, *f*, little basket

spūma, ae, *f*, froth, foam

spūmĕus, a, um, *adj*, foaming

spūmifer, ĕra, ĕrum, *adj*, foaming

spūmiger, ĕra, ĕrum, *adj*, foaming

spūmo, *v.i.* 1, to foam, froth

spūmōsus, a, um, *adj*, foaming

spŭo, ŭi, ūtum, *v.i.t.* 3, to spit

spūtum, i, *n*, spit

spurcus, a, um, *adj*, dirty

squālĕo, *v.i.* 2, to be stiff or rough, to be neglected, filthy

squālidus, a, um, *adj*, stiff, dirty, neglected

squālor, ōris, *m*, filthiness

squāma, ae, *f*, scale (of fish)

squāmĕus, a, um, *adj*, scaly

squāmiger, ĕra, ĕrum, *adj*, scaly

squāmōsus, a, um, *adj*, scaly

stăbĭlĭo, *v.t.* 4, to fix

stăbĭlis, e, *adj*, firm, steadfast

stăbĭlĭtas, ātis, *f*, firmness

stăbŭlo, *v.i.* (stăbŭlor, *v.i. dep*,) 1, to have a home, resting-place

stăbŭlum, i, *n*, stable, hut

stădĭum, ii, *n*, stade (distance of 200 yds. approx.), racecourse

stagnans, ntis, *adj*, stagnant

stagno, *v.i.* 1, to stagnate

stagnum, i, *n*, pool, pond

stălagmĭum, i, *n*, pendant

stāmen, ĭnis, *n*, thread

stătārĭus, a, um, *adj*, firm, calm

stătim, *adv*, immediately

stătĭo, ōnis, *f*, post, station, outposts, sentries

stătīva, ōrum, *n. pl*, permanent camp

stătīvus, a, um, *adj*, stationary

stător, ōris, *m*, messenger

stătŭa, ae, *f*, statue

stătŭo, ŭi, ūtum, *v.t.* 3, to set up, place, build, establish, settle, decide

stătūra, ae, *f*, stature

stătus, ūs, *m*, posture, position, condition, state, circumstance

stătus, a, um, *adj*, fixed

stella, ae, *f*, star

stellātus, a, um, *adj*, starry

stelliger, ĕra, ĕrum, *adj*, starry

stellio, ōnis, *m*, newt

stemma, ătis, *n*, garland, pedigree

stercus, ōris, *n*, manure

stĕrĭlis, e, *adj*, barren

stĕrĭlĭtas, ātis, *f*, sterility

sternax, ācis, *adj*, bucking (horse)

sterno, strāvi, strātum, *v.t.* 3, to scatter, extend, smooth, arrange, cover, overthrow, pave

sternūmentum, i, *n*, sneezing

sternŭo, ŭi, *v.i.t.* 3, to sneeze

sterto, ŭi, *v.i.* 3, to snore

stigma, ătis, *n*, brand

stillĭcĭdĭum, ii, *n*, dripping rain-water

stillo, *v.i.t.* 1, to drip; distil

stĭlus, i, *m*, pen, style

stĭmŭlo, *v.t.* 1, to torment, incite

stĭmŭlus, i, *m*, goad, sting, incentive

stīpātor, ōris, *m*, attendant

stīpendĭārĭus, a, um, *adj*, tribute-paying

stīpendĭum, ii, *n*, tax, dues, pay, military service, campaign

stīpes, ĭtis, *m*, log, post

stīpo, *v.t.* 1, to compress, surround, accompany

stips, stĭpis, *f*, donation

stĭpŭla, ae, *f*, stalk, stem

stĭpŭlātĭo, ōnis, *f*, agreement

stĭpŭlor, *v.i.t.* 1, *dep*, to bargain; demand

stīrĭa, ae, *f*, icicle

stirps, pis, *f*, root, stem, plant, race, family

stīva, ae, *f*, plough-handle

sto, stĕti, stătum, *v.i.* 1, to stand, remain, endure, persist, cost

stŏĭcus, a, um, *adj*, stoic

stŏla, ae, *f*, gown, robe

stŏlĭdus, a, um, *adj*, dull, stupid

stŏmāchor, *v.i.* 1, *dep*, to be angry

stŏmāchōsus, a, um, *adj*, irritable

stŏmāchus, i, *m*, gullet, stomach, taste, distaste

stŏrĕa, ae, *f*, straw-mat

strābo, ōnis, *m*, one who squints

strāges, is, *f*, destruction, massacre, slaughter

strāgŭlum, i, *n*, rug

strāgŭlus, a, um, *adj*, covering

strāmen, ĭnis, *n*, straw

strāmentum, i, *n*, straw

strāmĭnĕus, a, um, *adj*, of straw

strangŭlo, *v.t.* 1, to strangle

strătēgēma, ătis, *n*, stratagem

strātum, i, *n*, blanket, quilt, pillow, bed

strātus, a, um, *adj*, stretched out

strēnŭus, a, um, *adj*, *adv*, ē, brisk, quick, vigorous

strĕpĭto, *v.i.* 1, to rattle

strĕpĭtus, ūs, *m*, din

strĕpo, ŭi, *v.i.* 3, to rattle, rumble, roar

strictim, *adv*, briefly

strictūra, ae, *f*, iron bar

strictus, a, um, *adj*, tight

strīdĕo, di (strīdo, di, 3), *v.i.* 2, to creak, hiss, rattle

strīdor, ōris, *m*, creaking, hissing

strīdŭlus, a, um, *adj*, creaking, hissing

strĭgĭlis, is, *f*, scraper used by bathers for cleaning the skin

stringo, nxi, ctum, *v.t.* 3, to draw tight, graze, strip off, draw (sword)
stringor, ōris, *m,* touch, shock
strix, strigis, *f,* screech-owl
structor, ōris, *m,* builder
structūra, ae, *f,* construction
strŭes, is, *f,* heap, pile
strŭo, xi, ctum, *v.t.* 3, to pile up, build, contrive
strūthĭŏcămēlus, i, *m,* ostrich
stŭdĕo, *v.i.t.* 2, *with dat,* to be eager about, strive; pursue, favour
stŭdĭōsus, a, um, *adj, adv,* ē, eager, anxious, friendly
stŭdĭum, ii, *n,* eagerness, endeavour, affection, devotion, study
stultĭtĭa, ae, *f,* foolishness
stultus, a, um, *adj, adv,* ē, foolish
stūpa, ae, *f,* flax, tow
stŭpĕfăcĭo, fēci, factum, *v.t.* 3, to stun, daze
stŭpĕfactus, a, um, *adj,* stunned
stŭpĕo, *v.i.t.* 2, to be stunned, amazed; be astonished at
stŭpēus, a, um, *adj,* made of tow
stŭpĭdus, a, um, *adj,* amazed
stŭpor, ōris, *m,* astonishment, stupidity
stupp . . . see **stŭp. . . .**
stŭpro, *v.t.* 1, to ravish
stŭprum, i, *n,* disgrace, lewdness
sturnus, i, *m,* starling
suādĕo, si, sum, *v.i.t.* 2, *with dat,* to urge, persuade, recommend
suāsĭo, ōnis, *f,* recommendation
suāsor, ōris, *m,* adviser
suāvĭlŏquens, ntis, *adj,* pleasant-speaking
suāvĭor, *v.t.* 1, *dep,* to kiss
suāvis, e, *adj, adv,* ĭter, agreeable, pleasant
suāvĭtas, ātis, *f,* pleasantness
suāvĭum, ii, *n,* kiss
sub, *prep. with acc. and abl,* under, beneath, near, during, towards, just after
sŭbactĭo, ōnis, *f,* preparation
sŭbausculto, *v.t.* 1, to eavesdrop
subcentŭrĭo, ōnis, *m,* subaltern
subdĭtĭvus, a, um, *adj,* counterfeit
subdo, dĭdi, dĭtum, *v.t.* 3, to place under, subdue
subdŏlus, a, um, *adj,* crafty
subdūco, xi, ctum, *v.t.* 3, to pull up, haul up, remove, calculate, balance (accounts)
sŭbĕo, *v.i.t.* 4, to come up to, spring up, occur; enter, submit to, suffer, incur
sŭber, ĕris, *n,* cork-tree

subflāvus, a, um, *adj,* yellowish
sŭbĭcĭo, ĭēci, iectum, *v.t.* 3, to throw or place under or near, counterfeit, subject, affix, prompt
subiectĭo, ōnis, *f,* placing under, forging
subiecto, *v.t.* 1, to throw up
subiectus, a, um, *adj,* lying near, subject
sŭbĭgo, ēgi, actum, *v.t.* 3, to bring up, plough, conquer, subdue, compel, rub down
sŭbinde, *adv,* immediately, now and then
sŭbĭtō, *adv,* suddenly
sŭbĭtus, a, um, *adj,* sudden
subiungo, nxi, nctum, *v.t.* 3, to subordinate, subdue
sublābor, lapsus, *v.i.* 3, *dep,* to glide away
sublātus, a, um, *adj,* proud
sublĕgo, lēgi, lectum, *v.t.* 3, to gather up, kidnap
sublĕvo, *v.t.* 1, to lift up, support, alleviate
sublĭca, ae, *f,* stake, palisade
sublĭgo, *v.t.* 1, to tie on
sublīme, *adv,* aloft, on high
sublīmis, e, *adj,* high, eminent
sublūcĕo, *v.i.* 2, to glimmer
sublŭo, no perf, lūtum, *v.t.* 3, to flow along, wash
sublustris, e, *adj,* glimmering
subm . . . see **summ. . . .**
subnecto, xŭi, xum, *v.t.* 3, to tie on underneath
subnixus, a, um, *adj,* propped up
sŭbŏles, is, *f,* offspring, race
sŭborno, *v.t.* 1, to equip, fit out, instigate
subr . . . see **surr. . . .**
subscrībo, psi, ptum, *v.t.* 3, to write underneath, note down
subscrĭptĭo, ōnis, *f,* anything written underneath
subsĕco, ŭi, ctum, *v.t.* 1, to clip
subsellĭum, ii, *n,* seat, law-court
subsĕquor, sĕcūtus, *v.i.t.* 3, *dep,* to follow, ensue; follow closely, imitate
subsĭcīvus, a, um, *adj,* remaining
subsĭdĭārĭus, a, um, *adj,* reserve
subsĭdĭum, ii, *n,* reserve-ranks, assistance, aid, protection
subsĭdo, sēdi, sessum, *v.i.t.* 3, to settle down, lie in ambush; waylay
subsisto, stĭti, *v.i.* 3, to stop, halt, remain, withstand
subsortĭor, *v.t.* 4, *dep,* to choose as a substitute
substerno, strāvi, strātum, *v.t.* 3, to spread underneath, cover

For List of Abbreviations used, turn to pages 3, 4

substĭtŭo, ŭi, ŭtum, *v.t.* 3, to put under, substitute

substringo, nxi, ctum, *v.t.* 3, to tie; aurem prick up the ear

substructio, ōnis, *f*, foundation

substrŭo, xi, ctum, *v.t.* 3, to lay foundations

subsum, esse, *v, irreg*, to be under or near, to be at hand

subtēmen, ĭnis, *n*, texture, weft

subter, *adv. and prep. with abl*, beneath, below

subterfŭgio, fŭgi, *v.t.* 3, to avoid

subterlābens, ntis, *adj*, gliding under

subterlābor, *v.i.* 3, *dep*, to glide under

subterrānĕus, a, um, *adj*, underground

subtexo, ŭi, xtum, *v.t.* 3, to veil

subtilis, e, *adj, adv*, iter, slender, delicate, precise

subtīlĭtas, ātis, *f*, exactness, subtlety

subtrăho, xi, ctum, *v.t.* 3, to remove stealthily, carry off

sŭbūcŭla, ae, *f*, shirt

sŭbulcus, i, *m*, pig-keeper

sŭburbānus, a, um, *adj*, suburban

sŭburbĭum, ii, *n*, suburb

subvectio, ōnis, *f*, conveyance

subvecto, *v.t.* 1, to convey

subvĕho, xi, ctum, *v.t.* 3, to convey

subvĕnio, vĕni, ventum, *v.i.* 4, *with dat*, to help, aid, occur to the mind

subverto, ti, sum, *v.t.* 3, to overthrow

subvŏlo, *v.i.* 1, to fly up

subvolvo, *v.t.* 3, to roll up

succēdo, cessi, cessum, *v.i.t.* 3, to go under, advance, enter; ascend, follow after, succeed

succendo, di, sum, *v.t.* 3, to kindle

succensĕo, ŭi, sum, *v.i.* 2, to be angry

successio, ōnis, *f*, succession

successor, ōris, *m*, successor

successus, ūs, *m*, advance, success

succĭdo, di, *v.i.* 3, to sink

succĭdo, di, sum, *v.t.* 3, to cut down

succingo, nxi, nctum, *v.t.* 3, to surround, girdle, tuck up

succlāmo, *v.t.* 1, to shout out

succumbo, cŭbŭi, cŭbĭtum, *v.i.* 3, to surrender

succurro, curri, cursum, *v.i.* 3, *with dat*, to help, aid, occur

sūcĭnum, i, *n*, amber

sŭcōsus, a, um, *adj*, juicy

suctus, ūs, *m*, sucking

sūcus, i, *m*, juice, energy, life

sūdārĭum, ii, *n*, handkerchief

sūdis, is, *f*, stake, pile

sūdo, *v.i.t.* 1, to sweat, toil; exude

sūdor, ōris, *m*, sweat, toil

sūdum, i, *n*, clear weather

sūdus, a, um, *adj*, clear, bright

sŭesco, sŭēvi, sŭētum, *v.i.t.* 3, to be accustomed

sŭētus, a, um, *adj*, accustomed

suffĕro, ferre, sustŭli, sublātum, *v, irreg*, to undergo, suffer

suffĭcio, fēci, fectum, *v.i.t.* 3, to be sufficient; impregnate, supply, substitute, elect

suffīgo, xi, xum, *v.t.* 3, to fix

suffīmentum, i, *n*, incense

suffĭo, *v.t.* 4, to perfume

sufflāmen, ĭnis, *n*, drag-chain

sufflātus, a, um, *adj*, puffed up

sufflo, *v.t.* 1, to inflate

suffōco, *v.t.* 1, to strangle

suffŏdĭo, fōdi, fossum, *v.t.* 3, to pierce underneath

suffrāgātio, ōnis, *f*, support

suffrāgātor, ōris, *m*, supporter

suffrāgĭum, ii, *n*, vote, ballot

suffrāgor, *v.i.* 1, *dep, with dat.* to vote for, support

suffundo, fūdi, fūsum, *v.t.* 3, to spread over, tinge

suffulcio, fulsi, fultum, *v.t.* 4, to prop up

suffūsus, a, um, *adj*, spread over

suggĕro, gessi, gestum, *v.t.* 3, to carry up, supply

suggestum, i, *n*, platform

suggestus, ūs, *m*, platform

sūgo, xi, ctum, *v.t.* 3, to suck

sŭi, *genit. of reflexive pron,* of himself, herself, itself, etc.

sulco, *v.t.* 1, to plough

sulcus, i, *m*, furrow, ditch

sulfur, ŭris, *n*, sulphur

sulfūrāta, ōrum, *n. pl*, matches

sulfūrĕus, a, um, *adj*, sulphurous

sum, esse, fŭi, *v, irreg*, to be, exist, happen

summa, ae, *f*, top, chief point, perfection, amount, sum

summātim, *adv*, briefly

summē, *adv*, extremely

summergo, si, sum, *v.t.* 3, to submerge, overwhelm

sumministro, *v.t.* 1, to supply

summissus, a, um, *adj, adv*, ē, gentle, soft, low, mean

summitto, mĭsi, missum, *v.t.* 3, to send up, produce, rear, raise, lower, submit, supply, send

summŏvĕo, mōvi, mōtum, *v.t.* 2, to drive away, remove

summus, a, um, *adj*, highest, topmost

sūmo, mpsi, mptum, *v.t.* 3, to take hold of, assume, inflict, choose, claim, suppose, spend, use, buy

sumptio, ōnis, *f*, assumption

sumptŭōsus, a, um, *adj*, *adv*, ē, expensive, lavish

sumptus, ūs, *m*, expense

sŭo, sŭi, sūtum, *v.t.* 3, to sew

sŭpellex, lectĭlis, *f*, furniture

sŭper, *adv. and prep. with acc. and abl*, above, over, on, besides, concerning

sŭpĕrābĭlis, e, *adj*, able to be overcome

sŭperbia, ae, *f*, pride, arrogance

sŭperbio, *v.i.* 4, to be proud

sŭperbus, a, um, *adj*, *adv*, ē, proud, haughty, delicate, squeamish, magnificent

sŭpercĭlium, ii, *n*, eye-brow, ridge, summit, arrogance

sŭpercresco, crēvi, *v.i.* 3, to grow up

sŭpērēmĭnĕo, *v.t.* 2, to overtop

sŭperficies, ēi, *f*, top, surface

sŭperfundo, fūdi, fūsum, *v.t.* 3, to pour over

sŭpĕri, ōrum, *m.pl*, the gods

sŭpĕrimmĭnĕo, *v.i.* 2, to overhang

sŭpĕrimpōno, *no perf*, pŏsĭtum, *v.t.* 3, to place upon

sŭpĕrinicio, *no perf*, iectum, *v.t.* 3, to throw over or upon

sŭperiācio, iēci, iectum, *v.t.* 3, to throw over, overflow

sŭpĕrior, ius, *comp. adj*, higher, previous, former, superior

sŭperlātio, ōnis, *f*, exaggeration, hyperbole

sŭpernus, a, um, *adj*, *adv*, ē, upper, on high ground

sŭpĕro, *v.i.t.* 1, to have the upper hand, remain; ascend, outstrip, conquer

sŭpersĕdĕo, sēdi, sessum, *v.i.t.* 2, *with abl*, to refrain (from)

sŭperstĕs, ĭtis, *adj*, surviving

sŭperstĭtio, ōnis, *f*, excessive fear of the gods

sŭperstĭtĭōsus, a, um, *adj*, superstitious

sŭpersto, *v.i.t.* 1, to stand over

sŭpersum, esse, fŭi, *v.i.*, *irreg*, to remain, survive

sŭpĕrus, a, um, *adj*, upper, higher

sŭpervācānĕus, a, um, *adj*, unnecessary

sŭpervăcŭus, a, um, *adj*, unnecessary

sŭpervĕnio, vēni, ventum, *v.i.t.* 4, to come up, arrive; fall upon

sŭpervŏlo, *v.i.t.* 1, to fly over

sŭpīno, *v.t.* 1, to bend backwards

sŭpīnus, a, um, *adj*, lying on the back, sloping

suppĕdĭto, *v.i.t.* 1, to be enough, plenty; to supply

suppĕto, īvi, ītum, *v.i.* 3, to be at hand, to be enough

supplanto, *v.t.* 1, to trip up

supplēmentum, i, *n*, reinforcements

supplĕo, ēvi, ētum, *v.t.* 2, to complete, fill up

supplex, ĭcis, *c*, suppliant

supplex, ĭcis, *adj*, beseeching

supplicātio, ōnis, *f*, public thanksgiving

supplicium, ii, *n*, punishment

supplico, *v.i.* 1, to implore

supplōdo, si, *v.i.t.* 3, to stamp

suppōno, pŏsŭi, pŏsĭtum, *v.t.* 3, to put under, substitute

supporto, *v.t.* 1, to convey

supprimo, pressi, pressum, *v.t.* 3, to sink, suppress

suppūro, *v.i.* 1, to suppurate

sŭprā, *adv. and prep. with acc*, above, over, beyond, before

sŭprēmus, a, um, *adj*, highest, last

sūra, ae, *f*, calf of the leg

surcŭlus, i, *m*, shoot, twig

surdĭtas, ātis, *f*, deafness

surdus, a, um, *adj*, deaf

surgo, surrexi, rectum, *v.i.t.* 3, to rise, stand up; raise

surrēgŭlus, i, *m*, subordinate ruler

surrēmigo, *v.i.* 1, to row along

surrēpo, psi, ptum, *v.i.t.* 3, to creep under

surrīdĕo, si, sum, *v.i.* 2, to smile

surrĭpio, ŭi, reptum, *v.t.* 3, to snatch away, steal

surrŏgo, *v.t.* 1, to substitute

surrŭo, ŭi, ŭtum, *v.t.* 3, to undermine, overthrow

sursum, *adv*, upwards, on high

sūs, sŭis, *c*, pig

susceptio, ōnis, *f*, undertaking

suscipio, cēpi, ceptum, *v.t.* 3, to undertake, acknowledge, undergo

suscĭto, *v.t.* 1, to raise, arouse

suspectus, a, um, *adj*, mistrusted

suspectus, ūs, *m*, height

suspendium, ii, *n*, hanging

suspendo, di, sum, *v.t.* 3, to hang up, lift up, keep in suspense, interrupt

suspensus, a, um, *adj*, raised, hesitating

suspĭcio, spexi, ctum, *v.i.t.* 3, to look up; admire, suspect

suspĭcio, ōnis, *f*, suspicion

suspiciōsus, a, um, *adj*, *adv*, ē, suspicious

suspicor, *v.t.* 1, *dep*, to suspect, suppose

suspīritus, ūs, *m*, sigh

suspīrium, ii, *n*, sigh

suspīro, *v.i.t.* 1, to sigh; long for

sustento, *v.t.* 1, to support, maintain, endure

sustīnĕo, ūi, tentum, *v.t.* 2, to support, restrain, withstand, maintain

sŭsurro, *v.i.t.* 1, to hum; mutter

sŭsurrus, i, *m*, humming

sŭsurrus, a, um, *adj*, whispering

sūta, ōrum, *n. pl*, joints

sūtilis, e, *adj*, sewed together.

sūtor, ōris, *m*, cobbler

sūtōrius, a, um, *adj*, of a cobbler

sūtūra, ae, *f*, seam

sŭus, a, um, *adj*, his, hers, its, their

sўcŏmŏrus, i, *f*, sycamore

sўcŏphanta, ae, *m*, sycophant, cheat

syllăba, ae, *f*, syllable

syllăbātim, *adv*, by syllables

symphōnia, ae, *f*, harmony

symphōniăcus, i, *m*, chorister

sўnăgōga, ae, *f*, synagogue

syngrăpha, ae, *f*, promissory note

syngrăphus, i, *m*, passport

syntaxis, is, *f*, syntax

T

tăbānus, i, *m*, gad-fly

tăbella, ae, *f*, small board or table, writing-tablet, letter, ballot-paper, small picture

tăbellārius, ii, *m*, letter-bearer

tābĕo, *v.i.* 2, to melt away

tăberna, ae, *f*, hut, shop, inn

tăbernācŭlum, i, *n*, tent

tăbernārius, ii, *m*, shop-keeper

tābes, is, *f*, wasting-away, disease

tābesco, bŭi, *v.i.* 3, to melt away

tābĭdus, a, um, *adj*, decaying

tăbŭla, ae, *f*, plank, writing-tablet, letter, account-book, picture, painting, map, table

tăbŭlāria, ae, *f*, record-office

tăbŭlārium, ii, *n*, archives

tăbŭlārius, ii, *m*, registrar

tăbŭlātum, i, *n*, floor, storey

tābum, i, *n*, pus, matter, infectious disease

tăcĕo, *v.i.t.* 2, to be silent; to be silent about

tăcĭturnĭtas, ātis, *f*, silence

tăcĭturnus, a, um, *adj*, silent

tăcĭtus, a, um, *adj*, *adv*, ē, secret, silent

tactus, ūs, *m*, touch, feel, influence

taeda, ae, *f*, pine-tree, torch

taedet, taedŭit, *v.* 2, *impers. with acc. of person*, it offends, disgusts, wearies

taedium, ii, *n*, weariness, disgust

taenia, ae, *f*, hair-ribbon

taeter, tra, trum, *adj*, hideous

taetricus, a, um, *adj*, harsh

tālāris, e, *adj*, ankle-length

tālĕa, ae, *f*, stick, stake

tălentum, i, *n*, sum of money (app. £400–£500); weight (½ cwt.)

tālio, ōnis, *f*, similar punishment, reprisal

tālis, e, *adj*, of such a kind

talpa, ae, *f*, mole

tālus, i, *m*, ankle-bone, heel, die (marked on four sides)

tam, *adv*, so, as, equally

tamdiū, *adv*, so long

tămen, *adv*, nevertheless, however, still

tămetsi, *conj*, although

tamquam, *adv*, as much as, just as, as if, for example

tandem, *adv*, at length

tango, tĕtigi, tactum, *v.t.* 3, to touch, taste, reach, strike, affect, impress ence, mention

tanquam, see tamquam

tantisper, *adv*, so long, meanwhile

tantŏpĕre, *adv*, so greatly

tantŭlus, a, um, *adj*, so little

tantum, *adv*, so much, only

tantummŏdo, *adv*, only, merely

tantundem, *adv*, just as much

tantus, a, um, *adj*, so great; tanti esse, to be worth so much; tantō, by so much

tăpēte, is, *n*, tapestry

tardĭtas, ātis, *f*, slowness

tardo, *v.i.t.* 1, to delay; hinder

tardus, a, um, *adj*, *adv*, ē, slow

tăta, ae, *m*, dad, daddy

taurĕus, a, um, *adj*, of a bull

taurīnus, a, um, *adj*, of a bull

taurus, i, *m*, bull, ox

taxus, i, *f*, yew-tree

tē, *acc. or abl. of* tū

tector, ōris, *m*, plasterer

tectōrium, ii, *n*, plaster

tectum, i, *n*, roof, house

tectus, a, um, *adj*, *adv*, ō, covered, hidden, secret

tĕges, ĕtis, *f*, mat

tĕgimen, inis, *n*, cover

tĕgo, xi, ctum, *v.t.* 3, to cover, hide, protect

tĕgŭla, ae, *f*, tile

tĕgŭmen, see tĕgĭmen

tĕgūmentum, i, n, cover

tēla, ae, f, web, warp, loom

tellūs, ūris, f, earth, globe, land, region

tēlum, i, n, weapon, javelin

tĕmĕrārius, a, um, adj, rash

tĕmĕrē, adv, by chance, rashly

tĕmĕrĭtas, ātis, f, rashness

tĕmĕro, v.t. 1, to defile, disgrace

tēmētum, i, n, wine

temno, v.t. 3, to despise

tēmo, ōnis, m, pole, beam

tempĕrans, ntis, adj, moderate

tempĕrantĭa, ae, f, moderation

tempĕrātĭo, ōnis, f, symmetry, temperament

tempĕrātus, a, um, adj, moderate

tempĕrĭes, ēi, f, mildness

tempĕro, v.i.t. 1, to abstain, be moderate, be indulgent; mix properly, regulate, govern

tempestas, ātis, f, time, period, weather, storm

tempestīvus, a, um, adj, adv, ē, suitable, timely, early

templum, i, n, temple, open space

tempto, see tento

tempus, ŏris, n, time, opportunity; tempŏra, times, temples (of the head); ad tempus, (adv. phr.) at the right time, for the time being

tēmŭlentus, a, um, adj, drunk

tĕnācĭtas, ātis, f, tenacity

tĕnax, ācis, adj, holding tight, firm, stingy

tendo, tĕtendi, tentum, v.i.t. 3, to aim, go, march, stretch, strive, encamp; stretch, extend

tĕnĕbrae, ārum, f. pl, darkness

tĕnĕbrĭcōsus, a, um, adj, dark, gloomy

tĕnĕbrōsus, a, um, adj, dark, gloomy

tĕnĕo, ŭi, tentum, v.i.t. 2, to hold a position, sail, continue; hold, have, keep, restrain, uphold, maintain, control, comprehend, include

tĕner, ĕra, ĕrum, adj, tender

tĕnor, ōris, m, course, career

tensa, ae, f, triumphal chariot

tentāmentum, i, n, attempt

tentātĭo, ōnis, f, trial, attempt

tentātor, ōris, m, tempter

tento (tempto), v.t. 1, to handle, attack, attempt, tempt, excite

tentōrium, ii, n, tent

tentus, a, um, adj, extended

tĕnŭis, e, adj, adv, ĭter, thin, fine, meagre, poor, subtle

tĕnŭĭtas, ātis, f, slenderness, poverty

tĕnŭo, v.t. 1, to make thin, reduce, weaken, degrade

tĕnus, prep. with abl, as far as, according to

tĕpĕfăcĭo, fēci, factum, v.t. 3, to warm

tĕpĕo, v.i. 2, to be warm

tĕpesco, pŭi, v.i. 3, to grow warm

tĕpĭdus, a, um, adj, warm

tĕpor, ōris, m, warmth

tĕr, adv, three times

tĕrĕbinthus, i, f, terebinth tree

tĕrĕbra, ae, f, tool

tĕrĕbro, v.t. 1, to bore through

tĕrĕs, ĕtis, adj, rounded, smooth, polished

tergĕminus, a, um, adj, triple

tergĕo, si, sum, v.t. 2, to clean, polish

tergiversātĭo, ōnis, f, backsliding

tergiversor, v.i. 1, dep, to shuffle, refuse

tergo, si, sum, see tergĕo

tergum, i, n, back, rear, skin; a tergo, (adv. phr.) at the rear

terminālĭa, ium, n. pl, festival of Terminus (God of boundaries)

terminātĭo, ōnis, f, fixing

termino, v.t. 1, to limit, fix, define, determine, end

terminus, i, m, boundary, end

terni, ae, a, pl. adj, three each

tĕro, trīvi, trītum, v.t. 3, to rub, grind, smooth, polish, wear out, spend or waste time

terra, ae, f, earth, land, ground, region

terrēnus, a, um, adj, made of earth, terrestrial

terrĕo, v.t. 2, to frighten

terrestris, e, adj, of earth or land

terrēus, a, um, adj, of earth or land

terrĭbĭlis, e, adj, dreadful

terrĭcŭla, ōrum, n. pl, scarecrow bugbear

terrĭfĭco, v.t. 1, to terrify

terrĭfĭcus, a, um, adj, frightful

terrĭgĕna, ae, c, earthborn

terrĭto, v.t. 1, to terrify

terror, ōris, m, terror, dread

tertĭus, a, um, adj, adv, ō, third

tĕruncĭus, ii, m, trifling sum

tessellātus, a, um, adj, tesselated, mosaic

tessĕra, ae, f, stone or wooden cube, die, watchword, ticket

testa, ae, f, jug, broken piece of pottery, shell-fish

testāmentum, i, n, will, testament

testātor, ōris, m, testator

testātus, a, um, adj, manifest

testĭfĭcātĭo, ōnis, f, evidence

testĭfĭcor, *v.t.* 1, *dep*, to give evidence, demonstrate

testĭmōnĭum, ii, *n*, evidence

testis, is, *c*, witness

testor, *v.t.* 1, *dep*, to call a witness, prove, declare

testu(m), i, *n*, lid, earthen pot

testūdĭnĕus, a, um, *adj*, of a tortoise

testūdo, ĭnis, *f*, tortoise, lute, military shelter

tĕtānus, i, *m*, tetanus

tēter, tra, trum, *adj*, hideous

tĕtrarches, ae, *m*, petty princeling

tĕtrĭcus, a, um, *adj*, harsh

texo, ŭi, xtum, *v.t.* 3, to weave, build, devise

textile, is, *n*, fabric

textĭlis, e, *adj*, woven

textor, ōris, *m*, weaver

textum, i, *n*, web, fabric

textus, ūs, *m*, texture

thălămus, i, *m*, apartment, bedroom, marriage

thĕātrālis, e, *adj*, theatrical

thĕātrum, i, *n*, theatre

thēca, ae, *f*, envelope

thĕŏlŏgĭa, ae, *f*, theology

thĕŏlŏgus, i, *m*, theologian

thĕŏrēma, ătis, *n*, theorem

thermae, ārum, *f. pl*, warm baths

thēsaurus, i, *m*, store, hoard, treasure, treasure-house

thĭāsus, i, *m*, dance in honour of Bacchus

thŏlus, i, *m*, dome

thōrax, ācis, *m*, breastplate

thunnus, i, *m*, tunny-fish

thūs, thūris, *n*, incense

thymbra, ae, *f*, savory (plant)

thymum, i, *n*, thyme

thyrsus, i, *m*, stem of plant, staff carried by Bacchus

tĭāra, ae, *f*, tiara

tĭbia, ae, *f*, flute

tĭbĭāle, is, *n*, stocking

tĭbīcen, ĭnis, *m*, flute-player

tĭbīcĭna, ae, *f*, flute-player

tĭbĭcĭnĭum, ii, *n*, flute-playing

tignum, i, *n*, timber, log

tigris, is (ĭdis), *c*, tiger

tĭlĭa, ae, *f*, linden or lime tree

tĭmĕo, *v.i.t.* 2, to fear

tĭmĭdĭtas, ātis, *f*, cowardice

tĭmĭdus, a, um, *adj*, *adv*, ē, afraid, cowardly

tĭmor, ōris, *m*, fear, alarm, object of fear

tĭnĕa, ae, *f*, moth, book-worm

tingo, nxi, nctum, *v.t.* 3, to moisten, dye

tinnĭo, *v.i.t.* 4, to ring; tinkle

tinnītus, ūs, *m*, ringing

tinnŭlus, a, um, *adj*, tinkling

tintinnābŭlum, i, *n*, bell

tīro, ōnis, *m*, recruit, novice

tīrōcĭnĭum, ii, *n*, first campaign, inexperience

tĭtillātĭo, ōnis, *f*, tickling

tĭtillo, *v.t.* 1, to tickle

tĭtŭbo, *v.i.* 1, to stagger, hesitate, be perplexed

tĭtŭlus, i, *m*, title, placard, notice, honour, glory

tōfus, i, *m*, tufa (rock)

tŏga, ae, *f*, toga: the long outer garment of the Romans

tŏgātus, a, um, *adj*, wearing the toga

tŏlĕrābĭlis, e, *adj*, endurable

tŏlĕrantĭa, ae, *f*, tolerance

tŏlĕro, *v.t.* 1, to bear, endure

tollēno, ōnis, *m*, a swing-beam

tollo, sustŭli, sublātum, *v.t.* 3, to lift, raise, remove, destroy, educate, acknowledge

tŏnans, ntis, *m*, god of thunder

tondĕo, tŏtondi, tonsum, *v.t.* 2, to shave, crop, prune, graze

tŏnĭtrus, ūs, *m*, thunder

tŏnĭtrŭum, i, *n*, thunder

tŏno, ŭi, *v.i.t.* 1, to thunder; thunder out

tonsa, ae, *f*, oar

tonsillae, ārum, *f. pl*, tonsils

tonsor, ōris, *m*, barber

tonsōrĭus, a, um, *adj*, of shaving

tonsūra, ae, *f*, shearing

tŏpĭārĭus, ii, *m*, landscape-gardener

tŏreuma, ătis, *n*, embossed work

tormentum, i, *n*, missile, rope, missile-launcher, instrument of torture, rack, pain

tormĭna, um, *n. pl*, the gripes

torno, *v.t.* 1, to round off

tornus, i, *m*, lathe

tŏrōsus, a, um, *adj*, muscular

torpĕfăcĭo, fēci, factum, *v.t.* 3, to numb

torpens, ntis, *adj*, numb

torpĕo, *v.i.* 2, to be stiff, numb, sluggish, listless

torpesco, pŭi, *v.i.* 3, to become stiff or listless

torpor, ōris, *m*, numbness

torquātus, a, um, *adj*, wearing a collar

torquĕo, torsi, sum, *v.t.* 2, to twist, bend, wield, hurl, rack, torture torquis (torques), is, *m*, *f*, collar, necklace, wreath

torrens, ntis, *adj*, burning

torrens, ntis, *m*, torrent

torrĕo, ŭi, tostum, *v.t* 2, to dry, bake, scorch, burn

torrĭdus, a, um, *adj*, parched

torris, is, *m*, firebrand

tortĭlis, e, *adj*, twined

tortor, ōris, *m*, torturer

tortŭōsus, a, um, *adj*, winding, complicated

tortus, a, um, *adj*, twisted

tortus, ūs, *m*, twisting

tŏrus, i, *m*, muscle, knot, cushion, sofa, bed

torvus, a, um, *adj*, wild, grim

tŏt, *indecl. adj*, so many

tŏtĭdem, *indecl. adj*, just as many

tŏtĭens (tŏtĭes), *adv*, so often

tōtum, i, *n*, whole

tōtus, a, um, *adj*, the whole

trăbālis, e, *adj*, of a beam

trăbĕa, ae, *f*, robe of state

trabs, trăbis, *f*, beam, timber, tree, ship

tractābĭlis, e, *adj*, manageable, pliant, flexible

tractātĭo, ōnis, *f*, handling, treatment

tractātus, ūs, *m*, handling, treatment

tractim, *adv*, little by little

tracto, *v.t.* 1, to handle, manage, practise, discuss, drag

tractus, ūs, *m*, dragging, track, district, course, progress

trādĭtĭo, ōnis, *f*, surrender

trādo, dĭdi, dĭtum, *v.t.* 3, to hand over, commit, bequeath, relate

trādūco, xi, ctum, *v.t.* 3, to bring over, degrade, spend (time)

trāductĭo, ōnis, *f*, transferring

trăgĭcus, a, um, *adj*, tragic, fearful, grand

trăgoedĭa, ae, *f*, tragedy

trăgoedus, i, *m*, tragic actor

trăgŭla, ae, *f*, javelin, dart

trăhĕa, ae, *f*, sledge

trăho, xi, ctum, *v.t.* 3, to drag, extract, inhale, quaff, drag away, plunder, spin, influence, delay, protract

trāĭcĭo, iēci, iectum, *v.t.* 3, to throw across, transport, transfix

trāĭectĭo, ōnis, *f*, crossing over, passage

trāĭectus, ūs, *m*, crossing

trāmĕs, ĭtis, *m*, footpath, way

trāno, *v.t.* 1, to swim across

tranquillĭtas, ātis, *f*, calmness

tranquillo, *v.t.* 1, to calm

tranquillum, i, *n*, a calm

tranquillus, a, um, *adj*, *adv*, ē, calm, placid, serene

trans, *prep. with acc*, across, beyond, on the further side of

transābĕo, *v.t.* 4, to transfix

transādĭgo, ēgi, actum, *v.t.* 3, to thrust through

transalpīnus, a, um, *adj*, beyond the Alps

transcendo, di, sum, *v.i.t.* 3, to climb over, surmount; exceed

transcrībo, psi, ptum, *v.t.* 3, to transcribe, forge, transfer

transcurro, curri, cursum, *v.i.t.* 3, to run across; pass through

transĕo, *v.i.t.* 4, to go over or across, pass by, surpass

transfĕro, ferre, tŭli, lātum, *v.t*, *irreg*, to bring across, carry along, transfer, translate

transfīgo, xi, xum, *v.t.* 3, to pierce through

transfŏdĭo, fōdi, fossum, *v.t.* 3, to pierce through

transformo, *v.t.* 1, to transform

transfŭga, ae, *c*, deserter

transfŭgĭo, fūgi, *v.t.* 3, to desert

transfundo, fūdi, fūsum, *v.t.* 3, to transfer

transgrĕdĭor, gressus, *v.i.t.* 3, *dep*, to pass or climb over, across

transgressĭo, ōnis, *f*, passage

transĭgo, ēgi, actum, *v.t.* 3, to complete, transact, settle (a difference)

transĭlĭo, ŭi, *v.i.t.* 4, to leap across

transĭtĭo, ōnis, *f*, going over, passage

transĭtus, ūs, *m*, going over, passage

translātĭcĭus, a, um, *adj*, handed down

translātĭo, ōnis, *f*, transferring

translātus, a, um, *adj*, transferred, copied, figurative

translūcĕo, *v.i.* 2, to shine through

transmărīnus, a, um, *adj*, across the sea

transmĭgro, *v.i.* 1, to migrate

transmissus, ūs, *m*, transferring

transmitto, mīsi, missum, *v.i.t.* 3, to go across; send across, transfer, hand over

transmūto, *v.t.* 1, to change

transnăto, *v.i.* 1, to swim over

transpădānus, a, um, *adj*, beyond the river Po

transporto, *v.t.* 1, to carry across

transtrum, i, *n*, rowing-bench

transvĕho, xi, ctum, *v.t.* 3, to carry over

transverbĕro, *v.t.* 1, to transfix

transversārĭus, a, um, *adj*, crosswise

transversus, a, um, *adj*, crosswise

transvŏlo, *v.i.t.* 1, to fly across

trĕcēni, ae, a, *pl. adj*, three hundred each

trecentensĭmus, a, um, *adj*, three hundredth

trĕcenti, ae, a, *pl. adj*, three hundred

trēdĕcim, *indecl. adj*, thirteen

trĕmĕbundus, a, um, *adj*, trembling

trĕmĕfăcio, fēci, factum, *v.t.* 3, to cause to tremble

trĕmendus, a, um, *adj*, dreadful

trĕmesco, *v.i.t.* 3, to tremble; tremble at

trĕmo, ŭi, *v.i.t.* 3, to tremble; tremble at

trĕmor, ōris, *m*, shuddering

trĕmŭlus, a, um, *adj*, trembling

trĕpĭdans, ntis, *adj*, trembling

trĕpĭdātio, ōnis, *f*, confusion

trĕpĭdo, *v.i.t.* 1, to be alarmed; tremble at

trĕpĭdus, a, um, *adj*, alarmed

trēs, tria, *adj*, three

triangŭlum, i, *n*, triangle

triangŭlus, a, um, *adj*, triangular

triārii, ōrum, *m. pl*, veteran soldiers who fought in the third rank

trĭbŭārius, a, um, *adj*, of a tribe

trĭbūlis, e, *adj*, of the same tribe

trĭbŭlum, i, *n*, threshing-platform

trĭbŭlus, i, *m*, thistle

trĭbūnal, ālis, *n*, platform, judgement-seat

trĭbūnātus, ūs, *m*, position of tribune

trĭbūnicius, a, um, *adj*, of a tribune

trĭbūnus, i, *m*, tribune; 1. army officer; 2. magistrate to defend the rights of the people

trĭbŭo, ŭi, ŭtum, *v.t.* 3, to allot, give, attribute

trĭbus, ūs, *f*, tribe

trĭbus, see trēs

trĭbūtim, *adv*, by tribes

trĭbūtum, i, *n*, tribute, tax

trīcae, ārum, *f. pl*, tricks

trĭcēni, ae, a, *pl. adj*, thirty each

trĭceps, cĭpĭtis, *adj*, three-headed

trĭcēsĭmus, a, um, *adj*, thirtieth

trĭcies, *adv*, thirty times

trĭclīnium, ii, *n*, dining-couch, dining-room

trĭcorpor, ōris, *adj*, three-bodied

trĭdens, ntis, *adj*, three-pronged; *as nn*, trident

trīdŭum, i, *n*, three days

triennium, ii, *n*, three years

triens, ntis, *m*, a third part

triĕtērĭca, ōrum, *n. pl*, festival of Bacchus

trĭfaux, cis, *adj*, with three throats

trĭfĭdus, a, um, *adj*, three-forked

trĭfŏlium, ii, *n*, shamrock

trĭformis, e, *adj*, three-fold

trĭgĕmĭnus, a, um, *adj*, triple

trĭgēsĭmus, a, um, *adj*, thirtieth

trĭginta, *indecl. adj*, thirty

trĭgōn, ōnis, *m*, ball

trĭlĭbris, e, *adj*, weighing three pounds

trĭlinguis, e, *adj*, three-tongued

trĭlix, ĭcis, *adj*, with three thongs

trĭmestris, e, *adj*, of three months

trīmus, a, um, *adj*, three years old

trīni, ae, a, *pl. adj*, three each

trĭnōdis, e, *adj*, three-knotted

triōnes, um, *m. pl*, constellation of the Great and Lesser Bear

trĭpartītus, a, um, *adj, adv*, ō, three-fold

trĭpēs, ĕdis, *adj*, three-footed

trĭplex, ĭcis, *adj*, triple

trĭplĭco, *v.t.* 1, to treble

trĭpŭdium, ii, *n*, religious dance, favourable omen

trĭpūs, ŏdis, *m*, tripod

trĭquĕtrus, a, um, *adj*, triangular

trĭrēmis, e, *adj*, with three banks of oars

tristis, e, *adj*, sad, gloomy, harsh, disagreeable

tristĭtia, ae, *f*, sadness, gloominess, harshness

trĭsulcus, a, um, *adj*, three-forked

trītĭcĕus, a, um, *adj*, of wheat

trītĭcum, i, *n*, wheat

trītūra, ae, *f*, threshing (of grain)

trītus, a, um, *adj*, beaten, common, worn, familiar

triumphālis, e, *adj*, triumphal

triumpho, *v.i.t.* 1, to celebrate a triumph; triumph over

triumphus, i, *m*, triumphal procession after a victory

triumvĭrātus, ūs, *m*, triumvirate

triumvĭri, ōrum, *m. pl*, board of three men

trĭvium, ii, *n*, cross-road

trŏchaeus, i, *m*, metrical foot

trochlĕa, ae, *f*, pulley

trŏchus, i, *m*, hoop

trŏpaeum, i, *n*, trophy, victory

trŏpĭcus, a, um, *adj*, tropical

trŭcīdātio, ōnis, *f*, butchery

trŭcīdo, *v.t.* 1, to slaughter

trŭcŭlentus, a, um, *adj*, harsh

trŭdis, is, *f*, pole, pike

trūdo, si, sum, *v.t.* 3, to push, drive, put out

trulla, ae, *f*, ladle

truncātus, a, um, *adj*, maimed

trunco, *v.t.* 1, to maim, cut off

truncus, a, um, *adj*, maimed

truncus, i, *m*, trunk, stem

trŭtina, ae, *f*, pair of scales

trux, ŭcis, *adj*, harsh, stern

tū, *pron*, you (singular)

tŭba, ae, *f*, trumpet

tūber, ĕris, *n*, swelling, tumour

tŭbicen, ĭnis, *m*, trumpeter

tŭbŭlātus, a, um, *adj*, tubular

tŭbŭlus, i, *m*, tube

tŭĕor, *v.t.* 2, *dep*, to look at, gaze at, consider, guard, maintain, support

tŭgŭrium, ii, *n*, cottage

tŭli, see fero

tum, *adv, and conj*, then

tŭmĕfăcio, fēci, factum, *v.t.* 3, to cause to swell

tŭmĕo, *v.i.* 2, to swell, be puffed up

tŭmesco, mui, *v.i.* 3, to become swollen, be puffed up

tŭmĭdus, a, um, *adj*, swollen, excited, enraged

tŭmor, ōris, *m*, swelling, commotion

tŭmŭlo, *v.t.* 1, to bury

tŭmultŭārius, a, um, *adj*, hurried, hurriedly raised (troops)

tŭmultŭor, *v.i.* 1, *dep*, to be confused

tŭmultŭōsus, a, um, *adj, adv*, ē, restless, confused, turbulent

tŭmultus, ūs, *m*, uproar, tempest, rebellion

tŭmŭlus, i, *m*, hill, mound

tunc, *adv*, then

tundo, tŭtŭdi, tunsum (tusum), *v.t.* 3, to beat, strike, pound

tŭnica, ae, *f*, tunic, husk

tŭnicātus, a, um, *adj*, dressed in a tunic

tŭnicopallium, i, *n*, short cloak

tūrārius, ii, *m*, a dealer

turba, ae, *f*, hubbub, uproar, crowd, band, quarrel, confusion

turbātor, ōris, *m*, disturber

turbātus, a, um, *adj*, disturbed

turbĭdus, a, um, *adj, adv*, ē, confused, troubled, violent

turbo, *v.t.* 1, to confuse, disturb, make thick

turbo, ĭnis, *m*, hurricane, spinning-top, revolution

turbŭlentus, a, um, *adj, adv*, ē, nter, restless, boisterous, troublesome

turdus, i, *m*, thrush

tūrĕus, a, um, *adj*, of incense

turgĕo, rsi, *v.i.* 2, to swell

turgesco, *v.i.* 3, to swell up

turgidŭlus, a, um, *adj*, swollen

turgĭdus, a, um, *adj*, swollen

tūrĭbŭlum, i, *n*, incense-vessel

tūrĭcrĕmus, a, um, *adj*, for burning incense

tūrĭfer, ĕra, ĕrum, *adj*, incense-producing

turma, ae, *f*, cavalry-troop, crowd

turmālis, e, *adj*, of a squadron

turmātim, *adv*, by squadrons

turpis, e, *adj, adv*, iter, filthy, ugly, disgraceful, scandalous

turpĭtūdo, ĭnis, *f*, disgrace, baseness

turpo, *v.t.* 1, to pollute, soil

turriger, ĕra, ĕrum, *adj*, turreted

turris, is, *f*, tower

turrītus, a, um, *adj*, turreted

turtur, ŭris, *m*, turtle-dove

tūs, tūris, *n*, incense

tussio, *v.i.* 4, to cough

tussis, is, *f*, cough

tūtāmen, ĭnis, *n*, defence

tūtēla, ae, *f*, safeguard, defence, position of guardian, object under guardianship

tūtō, *adv*, safely

tūtor, ōris, *m*, guardian

tūtor, *v.t.* 1, *dep*, to guard, watch

tūtus, a, um, *adj*, safe, prudent

tŭus, a, um, *adj*, your(s)

tympănum, i, *n*, tambourine, door panel

tўrannĭcus, a, um, *adj*, tyrannical

tўrannis, ĭdis, *f*, despotic rule

tўrannus, i, *m*, sovereign, ruler, despot

U

ūber, ĕris, *n*, teat, udder, breast

ūber, ĕris, *adj*, fertile, rich

ūbertas, ātis, *f*, fertility, richness

ŭbī, *adv*, where, when, as soon as

ŭbīcumque, *adv*, wherever

ŭbīque, *adv*, everywhere, anywhere

ŭbīvis, *adv*, everywhere, anywhere

ūdus, a, um, *adj*, moist, wet

ulcĕrātio, ōnis, *f*, ulceration

ulcĕro, *v.t.* 1, to make sore

ulcĕrōsus, a, um, *adj*, ulcerous

ulcīscor, ultus, *v.t.* 3, *dep*, to avenge, punish, take vengeance on

ulcus, ĕris, *n*, sore, ulcer

ulex, ĭcis, *m*, furze

ūlīgĭnōsus, a, um, *adj*, moist, marshy

ūlīgo, ĭnis, *f*, moisture

ullus, a, um, *adj*, (genit, ullīus, dat, ulli), any

ulmĕus, a, um, *adj*, of elm

ulmus, i, *f*, elm, elm-tree

ulna, ae, *f*, elbow, arm, ell

ultĕrior, ius, *comp. adj*, beyond, on the farther side

For List of Abbreviations used, turn to pages 3, 4

ultĕrius, *comp. adv*, beyond, farther

ultĭmus, a, um, *sup. adj*, farthest, extreme, last

ultĭo, ōnis, *f*, revenge

ultor, ōris, *m*, avenger

ultrā, *adv. and prep. with acc*, beyond, past, farther, besides

ultrix, īcis, *adj*, avenging

ultrō, *adv*, on the other side, moreover, spontaneously

ŭlŭla, ae, *f*, screech-owl

ŭlŭlātus, ūs, *m*, wailing

ŭlŭlo, *v.i.t.* 1, to howl; cry out to

ulva, ae, *f*, sedge

umbella, ae, *f*, parasol

umbĭlicus, i, *m*, navel, centre, end of rod on which Roman books were rolled

umbo, ōnis, *m*, shield, knob

umbra, ae, *f*, shadow, shade, ghost, trace, shelter

umbrăcŭlum, i, *n*, shady spot, school

umbrātĭlis, e, *adj*, private, retired

umbrĭfer, ĕra, ĕrum, *adj*, shady

umbro, *v.t.* 1, to shade, cover

umbrōsus, a, um, *adj*, shady

ūmecto, *v.t.* 1, to moisten

ūmĕo, *v.i.* 2, to be damp

ŭmĕrus, i, *m*, shoulder, arm

ūmesco, *v.i.* 3, to grow wet

ūmĭdus, a, um, *adj*, wet, damp

ūmor, ōris, *m*, moisture, liquid

umquam, *adv*, ever

ūnā, *adv*, at the same time, in the same place, together

ūnănĭmus, a, um, *adj*, of one mind

ūnănĭmitas, ātis, *f*, unanimity

uncĭa, ae, *f*, a twelfth, ounce

unctĭo, ōnis, *f*, anointing

unctus, a, um, *adj*, oiled, rich, luxurious

uncus, i, *m*, hook

uncus, a, um, *adj*, hooked

unda, ae, *f*, wave, tide

undĕ, *adv*, from where, whence

undĕ ... (with number) one from. ...
e.g. undēvīginti (one from 20) 19

undēcĭes, *adv*, eleven times

undĕcĭm, *indecl. adj*, eleven

undēcĭmus, a, um, *adj*, eleventh

undēni, ae, a, *pl. adj*, eleven each

undĭquĕ, *adv*, from all sides, everywhere

undo, *v.i.* 1, to surge, undulate

undōsus, a, um, *adj*, billowy

ungo (unguo), unxi, unctum, *v.t.* 3, to besmear, oil

unguen, ĭnis, *n*, ointment

unguentārius, ii, *m*, perfume-seller

unguentum, i, *n*, ointment, perfume

unguis, is, *m*, finger or toe nail

ungŭla, ae, *f*, hoof, claw

unguo (3), see ungo

ūnĭcŏlor, ōris, *adj*, of one colour

ūnĭcus, a, um, *adj, adv*, ē, only, single, singular, unique

ūnĭo, ōnis, *m, f*, unity

ūnĭversitas, ātis, *f*, universe

ūnĭversum, i, *n*, whole world

ūnĭversus, a, um, *adj, adv*, ē, entire, all together

unquam, *adv*, ever

ūnus, a, um, *adj*, one, only

ūnusquisque, *pron*, each

ūpĭlio, ōnis, *m*, shepherd

urbānĭtas, ātis, *f*, city-life, elegance, courtesy, refinement

urbānus, a, um, *adj, adv*, ē, of the city, refined, elegant, courteous, humorous

urbs, urbis, *f*, city

urcĕus, i, *m*, water-jug

urgĕo, ursi, *v.t.* 2, to press, push, oppress, urge, crowd

ūrīna, ae, *f*, urine

ūrīnātor, ōris, *m*, diver

urna, ae, *f*, water-jar, urn (for voting-tablets or ashes of the dead)

ūro, ussi, ustum, *v.t.* 3, to burn, destroy by fire, scorch, nip with cold

ursa, ae, *f*, she-bear

ursus, i, *m*, bear

urtīca, ae, *f*, nettle

ūrus, i, *m*, wild-ox

ūsĭtātus, a, um, *adj*, usual

uspĭam, *adv*, anywhere, somewhere

usquam, *adv*, anywhere

usquĕ, *adv*, all the way, all the time, as far as, until

ustor, ōris, *m*, corpse-burner

ūsūra, ae, *f*, money-lending, interest

ūsurpātĭo, ōnis, *f*, using, use

ūsurpo, *v.t.* 1, to use, practise, exercise, acquire

ūsus, ūs, *m*, using, use, practice, custom, habit, familiarity, advantage

ut (ŭti), *conj*, so that, that, in order to, to; *adv*, now, as, when, as soon as, where

utcumquĕ (utcunquĕ), *adv*, in whatever way, however, whenever

ūter, tris, *m*, bottle, bag

ūter, tra, trum, *interr. pron*, which of the two

ŭtercumquĕ, utrăcumque, utrumcumque, *pron*, whichever of the two

ŭterlĭbet, utrălĭbet, utrumlĭbet, *pron*, which of the two you please

ŭterque, utrăque, utrumque, *pron*, each of the two, both

ŭtĕrus, i, *m*, womb, belly

ŭtervīs, utrāvīs, utrumvīs, *pron*, which of the two you please

ŭti, see ut

ŭti, see ŭtor

ŭtĭlis, e, *adj, adv*, ĭter, useful, suitable, advantageous

ŭtĭlĭtas, ātis, *f*, usefulness, advantage

ŭtĭnam, *adv*, if only! would that!

ŭtĭquĕ, *adv*, at any rate, at least, certainly

ŭtor, ūsus, *v*. 3, *dep, with abl*, to use, practise, be familiar with

utpŏtĕ, *adv*, namely, as, since

ŭtrimquĕ, *adv*, on both sides

ŭtrōbīquĕ (ŭtrŭbīquĕ), *adv*, on both sides

ŭtrōquĕ, *adv*, in both directions

ŭtrum, *adv, used to form an alternative question*, is it this . . . or that?

ūva, ae, *f*, grape, cluster

ūvĭdus, a, um, *adj*, moist, damp

uxor, ōris, *f*, wife

uxōrius, a, um, *adj*, of a wife

V

văcans, ntis, *adj*, unoccupied

văcātĭo, ōnis, *f*, exemption

vacca, ae, *f*, cow

vaccĭnĭum, ii, *n*, whortleberry

văcillātĭo, ōnis, *f*, vacillation

văcillo, *v.i.* 1, to stagger, sway, hesitate

văco, *v.i.* 1, to be empty, free from, have leisure (for)

văcŭĕfăcĭo, fēci, factum, *v.t.* 3, to empty, clear

văcŭĭtas, ātis, *f*, exemption

văcŭus, a, um, *adj*, empty, free, without, unoccupied, worthless

vădĭmōnĭum, ii, *n*, bail, security

vădo, *v.i.* 3, to go, walk, rush

vădor, *v.t.* 1, *dep*, to bind over by bail

vădōsus, a, um, *adj*, shallow

vădum, i, *n*, a shallow, ford (*often in pl.*)

vae, *interj*, ah! alas!

văfer, fra, frum, *adj*, sly

văgātĭo, ōnis, *f*, wandering

văgīna, ae, *f*, sheath, scabbard

văgĭo, *v.i.* 4, to cry, bawl

văgītus, ūs, *m*, crying, bawling

văgor, *v.i.* 1, *dep*, to wander, roam

văgus, a, um, *adj*, wandering, roaming, uncertain, vague

valdē, *adv*, energetically, very much, very

văle, *imperative*, (*pl*, vălēte), farewell!

vălens, ntis, *adj*, powerful, strong, healthy

vălĕo, *v.i.* 2, to be strong, vigorous or healthy, to have power or influence, to be capable or effective, be worth

vălesco, *v.i.* 3, to grow strong

vălētūdĭnārĭum, ii, *n*, hospital

vălētūdĭnārĭus, i, *m*, invalid

vălētūdo, ĭnis, *f*, health (good or bad)

vălĭdus, a, um, *adj*, strong, powerful, healthy

valles (vallis), is, *f*, valley

vallo, *v.t.* 1, to fortify with a rampart, protect

vallum, i, *n*, rampart, palisade

vallus, i, *m*, stake, palisade

valvae, ārum, *f. pl*, folding-doors

vānesco, *v.i.* 3, to disappear

vānĭtas, ātis, *f*, emptiness, uselessness, vanity

vannus, i, *f*, fan

vānus, a, um, *adj*, empty, groundless, false, deceptive

văpĭdus, a, um, *adj*, spoiled, flat

văpor, ōris, *m*, steam, vapour

văpōro, *v.t.* 1, to fumigate, warm

vappa, ae, *f*, flat wine; *m*, a good-for-nothing

văpŭlo, *v.i.* 1, to be flogged

vărĭco, *v.i.* 1, to straddle

vărĭcōsus, a, um, *adj*, varicose

vărĭĕtas, ātis, *f*, variety

vărĭo, *v.i.t.* 1, to vary; diversify, change

vărĭus, a, um, *adj, adv*, ē, variegated, changing, varying

vărix, ĭcis, *m, f*, varicose vein

vărus, a, um, *adj*, knock-kneed

văs, vădis, *m*, bail, security

văs, văsis, *n*, dish, utensil, military equipment

văsārĭum, ii, *n*, expense-account

vascŭlārĭus, ii, *m*, metal-worker

vastātĭo, ōnis, *f*, devastation

vastātor, ōris, *m*, destroyer

vastĭtas, ātis, *f*, desert, destruction, ruin

vasto, *v.t.* 1, to devastate, destroy, leave vacant

vastus, a, um, *adj*, deserted, desolate, rough, devastated, enormous, vast

vātes, is, *c*, forecaster, poet

vātĭcĭnātĭo, ōnis, *f*, prediction

vātĭcĭnātor, ōris, *m*, prophet

vāticĭnor, *v.i.t.* 1, *dep*, to predict

vătius, a, um, *adj*, bow-legged

vĕ, *conj*, or

vēcordia, ae, *f*, folly, madness

vēcors, dis, *adj*, foolish, mad

vectīgal, ālis, *n*, tax, income

vectīgālis, e, *adj*, tax-paying

vectis, is, *m*, pole, bar, lever

vecto, *v.t.* 1, to convey

vector, ōris, *m*, carrier, traveller, passenger

vectōrius, a, um, *adj*, for carrying

vectūra, ae, *f*, transportation, fare

vectus, a, um, *adj*, conveyed, carried

vĕgĕtus, a, um, *adj*, lively

vēgrandis, e, *adj*, small

vĕhĕmens, ntis, *adj, adv*, nter, violent, powerful, strong

vĕhĭcŭlum, i, *n*, vehicle

vĕho, xi, ctum, *v.t.* 3, to convey; *in passive, or with reflexive pron*, to ride, sail, go

vĕl, *conj*, either, or, indeed

vēlāmen, ĭnis, *n*, cover, garment

vēlāmentum, i, *n*, olive-branch

vēles, ĭtis, *m*, light-armed soldier

vēlifer, ĕra, ĕrum, *adj*, carrying sails

vēlĭfĭcātĭo, ōnis, *f*, sailing

vēlĭfĭcor, *v.i.* 1, *dep*, to sail, gain, procure

vēlĭvŏlus, a, um, *adj*, sail-winged; (mǎre) dotted with ships

vellĭco, *v.t.* 1, to nip, taunt

vello, vulsi, vulsum, *v.t.* 3, to tear out, pluck off

vellus, ĕris, *n*, fleece, hide

vēlo, *v.t.* 1, to cover, wrap up

vēlōcĭtas, ātis, *f*, speed

vēlox, ōcis, *adj, adv*, ĭter, swift, fast, fleet

vēlum, i, *n*, sail, covering

vēlut, *adv*, just as, like

vēna, ae, *f*, vein, disposition

vēnābŭlum, i, *n*, hunting-spear

vēnālĭcĭum, ii, *n*, slave-dealing

vēnālĭcĭus, ii, *m*, slave-dealer

vēnālis, e, *adj*, for sale, able to be bribed, corrupt

vēnālis, is, *m*, slave for sale

vēnātĭcus, a, um, *adj*, of hunting

vēnātĭo, ōnis, *f*, hunting, a hunt, combat of wild beasts

vēnātor, ōris, *m*, hunter

vēnātrix, īcis, *f*, huntress

vēnātus, ūs, *m*, hunting

vendĭbĭlis, e, *adj*, saleable

vendĭtātĭo, ōnis, *f*, boasting

vendĭtĭo, ōnis, *f*, sale

vendĭto, *v.t.* 1, to try to sell

vendĭtor, ōris, *m*, salesman

vendo, dĭdi, dĭtum, *v.t.* 3, to sell, betray, praise

vĕnēfĭca, ae, *f*, witch

vĕnēfĭcĭum, ii, *n*, poisoning, magic

vĕnēfĭcus, a, um, *adj*, poisonous, magic

vĕnēfĭcus, i, *m*, poisoner, sorcerer

vĕnēnātus, a, um, *adj*, poisonous

vĕnēnĭfer, ĕra, ĕrum, *adj*, poisonous

vĕnēno, *v.t.* 1, to poison, dye

vĕnēnum, i, *n*, poison, magic charm, drug

vēnĕo, ii, ĭtum, *v.i.* 4, to be sold

vĕnĕrābĭlis, e, *adj*, worthy of respect

vĕnĕrābundus, a, um, *adj*, devout

vĕnĕrātĭo, ōnis, *f*, great respect

vĕnĕrĕus, a, um, *adj*, venereal

vĕnĕror, *v.t.* 1, *dep*, to worship, revere, honour, entreat

vĕnia, ae, *f*, indulgence, mercy, permission, pardon

vĕnio, vēni, ventum, *v.i.* 4, to come

vēnor, *v.i.t.* 1, *dep*, to hunt

venter, tris, *m*, belly

ventĭlo, *v.t.* 1, to wave, fan

ventĭto, *v.i.* 1, to keep coming

ventōsus, a, um, *adj*, windy, swift, light, changeable, vain

ventrĭcŭlus, i, *m*, ventricle

ventūrus, *fut. partic.* from **vĕnĭo**

ventus, i, *m*, wind

vēnūcŭla (uva), a preserving grape

vēnundo, dĕdi, dătum, *v.t.* 1, to sell

vĕnus, ĕris, *f*, love, beauty, highest throw of the dice

vēnus, ūs, *m*, (vēnum, i, *n*), sale

vēnustas, ātis, *f*, charm, beauty

vĕnustus, a, um, *adj, adv*, ē, charming, graceful, beautiful

vĕprēcŭla, ae, *f*, small thorn-bush

vĕpres, is, *m*, thorn-bush

vēr, vēris, *n*, spring

vēra, see **vērus**

vērācĭtas, ātis, *f*, veracity

vērax, ācis, *adj*, true

verbēna, ae, *f*, foliage, branches

verber, ĕris, *n*, lash, whip, flogging, blow

verbĕrātĭo, ōnis, *f*, punishment

verbĕro, *v.t.* 1, to whip, strike

verbōsus, a, um, *adj*, effusive

verbum, i, *n*, word, language, conversation; **verba dare** to deceive

vērē, *adv*, really, truly

vērēcundĭa, ae, *f*, shyness

vērēcundor, *v.i.* 1, *dep*, to be shy

vērēcundus, a, um, *adj, adv*, ē, shy, modest

vĕrendus, a, um, *adj*, venerable, terrible

vĕrĕor, *v.i.t.* 2, *dep*, to fear, respect

vergo, *v.i.* 3, to turn, bend, lie, be situated

vēridĭcus, a, um, *adj*, truthful

vērīsimĭlis, e, *adj*, probable

vērĭtas, ātis, *f*, truth, reality

vermĭcŭlus, i, *m*, worm, grub

verminōsus, a, um, *adj*, worm-eaten

vermis, is, *m*, worm

verna, ae, *c*, slave born in his master's house

vernācŭlus, a, um, *adj*, domestic

vernīlĭter, *adv*, slavishly

verno, *v.i.* 1, to flourish, bloom

vernus, a, um, *adj*, of spring

vērō, *adv*, in fact, certainly, but indeed, however

verres, is, *m*, pig

verro, verri, versum, *v.t.* 3, to sweep, brush, impel, take away

verrūca, ae, *f*, wart, blemish

versātĭlis, e, *adj*, movable

versĭcŏlor, ōris, *adj*, of different colours

versĭcŭlus, i, *m*, single line of verse (or prose)

verso, *v.t.* 1, to turn, twist, whirl, consider

versor, *v.i.* 1, *dep*, to live, stay, be situated, be engaged on

versūra, ae, *f*, borrowing, loan

versus, *adv*, towards

versus, ūs, *m*, row, line, verse

versūtus, a, um, *adj*, *adv*, ē, clever, shrewd, cunning, sly

vertĕbra, ae, *f*, vertebra

vertex, ĭcis, *m*, whirlpool, whirlwind, flame, crown of the head, summit, peak

vertĭcōsus, a, um, *adj*, eddying

vertĭgĭnōsus, a, um, *adj*, suffering from giddiness

vertĭgo, ĭnis, *f*, dizziness

vēro, see vērus

verto, ti, sum, *v.i.t.* 3, to turn, change; turn, change, alter, overthrow, translate

vĕru, ūs, *n*, roasting-spit, javelin

vĕrŭcŭlum, i, *n*, skewer, small javelin

vērum, *adv*, but, yet, still

vērum, i, *n*, truth, reality, fact

vērumtămen, *conj*, nevertheless

vērus, a, um, *adj*, *adv*, ō, ē, true, real, proper, right

vĕrūtum, i, *n*, javelin

vĕrūtus, a, um, *adj*, armed with a javelin

vervex, ēcis, *m*, wether, sheep

vēsānia, ae, *f*, insanity

vēsānus, a, um, *adj*, mad, fierce

vescor, *v.i.t.* 3, *dep. with abl*, to feed on

vescus, a, um, *adj*, thin, weak

vēsīca, ae, *f*, bladder

vespa, ae, *f*, wasp

vesper, ĕris (ĕri), *m*, evening, the West

vespĕra, ae, *f*, evening, the West

vespĕrasco, āvi, *v.i.* 3, to draw towards evening

vespertīnus, a, um, *adj*, of evening, western

vespillo, ōnis, *m*, undertaker

vesta, ae, *f*, fire

vestālis, e, *adj*, of Vesta, the Goddess of Fire, Hearth, Home

vestālis, is, *f*, priestess of Vesta

vester, tra, trum, *adj*, your

vestiārium, ii, *n*, wardrobe

vestibŭlum, i, *n*, entrance-hall

vestigium, ii, *n*, footstep, track, sole of foot, mark, moment, instant; ē vestigio, instantly

vestigo, *v.t.* 1, to search out, investigate

vestimentum, i, *n*, clothing

vestio, *v.t.* 4, to clothe, cover

vestis, is, *f*, clothing, clothes, carpet, curtain

vestītus, ūs, *m*, clothes, dress

vĕtĕrānus, a, um, *adj*, old, veteran

vĕtĕrānus, i, *m*, veteran soldier

vĕtĕrātor, ōris, *m*, crafty, wily or sly person

vĕtĕrātōrius, a, um, *adj*, sly

vĕtĕres, um, *m. pl*, ancestors

vĕtĕrīnārius, a, um, *adj*, veterinary

vĕternus, i, *m*, sluggishness

vĕtĭtum, i, *n*, something forbidden, prohibition

vĕtĭtus, a, um, *adj*, forbidden

vĕto, ŭi, ĭtum, *v.t.* 1, to forbid

vĕtŭlus, a, um, *adj*, old

vĕtus, ĕris, *adj*, old, former

vĕtustas, ātis, *f*, old age, antiquity, posterity

vĕtustus, a, um, *adj*, old

vexātĭo, ōnis, *f*, distress

vexillārius, ii, *m*, standard-bearer

vexillum, ii, *n*, standard, ensign

vexo, *v.t.* 1, to shake, injure, molest, harass, torment

via, ae, *f*, road, street, way, method

viātĭcum, i, *n*, travelling-expenses, soldier's savings

viātor, ōris, *m*, traveller

vībex, ĭcis, *f*, weal

vībro, *v.i.t.* 1, to quiver; brandish, shake

vĭcārius, ii, *m*, deputy

For List of Abbreviations used, turn to pages 3, 4

vīcēni, ae, a, *pl. adj*, twenty each

vicēsimus (vicensimus), a, um, *adj*, twentieth

vicia, ae, *f*, vetch

vicies (viciens), *adv*, twenty times

vicinia, ae, *f*, neighbourhood

vicīnitas, ātis, *f*, proximity, neighbourhood

vicīnus, a, um, *adj*, neighbouring, similar

vicīnus, i, *m*, neighbour

vicis (*genitive*), vicem, vice, change, alternation, recompense, lot, misfortune, position, duty; in vicem, per vices, alternately; vicem, vice, instead of

vicissim, *adv*, in turn

vicissitūdo, inis, *f*, change

victima, ae, *f*, victim for sacrifice

victor, ōris, *m*, conqueror

victōria, ae, *f*, victory

victrix, icis, *f*, female conqueror

victrix, icis, *adj*, victorious

victus, ūs, *m*, nutriment, diet

vicus, i, *m*, street, village

vidēlicet, *adv*, obviously

vidĕo, vidi, vīsum, *v.t.* 2, to see, perceive, understand, consider, take care, see to it

vidĕor, visus, *v.* 2, *dep*, to seem; *impers*, it seems right or good

vidŭa, ae, *f*, widow

vidŭitas, ātis, *f*, bereavement

vidŭlus, i, *m*, valise

vidŭo, *v.t.* 1, to deprive

vidŭus, a, um, *adj*, robbed, widowed

viētus, a, um, *adj*, withered

vigĕo, *v.i.* 2, to flourish, thrive

vigesco, gŭi, *v.i.* 3, to flourish, thrive

vigil, ilis, *adj*, alert, watching

vigil, ilis, *m*, watchman

vigilans, ntis, *adj, adv*, nter, watchful, careful

vigilantia, ae, *f*, watchfulness

vigilia, ae, *f*, wakefulness, vigilance, guard, watch

vigilo, *v.i.t.* 1, to keep awake, be vigilant; spend (time) in watching

viginti, *indecl. adj*, twenty

vigor, ōris, *m*, liveliness

vilico, *v.i.t.* 1, to superintend

vilicus (villicus), i, *m*, superintendent

vilis, e, *adj*, cheap, mean

vilitas, ātis, *f*, cheapness

villa, ae, *f*, country-house

villāticus, a, um, *adj*, of a villa

villicus see vilicus

villōsus, a, um, *adj*, hairy, shaggy

villŭla, ae, *f*, small villa

villus, i, *m*, tuft of hair

vīmen, inis, *n*, pliant branch

Vīminālis (collis), the Viminal, one of the seven hills of Rome

vīminĕus, a, um, *adj*, of wickerwork

vīnārium, ii, *n*, wine-bottle

vīnārius, a, um, *adj*, of wine

vīnārius, i, *m*, vintner

vincio, nxi, nctum, *v.t.* 4, to bind, tie, surround

vinco, vici, victum, *v.i.t.* 3, to prevail; conquer, overcome, prove conclusively

vincŭlum (vinclum), i, *n*, cord, bond, fetter; *pl*, prison

vindēmia, ae, *f*, grape-gathering, wine

vindēmiātor, ōris, *m*, grape-gatherer

vindex, icis, *c*, claimant, defender, liberator, avenger

vindiciae, ārum, *f. pl*, legal claim

vindico, *v.t.* 1, to claim, appropriate, set free, protect, avenge

vindicta, ae, *f*, rod used to set free a slave

vinĕa, ae, *f*, vineyard, protective shed for soldiers

vinētum, i, *n*, vineyard

vīnitor, ōris, *m*, vine-pruner

vīnōlentia, ae, *f*, wine-drinking

vīnōlentus, a, um, *adj*, drunk

vīnōsus, a, um, *adj*, drunken

vīnum, i, *n*, wine

viōla, ae, *f*, violet

viōlābilis, e, *adj*, able to be injured or harmed

viōlārium, ii, *n*, bed of violets

viōlātio, ōnis, *f*, violation, profanation

viōlātor, ōris, *m*, injurer

viōlens, ntis, *adj, adv*, nter, impetuous, furious

viōlentia, ae, *f*, ferocity

viōlentus, a, um, *adj*, violent, impetuous

viōlo, *v.t.* 1, to injure, outrage, break

vipĕra, ae, *f*, viper

vipĕrĕus, a, um, *adj*, of a viper or snake

vipĕrinus, a, um, *adj*, of a viper or snake

vir, viri, *m*, man, husband

virāgo, inis, *f*, female soldier, heroine

virectum, i, *n*, glade, turf

virĕo, *v.i.* 2, to be green, flourish

vires, see vis

viresco, *v.i.* 3, to become green, flourish

virētum, i, *n*, glade, turf

virga, ae, *f*, twig, rod

virgātus, a, um, *adj*, striped

virgĕus, a, um, *adj*, made of rods

virgīnālis, e, *adj*, girl-like

virgīnĕus, a, um, *adj*, of a virgin

virgīnitas, ātis, *f*, virginity

virgo, inis, *f*, virgin, girl

virgŭla, ae, *f*, small twig

virgultum, i, *n*, shrubbery

virgultus, a, um, *adj*, bushy

virīdārium, ii, *n*, park

virĭdis, e, *adj*, green, fresh, young, blooming

virĭditas, ātis, *f*, greenness, freshness

virĭdo, *v.i.t.* 1, to be green; make green

virīlis, e, *adj*, male, manly, full-grown, vigorous

virītim, *adv*, individually

virōsus, a, um, *adj*, stinking

virtūs, ūtis, *f*, courage, manhood, military skill, goodness, moral perfection

vīrus, i, *n*, slime, poison, virus

vis, (*no genit*), vim, vi, *f*, force, power, violence, quantity, meaning; vīres, ium, *pl*, strength, power

viscātus, a, um, *adj*, sprinkled with lime

viscĕra, um, *n. pl*, inwards, flesh, bowels

viscum, i, *n*, mistletoe, birdlime

vīsio, ōnis, *f*, idea, notion

vīsĭto, *v.t.* 1, to visit

vīso, si, sum, *v.t.* 3, to survey, visit

vīsum, i, *n*, appearance, sight

vīsus, ūs, *m*, look, sight, appearance

vīta, ae, *f*, life

vītābĭlis, e, *adj*, to be avoided

vītālis, e, *adj*, of life, vital

vītātio, ōnis, *f*, avoidance

vītellus, i, *m*, small calf, egg-yolk

vītĕus, a, um, *adj*, of the vine

vĭtio, *v.t.* 1, to spoil, mar, infect

vĭtiōsitas, ātis, *f*, vice

vĭtiōsus, a, um, *adj, adv*, ē, faulty, defective, wicked

vītis, is, *f*, vine, vine-branch

vītisātor, ōris, *m*, vine-planter

vĭtium, ii, *n*, fault, defect, blemish, error, crime

vīto, *v.t.* 1, to avoid

vĭtrĕus, a, um, *adj*, made of glass, transparent, shining

vītrĭcus, i, *m*, step-father

vĭtrum, i, *n*, glass, woad

vitta, ae, *f*, hair-ribbon

vittātus, a, um, *adj*, bound with a hair-ribbon

vĭtŭlīnus, a, um, *adj*, of a calf

vĭtŭlus, i, *m* (vĭtŭla, ae, *f*), calf

vĭtŭpĕrātio, ōnis, *f*, blame, censure

vĭtŭpĕro, *v.t.* 1, to blame, censure

vīvārium, ii, *n*, fish-pond, game-reserve

vīvācitas, ātis, *f*, vigour or length of life

vīvax, ācis, *adj*, long-lived

vīvĭdus, a, um, *adj*, lively, animated

vīvo, xi, ctum, *v.i.* 3, to live

vīvus, a, um, *adj*, alive, fresh, natural, life-like

vix, *adv*, scarcely, barely

vixdum, *adv*, scarcely then

vōcābŭlum, i, *n*, name

vōcālis, e, *adj*, vocal

vōcātu, *abl*, at the bidding

vōcĭfĕrātio, ōnis, *f*, outcry

vōcĭfĕror, *v.i.t.* 1, *dep*, to cry out

vōcĭto, *v.i.t.* 1, to call out; name

vŏco, *v.i.t.* 1, to call; summon, urge, challenge, arouse, name

vōcŭla, ae, *f*, feeble voice

vŏlantes, ium, *c, pl*, birds

vŏlātĭcus, a, um, *adj*, flighty, fleeting

vŏlātĭlis, e, *adj*, flying, swift

vŏlātus, ūs, *m*, flight

vŏlens, ntis, *adj*, willing, favourable

volg . . . see vulg. . . .

vŏlĭto, *v.i.* 1, to fly about, flit, flutter

vŏlo, velle, vŏlŭi, *v.i.t.* (*irreg*), to wish, mean

vŏlo, *v.i.* 1, to fly

volp . . . see vulp. . . .

volsella, ae, *f*, tweezers

volt, see vult. . . .

vŏlūbĭlis, e, *adj*, turning, spinning, changeable

vŏlūbĭlitas, ātis, *f*, whirling motion, fluency

vŏlūcer, cris, cre, *adj*, flying, swift, transient

vŏlūmen, ĭnis, *n*, book, roll, fold

vŏluntārius, a, um, *adj*, voluntary; (of soldiers) volunteers

vŏluntas, ātis, *f*, wish, choice, will, affection, good-will

vŏluptārius, a, um, *adj*, sensual

vŏluptas, ātis, *f*, pleasure, delight

vŏlūto, *v.i.t.* 1, to roll, twist, writhe about; ponder, consider

volva (vulva), ae, *f*, womb

volvo, volvi, vŏlūtum, *v.t.* 3, to roll, unroll, turn, ponder, consider

vōmer, ĕris, *m*, ploughshare

vŏmĭca, ae, *f*, abscess, boil

vŏmĭtio, ōnis, *f*, vomiting

vŏmo, ŭi, ĭtum, *v.i.t.* 3, to vomit; throw up, pour out

vŏrāgo, ĭnis, *f*, abyss, whirlpool

vŏrax, ācis, *adj*, greedy, destructive

vŏro, *v.t.* 1, to devour, destroy

vortex, see vertex

vos, *pron*, you (*plural*)

vŏtīvus, a, um, *adj*, concerning a promise or vow

vŏtum, i, *n*, promise, vow, offering, wish, longing

vŏvĕo, vōvi, vōtum, *v.t.* 2, to promise, vow, dedicate

vox, vōcis, *f*, voice, sound, speech, saying, proverb

vulgāris, e, *adj*, general, ordinary, common

vulgātor, ōris, *m*, a gossip

vulgātus, a, um, *adj*, ordinary, notorious

vulgo, *v.t.* 1, to divulge, spread about

vulgō, *adv*, everywhere, openly

vulgus, i, *n*, the public, crowd, rabble

vulnĕrātus, a, um, *adj*, wounded

vulnĕro, *v.t.* 1, to wound, hurt

vulnifĭcus, a, um, *adj*, wounding

vulnus, ĕris, *n*, wound, blow

vulpēcŭla, ae, *f*, small fox

vulpes, is, *f*, fox

vulsus, a, um, *adj*, hairless, effeminate

vultur, ŭris, *m*, vulture

vultŭrĭus, ii, *m*, vulture

vultus, ūs, *m*, expression, look, features, aspect, face

X

xĭphĭas, ae, *m*, sword-fish

xystus, i, *m* (xystum, i, *n*), open colonnade

Z

zĕphўrus, i, *m*, west wind

zōdĭăcus, i, *m*, zodiac

zōna, ae, *f*, belt, girdle, zone

PROPER NAMES

For List of Abbreviations used, turn to pages 3, 4

A

Ăcădēmĭa, ae, *f*, the Academy, a gymnasium near Athens where Plato taught

Ăcădēmus, i, *m*, a Greek hero

Ăcestes, ae, *m*, a king of Sicily

Ăchaemĕnes, is, *m*, a king of Persia

Ăchaĭa, ae, *f*, a Roman province in the northern part of the Peloponnessus

Ăchātes, ae, *m*, 1, a river in Sicily; 2, a friend of Aeneas

Ăchĕron, ntis, *m*, 1, a river in Epirus; 2, a river in the Lower World

Ăchilles, is, *m*, the Greek hero, son of Peleus and Thetis

Achīvus, a, um, *adj*, Achaean, Greek

Ăcrŏcĕraunĭa, ōrum, *n.pl*, a rocky headland in Epirus

Actē, es, *f*, an old name of Attica

Actĭum, ĭi, *n*, a town in Epirus

Adherbal, ălis, *m*, a Numidian prince

Ădōnis, is, *m*, a beautiful youth, beloved of Venus

Ădŭātŭci, ōrum, *m, pl*, a Gallic tribe

Aeăcus, i, *m*, a king of Aegina who became a judge in the Lower World

Aedŭi, ōrum, *m. pl*, a Gallic tribe

Aeētēs, ae, *m*, a king of Colchis, father of Medea

Aegaeum mare, *n*, the Aegean Sea

Aegātes, um, *f. pl*, three islands off the west coast of Sicily

Aegeus, i, *m*, a king of Athens, father of Theseus

Aegīna, ae, *f*, an island near Athens

Aegyptus, i, *f*, Egypt

Aemilĭus, a, um, *adj*, the name of a Roman patrician "gens"

Aenēas, ae, *m*, the hero of Vergil's Aeneid, son of Venus and Anchises

Aeŏlus, i, *m*, the god of the winds

Aequi, ōrum, *m.pl*, an Italian people

Aeschўlus, i, *m*, the Athenian tragic poet

Aesōpus, i, *m*, the Greek writer of fables (sixth century B.C.)

Aethĭŏpĭa, ae, *f*, Ethiopia

Aethĭŏpissa, ae, *f*, Ethiopian, negress

Aethĭops, ŏpis, *m*, Ethiopian, negro

Aetna, ae, *f*, Etna, the volcano in Sicily

Ăfer, fra, frum, *adj*, African

Ăfrica, ae, *f*, Africa

Ăfricus, i, *m*, the south-west wind

Ăgămemnon, ŏnis, *m*, a king of Mycenae

Ăgăthŏclēs, is, *m*, a king of Sicily

Ăgēnor, ŏris, *m*, king of Phoenicia

Ăgēsĭlāus, i, *m*, a king of Sparta

Ăglāĭa, ae, *f*, one of the Graces

Agrĭcŏla, ae, *m*, (A.D. 37–93) governor of Britain, father-in-law of Tacitus

Agrĭgentum, i, *n*, a city on the south coast of Sicily

Agrippa, ae, *m*, a Roman family name; Marcus Vipsanius A., the friend of Augustus

Agrippīna, ae, *f*, mother of Nero

Ăhēnŏbarbus, i, *m*, the name of a Roman family ("red-beard")

Ăjax, ăcis, *m*, the name of a Greek hero

Alba Longa, *f*, the founder city of Rome

Alcaeus, i, *m*, the Greek lyric poet (c. 600 B.C.)

Alcestis, is, *f*, the wife of Admetus, whose life she saved by her own death

Alceus, ĕi, *m*, grandfather of Hercules

Alcĭbĭădes, is, *m*, an Athenian general

Alcmēne, es, *f*, the mother of Hercules by Juppiter

Alecto (Allecto),us, *f*, one of the three Furies

Ălēmanni, ōrum, *m. pl*, a German tribe

Alexander, dri, *m* (the Great: 356–323 B.C.), king of Macedonia

Alexandrĭa, ae, *f*, a city on the coast of Egypt

Allĭa, ae, *f*, a small river north of Rome

Allŏbrŏges, um, *m. pl*, a Gallic tribe

Alpēs, ĭum, *f. pl*, the Alps

Ămāryllis, idis, *f*, a shepherdess

Ămastris, is, *f*, a town in Paphlagonia

Ămāzon, ŏnis, *f*, an Amazon; (*pl*.) a race of warlike women

Ambĭŏrix, rĭgis, *m*, a chief of the Eburones

Ammōn, ōnis, *m,* a name of Juppiter

Amphiārāus, i, *m,* a famous Greek prophet

Amphīŏn, ŏnis, *m,* a king of Thebes

Amphītrŭo, ōnis, *m,* a king of Thebes

Amūlius, i, *m,* a king of Alba Longa

Ănăcrĕŏn, ontis, *m,* a Greek lyric poet

Anchīses, ae, *m,* the father of Aeneas

Ancus Martius, i, *m,* the fourth king of Rome (640–616 B.C.)

Andrŏmăchē, es, *f,* wife of Hector

Andrŏmĕda, ae, *f,* daughter of Cepheus, rescued from a sea-monster by Perseus became a star

Andrŏnīcus, i, *m,* L. Livius A., the first Roman poet

Andros, i, *f,* one of the Cyclades Islands

Angli, ōrum, *m. pl,* a German tribe

Antīgŏnē, es, *f,* daughter of Oedipus

Antiŏchīa, ae, *f,* Antioch

Antiŏchus, i, *m,* a king of Syria

Antipăter, tri, *m,* 1, one of Alexander's generals; 2, L. Caelius A. a Roman annalist

Antōnīnus, i, *m,* the name of two Roman emperors

Antōnius, a, um, *adj,* the name of a Roman "gens": Marcus Antonius, the triumvir, opponent of Octavianus

Ănūbis, bis, *m,* an Egyptian god

Anxur, ŭris, *n,* an ancient Volscian town

Ăornos, i, *m,* ("birdless"), Lake Avernus

Ăpennīnus, i, *m,* the Apennine Mts.

Āpis, is, *m,* the ox worshipped as a god by the Egyptians

Ăpollo, inis, *m,* Apollo, the sun god, also the god of archery, music and poetry

Ăpollōnius Rhŏdĭus, ii, *m,* a Greek poet

Appius, ii, *m,* a Roman praenomen; **Appia Via,** *f,* the Appian Way from Rome to Capua, begun by Appius Claudius, the censor (312 B.C.)

Apūlia, ae, *f,* a region of south Italy

Ăquilēia, ae, *f,* a town of north Italy

Ăquilo, ōnis, *m,* the north wind

Ăquinum, i, *n,* a town in Latium

Ăquitānia, ae, *f,* a province in south-west Gaul

Ărăbia, ae, *f,* Arabia

Ărabs, ăbis, *adj,* Arabian

Ărar, ăris, *m,* a river in Gaul

Arcădia, ae, *f,* a region of the Peloponnesus

Arcas, ădis, *m,* an Arcadian

Archĭlŏchus, i, *m,* a Greek poet

Archĭmēdēs, is, *m,* a famous mathematician

Ardĕa, ae, *f,* a town in Latium

Ardŭenna, ae, *f,* the Ardennes

Ărĕŏpăgus, i, *m,* Ares' hill at Athens, seat of the supreme court

Ārēs, is, *m,* the Greek war god

Argīlētum, i, *n,* a district of Rome

Argō, us, *f,* the ship in which Jason sailed to recover the Golden Fleece

Argŏlis, idis, *f,* a district of the Peloponnesus

Argos, *n,* the capital of Argolis

Ăriadne, es, *f,* daughter of Minos, king of Crete, who helped Theseus to kill the Minotaur

Ărīcia, ae, *f,* an old town in Latium

Ărīminum, i, *n,* a town in Umbria

Ărīon, ōnis, *m,* a famous poet who was saved from drowning by a dolphin

Ariŏvistus, i, *m,* a German chieftain

Ăristŏphănēs, is, *m,* a Greek comic poet

Ăristŏtĕles, is, *m,* the famous Greek philosopher

Armĕnia, ae, *f,* a country in Asia

Armīnius, i, *m,* a German prince

Armŏrīcae, ārum, *f. pl,* states in north-west Gaul

Arnus, i, *m,* a river of Etruria

Arpīnum, i, *n,* a town in Latium

Artaxăta, ōrum, *n.pl,* capital of Armenia

Artaxerxēs, is, *m,* name of four Persian kings

Arverni, ōrum, *m. pl,* a Gallic tribe

Ascānius, i, *m,* the son of Aeneas

Ăsia, ae, *f,* Asia

Assărăcus, i, *m,* a king of Troy

Assўria, ae, *f,* a country of Asia

Ătălanta, ae, *f,* a Boeotian girl famous for the speed of her running

Ăthēnae, ārum, *f. pl,* Athens

Ăthos, *m,* a mountain in Macedonia

Ătīlius, a, um, *adj,* the name of a Roman "gens"

Atlas, antis, *m,* a mountain in Africa

Ătrĕbătes, um, *m. pl,* a Gallic tribe

Ătreus, ei, *m.* the son of Pelops

Attălus, i, *m.* the name of several kings of Pergamum

Attĭca, ae, *f,* the region around Athens

Attĭcus, a, um, *adj,* Athenian, Attic

Ătўs, yos, *m,* the son of Hercules

Augustus, i, *m,* surname of Octavius, and all Roman emperors

Aulis, idis, *f,* a port in Boeotia

Avāricum, i, *n*, a Gallic town

Aventīnus, i, *m*, one of the seven hills of Rome

Avernus lacus, i, *m*, a lake near Cumae

Axius, ii, *m*, a river in Macedonia

B

Băbўlōn, ōnis, *f*, Babylon

Baccha, ae, *f*, a female worshipper of Bacchus

Bacchus, i, *m*, the god of wine

Bāiae, ārum, *f. pl*, a town and Roman holiday-resort on the Campanian coast

Bălĕāres insulae, *f. pl*, the Balearic Islands (Majorca)

Barcas, ae, *m*, the founder of the famous Carthaginian family to which Hannibal belonged

Bătāvi, ōrum, *m. pl*, a tribe inhabiting what is now Holland

Belgae, ārum, *m. pl*, a tribe inhabiting northern Gaul

Bellĕrŏphon, ontis, *m*, the rider of Pegasus who went to kill the Chimaera

Bellōna, ae, *f*, the goddess of War

Bĕnĕventum, i, *n*, a town in Samnium

Bibractĕ, is, *n*, capital of the Gallic tribe, the Aedui

Bĭthўnĭa, ae, *f*, a country in Asia Minor

Bĭtŭrĭges, um, *m. pl*, a tribe of Aquitania

Boadicĕa (or Boudicca), ae, *f*, a queen of the Iceni

Bocchus, i, *m*, a king of Mauritania

Boeōtĭa, ae, *f*, a district in northern Greece

Bōii, ōrum, *m, pl*, a Celtic people

Bōla, ae, *f*, a town of the Aequi

Bŏmilcar, āris, *m*, a Carthaginian general

Bŏnōnĭa, ae, *f*, a town in Cisalpine Gaul

Bŏōtes, ae, *m*, a constellation (from "bos", an ox)

Bŏrĕās, ae, *m*, the north wind

Bosphŏrus, i, *m*, the Straits between Thrace and Asia Minor

Brennus, i, *m*, a Gallic leader who defeated the Romans at the river Allia, 390 B.C.

Brĭāreus, i, *m*, a hundred-armed giant

Brĭgantes, um, *m. pl*, a British tribe

Brīsēis, ĭdis, *f*, Hippodamia, the slave of Achilles

Britanni, ōrum, *m. pl*, the Britons

Britannus, Brĭtannĭcus, a, um, British

Brundĭsĭum, ii, *n*, a town in Calabria and a Roman port

Brutii, ōrum, *m. pl*, a tribe in the southern tip of Italy

Brūtus, i, *m*, a Roman surname; 1, L. Junius B. the first Roman consul; 2, M. Junius B. the murderer of Caesar

Bўzantĭum, ii, *n*, a Greek city in Thrace

C

Cācus, i, *m*, a giant, son of Vulcan, slain by Hercules

Cadmus, i, *m*, the son of Agenor

Caelĭus mons, one of the seven hills of Rome

Caerĕ, itis, *n*, an Etruscan city

Caesar, āris, *m*, a Roman family name; Caius Julius C. general, statesman author and dictator

Caesărĕa, ae, *f*, a town in Palestine

Caius, i, *m*, a Roman "praenomen"

Călābria, ae, *f*, the south-eastern part of Italy

Călēdōnĭa, ae, *f*, the Highlands of Scotland

Călĭgŭla, ae, *m*, the nickname of Gaius, the third Roman emperor, ("little-boots")

Callĭmachus, i, *m*, a Greek poet

Callĭŏpē, ēs, *f*, the Muse of poetry

Cāmillus, i, *m*, M. Furius C. a Roman statesman and general

Campānĭa, ae, *f*, a district of Central Italy, famous for its fertility

Camŭlŏdūnum, i, *n*, a town in Britain (now Colchester)

Cannae, ārum, *f. pl*, a village in Apulia, scene of a great defeat of the Romans by Hannibal

Cantābrĭa, ae, *f*, a region in north-west Spain

Cantĭum, ii, *n*, a district in Britain (now Kent)

Cănŭsĭum, ii, *n*, a town in Apulia

Căpĭtōlĭum, ii, *n*, the Capitol and the Capitol Hill at Rome

Cappădŏcĭa, ae, *f*, a district of Asia Minor

Caprĕae, ārum, *f. pl*, an island off the Campanian coast (now Capri)

Căpŭa, ae, *f*, a city of Campania

Cărăcalla, ae, *m*, a Roman emperor

Caratācus, i, *m*, a British king

Cāria, ae, *f*, a province of Asia Minor

Carnūtes, um, *m. pl*, a Gallic tribe

Carrhae, ārum, *f. pl*, a town in Mesopotamia

For List of Abbreviations used, turn to pages 3, 4

Carthāgo, ĭnis, *f,* Carthage, a city in North Africa

Cassander, dri, *m,* a king of Macedonia

Cassandra, ae, *f,* the daughter of Priam, gifted with prophecy

Cassius, a, um, *adj,* the name of a Roman "gens": C. Cassius Longinus, one of Caesar's murderers

Cassivellaunus, i, *m,* a British chief

Castor, ŏris, *m,* twin-brother of Pollux; a twin-star and a guide to sailors

Cătilīna, ae, *m,* L. Sergius C., an impoverished patrician who led a conspiracy against the state

Căto, ōnis, *m,* a Roman family name; M. Porcius C., famous for his attacks on Roman luxury and indulgence

Cătullus, i, *m,* a Roman lyric poet

Cătŭlus, i, *m,* a Roman family name

Caucāsus, i, *m,* the Caucasus Mts.

Caudĭum, ii, *n,* a city in Samnium

Caurus, i, *m,* the north-west wind

Cēbenna, ae, *f,* a mountain range in Gaul (now the Cevennes)

Cēcrops, ŏpis, *m,* the first king of Athens

Celtae, ārum, *m. pl,* the Celts

Celtibēri, ōrum, *m. pl,* a people of central Spain, originally Celts

Cēphīsus, i, *m,* a river (god)

Cerbĕrus, i, *m,* the three-headed dog guarding the entrance to Hades

Cĕrēs, ĕris, *f,* the goddess of agriculture

Chaerōnēa, ae, *f,* a town in Boeotia

Chalcēdon, ŏnis, *f,* a town in Bithynia

Chalcis, ĭdis, *f,* a town of Euboea

Chaldaei, ōrum, *m. pl,* an Assyrian people

Chăŏs, i, *n,* the Lower World

Chăron, ontis, *m,* the ferryman who took the dead across the Styx

Chărybdis, is, *f,* a whirlpool off Sicily

Chatti, ōrum, *m. pl,* German tribe

Chauci, ōrum, *m. pl,* German tribe

Cherusci, ōrum, *m. pl,* German tribe

Chimaera, ae, *f,* a fire-breathing monster

Chĭos, ii, *f,* an island in the Aegean Sea

Chrȳsippus, i, *m,* a Stoic philosopher

Cicĕro, ōnis, *m,* M. Tullius C., the great Roman statesman and orator

Cilicia, ae, *f,* a province in Asia Minor

Cimbri, ōrum. *m. pl,* a German tribe who invaded Italy

Cīmon, ōnis, *m,* an Athenian statesman and general

Cincinnātus, i, *m,* a Roman family name: L. Quinctius C. dictator in 458 B.C.

Cīnĕas, ae, *m,* the friend of Pyrrhus

Cingĕtŏrix, ĭgis, *m,* a chief of the Treveri

Cinna, ae, *m,* a Roman family name; L. Cornelius C., one of Marius' lieutenants

Circē, es, *f,* an enchantress, daughter of the sun

Cirta, ae, *f,* a Numidian city

Claudius, a, um, *adj,* the name of two Roman "gentes": the fourth Roman emperor

Clĕon, ōnis, *m,* an Athenian demagogue

Clĕŏpātra, ae, *f,* Queen of Egypt

Clisthĕnes, is, *m,* an Athenian statesman

Clītumnus, i, *m,* a river in Umbria

Clōdĭus, P. Clodius Pulcher, tribune of the People, killed by Milo

Clūsĭum, ii, *n,* an Etruscan town

Clȳtaemnēstra, ae, *f,* the wife of Agamemnon

Cōcȳtus, i, *m,* a river in the Lower World

Cōdrus, i, *m,* an Athenian king

Colchis, ĭdis, *f,* a country on the Black Sea

Collātĭa, ae, *f,* a town in Latium

Collīna porta, *f,* a gate of Rome

Commŏdus, i, *m,* a Roman emperor

Cōmum, i, *n,* a town of Cisalpine Gaul

Concordia, ae, *f,* the goddess of Concord

Cŏnōn, ōnis, *m,* an Athenian general

Constantīnus, i, *m,* a Roman emperor

Constantĭus, i, *m,* the name of three Roman emperors

Corbŭlo, ōnis, *m,* a Roman general

Corcȳra, ae, *f,* an island in the Ionian Sea (now Corfu)

Corfīnĭum, ii, *n,* capital of the Paeligni

Coriŏtanus, i, *m,* an early Roman hero

Cornēlia, ae, *f,* the daughter of P. Scipio Africanus, and mother of the Gracchi

Cornēlĭus, ii, *m,* the name of a Roman "gens", to which belonged the Scipios, and Sulla

Corsica, ae, f, Corsica

Cōs, Cŏi, f, an island in the Aegean

Cotta, ae, m, a Roman family name

Crassus, i, m, a Roman family name; I, L. Licinius C., the orator; 2, M. Licinius C., the triumvir

Crĕmōna, ae, f, a town in Cisalpine Gaul

Crĕon, ontis, m, a king of Corinth

Crēta, ae, f, Crete

Crĕūsa, ae, f, the wife of Aeneas

Croesus, i, m, a king of Lydia, famous for his riches

Crŏtōn, ōnis, c, (Crotona, ae, f), a Greek settlement in Bruttium

Cūmae, ārum, f. pl, an ancient city of Campania, the home of the Sibyl

Cŭpīdo, ĭnis, m, the god of love

Cūres, ium, f. pl, an ancient town of the Sabines

Cŭriātii, ōrum, m. pl, an Alban family, from which came the three brothers who fought with the Roman Horatii

Cŭrius, a, um, adj, the name of a Roman "gens"

Curtius, a, um, adj, the name of a Roman "gens"

Cўbĕlē, es, f, a Phrygian goddess, worshipped in Rome

Cўclădes, um, f. pl, a group of islands in the Aegean Sea

Cyclōpes, um, m. pl, a race of one-eyed giants

Cydnus, i, m, a river in Cilicia

Cynthia, ae, f, Diana

Cŷprus, i, f, Cyprus

Cŷrēne, es, f, a Greek city of north Africa

Cŷrus, i, m, the founder of the Persian Empire

Cŷthērēia, ae, f, Venus

Cŷtōrus, i, m, a mountain-range of Paphlagonia

D

Dāci, ōrum, m. pl, the Dacians, a tribe of Thracian origin

Daedălus, i, m, an Athenian craftsman and architect

Dalmātae, ārum, m. pl, the Dalmatians, a tribe on the east coast of the Adriatic

Dămascus, i, f, Damascus

Dămŏclēs, is, m, a courtier of Dionysius

Dāmōn, ōnis, m, a Pythagorean

Dănăi, ōrum, m. pl, the Greeks

Dănūbius, i, m, the Danube

Daphne, as, f, the daughter of the river-god Peneus

Dardănus, i, m, the ancestor of the Trojans

Dārēus (or Darius), i, m, a king of Persia

Dĕcius, a, um, adj, the name of a Roman "gens"

Dēiŏtărus, i, m, a king of Galatia

Dēiphŏbus, i, m, the son of Priam and husband of Helen

Dēlos, i, f, an island in the Aegean, birthplace of Apollo and Diana

Delphi, ōrum, m. pl, a town in Phocis, famous for its oracle

Dēmosthĕnēs, is, m, I. a famous Athenian orator; 2. an Athenian general

Deucăliōn, ōnis, m, he was saved from the Flood with his wife Pyrrha

Diāna, ae, f, the goddess of the moon and of hunting

Dictē, es, f, a mountain in Crete

Dīdō, ūs, f, the founder-queen of Carthage

Dioclētiānus, i, m, a Roman emperor

Diŏgĕnes, is, m, a Greek philosopher of the fourth century B.C.

Diŏmēdes, is, m, a Greek hero of the siege of Troy

Diŏnŷsius, ii, m, a tyrant of Syracuse

Diŏnŷsus, i, m, the god of wine

Dis, Dītis, m, Pluto, king of the Lower World

Dōdōna, ae, f, a city of Epirus

Dŏlābella, ae, m, a Roman family name

Dŏlōpes, um, m. pl, a people of Thessaly

Dŏmĭtiānus, i, m, a Roman emperor

Dŏmĭtius, a, um, adj, the name of a Roman "gens"

Dōres, um, m. pl, the Dorians, a Greek people

Drāco, ōnis, m, an Athenian lawgiver

Drĕpăna, ōrum, n.pl, a town in Sicily

Drŭides, um, m. pl, the Druids

Drūsus, i, m, a Roman surname

Drўas, ădis, f, a wood-nymph

Dŭillius, ii, m, a Roman consul who won a naval victory over the Carthaginians in 260 B.C.

Dyrrăchium, ii, n, a town in Illyria

E

Eborăcum, i, n, York

Ebŭrōnes, um, m. pl, a German tribe

Ĕdessa, ae, *f,* a town in Macedonia

Ĕdōni, ōrum, *m. pl,* a Thracian people

Ĕlectra, ae, *f,* daughter of Agamemnon

Ĕleusis, īnis, *f,* a city of Attica where the mysteries of Ceres were held

Ĕlis, ĭdis, *f,* a country in the Peloponnesus

Ĕlўsium, i, *n,* the dwelling-place of the Blessed in the Lower World

Ĕmăthĭa, ae, *f,* a district of Macedonia

Encĕlădus, i, *m,* a giant slain by Iuppiter and buried under Etna

Ennĭus, i, *m,* the father of Roman poetry

Ĕōs, *f,* the dawn

Ĕphĕsus, i, *f,* an Ionian city of Asia Minor

Ĕpicūrus, i, *m,* an Athenian philosopher (342–270 B.C.)

Ĕpīrus, i, *f,* a region of northern Greece

Ĕrĕbus, i, *m,* a god of the Lower World

Ĕrectheus, ĕi, *m,* a king of Athens

Ĕrĕtrĭa, ae, *f,* a town of Euboea

Ĕridănus, i, *m,* one of the names of the river Po

Ĕrīnys, ўos, *f,* one of the Furies

Ĕrўmanthus, i, *m,* a chain of mountains in Arcadia

Ĕrўthēa, ae, *f,* an island near Gades

Ĕryx, ўcis, *m,* a mountain on the N.W. coast of Sicily

Esquĭliae, ārum, *f. pl,* the Esquiline, the largest of the hills of Rome

Ĕtrūrĭa, ae, *f,* a district of western Italy

Euboea, ae, *f,* an island in the Aegean

Euclĭdēs, is, *m,* the famous mathematician of Alexandria

Eumĕnĭdes, um, *f.pl,* a name of the Furies

Euphrātēs, is, *m,* the Euphrates

Euripĭdes, is, *m,* the famous Athenian poet (480–406 B.C.)

Eurīpus, i, *m,* the strait between Boeotia and Euboea

Eurōpa, ae, *f,* 1. the daughter of king Agenor; 2. the continent of Europe

Eurўălus, i, *m,* friend of Nisus (in Vergil's Aeneid)

Eurўdice, es, *f,* the wife of Orpheus

Eurystheus, ĕi, *m,* a king of Mycenae, who imposed on Hercules his Twelve Labours

Euxīnus Pontus, i, *m,* the Black Sea

Ĕvander, dri, *m,* the son of Mercury, who founded a colony on the Tiber

F

Făbĭus, a, um, *adj,* the name of a Roman "gens"; Q. Fabius Maximus Cunctator, the famous Roman general of the second Punic War

Fābrĭcĭus, a, um, *adj,* the name of a Roman "gens"

Faesŭlae, ārum, *f.pl,* an Etruscan town

Fălernus ager, *m,* the territory of Falernus in Campania, famous for its wine

Faunus, i, *m,* a forest god

Faustŭlus, i, *m,* the shepherd who found Romulus and Remus

Faustus, i, *m,* a Roman surname

Făvōnĭus, i, *m,* the west wind

Flaccus, i, *m,* a Roman surname

Flāminĭus, a, um, *adj,* the name of a Roman "gens"

Flāvĭus, a, um, *adj,* the name of a Roman "gens"

Flōra, ae, *f,* the goddess of Flowers

Flōrentĭa, ae, *f,* an Etruscan town (now Florence)

Fŏrentum, i, *n,* a town in Apulia

Formĭae, ārum, *f. pl,* a town in Latium

Frĕgellae, ārum, *f. pl,* a town in Latium

Frīsĭi, ōrum, *m. pl,* the Frisians, a north German tribe

Fulvĭa ae, *f,* 1. mistress of Curius 2. wife of M. Antony.

G

Găbăli, ōrum, *m. pl,* a Gallic tribe

Găbĭi, ōrum, *m. pl,* a city of Latium

Găbīnĭus, a, um, *adj,* the name of a Roman "gens"

Gādēs, ĭum, *f. pl,* a town in Spain

Gaetŭli, ōrum, *m. pl,* a people of north-west Africa

Gāĭus (Caius), i, *m,* a Roman "praenomen"

Galba, ae, *m,* a Roman family name; Servius Sulpicius G. a Roman emperor

Galli, ōrum, *m, pl,* the Gauls

Gallĭa, ae, *f,* Gaul; **Gallia Cisalpina,** Gaul on the Roman side of the Alps; **Gallia Transalpina,** Gaul on the further side of the Alps

Gallĭcus, a, um, *adj,* Gallic

Gangēs, is, *m,* the river Ganges

Gănўmēdes, is, *m,* a youth who was carried off to be Juppiter's cupbearer

Gărămantes, um, *m. pl,* a people of Africa

Gărumna, ae, *m,* a river of Gaul

Gēla, ae, *f,* a town of Sicily

Gēlon, ōnis, *m,* a king of Syracuse

Gĕnēva, ae, *f,* Geneva

Gĕnŭa, ae, *f,* a town in Liguria (now Genoa)

Gergŏvia, ae, *f,* a town of the Arverni in Aquitania

Germāni, ōrum, *m. pl,* the Germans

Germānia, ae, *f,* Germany

Germānus, a, um, *adj,* German

Gēryon, ōnis, *m,* a king of Spain slain by Hercules

Gĭgantes, um, *m. pl,* the Giants, who attacked Olympus and were killed by the thunder-bolts of Juppiter

Glaucus, i, *m,* 1. the son of Sisyphus; 2, the leader of the Lycians in the Trojan War

Gnossos, i, *f,* an ancient city of Crete

Gordĭum, ii, *n,* a city of Phyrgia

Gorgĭas, ae, *m,* a Greek sophist

Gorgo, ŏnis, *f,* a daughter of Phorcus whose look turned people to stone

Gŏthi, ōrum, *m. pl,* the Goths

Gracchus, i, *m,* a Roman family name

Graeci, ōrum, *m. pl,* the Greeks

Grāii, ōrum, *m. pl,* the Greeks

Grampius mons, *m,* the Grampian mountains

Grātiae, ārum, *f. pl,* the Graces

Gyās, ae, *m,* a hundred-armed giant

Gygēs, is, *m,* a wealthy king of Lydia

H

Hădrĭa, ae, *f,* the Adriatic Sea

Hadriānus, i, *m,* a Roman emperor

Hălicarnassus, i, *f,* a town in Caria

Hămilcar, ăris, *m,* a famous Carthaginian general of the first Punic War, father of Hannibal

Hannĭbal, ălis, *m,* a famous Carthaginian general of the second Punic War, son of Hamilcar

Harpyĭae, ārum, *f. pl,* the Harpies, monsters half-vulture, half-woman

Hasdrŭbal, ălis, *m,* a Carthaginian general, brother of Hannibal

Hēbē, is, *f,* the daughter of Iuppiter, and wife of Hercules

Hēbrus, i, *m,* a river in Thrace

Hĕcăte, es, *f,* the goddess of magic

Hector, ŏris, *m,* the son of Priam, hero of the Trojans

Hĕcŭba, ae, *f,* the wife of Priam

Hĕlĕna, ae, *f,* the wife of Menelaus; she was carried off to Troy by Paris, thus causing the Trojan War

Hĕlice, es, *f,* the Great Bear

Hĕlicon, ōnis, *m,* a mountain in Boeotia

Hellas, ădis, *f,* Greece

Hellespontus, i, *m,* the Hellespont (now the Dardanelles)

Hĕlōtes, um, *m. pl,* the slaves of the Spartans

Helvētii, ōrum, *m. pl,* a Celtic people inhabiting the region of Switzerland

Helvii, ōrum, *m. pl,* a Gallic tribe

Henna, ae, *f,* a city in Sicily

Hēra, ae, *f,* a Greek goddess

Hēraclēa, ae, *f,* the name of several Greek towns

Hērāclēum, i, *n,* a town in Macedonia

Hercŭlānĕum, i, *n,* a town of Campania, buried in A.D. 79 by an eruption of Vesuvius

Hercŭles, is, *m,* Hercules

Hercўnia silva, *f,* the Hercynian forest in Germany

Hermes, ae, *m,* a Greek god identified with the Roman Mercury

Hermĭŏne, es, *f,* the daughter of Menelaus and Helen

Hernĭci, ōrum, *m. pl,* a people of Latium, Sabine in origin

Hēro, us, *f,* a priestess of Aphrodite

Hērŏdŏtus, i, *m,* the first Greek historian

Hēsiŏdus, i, *m,* a Greek poet

Hespĕrus, i, *m,* the Evening Star

Hibēri, ōrum, *m. pl,* the Spaniards

Hibēria, ae, *f,* Spain

Hibērus, a, um, *adj,* Spanish

Hibērus, i, *m,* the Ebro

Hiempsal, ălis, *m,* son of Micipsa, king of Numidia

Hiēro, ōnis, *m,* king of Syracuse

Hippocrătes, is, *m,* a Greek physician

Hippŏdămus, i, *m,* the horse-tamer, i.e. Castor

Hippŏlўte, es, *f,* the Queen of the Amazons, taken captive by Theseus

Hippŏlўtus, i, *m,* the son of Theseus

Hirpīni, ōrum, *m. pl,* a people of Central Italy

Hispāni, ōrum, *m. pl,* the Spaniards

Hispānia, ae, *f,* Spain

Hispānus, a, um, *adj,* Spanish

Hŏmērus, i, *m,* Homer

Hōrae, ārum, *f. pl,* the Hours

Hŏrātius, a, um, *adj,* the name of a Roman "gens"

Hortensius, a, um, *adj,* the name of a Roman "gens"

For List of Abbreviations used, turn to pages 3, 4

Hostilius, a, um, *adj,* the name of a Roman "gens"

Hyădes, um, *f. pl,* a group of seven stars

Hydra, ae, *f,* a many-headed water snake

Hymen, ĕnis, *m,* the god of Marriage

Hypĕrion, ŏnis, *m,* 1. the father of the sun; 2. the sun god

Hypermnestra, ae, *f,* the only daughter of Danaus who did not kill her husband

I

Iacchus, i, *m,* a name of Bacchus

Iăpĕtus, i, *m,* a Titan, father of Prometheus

Iāpix, -pygis, *m,* 1. son of Daedalus; 2. a west wind

Icărus, i, *m,* son of Daedalus

Icēni, ōrum, *m. pl,* a British tribe in East Anglia

Ida, ae, *f,* a mountain in Crete

Idŏmĕneus, i, *m,* a king of Crete

Idūmaea, ae, *f,* a region of Palestine

Ilerda, ae, *f,* a town in Spain

Ilia, ae, *f,* a name of Rhea Silvia

Ilium (or Ilion), ii, *n,* a name of Troy

Illyria, ae, *f,* a region on the Adriatic Sea

Illyrii, ōrum, *m. pl,* a people on the Adriatic Sea

Inăchus, i, *m,* the first king of Argos

Indus, i, *m,* a river in India

Insŭbres, ium, *m. pl,* a people of Cisalpine Gaul

Io, see **Ion**

Iolcus, i, *m,* a town in Thessaly

Ion, ōnus, *f,* daughter of Inachus, beloved by Juppiter

Iōnia, ae, *f,* a country of Asia Minor, on the W. Coast

Iphigĕnia, ae, *f,* the daughter of Agamemnon

Iris, idis, *f,* the messenger of the gods

Isis, idis, *f,* an Egyptian goddess

Isŏcrătes, is, *m,* an Athenian orator

Isthmus, i, *m,* the Isthmus of Corinth

Itălia, ae, *f,* Italy

Ităli, ōrum, *m. pl,* the Italians

Itălicus, a, um, *adj,* Italian

Itălus, a, um, *adj,* Italian

Ithăca, ae, *f,* an island in the Ionian Sea

Itius Portus, ūs, *m,* a port in Belgic Gaul

Itys, yos, *m,* son of Tereus and Procne

Ixīon, ŏnis, *m,* a king of the Lapithae

J

Iăcētāni, ōrum, *m. pl,* a people of Spain

Iānicŭlum, i, *n,* one of the seven hills of Rome

Iānus, i, *m,* an Italian god

Iāsōn, ŏnis, *m,* leader of the Argonauts

Iūdaea, ae, *f,* the country of the Jews, Palestine

Iūdaei, ōrum, *m. pl,* the Jews

Iŭgurtha, ae, *m,* a king of Numidia

Iūliānus, a, um, *adj,* of Julius Caesar

Iūlius, a, um, *adj,* the name of a famous Roman "gens"; C. Julius Caesar, statesman, soldier, author

Iūnius, a, um, *adj,* the name of a Roman "gens"

Iūno, ŏnis, *f,* a goddess, daughter of Saturn, wife of Juppiter

Iūppiter, Jovis, *m,* the chief god of the Romans

Iūra, ae, *m,* Mt. Jura, in Gaul

Iustiniānus, i, *m,* a Roman emperor

Iūturna, ae, *f,* sister of Turnus

Iŭvĕnālis, is, *m,* D. Junius J., a Roman satirist

K

Karthāgo, ĭnis, *f,* see **Carthago**

L

Lābiēnus, i, *m,* a lieutenant of Julius Caesar

Lăcaena, ae, *adj,* Spartan

Lăcĕdaemon, ŏnis, *f,* Sparta

Lăcĕdaemŏnius, a, um, *adj,* Spartan

Lacĕtāni, ōrum, *m. pl,* a people of Spain

Lăco, ōnis, *m,* a Spartan

Laelius, a, um, *adj,* the name of a Roman "gens"

Lāertes, ae, *m,* the father of Ulysses

Laestrygŏnes, um, *m. pl,* a race of giants in Sicily

Lampsăcus, i, *f,* a city on the Hellespont

Lāŏcŏōn, ontis, *m,* a Trojan priest

Lāŏmĕdōn, ontis, *m,* the father of Priam, king of Troy

Lăpithae, ārum, *m. pl,* a people of Thessaly

Lăres, um, *m. pl,* household gods

Largus, i, *m,* a Roman surname

Lārissa, ae, *f,* a city in Thessaly

Lătīnus, i, *m,* a king of the Laurentines

Lătīnus, a, um, *adj,* Latin

Lătĭum, ii, *n,* Latium, the country of Italy in which Rome was situated

Lātōna, ae, *f,* the mother of Apollo and Diana

Laurentum, i, *n,* a town in Latium

Lāvīnia, ae, *f,* daughter of Latinus, wife of Aeneas

Lāvīnĭum, ii, *n,* a city of Latium

Lēander, dri, *m,* a youth who swam the Hellespont every night to visit Hero in Sestos

Lēda, ae, *f,* mother of Castor, Pollux, Helen and Clytemnestra

Lĕmannus, i, *m,* Lake Geneva

Lemnos, i, *f,* an island in the Aegean

Lĕōnĭdās, ae, *m,* a king of Sparta

Lĕpĭdus, i, *m,* a Roman family name; 1, M. Aemilius L. enemy of Sulla, consul 79 B.C.; 2. M. Aemilius L. triumvir 43 B.C.

Lerna, ae, *f,* a river and marsh near Argos

Lesbos, i, *f,* an island in the Aegean

Lēthē, ēs, *f,* a river in the Lower World, where departed souls drank "forgetfulness" of their past lives

Lexovii, ōrum, *m. pl,* a Gallic tribe

Lĭber, ĕri, *m,* an Italian god, identified with Bacchus

Lĭbĕra, ae, *f,* Proserpina, sister of Liber, daughter of Ceres

Lĭburni, ōrum, *m. pl,* a people of N. Illyria

Lĭbўa, ae, *f,* Libya

Lĭcĭnĭus, a, um, *adj,* the name of a Roman "gens"

Lĭger, ĕris, *m,* a river in Gaul (now the Loire)

Lĭgŭres, um, *m. pl,* a people of north-west Italy

Lingŏnes, um, *m. pl,* a Gallic tribe

Lĭpăra, ae, *f,* an island north of Sicily

Lĭvĭus, a, um, *adj,* the name of a Roman "gens"; T. Livius Patavinus, the Roman historian

Lōcusta, ae, *f,* a Roman woman skilled in poisoning

Lollĭus, a, um, *adj,* the name of a Roman "gens"

Londĭnĭum, ii, *n,* London

Lūcāni, ōrum, *m. pl,* a people of South Italy

Lūcānĭa, ae, *f,* a region of South Italy

Lūcānus, i, *m,* a Roman poet

Lŭcrētĭus, a, um, *adj,* the name of a Roman "gens"; T. Lucretius Carus, a Roman poet

Lŭcrīnus, i, *m,* a lake of Campania

Lūcullus, i, *m,* a Roman family name; Lucius Licinius L., conqueror of Mithridates

Lugdūnum, i, *n,* a city of Gaul (now Lyons)

Lūna, ae, *f,* the moon-goddess

Lŭpercālĭa, ōrum, *n. pl,* a Roman festival celebrated in February

Lŭpercus, i, *m,* a pastoral god who protected flocks from wolves

Lūsĭtānĭa, ae, *f,* the western part of Spain (now Portugal)

Lўcēum, i, *n,* a gymnasium at Athens where Aristotle taught

Lўcĭa, ae, *f,* a country of Asia Minor

Lўcurgus, i, *m,* a Spartan lawgiver

Lўdĭa, ae, *f,* a country of Asia Minor

Lynceus, i, *m,* 1. one of the Argonauts; 2. son of Aegyptus and husband of Hypermnestra

Lўsander, dri, *m,* a Spartan general

Lўsĭas, ae, *m,* a Greek orator

Lўsĭmăchus, i, *m,* one of Alexander's generals

M

Măcĕdŏnes, um, *m. pl,* the Macedonians

Măcĕdŏnĭa, ae, *f,* Macedonia

Maecēnas, ātis, *m,* the friend of Augustus and patron of Horace and Vergil

Magnēsĭa, ae, *f,* a district in Thessaly

Māgo, ōnis, *m,* brother of Hannibal

Maharbal, ălis, *m,* a Carthaginian general

Māia, ae, *f,* daughter of Atlas and mother of Mercury

Māmers, ertis, *m,* a name of Mars

Māmertīni, ōrum, *m. pl* (sons of Mars), the name adopted by the mercenary troops who seized Messana in Sicily in 289 B.C.

Mandūbii, ōrum, *m. pl,* a Gallic tribe

Mānĭlĭus, a, um, *adj,* the name of a Roman "gens"

Mantŭa, ae, *f,* a city in north Italy

Mărăthōn, ōnis, *f,* a village in Attica, where the Athenians defeated the Persian army in 490 B.C.

Marcellus, i, *m,* a Roman family name: Marcus Claudius M. conqueror of Syracuse, Roman general against Hannibal

Marcĭus, a, um, *adj,* the name of a Roman "gens"; Ancus M. the fourth king of Rome

Marcus, i, *m,* a Roman praenomen

Mărĭus, a, um, *adj,* the name of a Roman "gens"; C. Marius, conqueror of Jugurtha and the Cimbri, leader of the Popular Party against Sulla

Măro, ōnis, *m,* the surname of Vergil

Mars, tis, *m,* the god of War

Marsi, ōrum, *m. pl,* a people of Latium

Martĭālis, is, *m,* Marcus Valerius M., a Roman epigrammatic poet

Martĭus, a, um, *adj,* from Mars

Măsĭnissa, ae, *m,* a king of Numidia

Massĭlia, ae, *f,* seaport of Gaul (now Marseilles)

Mātūta, ae, *f,* the goddess of morning

Mauri, ōrum, *m. pl,* the Moors

Maurĭtānĭa, ae, *f,* a country in northwest Africa

Mausōlus, i, *m,* a king of Caria

Māvors, ortis, *m,* Mars

Mēdĕa, ae, *f,* daughter of king Aeetes

Mēdi, ōrum, *m. pl,* the Medes, a people of Asia

Mĕdullĭa, ae, *f,* a town of Latium

Mĕdūsa, ae, *f,* one of the Gorgons; everything she looked at turned to stone

Mĕgălŏpŏlis, is, *f,* a town in Arcadia

Mĕgăra, ae, *f* (or **ōrum,** *n.pl*), a city of Megaris

Mĕgăris, ĭdis, *f,* a country of Greece

Mĕlĭta, ae, *f,* Malta

Mēlos, i, *f,* an island in the Aegean

Melpŏmĕnē, es, *f,* the muse of tragic poetry

Memmĭus, a, um, *adj,* the name of a Roman "gens"

Memnon, ōnis, *m,* a king of Ethiopia, killed by Achilles in the Trojan War

Memphis, is, *f,* a city of Egypt

Mĕnander, dri, *m,* a Greek poet

Mĕnăpĭi, ōrum, *m. pl,* a Gallic tribe

Mĕnēlāus, i, *m,* brother of Agamemnon and husband of Helen

Mentor, ōris, *m,* a friend of Ulysses

Mercŭrĭus, ii, *m,* Mercury, the messenger of the gods

Mĕsŏpŏtămĭa, ae, *f,* a country of Asia

Messălĭna, ae, *f,* the wife of the emperor Claudius

Messalla, ae, *m,* a Roman family name

Messāna, ae, *f,* a Sicilian city (now Messina)

Mĕtaurus, i, *m,* a river in Umbria where Hasdrubal was defeated

Mĕtellus, i, *m,* a Roman family name; 1. Q. Metellus Macedonicus, who made Macedonia a Roman province; 2. Q. Caecilius Metellus Numidicus, who defeated Jugurtha

Mĕthymna, ae, *f,* a city of Lesbos

Mĕtiscus, i, *m,* the charioteer of Turnus

Mezentĭus, ii, *m,* a tyrant of Caere

Mĭcipsa, ae, *m,* a king of Numidia

Mĭdās, ae, *m,* a king of Phrygia who received from Bacchus the gift of turning everything he touched to gold

Mĭlētus, i, *f,* a town in Asia Minor

Milo, ōnis, *m,* 1. famous athlete of Crotona; 2, T. Annius M. the enemy of Clodius

Miltĭădes, is, *m,* the famous general of the Athenians at Marathon

Mincĭus, ii, *m,* a river in Gaul

Mĭnerva, ae, *f,* the Roman goddess of wisdom, the arts and sciences

Mīnos, ōis, *m,* a king of Crete

Mīnōtaurus, i, *m,* a monster with a bull's head and a man's body, slain by Theseus with the help of Ariadne

Mĭsēnum, i, *n,* a promontory and town in Campania

Mĭsēnus, i, *m,* the trumpeter of Aeneas

Mithras, ae, *m,* the Persian sun-god

Mithrĭdātes, is, *m,* a king of Pontus who fought the Romans and was finally defeated by Pompey

Mĭtўlēnē, es, *f,* the capital of Lesbos

Mŏlossi, ōrum, *m. pl,* a people of Epirus

Mŏlossus, i, *m,* a Molossian hound (famous for hunting)

Mŏna, ae, *f,* the Isle of Man

Mŏnēta, ae, *f,* a surname of Juno in whose temple money was minted

Mŏrini, ōrum, *m. pl,* a Gallic tribe

Mŏsa, ae, *m,* a river in Gaul (now the Meuse)

Mŏsella, ae, *m,* a river in Gaul (now the Moselle)

Mōses, is, *m,* Moses

Mŭcĭus, a, um, *adj,* the name of a Roman "gens"; C. Mucius Scaevola, who tried to assassinate Porsenna

Mulcĭber, bĕri, *m,* a surname of Vulcan

Mulvĭus pons, *m,* a bridge across the Tiber

Mummĭus, a, um, *adj,* the name of a Roman "gens"

Munda, ae, *f,* a city in Spain where Julius Caesar defeated Pompey's son

Mūsa, ae, *f,* a goddess of the Arts

Mūsaeus, i, *m,* a Greek poet

Mўcēnae, ārum, *f. pl,* a famous city of Argolis where Agamemnon was king

Mȳlae, ārum, *f. pl,* a city in Sicily

Myrmĭdōnes, um, *m. pl,* a people of Thessaly, under the rule of Achilles

Mȳsĭa, ae, *f,* a country of Asia Minor

N

Naevĭus, a, um, *adj,* the name of a Roman "gens"

Nāĭäs, ädis, *f,* a water-nymph

Namnētes, um, *m. pl,* a Gallic tribe

Nantŭātes, um, *m. pl,* a Gallic tribe

Narbo, ōnis, *m,* a city of southern Gaul

Narcissus, i, *m,* son of Cephisus, who fell in love with his own reflection and was changed into a flower

Nāsĭca, ae, *m,* a Roman family name

Naxos, i, *f,* an island in the Aegean Sea

Nĕāpŏlis, is, *f,* a sea-port of Campania (now Naples)

Nĕmĕa, ae, *f,* a city in Argolis

Nĕmĕsis, is, *f,* the goddess of justice

Nĕpos, ōtis, *m,* C. Cornelius N., a Roman historian

Neptūnus, i, *m,* Neptune, god of the sea

Nēreus, ei, *m,* a sea-god

Nēro, ōnis, *m,* a Roman family name; C. Claudius N., the fifth Roman emperor

Nerva, ae, *m,* a Roman family name; M. Cocceius N., a Roman emperor

Nervii, ōrum, *m. pl,* a Gallic tribe

Nestōr, ōris, *m,* a king of Pylos who fought with the Greeks at Troy

Nĭcŏmēdēs, is, *m,* a king of Bithynia

Nīlus, i, *m,* the river Nile

Nĭŏbē, es, *f,* daughter of Tantalus, wife of Amphion

Nīsus, i, *m,* 1. king of Megara; 2, a friend of Euryalus (in Vergil's Aeneid)

Nōla, ae, *f,* a town in Campania

Nōrĭcum, i, *n,* a country between the Danube and the Alps

Nŏtus, i, *m,* the south wind

Nŏvĭŏdūnum, i, n, 1, a town of the Aedui; 2. a town of the Bituriges; 3. a town of the Sessiones

Nŭma, ae, *m,* N. Pompilius, the second king of Rome

Nŭmantĭa, ae, *f,* a city in northern Spain

Nŭmĭdae, ārum, *m. pl,* the Numidians, a people of N. Africa

Nŭmĭdĭa, ae, *f,* Numidia

Nŭmĭtor, ōris, *m,* king of Alba Longa, grandfather of Romulus and Remus

Nȳsa, ae, *f,* a city in India, where Bacchus was born

O

Ocrĭcŭlum, i, *n,* a town in Umbria

Octāvĭānus, i, *m,* the surname of the Emperor Augustus

Octāvĭus, a, um, *adj,* the name of a Roman "gens"; C. Octavius, the father of the emperor Augustus

Oebălus, i, *m,* a king of Sparta

Oedĭpus, i, *m,* a king of Thebes, who killed his father and married his mother

Oenōnē, es, *f,* a Phrygian nymph, loved and then deserted by Paris

Ŏlympĭa, ae, *f,* a sacred plain in Elis where the Olympic Games were held

Ŏlympĭa, ōrum, *n. pl,* the Olympic Games

Ŏlympĭas, ädis, *f,* 1, an Olympiad, a four-year period which elapsed between Olympic Games; 2. wife of Philip of Macedon, and mother of Alexander the Great

Ŏlympĭcus, a, um, *adj,* Olympic

Ŏlympus, i, *m,* a mountain on the borders of Macedonia and Thessaly, the abode of the gods

Orbĭlius, i, *m,* a famous Roman grammarian and schoolmaster

Orcădes, um, *f. pl,* the Orkney Islands

Orchŏmĕnus, i, *m,* the name of two cities, one in Boeotia, one in Thessaly

Orcus, i, *m,* the Lower World

Ordŏvĭces, um, *m. pl,* a British tribe

Ŏrēās, ädis, *f,* a mountain-nymph

Ŏrestēs, is, *m,* the son of Agamemnon

Ŏrĭcum, i, *n,* a seaport in Illyria

Ŏrīon, ōnis, *m,* a hunter who was changed into a constellation

Ŏrōdēs, is, *m,* a king of Parthia

Ŏrontēs, is, *m,* a river in Syria

Orpheus, i, *m,* a famous Thracian singer

For List of Abbreviations used, turn to pages 3, 4

Osci, ōrum, *m. pl*, an ancient Italian tribe of Campania

Ŏsīris, is, *m*, an Egyptian god

Ossa, ae, *f*, a mountain range in Thessaly

Ostia, ae, *f*, a seaport at the mouth of the Tiber

Ostŏrius, i, *m*, P. Ostorius Scapula, governor of Britain

Ŏtho, ōnis, *m*, a Roman surname; M. Salvius O., a Roman emperor

Othrys, ўos, *m*, a mountain in Thessaly

Ŏvĭdius, a, um, *adj*, the name of a Roman "gens" P. Ovidius Naso, the Roman poet

Oxos, i, *m*, a river in Asia

P

Păcŏrus, i, *m*, a king of Parthia

Păcŭvius, i, *m*, a Roman poet

Pădus, i, *m*, the river Po

Paeligni, ōrum, *m. pl*, an Italian tribe

Pălaestīna, ae, *f*, Palestine

Pălātium, ii, *n*, the Palatine, one of the seven hills of Rome

Pălīnūrus, i, *m*, Aeneas' pilot who fell into the sea off the coast of Lucania

Pallăs, ădis, *f*, a surname of Athene, the Greek goddess of Wisdom

Pallăs, antis, *m*, son of Pandion

Pamphўlia, ae, *f*, a district of Asia Minor

Pān, Pānos, *m*, the god of woods and flocks

Panchāia, ae, *f*, a region of Arabia

Pandīŏn, ōnis, *m*, a king of Athens

Pandōra, ae, *f*, the first woman

Pannōnia, ae, *f*, a country on the Danube

Pănŏpēa, ae, *f*, a sea-nymph

Pănormus, i, *f*, a city in Sicily

Paphlăgŏnia, ae, *f*, a district in Asia Minor

Păpīrius, a, um, *adj*, the name of a Roman "gens"

Parca, ae, *f*, the goddess of fate

Păris, ĭdis, *m*, the son of Priam and Hecuba who carried away Helen from her husband Menelaus and thus caused the Trojan War

Părīsii, ōrum, *m. pl*, a Gallic tribe

Parma, ae, *f*, a town in Gaul

Parmĕnio, ōnis, *m*, one of Alexander's generals

Parnāsus, i, *m*, a mountain in Phocis, sacred to Apollo

Păros, i, *f*, an island in the Aegean

Parrhăsius, i, *m*, a Greek painter

Parthĕnon, ōnis, *m*, the temple of Athene at Athens

Parthĕnŏpē, es, *f*, a Siren who gave her name to Neapolis (Naples)

Parthi, ōrum, *m. pl*, the Parthians, a Scythian people, famous archers

Pāsĭphae, es, *f*, daughter of Helios, mother of the Minotaur

Pāsithĕa, ae, *f*, one of the three Graces

Pătăvium, i, *n*, a town in North Italy, birthplace of Livy

Pătrŏclus, i, *m*, friend of Achilles

Paulus, i, *m*, a Roman surname

Pausănias, ae, *m*, the leader of the Spartans in the battle of Plataea

Pēgăsus, i, *m*, the winged horse of the Muses

Pēlasgi, ōrum, *m. pl*, the oldest inhabitants of Greece

Pēleus, i, *m*, a king of Thessaly

Pēligni, ōrum, *m. pl*, a people of Central Italy

Pēlion, ii, *n*, a mountain in Thessaly

Pella, ae, *f*, a city in Macedonia

Pēlŏponnēsus, i, *f*, the southern part of Greece

Pĕlops, ŏpis, *m*, son of Tantalus, king of Phrygia

Pēlūsium, i, *n*, a town in Egypt

Pēnātes, ium, *m. pl*, Roman guardian deities of the household

Pēnĕlŏpē, es, *f*, the wife of Ulysses

Pentheus, ĕi, *m*, a king of Thebes

Pergămum, i, *n*, a city of Asia

Pĕricles, is, *m*, an Athenian statesman of the fifth century B.C.

Persae, ārum, *m. pl*, the Persians

Persia, ae (or Persis, ĭdis), *f*, Persia

Persĕphŏnē, es, *f*, Proserpine, daughter of Ceres

Persēs, ae, *m*, the last king of Macedonia

Perseus, ĕi, *m*, son of Iuppiter and Danae who killed Medusa

Phaedo, ōnis, *m*, a pupil of Socrates and friend of Plato

Phaedra, ae, *f*, daughter of Minos and wife of Theseus

Phaedrus, i, *m*, a pupil of Socrates

Phaethōn, ontis, *m*, son of Helios (the sun-god)

Phălērum, i, *n*, the oldest part of Athens

Pharsālus, i, *f*, a town of Thessaly where Pompey was defeated by Caesar

Phăros, i, *f,* an island near Alexandria with a famous light-house

Phīdias, ae, *m,* a famous Athenian sculptor

Philippi, ōrum, *m. pl,* a city in Macedonia

Philippus, i, *m,* the name of four kings of Macedonia

Philoctētēs, ae, *m,* a famous archer, and a friend of Hercules

Philŏmēla, ae, *f,* daughter of Pandion, she was changed into a nightingale

Philŏpoemen, ĕnis, *m,* a famous Greek general

Phlĕgĕthon, ontis, *m,* a river in the Lower World

Phōcaea, ae, *f,* a sea-port of Ionia

Phōcis, ĭdis, *f,* a country of northern Greece

Phoebē, es, *f,* the moon-goddess

Phoebus, i, *m,* the name of Apollo

Phoenicē, es, *f,* Phoenicia, a country of Syria

Phorcus, i, *m,* a sea-god

Phrўges, um, *m. pl,* the Phrygians, a people of Asia Minor

Phthĭa, ae, *f,* a region of Thessaly

Phўlăcē, ēs, *f,* a city of Thessaly

Pīcēnum, i, *n,* a district on the eastern side of Italy

Picti, ōrum, *m. pl,* a British tribe

Pictōnes, um, *m. pl,* a Gallic tribe

Pīcus, i, *m,* son of Saturn

Pīlumnus, i, *m,* ancestor of Turnus

Pindărus, i, *m,* Pindar, the lyric poet of Thebes

Pīraeus, i, *m,* the port of Athens

Pīrĭthŏus, i, *m,* son of Ixion, friend of Theseus

Pīsa, ae, *f.* a town in Elis

Pīsae, ārum, *f. pl,* an Etruscan city

Pīsistrătus, i, *m,* a tyrant of Athens

Plăcentĭa, ae, *f,* a city on the river Po

Plancus, i, *m,* a Roman surname

Plătaeae, ārum, *f. pl,* a town in Boeotia, where the Greeks defeated the Persians in 479 B.C.

Plăto, ōnis, *m,* the famous Greek philosopher, pupil of Socrates

Plautus, i, *m,* T. Maccius P. the famous Roman comic poet

Plīnius, a, um, *adj,* the name of a Roman "gens", 1. C. Plinius Secundus (the "Elder"), author of a work on Natural History; 2. C. Plinius Caecilius (the "Younger"), author of letters

Plūto, ōnis, *m,* the king of the Lower World

Poeni, ōrum, *m. pl,* the Carthaginians

Pollĭo, ōnis, *m,* a Roman surname; C. Asinius P., a Roman orator

Pollux, ūcis, *m,* twin brother of Castor

Pŏlўbius, ii, *m,* a famous Greek historian

Pŏlўclītus, i, *m,* a famous Greek sculptor

Pŏlyxĕna, ae, *f,* daughter of Priam

Pompēii, ōrum, *m. pl,* a city in the south of Campania

Pompēius, a, um, *adj,* the name of a Roman "gens"; Cn. P. Magnus, the triumvir, opponent of Julius Caesar

Pompīlius, a, um, *adj,* Numa Pompilius, the second king of Rome

Pomptīnus, a, um, *adj* (paludes), the Pomptine Marshes, in Latium

Pontius, a, um, *adj,* the name of a Roman "gens"; Pontius Pilatus governor of Judaea at the time of Christ's crucifixion

Pontus, i, *m,* the Black Sea

Porcius, a, um, *adj,* the name of a Roman "gens"; M. Porcius Cato, the Censor

Porsenna, ae, *m,* an Etruscan king

Portūnus, i, *m,* god of harbours

Pōrus, i, *m,* a king of India

Praeneste, is, *n,* a town in Latium

Praxĭtēles, is, *m,* an Athenian sculptor

Priămus, i, *m,* the last king of Troy

Prŏcas, ae, *m,* a king of Alba

Procnē, es, *f,* a daughter of Pandion who was changed into a swallow

Prŏmētheus, ei, *m,* son of Iapetus, father of Deucalion; he brought fire from heaven for mankind

Prŏpertius, i, *m,* Sextus Aurelius P. a Roman elegiac poet

Prŏpontis, ĭdis, *f,* the Sea of Marmora

Prŏserpĭna, ae, *f,* daughter of Ceres

Prŏtăgŏras, ae, *m,* a Greek sophist

Prōteus, ei, *m,* a sea-god

Prūsias, ae, *m,* a king of Bithynia

Ptŏlĕmaeus, i, *m,* Ptolemy, the name of a dynasty of Egyptian kings

Publius, ii, *m,* a Roman praenomen

Pŭtĕŏli, ōrum, *m. pl,* a city on the coast of Campania

Pydna, ae, *f,* a town in Macedonia

Pygmaei, ōrum, *m. pl,* a race of dwarfs

Pygmălion, ōnis, *m,* grandson of Agenor, who fell in love with a statue, to which Venus later gave life

Pўlos, i, *f,* the name of three towns of the Peloponnesus

Pўrēnē, es, *f,* the Pyrenees

Pўrŏis, entis, *m*, the planet Mars

Pyrrha, ae, *f*, the wife of Deucalion

Pyrrhus, i, *m*, 1. son of Achilles and founder of a kingdom in Epirus; 2. a king of Epirus who invaded Italy and fought the Romans

Pўthăgŏras, ae, *m*, the famous Greek philosopher (550 B.C.)

Pўtho, us, *f*, the old name of Delphi

Q

Quinctius, a, um, *adj*, the name of a Roman "gens"; L. Quinctius Cincinnatus, who came from the plough to be dictator of Rome

Quintiliānus, i, *m*, a Roman surname; L. Fabius Q., teacher and rhetorician

Quirīnus, i, *m*, a name of Romulus after he became a god

R

Raetia, ae, *f*, a country between the Alps and the Danube

Rāvenna, ae, *f*, a Gallic town on the Adriatic

Rēgillus, i, *m*, a lake in Latium

Rēgĭum, i, *n*, a town of south Calabria

Rēgŭlus, i, *m*, a Roman family name; M. Atilius R. a famous Roman general of the first Punic War

Rēmi, ōrum, *m. pl*, a Gallic tribe

Rēmus, i, *m*, the brother of Romulus

Rhădămanthus, i, *m*, son of Juppiter, a judge in the Lower World

Rhēa Silvia, she became, by Mars, mother of Romulus and Remus

Rhēnus, i, *m*, the Rhine

Rhŏdănus, i, *m*, the Rhone

Rhŏdos, i, *f*, the island of Rhodes

Rhoetēum, i, *n*, a promontory in the Hellespont

Rōma, ae, *f*, Rome

Rŏmŭlus, i, *m*. son of Mars, founder and first king of Rome

Roscius, a, um, *adj*, the name of a Roman "gens"

Rŭbi, ōrum, *m. pl*, a town in Apulia

Rŭbico, ōnis, *m*, a river which marked the boundary between Italy and Gaul

Rŭdiae, ārum, *f. pl*, a town in Apulia

Rŭtilius, a, um, *adj*, the name of a Roman "gens"

Rŭtŭli, ōrum, *m. pl*, a people of Latium

S

Săbelli, ōrum, *m. pl*, a name of the Sabines

Săbīni, ōrum, *m. pl*, a people of Central Italy, the Sabines

Săgittārius, i, *m*, a constellation

Săguntum, i, *n*, a town on the coast of Spain

Sălămis, mīnis, *f*, an island near Eleusis

Sălentīni, ōrum, *m. pl*, a people of southern Italy

Sălernum, i, *n*, a town of Campania (now Salerno)

Sălii, ōrum, *m. pl*, a Roman college of priests

Sallustius, a, um, *adj*, the name of a Roman "gens"; C. Sallustius Crispus, the famous Roman historian

Sămărŏbrīva, ae, *f*, a town in Gaul

Samnium, ii, *n*, a region of Central Italy

Sămos, i, *f*, an island in the Aegean

Santōnes, um, *m. pl*, a Gallic tribe

Sappho, ūs, *f*, the famous Greek lyric poetess

Sardes, ium, *f. pl*, the capital of Lydia

Sardi, ōrum, *m. pl*, the inhabitants of Sardinia

Sarmătia, ae, *f*, a country in South Russia

Săturnālia, ōrum, *n. pl*, the festival of Saturn, held in December

Săturnīnus, i, *m*, a Roman surname

Săturnus, i, *m*, father of Juppiter

Scaevŏla, ae, *m*, a Roman family name; C. Mucius Sc., opponent of Porsenna

Scămander, dri, *m*, a river at Troy

Scăpŭla, ae, *m*, a Roman family

Scīpio, ōnis, *m*, a Roman family name; 1. P. Cornelius Scipio Africanus; 2. P. Cornelius Scipio Aemilienus Africanus, two conquerors of the Carthaginians

Scŏpas, ae, *m*, a famous Greek sculptor

Scylla, ae, *f*, a rock in the straits between Italy and Sicily

Scythae, ārum, *m. pl*, the Scythians

Scўthia, ae, *f*, a region to the north of the Black Sea

Sĕgesta, ae, *f*, a city of Sicily

Sējānus, i, *m*, the prefect of the Praetorian Guard under Tiberius

Sĕleucus, i, *m*, the name of several kings of Syria

Sĕlīnus, untis, *f*, a port in Sicily

Sĕmĕlĕ, es, *f,* daughter of Cadmus, mother of Bacchus

Semprōnïus, a, um, *adj,* the name of a Roman "gens", to which belonged the brothers Tiberius and Gaius Sempronius Gracchus

Sĕnĕca, ae, *m,* a Roman family name; 1. M. Annaeus S., a famous rhetorician from Spain; 2. L. Annaeus S., his son, Stoic philosopher and tutor of Nero

Sĕnŏnes, um, *m. pl,* a Gallic tribe

Sēquăna, ae, *f,* the river Seine

Sēquăni, ōrum, *m. pl,* a Gallic tribe

Sertōrïus, i, *m,* a general of Marius

Servīlïus, a, um, *adj,* the name of a Roman "gens"

Servïus Tullïus, *m,* the sixth king of Rome

Sestos, i, *f,* a city in Thrace

Sĕvērus, i, *m,* a Roman family name

Sextīlis (mensis), another name for the month of August

Sïbylla, ae, *f,* a priestess of Apollo

Sĭcāni, ōrum, *m. pl,* a people of Italy

Sĭchaeus, i, *m,* the husband of Dido

Sĭcŭli, ōrum, *m. pl,* the Sicilians

Sīdon, ōnis, *f,* a Phoenician city

Sĭgēum, i, *n,* a promontory in Troas

Sĭlēnus, i, *m,* the attendant of Bacchus

Sĭlïus, a um, *adj,* the name of a Roman "gens"

Sĭlŭres, um, *m. pl,* a British tribe

Silvānus, i, *m,* the god of woods

Sĭmōnĭdes, is, *m,* a famous lyric poet of Ceos

Sĭnōpē, es, *f,* a town on the Black Sea

Sïrēnes, um, *f. pl,* nymphs who lived off the coast of south Italy and lured sailors to their death

Sīsÿphus, i, *m,* son of Aeolus, king of Corinth, a robber

Smyrna, ae, *f,* a trading city of Iona

Sōcrătes, is, *m,* the famous Athenian philosopher

Sŏlon, ōnis, *m,* one of the seven wise men of Greece (*c.* 600 B.C.)

Sontïātes, um, *m. pl,* a Gallic tribe

Sŏphŏcles, is, *m,* the famous Greek tragic poet

Sŏphŏnisba, ae, *f,* daughter of Hasdrubal

Sōracte, is, *n,* a mountain in Etruria

Sparta, ae, *f,* the capital of Laconia

Spartăcus, i, *m,* leader of the gladiators against Rome

Stōïcus, i, *m,* a Stoic philosopher

Styx, ÿgis, *f,* a river of the Lower World

Sŭessïōnes, um, *m. pl,* a Gallic tribe

Sŭētōnïus, Gaius S. Tranquillus, the biographer of the Caesars

Suēvi, ōrum, *m. pl,* a German tribe

Sŭgambri, ōrum, *m. pl,* a German tribe

Sullc, ae, *m,* a Roman family name; L. Cornelius S., dictator, opponent of Marius

Sulmo, ōnis, *m,* a town of the Paeligni

Sulpïcïus, a, um, *adj,* the name of a Roman "gens"

Sūnïum, i, *n,* a town of Attica

Sÿbăris, is, *f,* a town of Lucania

Sychaeus, see Sïchaeus

Sÿphax, ăcis, *m,* a king of Numidia

Sÿrācūsae, ārum, *f. pl,* Syracuse

Sÿria, ae, *f,* Syria

Syrtes, ïum, *f. pl,* two sandbanks on the north coast of Africa

T

Tăburnus, i, *m,* a range of mountains between Samnium and Campania

Tăcĭtus, i, *m,* Cornelius T. the famous Roman historian

Taenăros, i, *c,* a town in Laconia, near which was thought to be an entrance to the Lower World

Tăges, is, *m,* an Etruscan god

Tăgus, i, *m,* a river in Lusitania

Tămĕsis, is, *m,* the river Thames

Tănăis, is, *m,* the river Don

Tănăquil, ïlis, *f,* the wife of Tarquinius Priscus

Tantălus, i, *m,* a son of Juppiter

Tarbelli, ōrum, *m. pl,* a tribe of Aquitania

Tărentum, i, *n,* a Greek city on the south coast of Italy

Tarpēïus, a, um, *adj,* 1. the name of a Roman "gens"; Tarpeia, who betrayed the citadel to the Sabines; 2. The Tarpeian Rock at Rome from which criminals were thrown

Tarquĭnïi, ōrum, *m. pl,* an Etruscan town

Tarquĭnïus, ii, *m,* the name of two Etruscan kings of Rome

Tarsus, i, *f.* the capital of Cilicia

Tartărus, i, *m.* the Lower World

Tătïus, i, *m,* Titus T., a king of the Sabines

Taurus, i, *m,* a mountain range in Asia Minor

Tĕgĕa, ae, *f,* a town in Arcadia

Tĕlămon, ōnis, *m,* an Argonaut

Tĕlĕmăchus, i, *m,* son of Ulysses and Penelope

For List of Abbreviations used, turn to pages 3, 4

Tempē, *n. pl*, a valley in Thessaly

Tenctēri, ōrum, *m. pl*, a German tribe

Tĕnĕdos, i, *f*, an island in the Aegean

Tĕrentius, a, um, *adj*, the name of a Roman "gens"; M. Terentius Afer a "freed man" and famous dramatist

Tēreus, i, *m*, a king of Thrace

Teucer, cri, *m*, the first king of Troy

Teutŏnes, um, *m. pl*, a German people

Thapsus, i, *f*, 1. a city in Africa; 2. a city in Sicily

Thēbae, ārum, *f. pl*, the capital of Boeotia

Thĕmistŏcles, is, *m*, a famous Athenian general and statesman

Theŏcrĭtus, i, *m*, the famous Greek pastoral poet

Thĕophrastus, i, *m*, a Greek philosopher

Thermŏpўlae, ārum, *f. pl*, a famous mountain-pass on the borders of Thessaly

Thēseus, ei, *m*, king of Athens and slayer of the Minotaur

Thessălia, ae, *f*, Thessaly, a region of north Greece

Thessălŏnīca, ae, *f*, a town of Macedonia

Thĕtis, ĭdis, *f*, a sea-nymph

Thisbē, es, *f*, a Babylonian maiden

Thrācia, ae, *f*, Thrace, a country to the north of the Propontis

Thūcўdĭdes, is, *m*, the famous Athenian historian

Thūlē, es, *f*, an island of northern Europe (perh. Iceland)

Thūrii, ōrum, *m. pl*, a city of Lucania

Thўăs, ădis, *f*, a female attendant of Bacchus

Thўestes, ae, *m*, son of Pelops and brother of Atreus

Thўni, ōrum, *m. pl*, a Thracian people who emigrated to Bithynia

Tĭbĕris, is, *m*, the river Tiber

Tĭbĕrius, i, *m*, a Roman praenomen; Ti. Claudius Nero Caesar, the second Roman emperor

Tĭbullus, i, *m*, a Roman poet

Tĭbur, ŭris, *n*, a town in Latium

Tĭcīnus, i, *m*, a river in Cisalpine Gaul

Tĭgrānes, is, *m*, a king of Armenia

Tĭgris, ĭdis, *m*, a river of Asia

Tĭrĭdātes, is, *m*, the name of several Armenian kings

Tĭryns, ntis, *f*, a town of Argolis

Tĭsiphŏnē, es, *f*, one of the Furies

Tītan, ānis, *m*, ancestor of the Titans

Tīthŏnus, i, *m*, the wife of Aurora who received the gift of immortality

Tĭtus, i, *m*, a Roman praenomen

Tĭtўos, i, *m*, giant son of Juppiter, slain by Apollo

Tŏlōsa, ae, *f*, a city of southern Gaul

Tŏlumnius, i, *m*, a Rutulian soothsayer

Tŏmi, ōrum, *m. pl*, a town on the Black Sea

Torquātus, i, *m*, surname gained by T. Manlius who slew a Gaul and took his neck-chain

Trāiānus, i, *m*, a Roman emperor

Tralles, ium, *f. pl*, a town in Western Asia

Trāsĭmēnus, i, *m*, Lake Trasimene, where Hannibal gained a victory over the Romans (217 B.C.)

Trĕbia, ae, *m*, a river of Cisalpine Gaul, where Hannibal defeated the Romans (218 B.C.)

Trēvĕri, ōrum, *m. pl*, a Belgian tribe

Trinŏbantes, um, *m. pl*, a British tribe

Triptŏlĕmus, i, *m*, the inventor of agriculture

Triton, ōnis, *m*, a sea-god son of Neptune

Troezēn, ēnis, *f*, a town of Argolis

Trōia, ae, *f*, Troy

Trōiānus, a, um, Trojan

Trōicus, a, um, Trojan

Trōius, a, um, Trojan

Trōs, ōis, *m*, a king of Phrygia, after whom Troy was named

Tullius, a, um, *adj*, the name of a Roman "gens"; 1. Servius T., sixth king of Rome; 2. Marcus T. Cicero, famous orator and statesman

Turnus, i, *m*, a Rutulian prince killed by Aeneas

Tusci, ōrum, *m. pl*, the Etruscans

Tuscŭlum, i, *n*, a town of Latium

Tyndāreus, ĕi, *m*, a king of Sparta

Tўphōeus, ĕos, *m*, a giant buried beneath Mount Etna

Tўphōn, ōnis, *m*, another name for Typhoeus

Tyrrhēni, ōrum, *m. pl*, a Pelasgian colony which came to Italy

Tўrus, i, *f*, Tyre, a famous Phoenician city

U

Ubii, ōrum, *m. pl*, a German tribe

Ūcălĕgŏn, ontis, *m*, a Trojan, mentioned in Vergil's Aeneid

Ūfens, ntis, *m*, a river of Latium

Ŭlysses (Ŭlixes), is, *m*, Ulysses (or Odysseus) king of Ithaca and husband of Penelope

Umbri, ōrum, *m. pl*, a people of Italy

Ŭsĭpĕtes, um, *m. pl*, a German tribe

Ŭtĭca, ae, *f*, a city of North Africa

V

Vălĕrĭus, a, um, *adj*, the name of a Roman "gens"

Varro, ōnis, *m*, a Roman surname; M. Terentius V., a Roman writer

Vātĭcānus mons, the Vatican hill at Rome

Vectis, is, *f*, the Isle of Wight

Vēii, ōrum, *m. pl*, an Etruscan city

Vellēius, a, um, *adj*, the name of a Roman "gens"

Vĕnĕti, ōrum, *m. pl*, 1. a people of north-east Italy; 2. a people of north-west Gaul

Vĕnus, ĕris, *f*, the goddess of love

Vĕnŭsia, ae, *f*, a town on the border of Apulia

Vercellae, ārum, *f. pl*, a town of Cisalpine Gaul

Vercingĕtŏrix, ĭgis, *m*, a Gallic chieftain

Vergĭlius, i, *m*, P. Vergilius Maro, the Roman poet, author of the Aeneid and the Georgics

Verginius, a, um, *adj*, the name of a Roman "gens"

Vērōna, ae, *f*, a town of north Italy

Verres, is, *m*, C. Cornelius V., the notorious praetor of Sicily

Vertumnus, i, *m*, the god of the changing seasons

Vĕrŭlāmĭum, ii, *n*, St Albans

Vespāsiānus, i, *m*, Ti. Flavius V., a Roman emperor

Vesta, ae, *f*, the goddess of the hearth

Virgĭlius, see Vergilius

Volcae, ārum, *m. pl*, a Gallic tribe

Volcānus, i, *m*, son of Iuppiter and Juno, god of fire

Volsci, ōrum, *m. pl*, a people of Latium

Vulcānus, see Volcanus

Vulturnus, i, *m*, a river in Campania

X

Xantho, ūs, *f*, a sea-nymph

Xanthus, i, *m*, a river in Lycia

Xĕno, ōnis, *m*, an Epicurean philosopher

Xĕnŏphon, ontis, *m*, the famous Athenian historian, philosopher and general

Xerxes, is, *m*, a Persian king

Z

Zăma, ae, *f*, a town in Numidia where Scipio defeated Hannibal

Zanclē, ēs, *f*, another name of Messana in Sicily

Zēno, ōnis, *m*, a Greek philosopher

Zĕphўrus, i, *m*, the west wind

ENGLISH—LATIN

For List of Abbreviations used, turn to pages 3, 4

A

a, an, (*indefinite article*), no equivalent in Latin

abandon, *v.t,* rĕlinquo (3), dēsĕro (3)

abandoned, dērĕlictus, dēsertus; **(person),** perdĭtus

abandonment, rĕlictĭo, *f*

abase, *v.t,* dēprĭmo (3)

abasement, hŭmĭlĭtas, *f,* dēmĭssĭo, *f*

abash, *v.t,* confundo (3), perturbo (1)

abashed, pŭdōre confūsus **(perplexed with shame)**

abate, *v.t,* immĭnŭo (3), rĕmitto (3)

abatement, dēcessus, *m,* dēcessĭo, *f,* dēmĭnūtĭo, *f*

abbot, pontĭfex, *m,* **(high-priest),** săcerdos, *c*

abbreviate, *v.t,* immĭnŭo (3), contrăho (3)

abbreviation, compendĭum, *n,* contractĭo, *f*

abdicate, *v.i,* se abdĭcare (1. *reflex*)

abdication, abdĭcātĭo, *f*

abdomen, venter, *m,* abdōmen, *n*

abduction, raptus, *m,* raptĭo, *f*

abet, *v.i,* adsum (*irreg. with dat. of person*), adiŭvo (1)

abettor, mĭnister, *m,* adiŭtor, *m*

abeyance (to be in —), *v.i,* iăcĕo (2)

abhor, ăbhorrĕo (2) (*with acc. or ab and abl*), ōdi. (*v. defect*)

abhorrence, ŏdĭum, *n*

abide, *v.i,* mănĕo (2), hăbĭto (1)

abide, *v.t,* **(wait for),** exspecto (1)

abiding, *adj,* **(lasting),** mansūrus

ability (mental —), ingĕnĭum, *n;* **(power),** pŏtestas, *f*

abject, abiectus, hŭmĭlis

abjectness, hŭmĭlĭtas, *f*

abjure, *v.t,* abiūro (1), ēiūro (1)

ablaze, *adj,* flăgrans

able, *use* possum **(be able),** pŏtens

able (to be —), *v.i,* possum (*irreg*)

able-bodied, vălĭdus

ablution, lăvātĭo, *f,* ablūtĭo, *f*

ably, *adv,* ingĕnĭōse

abnegation, nēgātĭo, *f,* mŏdĕrātĭo, *f*

abnormal, abnormis, ĭnŭsĭtātus

aboard, in nāve; **(to go —),** *v.i,* nāvem conscendo (3); **(to put —),** *v.t,* in nāvem impōno (3)

abode, dŏmus, *f,* dŏmĭcĭlĭum, *n,* sēdes, *f,* hăbĭtātĭo, *f*

abolish, *v.t,* tollo (3), ăbŏlĕo (2), dissolvo (3)

abolition, dissŏlūtĭo, *f,* ăbŏlĭtĭo, *f*

abominable, infandus, dētestābĭlis

abominate, *v.t,* ōdi (*defect*), ăbhorrĕo (2)

abomination (hatred), ŏdĭum, *n;* **(crime),** flăgĭtĭum, *n*

aborigines, indĭgĕnae, *m. pl*

abortion, ăbortus, *m,* ăbortĭo, *f*

abortive (unsuccessful), irrĭtus

abound (in), *v.i,* ăbundo (1), sŭpĕro (1), circumflŭo (3), suppĕdĭto (1)

abounding, ăbundans, afflŭens, fēcundus

about, *prep,* circā, circum, ăd, sŭb (*with acc*), dē (*with abl*); **(of time),** circĭter (*with acc*)

about, *adv,* **(nearly),** circĭter, fermē, fērē

above, *prep,* sŭper, sŭprā (*with acc*); **(more than),** amplĭus

above, *adv,* sŭprā, insŭper; **(from above),** dēsŭper, sŭpernē

abrasion, attrītus, *m*

abreast, *adv,* părĭter

abridge, *v.t,* contrăho (3)

abridgement, ĕpĭtŏmē, *f,* ĕpĭtŏma, *f*

abroad, *adv,* **(in a foreign country),** pĕrĕgrē

abroad (to be —), *v.i,* pĕrĕgrīnor (1. *dep*)

abrogate, *v.t,* abrŏgo (1); rescindo (3)

abrogation, abrŏgātĭo, *f*

abrupt (sudden), sŭbĭtus; **(steep),** praeruptus

abruptly, *adv,* sŭbĭto, praerupte

abscess, vŏmĭca, *f*

abscond, *v.i,* lătĕo (2)

abscence, absentĭa, *f*

absent, absens

absent (to be —), *v.i,* absum (*irreg*)

149

absinth, absinthĭum, *n*
absolute, absŏlūtus
absolute power, tўrannis, *f*, impĕrĭum, *n*, dŏmĭnātĭo, *f*
absolutely (completely), *adv*, prorsum, prorsus
absolve, *v.t,* absolvo (3), lībĕro (1)
absorb, *v.t,* bĭbo (3), haurĭo (4), absorbĕo (2)
absorbent, *adj,* bĭbŭlus
abstain, *v.i,* abstĭnĕo (2)
abstemious, tempĕrātus
abstinence, abstĭnentĭa, *f*
abstinent, abstĭnens, mŏdĕrātus
abstract, *nn,* ĕpĭtŏme, *f*
abstract, *adj,* abstractus
abstract, *v.t,* abstrāho (3)
abstruse, rĕcondĭtus, obscūrus
absurd, ĭneptus, absurdus
absurdity, ĭneptĭa, *f*, insulsĭtas, *f*
absurdly, *adv,* ĭneptē, absurdē
abundance, cōpĭa, *f*, ăbundantĭa, *f*
abundant, largus, fēcundus
abuse, *nn,* (insult), contŭmēlĭa
abuse, *v.t,* (revile), mălēdīco (3); (misuse), ăbūtor (3 *dep*)
abusive, contŭmēlĭōsus
abut, *v.i,* adiăcĕo (2)
abutting, adiunctus
abyss, gurges, *m,* vŏrāgo, *f*
acacia, ăcācĭa, *f*
academic, ăcădēmĭcus
academy, ăcădēmĭa, *f*
accede, *v.i,* consentĭo (4)
accelerate, *v.t,* accĕlĕro (1)
accent, vox, *f*
accentuate, *v.t,* ăcŭo (3)
accentuation, accentus, *m*
accept, *v.t,* accĭpĭo (3), rĕcĭpĭo (3)
acceptability, suāvĭtas, *f,* făcĭlĭtas, *f*
acceptable, grātus
acceptance, acceptĭo, *f*
access (approach), ădĭtus, *m,* accessus, *m*
accessible, făcĭlis; (to be —), *v.i,* pătĕo (3)
accession (— to the throne), ĭnĭtĭum (*n*) regni (beginning of reign); *or use phr. with* incipio (to begin) *and* regno (to reign)
accessory (of crime), *adj,* conscĭus; (helper), auctor, *m*
accident, cāsus, *m*
accidental, fortŭĭtus
accidentally, *adv,* cāsū, fortē
acclaim, *v.t,* clāmo (1)
acclamation, clāmor, *m*
acclimatized, assŭētus
accommodate, *v.t,* accommŏdo (1)
accommodating, obsĕquens

accommodation (lodging), hospĭtĭum, *n*; (loan), commŏdum, *n*
accompaniment (musical), cantus, *m*
accompany, *v.t,* prōsĕquor (3 *dep*), cŏmĭtor (1 *dep*); (— in singing), oblŏquor (3 *dep*)
accomplice, *adj,* conscĭus, partĭceps
accomplish, *v.t,* confĭcĭo (3)
accomplished (learned), ērŭdītus
accomplishment (completion), confectĭo, *f*
accord (of my (your) own —), mĕā (tŭā) spontĕ, ultrō
accord, *v.t,* concēdo (3); *v.i,* consentĭo (4)
accordance (in — with), *prep,* ex, dē, prō (*with abl*)
according to, *as above*
accordingly, *adv,* ĭtăque
accost, *v.t,* compello (1); allŏquor (3 *dep*)
account, *nn,* rătĭo, *f*; (statement), mĕmŏrĭa, *f*
on account of, *prep,* propter, ŏb (*with acc*)
to render account for, rătĭonem reddo (3)
accountant, calcŭlātor, *m,* scrība, *m*
account-book, tăbŭlae, *f. pl*
accoutre, *v.t,* orno (1); armo (1)
accoutrements, arma, *n. pl*
accredit, *v.t,* (establish), confirmo (1)
accrue, *v.i,* accēdo (3)
accumulate, *v.t,* cŭmŭlo (1), cŏăcervo (1); *v.i,* cresco (3)
accumulation (bringing together), collātĭo, *f*
accuracy (exactness), subtīlĭtas, *f*; (carefulness), cūra, *f*
accurate (exact), subtīlis, vērus; (careful), dīlĭgens
accursed, exsĕcrābĭlis
accusation, crīmen, *n,* accūsātĭo, *f*
accuse, *v.t,* accūso (1); arcesso (3), nōmen dēfĕro (*v. irreg*)
accused person, rĕus, *m*
accuser, accūsātor, *m,* dēlātor, *m*
accustom, *v.t,* assŭēfăcĭo (3)
to be accustomed, *v.i,* sŏlĕo (2)
to become accustomed, *v.i,* assŭesco (3)
accustomed, assŭētus, sŏlĭtus
ache, *v.i,* dŏlĕo (2)
ache, *nn,* dŏlor, *m*
achieve, *v.t,* confĭcĭo (3), perfĭcĭo (3)
achievement, res gesta, *f,* făcĭnus, *n*
acid, *adj,* ăcerbus, ăcĭdus
acknowledge, *v.t,* (confess), confĭtĕor (2 *dep*), agnosco (3); (accept), tollo (3)

acknowledgement, confessĭo, *f*
acme, summa, *f*
aconite, ăcŏnītum, *n*
acorn, glans, *f*
acquaint, *v.t,* certĭōrem făcĭo (3)
(*with acc. of person, and* dē *with abl*)
to become acquainted with, *v.t,*
nosco (3), cognosco (3)
acquaintance (knowledge of), scĭentĭa,
f; (**with a person**), consŭētūdo, *f*; (**a**
person), nōtus, *m*
acquiesce, *v.i,* acquĭesco (3)
acquire, *v.t,* acquīro (3)
acquirement (obtaining), ădeptĭo, *f*
acquit, *v.t,* absolvo (3), lībĕro (1)
acquittal, absŏlūtĭo, *f,* lībĕrātĭo, *f*
acre, iūgĕrum, *n*
acrid, asper, ācer
acrimonious, ăcerbus, asper, ămārus
acrimony, ăcerbĭtas, *f*
across, *prep,* trans (*with acc*)
act, *v.i,* ăgo (3), gĕro (3)
act, *v.t.* (**a part in a play**), ăgo (3)
act, *nn,* factum, *n*; (**law**) lex, *f*
action (carrying out), actĭo, *f,* actus,
m; (**at law**) lis, *f,* (**battle**), proelĭum,
n
active, impĭger, ălăcer
actively, impĭgrē
activity (energy), industrĭa, *f*; (**agility,**
mobility) ăgĭlĭtas, *f*
actor, actor, *m*
actual, vērus
actually, *adv,* rē vērā
actuary, actŭārĭus, *m*
actuate, *v.t,* mŏvĕo (2), impello (3)
acumen, ăcūmen, *n*
acute, ācer, ăcūtus
acuteness, ăcĭes, *f,* ăcūmen, *n*
adage, dictum, *n*
adapt, *v.t,* accommŏdo (1), compōno
(3)
adapted, accommŏdātus, aptus
add, *v.t,* addo (3), adĭcĭo (3)
adder, vīpĕra, *f*
addict, *v.t,* dēdo (3) (*with dat*)
addicted, dedĭtus
addition (numerical), *use verb* addo
(3); (**increase**) accessĭo, *f*
additional (more, new, fresh), nŏvus
address, *v.t.* (**a letter**), inscrībo (3);
(**person**) allŏquor (3 *dep*)
address, *nn,* (**letter**), inscriptĭo, *f*;
(**speaking**) allŏquĭum, *n*
adduce, *v.t,* prōdūco (3), prōfĕro (*v.*
irreg)
adept, pērītus
adequacy, *use* sătis (**enough**) (*with nn.*
in genit)
adequate, sătis (*with genit*)

adhere, *v.i,* (**cling**) haerĕo (2)
adherent, clĭens, *m,* sectātor, *m*
adhesive, tĕnax
adjacency, vīcīnĭtas, *f*
adjacent, fīnĭtĭmus, vīcīnus, contermĭnus
adjoin, *v.i,* adiăcĕo (2)
adjoin, *v.t,* adiungo (3)
adjoining, conĭunctus, contĭgŭus
adjourn, *v.t,* diffĕro (*v. irreg*)
adjournment, dīlātĭo, *f*
adjudge (adjudicate), *v.t,* adiūdĭco
adjudication, addictĭo, *f*
adjure, *v.t,* obtestor (1 *dep*), obsĕcro
(1)
adjust, *v.t,* apto (1), compōno (3)
adjustment, compŏsĭtĭo, *f*
adjutant, optĭo, *m*
administer, *v.t,* admĭnistro (1)
administration, admĭnistrātĭo, *f,* prōcūrātĭo, *f*
administrator, procūrātor, *m*
admirable, mīrābĭlis
admirably, *adv,* praeclārē
admiral, praefectus, (*m*) classis
admiration, admīrātĭo, *f*
admire, *v.t,* admīror (1 *dep*), mīror (1
dep)
admirer, laudātor, *m*
admissible, accĭpĭendus, a, um
admission, (letting in), ădĭtus, *m*;
(**acknowledgement**) confessĭo, *f*
admit, *v.t.* (**let in**) admitto (3); (**grant**)
dō (1), concēdo (3); (**confess**)
confĭtĕor (2 *dep*)
admonish, *v.t,* mŏnĕo (2)
admonition, admŏnĭtĭo, *f*
adolescence, ădŏlescentĭa, *f*
adolescent, ădŏlescens, *c*
adopt, *v.t,* (**person**) ădopto (1);
(**custom**) ascisco (3)
adoption, ădoptĭo, *f*
adorable, cŏlendus
adoration, cultus, *m,* ădōrātĭo, *f*
adore, *v.t,* cŏlo (3), ădōro (1)
adorn, *v.t,* orno (1)
adorned, ornātus
adornment (as an act), exornātĭo, *f*;
(**a decoration**) ornāmentum, *n*
adrift, *adj,* in mări iactātus (**driven**
about on the sea)
adroit, callĭdus, sollers
adroitness, dextĕrĭtas, *f*
adulation, ădūlātĭo, *f*
adult, *adj,* ădultus
adulterate, *v.t,* vĭtĭo (1)
adulteration, adultĕrātĭo, *f*
adulterer(-ess), ădulter, *m,* (-era, *f*)
adultery, ădultĕrĭum, *n*
advance, *nn,* prōgressus, *m*

For List of Abbreviations used, turn to pages 3, 4

advance, *v.i*, prōcēdo (3), prōgrĕdĭor (3 *dep*), incēdo (3), pĕdem infĕro (*irreg*)
advance, *v.t*, infĕro (*irreg*), prōmŏvĕo (2)
in advance, *adv*, prae, *compounded with vb: e.g.* **send in advance**, praemitto (3)
advance-guard, prīmum agmen, *n*
advantage, commŏdum, *n*
to be advantageous, *v.i*, prōsum (*irreg*), ūsui esse (*irreg*) (*with dat*)
advantageous, ūtĭlis
advantageously, *adv*, ūtĭlĭter
advent, adventus, *m*
adventure, făcĭnus, *n*
adventurous, audax
adventurously, *adv*, audacter
adversary, hostis, *c*
adverse, adversus
adversity, res adversae, *f. pl*
advert to, *v.t*, attingo (3)
advertise, *v.t*, prōscrībo (3), prōnuntĭo (1)
advertisement, prōscriptĭo, *f*
advice, consĭlĭum, *n*
advisable (advantageous), ūtĭlis
advise, *v.t*, mŏnĕo (2), suādĕo (2), censĕo (2)
advisedly, *adv*, consultō
adviser, suāsor, *m*, auctor, *m*
advocate, *nn*, patrōnus, *m*
advocate, *v.t*, suādĕo (2)
adze, ascĭa, *f*
aedile, aedĭlis, *m*
aedileship, aedĭlĭtas, *f*
aerial, *adj*, (of the air), āĕrĭus
afar, *adv*, prŏcŭl
affability, cōmĭtas, *f*
affable, cōmis
affably, *adv*, cōmĭter
affair, rēs, *f*, nĕgōtĭum, *n*
affect, *v.t*, affĭcĭo (3); (the feelings) mŏvĕo (2)
affectation (show), sĭmŭlātĭo, *f*
affected, pūtĭdus
affection (love), ămor, *m*
affectionate, ămans
affiance, *v.t*, spondĕo (2)
affianced, sponsus
affidavit, testĭmōnĭum, *n*
affiliate, *v.t*, cŏ-opto (1)
affinity, cognātĭo, *f*
affirm, *v.t*, affirmo (1)
affix, *v.t*, affīgo (3)
afflict, *v.t*, affĭcĭo (3)
afflicted (with grief), mĭser
affliction (with grief etc), mĭsĕrĭa, *f*; (a bad thing), mălum, *n*

affluence, dīvĭtĭae, *f. pl*
affluent, dīves
afford, *v.t*. (give), praebĕo (2); *otherwise use phr. with* satis pecuniae habere ut . . . **(to have enough money to. . . .)**
affright, *v.t*, terrĕo (2)
affront, contŭmēlĭa, *f*
affront, *v.t*, contŭmēlĭam facĭo (3) (*with dat*)
afire, *adj*, flăgrans
afloat, (*use phr. with* in aquā (**on the water**))
afoot, *adv*, pĕdĭbus
afore, *adv*, sŭprā
aforementioned, sŭprā scriptus
aforesaid, sŭprā scriptus
afraid, tĭmĭdus
afraid (to be —), *v.i. and v.t*, tĭmĕo (2), vĕrĕor (2 *dep*), mĕtŭo (3)
afresh, *adv*, rursus
aft, *nn*, puppis, *f*
after, *prep*, post (*with acc*)
after, *conj*, postquam
after, *adv*, post, postĕa
after all (nevertheless), *adv*, tămen
afternoon, *adv*, post mĕrīdĭem
afternoon, *adj*, pōmĕrīdĭānus
afterwards, *adv*, post, postĕa
again, *adv*, ĭtĕrum, rursus
again and again, *adv*, ĭdentĭdem
against, *prep*, contra, in (*with acc*)
agape, *adj*, hĭans
age, aetas, *f*, aevum, *n*, (**old —**) sĕnectus, *f*
aged (old), sĕnex
aged (three) years, nātus (tres) annos
agency (doing, action), ŏpĕra, *f*
agent, actor, *m*
aggrandize, *v.t*, amplĭfĭco (1)
aggrandizement, amplĭfĭcātĭo, *f*
aggravate, *v.t*, grăvo (1); (annoy) aspĕro (1); (increase) augĕo (2)
aggregate, *nn*, summa, *f*
aggression, incursĭo, *f*
aggressive, hostīlis
aggressor, *use phr.* suā sponte bellum infĕrre *irreg*, (**inflict war of one's own accord**)
aggrieve, *v.t*, *use* affĭcĭo (3) (**affect**)
aghast, stŭpĕfactus
agile, ăgĭlis
agility, ăgĭlĭtas, *f*
agitate, *v.t*, ăgĭto (1), commŏvĕo (2)
agitated, sollĭcĭtus
agitation (violent movement), ăgĭtātĭo, *f*; (of the mind), commōtĭo, *f*
agitator (political), turbātor, *m*

ago, *adv*, ăbhinc *(with acc)* e.g. **two years** —, ăbhinc duos annos

agonize, *v.t*, crŭcĭo (1)

agony, dŏlor, *m*

agrarian, ăgrārĭus

agree with, *v.i*, consentĭo (4) *(with cum and abl)*; *v.t* compōno (3); **(it is — by all)** constat inter omnes

agreeable, grātus

agreeableness, dulcēdo, *f*

agreed upon (it is —), constat, convēnit, *v. impers*

agreeing, congrŭens, convĕnĭens

agreement (the — itself), pactum, *n*; **(of opinions, etc)** consensĭo, *f*

agricultural, rustĭcus

agriculture, agrĭcultūra, *f*

agriculturist, agrĭcŏla, *m*

aground (to run —) *use phr.* in vădo haerĕo (2) **(stick fast in a shallow place)**

ague, horror, *m*

ah! (alas!), eheu!

ahead, *adv*, *use* prae, pro, *compounded with verbs*, *e.g.* **send ahead**, praemitto (3)

aid, auxĭlĭum, *n*, subsĭdĭum, *n*

aid, *v.t*, adiŭvo (1), subvĕnĭo (4) *(with dat)*

ail, *v.i*, aegresco (3)

ailing, aeger, aegrōtus

aim, *v.t*. **(point a weapon, etc.)** dĭrĭgo (3); **(to aim at)** pĕto (3)

aim, *nn*, **(purpose)** finis, *m*; **(throwing)** conĭectus, *m*

air, āēr, *m*; **(manner)** spĕcĭes, *f*

air, *v.t*, ventĭlo (1)

air-hole, spīrācŭlum, *n*

airy, āĕrĭus

akin, *adj*, **(similar)** fīnītĭmus

alabaster, ălăbastrītes ae, *m*

alacrity, ălăcrĭtas, *f*

alarm (fear), păvor, *m*, trĕpĭdātĭo, *f*; **(confusion)** tŭmultus, *m*

alarm, *v.t*, perturbo (1), terrĕo (2)

alarmed, trĕpĭdus

alas!, heu!

alcove, angŭlus, *m* **(corner)**

alder, alnus, *f*

alderman, măgistrātus, *m*

ale, cerevisia, *f*

ale-house, caupona, *f*

alert, ălăcer

alertness, ălăcrĭtas, *f*

alien *(adj and nn)* **(foreign)**, pĕrĕgrīnus

alienate, *v.t*, ălĭēno (1)

alienation, ălĭēnātĭo, *f*

alight, *v.i*, dēsĭlĭo (4)

alike, *adj*, sĭmĭlis

alike, *adv*, sĭmĭlĭter

alive, vīvus

alive (to be —), vīvo (3)

all, *adj*, **(every)** omnis; **(the whole)** tōtus; *(with superlative*, e.g. **all the best people)** optĭmus quisque; **(at all, in all)**, *adv*, omnīno

all-powerful, omnĭpŏtens

allay, *v.t*, sēdo (1)

allegation, affirmātĭo, *f*

allege, *v.t*. **(assert)**, argŭo (3), affĕro *(irreg)*

allegiance fĭdes, *f*, offĭcĭum, *n*

allegory, allēgŏrĭa, *f*

alleviate, *v.t*, lĕvo (1)

alleviation, **(as an act)**, lĕvātĭo, *f*; **(something which brings —)** lĕvāmen, *n*

alley, angĭportus, *m*

alliance, sŏcĭĕtas, *f*, foedus, *n*; **(to make an —)** foedus făcĭo (3)

allied (states), foedĕrātus

allot, *v.t*, distrĭbŭo (3), assigno (1)

allotment (of land), ăger assignātus, *m*

allow, *v.t*. **(permit)**, pătĭor (3 *dep*), sĭno (3), concēdo (3); *or use impers. vb.* lĭcet *(with dat. of person allowed)*

allowable, *use* făs, **(indecl.** *nn***) (right)**

allowance (to make —), ignosco (3), rĕmitto (3)

allude to, *v.t*, signĭfĭco (1)

allure, *v.t*, allĭcĭo (3)

allurement, blandītĭa, *f*, illĕcĕbra, *f*

alluring, blandus

allusion, signĭfĭcātĭo, *f*

alluvium, allŭvĭo, *f*

ally, *nn*, sŏcĭus, *m*

ally, *v.t*, **(unite)**, iungo (3); **(— oneself)** se conĭungere *(with dat)*

almanack, fasti, *m. pl*

almighty, omnĭpŏtens

almond, ămygdălum, *n*; **(tree)** ămygdăla, *f*

almost, *adv*, paenĕ, prŏpĕ, fĕrĕ, fermē

alms, stips, *f*

aloe, ălŏē, *f*

aloft, *adv*, sublĭmĕ; *adj*, sublīmis

alone, *adj*, sōlus

alone, *adv*, sōlum

along, *prep*, sĕcundum, praeter *(with acc)*

aloof, *adv*, prŏcŭl; **(to stand — from)**, discēdo (3)

aloud, *adv*, magnā vōce

alphabet, *use* litterae *f. pl* **(letters)**

already, *adv*, iam

also, *adv*, ĕtĭam, quŏque, ĭtem; **(likewise)**, necnōn

altar, āra, *f*

alter, *v.t*, mŭto (1), verto (3), corrĭgo (3)

alter, *v.i*, mūtor (1 *dep*)

alteration, mūtātĭo, *f*

altercation, rixa, *f*

alternate, *v.t*, alterno (1)

alternate, *adj*, alternus

alternately, *adv*, invĭcem

alternation, vĭcissĭtūdo, *f*

alternative, *use phr. with* ălĭus mŏdus (other way)

although, *conj*, quamquam (*indicating fact*); quamvīs (*indicating a supposition*); etsi, tămetsi

altitude, altĭtūdo, *f*

altogether, *adv*, omnīno

always, *adv*, semper

amalgamate, *v.t*, iungo (3), miscĕo (2)

amalgamation, coniunctĭo, *f*

amass, *v.t*, cŏăcervo (1), cŭmŭlo (1)

amatory, ămātōrĭus

amaze, *v.t*, obstŭpĕfăcĭo (3)

amazed, stŭpĭdus, stŭpĕfactus

amazement, stŭpor, *m*

amazing, mīrus

amazingly, *adv*, mīris mŏdis

amazon, vīrāgo, *f*

ambassador, lēgātus, *m*

amber, sŭcĭnum, *n*

ambiguity, ambāges, *f. pl*

ambiguous, ambĭgŭus, anceps

ambiguously, *adv*, per ambāges

ambition, glōrĭa, *f*, ambĭtĭo, *f*

ambitious, *use phr.* cŭpĭdus glōrĭae (keen on glory)

amble, *v.i*, lēnĭter ambŭlo (1) (walk quietly)

ambrosia, ambrŏsĭa, *f*

ambrosial, ambrŏsĭus

ambush, insĭdĭae, (*f. pl*); (to ambush) insĭdĭor (1 *dep*)

ameliorate, *v.t*, mĕlĭōrem făcĭo (3)

amen! fĭat! (let it be)

amenable, ŏbēdĭens

amend, *v.t*, ēmendo (1), corrĭgo (3)

amendment (correction), ēmendātĭo, *f*

amends, *use* expĭo (1) (to make —s)

amenity, ămoenĭtas, *f*

amethyst, ămĕthystus, *f*

amiability, suāvĭtas, *f*

amiable, suāvis

amiably, *adv*, suāvĭter

amicable, ămīcus

amid(st), *prep*, inter (*with acc*)

amiss, *adv*, măle; (to take —) aegre fĕro (*irreg*)

amity, ămīcĭtĭa, *f*

ammunition, arma, *n. pl*

amnesty, vĕnĭa, *f*

among, *prep*, inter, ăpud (*with acc*)

amorous, ămans

amount, summa, *f*, fīnis, *m*

amount to, *v.t, use* esse (to be)

amphitheatre, amphĭthĕātrum, *n*

ample, amplus, cōpĭōsus

amplify, *v.t*, amplĭfĭco (1), dīlāto (1)

amplitude, amplĭtūdo, *f*

amply, *adv*, amplē

amputate, *v.t*, sĕco (1), ampŭto (1)

amputation, ampŭtātĭo, *f*

amuse, *v.t*, dēlecto (1)

amusement, dēlectātĭo, *f*

amusing, făcētus

anaesthetic, *adj*, sŏpōrĭfer

analogy (comparison), compărātĭo, *f*

analyse, *v.t*, discerpo (3), explĭco (1)

analysis, explĭcātĭo, *f*

anarchical, turbŭlentus

anarchy, lĭcentĭa, *f*

anathema, exsecrātĭo, *f* (curse)

anatomy, incīsĭo (*f*) corpŏris (incision of the body)

ancestor, auctor, *m*; (*in pl*), māiōres, *m. pl*

ancestral, proăvītus

ancestry (descent, origin), gĕnus, *n*

anchor, ancŏra, *f*

anchor, *v.i, use phr.* nāvem ad ancŏras dēlĭgo (1) (fasten a ship to the anchors)

anchorage, stătĭo, *f*

ancient, antīquus, vĕtus

and, et, atque, ac; quĕ (*joined to the second of two words, e.g.* I and you: ego tuque); (and . . . not) nĕque

anecdote, fābella, *f*

anew, *adv*, dēnŭo, dē intĕgro

anger, īra, *f*, īrācundĭa, *f*

anger, *v.t*, irrīto (1), lăcesso (3)

angle, angŭlus, *m*

angle, *v.i* (fish), piscor (1 *dep*)

angler, piscātor, *m*

angrily, *adv*, īrācundē, īrātē

angry, īrātus; (irascible) īrācundus

anguish, angor, *m*, dŏlor, *m*, ăcerbĭtas, *f*

angular, angŭlātus, angŭlāris

animal, ănĭmal, *n*, pĕcus, *f*

animal, *adj*, ănĭmālis

animate, *v.t*, ănĭmo, excĭto (1)

animated, ănĭmans; (lively) vĕgĕtus, ălăcer, vĕhĕmens

animation (liveliness), vĭgor, *m*

animosity, sĭmultas, *f*

ankle, tālus, *m*

annalist, annālĭum scriptor, *m*

annals, annāles, *m. pl*

annex, *v.t*, addo (3), iungo (3)

annihilate, *v.t*, dēlĕo (2)

annihilation, exĭtĭum, *n*, exstinctĭo, *f*

anniversary, *adj,* annĭversārĭus

anniversary, *nn,* dĭes annĭversārĭus, *m*

annotate, *v.t,* annŏto (1)

annotation, annŏtātĭo, *f*

announce, *v.t,* nuntĭo (1)

announcement, prōnuntĭātĭo, *f*

announcer, nuntĭus, *m,* praeco, *m*

annoy, *v.t,* irrīto (1), lăcesso (3)

annoyance, mŏlestĭa, *f,* vexātĭo, *f*

annual, annĭversārĭus

annually, *adv,* quŏtannis

annuity, annŭa, *n. pl*

annul, *v.t,* abrŏgo (1), tollo (3)

annulment, ăbŏlĭtĭo, *f*

anoint, *v.t,* unguo (3)

anointing, *nn,* unctĭo, *f*

anomaly, ănōmălĭa, *f*

anon, *adv* (immediately), stătim; (in a short time) brĕvi tempŏre

anonymously, (*adv. phr*), sĭne. nōmĭne

another, ălĭus; (the other of two), alter; (another's), *adj,* ălĭēnus

answer, *nn,* responsum, *n*

answer, *v.t,* respondĕo (2); (in writing) rescrībo (3); (to — for, be surety for), praesto (1)

answerable, *use phr,* rătĭonem reddo (3) (to render an account)

ant, formīca, *f*

antagonism, ĭnĭmīcĭtĭa, *f*

antagonist, adversārĭus, *m*

antagonistic, contrārĭus

antecedent, *adj,* antĕcēdens

antechamber, ātrĭŏlum, *n*

anterior, prĭor

ante-room, ātrĭŏlum, *n*

anticipate, *v.t,* occŭpo (1), antĕverto (3), praecĭpĭo (3); (expect), expecto (1)

anticipation (expectation), exspectātĭo, *f*

antics, lūdi, *m, pl*

antidote, rĕmĕdĭum, *n,* antĭdŏtum, *n*

antipathy rĕpugnantĭa, *f;* (of people) ŏdĭum, *n*

antipodes, antĭpŏdes, *m. pl*

antiquarian, *adj,* antĭquĭtatis stŭdĭōsus (keen on antiquity)

antiquated, priscus

antique, *adj,* vĕtus, antīquus

antiquity, antīquĭtas, *f,* vĕtustas, *f*

antithesis (opposite), contrārĭum, *n;* (in argument), contentĭo, *f*

antler, rāmus, *m,* cornu, *n*

anvil, incūs, *f*

anxiety, anxĭĕtas, *f,* sollĭcĭtūdo, *f,* cūra, *f;* (alarm) păvor, *m*

anxious, anxĭus, sollĭcĭtus; (alarmed) trĕpĭdus

anxiously, *adv,* anxĭē

any, *adj,* ullus (*after negatives, and in questions, and comparisons*); quisquam (*pron. used like* ullus); qui, quae, quod (*after* si, nisi, ne num)

anyone, anybody, *pron,* quis (*after* si, nisi, ne, num); quisquam (*after a negative*)

anything, *use neuter of prons. given above*)

anywhere, *adv,* (in any place), usquam; (to any place), quō, quōquam; (in any place) ŭbīquĕ

apace, *adv,* (quickly), cĕlĕrĭtĕr

apart, *adv,* sēorsum; (*adj*) dīversus

apartment, conclāve, *n*

apathetic, lentus, pĭger

apathy, ignāvĭa, *f,* lentĭtūdo, *f*

ape, sĭmĭa, *f*

aperture, fŏrāmen, *n*

apex, căcūmen, *n,* ăpex, *m*

aphorism, sententĭa, *f*

apiary, alvĕārĭum, *n*

apiece, *use distributive numeral, e.g.* two each, bīni

apologize, *v.i,* excūso (1), dēfendo (3)

apology, excūsātĭo, *f*

appal, *v.t,* perterrĕo (2)

apparatus, appărātus, *m*

apparel, vestis, *f,* vestīmentum, *n*

apparent, mănĭfestus, ăpertus

apparently, *adv,* per spĕcĭem

apparition (ghost), spĕcĭes, *f,* ĭmāgo *f*

appeal, *v.i,* appello (1), prōvŏco (1), (to — to) *v.t,* obtestor (1 *dep*)

appeal, *nn,* appellātĭo, *f,* obsecrātĭo, *f*

appear, *v.i,* appārĕo (2), conspĭcĭor (3 *pass*); (to seem) vĭdĕor (2 *pass*); (to come forward) prōdĕo (4)

appearance (looks), spĕcĭes, *f,* aspectus, *m;* (show), spĕcĭes, *f;* (image), sĭmŭlācrum, *n*

appeasable, plācābĭlis

appease, *v.t,* (people), plāco (1); (feelings), sēdo (1)

appeasement, plācātĭo, *f*

appellant, appellātor, *m*

append, *v.t,* (attach), addo (3)

appendage, appendix, *f*

appertain, *v.i,* pertĭnĕo (2)

appetite, appĕtītus, *m;* (hunger), fămes, *f*

applaud, *v.t,* plaudo (3), laudo (1)

applause (clapping), plausus, *m;* (cheers), clāmor, *m*

apple, mālum, *n;* (— tree), mālus, *f*

appliance (apparatus), appărātus, *m*

applicable to, commŏdus (*with dat*)

applicant, pĕtītor, *m*

application (asking), pĕtītĭo, *f;* (mental), stŭdĭum, *n,* dīligentĭa, *f*

For List of Abbreviations used, turn to pages 3, 4

apply, *v.t*, adhĭbĕo (2), admŏvĕo (2); (**to — oneself to**) se, dēdĕre (3 *with dat*); *v.i*, (**refer to**), pertĭnĕo (2); (**— for**), flāgĭto (1)

appoint, *v.t*, constĭtŭo (3) (**people to office, etc.**), crĕo (1); (**to appoint to a command**) praefĭcĭo (3) (*acc. of person appointed, dat. of person or thing commanded*)

appointment (**office**), mūnus, *n*; (**creation**), crĕātĭo, *f*; (**agreed meeting**), constĭtūtum, *n*

apportion, *v.t*, dīvĭdo (3), distrĭbŭo (3)

apposite, aptus

appraise, *v.t*, (**evaluate**), aestĭmo (1)

appraisement, aestĭmātĭo, *f*

appreciate, *v.t*, (**value**), aestĭmo (1) magni

appreciation, aestĭmātĭo, *f*

apprehend, *v.t*, (**arrest**), comprĕhendo (3); (**understand**), intellĕgo (3), percĭpĭo (3)

apprehension (**fear**), formīdo, *f*; (**arrest**) comprĕhensĭo, *f*; (**understanding**), intellĕgentĭa, *f*

apprehensive (**fearful**), tĭmĭdus

apprentice, tĭro, *m*

approach, *v.i*, apprŏpinquo (1) (*with ad and acc. or dat*), accēdo (3)

approach, *nn*, ădĭtus, *m*, adventus, *m*, accessus, *m*

approbation, apprŏbātĭo, *f*, laus, *f*

appropriate, *adj*, aptus, accommŏdātus (*with dat*)

appropriate, *v.t*, sūmo (3)

appropriately, *adv*, aptĕ

approval, apprŏbātĭo, *f*

approve (**of**), *v.t*, apprŏbo (1)

approved, spectātus, prŏbātus

approximate, proxĭmus

approximate, *v.i*, accēdo (3)

April, Aprīlis (mensis)

apron, ŏpĕrĭmentum, *n*

apt, aptus, ĭdŏnĕus; (**inclined**), prōnus, prŏpensus

aptitude (**ability**), ingĕnĭum, *n*

aptly, *adv*, aptē

aptness, *use adj*, aptus (**suitable**)

aquatic, ăquātĭlis

aqueduct, ăquae ductus, *m*

aquiline, ăquĭlīnus, ăduncus

arable land, arvum, *n*

arbiter, arbĭter, *m*

arbitrarily, *adv*, (**according to whim**), ad libīdĭnem

arbitrary (**capricious**), lĭbīdĭnōsus

arbitrate, *v.t*, discepto (1)

arbitration, arbĭtrĭum, *n*

arbitrator, arbĭter, *m*

arbour, umbrācŭlum, *n*

arc, arcus, *m*

arcade, portĭcus, *f*

arch, fornix, *m*, arcus, *m*

arch, *adj*, (**playful**), lascīvus

archaeology, investĭgātĭo, (*f*) rērum antīquārum (**search for ancient things**)

archaism, verbum obsŏlētum, *n*

archer, săgittārĭus, *m*

archipelago, *use phr*, māre, (*n*) insŭlis consĭtum (**sea set with islands**)

architect, archĭtectus, *m*, ŏpĭfex, *c*

architecture, archĭtectūra, *f*

archives, tăbŭlae, *f. pl*

arctic, septentrĭōnālis

ardent, ardens, fervĭdus

ardently, *adv*, ardenter, vĕhĕmenter

ardour, ardor, *m*, călor, *m*, fervor, *m*

arduous, ardŭus

area, spătĭum, *n*

arena, hărēna, *f*, ărēna, *f*

argue, *v.i*, discepto (1), dissĕro (3)

argument (**quarrel**), rixa, *f*, argūmentum, *n*; (**discussion**), dispŭtātĭo, *f*

arid, ārĭdus, siccus

aridity, ārĭdĭtas, *f*, siccĭtas, *f*

aright, *adv*, rectē

arise, *v.i*, surgo (3); (**heavenly bodies**), ŏrĭor (4 *dep*)

aristocracy (**aristocratic party**), optĭmātes, *c. pl*; (**govt.**) optĭmātĭum dŏmĭnātus, *m*

aristocratic, patrĭcĭus

arithmetic, ārĭthmētĭca, *n. pl*

ark, arca, *f*

arm (**fore —**), brācchĭum, *n*; (**upper —**), lăcertus, *m*; (**weapon**), telum, *n*

arms (**weapons**), arma, *n. pl*, tēla, *n. pl*; (**call to —**), ad arma vŏco (1); (**to take —s**), arma căpĭo (3); (**to lay down —s**), arma dēdo (3)

arm, *v.t*, armo (1); (**to take —s**), arma căpĭo (3)

armament (**forces**), cōpĭae, *f, pl*; (**weapon**), tēlum, *n*

armed, armātus

armistice, indūtĭae, *f. pl*

armour, arma, *n. pl*

armourer, făber, *m*

armour-bearer, armĭger, *m*

armoury, armāmentārĭum, *n*

army, exercĭtus, *m*; (**marching —**), agmen, *n*; (**drawn up for battle**), ăcĭes, *f*

around, *adv. and prep. with acc,* circā, circum
arouse, *v.t,* suscĭto (1), excĭto (1)
arraign, *v.t,* accūso (1)
arrange, *v.t,* compōno (3), constĭtŭo (3), collŏco (1), instrŭo (3)
arrangement (as an act), collŏcātĭo, *f* (order), ordo, *m*
array, *nn,* **(clothing),** vestis, *f,* vestĭmenta, *n. pl;* (battle —), ăcĭes, *f*
array, *v.t,* compōno (3)
arrears, rĕlĭquae pĕcūnĭae, *f. pl* (money remaining)
arrest, *v.t,* comprĕhendo (3)
arrest, *nn,* comprĕhensĭo, *f*
arrival, adventus, *m*
arrive, *v.i,* advĕnĭo (4), pervĕnĭo (4)
arrogance, arrŏgantĭa, *f*
arrogant, arrŏgans
arrogate, *v.t,* arrŏgo (1) *(with dat)*
arrow, săgitta, *f*
arsenal, armāmentārĭum, *n*
art, ars, *f*
artery, vēna, *f*
artful, callĭdus, văfer
artfully, *adv,* callĭde
artfulness, callĭdĭtas, *f*
article (thing), rēs, *f;* (term of a treaty, etc.), condĭcĭo, *f*
articulate, *adj,* clārus, distinctus
articulate, *v.t,* exprĭmo (3)
articulation, explānātĭo, *f*
artifice, ars, *f*
artificer (craftsman), artĭfex, *m,* ŏpĭfex, *c*
artificial, artĭfĭcĭōsus
artificially, *adv,* mănu, artĕ
artillery, tormenta, *n. pl*
artisan, făber, *m,* ŏpĭfex, *c*
artist, artĭfex, *m;* (painter), pictor, *m*
artistic, artĭfĭcĭōsus
artless (person), simplex; (work), incomptus
artlessness, simplĭcĭtas, *f*
as, *conj,* (because), quod, cum, quĭa; (*in a comparative phr, e.g.* as strong as) tam fortis quam; (the same as) īdem atque; (as . . . as possible) quam *with the superlative, e.g.* as quickly as possible; quam cĕlerrĭme; (as if) tamquam, quăsĭ, vĕlut
ascend, *v.t,* ascendo (3)
ascendant (to be in the —), *v.i,* praesto (1)
ascendancy, praestantĭa, *f*
ascent, ascensus, *m*
ascertain, *v.t,* (find out), cognosco (3), compĕrĭo (4)
ascetic, *adj,* abstĭnens

ascribe, *v.t,* ascrībo (3), assigno (1), attrĭbŭo (3)
ash (tree), fraxĭnus, *f,* (*adj*), fraxĭnĕus
ashamed (to be —), pŭdet; *impers. with acc. and genit,* (*e.g.* I am ashamed of my brother), pŭdet me frātris
ashes, cĭnis, *m*
ashore, *adv,* (on shore), in lītŏre; (to shore), in lītus
aside, *use* se, *compounded with verb, e.g.* to put aside, sēcerno (3)
ask, *v.t,* rŏgo (1) (*with 2 accs*) e.g. I ask you for a sword, tē glădĭum rōgo
askance (to look — at), līmis ŏcŭlis aspĭcĭo (3) (look with a sidelong glance)
aslant, *adv,* oblīque
asleep (to be —), *v.i,* dormĭo (4); (to fall —) obdormĭo (4)
asp, aspis, *f*
aspect (appearance), aspectus, *m,* făcĭes, *f*
asperity, ăcerbĭtas, *f*
asperse, *v.t,* aspergo (3)
aspersion, călumnĭa, *f*
asphalt, bĭtūmen, *n*
aspirate, *nn,* aspīrātĭo, *f*
aspiration (desire), affectātĭo, *f;* (hope) spes, *f*
aspire to, affecto (1)
ass, ăsĭnus, *m*
assail, *v.t,* appĕto (3), oppugno (1)
assailant, oppugnātor, *m*
assassin, percussor, *m,* sīcārĭus, *m*
assassinate, *v.t,* trŭcīdo (1)
assassination, caedes, *f*
assault, *nn,* impĕtus, *m,* oppugnātĭo, *f*
assault, *v.t,* oppugno (1), ădŏrĭor (4 *dep*)
assemble, *v.i,* convĕnĭo (4); *v.t,* cōgo (3)
assembly, coetus, *m,* conventus, *m;* (— of the Roman people), cŏmĭtĭa, *n. pl*
assent, *nn,* assensĭo, *f*
assent to, *v.i,* assentĭor (4 *dep*) (*with dat*)
assert, *v.t,* affirmo (1), confirmo (1)
assertion, affirmātĭo, *f,* dēfensĭo, *f*
assess, *v.t* (evaluate), aestĭmo (1)
assessment (valuation), aestĭmātĭo, *f,*
assessor, censor, *m*
assets, bŏna, *n. pl*
assiduity, assidŭĭtas, *f,* sēdŭlĭtas, *f*
assiduous, assidŭus, sēdŭlus
assiduously, *adv,* assĭdŭe, sēdŭlō
assign, *v.t,* assigno (1), trĭbŭo (3)
assignation, constĭtūtum, *n*

assimilate, v.t, sĭmĭlem făcĭo (3)

assist, v.t, iŭvo (1), auxĭlĭor (1 dep), subvĕnĭo (4) (with dat)

assistance, auxĭlĭum, n, ŏpem (no nomin), f

assistant, adiŭtor, m

assize (provincial law-court), conventus, m

associate, nn, sŏcĭus, m

associate, v.t (join), coniungo (3); v.i, ūtor (3 dep. with abl)

association, sŏcĭĕtas, f, consortĭo, f

assort, v.t. (arrange), dĭgĕro (irreg)

assortment (heap), ăcervus m.

assuage, v.t, lēvo (1), mītĭgo (1)

assume, v.t, pōno (3), sūmo (3); (take on) suscĭpĭo (3)

assumption (hypothesis), sumptĭo, f

assurance (promise), fĭdes, f; (confidence) fĭdūcĭa, f

assure, v.t, confirmo (1)

assured (certain), explōrātus

assuredly, adv, (certainly), prōfecto

astern, adv, ă puppi

asthma, dyspnoea, f

astonish, v.t, obstŭpĕfăcĭo (3)

astonished, stŭpĕfactus; (to be —), v.i, obstŭpesco (3)

astonishing, mīrĭfĭcus, admīrābĭlis

astonishingly, adv. phr, mirum in mŏdum

astonishment, stŭpor, m

astound, v.t, obstŭpĕfăcĭo (3)

astray (to go —), v.i, erro (1); (to lead —), v.t, indūco (3)

astrologer, măthēmătĭcus, m

astrology, astrŏlŏgĭa, f

astronomy, astrŏlŏgĭa, f

astute, callĭdus

astuteness, callĭdĭtas, f

asylum (refuge), perfŭgĭum, n

at, (of place) in (with abl), ad, ăpŭd (with acc); with proper names and dŏmus use locative case, e.g. at Rome, Rōmae, at home, dŏmi; (of time) use abl. case, e.g. at the third hour, tertĭa hōra; or sometimes ăd with the acc. case

atheist, ăthĕŏs, m

athlete, ăthlēta, c

athletic (strong), fortis

athwart, prep (across), trans (with acc)

Atlantic, Ocĕănus, m

atmosphere, āēr, m

atom, ătŏmus, f, sēmĭna (n.pl) rērum (seeds of things)

atone for, v.t, expĭo (1)

atonement, expĭātĭo, f

atrocious, nĕfărĭus

atrociousness, fĕrĭtas, f

atrocity, nĕfas, n

atrophy, tābes, f

atrophy, v.i, tābesco (3)

attach, v.t. (fasten), affīgo (3), applīco (1); (connect) adiungo (3)

attached (fastened), fixus, aptus; (fond) dēvinctus, ămans

attachment (affection), stŭdĭum, n, ămor, m

attack, nn, impĕtus, m, oppugnātĭo, f

attack, v.t, oppugno (1), aggrĕdĭor (3 dep), ădŏrĭor (4 dep), invādo (3), pĕto (3)

attacker, oppugnātor, m

attain, v.i. (reach), pervĕnĭo (4) (with ad and acc); v.t. (obtain), consĕquor (3 dep)

attainable, impĕtrābĭlis

attainment (obtaining), ădeptĭo, f; (learning) ērŭdĭtĭo, f

attempt, nn, inceptum, n, cōnātum, n

attempt, v.i, cōnor (1 dep)

attend, v.i. (be present at), intersum (irreg. with dat); v.t. (accompany), cŏmĭtor (1 dep), prōsĕquor, (3 dep); (pay attention) ŏpĕram do (1), ănĭmadverto (3)

attendance (being present), use vb. adsum (irreg) (to be present); (of crowds), frĕquentĭa, f; (service), appārĭtĭo, f

attendant, nn, (servant) mĭnister, m; (of a nobleman) sectātor, m, sătellĕs, c

attention (concentration), attentĭo (f) ănĭmi; (to pay —); ŏpĕram, (f) do (1)

attentive (alert), intentus, attentus; (respectful), observans

attentively, adv, sēdŭlo

attenuate, v.t, attĕnŭo (1)

attest, v.t, testor (1 dep)

attestation, testĭfĭcātĭo, f

attire, nn, vestis, f

attire, v.t, vestĭo (4)

attitude (of mind), ănĭmus, m; (of body), gestus m, hăbĭtus, m

attract, v.t, attrăho (3), allĭcĭo (3)

attraction (charms), illĕcĕbrae (f. pl)

attractive, blandus, iūcundus

attribute, v.t, attrĭbŭo (3), assigno (1)

attune, v.t, (adjust), consŏnum (aptum) reddo (3) (make harmonious (suitable))

auburn, flāvus

auction, auctĭo, f; (to sell by public—), sub hastā vendo (3) (sell under the spear)

auctioneer, praeco, *m*
audacious, audax
audacity, audācĭa, *f*, confīdentĭa, *f*
audibly, *use phr.* quod audīri pŏtest (that can be heard)
audience (of people), audītōres, *m,pl* (hearing), ădītus, *m*
audit, *v.t*, inspĭcĭo (3)
auditorium, auditorĭum, *n*
augment, *v.t*, augĕo (2)
augur, *nn*, augur, *c*
augur, *v.t*, vātĭcĭnor (1 *dep*)
augury, augŭrĭum, *n*, auspĭcĭum, *n*
August, Sextīlis or Augustus (mensis)
august, *adj*, augustus
aunt (paternal), ămĭta, *f*; (maternal), mātertĕra, *f*
auspices, auspĭcĭum, *n*
auspicious, faustus, sĕcundus
auspiciously, *adv*, fēlīcĭter
austere (severe), sĕvērus
austerity, sĕvērĭtas, *f*
authentic, vērus, certus
authentically, *adv*, certō
authenticate, *v.t*, rĕcognosco (3)
authenticity, auctōrĭtas, *f*
author (writer), scriptor, *m*; (instigator), auctor, *m*
authoritative, grăvis, impĕrĭosus
authority, auctōrĭtas, *f*, pŏtestas, *f*, impĕrĭum, *n*
authorize (give permission to), *v.i*, pŏtestātem (auctōrĭtātem), făcĭo (3) (*with dat*)
autocracy, tўrannis, *f*
autocrat, dŏmĭnus, *m*,
autograph, mănus, *f*
autumn, auctumnus, *m*
autumnal, auctumnālis
auxiliary, *adj*, auxĭlĭāris, auxĭlĭārĭus; *nn* adiūtor, *m*; (—forces) auxĭlĭa, *n.pl*
avail, *v.t* (assist), prōsum (*irreg*) (*with dat.*); (make use of), ūtor (3 *dep. with abl*)
available (ready), expĕdītus, părātus
avarice, ăvārĭtĭa, *f*
avaricious, ăvārus
avenge, *v.t*, ulciscor (3 *dep*)
avenger, ultor, *m*,
avenging, *adj*, ultrix
avenue, xystus, *m*
aver, *v.t* (affirm), affirmo (1)
average, *adj*, mĕdĭus (middle)
averse, ăversus
aversion, ŏdĭum, *n*,
avert, *v.t*, āverto (3), dēpello (3)
aviary, ăvĭārĭum, *n*
avid, ăvĭdus
avidity, ăvĭdĭtas, *f*

avoid, *v.t*, vīto (1), fŭgĭo (3)
avoidance, vītātĭo, *f*, fŭga, *f*
avow, *v.t*, fătĕor (2 *dep*)
avowal, confessĭo, *f*
avowed, prŏfessus, ăpertus
await, *v.t*, exspecto (1)
awake, *adj*, vĭgĭlans; (to be —), *v.i*, vĭgĭlo (1); (to awake), *v.t*, excĭto (1)
award, *nn*, (judicial decision); arbĭtrĭum, *n* (prize), palma, *f*
award, *v.t*, trĭbŭo (3), adiūdĭco (1)
aware, gnārus; (to be —), sentĭo (4); (know), scĭo (4)
away, *use* a, ab *compounded with a verb*, *e.g.* (ăbĕo) go away (4)
awe, formīdo, *f*, mĕtus, *m*, rĕvĕrentĭa, *f*
awe (be in —) vĕrĕor, (2 *dep.*)
awful, vĕrendus
awestruck, păvĭdus
awhile, *adv*, paulisper, părumper
awkward, rŭdis, impĕrītus
awkwardness, inscītĭa, *f*
awning, vēlum, *n*
awry, *adj*, perversus; *adv*, perversē
axe, sĕcūris, *f*
axiom, sententĭa, *f*
axis, axle, axis, *m*
ay, aye, *adv*, ĭta, vērō; (forever) in perpĕtŭum
azure, *adj*, caerŭlĕus

B

babble, *v.i*, garrĭo (4), blătĕro (1)
babbler, babbling, *adj*, garrŭlus
baby, infans, *c*
babyhood, infantĭa, *f*
bacchanalian, bacchānālis
bachelor, *adj*, caelebs
back, *nn*, tergum, *n*, dorsum, *n*; (at the —) a tergo; (to move something —), rĕtro mŏvĕo (2), rēĭcĭo (3); (to go —) se rĕcĭpĕre (3 *reflex*)
backbite, *v.t*, obtrecto (1)
backwards, *adj*, (dull) pĭger
backwards, *adv*, rĕtro
bacon, lārīdum, *n*
bad, mălus; (of health), aeger; (of weather), ădversus
badge, insigne, *n*
badger, mēles, *f*
badly, *adv*, mălĕ, prāvĕ, imprŏbē
badness (worthlessness), nēquĭtĭa, *f*
baffle, *v.t*, ēlūdo (3)
bag, saccus, *m*
baggage (military), impĕdīmenta, *n.pl*; (individual packs), sarcĭnae, *f. pl*
bail, *nn*, (person), văs, *m*; (security) vădīmōnĭum, *n*

For List of Abbreviations used, turn to pages 3, 4

bail (to give — for), *v.t*, spondĕo (2) prō (*with abl*)

bailiff (estate manager), villīcus, *m*; (official), appārītor, *m*

bait, *nn*, esca, *f*

bait, *v.t*, (tease), lăcesso (3), illūdo (3)

bake, *v.t*, torrĕo (2), cŏquo (3)

baker, pistor, *m*

bakery, pistrīnum, *n*

balance, *nn*, (scales), lībra, *f*; (equilibrium), lībrāmentum, *n*

balance, *v.t*, libro (1), compenso (1)

balcony, maenĭāna, *n.pl*

bald, calvus, glăber; (unadorned), ārĭdus

baldness, calvĭtĭum, *n*

bale out, *v.t*, (discharge), ēgĕro (3)

bale (bundle), fascis, *m*

baleful, pernĭcĭōsus

balk (beam), trabs, *f*

balk, *v.t*, frustror (1 *dep*)

ball (for play), pĭla, *f*; (globe, sphere), glŏbus, *m*

ballad, carmen. *n*

ballad-singer, cantātor, *m*

ballast, săbura, *f*

ballet, *use vb.* salto (1) (dance)

ballista, ballista, *f*

ballot, suffrāgĭum, *n*

ballot-box, cista, *f*, urna, *f*

balm, balsămum, *n*, unguentum, *n*

balmy (soothing), mollis, lēnis

balustrade (railings), cancelli, *m. pl*

bamboo, hărundo, *f* (reed)

ban, *v.t*, vĕto (1)

band (bond), vincŭlum, *n*; (of people), mănus, *f*, grex, *m*

band together, *v.i*, conĭūro (1)

bandage, fascĭa, *f*

bandage, *v.t*, lĭgo (1)

bandit, lătro, *m*

bandy (to — words), *v.i*, altercor (1 *dep*)

bandy-legged, lōrĭpes

bane (injury), pernĭcĭes, *f*; (poison), vĕnēnum, *n*

baneful, pernĭcĭōsus

bang, crĕpĭtus, *m*

bang, *v.t.* (beat), tundo (3)

banish, *v.t*, *use phr.* ăquā et ĭgni interdīco (3) (*with dat*) (forbid one the use of fire and water), expello (3)

banishment, rĕlēgātĭo, *f*, exsĭlĭum, *n*

bank, *nn*, (of earth), tŏrus, *m*; (of a river), rīpa, *f*; (for money), argentārĭa tăberna (money shop)

banker, argentārĭus, mensārĭus, *m*

bankrupt, *nn*, dēcoctor, *m*, (to be —), *v.i*, solvendo non esse

bankruptcy (personal), rŭīna, *f* (downfall)

banner, vexillum, *n*

banquet, convīvĭum, *n*, ĕpŭlae, *f. pl*

banter, *nn*, căvillātĭo, *f*

banter, *v.i*, căvillor (1 *dep*)

bar (wooden), asser, *m*; (lock), claustra, *n. pl*; (bolt), sĕra, *f*; (barrier), rĕpāgŭla, *n. pl*

bar, *v.t* (fasten), obsĕro (1); (— the way), obsto (1) (*with dat*)

barb (hook), uncus, *m*

barbarian, barbărus, *m*

barbaric (barbarous), barbărus, crūdēlis, immānis

barbarity, barbărĭa, *f*

barbarously, *adv*, (cruelly), crūdēlĭter

barbed, hāmātus

barber, tonsor, *m*

bard (poet, etc.), poēta, *m*

bare, nūdus; (to make —), *v.t*, ăpĕrĭo (4), nūdo (1)

barefaced, (shameless), impŭdens

barefoot, *adv*, nūdo pĕde

barely, *adv*, vix

bargain, *nn*, pactum, *n*

bargain, *v.i*, (make a — with), paciscor (3 *dep*) (*with cum and abl. of person*)

barge, linter, *f*; (— man), nauta, *m*

bark, *nn*, (of trees), cortex, *m*; (of dogs), lātrātus, *m*; (boat), rătis, *f*

bark, *v.i*, lātro (1)

barley, hordĕum, *n*

barley-water, ptĭsăna, *f*

barn, horrĕum, *n*

baron, princeps, *m*

barque, rătis, *f*

barracks, castra, *n. pl*

barrel, dōlĭum, *n*

barren, stĕrĭlis

barrenness, stĕrĭlĭtās, *f*

barricade, *nn*, agger, *m*

barricade, *v.t*, obsaepĭo (4)

barrier, impĕdīmentum, *n*, claustra, *n. pl*

barrister, pătrōnus, *m*

barrow, fercŭlum, *n*

barter, *v.t*, (exchange), mūto (1);

barter, *nn*, permūtātĭo, (*f*,) mercĭum (exchange of goods)

base, *nn*, băsis, *f*, fundāmentum, *n*

base, *adj*, (worthless), turpis; (lowborn), hŭmĭlis

baseless, *adj*, falsus

basely, *adv*, turpĭter

basement, băsis, *f*
baseness, turpĭtūdo, *f*
bashful, vĕrēcundus
bashfulness, vĕrēcundĭa, *f*
basin, pelvis, *f*
basis, băsis, *f*, fundāmentum, *n*
bask, *v.i*, ăprīcor (1 *dep*)
basket, călăthus, *m*, corbis, *f*, quālum, *n*
bass, *adj*, grăvis
bastard, *adj*, nŏthus
bastion, turris, *f*
bat (animal), vespertīlĭo, *m*; (club, stick), clāva, *f*
bath, *nn*, balnĕum, *n*; (public —) balnĕae, *f. pl*
bath, bathe *v.i*, lăvor (1 *pass*); v.t, lăvo (1)
bathing, *nn*, lăvātĭo, *f*
baton, scīpĭo, *m*
battalion, cŏhors, *f*
batter, v.t, pulso (1), verbĕro (1)
battering-ram, ărĭes, *m*
battery (assault), vīs, *f*; (cannon), tormenta, *n. pl*
battle, proelĭum, *n*; (—line), ăcĭes, *f*; (—cry), clāmor, *m*; (—field), lŏcus (*m*) pugnae
battlement, pinna, *f*, mūnītĭōnes, *f. pl*
bawd, lēna, *f*
bawl, *v.i*, clāmĭto (1)
bawling, *nn*, clāmor, *m*
bay (of the sea), sĭnus, *m*; (tree) laurus, *f*; (at bay) (*adj*) părātus ad pugnam (**ready for a fight**)
bay, *v.i*, lātro (1)
bayonet, pūgĭo, *m*
be, *v.i*, sum (*irreg*)
beach, lītus, *n*
beacon (fire), ignis, *m*
bead, bāca, *f*
beak, rōstrum, *n*
beaker, pōcŭlum, *n*
beam (of timber), tignum, *n*, trabs, *f*; (cross —), transtrum, *n*; (ray) rădĭus, *m*
bean, fāba, *f*
bear, *nn*, ursus, *m*, ursa, *f*; (constellation), septentrĭōnes, *m. pl*; (The Great —), ursa maior; (The Little —) septentrĭo minor
bear, *v.t*, fĕro (*irreg*), gĕro (3); (carry), porto (1); (produce), părĭo (3); (— away) aufĕro (*irreg*)
bearable, *adj*, tŏlĕrābĭlis
beard, barba, *f*; (bearded), barbātus
bearer (carrier), bāĭŭlus, *m*, portĭtor, *m*
bearing (posture), gestus, *m*

beast (wild), bestĭa, *f*, fĕra, *f*; (domestic), pĕcus, *f*
beastly (filthy), obscēnus
beat (in music, poetry), ictus, *m*
beat, *v.t*, caedo (3), fĕrĭo (4), verbĕro (1); (conquer), sŭpĕro (1), vinco (3); (— back), rĕpello (3); (— down) sterno (3); (be beaten),*v.i*, vāpŭlo (1)
beating, *nn*, verbĕra, *n. pl*
beautiful, pulcher
beautifully, *adv*, pulchre
beautify, *v.t*, orno (1)
beauty, pulchrĭtūdo, *f*, forma, *f*
beaver, castor, *m*
becalmed, vento dēstĭtūtus (**deserted by the wind**)
because, *conj*, quod, quĭa, cum; (because of) *prep*, propter, ŏb (*with acc*)
beckon, *v.t*, innŭo (3) (*with dat*)
become, *v.i*, fīo (*irreg*); *v.t* (to suit, adorn), dĕcet (2 *impers. with acc. of person*)
becoming, *adj*, dĕcōrus
bed, lectus, *m*; (go to —), cŭbĭtum ĕo (4)
bedroom, cŭbĭcŭlum, *n*
bedaub, *v.t*, līno (3)
bedeck, *v.t*, orno (1); (bedecked), ornātus
bedew, *v.t*, irrōro (1)
bee, ăpis, *f*
bee-hive, alvĕārĭum, *n*
beech-tree, fāgus, *f*
beef, căro būbŭla, *f*, (ox flesh)
beer, cerevisia, *f*
beetle, scărăbaeus, *m*
befall, *v.i*, accĭdo (3)
befit, *v.i* (suit), convĕnĭo (4)
before, *prep*, (time and place), antĕ (*with acc*); (place), prae, prō (*with abl*); (in the presence of), cōram (*with abl*); before, *adv*, (time), antĕ, prĭus; (space) prae; before, *conj*, antĕquam, prĭusquam
befoul, *v.t*, inquĭno (1)
befriend, *v.t*, adiŭvo (1)
beg, *v.t* (request), pĕto (3), ōro (1); (be a beggar), *v.i*, mendīco (1)
beget, *v.t*, gigno (3)
begetter, gĕnĭtor, *m*
beggar, mendīcus, *m*
begin, *v.i*, incĭpĭo (3), coepi (3 *defect*)
beginner (originator), auctor, *m* (learner), tīro, *m*
beginning, *nn*, ĭnĭtĭum, *n*, prĭncĭpĭum, *n*, inceptum, *n*
begone! ăpăgĕ!
begrudge, *v.t* (envy), invĭdĕo (2) (*with dat*)

beguile, v.t, fallo (3), dēcĭpĭo (3)

behalf (on — of), (prep), prō (with abl)

behave oneself, v. reflex, se gĕrĕre (3)

behaviour (manners), mōres, m. pl

behead, v.t, sĕcūri fĕrĭo (4) (strike with an axe)

behest (command), iussum, n

behind (prep), post (with acc)

behind, adv, post, ā tergo

behold, v.t, conspĭcĭo (3)

behold! (exclamation), eccĕ!

being (human —), hōmo, c

belabour, v.t, verbĕro (1)

belated, sērus

belch, v.i, and v.t, ructo (1)

belch, nn, ructus, m

beleaguer, v.t, obsĭdĕo (2)

belfry, turris, f

belie, v.t, (conceal), dissĭmŭlo (1)

belief, fĭdes, f; (impression), ŏpīnĭo, f, persuāsĭo, f

believe, v.t, crēdo (3) (with dat. of person), pŭto (1), arbĭtror (1 dep), censĕo (2)

believer, crēdens, c

bell, tintinnābŭlum, n

belligerent, bellans, belli cŭpĭdus (keen on war)

bellow, v.i, mūgĭo (4)

bellowing, nn, mūgītus, m

bellows (pair of —), follis, m

belly, venter, m, abdōmen, n

belong to, v.i, use esse (irreg) (to be) with genit. of person

beloved, cārus, dilectus

below, prep, infrā, subter (with acc) sub (with abl. or acc)

below, adv, infrā, subter

belt, baltĕus, m

bemoan, v.t, gĕmo (3)

bench, scamnum, n; (for rowers) transtrum, n

bend, v.t, flecto (3), curvo (1); v.i, se flectĕre (3 pass)

bend, bending, nn, flexus, m

beneath, see below

benefactor, phr, qui bĕnĕfĭcĭa confert (who confers favours)

beneficence, bĕnĕfĭcentĭa, f

beneficent, bĕnĕfĭcus

beneficial, sălūtāris, ūtĭlis; (to be —) v.i, prōsum (irreg) (with dat)

benefit, v.i, prōsum (irreg) (with dat), adiŭvo (1)

benefit, nn, bĕnĕfĭcĭum, n

benevolence, bĕnĕfĭcentĭa, f, bĕnĕvŏlentĭa, f

benevolent, bĕnĕfĭcus, bĕnĕvŏlus

benign, bĕnignus

benignity, bĕnignĭtas, f

bent, adj, curvus; (— on) attentus; (— back) rĕsŭpīnus; (— forward) prōnus

benumb, v.t, phr torpōre affĭcĭo (3) (affect with numbness)

bequeath, v.t, lēgo (1)

bequest, lēgātum, n

bereave, v.t, orbo (1)

bereaved, orbus

bereavement, orbĭtas, f, damnum, n

berry, bāca, f

berth (for a ship), stătĭo, f

beseech, ōro (1), obsecro (1), quaeso (3)

beseem (become), dĕcet (2 impers. with acc. of person)

beset, v.t, obsĭdĕo (2), circumvĕnĭo (4)

beside, prep, (near), prŏpē (with acc); (except), praeter (with acc)

besides, prep, praeter (with acc)

besides, adv or conj, praeterquam

besides, adv, (further), praetĕrĕā, insŭper

besiege, v.t, obsĭdĕo (2), circum sĕdĕo (2)

besieger, obsessor, m

besmear, v.t, illĭno (3)

bespatter, v.t, aspergo (3)

bespeak, v.t, (hire) condūco (3)

besprinkle, v.t, aspergo (3)

best, adj, optĭmus; (to the best of (one's) ability) prō (vĭrīli) parte;

best, adv, optĭmē

bestial, use phr, bestĭārum mōre (after the manner of beasts)

bestir (to — oneself), v.i, expergiscor (3 dep)

bestow, v.t, do (1), trĭbŭo (3), confĕro (irreg)

bestowal, largītĭo, f

bet, nn, pignus, n

bet, v.t, pignŏre contendo (3)

betake, v.t, conferre (irreg)

betimes, adv, mātūrē

betray, v.t, prōdo (3)

betrayal, prōdĭtĭo, f

betrayer, prōdĭtor, m

betroth, v.t, spondĕo (2)

betrothal, sponsālĭa, n. pl

better, adj, mĕlĭor; (of health), sānus; better, adv, mĕlĭus

better, v.t, (improve), corrĭgo (3); ēmendo (1)

between, prep, inter (with acc)

beverage, pōtĭo, f, pōtus, m

bevy, cătĕrva, f

bewail, v.t, dēplōro (1), lūgeo (2)

beware, v.i and v.t, căvĕo (2)

bewilder, v.t, perturbo (1), distrăho (3)

bewildered, turbātus, distractus

bewitch, *v.t,* fascīno (1); **(charm),** căpĭo (3)

beyond, *prep,* ultrā, trans, sŭprā, extrā *(with acc)*

beyond, *adv,* ultrā, sŭprā

bias, inclīnātĭo, *f*

bias, *v.t,* inclīno (1)

Bible, *use phr.* scripta săcra, *n. pl* **(sacred writings)**

bicker, *v.i,* altercor (1 *dep*)

bid, *nn,* **(of a price)** lĭcĭtātĭo, *f*

bid, *v.t* **(tell, order),** iŭbĕo (2)

bide, *v.i* **(stay),** mănĕo (2)

bier, fĕrētrum, *n,* fercŭlum, *n*

big, magnus, vastus, ingens

bigotry, obstĭnātĭo, *f*

bile, bĭlis, *f*

bilge-water, sentīna, *f*

bilious, bĭlĭōsus

bill (written, financial), lĭbellus, *m,* rātĭo, *f,* syngrăpha, *f;* **(proposal in Parliament),** rŏgātĭo, *f;* **(a law),** lex, *f;* **(of a bird),** rōstrum, *n*

billet (of wood), lignum, *n;* **(lodging of soldiers),** hospĭtĭum, **(n)** mīlĭtum

billet, *v.t* **(soldiers),** per hospĭtĭa dispōno (3) **(distribute through lodgings)**

billow, fluctus, *m*

billowy, fluctŭosus

bind, *v.t,* līgo (1), vincĭo (4); **(oblige),** oblĭgo (1); **(— together),** collĭgo (1)

biographer, scriptor rērum gestārum **(writer of exploits)**

biography, vīta, *f*

birch (tree), bĕtŭla, *f*

bird, ăvis, *f;* **(— cage),** căvĕa, *f;* **(— nest),** nīdus, *m*

birth, ortus, *m,* gĕnus, *n*

birthday, (dĭes) nātālis

birth-place, sŏlum, **(n)** nātāle

bishop, pontĭfex, *m*

bit (bite), offa, *f;* **(small piece of food),** frustrum, *n;* **(for a horse),** frēnum, *n*

bitch, cănis, *f*

bite, *nn,* morsus, *m*

bite, *v.t,* mordĕo (2)

biting, *adj,* mordax, asper

bitter, ămārus, ăcerbus, asper

bitterness, ăcerbĭtas, *f*

bitumen, bĭtūmen, *n*

bivouac, *nn,* excŭbĭae, *f. pl*

bivouac, *v.i,* excŭbo (1)

blab, *v.i,* blătĕro (1)

black, nĭger; **(— art),** măgĭce, *f*

blackberry, mōrum, *n,* rŭbus, *m*

blackbird, mĕrŭla, *f*

blacken, *v.t,* nigrum reddo (3)

blackguard, nĕbŭlo, *m*

Black Sea, Pontus Euxīnus, *m*

blacksmith, făber, *m*

bladder, vēsīca, *f*

blade (of grass), herba, *f;* **(of sword, knife),** lāmĭna, *f*

blame, *nn,* culpa, *f*

blame, *v.t,* culpo (1)

blameable, culpandus

blameless, innŏcens, intĕger

blamelessness, innocentĭa, *f*

bland, blandus

blandishment, blandītĭa, *f,* blandīmentum, *n*

blank, *adj,* **(empty),** văcŭus; **(paper),** pūrus

blank, *nn,* ĭnāne, *n*

blanket, lōdix, *f*

blaspheme, *v.t,* blasphēmo (1)

blast, *nn,* flāmen, *n,* flātus, *m*

blast, *v.t,* ūro (3)

blatant, *adj,* **(manifest),** ăpertus

blaze, *nn,* flamma, *f*

blaze, *v.i,* ardĕo (2), flăgro (1)

bleach, candĭdum reddo (3)

bleak, algĭdus, frīgĭdus

blear-eyed, lippus

bleat, bleating, bālātus, *m*

bleat, *v.i,* bālo (1)

bleed, *v.i,* sanguĭnem effundo (3); *v.t,* sanguĭnem mitto (3)

bleeding, *adj,* **(wound),** crūdus

bleeding, *nn, use phr* effūsĭo, **(f),** sanguĭnis **(shedding of blood)**

blemish, *nn,* **(physical),** vĭtĭum, *n,* **(moral),** măcŭla, *f*

blemish, *v.t,* măcŭlo (1)

blend, *v.t,* miscĕo (2)

bless, *v.t,* **(favour, make successful),** sĕcundo (1), bĕnēdīco (3)

blessed, beātus; **(of the dead),** pĭus

blessedness, bĕătĭtūdo, *f,* fēlĭcĭtas, *f*

blessing, *nn,* bĕnēdictĭo, *f,* bŏnum, *n*

blight, *nn,* rōbīgo, *f*

blight, *v.t,* ūro (3); **(— of hopes),** frustror (1 *dep*)

blind, *adj,* caecus

blind, *v.t,* caeco (1)

blindly (rashly), *adv,* tĕmĕre

blindness, caecĭtas, *f*

blink, *v.i,* connīvĕo (2)

bliss, fēlĭcĭtas, *f*

blissful, *adj,* fēlix

blister, pustŭla, *f*

blithe, hĭlăris

blizzard, imber, *m*

bloated, sufflātus

block, *nn,* **(of wood),** stīpes, *m,* massa, *f*

block, *v.t,* obstrŭo (3), obsaepĭo (4)

For List of Abbreviations used, turn to pages 3, 4

blockade, *nn*, obsĭdĭo, *f*
blockade, *v.t*, obsĭdĕo (2)
blockhead, caudex, *m*
blood, sanguis, *m*; (gore), crŭor, *m*
blood-letting, *nn*, missĭo, (*f*) sanguĭnis
bloodshed, caedes, *f*
bloodshot, crŭore suffusus (spread over with blood)
blood-stained, crŭentus
blood-thirsty, sanguĭnārĭus
bloody, crŭentus, sanguĭnĕus
bloom, *nn*, flōs, *m*
bloom, *v.i*, flōrĕo (2)
blooming, flōrens
blossom, etc., *see* bloom
blot, *v.t*, măcŭlo (1); (— out, obliterate), dēlĕo (2)
blot, *nn*, măcŭla, *f*
blow, *nn*, (stroke), plāga, *f*, ictus, *m*
blow, *v.i and v.t*, flo (1)
blowing, *nn*, flātus, *m*
bludgeon, fustis, *m*
blue, *adj*, caerŭlĕus
bluff, *v.t*, illūdo (3)
blunder, *nn*, mendum, *n*, error, *m*
blunder, *v.i*, offendo (3), erro (1)
blunt, *adj*, hēbes; (frank), lĭber
blunt, *v.t*, hĕbĕto (1), obtundo (3)
bluntly, *adv*, lĭbĕrē, plānē
blush, *nn*, rŭbor, *m*
blush, *v.i*, ērŭbesco (3)
bluster, *v.i*, dēclāmo (1)
bluster, *nn*, dēclāmātĭo, *f*
blusterer, iactātor, *m*
boar, verres, *m*, ăper, *m*
board, *nn*, tăbŭla, *f*; (council), concĭlĭum, *n*
board, *v.t* (ship), conscendo (3); (to — up), contăbŭlo (1); (provide food), victum praebĕo (2)
boast, *v.i*, glōrĭor (1 *dep.*), se iactare (1 *reflex*)
boasting, *nn*, glōrĭātĭo, *f*, iactātĭo, *f*
boat, scăpha, *f*, linter, *f*
boatman, nauta, *m*
bode, *v.t* (predict), praesāgĭo (4)
bodily, *adj*, corpŏrĕus
bodkin, ăcus, *f*
body, corpus, *n*; (— of soldiers, etc.), mănus, *f*, nŭmĕrus, *m*, multĭtūdo, *f*
body-guard, stĭpātōres, *m. pl*
bog, pălus, *f*
boggy, păluster
boil, *nn*, vŏmĭca, *f*
boil, *v.t*, cŏquo (3); *v.i*, fervĕo (2)
boiled, *adj*, ēlixus
boiler, caldārĭum, *n*
boisterous, prŏcellōsus, turbĭdus

bold, audax, ănĭmōsus, fortis
boldly, *adv*, audacter, ănĭmōse, fortĭter
boldness, audācĭa, *f*, fĭdentĭa, *f*
bolster, cervīcal, *n*, pulvīnus, *m*
bolt, *nn* (door, etc.), ŏbex, *m*, rĕpăgŭla, *n.pl*
bolt, *v.t* (door, etc.), obsĕro (1), claudo (3); (food), obsorbĕo (2)
bombastic, inflātus
bond, vincŭlum, *n*, cătēna, *f*; (legal), syngrăpha, *f*
bondage, servĭtus, *f*
bone, ŏs, *n*
book, lĭber, *m*, lĭbellus, *m*
bookbinder, glūtĭnātor, *m*
bookcase, armārĭum, *n*
book-keeper, actŭārĭus, *m*
bookseller, bĭblĭŏpōla, *m*
boom, *v.i*, sŏno (1)
boon (good thing), bŏnum, *n*
boor, hŏmo ăgrestis
boorish, agrestis
boot, calcĕus, *m*; (heavy —), călĭga, *f*
bootless (unsuccessful), *adj*, irrĭtus
booth, tăberna, *f*
booty, praeda, *f*, spŏlĭa, *n.pl*
booze, *v.i. and v.t*, pōto (1)
border, margo, *m*, *f*; (of a country), fīnis, *m*
border, *v.i*, attingo (3)
bordering, *adj*, fīnĭtĭmus
bore (person) use, *adj*, importūnus (rude)
bore, *v.t*, perfŏro (1), tĕrĕbro (1); (— someone), fătīgo (1)
boredom, taedĭum, *n*
born, *adj*, nātus; (to be —), *v.i*, nascor (3 *dep.*)
borough, mūnĭcĭpĭum, *n*
borrow, mūtŭor (1 *dep.*)
bosom, sĭnus, *m*, pectus, *n*
boss (of a shield), umbo, *m*
botany, ars herbārĭa, *f*
botch, *v.t*, măle sarcĭo (4), (patch badly)
both, ambo; (each of two), ŭterquĕ; (both . . . and), et . . . et
bother, *nn*, use adj, mŏlestus (troublesome)
bother, *v.t*, lăcesso (3), vexo (1)
bottle, ampulla, *f*, lăgēna, *f*
bottom, fundus, *m*, *or use adj.* īmus *in agreement with noun, e.g.* at the bottom of the tree, ad īmam arbŏrem
bottomless (very deep), prŏfundus
bough, rāmus, *m*
boulder, saxum, *n*

bounce, *v.i*, rĕsĭlĭo (4)
bound (limit), fīnis, *m*, mŏdus, *m*; (leap), saltus, *m*
bound, *v.i*, (leap), sălĭo (4); *v.t*, (limit), contĭnĕo (2)
boundary, fīnis, *m*
boundless, infīnītus
bountiful, largus, bĕnignus
bounty, largĭtas, *f*, bĕnignĭtas, *f*
bouquet, serta, *n.pl*
bout (contest), certāmen, *n*
bow (archery), arcus, *m*; (of a ship), prōra, *f*; (of salutation), sălūtātĭo, *f*
bow, *v.t*, inclīno (1), dēmitto (3); *v.i*, se dēmittĕre (3 *reflex*)
bow-legged, vātĭus
bowman, săgittārĭus, *m*
bowels, viscĕra, *n.pl*
bower, umbrācŭlum, *n*
bowl, crātēra, *f*
box, arca, *f*, cista, *f*; (tree), buxus, *f*; (slap), cōlăphus, *m*
box, *v.i*, pugnis certo (1), (fight with the fists)
boxer, pŭgil, *m*
boxing, *nn*, pŭgĭlātĭo, *f*
boy, pŭer, *m*
boyhood, pŭĕrĭtĭa, *f*
boyish, pŭĕrīlis
brace (support), fascĭa, *f*; (in architecture), fĭbŭla, *f*
brace, *v.t*, lĭgo (1), firmo (1)
bracelet, armilla, *f*
bracket, mūtŭlus, *m*
brackish, ămārus
brag, *v.i*, glōrĭor (1 *dep*.)
braggart, iactātor, *m*
braid, *nn*, (of hair), grădus, *m*
braid, *v.t*, necto (3)
brain, cĕrĕbrum, *n*
brainless (stupid), sōcors
bramble, dūmus, *m*
bran, furfur, *m*
branch, rāmus, *m*
branch, *v.i*, (separate), dīvĭdor (3 *pass*)
branching, *adj*, rāmōsus
brand (fire —), fax, *f*, torris, *m*; (burn-mark), nŏta, *f*; (stigma), stigma, *n*
brand, *v.t*, īnūro (3), nŏto (1)
brandish, *v.t*, vibro (1)
brass, ōrĭchalcum, *n*
brave, fortis, ănĭmōsus, ăcer
bravely, *adv*, fortĭter, ănĭmōsē
bravery, fortĭtūdo, *f*
brawl, *v.i*, rixor (1 *dep*.)
brawl, *nn*, rixa, *f*
brawny, lăcertōsus
bray, *v.i*, rŭdo (3)

brazen (made of brass), aēnĕus, aerĕus; (impudent), impŭdens
breach, rūīna, *f*, *or use vb*. rumpo (3) (to burst); (— in a treaty, etc.) *use* vĭŏlo (1) (to violate)
bread, pānis, *m*
breadth, lātĭtūdo, *f*
break, *v.t*, frango (3); (treaty, etc.) vĭŏlo (1); (— promise), fīdem fallo (3); (— down), *v.t*, rēscindo (3); (— in), *v.t*, (horses), dŏmo (1); (— into), *v.t*, irrumpo (3); (— loose), ērumpo (3)
break (of day), prīma lux, *f*, (first light); (fracture), fractūra, *f*
breakfast, ientācŭlum, *n*
breakfast, *v.i*, iento (1)
breakwater, mōles, *f*
breast, pectus, *n*, mamma, *f*
breast-plate, lōrīca, *f*
breath, spīrĭtus, *m*, ănĭma, *f*; (out of —), exănĭmātus; (to hold one's —), ănĭmam comprĭmo (3)
breathe, *v.i*, spīro (1); (— out), exspīro (1)
breathing, *nn*, aspīrātĭo, *f*
breathless, exănĭmātus
breed, *v.t*, gĕnĕro (1); *v.i*, nascor (3 *dep*.) (to be born)
breed, *nn*, gĕnus, *n*
breeding, *nn*, (giving birth) partus, *m*; (manners), hūmānĭtas, *f*
breeze, aura, *f*
breezy, ventōsus
brevity, brĕvĭtas, *f*
brew, *v.t*, cŏquo (3); *v.i* (overhang) impendĕo (2)
bribe, *nn*, praemĭum, *n*
bribe, *v.t*, corrumpo (3)
bribery, ambĭtus, *m*
brick, lăter, *m*; (made of —), *adj*, lătĕrĭcĭus
bricklayer, structor, *m*
bridal, nuptĭālis
bride (before marriage), sponsa, *f* (after marriage), nupta, *f*
bridegroom (before marriage), sponsus, *m*; (after marriage), nuptus, *m*, mărītus, *m*
bridge, pons, *m*
bridle, frēnum, *n*
brief, *adj*, brĕvis
briefly, *adv*, brĕvĭter
briar, dūmus, *m*
brigade, lĕgĭo, *f*
bright, clārus
brighten, *v.t*, illustro (1); *v.i*, clāresco (3)
brightly, *adv*, clāre
brilliance, splendor, *m*, nĭtor, *m*

brilliant, splendĭdus; **(famous),** prae-clārus

brim, margo, *m, f,* labrum, *n*

brimstone, sulfur, *n*

brine, salsāmentum, *n*

bring, *v.t,* fĕro, affĕro *(irreg),* addūco (3) apporto (1); **(— about),** confĭcĭo (3); **(— back, — before),** rĕfĕro *(irreg);* **(— down),** dēfĕro *(irreg);* **(— forward),** prōfĕro *(irreg);* **(— in),** infĕro *(irreg);* **(— out),** effĕro *(irreg);* **(— over),** perdūco (3); **(— together),** cōgo (3); **(— up) (children),** ēdūco (1)

brink (river, etc.), rīpa, *f;* **(of `cliff,** etc.)** use *adj,* summus **(highest)**

brisk, ălăcer

briskness, ălacrĭtas, *f*

bristle, saeta, *f*

bristle, *v.i,* horrĕo (2)

brittle, frăgĭlis

broach, *v.t,* ăpĕrĭo (4); prōfĕro *(irreg)*

broad, lātus

broadly (widely), *adv,* lātē

broil (quarrel), rixa, *f*

broil, *v.t,* torrĕo (2)

broken, fractus; **(disabled),** confectus

broker, interpres, *c* **(agent)**

bronze, aes, *n; (adj),* aēnĕus, aerĕus

brooch, fĭbŭla, *f*

brood, *v.i,* incŭbo (1)

brood (of young, etc.), fētus, *m*

brook, rīvus, *m*

brook (no interference etc), pătĭor (3 *dep)*

broom, scōpae, *f. pl*

broth, ius, *n*

brothel, gănĕa, *f*

brother, frāter, *m*

brotherhood sŏcĭĕtas, *f*

brow (forehead), frons, *f;* **(eye-brow),** sŭpercĭlĭum, *n;* **(of hill),** căcūmen, *n*

brown, fuscus

browse, *v.t* **(read),** perlĕgo (3)

bruise, *nn,* contūsum, *n*

bruise, *v.t,* contundo (3)

brunt (bear the — of), use sustĭnĕo (2) **(to bear)**

brush, *nn,* pēnĭcŭlus, *m*

brush, *v.t,* dētergĕo (2)

brushwood, sarmenta, *n.pl*

brutal, fĕrus, ătrox

brutality, immānĭtas, *f*

brutally, *adv,* immānĭter

brute, bestĭa, *f,* fĕra, *f*

bubble, bulla, *f*

bubble, *v.i,* bullo (1)

buccaneer, pīrăta, *m*

buck (male stag), cervus, *m*

bucket, sĭtŭla, *f*

buckle, fĭbŭla, *f*

buckle, *v.t,* fĭbŭlā necto (3) **(fasten with a buckle)**

buckler (shield), scūtum, *n*

bud, *nn,* gemma, *f*

bud, *v.i,* gemmo (1), germĭno (1)

budge, *v.i,* cēdo (3); *v.t,* mŏvĕo (2)

budget, rătĭo, *f* **(reckoning, account)**

buff, lŭtĕus

buffet (blow), cŏlăphus, *m*

buffoon, scurra, *m*

bug, cīmex, *m*

bugbear, terrĭcŭla, *n.pl*

bugle, būcĭna, *f*

build, *v.t,* aedĭfĭco (1)

builder, aedĭfĭcător, *m*

building (act of —), aedĭfĭcātĭo, *f,* **(structure itself),** aedĭfĭcĭum, *n*

bulb, bulbus, *m*

bulk, magnĭtūdo, *f,* mōles, *f*

bulky, ingens, grandis

bull, taurus, *m*

bullet, glans, *f*

bullion, aurum, *n*

bullock, iŭvencus, *m*

bulrush, iuncus, *m*

bulwark, mūnīmentum, *n*

bump, *nn,* tūber, *n,* tŭmor, *m*

bump, *v.i,* offendo (3)

bumpkin, rustĭcus, *m*

bunch, ūva, *f,* răcēmus, *m*

bundle, fascis, *m*

bung (stopper), obtūrāmentum, *n*

bungle, *v.i,* inscītē ăgo (3) **(do un-skilfully)**

bungler, *adj,* impĕrītus

buoyancy, lĕvĭtas, *f*

buoyant, lĕvis

burden, ŏnus, *n*

burden, *v.t,* ŏnĕro (1)

burdensome, grăvis

bureau, scrīnĭum, *n,* armărĭum, *n*

burgess, cīvis, *c*

burglar, fūr, *c*

burglary, furtum, *n*

burgle, *v.t,* fūror (1 *dep.*) **(steal)**

burial, fūnus, *n,* sĕpultūra, *f*

burial-place, lŏcus, *(m)* sĕpultūrae

burly, lăcertōsus

burn, *v.t,* ūro (3), incendo (3); *v.i,* ardĕo (2), flagro (1)

burn, *nn,* ambustum, *n*

burning, *adj,* ardens

burnish, *v.t,* pŏlĭo (4)

burrow, cŭnīcŭlum, *m*

burst, *v.t,* rumpo (3); *v.i,* rumpor (3 *pass)*

burst out, *v.i,* ērumpo (3)

bursting out, *nn,* ēruptĭo, *f*

bury, *v.t,* sĕpĕlĭo (4), abdo (3)

bush, dūmus
bushel, mědĭmnum, *n*
bushy, frŭtĭcōsus
busily, *adv*, sēdŭlō
business, něgōtĭum, *n*, res, *f*
bust (statue), ĭmāgo, *f*
bustle, *nn*, festīnātĭo, *f*
bustle, *v.i*, festīno (1)
busy, occŭpātus
but, *conj*, sed, vērum, at (*first word in clause*): autem, vēro (*second word in clause*); (except), praeter (*with acc*)
butcher, lănĭus, *m*
butcher, *v.t* (murder), trŭcīdo (1)
butchery, trŭcīdātĭo, *f*
butler, prōmus, *m*
butt (laughing stock), lūdĭbrĭum, *n*
butt, *v.t*, cornū fěrĭo (4) (strike with the horn)
butter, būtȳrum, *n*
butterfly, păpīlĭo, *m*
buttock, clūnis, *m, f*
buttress, antēris, *f*
buxom, věnustus
buy, *v.t*, ěmo (3)
buyer, emptor, *m*
buying, *nn*, emptĭo, *f*
by, *prep*, (of place, near), ad, prŏpe (*with acc*); (of time) *often expressed by abl. of noun, e.g.* by night, nocte; (— means of), per (*with acc*) (by an agent, *e.g.* by a man), ab (*with abl*), ab hŏmĭne; (by an instrument, *e.g.* by a spear, *abl. case alone*), hastā; (— chance), *adv*, fortě
by-gone, *adj*, praetěrĭtus
by-stander, spectātor, *m*
by-way, trāmes, *m*

C

cab, raeda, *f*, cĭsĭum, *n*
cabal (faction), factĭo, *f*
cabbage, brassĭca, *f*
cabin (hut), căsa, *f*
cabinet (furniture), armārĭum, *n*; (council), summum consĭlĭum, *n*
cable (anchor —), ancŏrāle, *n*
cackle, cackling, *nn*, strěpĭtus, *m*
cackle, *v.i*, strěpo (3)
cadaverous, cădāvěrōsus
cadence, cursus, *m*
cadet, discĭpŭlus, *m*, tīro, *m*
cage, căvěa, *f*
cajole, *v.t*, blandĭor (4 *dep. with dat*)
cajolery, blandĭtĭae, *f. pl*
cake, *nn*, plăcenta, *f*, lībum, *n*
calamitous, exĭtĭōsus
calamity, clādes, *f*, mălum, *n*

calculate, *v.t*, compŭto (1), aestĭmo (1)
calculation, rătĭo, *f*
calendar, fasti, *m. pl*
calf, vĭtŭlus, *m*; (of the leg), sūra, *f*
call, *v.t*, (name), vŏco (1), appello (1); dīco (3); (— back), rěvŏco (1); (— to, summon), advŏco (1); (— together), convŏco (1); (— up or out), suscĭto (1)
call, *nn* (cry), clāmor, *m*; (visit) sălūtātĭo, *f*
caller, sălūtātor, *m*
calling, *nn* (vocation), ars, *f*, artĭfĭcĭum, *n*
callous, callōsus
callow, implūmis
calm, *adj*, plăcĭdus, tranquillus
calm, *nn*, tranquillĭtas, *f*, mălăcĭa, *f*
calm, *v.t*, sēdo (1), plāco (1)
calmly, *adv*, tranquille, plăcĭde
calumniate, *v.t*, crīmĭnor (1 *dep.*)
calumnious, crīmĭnōsus
calumny, crīmĭnātĭo, *f*
camel, cămēlus, *m*
camp, castra, *n.pl*; (to pitch —), castra pōno (3); (to move —), castra mŏvěo (2); (a winter —), hīberna, *n.pl*
campaign, stipendĭum, *n*
campaign, *v.i*, stīpendĭum měrěor (2 *dep.*)
can, *nn*, urcěus, *m*
can, *v.i* (to be able), possum (*irreg*)
canal, fossa, *f*
cancel, *v.t*, dēlěo (2), abrŏgo (1)
cancer (sign of Zodiac), cancer, *m*
candid, ăpertus, līber
candidate, candĭdātus, *m*
candle, candēla, *f*
candlestick, candēlābrum, *n*
candour, lībertas, *f*
cane, hărundo, *f*, băcŭlum, *n*, virga, *f*
cane, *v.t*, verběro (1)
canister, arca, *f*, pyxis, *f*
canker, rōbīgo, *f*
canker, *v.t*, corrumpo (3)
cannibal, anthrōpŏphăgus, *m*
cannon, tormentum, *n*
canoe, scăpha, *f*
canon (rule), rēgŭla, *f*
canopy, vēla, *n.pl*
cant, ostentātĭo, *f*
canter, *v.i*, lēnĭter curro (3) (run smoothly)
canton, pāgus, *m*
canvas, vēla, *n.pl*, carbăsus, *f*
canvass, *v.i*, ambĭo (4)
canvass, *nn*, ambĭtĭo, *f*; (illegal), ambĭtus, *m*
cap, pillěus, *m*

For List of Abbreviations used, turn to pages 3, 4

capability, făcultas, *f*
capable, căpax
capacious, căpax
capacity, căpăcĭtas, *f*; (mental —), ingĕnĭum, *n*
cape, prōmontŭrĭum, *n*
caper, *v.i*, exsulto (1), salĭo (4)
capital, *nn*, (city), căput, *n*
capital, *adj* (crime, etc.), căpĭtālis; (chief), princeps
capitulate, *v.t*, dēdo (3); *v.i*, se dēdĕre (3 *reflex*)
caprice, lĭbīdo, *f*
capricious, lĕvis
captain, dux, *m*, princeps, *m*; (of a ship), măgister, *m*, nauarchus, *m*
captivate, *v.t*, căpĭo (3), dēlēnĭo (4)
captive, *adj. and nn*, captīvus, *m*.
captivity, captīvĭtas, *f*
capture, *nn*, (of city, camp, etc.), expugnātĭo, *f*; (of persons), *use vb*, căpĭo (3) (to capture)
capture, *v.t*, căpĭo (3)
car, currus, *m*, plaustrum, *n*
caravan (convoy), commĕātus, *m*, (vehicle), raeda, *f*
carbuncle, fūruncŭlus, *m*
carcass, cădāver, *n*, corpus, *n*
card, charta, *f*
cardinal, *adj*, prīmus, princeps
care, cūra, *f*, sollĭcĭtūdo, *f*
care, *v.t* (to — about or for), cūro (1)
career, currĭcŭlum, *n*
careful, dĭlĭgens; (carefully prepared) accūrātus; (cautious) cautus
carefully, *adv*, dīlĭgenter
careless, neglĕgens, indīlĭgens
carelessly, *adv*, neglegenter
carelessness, neglĕgentĭa, *f*
caress, blandīmenta, *n.pl*, complexus, *m*
caress, *v.t*, blandĭor (4 *dep*.) (*with dat*.)
caressing, *adj*, blandus
cargo, ŏnus, *n*
caricature, ĭmāgo, *f*
caricature, *v.t*, *use phr*. vultum dĕtorquĕo (2) (distort the features)
carnage, caedes, *f*, strāges, *f*
carnal, corpŏrĕus
carnival, fērĭae, *f.pl*
carnivorous, carnĭvŏrus
carol, cantus, *m*
carousal, cōmissātĭo, *f*
carouse, *v.i*, cōmissor (1 *dep*.)
carp at, *v.t*, carpo (3), mordĕo (2)
carpenter, făber, *m*
carpet, strāgŭlum, *n*

carriage (vehicle), raeda, *f*, carpentum, *n*; (transportation), vectūra, *f*; (poise), incessus, *m*
carrier, vector, *m*
carrion, căro, *f*, cădāver, *n*
carrot, pastīnăca, *f*
carry, *v.t*, porto (1), fĕro (*irreg*.), vĕho (3), gĕro (3); (— away or off), aufĕro (*irreg*.); (— back) rĕfĕro (*irreg*.); (— in) infĕro (*irreg*.); (— on) gĕro (3); (— over) transporto (1); (— out, perform) exsĕquor (3 *dep*.); (— through a law, etc.), perfĕro (*irreg*.)
cart, plaustrum, *n*
cart, *v.t*, vĕho (3)
cart-horse, iūmentum, *n*
cartilage, cartīlāgo, *f*
carve, *v.t*, caelo (1), sĕco (1), sculpo (3)
carver, sculptor, *m*
carving, *nn*, caelātūra, *f*
case (in law), causa, *f* (circumstances), cāsus, *m* (cover), thēca, *f*
casement, fĕnestra, *f*
cash, nummus, *m*, pĕcūnĭa nŭmĕrāta, *f*
cashier, *nn*, *use phr*. qui nummos dispensat (who dispenses the cash)
cashier, *v.t*, (from the army), exauctoro (1)
cask, cūpa, *f*
casket, arcŭla, *f*
cast, *nn*, (throw), iactus, *m*
cast, *v.t*, iăcĭo (3), mitto (3); (— down) dēĭcĭo (3); (— off) dēpōno (3); (— out) expello (3)
castaway, perdĭtus, *m*
caste, ordo, *m*
castigate, *v.t*, castīgo (1)
castle, castellum, *n*
castor-oil, cĭcīnum ŏlĕum, *n*
castrate, *v.t*, castro (1)
casual, fortŭĭtus
casually, *adv*, neglĕgenter
casualty (accident), cāsus, *m*; (killed) *adj*, interfectus
cat, fēles, *f*
catalogue, index *c*
catapault, cătăpulta, *f*,
cataract (waterfall), cătăracta, *f*
catarrh, grăvēdo, *f*
catastrophe, rŭīna, *f*
catch, căpĭo (3), comprĕhendo (3); (a disease), contrăho (3)
categorical (absolute), simplex, plānus
category, nŭmĕrus, *m*

cater, *v.t*, obsōno (1)

caterpillar, ērūca, *f*

catgut, chorda, *f*

cattle, pĕcus, *n*

cauldron, cortīna, *f*

cause, *nn*, causa, *f*

cause, *v.t*, făcĭo (3), efficĭo (3)

causeway, agger, *m*

caustic, *adj*, mordax (biting)

caution, cautĭo, *f*

caution, *v.t*, mŏnĕo (2)

cautious, cautus,

cavalry, ĕquĭtātus, *m*, ĕquĭtes, *m. pl*

cave, spēlunca, *f*, căverna, *f*, antrum, *n*

caw, *v.i*, crōcĭo (4)

cease, *v.i*, dēsĭno (3) (*with infin*)

ceaseless, perpĕtŭus

cedar, cedrus, *f*

ceiling, tectum, *n*

celebrate, *v.t*, căno (3), cĕlĕbro (1)

celebrated, clārus, illustris

celebration, cĕlĕbrātĭo, *f*

celebrity, fāma, *f*, glōrĭa, *f*; (person), vir praeclārus

celerity, cĕlĕrĭtas, *f*

celestial, caelestis

celibacy, caelĭbātus, *m*

cell, cellar, cella, *f*

cement, ferrūmen, *n*

cement, *v.t*, glūtĭno (1), ferrūmĭno (1)

cemetery, sĕpulcrētum, *n*

censor, censor, *m*

censure, vĭtŭpĕrātĭo, *f*

censure, *v.t*, vĭtŭpĕro (1) reprĕhendo (3)

census, census, *m*

per cent, *use nn*, centēsĭma, *f* (one hundredth part)

centaur, centaurus, *m*

central, mĕdĭus

centre (of) mĕdĭus, *in agreement with noun, e.g.* in the centre of the line, in mĕdĭā ăcĭe

centre on, *v.i* (depend on), pendĕo (2) (*with ab and abl*)

centurion, centŭrĭo, *m*

century, saecŭlum, *n*

ceremonial, rītus, *m*, caerĭmōnĭa, *f*

ceremonious, sollemnis

certain, certus, explōrātus; (a — person), *use pron*, quĭdam

certainly, *adv*, certo, certē, prŏfecto

certainty, res certa; *or use adj*, certus (certain)

certificate, scriptum testĭmōnĭum (written proof)

certify, *v.i*, rĕcognosco (3), confirmo (1)

cessation, intermissĭo, *f*

chafe, *v.t*, fŏvĕo (2), călĕfăcĭo (3); *v.i*, stŏmăchor (1 *dep.*) (be irritated)

chaff, pălĕa, *f*

chaffinch, fringilla,

chagrin, stŏmăchus, *m*

chain, cătēna, *f*, vincŭlum, *n*

chain, *v.t*, cătēnas inĭcĭo (3) (*with dat*)

chair, sella, *f*

chairman, măgister, *m*

chalk, crēta, *f*

chalk out (mark out), *v.t*, dēsigno (1)

challenge, *nn*, prŏvŏcātĭo, *f*

challenge, *v.t*, prŏvŏco (1)

chamber, conclāve, *n*; (bed —), cŭbĭcŭlum, *n*

chamberlain, cŭbĭcŭlārĭus, *m*

chamois, căprĕŏlus, *m*

champ, *v.t*, mando (3)

champion victor *m;* (defender), prōpugnātor, *m*

chance, *nn*, cāsus, *m*, fors, *f*, fortūna, *f*

by chance, *adv*, (happen), forte, cāsu

chance, *v.i*, accĭdo (3)

chandelier, candēlābrum, *n*

change, changing, *nn*, mūtātĭo, *f*, permūtātĭo, *f*

change, *v.t*, mūto (1), converto (3); *v.i*, mūtor (1 *pass*)

changeable, mūtābĭlis

channel, cănālis, *m*, alvĕus, *m*

chant, *v.i and v.t*, canto (1)

chaos, perturbātĭo, *f*

chaotic, perturbātus

chapel, săcellum, *n*

chapter, căpŭt, *n*

char, *v.t*, ambūro (3)

character, mōres, *m. pl*, ingĕnĭum, *n*; (reputation), existĭmātĭo, *f*, ŏpĭnĭo, *f*; (in a play), persōna, *f*

characteristic, *adj*, prŏprĭus

charcoal, carbo, *m*

charge, *nn*, (attack), impĕtus, *m*; (accusation), crīmen, *n*; (price), prĕtĭum, *n*; (care of), cūra, *f*

charge, *v.t*, (attack), impĕtum făcĭo (3); signa infĕro (*irreg*); (accuse), accūso (1); (of price), vendo (3) (sell) (3); (put in—) praefĭcĭo (3) (*with dat*); (be in—) praesum (*irreg.*) (*with dat*)

chariot, currus, *m*, essēdum, *n*

charioteer, aurīga, *c*

charitable, bĕnignus, mītis

charity, ămor *m*, bĕnĕfĭcentĭa, *f*

charm, blandīmentum, *n*, grātĭa, *f* (trinket), bulla, *f*

charm, *v.t*, fascĭno (1), dēlēnĭo (4), dēlecto (1)

charming, vĕnustus, lĕpĭdus

chart, tăbŭla, f

charter, v.t, (hire), condūco (3)

chase, nn, (hunt), vēnātĭo, f, vēnātus, m

chase, v.t, sector (1 dep.), vēnor (1 dep.)

chasm, hĭātus, m

chaste, castus

chastise, v.t, castīgo (1), pūnĭo (4)

chastisement, castīgātĭo, f

chastity, castĭtas, f

chat, v.i, fābŭlor (1 dep.)

chat, nn, sermo, m

chatter, v.i, garrĭo (4); (of teeth), crēpĭto (1)

chatter, nn, garrŭlĭtas, f

chattering, adj, garrŭlus

cheap, vīlis

cheapness, vīlĭtas, f

cheat, nn, (person), fraudātor, m

cheat, v.t, fraudo (1)

cheating, nn, fraudātĭo, f

check, nn, (hindrance), impedīmentum, n, incommŏdum, n; (set back), incommŏdum, n

check, v.t, cŏhĭbĕo (2), contĭnĕo (2), comprĭmo (3), cŏercĕo(2)

cheek, gĕna, f

cheer, nn, (shout), clāmor, m

cheer, v.i, (applaud), plaudo (3), clāmo (1)

cheerful, hĭlăris

cheerfulness, hĭlărĭtas, f

cheerless, tristis

cheese, cāsĕus, m

cheque, perscrīptĭo, f, (written entry)

chequered, vărĭus

cherish, v.t, fŏvĕo (2), cŏlo (3)

cherry, cherry-tree, cĕrăsus, f

chess, latruncŭli, m. pl

chest (box), amārĭum, n, cista, f; (body), pectus, n, thorax, m

chestnut, glans, f; (— tree), castănĕa, f

chew, mando (3)

chicken, pullus, m

chide, v.t, obiurgo (1), incrĕpĭto (1), rĕprĕhendo (3)

chiding, rĕprĕhensĭo, f

chief, nn, princeps, m, prŏcer, m

chief, adj, prīmus, princeps

chieftain, see chief

child, pŭer, m, infans, c; (pl.) lībĕri, m. pl

childbirth, partus, m

childhood, pŭĕrĭtĭa, f

childish, pŭĕrīlis

childless, orbus

chill, chilly, adj, frīgĭdus

chill, v.t, rĕfrīgĕro (1)

chime, nn, concentus, m

chime, v.i, (sound), căno (3)

chimney, camīnus, m

chin, mentum, n

chine, tergum, n

chink, rīma, f

chip, assŭla, f

chirp, chirping, nn, pīpātus, m

chirp, v.i, pīpĭo (4)

chisel, scalprum, n

chisel, v.t, sculpo (3)

chivalrous, magnănĭmus

chivalry, magnănĭmĭtas, f

choice, nn, dēlectus, m; (— between), optĭo, f

choice, adj, ēlectus

choir, chŏrus, m

choke, v.t, suffōco (1); v.i, suffōcor (1 pass)

choose, v.t, lĕgo (3), ēlĭgo (3)

chop, v.t, caedo (3); (cut off), abscīdo (3)

chord, use nervus, m, (string)

chorus, chŏrus, m

Christ, Christus, m

Christian, Christĭānus

chronic (long-lasting), dĭuturnus

chronicle, annāles, m. pl

chuckle, v.i, căchinno (1)

church, templum, n

church-yard, ārĕa, f

churl, hŏmo rustĭcus

churlish, rustĭcus

churn, v.t, (stir), ăgĭto (1)

cinder, cĭnis, m, făvilla, f

cipher (a nonentity), nŭmĕrus, m; (secret writing), nŏta, f

circle, orbis, m

circuit, circŭĭtus, m

circuitous (route, etc.), flexŭōsus

circular, rŏtundus

circulate, v.t, spargo (3), dīvulgo (1); v.i, diffundor (3 pass), percrĕbresco (3)

circulation, (to be in —) (of books etc.) in mănĭbus esse (irreg)

circumcise, v.t, circumcīdo (3)

circumference, ambĭtus, m

circumscribe, v.t, circumscrībo (3)

circumstance, res, f; or use neuter of an adj, e.g. adversa (adverse circumstances)

circumstantial evidence, conĭectūra, f

circumvent, v.t, circumvĕnĭo (4)

circus, circus, m

cistern, cisterna, f

citadel, arx, f

cite, v.t, (quote), prōfĕro (irreg)

citizen, cīvis, c

citizenship, cīvĭtas, f

city, urbs, *f*

civic, cīvīlis

civil (polite), urbānus; (civic) cīvīlis; (— war), bellum dŏmestĭcum

civilian (opp. military), tŏgātus, *m*

civilization, cultus, *m*, hūmānĭtas, *f*

civilize, *v.t*, excŏlo (3), expŏlĭo (4)

civilized, hūmānus, cultus

claim, *v.t*, postŭlo (1), rĕposco (3)

claim, *nn*, postŭlātĭo, *f*

claimant, pĕtītor, *m*

clammy, lentus

clamorous, clāmans

clamour, *nn*, clāmor, *m*, strĕpĭtus, *m*

clamour, *v.i*, vōcĭfĕror (1 *dep*)

clandestine, clandestīnus

clang, *nn*, clangor, *m*

clang, *v.i. and v.t*, strĕpo (3)

clank, crĕpĭtus, *m*

clank, *v.i*, crĕpo (1)

clap, *nn*, (hands), plausus, *m*; (thunder), frăgor, *m*

clap, *v.i. and v.t*, plaudo (3)

clash, *v.i.*, concrĕpo (1), crĕpĭto (1); (opinions) rĕpugno (1); (fight), confligo (3)

clash, *nn*, (noise), crĕpĭtus, *m*; (collision), concursus, *m*

clasp, *nn*, (embrace), complexus, *m*; (fastener), fībŭla, *f*

clasp, *v.t*, (fasten), fībŭlo (1); (embrace), complector (3 *dep*.)

class, classis, *f*, gĕnus, *n*

classic, classical (well-established), prŏbus

classify, *v.t*, dēscrībo (3) ordĭne

clatter, *nn*, strĕpĭtus, *m*

clatter, *v.i*, incrĕpo (1)

clause, membrum, *n*, căpŭt, *n*

claw, unguis, *m*

clay, argilla, *f*, lŭtum, *n*

clean, *adj*, mundus, pūrus

clean, *v.t*, purgo (1), mundo (1)

cleanliness, mundĭtĭa, *f*

cleanse, *v.t*, purgo (1)

clear, clārus, *f*; (weather), sĕrēnus; (matter), mănĭfestus

clear, *v.t*, (open up), expĕdĭo (4); (— oneself), sē purgāre (1 *reflex*); *v.i*, (of the weather), dissĕrēnat (1 *impers*)

clearing, *nn*, (open space), lŏcus ăpertus

clearly, *adv*, clārē, ăpertē, plānē

clearness, clārĭtas, *f*

cleave, *v.t*, (split), findo (3); *v.i* (stick to), adhaerĕo (2)

cleft, hiātus, *m*, rima, *f*

clemency, clēmentĭa, *f*

clement, clēmens, lēnis

clench (the fist), *v.t*, comprĭmo (3)

clerk, scrība, *m*

clever, callĭdus, astūtus

cleverness, *f*, callĭdĭtas, *f*

client, clĭens, *m*, consultor, *m*

cliff, cautes, *f*, scŏpŭlus, *m*, rūpes,

climate, caelum, *n*

climax, grădātĭo, *f*

climb, *v.i. and v.t*, ascendo (3), scando (3)

climb, *nn*, ascensus, *m*

cling to, *v.i*, ădhaerĕo (2) (*with dat*)

clip, *v.t*, tondĕo (2)

cloak, pallĭum, *n*, lăcerna, *f*

cloak, *v.t*, (hide), dissĭmŭlo (1)

clock, hŏrŏlŏgĭum, *n*

clod, glaeba, *f*

clog (hindrance), impĕdīmentum, *n*; (shoe), sculpōnĕa, *f*

clog, *v.t*, (impede), impĕdĭo (4)

close, *adj*, (near), vīcīnus; (packed together) confertus, densus; (at close quarters), commĭnus, *adv*

close, *nn*, (end), fīnis, *m*, termĭnus, *m*

close, *adv*, prŏpe, iuxta

close, *v.t*, claudo (3); *v.i*, claudor (3 *pass*)

close in on, *v.t*, prĕmo (3) (press)

closely, *adv*, prŏpe; (accurately), exacte

closeness, prŏpinquĭtas, *f*,

closet, cella, *f*

clot (of blood), crŭor, *m*

cloth, textum, *n*

clothe, *v.t*, vestĭo (4), indŭo (3)

clothes, vestis, *f*, vestīmenta, *n.pl*

cloud, nūbes, *f*

cloudy, nūbĭlus

cloven, bĭsulcus

clown, scurra, *m*

club (cudgel), clāva, *f*; (association), sŏdālĭtas, *f*

cluck, *v.i*, singultĭo (4)

clump, massa, *f*

clumsy, ĭnhăbĭlis, rustĭcus

cluster, *nn*, răcēmus, *m*; (people), glŏbus, *m*

clutch, *v.t*, arrĭpĭo (3)

coach, carpentum, *n*, raeda, *f*

coachman, raedārĭus, *m*

coagulate, *v.i*, concresco (3)

coal, carbo, *m*

coalition, coniunctĭo, *f*, conspīrātĭo, *f*

coarse, crassus; (manners), incultus

coarseness, crassĭtūdo, *f*, ĭnhūmānĭtas, *f*

coast, ōra, *f*, lītus, *n*

coast, *v.i*, praetervĕhor (3 *pass*)

coat, tŭnĭca, *f*, ămictus, *m*; (animal's), pellis, *f*

For List of Abbreviations used, turn to pages 3, 4

coat, *v.t*, illĭno (3)
coax, *v.t*, mulcĕo (2), blandĭor (4 *dep*)
cobble, *v.t*, sarcĭo (4)
cobbler, sūtor, *m*
cock, gallus, *m*
code, (method, system), rătĭo, *f*
coerce, *v.t*, cōgo (3), cŏercĕo (2)
coercion, cŏercĭtĭo, *f*
coffin, arca, *f*
cog, dens, *m*
cogent, vălĭdus
cogitate, *v.i*, cōgĭto (1)
cognizance, cognĭtĭo, *f*
cohabit, *v.i*, consŭesco (3)
cohere, *v.i*, cŏhaerĕo (2)
coherent, cŏhaerens
cohesion, cŏhaerentĭa, *f*
cohort, cŏhors, *f*
coil, *nn*, spīra, *f*
coil, *v.t*, glŏmĕro (1)
coin, *nn*, nummus, *m*
coin, *v.t*, cūdo (3)
coinage, nummi, *m. pl*
coincide, *v.i*, compĕto (3), concurro (3)
coincidence, concursătĭo, *f*, concursus, *m*
cold, *adj*, frīgĭdus, gĕlĭdus
cold (to be —), *v.i*, algĕo (2)
coldness, frīgus, *n*
collapse, *v.i*, collābor (3 *dep*.)
collar, torques, *m and f*
collation (comparison), collātĭo, *f*
colleague, collĕga, *m*
collect, *v.t*, collĭgo (3), cōgo (3)
collection (act of —), collātĭo, *f*; (heap, etc.), congĕrĭes, *f*
collector (of taxes, etc.), exactor, *m*
college, collēgĭum, *n*
collide, *v.i*, conflīgo (3), concurro (3)
collision, concursus, *m*
colloquial (speech), *use* sermo, *m*
collusion, collūsĭo, *f*
colon, cōlon, *n*
colonel, praefectus, *m*
colonist, cŏlōnus, *m*
colony, cŏlōnĭa, *f*
colonnade, portĭcus, *f*
colossal, ingens
colour, cŏlor, *m*; (flag), vexillum, *n*; (— bearer), signĭfer, *m*
colour, *v.t*, cŏlōro (1)
coloured, pictus
colourful, fūcātus
colt, equŭlĕus, *m*
column (pillar), columna, *f*; (military), agmen, *n*

comb, *nn*, pecten, *m*
comb, *v.t*, pecto (3)
combat, *nn*, proelĭum, *n*
combat, *v.i*, pugno (1), luctor (1 *dep*)
combat, *v.t*, (oppose), obsto (1)
combatant, pugnātor, *m*
combination, coniunctĭo, *f*
combine, *v.t*, coniungo (3)
come, *v.i*, vĕnĭo (4); (— about, happen), ēvĕnĭo (4); (— across, find), *v.t*, invĕnĭo (4); (— back), *v.i*, rĕvĕnĭo (4); (— by, obtain), *v.t*, ădĭpiscor (3 *dep*); (— down), *v.i*, dēscendo (3); (— in) incēdo (3); (— near) apprŏpinquo (1); (— on, advance), prōgrĕdĭor (3 *dep*); (— out) exĕo (4); (— to) advĕnĭo (4) (regain consciousness) ad se rĕdire (4); (— together) convĕnĭo (4); (— upon), *v.t*, sŭpervĕnĭo (4) (attack) incĭdo (3)
comedian, cōmoedus, *m*
comedy, cōmoedĭa, *f*
comely, pulcher
comet, cŏmētes, *m*
comfort, sōlācĭum, *n*, consōlātĭo, *f*
comfort, *v.t*, consōlor (1 *dep*.)
comfortable, commŏdus
comforter, consōlātor, *m*
comic, comical, cōmĭcus
coming, *adj*, ventūrus
coming, *nn*, adventus, *m*
command, *nn*, (power), impĕrĭum, *n*; (an order), iussum, *n*, mandātus, *m*; (to be in —) *v.i*, praesum (*with dat*)
command, *v.t*. impĕro (1) (*with dat*.), iŭbĕo (2)
commander, dux, *m*, impĕrātor, *m*
commemorate, *v.t*, cĕlĕbro (1)
commemoration, cĕlĕbrātĭo, *f*
commence, *v.i*, incĭpĭo (3)
commencement, ĭnĭtĭum, *n*
commend, *v.t*, commendo (1); (praise), laudo (1)
commendable, laudābĭlis
comment, *v.i*, dĭco (3), sententĭas dĭco (3) (declare one's opinion)
comment, *nn*, dicta, *n.pl*
commentary, commentārĭi, *m. pl*
commerce, commercĭum, *n*
commercial traveller, instĭtor, *m*
commiserate, *v.i. and v.t*, mĭsĕror (1 *dep*.)
commisariat, praefecti (*m. pl*.) rĕi frūmentārĭae (superintendents of corn supply), (provisions), commĕātus, *m*

commissary, prōcūrātor, *m*, lēgātus, *m*

commission (task), mandātum, *n*

commission, *v.t*, (give a task to), mando (1) (*dat. of person*)

commit, *v.t*, (crime, etc.), admitto (3); (entrust), committo (3), mando (1)

committee, dēlecti, *m. pl*, (selected ones)

commodious (opportune), commŏdus; (capacious), amplus

commodity (thing), res, *f*

common, *adj*, commūnis; (belonging to the public), pūblĭcus; (ordinary), vulgāris; (common land), āger pūblĭcus, *m*, (usual), ūsĭtātus

commonplace, *adj*, vulgāris, trītus

commonly, *adv*, (mostly), plērumque

commonwealth, respublĭca, *f*

commotion, mōtus, *m*, tŭmultus, *m*, commōtĭo, *f*

communicate, *v.t*, commūnĭco (1); (report), dēfĕro (*irreg*)

communication, commūnĭcātĭo, *f*; (reporting), nuntĭus, *m*

communicative, lĭber, lŏquax

communion, sŏcĭĕtas, *f*

community, cīvĭtas, *f*, sŏcĭĕtas, *f*

commute, *v.t*, mūto (1)

compact, *adj*, confertus, pressus

compact, *nn*, pactum, *n*, foedus, *n*

companion, sŏcĭus, *m*, cŏmes, *c*

companionable, făcĭlis

companionship, sŏdālĭtas, *f*

company, coetus, *m*, sŏcĭĕtas, *f*; (military body), mănĭpŭlus, *m*

comparable, confĕrendus

comparative, compărātīvus

compare, *v.t*, compăro (1), confĕro (*irreg*)

comparison, compărātĭo, *f*

compartment, lŏcŭlus, *m*

compass (range), fīnes, *m. pl*; (pair of compasses), circĭnus, *m*

compass, *v.t*, complector (3 *dep*)

compassion, mĭsĕrĭcordĭa, *f*

compassionate, mĭsĕrĭcors

compatability, congrŭentĭa, *f*

compatible, congrŭens

compatriot, cīvis, *c*

compel, *v.t*, cōgo (3), compello (3)

compensate for, *v.t*, compenso (1)

compensation, compensātĭo, *f*

compete, *v.i*, certo (1) (struggle)

competent, căpax; (to be — to), *v.i*, suffĭcĭo (3)

competition, certāmen, *n*

competitor, compĕtītor, *m*

complacent, sĭbi plăcens (pleasing to oneself)

complain, *v.i*, gĕmo (3); *v.t*, quĕror (3 *dep*.)

complaint, questŭs, *m*, quĕrēla, *f*; (disease), morbus, *m*

complement, complēmentum, *n*

complete, plēnus, perfectus

complete, *v.t*, complĕo (2), confĭcĭo (3)

completely, *adv*, omnīno

completion, perfectĭo, *f*, confectĭo, *f*

complex, multĭplex

complexion, cŏlor, *m*

compliance, obsĕquĭum, *n*

compliant, obsĕquens

complicated, invŏlūtus

complication, implĭcātĭo, *f*

compliment, *nn*, (esteem), hŏnor, *m*; (praise) laus, *f*; (greeting), sălūtātĭo, *f*

compliment, *v.t*, (praise), laudo (1)

complimentary, hŏnōrĭfĭcus

comply with, *v.i*, concēdo (3) (*with dat*)

component, *nn*, (part), ĕlĕmentum, *n*

compose, *v.t*, compōno (3)

composed (calm), sēdātus

composer, scriptor, *m*

composition (act of —), compŏsĭtĭo, *f*; (a literary —), ŏpus scriptum, *n*

composure, tranquillĭtas, *f*

compound, *adj*, compŏsĭtus

compound, *v.t*, compōno (3), miscĕo (2)

comprehend, *v.t*, (understand), intellĕgo (3)

comprehension, comprĕhensĭo, *f*

comprehensive, *use phr*, ad omnĭa pertĭnens (extending to everything)

compress, *v.t*, comprĭmo (3)

comprise, *v.t*, contĭnĕo (2)

compromise, *nn*, (agreement), compŏsĭtĭo, *f*

compromise, *v.t*, compōno (3); (implicate), implĭco (1)

compulsion, nĕcessĭtas, *f*

compunction, paenĭtentĭa, *f*

compute, *v.t*, compŭto (1)

comrade, sŏcĭus, *m*, cŏmes, *c*

concave, căvus

conceal, *v.t*, cēlo (1), abdo (3)

concede, *v.t*, cēdo (3)

conceit, arrŏgantĭa, *f*

conceited, arrŏgans

conceive, *v.t*, concĭpĭo (3)

concentrate (mentally), *v.i*, ănĭmum intendo (3); (bring together), *v.t*, contrăho (3), cōgo (3)

conception (mental), nōtĭo, *f*; (physical), conceptĭo, *f*

concern, *nn*, (affair, circumstance), rēs, *f*; (worry), sollīcītūdo, *f*

concern, *v.t*, pertīněo (2); (it concerns), rěfert (*irreg. impers*)

concerned (to be —), *v.i*, sollīcītus esse

concerning, *prep*, dē (*with abl. of nn. etc*)

concert, *v.t*, (plans, etc.), confěro (*irreg*), compōno (3)

concession, concessĭo, *f*

conciliate, *v.t*, concĭlĭo (1)

conciliation, concĭlĭātĭo, *f*

conciliatory, pācĭfĭcus

concise, brěvis

conciseness, brěvĭtas, *f*

conclude, *v.t*, (decide), stătŭo (3); (end), perfĭcĭo (3)

conclusion (end), exĭtus, *m*, fīnis, *m*; (decision), dēcrētum, *n*

conclusive, certus

concord, concordĭa, *f*

concourse, concursus, *m*

concubine, pellex, *f*

concupiscence, lĭbĭdo, *f*

concur, *v.i*, consentĭo (4)

concurrence, consensus, *m*

concurrent, *use adv*, sĭmŭl (at the same time)

concurrently, *adv*, sĭmŭl

condemn, *v.t*, damno (1) (*with acc. of person and genit. of crime or punishment*)

condemnation, damnātĭo, *f*

condense, *v.t*, denso (1), comprĭmo (3)

condensed, densus

condescend, *v.i*, dēscendo (3)

condescension, cōmĭtas, *f*, (friendliness)

condition, condĭcĭo, *f*, stătus, *m*

condole, *v.i*, dŏlěo (2) cum (*with abl*)

condone, *v.t*, condōno (1)

conduce, *v.t*, condūco (3)

conducive, ūtĭlis (advantageous)

conduct, *nn*, (personal, etc.), mōres, *m. pl*; (administration), admĭnis-trātĭo, *f*

conduct, *v.t* (lead), dūco (3); (administer), admĭnistro (1); (— oneself), sē gěrěre (3 *reflex*)

conductor, dux, *m*

conduit, cănālis, *m*

cone, cōnus, *m*

confectionery, crustum, *n*

confederacy, sŏcĭětas, *f*

confederate, foeděrātus

confer, *v.t*, confěro (*irreg*); (— with), collŏquor (3 *dep*); (— about), ăgo (3) dē

conference, collŏquĭum, *n*

confess, *v.t*, confĭtěor (2 *dep*)

confession, confessĭo, *f*

confide, *v.t*, confīdo (3), fīdo (3) (*with dat*)

confidence, fĭdes, *f*, fīdūcĭa, *f*

confident, fīdens

confidential (trusty), fīdus; (one's own, special), prŏprĭus; (secret), arcānus

confine, *v.t*, inclūdo (3), contĭněo (2)

confinement, inclūsĭo, *f*, custōdĭa, *f*; (childbirth), partus, *m*; pŭerpěrĭum, *n*

confirm, *v.t*, confirmo (1)

confiscate, *v.t*, pūblĭco (1), ădĭmo (3)

confiscation, pūblĭcātĭo, *f*

conflagration, incendĭum, *n*

conflict, *nn*, certāmen, *n*

conflict, *v.i*, certo (1); dissentĭo (4)

confluence, conflŭens, *m*

conform to, *v.i*, obtempěro (1) (*with dat*); *v.t*, accommŏdo (1)

conformity, convěnĭentĭa, *f*

confound, *v.t*, (disturb), turbo (1); (amaze), obstŭpěfăcĭo (3); (bring to nothing, thwart), frustor (1 *dep.*)

confront, *v.i*, obvĭam ěo (*irreg.*) (*with dat*)

confuse, *v.t*, turbo (1)

confused, perturbātus

confusion, perturbātĭo, *f*

congeal, *v.i, and v.t*, congělo (1)

congenial, concors

congested, frěquens

congratulate, *v.t*, grātŭlor (1 *dep*)

congratulation, grātŭlātĭo, *f*

congregate, *v.i*, sē congrěgare (1 *reflex.*)

congress, concĭlĭum, *n*, conventus, *m*

congruous, congrŭens

conjecture, *nn*, conĭectūra, *f*

conjecture, *v.i*, cōnĭcĭo (3)

conjugate, *v.t*, dēclīno (1)

conjunction (grammar), conĭunctĭo, *f*

conjure, *v.i* (perform tricks), prae-stĭgĭis ūtor (3 *dep.*); (image) cōgĭto (1)

conjurer, măgus, *m*

connect, *v.t*, conĭungo (3)

connected, conĭunctus

connection, conĭunctĭo, *f*; (by marriage), affīnĭtas, *f*

connive at, *v.i*, connīvěo (2) in (*with abl*)

connoisseur, *use vb*, stŭděo (2) (to be keen on)

conquer, *v.t*, vinco (3), sŭpěro (1)

conqueror, victor, *m*

conquest, victōrĭa, *f*

conscience, conscĭentĭa, f
conscientious, rēlĭgĭōsus
conscientiousness, fĭdes, f
conscious, conscĭus
consciously, *adv, use adj,* scĭens (knowing)
consciousness, conscĭentĭa, f, sensus, m
conscript (recruit), tīro, m
consecrate, v.t, conscĕro (1)
consecrated, săcer
consecutive, contĭnŭus
consent, nn, consensus, m; (by the — of), consensu
consent to, v.i, assentĭo (4)
consequence (result), exĭtus, m; (importance), mōmentum, n; (in — of), prep, propter (with acc)
consequent, sĕquens
consequently, adv, ĭgĭtur, ĭtăque
conserve, v.t, conservo (1)
consider, v.t, cōgĭto (1), dēlībĕro (1), existĭmo (1);(— with respect), respĭcĭo (3)
considerable, ălĭquantus
considerate, hūmānus
considerateness, hūmānĭtas, f
consideration, consĭdĕrātĭo, f; (regard), rătĭo, f
considering, conj, ut
consign, v.t, mando (1), committo (3)
consignment (of goods), merces, f.pl
consist of, v.i, consisto (3) in (with abl)
consistency, constantĭa, f
consistent (constant), constans; (consistent with), consentānĕus
console, v.t, consōlor (1 dep.)
consolidate, v.t, firmo (1), sōlĭdo (1)
consonant, consŏnans littĕra
consort (husband), mărītus, m; (wife), mărīta, f
consort with, v.i, ūtor (3 dep) (with abl)
conspicuous, mănĭfestus, insignis
conspiracy, conĭūrātĭo, f
conspirator, conĭūrātus, m
conspire, v.i, conĭūro (1)
constable, dĕcŭrĭo, m, lictor, m
constancy, fĭdes, f; (steadiness), constantĭa, f, fĭdēlĭtas, f
constant, fĭdēlis, constans
constellation, sīdus, n
consternation, păvor, m
constituent parts, ĕlĕmenta, n.pl
constitute, v.t, constĭtŭo (3), compōno (3), crĕo (1)
constitution (of a state), respūblĭca, f; (of a body), hăbĭtus, m
constitutional, lēgĭtĭmus

constrain, v.t, cōgo 3), compello (3)
construct, v.t, făbrĭcor (1 dep.), exstrŭo (3)
construction (act of —), făbrĭcātĭo, f; (method), fĭgūra, f, structūra, f
construe, v.t, interprĕtor (1 dep)
consul, consul, m
consulship, consŭlātus, m
consult, v.t, consŭlo (3); v.i, dēlībĕro (1); (— someone's interests), consŭlo (3) (with dat)
consultation, collŏquĭum, n
consume, v.t, consumo (3), confĭcĭo (3)
consummate, v.t, consummo (1), perfĭcĭo (3)
consummate, adj, summus
consummation, consummātĭo, f
consumption, consumptĭo, f
contact, tactus, m
contagion, contāgĭo, f
contain, v.t, contĭnĕo (2)
contaminate, v.t, contāmĭno (1)
contamination, contāgĭo, f, măcŭla, f
contemplate, v.t, contemplor (1 dep.)
contemplation (study), mĕdĭtātĭo, f
contempory, aequālis
contempt, contemptus, m
contemptible, contemnendus
contend, v.i, contendo (3), certo (1), pugno (1); (argue), v.t, affirmo (1)
content, contentus
content, v.t, sătĭsfăcĭo (3) (with dat.); v.i, (be content), sătis hăbĕo (2)
contentment, aequus ănĭmus, m
contest, nn, certāmen, n, pugna, f
contest, v.t, certo (1), contendo (3)
contestant, pugnātor, m, pĕtītor, m
contiguous, contĭgŭus, confĭnis
continent, adj, contĭnens
continent, nn, contĭnens, f
contingency, cāsus, m
continual, perpĕtuus, contĭnens
continually, adv, perpĕtuo, contĭnenter
continuation, perpĕtŭĭtas, f
continue, v.t, prōdūco (3), prōrŏgo (1); v.i, mănĕo (2)
continuity, perpĕtŭĭtas, f
continuous, contĭnens
contort, v.t, torquĕo (2)
contour, fĭgūra, f
contraband, adj, vĕtĭtus
contract, nn, pactum, n
contract, v.i, (grow smaller), sē contrăhĕre (3 reflex); v.t, contrăho (3)
contraction, contractĭo, f
contractor, conductor, m
contradict, v.t, contrādīco (3) (with dat)

For List of Abbreviations used, turn to pages 3, 4

contradiction, contrādictĭo, *f*; (**inconsistency**), rĕpugnantĭa, *f*
contradictory, rĕpugnans
contrary, *adj*, adversus, contrārĭus; (— **to**), *prep*, contrā (*with acc*); **the contrary,** *nn*, contrārĭum, *n*; (**on the** —), *adv*, contrā
contrast, *v.t*, confĕro (*irreg*); *v.i*, discrĕpo (1)
contravene, *v.t*, vĭŏlo (1)
contribute, *v.t*, confĕro (*irreg*)
contribution, collātĭo, *f*, trĭbūtum, *n*
contrivance (**gadget**), māchĭna, *f*
contrive, *v.t*, (**think out**), excōgĭto (1)
control, *v.t*, mŏdĕror (1 *dep*) (*with dat*); (**guide**), rĕgo (3)
control, *nn*, pŏtestas, *f*, tempĕrantĭa, *f*
controversy, contrōversĭa, *f*
contumacious, pertĭnax
contumacy, pertĭnācĭa, *f*
contumely, contŭmēlĭa, *f*
convalescent, convălescens
convenience, commŏdĭtas, *f*, opportūnĭtas, *f*
convenient, commŏdus, opportūnus
convention (**meeting**), conventus, *m*; (**agreement**), conventĭo, *f*
converge, *v.i*, ĕōdem vergo (3)
conversation, sermo, *m*, collŏquĭum, *n*
converse, *v.i*, collŏquor (3 *dep*)
conversion, commūtātĭo, *f*
convert, *v.t*, mūto (1), converto (3)
convex, convexus
convey, *v.t*, vĕho (3), porto (1)
conveyance (**act of** —), vectūra, *f*; (**vehicle**), vĕhĭcŭlum, *n*
convict, *v.t*, damno (1)
conviction (**belief**), *use phr*, persuāsum est (*with dat. of person*), e.g. persuāsum est mĭhi (**it is my conviction**); (**convicting**), damnātĭo, *f*
convince, *v.t*, persuādĕo (2) (*with dat.*)
conviviality, hĭlārĭtas, *f*
convoke, *v.t*, convŏco (1)
convoy, *nn*, commĕātus, *m*; (**escort**), praesĭdĭum, *n*
convulse, *v.t*, concŭtĭo (3), ăgĭto (1)
convulsion, tŭmultus, *m*, mōtus, *m*; (**medical**), convulsĭo, *f*
cook, *nn*, cŏquus, *m*
cook, *v.t*, cŏquo (3)
cool, frĭgĭdus; (**of mind**), lentus
cool, *v.t*, rĕfrĭgĕro (1); *v.i*, rĕfrĭgĕror (1 *pass*)
coolly, *adv*, frĭgĭde, lentē
coolness, frĭgus, *n*

co-operate with, *v.t*, adiŭvo (1)
co-operation, auxĭlĭum, *n*, (**help**)
cope with, *v.i*, congrĕdĭor (3 *dep*.)
copious, largus, cōpĭōsus
copper, aes, *n*
copper, *adj*, aēnĕus
coppice, dūmētum, *n*
copy, exemplum, *n*
copy, *v.t*, ĭmĭtor (1 *dep*), dēscrībo (3)
coral, cŏrālĭum, *n*
cord, fūnis, *m*
cordial, *adj*, bĕnignus
cordiality, bĕnignĭtas, *f*
cordon, cŏrōna, *f*
core, nuclĕus, *m*
cork, *nn*, cortex, *m*, *f*
corn, frūmentum, *n*; (-**crop**), sĕges, *f*; (**on the foot**), clāvus, *m*
corner, angŭlus, *m*
cornice, cŏrōna, *f*
coronation, *use* crĕo (1) (**elect to office**)
coroner, quaesĭtor, *m*
corporal, *adj*, corpŏrĕus
corporal, *nn*, dĕcŭrĭo, *m*
corps (**company**), mănus, *f*
corpse, cădāver, *n*, corpus, *n*
corpulence, ŏbēsĭtas, *f*
corpulent, ŏbēsus
correct, rectus, pūrus
correct, *v.t*, corrĭgo (3), ēmendo (1)
correction, ēmendātĭo, *f*; (**chastisement**), castīgātĭo, *f*
correctly, *adv*, rectē
correctness, vērĭtas, *f*
correspond, *v.i*, (**agree with**), convĕnĭo (4) (*with dat*); (**write**), littĕras mitto (3) et accĭpĭo (3) (**send and receive letters**)
correspondence, missĭo et acceptĭo ĕpistŏlārum (**sending and receiving of letters**)
corresponding, par, gĕmellus
corroborate, *v.t*, confirmo (1)
corrode, *v.t*, rōdo (3), ĕdo (3)
corrosive, mordax
corrupt, *v.t*, corrumpo (3)
corrupt, *adj*, corruptus
corruption, dēprāvātĭo, *f*
corselet, lōrīca, *f*
cost, *nn*, prĕtĭum, *n*, sumptus, *m*
cost, *v.i*, sto (1) (*with dat. of person and abl. or genit. of price*) e.g. **the victory cost the Carthaginians much bloodshed:** victōrĭa stĕtit Poenis multo sanguĭne
costly, *adj*, prĕtĭōsus
costume, hăbĭtus, *m*

cot, lectŭlus, *m*

cottage, căsa, *f*

cotton, gossўpĭum, *n*

couch, lectus, *m*

couch, *v.i*, subsīdo (3); *v.t* (— a weapon), intendo (3)

cough, *nn*, tussis, *f*

cough, *v.i*, tussĭo (4)

council, concĭlĭum, *n*

**counsel (advice), consĭlĭum, *n*; (lawyer), pătrōnus, *m*

count, *v.t*, nŭmĕro (1); (— upon, trust), confīdo (3) (*with dat*)

countenance, *nn*, vultus, *m*

countenance, *v.t*, permitto (3), făvĕo (2), indulgĕo (2)

counter (in shop), mensa, *f*; (for counting), calcŭlus, *m*

counter, *adv*, contra

counteract, *v.t*, obsisto (3) (*with dat.*)

counter-balance, *v.t*, exaequo (1)

counterfeit, *adj*, ădultĕrīnus, fictus

counterfeit, *v.t*, sĭmŭlo (1), fingo (3)

counterpart, res gĕmella (paired, twin thing)

countless, innŭmĕrābĭlis

country (fatherland), pătrĭă, *f*; (countryside), rūs, *n*; (region), rĕgĭo, *f*

country-house, villa, *f*

countryman (of the same country), cīvis, *c*; (living in the countryside), rustĭcus, *m*

couple, *nn*, (pair), pār *n*

couple, *v.t*, coniungo (3)

courage, virtus, *f*, ănĭmus, *m*

courageous, fortis, ācer, fĕrox

courier (messenger), nuntĭus, *m*

course (motion), cursus, *m*; (route), vĭa, *f*, ĭter *n*; (plan), rătĭo, *f*; (race —), circus, *m*; (of —), *adv*, nĭmīrum, certē

court (— of justice), iūdĭcĭum, *n*; (judges themselves), iūdĭces, *m. pl*; (palace), aula, *f*, dŏmus, (*f*) rēgis (the house of the king); (court-yard), ārĕa, *f*

court, *v.t*, cŏlo (3)

court-martial, *use phr.* in castris iudicare (1) (to try in camp)

courteous, cōmis, hūmānus

courtesy, cōmĭtas, *f*, hūmānĭtas, *f*

courtier, aulĭcus, *m*

courtship, ămor, *m*

cousin, consōrbrīnus, *m* (. . . a), *f*

covenant, pactum, *n*

cover, *v.t*, tĕgo (3); (conceal) occulto (1)

cover, covering, *nn*, tĕgŭmen; *n*; (lid), ŏpĕrīmentum, *n*

coverlet, străgŭlum, *n*

covert, *nn*, dūmētum, *n*

covet, *v.t*, cŭpĭo (3)

covetous, ăvārus, ăvĭdus, cŭpĭdus

covetousness, ăvārĭtĭa, *f*, cŭpĭditas, *f*

cow, vacca, *f*

cow, *v.t*, terrĕo (2), dŏmo (1) (tame)

coward, ignāvus, *m*

cowardice, ignāvĭa, *f*

cowardly, *adj*, ignāvus

cowl, cŭcullus, *m*

coy (bashful), vĕrēcundus

crab, cancer, *m*

crabbed, mōrōsus

crack, *nn*, (noise), crĕpĭtus, *m*; (chink), rīma, *f*

crack, *v.t*, findo (3), frango (3); *v.i*, (open up), dĕhisco (3); (sound), crĕpo (1)

cradle, cūnae, *f. pl.*

craft (deceit), dŏlus, *m*; (skill), artĭfĭcĭum, *n*; (boat), rătis, *f*, nāvis, *f*

craftsman, ŏpĭfex, *m*

crafty, callĭdus

crag, scŏpŭlus, *m*

cram, *v.t*, confercĭo (4)

cramp, *v.t*, comprĭmo (3)

crane (bird), grus, *m*, *f*; (machine), tollēno, *f*

crank, uncus, *m*

cranny, rīma, *f*

crash, *nn*, frăgor, *m*

crash, *v.i*, (noise), strĕpo (3); (bring into collision), *v.t*, collīdo (3)

crate, corbis, *m*

crater, crāter, *m*

crave for, *v.t*, ōro (1), appĕto (3)

craving, *nn*, dēsīdĕrĭum, *n*

crawl, *v.i*, rēpo (3)

crayon, crēta, *f*

crazy, cerrītus, dēmens

creak, *v.i*, crĕpo (1)

creaking, *nn*, strĭdor, *m*, crĕpĭtus, *m*

crease, *nn*, rūga, *f*

crease, *v.t*, rūgo (1)

create, *v.t*, crĕo (1)

creation (act of —), crĕātĭo, *f*; (making), făbrĭcātĭo, *f*; (universe), mundus, *m*

creator, auctor, *m*, crĕātor, *m*

creature, ănĭmal,-*n*

credence (belief), fĭdes, *f*

credible, crēdĭbĭlis

credit (belief or commercial credit), fĭdes, *f*; (reputation), existĭmātĭo, *f*

credit, *v.t*, (believe), crēdo (3); (— an account, person, etc.), acceptum rēfĕro (*irreg*) (*with dat. of person*)

creditable (honourable), hŏnestus

creditor, crēdĭtor, *m*
credulous, crēdŭlus, *m*
creek, sīnus, *m*
creep, *v.i*, serpo (3), rēpo (3)
crescent, lūna, *f*, (crescent moon)
crescent-shaped, lūnātus
crest, crista, *f*
crested, cristātus
crest-fallen, dēmissus
crevice, rīma, *f*
crew, nautae, *m*, *pl*, rēmĭges, *m*, *pl*
crib (child's bed), lectŭlus, *m*
cricket (insect), cĭcāda, *f*
crime, făcĭnus, *n*, scĕlus, *n*
criminal, *nn*, hŏmo sons, hŏmo nŏcens
criminal, *adj*, nĕfārĭus, scĕlestus
crimson, *adj*, coccĭnēus
cringe to, *v.i*, ădūlor (1 *dep*)
cripple, *nn*, hŏmo claudus
cripple, *v.t*, dēbĭlĭto (1); (— a person), claudum reddo (3)
crippled, dēbĭlis, claudus
crisis, discrīmen, *n*
crisp, frăgĭlis
critic, existĭmātor, *m*, censor, *m*
critical, ēlĕgans; (of a crisis, etc.), *use* discrīmen, *n* (crisis)
criticise, *v.t*, (find fault) rĕprĕhendo (3), iūdĭco (1)
croak, *nn*, quĕrēla, *f*, clāmor, *m*
croak, *v.i*, căno (3), crōcĭo (4)
crockery, fictĭlĭa, *n.pl*
crocodile, crŏcŏdīlus, *m*
crocus, crŏcus, *m*
crook (shepherd's —), pĕdum, *n*
crooked, curvus; (bad, etc.), prāvus
crop (of corn), sĕges, *f*, frūges, *f*, *pl*; (of a bird), inglŭvĭes, *f*
crop, *v.t*, tondĕo (2)
cross, *nn*, crux, *f*
cross, *adj*, transversus; (annoyed), īrātus
cross, *v.i. and v.t*, transĕo (4 *irreg*)
cross-examine, *v.t*, interrŏgo (1)
crossing (act of —), transĭtus, *m*; (cross-road), compĭtum, *n*
crouch, *v.i*, sē dēmittĕre (3 *reflex*)
crow (bird), cornix, *f*
crow, *v.i*, (of a cock), căno (3); (boast), sē iactare (1 *reflex*)
crowd, turba, *f*
crowd together, *v.i*, congrĕgor (1 *dep*); *v.t*, stipo (1), frĕquento (1)
crowded, confertus, cĕlĕber
crown, cŏrōna, *f*; (royal), dĭădēma, *n*; (of head, etc.), vertex, *m*
crown, *v.t*, cŏrōno (1)
crucifixion, *use phr. with* crux, *f*, (cross)

crucify, *v.t*, crŭce affĭcĭo (3)
crude, rŭdis
cruel, crūdēlis, atrox
cruelty, crūdēlĭtas, *f*
cruet, gutus, *m*
cruise, *nn*, nāvĭgātĭo, *f*
cruise, *v.i*, nāvĭgo (1)
crumb, mĭca, *f*
crumble, *v.t*, tĕro (3); *v.i*, corrŭo (3)
crumple, *v.t*, rūgo (1)
crush, *v.t*, contundo (3), opprĭmo (3)
crust, crusta, *f*
crutch, băcŭlum, *n*
cry, *nn*, clāmor, *m*, vox, *f*
cry, *v.i*, clāmo (1); (weep), lacrĭmo (1)
crystal, *nn*, crystallum, *n*
cub, cătŭlus, *m*
cube, tessĕra, *f*
cubic, cŭbĭcus
cuckoo, cŭcūlus, *m*, coccyx, *m*
cucumber, cŭcŭmis, *m*
cudgel, fustis, *m*
cudgel, *v.t*, verbĕro (1), mulco (1)
cue, signum, *n*
cuff, *nn*, (blow), cŏlăphus, *m*, ălăpa, *f*
cuff, *v.t*, incŭtĭo (3)
cuirass, lōrīca, *f*, thōrax, *m*
culminate, *use adj*, summus (topmost)
culpable, culpandus, nŏcens
culprit, hŏmo nŏcens
cultivate, *v.t*, cŏlo (3)
cultivation, cultus, *m*, cultūra, *f*
cultivator, cultor, *m*
culture, cultus, *m*, cultūra, *f*
cumbersome, inhăbĭlis
cunning, *adj*, callĭdus, dŏlōsus
cunning, *nn*, callĭdĭtas, *f*, dŏlus, *m*
cup, pōcŭlum, *n*
cupboard, armārĭum, *n*
cupidity, cŭpĭdĭtas, *f*
cupola, thŏlus, *m*
curate, săcerdos, *c*, (priest)
curator, cūrātor, *m*
curb, *v.t*, frēno (1), cŏhĭbĕo (2)
curdle, *v.t*, cōgo (3), cŏăgŭlo (1); *v.i*, concresco (3)
cure, *nn*, sānātĭo, *f*
cure, *v.t*, mĕdĕor (2 *dep*) (*with dat.*)
curiosity, stŭdĭum, *n*
curious (inquisitive), cūrĭōsus; (rare), rārus
curl, *v.t*, crispo (1)
curl, *nn*, cincinnus, *m*
curly, cincinnātus
currant, ăcĭnus, *m*
currency, mŏnēta, *f*, nummi, *m. pl*
current, *nn*, (of river), flūmen, *n*
current, *adj*, (present), hic; (general), ūsĭtātus

curse, *nn*, imprĕcātĭo, *f*, dīrae, *f. pl*
curse, *v.t*, exsĕcror (1 *dep*.)
cursed, exsĕcrābĭlis
cursorily, *adv*, summātim, brĕvĭter
curt, brĕvis
curtail, *v.t*, arto (1)
curtain, aulaeum, *n*
curve, *nn*, flexus, *m*
curve, *v.t*, flecto (3), curvo (1)
curved, curvātus
cushion, pulvīnar, *n*
custodian, cūrātor, *m*
custody (keeping), custōdĭa, *f*; (imprisonment), vincŭla, *n.pl*
custom, mos, *m*, consŭĕtūdo, *f*; (— duty), portōrĭum, *n*
customary, ūsĭtātus, sŏlĭtus
customer, emptor, *m*
cut, *nn*, (incision), incīsĭo, *f*; (blow), ictus, *m*, plāga, *f*
cut, *v.t*, sĕco (3); caedo (3); (— away), abscīdo (3); (— down), succīdo (3); (— off), praecīdo (3); (— off from communications, supplies, etc.) interclūdo (3); (— out), excīdo (3); (— short), praecīdo (3); (— to pieces), concīdo (3), trŭcīdo (1)
cutaneous, *use genit. of* cŭtis (skin)
cutlass, glădĭus, *m*
cutlery, cultri, *m. pl* (knives)
cutter (boat), phăsēlus, *m*, cĕlox, *f*
cutting, *adj*, (biting), mordax
cuttle-fish, sēpĭa, *f*
cycle (circle), orbis, *m*
cygnet, pullus, *m*
cylinder, cylindrus, *m*
cymbal, cymbălum, *n*
cynic, cynĭcus, *m*
cynical, mordax, difficĭlis
cynicism, dūrĭtĭa, *f*
cypress, cupressus, *f*

D

dab, *v.t*, illīdo (3)
dabble in, *v.t*, attingo (3)
daffodil, narcissus, *m*
dagger, pūgĭo, *m*
daily *adj*, quŏtīdĭānus
daily, *adv*, quŏtīdĭē
daintiness (of manners), fastīdĭum, *n*
dainty (things), dēlĭcātus; (people), fastīdĭōsus
daisy, bellis, *f*
dale, valles, *f*
dalliance, lūsus, *m*
dally, *v.i*, (delay), mŏror (1 *dep*)
dam (breakwater), mōles, *f*
dam, *v.t*, obstrŭo (3)

damage, *nn*, dētrīmentum, *n*, damnum, *n*
damage, *v.t*, laedo (3), affīgo (3)
dame, dŏmĭna, *f*, mātrōna, *f*
damn, *v.t*, damno (1)
damp, *adj*, hūmĭdus
damp, *v.t*, hūmecto (1); (enthusiasm, etc.), immĭnŭo (3) (lessen)
damp, *nn*, hūmor, *m*
dance, *v.i*, salto (1)
dance, *nn*, saltātus, *m*
dancer, saltātor, *m* (... trix, *f*)
dandy, hŏmo lēpĭdus, ēlĕgans, bellus
danger, pĕrĭcŭlum, *n*
dangerous, pĕrĭcŭlōsus
dangle, *v.i*, pendĕo (2)
dank, hūmĭdus, ūvĭdus
dapper (spruce), nĭtĭdus
dappled, măcŭlōsus
dare, *v.i*, audĕo (2 *semi-dep*) mōlĭor (4 *dep*)
daring, *adj*, audax
daring, *nn*, audācĭa, *f*
dark, *adj*, obscūrus tĕnĕbrōsus; (in colour), fuscus
dark, darkness, *nn*, tĕnĕbrae, *f. pl*
darken, *v.t*, obscūro (1), occaeco (1)
darling, *nn*, dēlĭcĭae, *f. pl*; *adj*, mellītus
darn, *v.t*, sarcĭo (4)
dart, *nn*, tēlum, *n*, iăcŭlum, *n*
dart, *v.i*, (rush), *use compound of* vŏlo (1) (to fly)
dash, *nn*, (rush), *use vb*, vŏlo (1) (to fly)
dash, *v.i*, prōvŏlo (1), rŭo (3); *v.t*, affīgo (3), impingo (3)
dashing, *adj*, ălăcer
dastardly, *adj*, ignāvus
date (fruit), palmŭla, *f*; (time), dĭes, *f*
date, *v.t*, (something), dĭem ascrībo (3) in (*with abl.*)
daub, *v.t*, oblīno (3)
daughter, fīlĭa, *f*; (— in-law), nŭrus, *f*
daunt, *v.t*, percello (3)
dauntless, impăvĭdus
dawdle, *v.i*, cesso (1)
dawn, prīma lux, aurōra, *f*
dawn, *v.i*, dīlūcesco (3)
day, dĭes, *m*, *f*; (at — break), *adv. phr*, prīmā lūce; (by —), *adv*, interdĭu; (every —), *adv*, quŏtīdĭe; (late in the —), multo dĭe; (on the — before), prīdĭe; (on the next —), postrīdĭe; (— time), tempus dĭurnum, *n*
daze, *v.t*, stŭpĕfăcĭo (3)
dazzle, *v.t*, perstringo (3)

For List of Abbreviations used, turn to pages 3, 4

dazzling, splendĭdus

dead, *adj*, mortŭus; (the dead or departed), mānes, *m. pl*; (a — body), corpus, *n*

deaden, *v.t*, (senses, etc.), hĕbĕto (1)

deadly, *adj*, mortĭfer, pernĭcĭōsus, fūnestus

deaf, surdus

deafen, *v.t*, exsurdo (1), obtundo (3)

deafness, surdĭtas, *f*

deal (a good-,), ălĭquantum, (business) nĕgōtĭum, *n*

deal, *v.t*, (distribute), distrĭbŭo (3); mētĭor (4 *dep*.); *v.i*, (deal with), ăgo (3) cum (*with abl*)

dealer, mercātor, *m*

dealings, *nn*, ūsus, *m*, commercĭum, *n*

dear, cārus; (of price), prĕtĭōsus

dearly, *adv*, (at a high price), magni

death, mors, *f*

death-bed (on his —), *use adj*, mŏrĭens (dying)

deathless, immortālis

debar, *v.t*, exclūdo (3)

debase, *v.t*, dēmitto (3), vĭtĭo (1)

debate, contrōversĭa, *f*

debate, *v.t*, dispŭto (1), discepto (1)

debater, dispŭtātor, *m*

debauch, *v.t*, corrumpo (3)

debauchery, stŭprum, *n*

debit, *nn*, expensum, *n*

debit, *v.t*, expensum fĕro (*irreg*) (*with dat*)

debt, aes ălĭēnum, *n*

debtor, dēbĭtor, *m*

debut, ĭnĭtĭum, *n*

decamp, *v.i*, castra mŏvĕo (2); discēdo (3)

decant, *v.t*, diffundo (3)

decanter, lăgēna, *f*

decapitate, *v.t*, sĕcūri fĕrĭo (4)

decay, *nn*, tābes, *f*, dēmĭnūtĭo, *f*

decay, *v.i*, dīlābor (3 *dep*), tābesco (3)

decease, dēcessus, *m*

deceased, *adj*, mortŭus

deceit, fraus, *f*, dŏlus, *m*

deceitful, fallax

deceive, *v.t*, dēcĭpĭo (3), fallo (3)

December, Dĕcember (mensis)

decency, dĕcōrum, *n*, hŏnestas, *f*

decent, dĕcōrus, hŏnestus

deception, fraus, *f*, dŏlus, *m*

deceptive, fallax

decide, *v.t*, constĭtŭo (3), stătŭo (3), dēcerno (3)

decided (persons), firmus; (things), certus

decidedly, *adv*, (assuredly), plānē, vēro

decimate, *v.t*, dĕcĭmo (1)

decision, arbĭtrĭum, *n*, dēcrētum *n*

deck, pons, *m*

deck, *v.t*, orno (1)

declaim, *v.t*, dēclāmo (1)

declaration, prŏfessĭo, *f* (— of war), dēnuntĭātĭo, *f* (belli)

declare, *v.i*, prŏfĭtĕor (2 *dep*), affirmo (1); *v.t*, dēclāro (1); (— war), dēnuntĭo (1) (bellum)

decline, *nn*, dēmĭnūtĭo, *f* (diminution)

decline, *v.t*, (refuse), rĕcūso (1); *v.i*, inclīno (1), dēcresco (3)

declivity, clīvus, *m*

decompose, *v.t*, solvo (3); *v.i*, solvor (3 *pass*)

decomposition, sŏlūtĭo, *f*

decorate, *v.t*, orno (1), dĕcŏro (1)

decoration (ornament), ornāmentum, *n*, dĕcus, *n*; (badge), insigne, *n*

decorous, dĕcōrus

decorum, dĕcōrum, *n*, pŭdor, *m*

decoy, illex, *m*; (bait), esca, *f*

decrease, *nn*, dēmĭnūtĭo, *f*

decrease, *v.i*, dēcresco (3); *v.t*, mĭnŭo (3)

decree, *nn*, dēcrētum, *n*; (— of the Senate), consultum, *n*

decree, *v.t*, dēcerno (3), censĕo (2)

decrepit, dēcrĕpĭtus, dēbĭlis

decry, *v.t*, vĭtŭpĕro (1), obtrecto (1)

dedicate, *v.t*, consĕcro (1)

deduce, *v.t*, conclūdo (3)

deduct, *v.t*, dēdūco (3)

deduction (taking away), dēductĭo, *f*

deed, factum, *n*, făcĭnus, *n*; (legal), tābŭla, *f*

deem, *v.t*, pŭto (1)

deep, *nn*, (the sea), altum, *n*

deep, altus; (of sound), grăvis

deepen, *v.t*, altĭōrem reddo (3)

deeply, *adv*, altē, pĕnĭtus (deep within)

deer, cervus, *m* cerva, *f*

deface, *v.t*, dēformo (1)

defame, *v.t*, mălēdīco (3) (*with dat*)

default, *v.i*, dēfĭcĭo (3) (fail to answer bail), vădĭmōnĭum dēsĕro (3)

defeat, *nn*, clādes, *f*

defeat, *v.t*, vinco (3), sŭpĕro (1)

defect, vĭtĭum, *n*

defective, vĭtĭōsus

defence (protection), praesĭdĭum, *n*; (legal), dēfensĭo, *f*

defenceless, ĭnermis

defend, v.t, dēfendo (3)
defendant (in a trial), rēus, m
defender, dēfensor, m; (in court),
pătrōnus, m
defer, v.t, (put off), diffĕro (irreg);
v.i, (show deference to), cēdo (3)
deference, observantĭa, f
defiance, prŏvŏcātĭo, f
defiant, fĕrox
deficiency, dēfectĭo, f
deficient, ĭnops, mancus
deficit, lăcūna, f
defile, v.t, contămĭno (1)
defile, nn, angustĭae, f, pl
define, v.t, circumscrībo (3)
definite, constĭtūtus, certus
definition, dēfinītĭo, f
deflect, v.t, dēflecto (3)
deform, v.t, dēformo (1)
deformity, dēformĭtas, f
defraud, v.t, fraudo (1)
defray, v.t, suppĕdĭto (1) (supply)
deft, doctus (skilled)
defy, v.t obsto (1), prŏvŏco (1)
degenerate, v.i, dēgĕnĕro (1)
degenerate, adj, dēgĕner
degradation, ignōmĭnĭa, f
degrade, v.t, mŏvĕo (2), dē or ex (with
abl), (move down from); dēhŏnesto
(1)
degree (interval, stage, rank), grădus,
m; (to such a degree), adv, ădĕo; (by
degrees), adv, (gradually), grădātim
deify, v.t, consēcro (1)
deign, v.t, dignor (1 dep)
deity, dĕus, m
deject, v.t, afflīgo (3)
dejected, dēmissus, afflictus
dejection, maestĭtĭa, f
delay, nn, mŏra, f
delay, v.i, mŏror (1 dep), cunctor (1
dep); v.t, mŏror (1 dep), tardo (1)
delegate, nn, lēgātus, m
delegate, v.t (depute), lēgo (1), mando
(1) (with acc. of thing and dat. of
person)
delegation, lēgātĭo, f
deliberate, adj, consĭdĕrātus
deliberate, v.t, consŭlo (3), dēlībĕro (1)
deliberately, adv, consultō
deliberation, dēlībĕrātĭo, f
delicacy, subtīlĭtas, f, suāvĭtas, f;
(food), cūpēdĭa, n.pl
delicate, subtīlis, tĕner; (of health),
infirmus
delicious, suāvis
delight, nn, (pleasure), vŏluptas, f
delight, v.t, dēlecto (1); v.i, gaudĕo (2)
delightful, iūcundus, ămoenus
delineate, v.t, dēscrībo (3)

delinquency, dēlictum, n
delinquent, nn, peccātor, m
delirious, dēlīrus
delirium, dēlīrĭum, n
deliver, v.t, (set free), lībĕro (1); (hand
over), do (1), trādo (3), dēdo (3);
(— a speech), hăbĕo (2), ōrātĭonem
deliverance (freeing), lībĕrātĭo, f
deliverer, lībĕrātor, m
delivery (freeing), lībĕrātĭo, f; (childbirth), partus, m; (of a speech),
ēlŏcūtĭo, f
delude, v.t, dēcĭpĭo (3)
deluge, dīlŭvĭum, n, ĭnundātĭo, f
delusion, error, m; (trick), fallācĭa,
f, fraus, f
delusive (deceitful), fallax; (empty),
vānus
demagogue, plēbĭcŏla, c
demand, nn, postŭlātĭo, f
demand, v.t, posco (3), postŭlo (1)
demean oneself, dēmittor (3 pass), sē
dēmittĕre (3 reflex)
demeanour, mōres, m. pl, hăbĭtus, m
demented, dēmens
demise, nn, (death), dēcessus, m,
mors, f
democracy, cīvĭtas pŏpŭlāris, f
democrat, plēbĭcŏla, c
demolish, v.t, dīrŭo (3), dēlĕo (2),
dēmōlĭor (4 dep.)
demolition, ēversĭo, f, rŭīna, f
demon, daemŏnĭum, n
demonstrate, v.t, dēmonstro (1)
demonstration, dēmonstrātĭo, f
demur, v.i, haesĭto (1)
demure, adj, vērēcundus
den, lătībŭlum, n
denial, nĕgātĭo, f
denominate, v.t, nōmĭno (1)
denote, v.t, indĭco (1), signĭfĭco (1),
nōto (1)
denounce, v.t, (nōmen) dēfĕro (irreg)
dense, densus, confertus
density, crassĭtūdo, f
dent, nŏta, f
dentist, dentĭum mĕdĭcus, m
denude, v.t, nūdo (1)
deny, v.t, nĕgo (1), abnŭo (3)
depart, v.i, ăbĕo (4), discēdo (3)
departed (dead), mortŭus
department (of administration, etc.),
prŏvincĭa, f; (part), pars, f
departure, discessus, m
depend on, v.i, pendĕo (2) ex or in
(with abl); (rely on), confīdo (3
semi-dep) (with dat)
dependant, nn, clĭens, c
dependence on, clĭentēla, f; (reliance),
fĭdes, f

dependency (subject state), prōvincĭa, f

depict, v.t, dēscrībo (3). effingo (3)

deplorable, mĭsĕrābĭlis

deplore, v.t, dēplōro (1)

deploy, v.t, explĭco (1)

depopulate, v.t, pŏpŭlor (1 dep); vasto (1)

deport, v.t, dēporto (1); **(behave oneself)**, se gĕrĕre (3 reflex)

deportment, hăbĭtus, m

depose, v.t, mŏvĕo (2) (with abl)

deposit, v.t, dēpōno (3)

deposit, nn, dēpŏsĭtum, n

deprave, v.t, dēprāvo (1), corrumpo (3)

depravity, prāvĭtas, f

deprecate, v.t, dēprĕcor (1 dep)

depreciate, v.t, dētrăho (3); v.i, mĭnŭor (3 pass) **(grow less)**

depreciation (decrease), dēmĭnūtĭo, f; **(disparagement)**, obtrectātĭo, f

depredation, expĭlātĭo, f, praedātĭo, f

depress, v.t, dēprĭmo (3); **(spirits, etc.)**, infringo (3)

depression (sadness), tristĭtĭa, f

deprive, v.t, privo (1) (with acc. of person deprived, and abl. of thing)

depth, altĭtūdo, f

deputation, lēgātĭo, f

depute, v.t, lēgo (1), mando (1) (with dat)

deputy, lēgātus, m

deputy-governor, prōcūrātor, m

derange, v.t, perturbo (1)

deride, v.t, dērīdĕo (2)

derision, irrīsĭo, f, risus, m

derive (from), v.t, **(deduce)**, dūco (3), ab (and abl)

derogate from, v.i, dērŏgo (1) dē (with abl)

derogatory (remark), noxĭus

descend, v.i, dēscendo (3)

descendant, prōgĕnĭes, f

descent (lineage), prōgĕnĭes, f; **(movement)**, dēscensus, m; **(slope)**, dēclive, n

describe, v.t, dēscrībo (3), expōno (3)

description, dēscriptĭo, f, narrātĭo, f

descry, v.t, conspĭcor (1 dep)

desecrate, v.t, prŏfāno (1)

desert (wilderness), sōlĭtūdo, f

desert, v.t, dēsĕro (3), rēlinquo (3)

deserted, dēsertus

deserter, perfŭga, m, transfŭga, m

deserve, v.t, mĕrĕor (2 dep); dignus esse (irreg) (with abl)

deservedly, adv, mĕrĭto

design, dēscriptĭo, f; **(plan)**, consĭlĭum, n

design, v.t, dēscrībo (3); **(intend)**, in ănĭmo hăbĕo (2)

designate, v.t, dēsigno (1)

designing, adj, callĭdus, dŏlōsus

desirable, optābĭlis

desire, nn, dēsīdĕrĭum, n, cŭpĭdĭtas, f

desire, v.t, cŭpĭo (3), opto (1)

desirous, cŭpĭdus

desist, v.i, dēsisto (3), dēsĭno (3)

desk, scrīnĭum, n

desolate, dēsertus, sōlus

despair, nn, dēspērātĭo, f

despair, v.i, dēspēro (1)

despatch, v.t mitto (3); **(kill)**, interfĭcĭo (3)

despatch, nn, **(sending)**, dīmissĭo, f; **(letter)**, littĕrae, f. pl; **(speed)**, cĕlĕrĭtas, f

desperate, dēspērātus; **(situation)**, extrēmus

desperation, dēspērātĭo, f

despicable, contemptus

despise, v.t, dēspĭcĭo (3), sperno (3)

despite, prep, contrā (with acc)

despoil, v.t, spŏlĭo (1)

despond, v.i, ănĭmum dēmitto (3)

despondent, use adv. phr, ănĭmo dēmisso

despot, dŏmĭnus, m

despotic, tўrannĭcus, m

despotism, dŏmĭnātĭo, m

dessert, mensa sĕcunda **(second table)**

destination, often quo? **(whither)**, or ĕo **(to that place)**

destine, v.t, dēstĭno (1), dēsigno (1)

destiny, fātum, n

destitute, ĭnops

destroy, v.t, perdo (3), dēlĕo (2), ēverto (3)

destroyer, vastātor, m

destruction, pernĭcĭes, f, ēversĭo, f, exĭtĭum, n

destructive, pernĭcĭōsus

desultory, inconstans

detach, v.t, sēiungo (3), sēpăro (1)

detached, sēpărātus

detachment (of troops, etc.), mănus, f

details, singŭla, n.pl

detail, v.t, explĭco (1)

detain, v.t, rĕtĭnĕo (2)

detect, v.t, dēprĕhendo (3), compĕrĭo (4)

deter, v.t, dēterrĕo (2), dēpello (3)

deteriorate, v.i, corrumpor (3 pass)

determinate, adj, certus

determination (resolution), constantĭa, f; **(intention)**, consĭlĭum, n

determine, v.i and v.t, constĭtŭo (3)

determined (resolute), firmus; **(fixed)**, certus

detest, *v.t*, ōdī (*v. defect*)

detestable, ŏdĭōsus

dethrone, *v.t*, regno pello (3) **(expel from sovereignty)**

detour, circŭĭtus, *m*

detract from, *v.t*, dētrăho (3) dē (*with abl*)

detriment, dētrīmentum, *n*

detrimental (to be —), *v.i*, esse (*irreg*) dētrīmento (*with dat*)

devastate, *v.t*, vasto (1)

devastation, vastātĭo, *f*

develop, *v.t*, explĭco (1), ēdūco (1); *v.i*, cresco (3) **(grow)**

development, prōlātĭo, *f*; **(unfolding)**, explĭcātĭo, *f*

deviate, *v.i*, dēclīno (1), discēdo (3)

deviation, dēclīnātĭo, *f*

device (contrivance), artĭfĭcĭum, *n*; **(emblem)**, insigne, *n*; **(plan)**, dŏlus, *m*

devil, daemŏnĭum, *n*

devilish, nĕfandus

devious, dēvĭus

devise, *v.t*, excōgĭto (1), fingo (3)

devoid, expers, văcŭus

devolve, *v.i*, obvĕnĭo (4); *v.t*, dēfĕro (*irreg*)

devote, *v.t*, dēdĭco (1), dēdo (3); **(consecrate)**, dēvŏvĕo (2)

devoted, dēdĭtus, dēvōtus

devotion, stŭdĭum, *n*; **(love)**, ămor, *m*

devour, *v.t*, dēvŏro (1), consūmo (3)

devouring, ĕdax

devout, pĭus, vĕnĕrābundus, rēlĭgĭōsus

dew, rōs, *m*

dexterity, sollertĭa, *f*, callĭdĭtas, *f*

dexterous, sollers, callĭdus

diadem, dĭădēma, *n*

diagonal, *adj*, dĭăgōnālis

diagram, forma, *f*

dial, sōlārĭum, *n*

dialect, dĭălectus, *f*

dialectics, dĭălectĭca, *n.pl*

dialogue, sermo, *m*; **(written)**, dĭălŏgus, *m*

diameter, crassĭtūdo, *f*

diamond, ădămas, *m*

diaphragm, praecordĭa, *n.pl*

diarrhoea, prōflŭvĭum, *n*

diary, commentārĭi dĭurni, *m. pl*

dice, tāli, *m. pl*; **(the game)**, ălĕa, *f*

dictate, *v.t*, dicto (1); *v.i*, impĕro (1) (*with dat*)

dictation, dictātĭo, *f*

dictator, dictātor, *m*

dictatorial, impĕrĭōsus

dictatorship, dictātūra, *f*

dictionary, glossārĭum, *n*

die, *v.i*, mŏrĭor (3 *dep*), cădo (3)

diet, victus, *m*

differ, *v.i*, discrĕpo (1), diffĕro (*irreg*)

difference, discrīmen, *n*, dīversĭtas, *f*; **(— of opinion)**, discrĕpantĭa, *f*

different, ălĭus, dīversus

difficult, diffĭcĭlis

difficulty, diffĭcultas, *f*; **(to be in —)**, lăbōro (1); **(with—)**, *adv*, aegrē

diffidence, diffīdentĭa, *f*

diffident, diffīdens

diffuse, *v.t*, diffundo (3)

dig, *v.t*, fŏdĭo (3)

digest, *v.t*, concŏquo (3)

digestion, concoctĭo, *f*

dignified, grăvis

dignify, *v.t*, hŏnesto (1)

dignity (of character), grăvĭtas, *f*, dignĭtas, *f*

digress, *v.i*, dīgrĕdĭor (3 *dep*)

digression, dīgressĭo, *f*

dike (ditch), fossa, *f*; **(mound)**, agger, *m*

dilapidated, rŭĭnōsus

dilate, *v.i*, sē dīlātāre (1 *reflex*); *v.t* **(— upon)**, dīlāto (1)

dilatory, ignāvus, lentus

dilemma (difficulty), angustĭae, *f. pl*

diligence, dīlĭgentĭa, *f*

dilute, *v.t*, dīlŭo (3), miscĕo (2)

dim, *adj*, **(light, etc.)**, obscūrus; **(dull, stupid)**, hĕbes

dim, *v.t*, obscūro (1)

dimension, mŏdus, *m*

diminish, *v.t*, mĭnŭo (3); *v.i*, mĭnŭor (3 *pass*)

diminution, dēmĭnūtĭo, *f*

diminutive, parvus, exĭgŭus

dimness, obscūrĭtas, *f*

dimple, lăcūna, *f*

din, strĕpĭtus, *m*

dine, *v.i*, cēno (1)

dingy, sordĭdus

dining-room, trīclīnĭum, *n*, cēnātĭo, *f*

dinner, cēna, *f*

by dint of, *prep*, per (*with acc*)

dip, *v.t*, mergo (3); *v.i*, mergor (3 *pass*)

diploma, dīplōma, *n*

diplomacy (by —), per lēgātos **(by means of diplomats)**

diplomat(ist), lēgātus, *m*

direct, *adj*, rectus

direct, *v.t*, dīrĭgo (3); **(order)**, praecĭpĭo (3) (*with dat. of person*); **(show)**, monstro (1)

direction (of motion), cursus, *m*; **(pointing out)**, monstrātĭo, *f*; **(affairs)**, admĭnistrātĭo, *f*; **(in different —s)**, (*pl. adj*), dīversi

director, cūrātor, *m*

dirt, sordes, *f*

For List of Abbreviations used, turn to pages 3, 4

dirty, sordĭdus, spurcus

dirty, v.t, inquĭno (1), foedo (1)

disable, v.t, dēbĭlĭto (1)

disabled, inhăbĭlis, confectus

disadvantage, incommŏdum, n

disadvantageous, incommŏdus

disaffected, ălĭēnātus

disaffection, ănĭmus āversus, m

disagree, v.i, discrĕpo (1), dissentĭo (4)

disagreeable (unpleasant), iniūcundus

disagreement, discrĕpantĭa, f, dissensĭo, f

disappear, v.i, ēvānesco (3), diffŭgĭo (3)

disappearance, exĭtus, m

disappoint, v.t, frustror (1 dep)

disappointment, incommŏdum, n

disapproval, rĕprĕhensĭo, f

disapprove, v.t, imprŏbo (1)

disarm, v.t, armis exŭo (3) (strip of arms)

disaster, clădes, f

disastrous, pernĭcĭōsus

disavow, v.t, diffĭtĕor (2 dep)

disavowal, infĭtĭātĭo, f

disband, v.t, dīmitto (3)

disbelieve, v.t, non crēdo (3), diffīdo (3) (with dat)

disburse, v.t, expendo (3)

disc, orbis, m

discard, v.t, rĕpŭdĭo (1)

discern, v.t, cerno (3)

discerning, adj, perspĭcax

discernment, intellĕgentĭa, f

discharge, v.t, (missiles, etc.), ēmitto (3), iăcŭlor (1 dep); (soldiers, etc.), dīmitto (3); (duties, etc.), fungor (3 dep) (with abl)

discharge, nn, ēmissĭo, f, dīmissĭo, f

disciple, discĭpŭlus, m

discipline, disciplĭna, f

discipline, v.t, instĭtŭo (3)

disclaim, v.t, nĕgo (1), rĕpŭdĭo (1)

disclose, v.t, ăpĕrĭo (4)

disclosure, indĭcĭum, n

discolour, v.t, dēcŏlōro (1)

discomfiture, clădes, f

discomfort, incommŏdum, n

disconcert, v.t, perturbo (1)

disconnect, v.t, sēiungo (3)

disconsolate, maestus

discontented, mălĕ contentus

discontinue, v.t, intermitto (3)

discord (strife), discordĭa, f, dissensĭo, f

discount, nn, dēcessĭo, f (decrease)

discourage, v.t, ănĭmum dēmitto (3)

discouragement, ănĭmi infractĭo, f, or dēmissĭo, f

discourse, v.i, dissĕro (3)

discourse, nn, sermo, m, contĭo, f

discover, v.t, invĕnĭo (4), rĕpĕrĭo (4), cognosco (3)

discovery inventĭo, f; (thing discovered), inventum, n

discredit, v.t, fĭdem abrŏgo (1)

discreditable, ĭnhŏnestus

discreet, consĭdĕrātus, prūdens

discretion, prūdentĭa, f

discriminate, v.t, discerno (3)

discuss, v.t, discepto (1), dispŭto (1)

discussion, dispŭtātĭo, f

disdain, v.t, sperno (3), dēspĭcĭo (3)

disdain, nn, fastĭdĭum, n

disdainful, fastĭdĭōsus

disease, morbus, m

diseased, aeger

disembark, v.t, expōno (3); v.i, ēgrĕdĭor (3 dep)

disengage, v.t, (release), solvo (3)

disengaged (at leisure), ōtĭōsus; (free, loose), sŏlūtus

disentangle, v.t, explĭco (1)

disfigure, v.t, dēformo (1)

disgrace, nn, dēdĕcus, n, ignōmĭnĭa, f

disgrace, v.t, dēdĕcŏro (1)

disgraceful, turpis, flăgĭtĭōsus

disguise, nn, persōna, f, intĕgŭmentum, n

disguise, v.t, vestem mūto (1) (change the clothes); dissĭmŭlo (1) (pretend, hide)

disgust, nn, fastĭdĭum, n, taedĭum, n

disgust, v.t, taedĭum mŏvĕo (2) (with dat)

disgusted (to be —), use impersonal vb, pĭget (2) (it disgusts)

disgusting, foedus

dish, nn, pătĭna, f

dishearten, v.t, exănĭmo (1), percello (3)

dishonest, imprŏbus, perfĭdus

dishonesty, f, imprŏbĭtas, f

dishonour, nn, dēdĕcus, n

dishonour, v.t, dēdĕcŏro (1)

dishonourable, ĭnhŏnestus

disinclination, dēclīnātĭo, f

disinherit, v.t, exhērēdo (1)

disintegrate, v.t, solvo (3); v.i, solvor (3 pass)

disinterested, neutri făvens (favouring neither side)

disjointed, ĭnordĭnātus

disk, orbis, m

dislike, nn, ŏdĭum, n

dislike, *v.t,* ăbhorrĕo (2) ab (*with abl*); displĭcĕo (2)
dislocate, *v.t,* extorquĕo (2)
dislodge, *v.t,* dēĭcĭo (3), pello (3)
disloyal, infīdēlis
dismal, āter, maestus
dismantle, *v.t,* dirĭpĭo (3)
dismay, *nn,* păvor, *m*
dismay, *v.t,* consterno (1), perturbo (1)
dismiss, *v.i,* dīmitto (3)
dismissal, dīmissĭo, *f*
dismount, *v.i,* ex ĕquo dēscendo (3)
disobedience, *use phr. with vb,* pārĕo (obey)
disobedient, măle pārens
disobey, *v.t,* măle pārĕo (*with dat*)
disoblige, *v.t,* offendo (3)
disorder, *nn,* perturbātĭo, *f*
disorderly, *adv,* turbātus; (**crowd**), turbŭlentus
disown, *v.t,* infĭtĭor (1 *dep*)
disparage, *v.t,* dētrăho (3), obtrecto (1)
dispatch, *v.t,* (see **despatch**)
dispel, *v.t,* dēpello (3), discŭtĭo (3)
dispense, *v.t* dispertĭor (4 *dep*) dis-trĭbŭo (3); (— **with**), dīmitto (3)
dispersal, dissĭpātĭo, *f*
disperse, *v.t,* dispergo (3), dissĭpo (1), *v.i,* diffŭgĭo (3)
dispirited, *use adv. phr,* dēmisso ănĭmo
display, *nn,* ostentātĭo, *f*
display, *v.t,* ostento (1)
displease, *v.t,* displĭcĕo (2) (*with dat*)
displeasing, ŏdĭōsus
displeasure, offensĭo, *f*
disposal, ēmissĭo, *f*; (**power**), arbĭtrĭum, *n*
dispose, *v.t,* (**arrange**), constĭtŭo (3), dispōno (3); (**induce**), inclīno (1); (**get rid of**), ēlŭo (3)
disposed, inclīnātus
disposition (**arrangement**), dispŏsĭtĭo, *f*; (**of mind, etc.**), nātūra, *f,* ingĕnĭum, *n*
dispossess, *v.t,* dēturbo (1), dētrūdo (3)
disproportion, dissĭmĭlĭtūdo, *f*; (**of parts, etc.**), inconcinnĭtas, *f*
disprove, *v.t,* rĕfello (3), rĕfūto (1)
dispute, *nn,* contrōversĭa, *f*
dispute, *v.t,* dispŭto (1)
disqualify, *v.t,* (**prevent**), prŏhĭbĕo (2)
disregard, *nn,* neglĕgentĭa, *f*
disregard, *v.t,* neglĕgo (3)
disreputable, infāmis
disrespectful, contŭmax, insŏlens
dissatisfaction, mŏlestĭa, *f*
dissatisfied (**to be** —), *use impers. vb,* paenĭtet (*with acc. of subject and genit. of object*)

dissect, *v.t,* insĕco (1), persĕco (1)
dissemble, *v.i,* dissĭmŭlo (1)
dissension, discordĭa, *f,* dissensĭo, *f*
dissent, *v.i,* dissentĭo (4)
dissimilar, dissĭmĭlis
dissipate, *v.t,* dissĭpo (1)
dissipated, dissŏlūtus, lĭbīdĭnōsus
dissipation, lĭcentĭa, *f*
dissolute, dissŏlūtus, lĭbīdĭnōsus
dissolve, *v.t,* solvo (3), lĭquĕfăcĭo (3), *v.i,* solvor (3 *pass*), lĭquesco (3)
dissuade, *v.t,* dissuādĕo (2) (*with dat*)
distaff, cŏlus, *f*
distance, spătĭum, *n*; (**remoteness**), longinquĭtas, *f*; (**at a** —), *adv,* longē, prŏcul
distant, rĕmōtus, distans; (**to be** —), absum (*irreg*)
distaste, fastīdĭum, *n*
distasteful, iniūcundus
distemper (**malady**), morbus, *m*
distend, *v.t,* tendo (3)
distil, *v.t,* stillo (1)
distinct (**separate**), sēpărātus; (**clear**), clārus, mănĭfestus
distinction (**difference**), discrīmen, *n*; (**mark of honour**), hŏnor, *m,* dĕcus, *n*
distinctive, prŏprĭus
distinguish, *v.t,* distinguo (3); *v.i,* (— **oneself**), clāresco (3), ēmĭnĕo (2)
distinguished, insignis, clārus
distort, *v.t,* dētorquĕo (2)
distortion, distortĭo, *f*
distract, *v.t,* distrăho (3)
distracted (**mentally**), āmens, turbātus
distraction (**mental**), āmentĭa, *f*
distress, mĭsĕrĭa, *f,* dŏlor, *m*
distress, *v.t,* sollĭcĭto (1)
distressed, sollĭcĭtus
distribute, *v.t,* distrĭbŭo (3), partĭor (4 *dep*)
distribution, partītĭo, *f*
district, rĕgĭo, *f*
distrust, *nn,* diffīdentĭa, *f*
distrust, *v.t,* diffīdo (3) (*with dat*)
distrustful, diffīdens
disturb, *v.t,* turbo (1)
disturbance, mōtus, *m,* tŭmultus, *m*
disunion, discordĭa, *f*
disunite, *v.t,* sēiungo (3), dissŏcĭo (1)
disused, dēsuētus
ditch, fossa, *f*
ditty, carmen, *n*
divan, lectŭlus, *m*
dive, *v.i,* sē mergĕre (3 *reflex*)
diver, ūrīnātor, *m*
diverge, *v.i,* discēdo (3)
divergence, dēclīnātĭo, *f*

diverse, ălĭus, dīversus

diversion, dērīvātĭo, f; (of thought, etc.), āvŏcātĭo, f

divert, v.t, āverto (3), āvŏco (1); (amuse), oblecto (1), prōlecto (1)

divide, v.t, dīvĭdo (3); (share out), partĭor (4 dep); v.i, sē dīvĭdĕre (3 reflex)

divine, dīvīnus

divine, v.t, dīvīno (1), augŭror (1 dep)

diviner, augur, m

divinity, dīvīnĭtas, f

divisible, dīvĭdŭus

division (act of —), dīvīsĭo, f; (a section), pars, f; (discord), discĭdĭum, n

divorce, dīvortĭum, n

divorce, v.i, dīvortĭum făcĭo (3), cum (and abl)

divulge, v.t, pătĕfăcĭo (3), ăpĕrĭo (4)

dizziness, vertīgo, f

dizzy, vertīgĭnōsus

do, v.t, făcĭo (3), ăgo (3); (to be satisfactory), v.i, sătĭs esse; (— away with), ăbŏlĕo (2); (— without), cărĕo (2) (with abl)

docile, făcĭlis, dŏcĭlis

dock, nāvālĭa, n.pl

doctor, mĕdĭcus, m

doctor, v.t, cūro (1)

doctrine, dogma, n, rătĭo, f

document, tăbŭla, f, littĕrae, f. pl

dodge, dŏlus, m

dodge, v.t, (elude), ēlūdo (3)

doe, cerva, f

dog, cănis, c

dog, v.t, insĕquor (3 dep.)

dogged (stubborn), pertĭnax, pervĭcax

dogged (by ill-luck, etc.), ăgĭtātus

dogma, dogma, n

dogmatic, arrŏgans

dole (small allowance), dĭurna, n.pl

dole out, v.t, dīvĭdo (3)

doleful, tristis, maestus

dolefulness, tristĭtĭa, f

doll, pūpa, f

dolphin, delphīnus, m

dolt, caudex, m

dome, thŏlus, m

domestic, dŏmestĭcus, fămĭlĭāris; (animals) villātĭcus

domestic, nn, (servant), fămŭlus, m

domicile, dŏmĭcĭlĭum, n

dominant, pŏtens

dominate, v.t, dŏmĭnor (1 dep)

domination, dŏmĭnātus, m

domineering, impĕrĭōsus

dominion, impĕrĭum, n, regnum, n

donation, dōnum, n

donkey, ăsĭnus, m

doom, fātum, n

doom, v.t, damno (1)

door, iānŭa, f; (out of -s), adv, fŏrīs

doorkeeper, iānĭtor, m

doorpost, postis, f

dormitory, cŭbĭcŭlum, n

dormouse, glīs, m

dot, nn, punctum, n

dotage, sēnĭum, n

dotard, sĕnex, m

dote upon, v.i, dĕpĕrĕo (4)

double, adj, dŭplex, gĕmĭnus

double, v.t, dŭplĭco (1); v.i, dŭplex fīo (irreg), ingĕmĭno (1)

double-dealing, nn, fraus, f

double-faced fallax

doubt, v.i, dŭbĭto (1)

doubt, nn, dŭbĭum, n, dŭbĭtātĭo,

doubtful, dŭbĭus, incertus

doubtless, adv, sīne dŭbĭo, nīmīrum

dough, fărīna, f

dove, cŏlumba, f

dove-coloured, cŏlumbīnus

dove-cot, cŏlumbārĭum, n

dowager, vĭdŭa, f

down, prep, dē (with abl); adv, use dē in a compound verb, e.g. run down, dēcurro (3)

down, nn (feathers, etc.), plūma, f; down, v.t, (put down), dēpōno (3)

downcast, dēiectus, dēmissus

downfall, occāsus, m, rŭīna, f

down-hearted, adv, dēmisso ănĭmo

downpour, imber, m

downright, dīrectus; (sheer), mĕrus

downward, adj, dēclīvis

downwards, adv, dĕorsum

downy, adj, plūmĕus

dowry, dos, f

doze, v.i, dormīto (1)

dozen (twelve), dŭŏdĕcim

dozing, adj, somnĭcŭlōsus

drab, cĭnĕrĕus (ash-coloured)

drag, v.t, trăho (3)

dragon, drăco, m

drain, nn, clŏāca, f, fossa, f

drain, v.t, (land), sicco (1); (a drink), haurĭo (4)

dram, cўăthus, m

drama, fābŭla, f, scēna, f

dramatic (theatrical), scēnĭcus

dramatist, pŏēta, m

drapery, vēlāmen, n

draught (of air), spīrĭtus, m; (water, etc.) haustus, m; (game of -s), lătruncŭli, m, pl

draw, v.t (pull), trăho (3); (portray), dēscrībo (3); (— a sword), glădĭum stringo (3); (— aside), sēdūco (3); (— water, etc.), haurĭo (4); v.i (—

back), pĕdem rĕfĕro (*irreg*); (— lots), sortes dūco (3); (— up troops, etc.), *v.t*, instrŭo (3)

drawback, *nn*, incommŏdum, *n*

drawbridge, pontĭcŭlus, *m*

drawing (picture), pictūra, *f*

drawl, *v.i*, lentē prōnuntĭo (1) (pronounce slowly)

dray, plaustrum, *n*

dread, *nn*, formīdo, *f*, păvor, *m*

dread, *v.t*, tĭmĕo (2), formīdo (1)

dreadful, terrĭbĭlis, ătrox

dream, *nn*, somnĭum, *n*

dream, *v.t*, somnĭo (1)

dreamy, somnĭcŭlōsus

dreary, tristis

dregs, faex, *f*

drench, *v.t*, mădĕfăcĭo (3)

dress, *nn*, vestis, *f*, hăbĭtus, *m*

dress, *v.t*, (clothe), vestĭo (4); (— a wound), cūro (1) (care for)

dressing, *nn*, (of wound), fōmentum, *n*

drift, *nn*, (heap), agger, *m*; (tendency), *use phr. with* quŏrsus (to what end?)

drift, *v.i*, dēfĕror (*irreg. pass*)

drill (military), exercĭtātĭo, *f*; (tool), tĕrēbra, *f*

drill, *v.t* (pierce), tĕrēbro (1); (train), exercĕo (2)

drink, *v.t*, bĭbo (3), pōto (1)

drink, *nn*, pōtĭo, *f*

drinker, pōtātor, *m*

drinking, pōtĭo, *f*; (— party), cōmissātĭo, *f*

drip, *v.i*, stillo (1)

dripping, *adj*, mădĭdus

drive, *nn* gestātĭo, *f*

drive, *v.t*, ăgo (3); (— away), fŭgo (1) pello (3); (— back), rĕpello (3); (— out), expello (3)

drive, *v.i*, (on horse-back, etc.), vĕhor (3 *pass*)

drivel ĭneptĭae, *f*, *pl*

drivel, *v.i*, dēlīro (1)

driver, aurīga, *c*

drizzle, *v.i*, rōro (1)

droll, rīdĭcŭlus, lĕpĭdus

drollery, făcētĭae, *f*. *pl*

dromedary, drŏmas, *m*

drone, *nn*, (bee), fūcus, *m*; (sound), murmur, *n*

drone, *v.i*, murmŭro (1)

droop, *v.i*, pendĕo (2), languesco (3)

drooping, *adj*, pendŭlus; (of spirits, etc.), dēmissus

drop, *nn*, gutta, *f*

drop, *v.t*, dēmitto (3); (leave off), omitto (3); *v.i*, cădo (3)

dropsy, hydrops, *m*

drought, siccĭtas, *f*

drove (flock), grex, *m*

drown, *v.t*, submergo (3); (of noise) obstrĕpo (3)

drowsy, somnĭcŭlōsus

drudge, *nn*, servus, *m*

drudge, *v.i*, servĭo (4); (weary oneself), *v.i*, sē fătīgāre (1 *reflex*)

drudgery, lăbor servīlis (servile labour)

drug, *nn*, mĕdĭcāmentum, *n*

drug, *v.t*, mĕdĭco (1)

drum, tympănum, *n*

drunk, *adj*, ēbrĭus

drunkenness, ēbrĭĕtas, *f*

dry, siccus, ārĭdus; (thirsty), sĭtĭens

dry (up), *v.t*, sicco (1); *v.i*, āresco (3)

dryness, siccĭtas, *f*, ārĭdĭtas, *f*

dubious, dŭbĭus

duck, *nn*, ănas, *f*

duck, *v.t*, mergo (3)

duckling, ănătĭcŭla, *f*

duct, fŏrāmen, *n*

due, *adj*, (owed), dēbĭtus; (just), iustus; (suitable), ĭdōnĕus, aptus

due, *nn*, (a right), ius, *n*; (taxes), vectīgal, *n*, portōrĭum, *n*

duel, certāmen, *n*

dull (person), hĕbes, obtūsus; (colour), obscūrus; (blunt), hĕbes; (weather), subnūbĭlus

dullness (of mind), tardĭtas, *f*

duly, *adv*, (established by precedent), rītē

dumb, mūtus

dumbfound, *v.t*, obstŭpĕfăcĭo (3)

dump, *v.t*, cŏăcervo (1)

dun, fuscus

dunce, hŏmo stŭpĭdus

dung, stercus, *n*

dungeon, carcer, *m*

dupe, *nn*, hŏmo crēdŭlus

dupe, *v.t*, dēcĭpĭo (3)

duplicate, exemplum, *n*

duplicity, fallācĭa, *f*

durability, firmĭtas, *f*

durable, firmus

duration, spătĭum, *n*; (long —), dĭūturnĭtas, *f*

during, *prep*, per (*with acc*)

dusk, crĕpuscŭlum, *n*

dusky, fuscus, nĭger

dust, *nn*, pulvis, *m*

dust, *v.t*, dētergĕo (2)

duster, pēnĭcŭlus, *m*

dusty, pulvĕrŭlentus

dutiful, pĭus

dutifulness, pĭĕtas, *f*

duty (moral), offĭcĭum, *n*; (given), mūnus, *n*; (tax), vectīgal, *n*; (it is my —), *use vb*. dēbĕo (2) (ought)

For List of Abbreviations used, turn to pages 3, 4

dwarf, pŭmĭlĭo, *c*
dwarfish, pŭsillus
dwell, *v.i*, hăbĭto (1), incŏlo (3); (— **on a theme**), commŏror (1 *dep*), haerĕo (2) in (*with abl*)
dweller, incŏla, *c*
dwelling (place), dŏmĭcĭlĭum, *n*
dwindle, *v.i*, dēcresco (3)
dye, *nn*, fūcus, *m*
dye, *v.t*, tingo (3), infĭcĭo (3)
dyer, infector, *m*
dying, *adj*, mŏrĭens
dynasty, dŏmus, *f*
dysentery, dўsentĕrĭa, *f*
dyspeptic, crūdus

E

each, ūnusquisque; (— **of two**), ūterque; (**one** —), *use distributive num*, singŭli, bĭni
eager, cŭpĭdus, ăvĭdus (*with genit*)
eagerness, cŭpĭdĭtas, *f*, ăvĭdĭtas, *f*
eagle, ăquĭla, *f*
ear, auris, *f*; (— **of corn**), spīca, *f*
early, *adj*, (**in the morning**), mātūtīnus; (**of time, etc.**), mātūrus
early, *adv*, (**in the morning**), māne; (**in time, etc.**), mātūrē
earn, *v.t*, mĕrĕo (2), mĕrĕor (2 *dep*)
earnest, intentus, ācer
earnestly, *adv* intentē
earth (land), terra, *f*; (**ground**), sŏlum, *n*; (**globe**), orbis, (*m*) terrārum
earthenware, fictĭlĭa, *n.pl*
earthly, *adj*, (**terrestrial**) terrestris
earthquake, terrae mōtus, *m*, (**movement of the earth**)
earth-work, agger, *m*
ease, quĭes, *f*, ōtĭum, *n*
ease, *v.t*, (**lighten**), lĕvo (1), exŏnĕro (1)
easily, *adv*, făcĭlē
easiness, făcĭlĭtas, *f*
east, *nn*, ŏrĭens, *m*
eastern, *use genit. of* ŏrĭens (**east**)
eastward, *adv. phr*, ăd ŏrĭentem
easy, făcĭlis
eat, *v.t*, ĕdo (3); (— **away**), rōdo (3)
eatable, escŭlentus
eating-house, pŏpīna, *f*
eaves, prōtectum, *n*
eaves-dropper, auceps, *c*
ebb, *v.i*, rēcēdo (3)
ebb-tide, rĕcessus aestus (**receding of the tide**)
ebony, ĕbĕnus, *f*
eccentric (of persons), nŏvus
echo, *nn*, ĭmāgo, *f*, ĕcho, *f*

echo, *v.t*, rĕfĕro (*irreg*), rĕsŏno (1)
echoing, *adj*, rĕsŏnus
eclipse, *nn*, dēfectĭo, *f*
eclipse, *v.t*, obscūro (1)
economical, parcus, dīlĭgens
economy, parsĭmōnĭa, *f*, (**frugality**)
ecstasy, fŭror, *m*
ecstatic, fŭrens
eddy, vertex, *m*
edge (of knife, etc.), ăcĭes, *f*; (**margin**), margo, *c*, ōra, *f*
edible, escŭlentus
edict, ēdictum, *n*
edifice, aedĭfĭcĭum, *n*
edify, *v.t*, instĭtŭo (3)
edit, *v.t*, ēdo (3)
edition, ēdĭtĭo, *f*
educate, *v.t*, ēdŭco (1)
education, ēdŭcātĭo, *f*, doctrīna, *f*
eel, anguilla, *f*
efface, *v.t*, dēlĕo (2)
effect, *v.t*, effĭcĭo (3)
effect, *nn*, (**influence, impression**), vīs, *f*; (**result**), effectus, *m*; (**consequence**), ēventus, *m*; (**without** —), (*adv*), nēquĭquem
effective (impressive), grăvis; *or use phr. with* confĭcĭo (3) (**to bring to a conclusion**)
effectual, effĭcax
effeminate, effēmĭnātus
effervescence (of spirit, etc.), fervor, *m*
efficacy, vīs, *f*
efficiency, vīs, *f*
efficient, hăbĭlis, effĭcĭens
effigy, ĭmāgo, *f*
effort, ŏpĕra, *f*
effrontery, ōs, *n*
effulgent, fulgens
effusion, effūsĭo, *f*
egg, ōvum, *n*
egg on, *v.t*, incĭto (1)
egoism, ămor, (*m*) sŭi (**fondness of oneself**)
egoist, ămātor, (*m*) sŭi
egregious, insignis
egress, exĭtus, *m*
eight, octo; (— **each**), octōni; (— **times**), *adv*. octĭens; (— **hundred**) octingenti
eighteen, dŭŏdēvīgĭnti
eighteenth, dŭŏdēvīcensĭmus
eighth, octāvus
eightieth, octōgēsĭmus
eighty, octōginta
either, *pron*, altĕrŭter; *conj*, aut
either ... or, aut ... aut, vel ... vel

ejaculate, *v.t*, ēmitto (3)
ejaculation (cry), vox, *f*, clāmor, *m*
eject, *v.t*, ēĭcĭo (3)
eke out, *v.t*, parco (3) (*with dat*)
elaborate, *adj*, ēlăbōrātus
elaborate, *v.t*, ēlăbōro (1)
elapse, *v.i*, (of time), intercēdo (3)
elate, *v.t*, effĕro (*irreg*)
elated (joyful), laetus
elbow, cŭbĭtum, *n*
elder, *adj*, māior nātu (greater by birth)
elder-tree, sambūcus, *f*
elderly, *adj*, prōvectus aetāte (advanced in age)
elect, *v.t*, crĕo (1), dēlĭgo (3)
elect, *adj*, dēsignātus
election, ēlectĭo, *f*, cōmĭtĭa, *n.pl*
elector, suffrāgātor, *m*
elegance, ēlĕgantĭa, *f*, vĕnustas, *f*
elegant, ēlĕgans, vĕnustus
elegy, ĕlĕgīa, *f*
element, ĕlĕmentum, *n*, prīncĭpĭa, *n.pl*
elementary, prīmus, simplex
elephant, ĕlĕphantus, *m*
elevate, *v.t*, tollo (3)
elevated, ēdĭtus; (mind) ēlātus
elevation, altĭtūdo, *f*, ēlātĭo, *f*
eleven, undĕcim; (— each), undēni
eleventh, undĕcĭmus
elicit, *v.t*, ēlĭcĭo (3)
eligible, ĭdōnĕus, opportūnus
elk, alces, *f*
ell, ulna, *f*
elm, ulmus, *f*
elocution, prōnuntĭātĭo, *f*
elope, *v.i*, aufŭgĭo (3) (run away
eloquence, ēlŏquentĭa, *f*
eloquent, ēlŏquens, dĭsertus
else, *adj*, ălĭus
else, *adv*, ălĭter
elsewhere, *adv*, ălĭbĭ
elude, *v.t*, ēlūdo (3)
emaciate, *v.t*, attĕnŭo (1)
emaciated, măcer
emaciation, măcĭes, *f*
emanate, *v.i*, ēmāno (1)
emancipate, *v.t*, lībĕro (1), mănūmitto (3)
embalm, *v.t*, condĭo (4)
embankment, mōles, *f*
embark, *v.t*, in nāvem impōno (3); *v.i*, nāvem conscendo (3)
embarrass, *v.t*, (entangle), impĕdĭo (4); (confuse), turbo (1)
embarrassment, scrūpŭlus, *m*; (difficulty), diffĭcultas, *f*
embassy (delegation), lēgāti, *m. pl*, (ambassadors)
embedded, sĭtus

embellish, *v.t*, orno (1)
embellishment, ornāmentum, *n*
embers, cĭnis, *m*
embezzle, *v.t*, āverto (3), pĕcŭlor (1 *dep*)
embezzlement, pĕcŭlātus, *m*
embezzler, āversor, (*m*) pĕcūnĭae
embitter, *v.t*, exăcerbo (1)
emblem, insigne, *n*, indĭcĭum, *n*
embody, *v.t*, inclūdo (3)
embolden, *v.t*, confirmo (1)
embrace, *nn*, amplexus, *m*, complexus, *m*
embrace, *v.t*, amplector (3 *dep*), complector (3 *dep*); (— an opportunity), arrĭpĭo (3)
embroidered (clothing, etc.), pictus
embroil, *v.t*, (entangle), implĭco (1)
emerald, smăragdus, *c*
emerge, *v.i*, ēmergo (3), prōdĕo (4)
emergency, discrīmen, *n*, tempus, *n*
emigrate, *v.i*, mĭgro (1)
emigration, mĭgrātĭo, *f*
eminence (high ground), tŭmŭlus, *m*; (of rank, etc.), lŏcus amplissĭmus
eminent, ēgrĕgĭus, insignis
emissary, lēgātus, *m*
emit, *v.t*, ēmitto (3)
emolument, lŭcrum, *n*
emotion, mōtus, (*m*,) ănĭmi (movement of the mind)
emperor, impĕrātor, *m*, prĭnceps, *m*
emphasize, *v.t*, prĕmo (3)
emphatic, grăvis
empire, impĕrĭum, *n*
empirical, empīrĭcus
employ, *v.t*, ūtor (3 *dep*) (*with abl*)
employed (of persons), occŭpātus
employer, conductor, *m*
employment (occupation), quaestus, *m*; (business), nĕgōtĭum, *n*; (using) ūsurpātĭo, *f*
emporium, empŏrĭum, *n*
empower (someone to do . . .), *v.i*, pŏtestātem făcĭo (3) (*with dat. of person and genit. of gerund(ive)*)
empty, *adj*, văcŭus, ĭnānis
empty, *v.t*, exĭnānĭo (4)
emulate, *v.t*, aemŭlor (1 *dep*)
emulous, aemŭlus
enable, *v.t*, făcultātem do (1) (*with dat*)
enact, *v.t*, (law), sancĭo (4), constĭtŭo (3)
enactment lex, *f*
enamoured (to be — of somone), *v.t*, ămo (1)
encamp, *v.i*, castra pōno (3)
enchant, *v.t*, fascĭno (1), dēlecto (1)

enchantment (allurement), blandīmentum, *n*
encircle, *v.t,* circumdo (1)
enclose, *v.t,* inclūdo (3), saepĭo (4)
enclosure, saeptum, *n*
encounter, *v.t,* incĭdo (3) in (*with
  acc*); concurro (3), obvĭam ĕo (4)
  (*irreg*) (*with dat*)
encounter, *nn,* congressus, *m*
encourage, *v.t,* hortor (1 *dep*)
encouragement, hortātŭs, *m*; con-
  fīrmātĭo, *f,* hortātĭo, *f*
encroach upon, *v.t,* occŭpo (1)
encumber, *v.t,* ŏnĕro (1), impĕdĭo (4)
encumbrance, impĕdīmentum, *n*
end, fīnis, *m*; *or use* extrēmus, *adj,
  agreeing with a noun; e.g.* **at the
  end of the bridge,** in extrēmo ponte
end, *v.t,* confĭcĭo (3), fīnĭo (4); *v.i,
  use phr. with* extrēmum, *n,* (**end**);
  (**turn out, result**), cēdo (3), ēvĕnĭo
  (4)
endanger, *v.t,* in pĕrīcŭlum addūco
  (3)
endear, *v.t,* dēvincĭo (4)
endeavour, *nn,* cōnātŭs, *m*
endeavour, *v.t,* cōnor (1 *dep*)
endless, infīnītus, perpĕtŭus
endorse, *v.t,* confīrmo (1)
endow, *v.t,* dōno (1)
endowed, praedītus
endurable, tŏlĕrābĭlis
endurance, pătĭentĭa, *f*
endure, *v.t,* pătĭor (3 *dep*), fĕro
  (*irreg*); *v.i,* dūro (1)
enemy (public), hostis, *c*; (**private**),
  ĭnĭmīcus, *m*
energetic, ācer, strēnŭus, impĭger
energy, vis, *f,* vĭgor, *m*
enervate, *v.t,* ēnervo (1)
enervation, dēbĭlĭtātĭo, *f*
enfeeble, *v.t,* dēbĭlĭto (1)
enforce, *v.t,* (**carry out**), exsĕquor
  (3 *dep*)
enfranchise, *v.t,* (**give the right of
  voting**), suffrāgĭum do (1) (*with dat*)
enfranchisement, cīvĭtātĭs dōnātĭo, *f,*
  (**granting of citizenship**)
engage, *v.t,* (**join**) iungo (3); (**hire**),
  condūco (3); (**— in battle**), signa
  conferre (*irreg*); (**enter into**), ingrĕdĭor (3 *dep*)
engaged, occŭpātus; (**betrothed**),
  sponsus
engagement (battle), proelĭum, *n*;
  (**agreement**), pactum, *n*; (**promise**),
  sponsĭo, *f*
engender, *v.t,* gĭgno (3), părĭo (3)
engine, māchĭna, *f*; (**military —**),
  tormentum, *n*

engineer, făber, *m*
England, Brĭtannĭa, *f*
English, Brĭtannus, Brĭtannĭcus
engrave, *v.t,* scalpo (3)
engraver, scalptor, *m*
engraving, *nn,* scalptūra, *f*
engross, *v.t,* occŭpo (1)
enhance, *v.t,* augĕo (2), orno (1)
enigma, aenigma, *n,* ambāges, *f, pl*
enigmatic, ambĭgŭus
enjoin, *v.t,* iŭbĕo (2), mando (1)
enjoy, *v.t,* frŭor (3 *dep*) (*with abl*);
  (**possess**), ūtor (3 *dep*) (*with abl*)
enjoyment (pleasure), gaudĭum, *n,*
  lībīdo, *f*
enlarge, *v.t,* augĕo (2), amplĭfĭco (1)
enlargement, prōlātĭo, *f*
enlighten, *v.t,* (**instruct**), dŏcĕo (2)
enlist, *v.t,* (**troops**), conscrībo (3);
  (**bring over**), concĭlĭo (1); *v.i,*
  nōmen do (1) (**give one's name**)
enliven, *v.t,* excĭto (1)
enmity, ĭnĭmīcĭtĭa, *f*
ennoble, *v.t,* (**make honourable**),
  hŏnesto (1)
enormity, immānĭtas, *f*; (**crime**),
  scĕlus, *n*
enormous, ingens
enough, *nn. and adv,* sătĭs; (*foll. by
  genit*), *e.g.* **enough water,** sătĭs
  ăquae
enquire, *v.t,* quaero (3) ab (*with abl*)
enrage, *v.t,* irrīto (1), inflammo (1)
enrapture, *v.t,* oblecto (1)
enrich, *v.t,* lŏcŭplēto (1)
enroll, *v.t,* scrībo (3)
ensign, signum, *n*; (**— bearer**), signĭfer,
  m
enslave, *v.t,* servĭtūtem iniungo (3)
  (*with dat*)
ensue, *v.i,* sĕquor (3 *dep*)
entail, *v.t,* affĕro (*irreg*)
entangle, *v.t,* impĕdĭo (4)
enter, *v.i, and v.t,* intro (1), ingrĕdĭor
  (3 *dep*), ĭnĕo (4 *irreg*); *v.t,* (**— write
  in**), inscrībo (3)
enterprise (undertaking), inceptum, *n*
enterprising, promptus, strēnŭus
entertain, *v.t,* (**people**), excĭpĭo (3)
  (**receive**); (**amuse**), oblecto (1); (**an
  idea, etc.**) hăbĕo (2)
entertainment (of guests), hospĭtĭum,
  n
enthusiasm, stŭdĭum, *n,* fervor, *m*
enthusiastic, fănātĭcus, stŭdĭōsus
entice, *v.t,* illĭcĭo (3)
entire, tōtus, intĕger
entirely, *adv,* omnīno
entitle, *v.t,* (**give the right to**), ius do
  (1) (*with dat*); (**name**), inscrībo (3)

entitled (to be — to), *v.i*, ius hăbĕo (2)

entrails, viscĕra, *n.pl*

entrance (act of —), ingressĭo, *f*; (door, etc), ădĭtus, *m*, ostĭum, *n*

entreat, *v.t*, obsĕcro (1), ōro (1)

entreaty, obsĕcrātĭo, *f*

entrust, *v.t*, crēdo (3) (*with dat*) committo (3) (*with dat*)

enumerate, *v.t*, nŭmĕro (1)

envelop, *v.t*, involvo (3)

envelope, *nn*, invŏlūcrum, *n*

enviable, fortūnātus

envious, invĭdus

envoy, lēgātus, *m*

envy, invĭdĭa, *f*

envy, *v.t*, invĭdĕo (2) (*with dat*)

ephemeral, brĕvis

epic, *adj*, ĕpĭcus

epidemic, pestĭlentĭa, *f*

epigram, ĕpĭgramma, *n*

epigrammatic, ĕpĭgrammătĭcus, a, um, *adj*

epilepsy, morbus cŏmĭtĭālis, *m*

episode (digression), excursus, *m*; res, *f*

epitaph, ĕlŏgĭum, *n*

epoch, aetas, *f*

equable. aequus

equal, *adj*, aequus, păr

equal, *nn*, use *adj*, păr

equal, *v.i and v.t*, aequo (1)

equality, aequālĭtas, *f*

equanimity, aequus ănĭmus, *m*

equator, aequĭnoctĭālis circŭlus, *m*

equestrian, ĕquester

equilibrium, aequĭlībrĭum, *n*

equinox, aequĭnoctĭum, *n*

equip, *v.t*, orno (1), armo (1)

equipment, arma, *n.pl*, armāmenta, *n.pl*

equitable, aequus

equity, aequĭtas, *f*; (justice), iustĭtĭa, *f*

equivalent, *adj*, (equal), păr; (to be —), *v.i*, use vălĕo (2) (to be worth) tanti

equivocal, ambĭgŭus

era, tempus, *n*, aetas, *f*.

eradicate, *v.t*, ēvello (3), exstirpo (1)

erase, *v.t*, dēlĕo (2)

ere (before), *conj*, prĭusquam

erect, *v.t*, ērĭgo (3); (build), exstrŭo (3)

erect, *adj*, rectus

erection (act of —), aedĭfĭcātĭo, *f*; (a building), aedĭfĭcĭum, *n*

err, *v.i*, erro (1), pecco (1)

errand, mandātum, *n*

erratic, văgus

erroneous, falsus

error, error, *m*

erudite, doctus

eruption, ērŭptĭo, *f*

escape, *nn*, fŭga, *f*

escape, *v.i*, *and v.t*, effŭgĭo (3), ēlābor (3 *dep*)

escarpment, praeruptus lŏcus, *m*

escort, *nn*, comĭtātus, *m*; (protective), praesĭdĭum, *n*

escort, *v.t*, cŏmĭtor (1 *dep*)

especial, praecĭpŭus

especially, *adv*, praecĭpŭē

espouse, *v.t*, (betroth), spondĕo (2); (marry), dūco (3), nūbo (3)

essay (attempt), cōnātus, *m*; (composition), lĭbellus, *m*

essence (nature), nātūra, *f*, vīs, *f*

essential (necessary), nĕcessārĭus

establish, *v.t*, constĭtŭo (3), confirmo (1)

establishment, constĭtūtĭo, *f*

estate (property), rēs, *f*, fundus, *m*

esteem, *nn*, existĭmātĭo, *f*

esteem, *v.t*, (think), aestĭmo (1), pŭto (1); (think highly of), magni aestĭmo (1)

estimable, laudātus

estimate, *nn*, aestĭmātĭo, *f*

estimate, *v.t*, aestĭmo (1)

estimation (opinion), ŏpĭnĭo, *f*

estrange, *v.t*, ălĭēno (1)

estrangement, ălĭēnātĭo, *f*

estuary, aestŭārĭum, *n*

eternal, aeternus

eternally, *adv. phr*, in aeternum

eternity, aeternĭtas, *f*

ether, aether, *m*

ethereal, aethĕrĭus

ethical (moral), mōrālis

eulogy, laudātĭo, *f*

evacuate, *v.t*, (— troops from a place), dēdūco (3); *v.i*, (depart from), excēdo (3), ex (*with abl*)

evade, *v.t*, ēlūdo (3)

evaporate, *v.i*, discŭtĭor (3 *pass*)

evasion, lătĕbra, *f*

evasive, ambĭgŭus

eve (evening), vesper, *m*

even, *adv*, ĕtĭam, *often use emphatic pron, e.g.* even Caesar, Caesar ipse; (not —), nĕ . . . quĭdem

even, *adj*, (level, equable), aequus; (— number), păr

even if, *conj*, etsi

evening, vesper, *m*, (in the —), sub vespĕrum

event (occurrence), rēs, *f*; (outcome), exĭtus, *m*

eventually, *adv*, ălĭquando

ever, *adv*, (at any time), umquam; (always), semper; (if —), si quando

evergreen, *adj*, semper vĭrĭdis

everlasting, aeternus

For List of Abbreviations used, turn to pages 3, 4

every (all), omnis; **(each)**, quisque;
(— day), *adv*, cottīdĭē; (— one),
omnes, *m.pl*; (— thing), omnĭa,
n.pl; (— where), *adv*, ŭbīque
evict, *v.t*, expello (3)
evidence, testĭmōnĭum, *n*; **(factual)**,
argūmentum, *n*
evident, mănĭfestus, perspĭcŭus; **(it
is —)**, appāret (2 *impers*)
evil, *adj*, mălus, prāvus
evil, *nn*, mălum, *n*
evil-doer, hŏmo nĕfārĭus
evoke, *v.t*, ēvŏco (1)
evolve, *v.t*, ēvolvo (3)
ewe, ŏvis, *f*
exact, *adj*, **(number, etc.)**, exactus;
(persons), dīlĭgens
exact, *v.t*, exĭgo (3)
exactness, subtīlĭtas, *f*
exaggerate, *v.t*, augĕo (2)
exaggeration, sŭperlātĭo, *f*
exalt, *v.t*, tollo (3), augĕo (2)
exalted, celsus
examination (test, etc.), prŏbātĭo, *f*;
(enquiry), investīgātĭo, *f*
examine, *v.t*, investīgo (1), interrŏgo
(1); **(test)**, prŏbo (1)
example, exemplum, *n*; **(for —)**,
verbi causā
exasperate, *v.t*, exăcerbo (1)
excavate, *v.t*, căvo (1)
excavation (cavity), căvum, *n*
exceed, *v.t*, sŭpĕro (1), excēdo (3)
exceedingly, *adv*, admŏdum; *or use
superlative of adj*, e.g. (— large),
maxĭmus
excel, *v.t*, praesto (1) *(with dat)*
excellence, praestantĭa, *f*
excellent, praestans, ēgrĕgĭus
except, *prep*, praeter *(with acc)*
except, *v.t*, excĭpĭo (3)
exception (everyone, without —),
omnes ad ūnum; **(take — to)** aegre
fĕro *(irreg)*
exceptional, rārus, insignis
excess (over-indulgence), intempĕrantĭa, *f*
excessive, nĭmĭus
exchange, *nn*, permūtātĭo, *f*
exchange, *v.t*, permūto (1)
exchequer, aerārĭum, *n*
excitable, fervĭdus, fĕrox
excite, *v.t*, excĭto (1), incendo (3)
excited, commōtus, incensus
excitement, commōtĭo, *f*
exclaim, *v.i*, clāmo (1), conclāmo (1)
exclamation, exclāmātĭo, *f*
exclude, *v.t*, exclūdo (3)

exclusion, exclūsĭo, *f*
exclusive (one's own), prŏprĭus
excrescence, tūber, *n*
excruciating (pain, etc.), ācer
excursion, ĭter, *n*
excusable, excūsābĭlis
excuse, *nn*, excūsātĭo, *f*
excuse, *v.t*, excūso (1); **(pardon)**,
ignosco (3) *(with dat)*
execrable, nĕfārĭus
execrate, *v.t*, dētestor (1 *dep*)
execute, *v.t*, **(carry out)**, exsĕquor (3
dep); **(inflict capital punishment)**,
nĕco (1)
execution (carrying out), *use vb*
exsĕquor; **(capital punishment)**,
supplĭcĭum, *n*
executioner, carnĭfex, *m*
exemplary, ēgrĕgĭus
exempt, *v.t*, excĭpĭo (3)
exempt, *adj*, inmūnis
exemption, immūnĭtas, *f*
exercise, exercĭtātĭo, *f*; **(set task)**,
ŏpus, *n*
exercise, *v.t*, exercĕo (2)
exert, *v.t*, contendo (3), ūtor (3 *dep*)
(with abl); **(to — oneself)**, *v.i*,
nītor (3 *dep)*
exertion, contentĭo, *f*, lăbor, *m*
exhale, *v.t*, exhālo (1)
exhaust, *v.t*, exhaurĭo (4); **(weary)**,
confĭcĭo (3), dēfătīgo (1)
exhausted (tired out), confectus
exhaustion, vīrĭum dēfectĭo, *f*, **(failing
of strength)**
exhibit, *v.t*, expōno (3)
exhibition (spectacle), spectācŭlum,
n
exhilarate, *v.t*, hĭlăro (1)
exhilaration, hĭlărĭtas, *f*
exhort, *v.t*, hortor (1 *dep*)
exhume, *v.t*, ērŭo (3)
exile, *nn*, **(person)**, exsul, *c*; **(banishment)**, exsĭlĭum, *n*; **(to be in —)**,
v.i, exsŭlo (1)
exile, *v.t*, in exsĭlĭum pello (3)
(drive into exile)
exist, *v.i*, sum *(irreg)*, exsisto (3)
existence (life), vīta, *f*
exit, exĭtus, *m*
exonerate, *v.t*, lībĕro (1)
exorbitant, nĭmĭus
exotic, externus
expand, *v.t*, extendo (3); *v.i*, ex-
tendor (3 *pass)*
expanse, spătĭum, *n*
expatiate (on a theme, etc.), *v.*,
permulta dissĕro (3) dē *(with abl.)*

expatriate, *v.t,* ēĭcĭo (3)

expect, *v.t,* exspecto (1)

expectation, exspectātĭo, *f*

expediency, ūtĭlĭtas, *f*

expedient, *adj,* ūtĭlis

expedient, *nn,* rătĭo, *f*

expedite, *v.t,* expĕdĭo (4)

expedition (military, etc.), expĕdĭtĭo, *f*

expeditious, cĕler

expel, *v.t,* expello (3)

expend, *v.t,* expendo (3)

expenditure, ērŏgātĭo, *f*

expense, impensa, *f,* sumptus, *m*

expensive, sumptŭōsus, prĕtĭōsus

experience, ūsus, *m,* pĕrĭtĭa, *f*

experience, *v.t,* expĕrĭor (4 *dep*), pătĭor (3 *dep*)

experienced, pĕrītus

experiment, expĕrīmentum, *n*

expert, *adj,* scĭens

expiate, *v.t,* expĭo (1)

expiation, expĭātĭo, *f*

expiatory, pĭăcŭlāris

expiration (breathing out), exspīrātĭo, *f*; (time), *use partic.* confectus (completed)

expire, *v.i,* (persons), exspīro (1); (time), exĕo (4), conficĭo (3)

explain, *v.t,* explĭco (1), expōno (3)

explanation, explĭcātĭo, *f*

explicit, ăpertus

explode, *v.i,* dīrumpor (3 *pass*)

explore, *v.t,* explōro (1)

export, *v.t,* exporto (1)

exports, merces, *f, pl*

expose, *v.t,* expōno (3), dētĕgo (3), nūdo (1); (— to danger, etc.), offĕro (*irreg*)

exposition (statement), expŏsĭtĭo, *f*

expostulate, *v.i,* expostŭlo (1)

expound, *v.t,* explĭco (1), expōno (3)

express, *v.t,* exprĭmo (3); (— in-writing), dēscrĭbo (3)

expression (verbal), vox, *f,* verba, *n.pl;* (facial), vultus, *m*

expressive, *use phr,* multam vim hăbens (having much significance)

expulsion, exactĭo, *f*

expunge, *v.t,* dēlĕo (2)

exquisite, conquīsītus

extant (to be —), *v.i,* exsto (1)

extemporary, extempŏrālis

extemporize, *v.i,* sŭbĭta dīco (3)

extend, *v.t,* extendo (3), distendo (3); *v.i,* pătĕo (2); (— to), pertĭnĕo (2) ad (*with acc*)

extension (act of), porrectĭo, *f;* (of boundaries, etc.), prŏpāgātĭo, *f*

extensive, amplus

extent, spătĭum, *n*

extenuate, *v.t,* lĕvo (1), mītĭgo (1)

exterior, *adj,* externus

exterior, *nn,* spĕcĭes, *f*

exterminate, *v.t,* interfĭcĭo (3), dēlĕo (2)

extermination, internĕcĭo, *f*

external, externus

extinct, exstinctus

extinguish, *v.t,* exstinguo (3)

extirpate, *v.t,* exstirpo (1), excīdo (3)

extol, *v.t,* laudo (1)

extort, *v.t,* (by force), extorquĕo (2)

extortion, res rĕpĕtundae, *f. pl*

extra, *adv,* praetĕrĕā

extract, *nn,* (from a book, etc.), exceptĭo, *f*

extract, *v.t,* extrăho (3), ēvello (3)

extraction (pulling out), ēvulsĭo, *f*

extraordinary, extraordĭnārĭus, ĭnsŏlĭtus

extravagance, sumptus, *m,* luxŭrĭa, *f,* intempĕrantĭa, *f*

extravagant, immŏdĭcus, sumptŭōsus

extreme, *adj,* extrēmus, ultĭmus

extremity, extrēmum, *n;* (top), căcūmen, *n,* vertex, *m; or use adj,* extrēmus (extreme)

extricate, *v.t,* expĕdĭo (4), solvo (3)

exuberance, luxŭrĭa, *f*

exuberant, luxŭrĭōsus, effūsus

exude, *v.i,* māno (1)

exult, *v.i,* exsulto (1), laetor (1 *dep*)

exultant, laetus, ēlātus

eye, ŏcŭlus, *m;* (— lash), palpĕbrae pĭlus, *m;* (— lid), palpĕbra, *f;* (— sight), ăcĭes, *f;* (— witness), arbĭter, *m*

F

fable, fābŭla, *f*

fabric (woven), textum, *n;* (building), aedĭfĭcĭum, *n*

fabricate, *v.t,* fabrĭcor (1 *dep*)

fabrication mendācĭum, *n*

fabulous, fictus, falsus

face, făcĭes, *f,* vultus, *m,* ōs, *n*

face, *v.t* (confront), obvĭam ĕo (4) (*with dat*); (look towards), specto (1) ad (*with acc*)

facetious, făcētus

facilitate, *v.t,* făcĭlĭorem reddo (3) (make easier)

facility (possibility), făcultas, *f;* (dexterity), făcĭlĭtas, *f*

facing, *prep,* adversus (*with acc*)

fact, rēs, *f;* (in —, truly), *conj,* ĕnim; *adv,* vērō

faction, factĭo, *f*

factious, factĭōsus

factory, officīna, *f*

faculty, făcultas, *f*, vīs, *f*

fade, *v.i*, pallesco (3)

faggot, sarmenta, *n.pl*

fail, *v.i*, cădo (3), dēficĭo (3), dēsum (*irreg*) (*with dat*)

failing, *nn* (defect), vĭtĭum, *n*

failure (of supplies, **strength**, etc.), dēfectĭo, *f*, *otherwise use* irrĭtus (vain, **unsuccessful**)

faint, *v.i*, collābor (3 *dep*), languesco (3)

faint, *adj*, (exhausted), dēfessus

faint-hearted, tĭmĭdus, imbellis

faintness (of body), languor, *m*

fair, *nn*, (market), nundĭnae, *f*, *pl* (ninth day)

fair, *adj*, (beautiful), pulcher; (just), aequus; (colour), candĭdus; (weather), sērēnus; (wind, etc.), sĕcundus; (fairly good), mĕdĭŏcris

fairly, *adv*, (justly), iustē; (moderately), mĕdĭŏcrĭter

fairness (justice), aequĭtas, *f*; (of complexion, etc.), candor, *m*

faith, fīdes, *f*; (to keep —), *v.i*, fĭdem servo (1)

faithful, fīdēlis, fidus

faithfulness, fĭdēlĭtas, *f*

faithless, infīdus, perfĭdus

faithlessness, perfĭdĭa, *f*

falcon, falco, *m*

fall, *nn*, cāsus, *m*, rŭīna, *f*

fall, *v.i*, cădo (3); (— back) rĕcĭdo (3); (retreat), pĕdem rĕfĕro (*irreg*); (— headlong), praecĭpĭto (1); (— in love with), ădāmo (1); (— off), dēlābor (3 *dep*); (— out, happen), cădo (3); (— upon, attack), *v.t*, invādo (3)

fallacious, fallax, falsus

fallacy, vĭtĭum, *n*

falling off, *nn*, (revolt), dēfectĭo, *f*

fallow, nŏvālis, ĭnārātus

false, falsus; (not genuine), fictus; (person), perfĭdus

falsehood, mendācĭum, *n*

falsify, *v.t*, vĭtĭo (1)

falter, *v.i*, haerĕo (2), haesĭto (1)

faltering, *adj*, haesĭtans

fame, glōrĭa, *f*, fāma, *f*

familiar, nōtus, fămĭlĭāris; (usual), consŭētus, *f*

familiarity, fămĭlĭārĭtas, *f*

familiarize, *v.t*, consŭesco (3)

family, *nn*, fămĭlĭa, *f*, dŏmus, *f*, gens, *f*

family, *adj*, fămĭlĭāris, gentīlis

famine, fămes, *f*

famished, făme confectus (**exhausted from hunger**)

famous, clārus

fan, flābellum, *n*

fan, *v.t*, ventĭlo (1)

fanatical, fānātĭcus

fanaticism, sŭperstĭtĭo, *f*

fancied (imaginary), fictus

fancy, *nn*, (notion), ŏpīnĭo, *f*; (liking for), lĭbīdo, *f*

fancy, *v.t*, (imagine), fingo (3); (think), ŏpīnor (1 *dep*); (want) cŭpĭo (3)

fang, dens, *m*

far, *adv*, (of distance), prŏcul, longē; (as — as), *prep*, tĕnus; *with comparatives*, multō, *e.g.* **far bigger**, multō māior; (how —), quātĕnus; (— and wide), longē lātēque

far-fetched, quaesītus

farce, mīmus, *m*

farcical, mīmĭcus

fare (food), cĭbus, *m*; (charge), vectūra, *f*

farewell!, ăvē; (*pl*) ăvete; vălē, vălete; (to bid —), vălēre iŭbĕo (2)

farm, *nn*, fundus, *m*

farm, *v.t*, cŏlo (3)

farmer, agrĭcŏla, *m*, cŏlōnus, *m*

farming, agrĭcultūra, *f*

farther, *adj*, ultĕrĭor

farther, *adv*, longĭus

farthest, *adj*, ultĭmus

farthest, *adv*, longissĭme

fascinate, *v.t*, fascĭno (1)

fascination, fascĭnātĭo, *f*

fashion, *nn*, mōs, *m*

fashion, *v.t*, fingo (3)

fashionable, ēlĕgans

fast, *nn*, iēiūnĭum, *n*

fast, *v.i*, iēiūnus sum (*irreg*) (be hungry)

fast, *adj*, (quick), cĕler; (firm), firmus; (make —), *v.t*, firmo (1), dēlĭgo (1)

fast, *adv*, (quickly), cĕlĕrĭter; (firmly), firme

fasten, *v.t*, fīgo (3), dēlĭgo (1); (doors, etc.), obtūro (1)

fastening, *nn*, vincŭlum, *n*

fastidious, dēlĭcātus

fat, *adj*, pinguis

fat, *nn*, ădeps, *c*

fatal (deadly), pernĭcĭōsus

fatality, cāsus, *m*

fate, fātum, *n*

fated, fātālis

father, păter, *m*; (-in-law), sŏcer, *m*

fatherland, pătrĭa, *f*

fatherless, orbus

fathom, *nn*, ulna, *f*

fatigue, *nn*, dēfătĭgātĭo, *f*

fatigue, *v.t*, fătīgo (1)

fatigued, fătīgātus

fatten, *v.t*, săgīno (1)

fault, culpa, *f*, vĭtĭum, *n*

faultless, intĕger, perfectus

faulty, mendōsus, vĭtĭōsus

favour, *nn*, grātĭa, *f*, făvor, *m*, stŭdĭum, *n*; (a benefit), grātĭa, *f*, bĕnĕfĭcĭum, *n*

favour, *v.t*, făvĕo (2) (*with dat*)

favourable, commŏdus; (of wind), sēcundus

favourite, *nn*, dēlĭcĭae, *f. pl*

favourite, *adj*, grātus

fawn, *nn*, hinnŭlĕus, *m*

fawn upon, *v.t*, ădūlor (1 *dep*)

fear, *nn*, tĭmor, *m*, mĕtus, *m*

fear, *v.t*, tĭmĕo (2), mĕtŭo (3), vĕrĕor (2 *dep*)

fearful, *adj*, (afraid), tĭmĭdus; (terrible), terrĭbĭlis

fearless, intrĕpĭdus

fearlessness, audācĭa, *f*

feasible, *use phr. with vbs*, posse (to be able) *and* effĭcĕre (to bring about)

feast, *nn*, daps, *f*, ĕpŭlae, *f. pl*; (— day), dĭes festus, *m*

feast, *v.i*, ĕpŭlor (1 *dep*); *v.t*, pasco (3)

feat, făcĭnus, *n*

feather, penna, *f*, plūma, *f*

feature (of face, etc.), lĭnĕāmentum, *n*; (peculiarity) *use adj*, prŏprĭus, (one's own)

February, Fĕbrŭārĭus (mensis)

fecundity, fēcundĭtas, *f*

federal, foedĕrātus

fee, merces, *f*, hŏnor, *m*

feeble, infirmus, imbēcillus

feebleness, infirmĭtas, *f*

feed, *v.t*, pasco (3), ălo (3); *v.i*, vescor (3 *dep*), pascor (3 *dep*)

feel, *v.t*, sentĭo (4); (with the hands), tempto (1)

feeler, cornĭcŭlum, *n*

feeling, *nn*, (sensation or emotion), sensus, *m*, tactus, *m*; (spirit, etc.), ănĭmus, *m*

feign, *v.t*, sĭmŭlo (1)

feigned, sĭmŭlātus

feint, sĭmŭlātĭo, *f*

felicitous, fēlix

felicity, fēlĭcĭtas, *f*

fell, *v.t*, excīdo (3), sterno (3)

fellow (companion), cŏmĕs, *c*; (— citizen), cīvis, *c*; (— feeling), consensĭo, *f*; (— soldier), commīlĭto, *m*; (worthless —), nēbŭlo, *m*

fellowship (companionship), sŏcĭĕtas, *f*

felt, *nn*, cŏactum, *n*

female, *nn*, fēmĭna, *f*

female, *adj*, mŭlĭĕbris

fen, pălus, *f*

fence, *nn*, saeptum, *n*, cancelli, *m*, *pl*

fence, *v.t*, saepĭo (4); (with swords), *v.i*, bāttŭo (3)

fencing (art of —), ars, (*f*) glădĭi

ferment, *nn*, (excitement), aestus, *m*

ferment, *v.i*, fervĕo (2)

fern, fĭlix, *f*

ferocious, saevus, fĕrus

ferocity, saevĭtĭa, *f*

ferry, *nn*, trāĭectus, *m*; (— boat), cymba, *f*

ferry, *v.t*, trāĭcĭo (3)

fertile, fēcundus, fertĭlis

fertility, fēcundĭtas, *f*

fervent, ardens, fervĭdus

fervour, ardor, *m*, fervor, *m*

festival (holidays), fērĭae, *f. pl*; (religious —, etc.), sollemne, *n*

festive (gay), hĭlăris

festivity (gaiety), hĭlărĭtas, *f*

fetch, *v.t*, pĕto (3), affĕro (*irreg*)

fetter, *nn*, vincŭlum, *n*

fetter, *v.t*, vincŭla ĭnĭcĭo (3) (*with dat*)

feud (quarrel), sĭmultas, *f*

fever, fĕbris, *f*

feverish, fĕbrĭcŭlōsus; (excited) commōtus

few, *adj*, pauci (*pl*)

fewness, paucĭtas, *f*

fib, mendācĭum, *n*

fibre, fibra, *f*

fickle, inconstans

fickleness, inconstantĭa, *f*

fiction, commentum, *n*, făbŭla, *f*

fictitious, commentĭcĭus

fiddle (instrument), fĭdes, *f. pl*

fidelity, fĭdēlĭtas, *f*

fidgety, inquĭētus

field, ăger, *m*; (plain), campus, *m*; (— of battle), lŏcus, (*m*) pugnae; (scope), lŏcus, *m*

fiendish, nĕfandus

fierce, fĕrox, fĕrus

fierceness, fĕrōcĭtas, *f*

fiery (of temper, etc.), ardens

fifteen, quindĕcim; (— times), *adv*, quindĕcĭes

fifteenth, quintus dĕcĭmus

fifth, quintus

fiftieth, quinquāgēsĭmus

fifty, quinquāginta

fig, **fig-tree**, fĭcus, *f*

fight, *nn*, pugna, *f*

fight, *v.i*, pugno (1)

fighter, pugnātor, *m*

figurative, translātus

figure, fĭgūra, *f*, forma, *f*

FIG   196   **FLI**

For List of Abbreviations used, turn to pages 3, 4

figure, *v.t*, (imagine), fingo (3)

figured, sĭgillātus

filch, *v.t*, surrĭpĭo (3)

file (tool), scŏbīna, *f*; (rank), ordo, *m*

file, *v.t*, (wood, metal), līmo (1)

filial (dutiful, respectful), pĭus

fill, *v.t*, implĕo (2), complĕo (2); (a post, etc.), fungor (3 *dep*) (*with abl*)

fillet (for the hair), vitta, *f*

film, membrāna, *f*

filter, *v.t*, cōlo (1)

filth, caenum, *n*

filthy, sordĭdus, foedus

fin, pinna, *f*

final, ultĭmus

finally, *adv*, postrēmo, dēnĭque, tandem

finance (of the state), aerārĭum, *n*

find, *v.t*, invĕnĭo (4), rĕpĕrĭo (4); (— out); cognosco (3), compĕrĭo (4); (— fault with), culpo (1); accūso (1)

fine, *v.t*, multo (1)

fine, *nn*, multa, *f*

fine, *adj*, (of texture), subtīlis; (handsome, etc.), praeclārus; (weather), sĕrēnus

finery, mundĭtĭa, *f*

finger, dĭgĭtus, *m*; (fore —), index dĭgĭtus

finger, *v.t*, tango (3)

finish, *nn*, (perfection), perfectĭo, *f*

finish, *v.t*, confĭcĭo (3); (limit), fīnĭo (4)

finished (complete, perfect), perfectus

fir, fir-tree, ăbĭes, *f*

fire, ignis, *m*; (ardour), vīs, *f*, ardor, *m*; (to be on —), *v.i*, ardĕo (2); (to set on —), *v.t*, incendo (3)

fire, *v.t*, incendo (3); (missiles), cōnĭcĭo (3)

fire-brand, fax, *f*

fire-place, fŏcus, *m*

fire-wood, lignum, *n*

firm, firmus; (constant), constans; (to make —), *v.t*, confirmo (1)

first, *adj*, prīmus

first, *adv*, prīmum, prīmō

fish, *nn*, piscis, *m*

fish, *v.i*, piscor (1 *dep*)

fisherman, piscātor, *m*

fishing, *nn*, piscātus, *m*

fishing-boat, hŏrĭŏla, *f*

fishing-net, rēte, *n*

fishmonger, cētārĭus, *m*

fishpond, piscīna, *f*

fissure, rīma, *f*

fist, pugnus, *m*

fit (violent seizure), accessĭo, *f*, impĕtus, *m*

fit, fitted, aptus, ĭdōnĕus, accommŏdātus

fit, *v.t*, accommŏdo (1), apto (1); (— out), exorno (1)

five, quinque; (— each), quīni; (— times), *adv*, quinquĭes

five hundred, quingenti

fix, *v.t*, fīgo (3); (determine), stătŭo (3), constĭtŭo (3)

fixed, certus

flabby, flaccĭdus

flag, vexillum, *n*

flag, *v.i*, (become weak), languesco (3)

flagrant (clear), mănĭfestus; (heinous), nĕfandus

flail, pertīca, *f*

flame, *nn*, flamma, *f*

flame, *v.i*, flagro (1)

flame-coloured, flammĕus

flank (of army, etc.), lătus, *n*; (of animal), īlĭa, *n. pl*

flap (of dress, etc.), lăcĭnĭa, *f*

flare, *v.i*, flăgro (1)

flash, *nn*, fulgor, *m*

flash, *v.i*, fulgĕo (2)

flask, ampulla, *f*

flat, aequus, plānus

flatness, plānĭtĭes, *f*

flatter, *v.t*, ădūlor (1 *dep*)

flatterer, ădūlātor, *m*

flattering, ădūlans

flattery, ădūlātĭo, *f*

flaunt, *v.t*, iacto (1)

flavour, săpor, *m*

flaw, vitĭum, *n*

flawless, ēmendātus

flax, līnum, *n*

flaxen, *adj*, līnĕus

flea, pūlex, *m*

flee, *v.i*, (flee from, *v.t.*), fŭgĭo (3)

fleece, *nn*, vellus, *n*

fleece, *v.t*, (rob), spŏlĭo (1)

fleecy, lānĭger

fleet, *nn*, classis, *f*

fleet, *adj*, cĕler

fleeting, fŭgax

flesh, căro, *f*

flesh-coloured, fleshy, carnōsus

flexibility, făcĭlĭtas, *f*

flexible, flexĭbĭlis

flicker, *v.i*, trĕpĭdo (1), cŏrusco (1)

flickering, trĕpĭdans, trĕmŭlus

flight (flying), vŏlātus, *m*; (escape) fŭga, *f*

flighty, mōbĭlis, lĕvis

fling, *v.t*, cōnĭcĭo (3)

flint, sīlex, *m*

flippant, făcētus

flirt, *v.i*, blandĭor (4 *dep*)

flit, *v.i*, vŏlĭto (1); (— in, or upon), inno (1) (*with dat*)

float, *v.i*, năto (1); (in the air), vŏlĭto (1)

flock, grex, *m*, pĕcus, *n*

flock, *v.i*, conflŭo (3), concurro (3)

flog, *v.t*, verbĕro (1)

flogging, verbĕra, *n. pl*

flood, dīlŭvĭes, *f*, *n*

flood, *v.t*, ĭnundo (1)

floor, sŏlum, *n*; (upper —) contăbŭlātĭo, *f*

florid, flōrĭdus

flotilla, classis, *f*

flounder, *v.i*, vŏlūtor (1 *pass*)

flour, fărīna, *f*

flourish, *v.i*, flōrĕo (2); *v.t*, vĭbro (1)

flourishes (of style), călămistri, *m*, *pl*

flow, *nn*, cursus, *m*, fluxĭo, *f*; (of the tide), accessus, *m*

flow, *v.i*, flŭo (3); (— past), praeterflŭo (3); (— together), conflŭo (3); (trickle), māno (1)

flower, *nn*, flos, *m*

flower, *v.i*, flōrĕo (2)

flowing, flŭens; (hair), fūsus

fluctuate, *v.i*, iactor (1 *pass*); aestŭo (1)

fluctuation, mūtātĭo, *f*

fluency, vŏlūbĭlĭtas, *f*

fluent, vŏlūbĭlis

fluid, *nn*, hūmor, *m*, lĭquor, *m*

fluid, *adj*, lĭquĭdus

flurry concĭtātĭo, *f*

flush, *nn*, rŭbor, *m*

flush, *v.i*, ērŭbesco (3)

fluster, *v.i*, ăgĭto (1)

flute, tībĭa, *f*; (— player), tībīcen, *m*

flutter, *nn*, trĕpĭdātĭo, *f*

flutter, *v.i*, vŏlĭto (1), (in fear), trĕpĭdo (1)

flux (flow), fluctus, *m*, fluxus, *m*

fly, *nn*, musca, *f*

fly, *v.i*, vŏlo (1)

flying, *adj*, vŏlātĭlis, vŏlūcer

flying, *nn*, vŏlātus, *m*

foal, ĕquŭlĕus, *m*, pullus, *m*

foam, *nn*, spūma, *f*

foam, *v.i*, spūmo (1)

foaming, foamy, spūmōsus

fodder, pābŭlum, *n*

foe, hostis, *c*

fog, cālīgo, *f*

foggy, cālīgĭnōsus

foil (sword), rŭdis, *f*; (metal leaf), lāmĭna, *f*

foil, *v.t*, (parry a blow, delude), ēlūdo (3)

fold, *nn*, (of garment, etc.), sīnus, *m*

fold, *v.t*, plĭco (1)

folding-doors, valvae, *f. pl*

foliage, frons, *f*

folk (people), hŏmĭnes, *c. pl*

follow, *v.i. and v.t*, sĕquor (3 *dep*); sector (1 *dep*); (succeed), succēdo (3) (*with dat*)

follower (attendant), assectātor, *m*; or use *adj*, *e.g.* (—of Caesar) Caesărĭānus

following, sĕquens, proxĭmus, sĕcundus

folly, stultĭtĭa, *f*

foment, *v.t*, fŏvĕo (2); (— trouble, etc.), sollĭcĭto (1)

fond, ămans (*with genit*)

fondle, *v.t*, mulcĕo (2)

food, cĭbus, *m*; (fodder), pābŭlum, *n*

fool, hŏmo stultus; (to act the —), *v.i*, dēsĭpĭo (3)

fool, *v.t*, lūdo (3)

foolhardy, tĕmĕrārĭus

foolish, stultus

foot, pes, *m*; (on —), *adj*, pĕdester; (— in length), *adj*, pĕdālis; (bottom of), use *adj*, īmus, *in agreement with noun*, *e.g.* īma quercus (foot of an oak)

footing, stătus, *m*, *or use vb*, consisto (3), (to stand)

footman, pĕdĭsĕquus, *m*

footpath, sēmĭta, *f*

footprint, vestīgĭum, *n*

footsoldier, pĕdes, *m*

for, *prep*, (on behalf of), prō (*with abl*); (on account of), propter, ŏb (*with acc*); (during a certain time), use *acc*, *e.g.* for two hours, dŭas hōras, *or* per (*with acc*); (expressing purpose), use ad (*with acc.*)

for, *conj*, nam, namque; ĕnim (*second word in clause*); (because), quippe, quod

forage, *nn*, pābŭlum, *n*

forage, *v.i. and v.t*, pābŭlor (1 *dep*)

forbear, *v.i. and v.t*, parco (3)

forbearance, contĭnentĭa, *f*

forbid, *v.t*, vĕto (1)

force, *nn*, vīs, *f*; (military forces), cōpĭae, *f*, *pl*

force, *v.t*, (compel), cōgo (3); (break through), perrumpo (3)

forced (unnatural), quaesītus; (a — march), magnum ĭter *n*

forcible, forcibly, use *adv. phr*, per vim

ford, *nn*, vădum, *n*

ford, *v.i. and v.t*, vădo transĕo (4) (cross by a ford)

forearm, bracchĭum, *n*
forebode, *v.t*, praesagĭo (4), portendo (3)
foreboding, *nn*, praesensĭo, *f*
forecast, *v.t*, praevĭdĕo (2)
forefather, prŏāvus, *m*; (*pl*) māiŏres *m. pl*
forehead, frons, *f*
foreign, externus, pĕrĕgrīnus
foreigner, pĕrĕgrīnus, *m*
foreman, qui (servis) praeest (who is in charge of (slaves))
foremost, prīmus
forensic, fŏrensis
forerunner, praenuntĭus, *m*
foresee, *v.t*, prōvĭdĕo (2)
foresight, prōvĭdentĭa, *f*
forest, silva, *f*
foretell, *v.t*, praedīco (3)
forethought, prōvĭdentĭa, *f*
forewarn, *v.t*, praemŏnĕo (2)
forfeit, *nn*, poena, *f*
forfeit, *v.t*, āmitto (3)
forge, *nn*, fornax, *f*
forge, *v.t*, fābrĭcor (1 *dep*), excūdo (3); (strike counterfeit coins), nummos ădultĕrīnos cūdo (3); (documents), suppōno (3)
forgery *use phr*. subiectĭo falsārum littĕrārum (substitution of counterfeit letters)
forget, *v.t*, oblīviscor (3 *dep*) (*with genit*)
forgetful, immĕmor
forgetfulness, oblīvĭo, *f*
forgive, *v.t*, ignosco (3) (*with dat of person*)
forgiveness, vĕnĭa, *f*
fork, furca, *f*
forked, bĭfurcus
forlorn, destĭtūtus, perdĭtus
form, forma, *f*, fĭgūra, *f*
form, *v.t*, (shape), formo (1), fingo (3); (— a plan), ĭnĕo (4), căpĭo (3); (troops, etc.), instrŭo (3)
formality, rītus, *m*
formally, *adv*, rĭtĕ
formation, conformātĭo, *f*
former, prĭor, sŭpĕrĭor; (the — and the latter), ille . . . hic
formerly, *adv*, antĕā, ōlim
formidable, grăvis, mĕtŭendus
formula, formŭla, *f*
forsake, *v.t*, rĕlinquo (3), dēsĕro (3)
forswear, *v.t*, (renounce), abĭūro (1); (swear falsely), perĭūro (1)
fort, castellum, *n*
forth, *adv, use compound vb. with* e *or* ex, e.g. exĕo, go forth; (of time), inde
forthwith, *adv*, stătim, extemplo

fortification, mūnītĭo, *f*
fortify, *v.t*, mūnĭo (4)
fortitude, fortĭtūdo, *f*
fortuitous, fortūĭtus
fortunate, fēlix, fortūnātus
fortune, fortūna, *f*, (property, etc.), rēs, *f*, ŏpes, *f. pl*
fortune-teller, hărĭolŭs, *m*
forty, quădrāginta
forum, fŏrum, *n*
forward, forwards, *adv*, porro, prorsum, ante; *or use compound verb with* pro, e.g. prōdūco, (lead forward)
forward, *adj*, praecox
forward, *v.t*, (send on), perfĕro (*irreg*)
foster, *v.t*, nūtrĭo (4)
foster-brother, collactĕus, *m*; (— child), ălumnus, *m*; (— father), altor, *m*; (— mother), nūtrix, *f*; (— sister), collactĕa, *f*
foul, *adj*, foedus
found, *v.t*, condo (3); (metal), fundo (3)
foundation, fundāmenta, *n, pl*
founder, condĭtor, *m*
founder, *v.i*, submergor (3 *pass*)
fountain, fons, *m*
four, quattŭor; (— times), *adv*, quătĕr; (— each), quăterni
fourteen, quattŭordĕcim; (-teenth), quartus dĕcĭmus
fourth, quartus; (— part, quarter), quădrans, *m*
fowl, ăvis, *f* gallīna, *f*
fowler, auceps, *c*
fox, vulpes, *f*
fraction (part) pars, *f*
fractious, diffĭcĭlis
fracture, *nn*, fractūra, *f*
fracture, *v.t*, frango (3)
fragile, frăgĭlis
fragment, fragmentum, *n*
fragrance, dulcis ŏdŏr, *m*, (pleasant smell)
fragrant, dulcis, suāvis
frail, frăgĭlis, dēbĭlis
frailty, frăgĭlĭtas, *f*, dēbĭlĭtas
frame, forma, *f*, compāges, *f*; (— of mind), ănĭmus, *m*, affectĭo, *f*
frame, *v.t*, (shape), fābrĭcor (1 *dep*), fingo (3); (form), compōno (3)
franchise (citizenship), cīvĭtas, *f*; (right of voting), suffrāgĭum, *n*
frank, lĭber, ăpertus
frantic, āmens
fraternal, frāternus
fraternity (association of men), sŏdālĭtas, *f*
fratricide (the person), frātrĭcīda, *m*; (the crime), fraternum parrĭcīdĭum, *n*

fraud, fraus, *f*, dŏlus, *m*
fraudulent, fraudŭlentus, dŏlōsus
fraught, opplētus (filled)
fray, certāmen, *n*, pugna, *f*
freak, (prodigy), prōdĭgĭum, *n*
freckle, lentīgo, *f*
free, līber; (generous), līberālis; (of one's will), sua sponte
free, *v.t.* lībēro (1), solvo (3)
free-born, ingĕnŭus
freedman, lībertus, *m*
freedom, lībertas, *f*; (— from a burden, tax, etc.), immūnĭtas, *f*
freehold, *nn*, praedĭum lībĕrum, *n*, (free estate)
freely, *adv.* lībĕrē; (generously), mūnĭfĭcē, largē; (of one's own free will), sŭā sponte
free-will, vŏluntas, *f*
freeze, *v.t.* glăcĭo (1); *v.i.* congĕlo (1)
freight, *nn*, ŏnus, *n*
freight, *adj.* ŏnustus
French, *adj.* Gallĭcus; (The French), Gallī, *pl*
frenzied, fŭrens, āmens
frenzy, fŭror, *m*, āmentĭa, *f*
frequent, *adj.* crēber, frĕquens
frequent, *v.t.* cĕlĕbro (1)
frequently, *adv.* saepe
fresh (new), rĕcens, nŏvus; (wind), vĕhĕmens
freshen, *v.t.* rĕcrĕo (1); *v.i.* (of wind), incrēbresco (3)
freshness, vĭrĭdĭtas, *f*
fret, *v.i.* dŏlĕo (2)
fretful, mōrōsus
fretfulness, mōrōsĭtas, *f*
friction, trītus, *m*
friend, ămīcus, *m*
friendless, ĭnops, ămīcōrŭm (destitute of friends)
friendliness, cōmĭtas, *f*
friendly, ămīcus, cōmis
friendship, ămīcĭtĭa, *f*
fright, terror, *m*, păvor, *m*; (to take —), *v.i.* păvesco (3)
frighten, *v.t.* terrĕo (2)
frightful, terrĭbĭlis, horrĭbĭlis
frigid, frĭgĭdus
frill, segmenta, *n.pl*
fringe, fimbrĭae, *f. pl*
frippery, nūgae, *f. pl*
frisk, *v.i.* lascīvĭo (4)
fritter away, *v.t.* dissĭpo (1)
frivolity, lĕvĭtas, *f*
frivolous, lĕvis; (opinion, etc.), fŭtĭlis
fro (to and —), *adv. phr*, hūc et illūc
frock, stŏla, *f*
frog, rāna, *f*
frolic, *nn*, lūdus, *m*

frolic, *v.i.* lūdo (3)
from, ā, ab, dē, ē, ex (all with abl) (with expressions of place, time and cause)
front, *nn*, frons, *f*, prĭor pars; (in —) ā fronte, *or use adj*, adversus; (in — of) *prep*, prō (with abl)
front, *adj.*, prĭor
frontage, frons, *f*
frontier, fīnis, *m*
frost, gĕlu, *n*; (— bitten), *adj.*, ambustus
frosty, gĕlĭdus
froth, *nn*, spūma, *f*
froth, *v.i.* spūmo (1)
frown, *nn*, contractĭo, (*f*) frontis (contraction of the forehead)
frown, *v.i.* frontem contrăho (3)
frowsy, incultus
frozen, rĭgĭdus, glăcĭālis
fructify, *v.t.* fēcundo (1)
frugal, frūgi, *indecl*
frugality, parsĭmōnĭa, *f*
fruit, fructus, *m*, pōmum, *n*
fruitful, fēcundus
fruitfulness, fēcundĭtas, *f*
fruition, fructus, *m*
fruitless (without result), irrĭtus
fruit-tree, pōmum, *n*, pōmus, *f*
frustrate, *v.t.* (an undertaking, etc.), ad vānum rĕdĭgo (3)
frustrated (to be —), *v.i.* frustrā esse
frustration, frustrātĭo, *f*
fry, *v.t.* frīgo (3)
frying-pan, sartāgo, *f*
fuel, ligna, *n. pl*
fugitive, *nn*, prŏfŭgus, *m*, fŭgĭtīvus, *m*
fugitive, *adj.* fŭgĭtīvus
fulfil, *v.t.* explĕo (2), exsĕquor (3 *dep*), fungor (3 *dep*) (with abl)
full, plēnus, replētus; (with people), frĕquens, crēber
full-grown, ădultus
fulminate, *v.i.* fulmĭno (1), intŏno (1)
fulness (abundance), ūbertas, *f*
fulsome, pūtĭdus
fumble, *v.t.* (handle), tento (1)
fume, *nn*, hālĭtus, *m*
fume, *v.i.* (with anger, etc.), fŭro (3)
fumigate, *v.t.* suffĭo (4)
fun, iŏcus, *m*, lūdus, *m*
function, offĭcĭum, *n*, mūnus, *n*
fund (of knowledge, etc.), cōpĭa, *f*, with nn . in genit.
fundamental, prīmus
funeral, fūnus, *n*, exsĕquĭae, *f*, *pl*
funeral, funereal, *adj.* fūnĕbris
fungus, fungus, *m*
funnel, infundĭbŭlum, *n*
funny, rĭdĭcŭlus

For List of Abbreviations used, turn to pages 3, 4

fur, pĭlus, *m*

furbish, *v.t,* interpŏlo (1)

furious, fŭrens, saevus; (to be —), *v.i,* saevĭo (4), fŭro (3)

furl, *v.t,* contrăho (3), lĕgo (3), sub-dūco (3)

furlough, commēātus, *m*

furnace, fornax, *f*

furnish, *v.t,* suppĕdĭto (1), orno (1)

furniture, sŭpellex, *f*

furrow, *nn,* sulcus, *m*

furrow, *v.t,* sulco (1)

further, *adj,* ultĕrĭor; *adv,* ultĕrĭus

further, *v.t,* (help), adiŭvo (1)

furthermore, *adv,* porro, praetĕrĕa

furthest, *adj,* ultĭmus

furtive, furtĭvus

fury, fŭror, *m*

fuse, *v.t,* (melt), lĭquĕfăcĭo (3); (— to-gether), miscĕo (2)

fuss, *nn,* perturbātĭo, *f*

fussy, nĭmis stŭdĭōsus

fusty, mŭcĭdus

futile, vānus, fūtĭlis

futility, fūtĭlĭtas, *f*

future, *adj,* fŭtūrus

future, *nn,* fŭtūra, *n.pl;* (in —), *adv,* in rĕlĭquum tempus

futurity, tempus fŭtūrum, *n*

G

gabble, *v.i,* blătĕro (1)

gabbler, blătĕro, *m*

gable, fastīgĭum, *n*

gad about, *v.i,* văgor (1 *dep*)

gadfly, tăbānus, *m*

gag, *v.t,* ōs obvolvo (3) *(with dat)* (muffle the mouth)

gage, pignus, *n*

gaiety, hĭlărĭtas, *f*

gaily, *adv,* hĭlăre

gain, *nn,* lŭcrum, *n,* quaestus, *m*

gain, *v.t,* (profit, etc.), lŭcror (1 *dep*); (obtain), consĕquor (3 *dep*), pŏtĭor (4 *dep*) *(with abl);* (— a victory), victōrĭam rĕporto (1) *or* părĭo (3)

gainsay, *v.t,* contrā dīco (3)

gait, incessus, *m*

gaiters, ŏcrĕae, *f. pl*

galaxy, *use* vĭa lactĕa, *f.* (milky way)

gale, ventus, *m,* prŏcella, *f*

gall, *nn,* fel, *n*

gall, *v.t,* (chafe), ūro (3); (annoy), sollĭcĭto (1); *or* pĭget (2 *impers*) (it irks)

gallant, fortis

gallant, *nn,* (lover), ămātor, *m*

gallantry, virtus, *f*

gallery, portĭcus, *f*

galley (ship), nāvis, *f*

galling, mordax

gallon, congĭus, *m*

gallop, *v.i,* ĕquo cĭtāto vĕhi (3 *pass*) (to be carried by a swift horse)

gallows, furca, *f,* crux, *f*

gamble, *v.i,* ălĕa lūdo (3) (play with dice)

gambler, ālĕātor, *m*

gambling, *nn,* ălĕa, *f*

gambol, *v.i,* lascĭvĭo (4),

game, lūdus, *m;* (wild beasts), fĕrae, *f. pl*

gamester, ālĕātor, *m*

gammon, perna, *f*

gander, anser, *m*

gang, grex, *m,* căterva, *f*

gangrene, gangraena, *f*

gangway, fŏrus, *m*

gaol, carcer, *m*

gaoler, custos, *m*

gap, lăcūna, *f,* hĭātus, *m*

gape, *v.i,* hĭo (1)

gaping, *adj,* hĭans

garb, vestītus, *m*

garbage, quisquĭlĭae, *f, pl*

garden, hortus, *m*

gardening, cūra, (*f*) hortōrum (care of gardens)

gargle, *v.i,* gargărĭzo (1)

garland, serta, *n.pl*

garlic, ālĭum, *n*

garment, vestīmentum, *n*

garner, *v.t,* (store), condo (3)

garnish, *v.t,* dĕcŏro (1)

garret, cēnācŭlum, *n*

garrison, praesĭdĭum, *n*

garrison, *v.t,* praesĭdĭum collŏco (1) in *(with abl)*

garrulity, lŏquācĭtas, *f*

garrulous, lŏquax

gas, spĭrĭtus, *m*

gash, *nn,* plāga, *f*

gash, *v.t,* percŭtĭo (3)

gasp, *nn,* ănhēlĭtus, *m*

gasp, *v.i,* ănhēlo (1)

gastric, *use genitive* stŏmăchi (of the stomach)

gate, porta, *f,* iānŭa, *f;* (-keeper), iānĭtor, *m*

gather, *v.t,* lĕgo (3), collĭgo (3); (pluck), carpo (3); *v.i,* convĕnĭo (4), congrĕgor (1 *dep*)

gathering, coetus, *m*

gaudy, fūcātus

gauge, *v.t,* mētĭor (4 *dep*)

gauge, *nn*, mŏdŭlus, *m*

gaunt, măcer

gay, hĭlăris

gaze at, *v.t*, tŭĕor (2 *dep*)

gaze, *nn*, obtūtus, *m*

gazelle, dorcas, *f*

gazette, acta dĭurna, *n. pl*, (daily events)

gear, appărātus, *m*

geld, *v.t*, castro (1)

gelding, cantērĭus, *m*

gem, gemma, *f*

gender, gĕnus, *n*

geneology (lineage), ŏrīgo, *f*, gĕnus, *n*

general, *adj*, (opp. to particular), gĕnĕrālis; (common, wide-spread), vulgāris, commūnis

general, *nn*, dux, *m*, impĕrātor, *m*

generality (majority), plērīque

generally (for the most part), *adv*, plērumque

generalship, ḍuctus, *m*

generate, *v.t*, gĕnĕro (1), gigno (3)

generation, saecŭlum, *n*

generosity, bĕnignĭtas, *f*

generous (with money, etc.), lībĕrālis

genial, cōmis

geniality, cōmĭtas, *f*

genius (ability), ingĕnĭum, *n*; (guardian spirit), gĕnĭus, *m*

genteel, urbānus

gentle (mild), mītis; (of birth), gĕnĕrōsus

gentleman, hŏmo ingĕnŭus

gentlemanly, *adj*, lībĕrālis, hŏnestus

gentleness, lēnĭtas, *f*

gently, *adv*, lēnĭter

gentry, nōbĭles, *m. pl*

genuine, sincērus

geography, gĕographĭa, *f*

geometry, gĕōmĕtrĭa, *f*

germ, germen, *n*

German, Germānus

germane, affīnis

germinate, *v.i*, germĭno (1)

gesticulate, *v.i*, sē iactāre (1 *reflex*)

gesture, gestus, *m*

get, *v.t*, (obtain), ădĭpiscor (3 *dep*), nanciscor (3 *dep*); (a request), impĕtro (1); (become), *v.i*, fio (*irreg*); (— about, or spread, etc.), percrēbesco (3); (— away), effŭgĭo (3); (— back), *v.t*, rĕcĭpĭo (3); (— the better of), sŭpĕro (1); (— down), *v.i*, dēscendo (3); (— out), exĕo (4); (— ready), *v.t*, păro (1); (— rid of), ămŏvĕo (2) in *or* ad (*with acc*); (— up, rise), surgo (3)

ghastly, exsanguis,

ghost, mānes, *m. pl*

giant, vir ingenti stătūra (man of huge stature)

gibbet, crux, *f*

giddy, vertīgĭnōsus

gift, dōnum, *n*

gifted (mentally, etc.), ingĕnĭōsus

gigantic, ingens

giggle, *v.i*, use rīdĕo (2), (to laugh)

gild, *v.t*, ĭnauro (1)

gills (of fish), branchĭae, *f. pl*

gimlet, tĕrēbra, *f*

gin, pĕdĭca, *f*

giraffe, cămēlŏpardălis, *f*

gird, *v.t*, cingo (3); (— oneself), sē accingĕre (3 *reflex*)

girder, trabs, *f*

girdle, cingŭlum, *n*

girl, pŭella, *f*, virgo, *f*

girlhood, aetas, (*f*) pŭellāris

girth, ambĭtus, *m*

give, *v.t*, do (1), dōno (1); (render), reddo (3); (— an opportunity), făcultātem do (1); (— back), reddo (3); (— in), *v.i*, cēdo (3); (— up, deliver), trādo (3); (abandon), dīmitto (3); (— up hope), *v.i*, dēspēro (1); (— orders), iŭbĕo (2)

glad, laetus, hĭlăris

gladden, *v.t*, hĭlăro (1)

glade, nĕmus, *n*, saltus, *m*

gladiator, glădĭātor, *m*

gladness, laetĭtĭa, *f*

glance at, *v.t*, aspĭcĭo (3); (graze) stringo (3)

glance, *nn*, aspectus, *m*

gland, glans, *f*

glare, *nn*, fulgor, *m*

glare, *v.i*, fulgĕo (2); (look with stern glance), torvis ŏcŭlis tŭĕor (2 *dep*)

glaring (conspicuous), mănifestus

glass, *nn*, vĭtrum, *n*; (drinking —), pōcŭlum, *n*

glass, *adj*, vĭtrĕus

gleam, *nn*, fulgor, *m*

gleam, *v.i*, fulgĕo (2)

glean, *v.t*, spīcas collĭgo (3) (collect ears of corn)

glee, laetĭtĭa, *f*

glen, valles, *f*

glib (of tongue), vŏlūbĭlis

glide, lābor (3 *dep*)

glimmer, *v.i*, sublūcĕo (2)

glimmering, *adj*, sublustris

glimpse (get a — of), *v.t*, dispĭcĭo (3)

glitter, *v.i*, fulgĕo (2)

glittering, *adj*, fulgĭdus, cŏruscus

gloat over, *v.t*, gaudens aspĭcĭo (3)

globe, glŏbus, *m*; (the earth), orbis, *m*

gloom, tĕnebrae, *f. pl*, tristĭtĭa, *f*

gloomy, tĕnebrōsus, tristis

glorify, v.t, laudo (1), extollo (3)

glorious, praeclārus, illustris

glory, glōrĭa, f, dĕcus, n, laus, f

gloss, nn, nĭtor, m

gloss over, v.t, praetĕrĕo (4)

glossy, nĭtĭdus

gloves, mănĭcae, f. pl

glow, nn, ardor, m

glow, v.i, ardĕo (2), candĕo (2)

glue, nn, glūten, n

glut, nn, sătĭĕtas, f

glut, v.t, explĕo (2), sătĭo (1)

glutton, hellŭo, m

gluttonous, ĕdax

gluttony, ĕdācĭtas, f

gnarled, nōdōsus

gnash (the teeth), v.t, frendĕo (2), (dentibus)

gnat, cŭlex, m

gnaw, v.t, rōdo (3)

gnawing, adj, mordax

go, v.i, ĕo (irreg), vādo (3); (depart), ăbĕo (4), prŏfĭciscor (3 dep); (— abroad), pĕrĕgre exĕo (4 irreg); (— away), ăbĕo (4 irreg); (— back), rĕdĕo (4 irreg); (— by, past), praetĕrĕo (4 irreg); (— down), dēscendo (3); (— in), ĭnĕo (4 irreg); (— over), transĕo (4 irreg); (— round), circumĕo (4 irreg) (— through), ōbĕo (4 irreg); (— up), ascendo (3); (— without), cărĕo (2) (with abl)

goad, v.t, stĭmŭlo (1)

goal, mēta, f

goat, căper, m

go-between, nn, interpres, c

goblet, pōcŭlum, n

god, dĕus, m

goddess, dĕa, f

godless, impĭus

godlike, dīvīnus

godly, adj, pĭus

gold, aurum, n

golden, aurĕus

goldsmith, aurĭfex, m

good, adj, bŏnus, prŏbus, hŏnestus, aptus, commŏdus

good, nn, bŏnum, n; (advantage), commŏdum, n; (goods, possessions), bŏna, n.pl; (— for nothing), adj, nēquam; (to do —), prōdesse (irreg) (with dat)

good-bye! vălē! (pl, vălete!)

good-humour, cōmĭtas, f

good-humoured, cōmis

good-looking, spĕcĭōsus

good-nature, cōmĭtas, f

good-natured, cōmis

goodness (virtue), virtus, f, prŏbĭtas, f; (excellence), bŏnĭtas, f

good-tempered, mītis

goose, anser, m

gore, nn, crŭor, m

gorge (throat), guttur, n, fauces, f. pl; (mountain pass), angustĭae, f. pl

gorge oneself, v.i, sē ingurgĭtāre (1 reflex)

gorgeous, spĕcĭōsus, splendĭdus

gorgeousness, magnĭfĭcentĭa, f

gory, crŭentus

gossip, v.i, garrĭo (4)

gossip, nn, (talk), rūmor, m; (person), garrŭlus, m

gouge, v.t, (— out eyes), ŏcŭlos ērŭo (3)

gourd, cŭcurbĭta, f

gout, morbus, (m) artĭcŭlōrum (disease of the joints)

gouty, arthrītĭcus

govern, v.t, gŭberno (1), impĕro (1), tempĕro (1), mŏdĕror (1 dep)

government (act of —), admĭnistrātĭo, f, cūra, f; (persons), use phr, ii qui summum impĕrĭum hăbent (those who hold supreme authority)

governor (supreme), gŭbernātor, m; (subordinate), prōcūrātor, m, lēgātus, m

gown (woman's), stŏla, f; (man's), tŏga, f

grace, grātĭa, f; (pardon), vĕnĭa, f; (charm), vĕnustas, f; (to say —), grātĭas ăgo (3)

grace, v.t, (adorn), dĕcŏro (1)

graceful, vĕnustus, lĕpĭdus

gracious, prŏpĭtĭus, bĕnignus

grade, grădus, m

gradient, clīvus, m

gradually, adv, paulātim

graft, v.t, insĕro (3)

grain, frumentum, n

grammar, grammătĭca, f

granary, horrĕum, n

grand, magnĭfĭcus, grandis

grandchild, nĕpos, m, f

granddaughter, neptis, f

grandeur, magnĭfĭcentĭa, f

grandfather, ăvus, m

grandiloquent, grandĭlŏquus

grandmother, ăvĭa, f

grandson, nĕpos, m

granite, (hard rock), use sĭlex, m, (flint stone)

grant, granting, nn, concessĭo, f

grant, v.t, concēdo (3), do (1)

grape, ăcĭnus, m, ūva, f

graphic, expressus

grapple, v.i, luctor (1 dep)

grappling-iron, harpăgo, m

grasp, nn, mănus, f; (of the mind), captus, m

grasp, *v.t*, prěhendo (3); (mentally), intellěgo (3); (snatch at, aim at), capto (1)

grass, grāmen, *n*, herba, *f*

grasshopper, gryllus, *m*

grassy, grāmĭnĕus

grate, crātĭcŭla, *f*

grate, *v.t*, těro (3); *v.i*, strīděo (2)

grateful, grātus

gratification, explētĭo, *f*, vŏluptas, *f*

gratify, *v.t*, grātĭfĭcor (1 *dep*) (*with dat*)

grating, *nn*, (noise), strīdor, *m*

gratitude, grātĭa, *f*, grātus ănĭmus, *m*

gratuitous, grātŭĭtus

gratuity, conglārĭum, *n*

grave, *nn*, sěpulcrum, *n*

grave, *adj*, grāvis,

gravel, glārĕa, *f*

gravity, grăvĭtas, *f*

gravy, iūs, *n*

gray, *see* grey

grayness, *see* grey, greyness

graze, *v.t*, (animals), pasco (3); *v.i*, pascor (3 *dep*); (touch lightly), *v.t*, stringo (3)

grease, *nn*, ădeps, *c*

grease, *v.t*, ungo (3)

greasy, unctus

great, magnus, grandis, amplus; (distinguished), illustris

greatcoat, lăcerna, *f*

great-grandfather, prŏăvus, *m*

great-grandson, prŏněpos, *m*

greatness, magnĭtūdo, *f*

greaves, ōcrĕae, *f. pl*

Greece, Graecĭa, *f*

greed, ăvārĭtĭa, *f*

greedy, ăvārus

Greek, Graecus

green, *adj*, vĭrĭdis; (unripe), crūdus; (to become —), *v.i*, vĭresco (3)

greet, *v.t*, sălūto (1)

greeting, sălūtātĭo, *f*

gregarious, grĕgālis

grey, caesĭus, rāvus; (of hair), cānus

greyness (of hair), cānĭtĭes, *f*

gridiron, crātĭcŭla, *f*

grief, dŏlor, *m*, luctus, *m*

grievance, quěrĭmōnĭa, *f*

grieve, *v.i. and v.t*, dŏlĕo (2)

grievous, grăvis, ăcerbus

grim, trux

grin, *v.i*, rīdĕo (2)

grind, *v.t*, contěro (3); mŏlo (3) (— down, oppress), opprĭmo (3);

grindstone, cōs, *f*

grip, *nn, use* mănus, *f*, (hand)

grip, *v.t*, arrĭpĭo (3)

gripes, tormĭna, *n.pl*

grisly, horrendus

grist, fărīna, *f*

gristle, cartĭlăgo, *f*

grit, glārĕa, *f*

groan, *nn*, gěmĭtus, *m*

groan, *v.i*, gěmo (3)

grocer, tūrārĭus, *m*

groin, inguen, *n*

groom, *nn*, ăgāso, *m*

groom, *v.t*, (look after), cūro (1)

groove, cănālis, *m*

grope, *v.i*, praetento (1)

gross, *adj*, crassus; (unseemly), indĕcōrus

grotto, antrum, *n*

grotesque, monstrŭōsus

ground (earth), hūmus, *f*, sŏlum, *n*, terra, *f*; (cause, reason), causa, *f*; (to give —), pědem rěfěro (*irreg*)

ground, *v.i*, (of ships), sīdo (3)

groundless, vānus

groundwork (basis), fundāmentum, *n*

group, glŏbus, *m*

group, *v.t*, dispōno (3)

grouse, lăgōpūs, *f*

grove, lūcus, *m*

grovel, *v.i*, serpo (3)

grow, *v.i*, cresco (3), augesco (3); (— up), ădŏlesco (3); (become), fīo (*irreg*); *v.t*, cōlo (3)

growl, *nn*, frěmĭtus, *m*

growl, *v.i*, frěmo (3)

growth, incrēmentum, *n*

grub, *nn*, vermĭcŭlus, *m*

grudge, *nn*, sĭmultas, *f*

grudge, *v.t*, invĭdĕo (2) (*with dat*)

grudgingly, *adv, use adj*, invĭtus

gruel, ptīsăna, *f*

gruff, asper

grumble, *v.i*, frěmo (3)

grunt, *nn*, grunnĭtus, *m*

grunt, *v.i*, grunnĭo (4)

guarantee, *nn*, fĭdes, *f*

guarantee, *v.t*, fĭdem do (1) (*with dat*)

guarantor, vas, *m*

guard (person), custos, *c*; (defence), custōdĭa, *f*, praesĭdĭum, *n*: (to keep —), *v.i*, custōdĭam ăgo (3)

guard, *v.t*, custōdĭo (4)

guarded (cautious), cautus

guardian, custos, *c*; (of child), tūtor, *m*

guardianship, custōdĭa, *f*; (of child), tūtēla, *f*

guess, *nn*, conĭectūra, *f*

guess, *v.t*, cōnĭcĭo (3), dīvĭno (1)

guest, hospes, *m*, hospĭta, *f*; (at a party, etc.), convīva, *c*

guidance (advice), consĭlĭum, *n*

For List of Abbreviations used, turn to pages 3, 4

guide, *nn*, dux, *c*
guide, *v.t*, dūco (3)
guild, collēgĭum, *n*
guile, dŏlus, *m*
guileful, dŏlōsus
guileless, simplex
guilt, culpa, *f*
guiltless, innŏcens, insons
guilty, sons, nŏcens
guise, hăbĭtus, *m*, spĕcĭes, *f*
gulf (bay), sĭnus, *m*; (abyss), gurges, *m*, vŏrāgo, *f*
gullet, guttur, *n*
gullible, crēdŭlus
gully (channel), cănālis, *m*, fossa, *f*
gulp, *v.t*, haurĭo (4)
gum (of the mouth), gingīva, *f*; (of plants, etc.), gummi, *n*
gurgle, *v.i*, singulto (1)
gush, *v.i*, prŏfundor (3 *pass*)
gust, flātus, *m*
gut, intestīna, *n.pl*
gutter, fossa, *f*, clŏāca, *f*
guttural, grăvis
gymnasium, gymnăsĭum, *n*
gymnastics, pălaestra, *f*

H

haberdasher, lintĕo, *m*
habit, consŭētūdo, *f*, mōs, *m*
habitable, hăbĭtābĭlis
habitation, dŏmĭcĭlĭum, *n*
habitual, ūsĭtātus
habituate, *v.t*, consŭēfăcĭo (3)
hack, căballus, *m*
hack, *v.t*, concīdo (3)
hackneyed, trītus
haft, mănūbrĭum, *n*
hag, ănus, *f*
haggard, măcĭe corruptus (marred by leanness)
haggle, *v.i*, dē prĕtĭo căvillor (1 *dep*) (to quibble about price)
hail, *nn*, grando, *f*
hail, *v.i*, (weather), grandĭnat (*impers.*); *v.t*, (greet), sălūto (1)
hair, căpillus, *m*, crīnis, *m*, caesărĭes, *f*
hair-dresser, tonsor, *m*
hairless (bald), calvus
hairy, pĭlōsus
halcyon, *adj*, alcўŏnēus
hale (healthy), vălĭdus
half, *nn*, dīmĭdĭum, *n*; *adj*, dīmĭdĭus; *adv*, *use prefix* sēmi-, *e.g.* half-asleep, sēmĭsomnus; (half-dead), sēmĭănĭmis, mŏrĭbundus;

(— hour), sēmĭhŏra, *f*; (— moon), lūna dīmĭdĭāta, *f*; (— yearly), sēmestris
hall (of house), ātrĭum, *n*; (public), concĭlĭābŭlum, *n*
hallo! heus!
hallow, *v.t*, consēcro (1)
hallucination, somnĭa, *n.pl*
halo, cŏrōna, *f*
halt, *nn*, *use vb*, consisto (3)
halt, *v.i*, consisto (3)
halter (horse), căpistrum, *n*; (noose), lăquĕus, *m*
halve, *v.t*, ex aequo dīvĭdo (3)
ham, perna, *f*
hamlet, vīcus, *m*
hammer, *nn*, mallĕus, *m*
hammer, *v.t*, contundo (3)
hamper, quălum, *n*
hamper, *v.t*, impĕdĭo (4)
hamstring, *v.t*, poplĭtem succīdo (3) (*with dat*)
hand, mănus, *f*; (left) —), mănus sĭnistra; (right —), dextra mănus; (to shake —s), dextras coniungĕre (3); (— cuffs), mănĭcae, *f*, *pl*; (— writing), chīrŏgrăphum, *n*; (on the one —, on the other —), et ... et, *or* quĭdem (*second word in clause*) ... autem (*second word in clause*); (— to— fighting, etc.), commĭnus, *adv*; (at hand), praesto, *adv*
hand, *v.t*, do (1), trādo (3); (—down or over), trādo (3)
handful (few), *use adj*, pauci
handicraft, artĭfĭcĭum, *n*
handiwork, ŏpus, *n*
handkerchief, sūdārĭum, *n*
handle, mănūbrĭum, *n*
handle, *v.t*, tracto (1)
handling (treatment), tractātĭo, *f*
handsome, spĕcĭōsus, pulcher
handy (manageable), hăbĭlis
hang, *v.t*, suspendo (3); (— the head), dēmitto (3); *v.i*, pendĕo (2); (— back, hesitate), dŭbĭto (1); (over-hang), impendĕo (2)
hanger-on, assecla, *c*
hanging (death by —), suspendĭum, *n*
hangman, carnĭfex, *m*
hanker after, *v.t*, opto (1)
haphazard, *use adv. phr.* nullo ordĭne (in no order)
happen, *v.i*, accĭdo (3), ēvĕnĭo (4)
happiness, fēlīcĭtas, *f*
happy, fēlix, bĕātus
harangue, *nn*, contĭo, *f*
harangue, *v.t*, contĭōnor (1 *dep.*)

harass, v.t, sollĭcĭto (1)

harbour, portus, m; (— **dues**), portōrĭum, n

harbour, v.t, (**shelter**), excĭpĭo (3)

hard, dūrus; (**difficult**), diffĭcĭlis

hard, adv, (**strenuously**), strēnŭē

harden, v.t, dūro (1); v.i, dūresco (3)

hard-hearted, dūrus

hardiness, rōbur, n

hardly, adv, vix; (**harshly**), crūdēlĭter

hardness, dūrĭtĭa, f

hardship, lăbor, m

hardware, ferrāmenta, n.pl

hardy, dūrus

hare, lĕpus, m

hark! heus!

harlot, mĕrĕtrix, f

harm, nn, damnum, n

harm, v.t, nŏcĕo (2) (with dat)

harmful, noxĭus

harmless, innŏcŭus, innŏcens

harmonious, concors

harmonize, v.i, concĭno (3)

harmony, concentus, m, consensus, m

harness, nn, ĕquestrĭa arma, n.pl, (**horse equipment**), frēnum, n

harness, v.t, iungo (3)

harp, fĭdes, f. pl; (**harpist**), fĭdĭcen, m

harrow, nn, irpex, m

harrow, v.t, occo (1)

harrowing, adj, horrendus, terrĭbĭlis

harsh, asper, ăcerbus

harshness, aspĕrĭtas, f

hart, cervus, m

harvest, messis, f

hasp, fĭbŭla, f

haste, nn, festĭnātĭo, f

hasten, v.i, prŏpĕro (1), festīno(1); v.t, mātūro (1), accĕlĕro (1)

hastily, adv, prŏpĕrē

hastiness (of temper), īrācundĭa, f

hasty, prŏpĕrus; (**of temper**), īrācundus

hat, pĕtăsus, m

hatch, v.t, (**eggs**), exclūdo (3); (**plans etc.**), ĭnĕo (4)

hatchet, sĕcūris, f

hate, nn, ŏdĭum, n

hate, v.t, ōdi (v.defect)

hateful, ŏdĭōsus

haughtiness, sŭperbĭa, f

haughty, sŭperbus, arrŏgans

haul, v.t, trăho (3)

haunt, nn, lătĕbrae, f. pl

haunt, v.t, (**visit frequently**), cĕlĕbro (1); (**trouble**), sollĭcĭto (1)

have, v.t, hăbĕo (2); or use esse (irreg) with dat. of possessor, e.g. **I have a brother,** est mĭhĭ frāter

haven, portus, m

haversack, saccus, m

havoc, strāges, f, vastātĭo,

hawk, nn, accĭpĭter, m,f

hay, faenum, n

hazard, nn, pĕrīcŭlum, n

hazardous, pĕrīcŭlōsus

haze, nĕbŭla, f

hazel, nn, cŏrўlus, f

hazy, nĕbŭlōsus

he, pron, If not emphatic, use 3rd pers. of verb; otherwise, ille, hic, is

head, căput, n, vertex, m; (**chief**), princeps, m; (**to be at the — of**) praesum (irreg) (with dat)

head, adj, (**of wind**), adversus

head, v.t, (**be in charge**), praesum (irreg) (with dat)

head-ache, căpĭtis dŏlor, m; (— **band**), vitta, f; (— **land**), prōmontōrĭum, n; (— **long**), adj, praeceps; (— **quarters**), praetōrĭum, n; (— **strong**), adj, pervĭcax

heal, v.t, sāno (1), mĕdĕor (2 dep) (with dat); v.i, consānesco (3)

healing, nn, sānātĭo, f

healing, adj, sălūtāris

health, vălētūdo, f

healthy, sānus, vălĭdus; (**of place or climate**), sălūbris

heap, nn, ăcervus, m

heap, v.t, cŭmŭlo (1), congĕro (3)

hear, v.t, audĭo (4); (**learn**), cognosco (3)

hearer, audītor, m

hearing, nn, (**sense of —**), audītus, m

hearsay, rūmor, m

heart, cor, n; (**interior**), use adj, intĭmus (**inmost**); (**feelings, etc.**), pectus, n, mens, f; (**courage**), ănĭmus, m; (— **ache**), sollĭcĭtūdo, f; (— **break**), dŏlor, m; (— **broken**) adj. phr, ănĭmo afflictus

hearth, fŏcus, m

heartiness, stŭdĭum, n

heartless, dūrus

heartlessness, crūdēlĭtas, f

hearty, ălăcer

heat, nn, călor, m, ardor, m, aestus, m, fervor, m

heat, v.t, călĕfăcĭo (3); (**excite**), incendo (3)

heath, lŏca obsĭta, n.pl, lŏca inculta, n.pl

heave, v.t, tollo (3); v.i, tŭmesco (3)

heaven, caelum, n; (— **dwelling**) adj, caelĭcŏla

heavenly, adj, dīvīnus

heaviness, grăvĭtas, f; (— **of mind**), tristĭtĭa, f

heavy, grăvis; (sad), tristis; (air, etc.), crassus

hectic (agitated, confused), turbŭlentus

hedge, saepes, f

hedge in, v.t, saepĭo (4)

hedgehog, ěchīnus, m

heed, v.t, (obey), pārěo (2) (with dat); (to take —), v.i, căvěo (2)

heedless, incautus

heedlessness, neglěgentĭa, f

heel, calx, f; (take to one's —s), fŭgĭo (3)

heifer, iŭvenca, f

height, altĭtūdo, f; (high ground) sŭpěrĭor lŏcus, m

heighten, v.t, use augěo (2) (increase)

heinous, ătrox

heir, heiress, hēres, c

hell, infěri, m. pl, Orcus, m

hellish, infernus

helm, gŭbernācŭlum, n

helmet, cassis, f, gălěa, f

helmsman, gŭbernātor, m

help, nn, auxĭlĭum, n

help, v.t, iŭvo (1), subvěnĭo (4) (with dat); (I cannot help coming), non possum făcěre quin věnĭam

helper, adiŭtor, m

helpful, ūtĭlis

helpless, ĭnops

helplessness, ĭnŏpĭa, f

helpmate, consors, m, f

hem, nn, limbus, m

hem in, v.t, circumsěděo (2), saepĭo (4)

hemisphere, hēmisphaerĭum, n

hemp, cannābis, f

hen, gallīna, f; (— house), gallīnārĭum, n

hence, adv, (place or cause), hinc; (time), posthāc

henceforth, adv, posthāc

her, pron, adj, eius; (if it refers to the subject of the sentence), sŭus, a, um

herald, praeco, m

herb, herba, f, hŏlus, n

herd, grex, m

herd together, v.i, congrěgor (1 pass)

herdsman, pastor, m

here, hīc; (hither), hūc; (to be —), v.i, adsum (irreg)

hereafter, adv, posthāc

hereby, adv, ex hōc

hereditary, hěrēdĭtārĭus

heredity, gěnus, n

heretical, prāvus

hereupon, adv, hīc

heritage, hěrēdĭtas, f

hermit, hŏmo sōlĭtārĭus

hernia, hernĭa, f

hero, vir fortissĭmus

heroic (brave), fortis

heroine, fēmĭna fortis, f

heroism, virtus, f

heron, arděa, f

hers, see her

herself, pron. reflexive, sē; (pron. emphatic), ipsa

hesitancy, hesitation, haesĭtātĭo, f

hesitate, v.i, dŭbĭto (1), haesĭto (1)

hew, v.t, caedo (3)

hey-day (youth), iŭventus, f

hibernate, v.i, condor (3 pass)

hiccough, singultus, m

hidden, occultus

hide, nn, (skin), cŏrĭum, n, pellis, f

hide, v.t, abdo (3), cēlo (1)

hideous, foedus

hideousness, foedĭtas, f

hiding-place, lătěbrae, f. pl

high, altus, celsus; (of rank), amplus; (of price), magnus, magni; (— born), gěněrōsus; (— handed), impěrĭōsus; (— lands), montes, m. pl; (— landers), montāni, m. pl; (— spirited), ănĭmōsus; (— treason), māiestas, f; (— way), vĭa, f; (— wayman), lătro, m

hilarity, hĭlărĭtas, f

hill, collis, m

hillock, tŭmŭlus, m

hilly, montŭōsus

hilt, căpŭlus, m

himself, pron. reflexive, sē; pron. emphatic, ipse

hind, adj, postěrĭor

hinder, v.t, impědĭo (4), obsto (1) (with dat)

hindrance, impědīmentum, n

hinge, nn, cardo, m

hinge on, v.i, vertor (3 dep), versor (1 dep) in (with abl)

hint, nn, signĭfĭcātĭo, f

hint at, v.t, signĭfĭco (1)

hip, coxendix, f

hippopotamus, hippŏpŏtāmus, m

hire (wages), merces, f

hire, v.t, condūco (3)

hired, conductus

his, pron, ēius, hūius, illĭus; or sŭus (referring to the subject of the sentence)

hiss, nn, sībĭlus, m

hiss, v.i. and v.t, sībĭlo (1)

historian, scriptor, (m) rērum

historic(al) use nn, histŏrĭa, f, (history)

history, histŏrĭa, f, rēs gestae, f. pl

hit, nn, (blow), plāga, f

hit, v.t, (strike), fěrĭo (4); (— upon), incĭdo (3)

hitch, impĕdīmentum, *n*

hitch, *v.t*, necto (3)

hither, *adv*, hūc; (— and thither), hūc illūc

hitherto, *adv*, ădhūc

hive, alvĕārĭum, *n*

hoard, *nn*, ăcervus, *m*

hoard, *v.t*, collĭgo (3), condo (3)

hoar-frost, prūīna, *f*

hoarse, raucus

hoary, cānus

hoax, *nn*, lūdus, *m*

hoax, *v.t*, lūdĭfĭcor (1 *dep*), lūdo (3)

hobble, *v.i*, claudĭco (1)

hobby, stŭdĭum, *n*

hob-nail, clāvus, *m*

hoe, *nn*, sarcŭlum, *n*

hoe, *v.t*, sarrĭo (4)

hog, porcus, *m*

hogshead, dōlĭum, *n*

hoist, *v.t*, tollo (3)

hold, *nn*, (grasp), *use* comprĕhendo (3), *or* mănus, *f*

hold, *v.t*, tĕnĕo (2), obtĭnĕo (2), hăbĕo (2); (— an office), obtĭnĕo (2), fungor (3 *dep*); (— elections, etc.), hăbĕo (2); (— back), *v.i*, cunctor (1 *dep*), *v.t*, rĕtĭnĕo (2); (— fast), rĕtĭnĕo (2); (— out), *v.t*, porrĭgo (3); (endure), sustĭnĕo (2), perfĕro (*irreg*); (— up, lift), tollo (3)

hold-fast, *nn*, fībŭla, *f*

hole, fŏrāmen, *n*, căvum, *n*

holiday, fērĭae, *f. pl*

holiness, sanctĭtas, *f*

hollow, *nn*, căvum, *n*, lăcūna, *f*; (— of the hand), căva mănus, *f*

hollow, *adj*, căvus; (false), vānus

hollow, *v.t*, căvo (1)

holm-oak, īlex, *f*

holy, săcer

homage (respect), observantĭa, *f*

home, *adj*, dŏmestĭcus; (homely), rustĭcus

home, dŏmus, *f*; (at —), dŏmi; (homewards), dŏmum; (from —), dŏmo; (— less), cărens tecto (lacking shelter)

homicide (deed), caedes, *f*; (person), hŏmĭcīda, *c*

honest, prŏbus

honesty, prŏbĭtas, *f*, intĕgrĭtas, *f*

honey, mel, *n*

honeycomb, fāvus, *m*

honorary, hŏnōrārĭus

honour, hŏnos, *m*; (glory), dĕcus, *n*; (integrity), hŏnestas, *f*, intĕgrĭtas, *f*; (repute), fāma, *f*

honour, *v.t*, cŏlo (3), hŏnesto (1)

honourable, hŏnōrātus, hŏnestus

hood, cŭcullus, *m*

hoof, ungŭla, *f*

hook, hāmus, *m*

hook, *v.t*, hāmo căpĭo (3), (catch by a hook)

hooked, hāmātus

hoop, circŭlus, *m*

hoot, *nn*, cantus, *m*

hoot, *v.i*, căno (3); *v.t*, (hoot at), explōdo (3)

hop, *v.i*, sălĭo (4)

hope, *nn*, spes, *f*

hope, *v.i. and v.t*, spēro (1)

hopeful (promising), *use genit. phr*, bŏnae spēi

hopefully, *adj*, *phr*, multa spērans

hopeless (desperate), dēspērātus

hopelessness, dēspērātĭo, *f*

horizon, orbis, (*m*) fīnĭens (limiting circle)

horizontal, lībrātus

horn, cornu, *n*; (made of —), *adj*, cornĕus

hornet, crābro, *m*

horrible, horrĭbĭlis, horrendus, ătrox, foedus

horrid, horrĭbĭlis, horrendus, ătrox, foedus

horrify, *v.t*, (dismay), percello (3), terrĕo (2)

horror, horror, *m*

horse, ĕquus, *m*

horseback (to ride on —), in ĕquo vĕhor (3 *pass*); (to fight on —), ex ĕquo pugno (1)

horse-fly, tăbānus, *m*

horse-race, certāmen ĕquestre, *n*

horse-shoe, sŏlĕa, *f*

horse-whip, flăgellum, *n*

horticulture, hortōrum cultus, *m*

hospitable, hospĭtālis

hospital, vălētūdĭnārĭum, *n*

hospitality, hospĭtĭum, *n*

host (one who entertains), hospes, *m*; (innkeeper), caupo, *m*; (large number), multĭtūdo, *f*

hostage, obses, *c*

hostess, hospĭta, *f*

hostile, hostīlis, infestus

hostility, ĭnĭmīcĭtĭa, *f*; (hostilities, war), bellum, *n*

hot, călĭdus, fervens; (of temper), ācer; (to be —), *v.i*, călĕo (2), fervĕo (2); (to become —), *v.i*, călesco (3); (— headed), *adj*, fervĭdus, fervens; (hotly), *adv*, ardenter

hotel, hospĭtĭum, *n*

hound, cănis, *m*, *f*

hound on, *v.t*, (goad on), instīgo (1), ăgĭto (1)

For List of Abbreviations used, turn to pages 3, 4

hour, hōra, *f*

hourly, *adv*, in hōras

hour-glass, hōrārĭum, *n*

house, dŏmus, *f*, aedes, *f*, *pl*; (**family**), gens, *f*; (— **hold**), dŏmus, *f*, fămĭlĭa, *f*; (— **keeper**), prōmus, *m*; (— **maid**), ancĭlla, *f*; (— **wife**), māterfămĭlĭas, *f*

house, *v.t,*(**store**), condo (3), rĕpōno, (3)

hovel, tŭgŭrĭum, *n*, căsa, *f*

hover, *v.i,* vŏlĭto (1), impendĕo (2)

how (in what way?), quōmŏdŏ?; *with adj. or adv*, quam?; (— **many**), quot?; (— **often**), quŏtĭes?; (— **great or big**), quantus?

however, *conj*, tămen; *adv*, quamvis; (**how big or great**), quantumvis

howl, *nn*, ŭlŭlātus, *m*

howl, *v.i,* ŭlŭlo (1)

hubbub, tŭmultus, *m*

huddle, *v.i,* (— **together**), congrĕgor (1 *dep*), confĕror (*irreg. pass*)

hue (colour), cŏlor, *m*

huff (to be in a — about), *v.t,* aegrē fĕro (*irreg*)

hug, *nn*, complexus, *m*

hug, *v.t,* amplector (3 *dep*)

huge, ingens, immānis

hull (of a ship), alvĕus, *m*

hum, *nn*, frēmĭtus, *m*

hum, *v.i,* frĕmo (3), strĕpo (3)

human, *adj*, hūmānus; (— **being**), hŏmo, *c*

humane (compassionate), mĭsĕrĭcors

humanity, hūmānĭtas, *f*; (**human race**), hŏmĭnes, *c. pl*; (**compassion**), mĭsĕrĭcordĭa, *f*

humble, hŭmĭlis, vĕrēcundus

humble, *v.t,* dēprĭmo (3); (— **in war**), dēbello (1); (— **oneself**), sē summittĕre (3 *reflex*)

humdrum, *adj*, mĕdĭŏcris, tardus

humid, hūmĭdus

humidity, hūmor, *m*

humiliate, *v.t,* dēprĭmo (3)

humility, mŏdestĭa, *f*

humorous, rīdĭcŭlus

humour, făcētĭae, *f. pl*; (**disposition**), ingĕnĭum, *n*. lĭbīdo, *f*; (**to be in the — to**), *use* lĭbet (*v*. 2 *impers*) (*with dat. of person*)

humour, *v.t,* obsĕquor (3 *dep*) (*with dat. of person*)

hump, gibber, *m*

humpbacked, *adj*, gibber

hunch, hunchbacked, *see* **humpbacked**

hundred, *adj*, centum; (— **times**), *adv*, centies; (— **fold**), *adj*, centŭplex

hundredth, centēsĭmus

hundredweight, centumpondĭum, *n*

hunger, fămes, *f*

hunger, *v.i,* ēsŭrĭo (4)

hungry, ēsŭrĭens, ăvĭdus (cĭbi)

hunt, *v.t,* vēnor (1 *dep*)

hunt, hunting, *nn*, vēnātĭo, *f*

hunter, vēnātor, *m*

huntress, vēnātrix, *f*

hurdle, crātes, *f. pl*

hurl, *v.t,* iăcŭlor (1 *dep*), cōnĭcĭo (3)

hurricane, tempestas, *f*, prŏcella, *f*

hurried, praeceps

hurriedly, *adv*, raptim

hurry, *v.i,* festīno (1), prŏpĕro (1); *v.t,* răpĭo (3); (**an action, etc.**), mātūro (1)

hurt, *nn*, (**wound**), vulnus, *n*

hurt, *v.t,* laedo (3), nŏcĕo (2) (*with dat*)

hurt, *adj*, (**wounded**), saucĭus

hurtful, nŏcens, noxĭus

husband, vir, *m*, mărītus, *m*

husbandry, agrĭcultūra, *f*

hush! tăcē; *pl*, tăcētĕ (*from* tăcĕo)

hush up, *v.t* (**conceal**), tĕgo (3), cēlo (1)

husk, follĭcŭlus, *m*

husky, fuscus, raucus

hustle, *v.t,* pulso (1), trūdo (3)

hut, căsa, *f*, tŭgŭrĭum, *n*

hutch, căvĕa, *f*

hyacinth, hўăcinthus, *m*

hybrid, hybrĭda, ae, *c*

hymn, carmen, *n*

hyperbole, hўperbŏlē, *f*

hyperchondriac, mĕlanchŏlĭcus

hypocrisy, sĭmŭlātĭo, *f*

hypocrite, sĭmŭlător, *m*

hypocritical, sĭmŭlātus

hypothesis, conĭectūra, *f*, condĭcĭo, *f*

hysteria, āmentĭa, *f*, perturbātĭo, *f*

I

I, *pron*, (**emphatic**), ĕgo; *otherwise use* 1st *pers. sing. of verb, e.g.* **I love,** ămo

iambic, *adj*, ĭambĕus

ice, glăcĭes, *f*

icicle, stīrĭa, *f*

icy, gĕlĭdus, glăcĭālis

idea, nōtĭo, *f*, ĭmāgo, *f*, sententĭa, *f*; (**to form an —**) *v.i,* cōgĭtātĭōne fingo (3)

ideal, *adj*, (**perfect**), perfectus, summus, optĭmus

ideal, *nn*, exemplar, *n*

identical, ĭdem (**the same**)

identify, *v.t,* agnosco (3)

identity (to find the — of), cognosco (3) quis sit . . .

ides, īdūs, *f. pl*

idiocy, fătŭĭtas, *f*

idiom, prŏprĭĕtas, *f.* (linguae) (peculiarity of language)

idiot, fătŭus, *m*

idiotic, fătŭus

idle (unemployed), ōtĭōsus; (lazy), ignāvus; (useless), vānus; (to be —), *v.i.*, cesso (1)

idleness, ignāvĭa, *f*, cessātĭo, *f*

idler, cessātor, *m*, cessātrix, *f*

idol (statue), sĭmŭlācrum, *n*; (something loved), dēlĭcĭae, *f. pl*

idolatry, vĕnĕrātĭo, (*f*) sĭmŭlācrōrum (worship of images)

idolize, *v.t*, cŏlo (3)

idyl, ĭdyllĭum, *n*

if, *conj*, sī; (— not), sīn; (*after a vb. of asking* — whether), num, ŭtrum; (whether . . . or if), sīve . . . sīve; (— only), dummŏdo

ignite, *v.i*, ardesco (3); *v.t*, accendo (3)

ignoble (of birth), ignōbĭlis; (dishonourable), turpis

ignominious, turpis

ignominy, ignōmĭnĭa, *f*, infāmĭa, *f*

ignorance, inscĭentĭa, *f*

ignorant, ignārus, inscĭus

ignore, *v.t*, praetĕrĕo (4)

ill, *adj*, aeger; (evil), mălus; (to be —), *v.i*, aegrōto (1); (to fall —), *v.i*, in morbum incĭdo (3)

ill, *adv*, mălē

ill, *nn*, (evil), mălum, *n*

ill-advised (reckless), tĕmĕrārĭus

ill-bred, inhūmānus

ill-disposed, mălĕvŏlus

illegal, illĭcĭtus

illegitimate, non lēgĭtĭmus

ill-favoured, dēformis, turpis

ill-health, vălētūdo, *f*

illicit, illĭcĭtus

illiterate, illittĕrātus

ill-natured, mălĕvŏlus

ill-omened, dīrus

ill-starred, infēlix

ill-temper, īrācundĭa, *f*

illness, morbus, *m*

illogical, absurdus, rĕpugnans

illuminate, *v.t*, illustro (1)

illusion, error, *m*

illusive, vānus

illustrate, *v.t*, illustro (1)

illustration, exemplum, *n*

illustrious, clārus, illustris

image, ĭmāgo, *f*, effĭgĭes, *f*

imaginable, *use phr*, quod concĭpi pŏtest (that can be imagined)

imaginary, commentĭcĭus

imagination, cōgĭtātĭo, *f*

imagine, *v.i*, ănĭmo concĭpĭo (3) *or* fingo (3)

imbecile, fătŭus

imbecility, imbēcillĭtas, (*f*) ănĭmi

imbibe, *v.t*, bĭbo (3), haurĭo (4)

imbue, *v.t*, infĭcĭo (3)

imitate, *v.t*, ĭmĭtor (1 *dep*)

imitation, ĭmĭtātĭo, *f*; (likeness), effĭgĭes, *f*

imitator, ĭmĭtātor, *m*

immaculate, intĕger

immaterial (unimportant), *use phr*, nullo mōmento

immature, immātūrus

immeasurable, immensus

immediate, praesens, proxĭmus

immediately, *adv*, stătim, confestim

immemorial (from time —), *ex* hŏmĭnum mĕmŏrĭa

immense, immensus, ingens

immensity, immensĭtas, *f*

immerse, *v.t*, immergo (3)

immigrant, advĕna, *m. f*

immigrate, *v.i*, immĭgro (1)

imminent, praesens; (to be —), *v.i*, immĭnĕo (2)

immobility, immōbĭlĭtas, *f*

immoderate, immŏdĕrātus, immŏdĭcus

immodest, impŭdĭcus

immodesty, impŭdĭcĭtĭa, *f*

immolate, *v.t*, immŏlo (1)

immoral, prāvus, turpis

immorality, mōres măli, *m. pl*

immortal, immortālis, aeternus

immortality, immortālĭtas, *f*

immovable, immōbĭlis

immunity, immūnĭtas, *f*, văcātĭo, *f*

immutable, immūtābĭlis

impair, *v.t*, mĭnŭo (3)

impale, *v.t*, transfīgo (3)

impart, *v.t*, impertĭo (4)

impartial, aequus, iustus

impartiality, aequĭtas, *f*

impassable, insŭpĕrābĭlis

impassioned, concĭtātus, fervens

impassive, pătĭens

impatience (haste), impătĭentĭa, *f*, festīnātĭo *f*

impatient, ăvĭdus

impeach, *v.t*, accūso (1)

impeachment, accūsātĭo, *f*

impeccable, impeccābĭlis

impede, *v.t*, impĕdĭo (4)

impediment, impĕdīmentum, *n*; (of speech), haesĭtantĭa, *f*

impel, *v.t*, impello (3), incĭto (1)

impend, *v.i*, impendĕo (2), immĭnĕo (2)

impending, fŭtūrus
impenetrable, impĕnĕtrābĭlis
imperfect, imperfectus
imperfection (defect), vĭtĭum, *n*
imperial (kingly), rēgĭus *or use genit.* of impĕrĭum, *n*, **(empire),** *or* impĕrātor, *m*, **(emperor)**
imperil, *v.t*, in pĕrīcŭlum addūco (3)
imperious impĕrĭōsus
impermeable, impervĭus
impersonate, *v.t*, partes sustĭnĕo (2) **(keep up a part)**
impertinence, insŏlentĭa, *f*
impertinent, insŏlens
imperturbable, immōtus, immōbĭlis
impetuosity, vīs, *f*
impetuous, vĕhĕmens
impetus, vīs, *f*, impĕtus, *m*
impious, impĭus
implacable, implācābĭlis
implant, *v.t*, insĕro (3)
implement, instrūmentum, *n*
implicate, *v.t*, implĭco (1)
implicit, *adj*, tăcĭtus; **(absolute),** omnis, tōtus
implore, *v.t*, implōro (1), ōro (1)
imply, *v.t*, signĭfĭco (1); **(involve),** hăbĕo (2)
impolite, inurbānus
import, *nn*, **(meaning),** signĭfĭcātĭo, *f*
import, *v.t*, importo (1)
importance, mōmentum, *n*; **(of position),** amplĭtūdo, *f*
important, grăvis; **(people),** amplus
importunate, mŏlestus
importune, *v.t*, flāgĭto (1)
impose, *v.t*, impōno (3)
imposition (fraud), fraus, *f*
impossible, *use phr*, quod fĭĕri nōn pŏtest **(which cannot be done)**
imposter, fraudātor, *m*
impotence, imbēcillĭtas, *f*
impotent, imbēcillus, infirmus
impoverish, *v.t*, in paupertātem rĕdĭgo (3)
impoverishment, paupertas, *f*
imprecation, exsēcrātĭo, *f*
impregnable, ĭnexpugnābĭlis
impregnate, *v.t*, ĭnĭcĭo (3)
impress, *v.t*, imprĭmo (3); **(the mind),** mŏvĕo (2)
impression (mental), mōtus, *(m)* ănĭmi; **(idea, thought),** ŏpīnĭo, *f*, ŏpĭnātĭo, *f*; **(mark),** vestīgĭum, *n*
impressive, grăvis
imprint, *nn*, signum, *n*; **(of a foot),** vestīgĭum, *n*
imprison, *v.t*, in vincŭla cōnĭcĭo (3) **(throw into chains)**
imprisonment, vincŭla, *n.pl*

improbable, nōn vērĭsĭmĭlis **(not likely)**
improper, indĕcōrus
improve, *v.t*, mĕlĭōrem făcĭo (3) *or* reddo; *v.i*, mĕlĭor fīo **(irreg)**
improvement, ēmendātĭo, *f*
improvident, neglĕgens, imprōvĭdus
imprudence imprūdentĭa, *f*
imprudent, inconsultus, imprūdens
impudence, impŭdentĭa, *f*
impudent, impŭdens
impulse, impĕtus, *m*, impulsus, *m*
impulsive, vĕhĕmens
impunity (with —), *adv*, impūnĕ
impure, impūrus, foedus
impurity, impūrĭtas, *f*, incestus, *m*
impute, *v.t*, attrĭbŭo (3)
in, *prep*, **(place),** in *(with abl.) or use locative case if available, e.g.* Londīnĭi, **in London; (time),** *use abl. or* in *(with abl.)*
inability (weakness), imbēcillĭtas, *f*
inaccessible, ĭnaccessus
inaccuracy (fault), error, *m*
inaccurate, (things), falsus
inactive, ĭners
inactivity, cessātĭo, *f*, ĭnertĭa, *f*
inadequate, impar
inadmissible, *use phr*, quod nōn līcet **(which is not allowed)**
inadvertent, imprūdens
inane, ĭnānis
inanimate, ĭnănĭmus
inappropriate, nōn aptus **(not suitable)**
inasmuch as, *conj*, quŏnĭam, quandōquĭdem
inattention, neglĕgentĭa, *f*
inattentive, neglĕgens
inaudible, *use phr*, quod audīri nōn pŏtest **(which cannot be heard)**
inaugurate, *v.t*, ĭnaugŭro (1)
inauguration, consēcrātĭo, *f*
inauspicious, infēlix
inborn, insĭtus
incalculable, *use phr*, quod aestĭmāri nōn pŏtest **(which cannot be estimated)**
incapable, inhābĭlis
incarcerate, *v.t*, in vincŭla cōnĭcĭo (3) **(throw into chains)**
incarnate, spĕcĭe hūmānā indūtus **(clothed with human form)**
incautious, incautus
incendiary, incendĭārĭus, *m*
incense, *nn*, tūs, *n*
incense, *v.t*, ad īram mŏvĕo (2) **(arouse to anger)**
incentive, stĭmŭlus, *m*
incessant, perpĕtŭus, assĭdŭus
incest, incestum, *n*

inch, uncĭa, *f*

incident, rēs, *f*

incidental (casual), fortŭĭtus

incipient, *use vb*, incĭpĭo **(begin)**

incision, incīsūra, *f*

incisive, mordax, ācer

incite, *v.t*, incĭto (1)

inclemency, aspĕrĭtas, *f*, sĕvērĭtas, *f*

inclement, asper, sĕvērus

inclination (desire), stŭdĭum, *n*, vŏluntas, *f*; **(leaning, bias)**, inclīnātĭo, *f*

incline, *v.t*, inclīno (1); *v.i*, inclīnor (1 *pass*)

incline, *nn*, **(slope)**, acclīvĭtas, *f*

inclined (disposed), prōpensus

include, *v.t*, rĕfĕro *(irreg)*, cŏmprĕhendo (3)

including (together with), cum *(with abl)*

incoherent; *use vb. phr. with* nōn *and* cŏhaerĕo (2) **(to hold together)**

income, fructus, *m*, stīpendĭum, *n*

incomparable, singŭlāris

incompatibility, rĕpugnantĭa, *f*

incompatible, rĕpugnans

incompetent, ĭnhăbĭlis

incomplete, imperfectus

incomprehensible, *use phr*, quod intellĕgi nōn pŏtest

inconceivable, *use phr*, quod ănĭmo fingi nōn pŏtest **(that cannot be conceived)**

inconclusive (weak), înfirmus

incongruous, rĕpugnans

inconsiderable, parvus

inconsiderate, inconsĭdĕrātus

inconsistency, inconstantĭa, *f*

inconsistent, inconstans; **(to be —)**, *v.i*, rĕpugno (1)

inconsolable, inconsōlābĭlis

inconspicuous, obscūrus

inconstancy, inconstantĭa, *f*

inconstant, inconstans

inconvenience, incommŏdum, *n*

inconvenient, incommŏdus

incorporate, *v.t*, constĭtŭo (3), iungo (3)

incorrect, falsus

incorrigible, perdĭtus

incorruptible, incorruptus

increase, *nn*, incrēmentum, *n*

increase, *v.t*, augĕo (2), *v.i*, cresco (1)

incredible, incrēdĭbĭlis

incredulous, incrēdŭlus

incriminate, *v.t*, implĭco (1)

inculcate, *v.t*, inculco (1)

incumbent upon (it is —), ŏportet *(v. 2 impers. with acc. of person)*

incur, *v.t*, sŭbĕo (4)

incurable, insānābĭlis

indebted, obnoxĭus

indecency, turpĭtūdo, *f*

indecent, turpis, obscēnus

indecisive, dŭbĭus, anceps

indeed, *adv*, *emphatic*, prŏfecto; **(yes —)**, vēro; *concessive*; quĭdem

indefatigible, assĭdŭus

indefensible, *use phr*, quod nōn pŏtest făcĭlĕ dēfendi **(that cannot be defended easily)**

indefinite, incertus

indemnify, *v.t*, damnum rēstĭtŭo (3) **(restore a loss)**

indentation, lăcūna, *f*

independence, lībertas, *f*

independent, līber

indescribable, ĭnēnarrābĭlis

indestructible (unfailing), pĕrennis

indeterminate, incertus

index, index, *m*

indicate, *v.t*, indĭco (1), signĭfĭco (1)

indication, indĭcĭum, *n*

indict, *v.t*, accūso (1)

indictment, accūsātĭo, *f*

indifference, lentĭtūdo, *f*

indifferent, neglĕgens; **(middling)**, mĕdĭŏcris

indifferently, *adv* **(moderately)**, mĕdĭŏcrĭter

indigenous, *adj*, indĭgĕna

indigestible, *adj*, grăvis

indigestion, crūdĭtas, *f*

indignant, īrātus; **(to be —)**, *v.i*, indignor (1 *dep*), īrātus esse

indignation, indignātĭo, *f*, ira, *f*

indignity, contŭmēlĭa, *f*

indirect, oblīquus; **(path, etc.)**, dēvĭus

indiscreet, inconsultus

indiscriminate, prōmiscŭus

indispensable, nĕcessārĭus

indispose, *v.t*, ălĭēno (1)

indisposed (not inclined), āversus; **(ill)**, aegrōtus

indisposition (unwillingness), ănĭmus āversus; **(sickness)**, vălētūdo, *f*

indisputable, certus

indistinct, obscūrus

individual, *nn*, hŏmo, *c*

individual, *adj*, prŏprĭus

indivisible, indivĭdŭus

indolence, ignāvĭa, *f*

indolent, ignāvus

indomitable, indŏmĭtus

indoor, *adj*, umbrātĭlis **(in the shade)**

indoors (motion), in tectum

indubitable, certus

induce, *v.t*, addūco (3)

inducement, praemĭum, *n*

indulge, *v.i. and v.t*, indulgĕo (2)

indulgence, indulgentĭa, *f*

For List of Abbreviations used, turn to pages 3, 4

indulgent, indulgens

industrious, industrius, dīligens

industry (diligence), industria, *f*, dīligentia, *f*

inebriated, ēbrius

ineffective, inūtilis

inefficient, *use phr*, qui rem cělěrĭter confĭcĕre nōn pŏtest (**who cannot complete a matter quickly**)

inelegant, inēlĕgans

inept, ĭneptus

inequality, dissĭmĭlĭtūdo, *f*

inert, iners, segnis

inertly, *adv*, segnĭter

inestimable, ĭnaestĭmābĭlis

inevitable, nĕcessārĭus

inexcusable, *use phr*, quod praetermitti nōn pŏtest (**that cannot be overlooked**)

inexhaustible, infinītus, sĭne fĭne

inexorable, ĭnexōrābĭlis

inexperience, impĕrĭtĭa, *f*, inscĭentĭa, *f*

inexperienced, impĕrĭtus

inexplicable, ĭnexplĭcābĭlis

inexpressible, ĭnēnarrābĭlis, *or phr*, quod exprĭmi nōn pŏtest (**that cannot be expressed**)

infallible, qui falli nōn pŏtest (**who cannot be mistaken**)

infamous, infāmis

infamy, infāmĭa, *f*

infancy, infantĭa, *f*

infant, *adj. and nn*, infans

infantry, pĕdĭtātus, *m*

infatuate, *v.t*, infătŭo (1)

infatuated, dēmens

infect, *v.t*, inficĭo (3)

infection, contāgĭo, *f*

infer, *v.t*, collĭgo (3)

inference, coniectūra, *f*

inferior, *adj*, infĕrĭor, dētĕrĭor

infernal, infernus

infested, infestus

infidelity, perfĭdĭa, *f*

infinite, infinītus

infinity, infinītas, *f*

infirm, invălĭdus, infirmus

infirmity, infirmĭtas, *f*

inflame, *v.t*, accendo (3)

inflammable, *use phr*, quod făcĭlĕ incendi pŏtest (**that can be set on fire easily**)

inflammation, inflammātĭo, *f*

inflate, *v.t*, inflo (1)

inflexible, rĭgĭdus

inflict, *v.t*, infligo (3); (**war, etc.**), infĕro (*irreg*) (*with dat of person*)

infliction, mălum, *n* (**trouble**)

influence, *nn*, vīs, *f*, mōmentum, *n*; (**authority**), auctōrĭtas, *f*; (**to have —**), *v.i*, vălĕo (2)

influence, *v.t*, mŏvĕo (2)

influential, grăvis

inform, *v.t*, certĭōrem făcĭo (3); (**— against someone**), nōmen dēfĕro (*irreg*) (*with genit*)

information (news), nuntĭus, *m*

informer, dēlātor, *m*

infrequency, rārĭtas, *f*

infrequent, rārus

infringe, *v.t*, vĭŏlo (1)

infringement, vĭŏlātĭo, *f*

infuriate, *v.t*, effĕro (1)

infuriated, īrā incensus

infuse, *v.t*, infundo (3), inĭcĭo (3)

ingenious, subtīlis

ingenuity, *f*, ars, *f*, callĭdĭtas, *f*

ingenuous, ingĕnŭus

inglorious, inglōrĭus

ingot, lāter, *m*

ingrained, insĭtus

ingratiate oneself with, *v.t*, concĭlĭo (1), sē grātum reddere (*with dat*)

ingratitude, ănĭmus ingrātus, *m*

ingredient, pars, *f*

inhabit, *v.t*, incŏlo (3), hăbĭto (1)

inhabitant, incŏla, *c*

inhale, *v.t*, (spīrĭtum) haurĭo (4)

inherent, insĭtus

inherit, *v.t, use phr. with*, hērес (**heir**), *and* accĭpĭo (**to receive**)

inheritance, hērēdĭtas, *f*

inherited, hērēdĭtārĭus

inhibit, *v.t*, interdīco (3)

inhospitable, ĭnhospĭtālis

inhuman, immānis, crūdēlis

inhumanity, immānĭtas, *f*, crūdēlĭtas, *f*

inimitable, nōn ĭmĭtābĭlis

iniquitous, ĭnĭquus, imprŏbus

iniquity, imprŏbĭtas, *f*

initial, *adj*, prīmus

initiate, *v.t*, ĭnĭtĭo (1)

initiative (take the —), *v.i*, occŭpo (1)

inject, *v.t*, inĭcĭo (3)

injudicious, inconsultus

injure, *v.t*, nŏcĕo (2) (*with dat*)

injurious, noxĭus, nŏcens

injury (of the body), vulnus, *n*; (**disadvantage**), dētrīmentum, *n*, iniūrĭa, *f*

injustice, ĭnĭquĭtas, *f*, iniūrĭa, *f*

ink, ātrāmentum, *n*

inland, mĕdĭterrānĕus

inlay, *v.t*, insĕro (3)

inlet, aestŭārĭum, *n*

inn, dēversōrĭum, *n,* caupōna, *f;* (keeper), caupo, *m*

innate, insĭtus, innātus

inner, intĕrĭor

innocence, innŏcentĭa, *f*

innocent, innŏcens, insons

innocuous, innŏcŭus

innovate, *v.t,* nŏvo (1)

innumerable, innŭmĕrābĭlis

inobservant, nōn perspĭcax

inoffensive, innŏcens

inopportune, ĭnopportūnus

inordinate, immŏdĕrātus

inquest, quaestĭo, *f*

inquire, *v.i,* quaero (3) ab (*with abl*) or dē (*with abl*)

inquiry, interrŏgātĭo, *f;* (official), quaestĭo, *f*

inquisitive, cūrĭōsus

inquisitor, quaesĭtor, *m*

inroad, incursĭo, *f*

insane, insānus, dēmens

insanity, insānĭa, *f,* dēmentĭa, *f*

insatiable, insătĭābĭlis

inscribe, *v.t,* inscrībo (3) in (*with abl*)

inscription, inscriptĭo, *f*

inscrutable, obscūrus

insect, bestĭŏla, *f*

insecure, intūtus **(unsafe)**

insecurity, *use adj,* intūtus

insensible (unfeeling), dūrus

inseparable, *use phr,* quod sēpărāri nōn pŏtest **(that cannot be separated)**

insert, *v.t,* insĕro (3)

inside, *prep,* intrā (*with acc*)

inside, *adv,* intus

inside, *nn,* intĕrĭor pars, *f*

insidious, insĭdĭōsus

insight (understanding), intellĕgentĭa, *f*

insignia, insignĭa, *n.pl*

insignificant, exĭgŭus, nullĭus mŏmenti

insincere, sĭmŭlātus

insincerity, fallācĭa, *f,* sĭmŭlātĭo, *f*

insinuate, *v.t,* insĭnŭo (1); (hint), signĭfĭco (1)

insinuating (smooth), blandus

insipid, insulsus

insist, *v.i,* insto (1); *v.t,* (— on, demand), posco (3), flāgĭto (1)

insolence, contŭmācĭa, *f,* insŏlentĭa, *f*

insolent, contŭmax, insŏlens

insoluble, *use phr,* quod explĭcāri nōn pŏtest **(that cannot be explained)**

insolvent (to be —), *v.i,* nōn esse solvendo

inspect, *v.t,* inspĭcĭo (3)

inspection, *use vb,* inspĭcĭo (3), *or* lustro (1)

inspector (superintendent), cūrātor, *m*

inspiration (divine, poetic, etc), instinctus, *m,* afflātus, *m*

inspire, *v.t,* ĭnĭcĭo (3) (*with acc. of thing inspired and dat. of person*); (rouse), accendo (3)

inspired (of persons), incensus

instal, *v.t,* ĭnaugŭro (1)

instalment, pensĭo, *f*

instance (example), exemplum, *n;* (for —), verbi grātĭā

instant, *adj,* praesens

instant, *nn,* mōmentum, *n*

instantly (at once), *adv,* stătim

instantaneous, praesens

instead, *adv,* măgis **(rather)**

instead of, *prep,* prō (*with abl*)*; with a clause, use* tantum ăbĕrat (ăbest) ut … ut

instigate, *v.t,* instīgo (1)

instill, *v.t,* instillo (1), ĭnītĭo (3)

instinct, nātūra, *f*

instinctive, nātūrālis

institute, *v.t,* instĭtŭo (3)

institute, institution, collĕgĭum *n;* instĭtūtum, *n*

instruct, *v.t,* dŏcĕo (2), ērŭdĭo (4); (order), praecĭpĭo (3)

instruction, dĭscĭplīna, *f,* institutio, *f;* (command), mandātum, *n*

instructor, măgister, *m*

instrument, instrūmentum, *n*

instrumental (in doing something), ūtĭlis

insubordinate, sēdĭtĭōsus

insufferable, intŏlĕrābĭlis

insufficiency, ĭnōpĭa, *f*

insufficient, haud sătis (*with genit*) **(not enough …)**

insult, *nn,* contŭmēlĭa, *f*

insult, *v.t,* contŭmēlĭam impōno (3) (*with dat*)

insulting, contŭmēlĭōsus

insuperable, *use phr,* quod sŭpĕrāri nōn pŏtest **(that cannot be overcome)**

insure against, *v.t,* praecăvĕo (2)

insurgent, rĕbellis, *m*

insurrection, mōtus, *m*

intact, intĕger

integral, nĕcessārĭus **(necessary)**

integrity, intĕgrĭtas, *f*

intellect, mens, *f,* ingĕnĭum, *n*

intellectual, ingĕnĭōsus

intelligence, ingĕnĭum, *n;* **(news),** nuntĭus, *m*

intelligent, săpĭens, intellĕgens

intelligible, perspĭcŭus
intemperate, intempĕrans
intend, v.t, in ănĭmo hăbĕo (2) (with infinitive)
intense, ācer
intensify, v.t, augĕo (2), incendo (3) (inflame, rouse)
intensity, vīs, f
intent, adj, intentus; (to be — on), ănĭmum intendo (3) in (with acc)
intention, consĭlĭum, n, prŏpŏsĭtum, n
intentionally, adv, consultō
inter, v.t, sĕpĕlĭo (4)
intercede (on behalf of), dēprĕcor (1 dep) pro (with abl)
intercept, v.t, (catch), excĭpĭo (3); (cut off), interclūdo (3)
intercession, dēprĕcātĭo, f
interchange, nn, permūtātĭo, f
interchange, v.t, permūto (1)
intercourse, commercĭum, n, ūsus, m
interest, nn, (zeal), stŭdĭum, n; (advantage), commŏdum, n; (it is in the — of), intĕrest (v. impers. with genit); (financial), fēnus, n, ūsūra, f
interest, v.t, tĕnĕo (2), plăcĕo (2); (— oneself in), stŭdĕo (2) (with dat)
interested, attentus
interesting, use vb. to interest
interfere, v.i, sē interpōnĕre (3 reflex)
interim, adv, (in the —), intĕrim
interior, adj, intĕrĭor; nn, pars intĕrĭor, f
interject, v.t, intĕrĭcĭo (3)
interlude, embŏlĭum, n
intermarriage, connūbĭum, n
intermediate, mĕdĭus
interminable, infīnītus
intermingle, v.t, miscĕo (2); v.i, sē miscēre (2 reflex)
intermission, intermissĭo, f
internal, intestīnus
international, use genit, gentĭum (of nations)
internecine, internĕcīnus
interpose, v.t, interpōno (3)
interpret, v.t, interprĕtor (1 dep)
interpretation, interprĕtātĭo, f
interpreter, interpres, c
interregnum, interregnum, n
interrogate, v.t, interrŏgo (1)
interrupt, v.t, interpello (1), interrumpo (3)
interruption, interpellātĭo, f
intersect, v.t, sĕco (1) (cut)
interval, intervallum, n, spătĭum, n
intervene, v.i, intercēdo (3), sē interpōnĕre (3 reflex) (both with dat)
intervention, intercessĭo, f

interview, collŏquĭum, n
interview, v.t, collŏquor (3 dep) cum (with abl) (speak with)
interweave, v.t, intertexo (3), implĭco (1)
intestines, intestīna, n.pl
intimacy, consŭētūdo, f, fămĭlĭărĭtas, f
intimate, adj, fămĭlĭāris
intimate, v.t, signĭfĭco (1)
intimidate, v.t, dēterrĕo (2)
intimidation, terror, m, mĭnae, f. pl
into, prep, in (with acc)
intolerable, intŏlĕrābĭlis
intolerance, sŭperbĭa, f
intolerant, sŭperbus
intone, v.t, căno (3)
intoxicate, v.t, ēbrĭum reddo (3) (make drunk)
intoxicated, ēbrĭus
intoxication, ēbrĭĕtas, f
intractable, diffĭcĭlis
intrepid, intrĕpĭdus
intricacy (difficulty), diffĭcultas, f
intricate, diffĭcĭlis
intrigue, dŏlus, m
intrigue, v.i, dŏlīs ūtor (3 dep)
introduce, v.t, intrōdūco (3)
introduction, intrŏductĭo, f; (letter of —) littĕrae commendātīcĭae, f. pl
intrude, v.i, sē inculcāre (1 reflex)
intrusive use phr, qui interpellāre sŏlet (who usually disturbs)
intuition, cognītĭo, f
inundate, v.t, ĭnundo (1)
inundation, ĭnundātĭo, f
inure, v.t, assŭēfăcĭo (3)
invade, v.t, bellum infĕro (irreg) (with dat), invādo (3) in (with acc)
invader, hostis, c
invalid, nn, aeger, m
invalid, adj, (of no avail), irrĭtus, infirmus
invalidate, v.t, infirmo (1)
invariable, constans
invasion, incursĭo, f
invective, convīcĭum, n
inveigh against, v.i, invĕhor (3 dep) in (with acc.)
inveigle, v.t, illĭcĭo (3)
invent, v.t, invĕnĭo (4)
invention (faculty), inventĭo, f; (thing invented), inventum, n
inventor, inventor, m
inverse, inversus
invert, v.t, inverto (3)
invest, v.t, (money), collŏco (1); (besiege), obsĭdĕo (2); (— someone with an office), măgistrātum committo (3) (with dat)

investigate, *v.t,* exquīro (3), cognosco (3)

investigation, investīgātĭo, *f,* cognĭtĭo, *f*

investiture, consĕcrātĭo, *f*

inveterate, invĕtĕrātus

invidious (envious, hateful), invĭdĭōsus

invigorate, *v.t,* vīres rĕfĭcĭo (3)

invincible, invictus

inviolability, sanctĭtas, *f* (sacredness)

inviolable, invĭŏlātus

invisible, caecus

invitation, invītātĭo, *f;* (at your —), tŭo invītātu

invite, *v.t,* invīto (1)

inviting, blandus

invoke, *v.t,* invŏco (1)

involuntary, nōn vŏluntārĭus,

involve, *v.t,* involvo (3), illĭgo (1), hăbĕo (2)

invulnerable, *use phr,* quod vulnĕrāri nōn pŏtest (that cannot be wounded)

inward, *adj,* intĕrĭor

inwardly, inwards, *adv,* intus

irascibility, īrācundĭa, *f*

irascible, īrācundus

iris, īris, *f*

irk (it —s), pĭget (*v. 2 impers.*) (*with acc. of person*)

irksome, grăvis, mŏlestus

iron, *nn,* ferrum, *n*

iron, *adj,* ferrĕus

ironical, *use nn,* īrōnĭa, *f* (irony)

ironmongery, ferrāmenta, *n.pl*

irony, īrōnĭa, *f,* dissĭmŭlātĭo, *f*

irradiate, *v.t,* illustro (1)

irrational, rătĭōnis expers (devoid of reason)

irreconcilable, rĕpugnans

irrefutable, firmus

irregular (out of the ordinary), inūsĭtātus, extrāordĭnārĭus; (not well regulated), nōn ordĭnātus

irregularity, vĭtĭum, *n; otherwise use adjs. above*

irrelevant, ălĭēnus

irreligious, impĭus

irremediable, insānābĭlis

irreparable, *use phr,* quod rĕfĭci nōn pŏtest (that cannot be repaired)

irreproachable, intĕger, invictus

irresistible, invictus

irresolute, dŭbĭus

irretrievable, irrĕpĕrābĭlis

irreverance,, impĭĕtas, *f*

irreverent, impĭus

irrevocable, irrĕvŏcābĭlis

irrigate, *v.t,* irrĭgo (1)

irrigation, irrĭgātĭo, *f*

irritable, stŏmăchōsus

irritate, *v.t,* irrīto (1); (make worse), pēius reddo (3)

irruption, (attack), incursĭo, *f*

island, insŭla, *f*

islander, insŭlānus, *m*

isolate, *v.t,* sēpăro (1)

isolation, sōlĭtūdo, *f*

issue, *nn,* (result), ēventus, *m;* (topic), rēs, *f;* (offspring), prōgĕnĭes, *f*

issue, *v.i,* (proceed), ēgrĕdĭor (3 *dep*); (turn out), ēvĕnĭo (4); *v.t* (give out), ēdo (3); (edicts, etc.) ēdīco (3)

isthmus, isthmus, *m*

it, *pron,* id, hoc, illud; *often expressed by 3rd person sing. of verb, e.g.* it is, est

itch, *nn,* prūrītus, *m;* (disease), scăbĭes, *f*

itch, *v.i,* prūrĭo (4)

item, rēs, *f*

itinerant, circumfŏrānĕus

itinerary, ĭter, *n* (route)

itself, *see* himself

ivory, *nn,* ĕbur, *n; adj,* ĕburnĕus

ivy, hĕdĕra, *f*

J

jab, *v.t,* fŏdĭo (3)

jabber, *v.i,* blătĕro (1)

jackass, ăsĭnus, *m*

jacket, tŭnĭca, *f*

jaded, dēfessus

jagged, asper

jail, carcer, *m*

jailer, custos, *c*

janitor, iānĭtor, *m*

January, Iānŭārĭus (mensis)

jar, olla, *f,* amphŏra, *f,* dōlĭum, *n*

jarring, dissŏnus

jaunt, excursĭo, *f*

javelin, pīlum, *n*

jaws, faucēs, *f. pl*

jealous, invĭdus

jealousy, invĭdĭa, *f*

jeer at, *v.t,* dērīdĕo (2)

jeering, *nn,* irrīsĭo, *f*

jejune, iēiūnus

jeopardize, *v.t,* pĕrīclĭtor (1 *dep*)

jeopardy, pĕrīcŭlum, *n*

jerk, *v.t,* quătĭo (3)

jerkin, tŭnĭca, *f*

jest, *nn,* iŏcus, *m*

jest, *v.i,* iŏcor (1 *dep*)

jester, scurra, *m*

jetty, mōles, *f*

Jew, *nn,* Jūdaeus, *m*

jewel, gemma, *f*

For List of Abbreviations used, turn to pages 3, 4

jeweller, gemmārĭus, *m*

jibe, convĭcĭum, *n*

jilt, *v.t*, rĕpŭdĭo (1)

jingle, *nn*, tinnītus *m*

jingle, *v.i*, tinnĭo (4)

job, ŏpus, *n*

jockey, ăgāso, *m*

jocose, ĭŏcōsus

jocular, ĭŏcŭlāris

jocund, hĭlăris, iūcundus

jog, *v.t*, fŏdĭco (1) (nudge)

join, *v.t*, iungo (3); *v.i*, sē coniungĕre (3 *reflex*); (— battle) committo (3)

joiner, lignārĭus, *m*

joint, commissūra, *f*

joist, tignum transversum, *n*

joke, *nn*, ĭŏcus, *m*

joke, *v.i*, ĭŏcor (1 *dep*)

joker, ĭŏcŭlātor, *m*

jollity, hĭlărĭtas, *f*

jolly, hĭlăris

jolt, *v.t*, concŭtĭo (3)

jostle, *v.t*, pulso (1)

jot, *v.t*, adnŏto (1)

journal, commentārĭi dĭurni, *m. pl*

journey, *nn*, ĭter, *n*

journey, *v.i*, ĭter făcĭo (3)

journey-man, ŏpĭfex, *c*

jovial, hĭlăris

jowl, gĕnae, *f. pl*

joy (outward), laetĭtĭa, *f*; (inner), gaudĭum, *n*

joyful, laetus

joyless, tristis

jubilant, gaudĭo (*or* laetĭtĭā) exsultans (exultant with joy)

judge, *nn*, iūdex, *m*

judge, *v.t*, iūdĭco (1), aestĭmo (1)

judgement, iūdĭcĭum, *n*

judicature, iūdĭces, *m. pl*

judicial, iūdĭcĭālis

judicious, săpĭens

judiciously, săpĭenter

judiciousness, prūdentĭa, *f*

jug, urcĕus, *m*

juggling-tricks, praestĭgĭae, *f. pl*

juice, sūcus, *m*

juicy, sūcōsus

July (before Caesar), Quīntīlis (mensis); (after Caesar), Iūlĭus (mensis)

jumble, *nn*, congĕrĭes, *f*

jumble, *v.t*, confundo (3)

jump, *nn*, saltus *m*

jump, *v.i*, sălĭo (4)

junction, coniunctĭo, *f*

juncture, tempus, *n*

June, Iūnĭus (mensis)

junior, mĭnor nātu, iūnĭor

juniper, iūnĭpĕrus, *f*

jurisconsult, iūrisconsultus, *m*

jurisdiction, iūrisdictĭo, *f*

juror, iūdex, *m*

jury, iūdĭces, *m. pl*

just, iustus

justice, iustĭtĭa, *f*

justification, sătisfactĭo, *f*

justify, *v.t*, purgo (1), excūso (1)

justly, *adv*, iustē

jut, *v.i*, exsto (1)

juvenile, iūvĕnīlis

K

keel, cărīna *f*

keen, ācer; (mentally), perspĭcax

keenness (eagerness), stŭdĭum, *n*; (sagacity), săgācĭtas, *f*; (sharpness, etc.), ăcerbĭtas, *f*

keep, *nn*, arx, *f*

keep, *v.t*, (hold), tĕnĕo (2), hăbĕo (2); (preserve), servo (1); (store), condo (3); (support, rear), ălo (3); (— apart), distĭnĕo (2); (— back), rĕtĭnĕo (2), dētĭnĕo (2); (— off), arcĕo (2); *v.i*, (remain), mănĕo (2)

keeper, custos, *c*

keeping (protection), tūtēla, *f*, custōdĭa, *f*

keg, dōlĭum, *n*, amphŏra, *f*

kennel, stăbŭlum, *n*

kerb (stone), crĕpĭdo, *f*

kernel, nŭclĕus, *m*

kettle, lēbes, *m*

key, clāvis, *f*

kick, *nn*, calcĭtrātus, *m*

kick, *v.i*, calcĭtro (1)

kid, haedus, *m*

kidnap, *v.t*, surrĭpĭo (3)

kidney, rēn, *m*

kidney-bean, phăsēlus, *m*, *f*

kill, *v.t*, nĕco (1), interfĭcĭo (3)

kiln, fornax, *f*

kind, *nn*, gĕnus, *n*; (of such a —), *adj*, tālis

kind, *adj*, bĕnignus

kindle, *v.t*, accendo (3), excĭto (1)

kindliness, bĕnignĭtas, *f*

kindness, bĕnĕfĭcĭum, *n*; (of disposition), bĕnignĭtas, *f*

kindred (relatives), consanguĭnĕi, *m. pl*; cognāti, *m. pl*

king, rex, *m*

kingdom, regnum, *n*

kingfisher, alcēdo, *f*

kinsman, nĕcessārĭus, *m*

kiss, *nn*, oscŭlum, *n*

kiss, v.t, oscŭlor (1 dep)

kitchen, cŭlīna, f

kitten, fēlis cătŭlus, m (the young of a cat)

knapsack, sarcĭna, f

knave, scĕlestus, m

knavery, nēquĭtĭa, f, imprŏbĭtas, f

knavish, nēquam (indeclinable); imprŏbus

knead, v.t, sŭbĭgo (3)

knee, gĕnu, n; (knock-kneed), adj, vārus

knee-cap, pătella, f

kneel, gĕnu (gĕnĭbus) nītor (3 dep) (rest on the knee(s))

knife, culter, m

knight, ĕques, m

knighthood, dignĭtas ĕquestris, f

knit, v.t, texo (3); (— the forehead) frontem contrăho (3)

knob, bulla, f, nōdus, m

knock, v.t, pulso (1); (— against), offendo (3); (— down), dēpello (3), dēĭcĭo (3)

knock, knocking pulsus, m, pulsātĭo, f

knoll, tŭmŭlus, m

knot, nn, nōdus, m

knot, v.t, nōdo (1)

knotty, nōdōsus

know, v.t, scĭo (4); (get to —), cognosco (3); (person, acquaintance) nosco (3); (not to —), nescĭo (4)

knowing, adj, (wise), prūdens

knowingly, adv, consultō

knowledge, scĭentĭa, f

known, nōtus; (to make —), dēclāro (1)

knuckle, artĭcŭlus, m

L

label, tĭtŭlus, m, pittācĭum, n

laborious, lăbōrĭōsus

labour, lăbor, m, ŏpus, n; (to be in —), v.i, partŭrĭo (4)

labour, v.i, lăbōro (1), ēnītor (3 dep)

labourer, ŏpĕrārĭus, m

labyrinth, lăbўrinthus, m

lace, rētĭcŭlāta texta, n.pl (net-like fabric)

lacerate, v.t, lăcĕro (1)

laceration, lăcĕrātĭo, f

lack, nn, inŏpĭa, f

lack, v.i, ĕgĕo (2), cărĕo (both with abl)

lackey, pĕdĭsĕquus, m

laconic, brĕvis

lad, pŭer, m

ladder, scālae, f. pl

ladle, trulla, f

lady, mātrōna, f, dŏmĭna, f

lady-like, lībĕrālis (gracious)

lag, v.i, cesso (1)

laggard, cessātor, m

lagoon, lăcus, m

lair, lătĭbŭlum, n

lake, lăcus, m

lamb, agnus, m ; (agna, f)

lame, claudus; (argument, etc.), lĕvis; (to be —), v.i, claudĭco (1)

lameness, claudĭcātĭo, f

lament, lāmentātĭo, f, complōrātĭo, f, ŭlŭlātus, m

lament, v.i, and v.t, lāmentor (1 dep), dēplōro (1), lūgĕo (2)

lamentable, lāmentābĭlis

lamented, dēplōrātus, flēbĭlis

lamp, lŭcerna, f

lampoon, carmen rīdĭcŭlum et fāmōsum (facetious defamatory verse)

lance, lancĕa, f, hasta, f

lancet, scalpellum, n

land (earth, etc.), terra, f; (region or country), rēgĭo, f, fīnes, m. pl; (native —), pătrĭa, f

land, v.t, expōno (3); v.i, ēgrĕdĭor (3 dep)

landing, nn, ēgressus, m

landlord (innkeeper), caupo, m; (owner), dŏmĭnus, m

landmark, lăpis, m

landslide, lapsus, (m) terrae

lane, sēmĭta, f,

language, lingua, f; (speech, style), ōrātĭo, f

languid, languĭdus, rĕmissus

languish, v.i, languĕo (2), tābesco (3)

languor, languor, m

lank, (hair), prōmissus; (persons), prōcerus

lantern, lanterna, f

lap, grĕmĭum, n, sĭnus, m

lap up, v.t, lambo (3)

lapse, nn, (mistake), peccātum, n; (of time), fŭga, f

lapse, v.i, (err), pecco (1); (time), praetĕrĕo (4)

larceny, furtum, n

larch, lărix, f

lard, ădeps, c, lārĭdum, n

larder, use cella, f, (store-room), or armārĭum, n, (food cupboard)

large, magnus

largeness, magnĭtūdo, f

largess, largītĭo, f

lark, ălauda, f

larynx, use guttur, n, (throat)

lascivious, lībidĭnōsus

lash (whip), lōrum, n, flăgellum, n; (eye —), pĭlus, m

lash, *v.t*, (whip), verběro (1); (bind), allĭgo (1)

lass, pŭella, *f*

last, *adj*, ultĭmus, postrēmus, extrēmus; (most recent), nŏvissĭmus, proxĭmus; (at —), *adv*, tandem

last, *v.i*, dūro (1), mănĕo (2)

lasting, *adj*, dĭuturnus

lastly, *adv*, postrēmo, dēnĭque

latch, pessŭlus, *m*

late, sērus, tardus; (dead), mortŭus; *adv*, sēro; (— at night) (*adv. phr.*), multā nocte

lately, *adv*, nūper

latent, occultus

lathe, tornus, *m*

Latin, Lătīnus; (— language), lingua Lătīna, *f*

latitude (freedom, scope), lībertas, *f*

latter (the —), hic

lattice, cancelli, *m. pl*

laud, *v.t*, laudo (1)

laudable, laudābĭlis

laugh, *nn*, rīsus, *m*; (loud —), căchinnus, *m*

laugh, *v.i*, cachinno (1)

laughing-stock, lūdĭbrĭum, *n*

launch, *v.t*, (a ship), dēdūco (3); *v.i*, (launch out), insĕquor (3 *dep*)

laurel, laurus, *f*; *adj*, laurĕus

lava, massa līquĕfacta, *f*, (molten mass)

lavish, *adj*, prŏdĭgus, prŏfūsus

lavish, *v.t*, prŏfundo (3)

law (a law), lex, *f*; (the law), iūs, *n*

lawful, lēgĭtĭmus

lawless, nĕfārĭus

lawn, prātum, *n*

lawsuit, līs, *f*

lawyer, iūrisconsultus, *m*

lax, dissŏlūtus

laxness, rēmissĭo, *f*, neglĕgentĭa, *f*

laxity, rēmissĭo, *f*, neglĕgentĭa, *f*

lay, *v.t*, pōno (3); (— aside), pōno (3); (— foundations), iăcĭo (3); (— an ambush), insĭdĭas collŏco (1); (— down arms), ab armis discēdo (3); (— eggs), ŏva părĭo (3)

layer, cŏrĭum, *n*, tăbŭlātum, *n*

laziness, ignāvĭa, *f*

lazy, ignāvus, pĭger

lead, *nn*, plumbum, *n*; *adj*, plumbĕus

lead, *v.t*, dūco (3); (— a life, etc.), ăgo (3); (— on, persuade), addūco (3)

leader, dux, *c*

leadership, ductus, *m*; *or use phr. in abl, e.g.* under the — of Brutus, Brūto dŭce (with Brutus leader)

leading, *adj*, princeps

leaf, frons, *f*, fŏlĭum, *n*; (paper) schēda, *f*

leafy, frondōsus

league, foedus, *n*, sŏcĭĕtas, *f*

league together, *v.i*, coniūro (1)

leak, *nn*, rīma, *f*

leak (let in water), ăquam per rīmas accĭpĭo (3)

leaky, rīmōsus

lean, *adj*, măcer, exĭlis

lean, *v.i*, innītor (3 *dep*); *v.t*, inclīno (1)

leanness, măcĭes, *f*

leap, *nn*, saltus, *m*

leap, *v.i*, sălĭo (4); (— down) dēsĭlĭo (4)

leap-year, bĭsextĭlis annus, *m*

learn, *v.t*, disco (3); (ascertain) cognosco (3)

learned, doctus

learning, doctrīna, *f*, ērŭdĭtĭo, *f*

lease, *nn*, conductĭo, *f*

lease, *v.t*, condūco (3)

leash, cōpŭla, *f*

least, *adj*, mĭnĭmus; *adv*, mĭnĭmē; (at —), *adv*, saltem

leather, cŏrĭum, *n*

leave, *nn*, (permission), pŏtestas, *f*, permissĭo, *f*; (— of absence) commĕātus, *m*

leave, *v.i*, discēdo (3); *v.t*, rĕlinquo (3), dēsĕro (3)

leave off, *v.i. and v.t*, dēsĭno (3)

leavings, *nn*, rĕlĭquĭae, *f. pl*

lecture, *nn*, audītĭo, *f*, (hearing)

lecture, *v.i*, schŏlas hăbĕo (2)

lecture-room, schŏla, *f*

ledge, *use adj*, ēmĭnens (projecting) *in agreement with a noun*

ledger, cōdex, *m*

leech, hīrūdo, *f*

leek, porrum, *n*

leering, *adj*, līmus

left, *adj*, (opp. to right), sĭnister, laevus; (remaining), rĕlĭquus

leg, crus, *n*

legacy, lēgātum, *n*

legal, lēgĭtĭmus

legalize, *v.t*, sancĭo (4)

legate, lēgātus, *m*

legation, lēgātĭo, *f*

legend, fābŭla, *f*

legendary, fābŭlōsus

leggings, ŏcrĕae, *f. pl*

legible, *use phr*, făcĭlis ad lĕgendum (easy for reading)

legion, lēgĭo, *f*

legislate, *v.i*, lēges făcĭo (3) (make laws)

legislator, lātor, (*m*) lēgum (proposer of laws)

legitimate, lēgĭtĭmus

leisure, ōtĭum, *n*; (to be at —), *v.i,*
ōtĭor (1 *dep*)
leisurely, *adj*, lentus
lend, *v.t*, mŭtŭum do (1) (give a loan),
commŏdo (1)
length, longĭtūdo, *f*; (of time), dĭūturnĭtas, *f*; (at —), *adv*, tandem
lengthen, *v.t*, prōdūco (3), longĭōrem
reddo (3)
leniency, clēmentĭa, *f*
lenient, mītis, clēmens
lentil, lens, *f*
leper, hŏmo lēprōsus, *m*
leprosy, lēprae, *f. pl*
less, *adj*, mĭnor; *adv*, mĭnus
lessen, *v.i. and v.t*, mĭnŭo (3)
lesson, dŏcŭmentum, *n*
lest, *conj*, nē
let, *v.t*, sĭno (3), permitto (3) (*with dat
of person*); (lease), lŏco (1);(— go),
dīmitto (3); (— in), admitto (3); (—
out), ēmitto (3)
lethal, mortĭfer
lethargic, lentus
letter (of the alphabet), littĕra, *f*;
(epistle), littĕrae, *f. pl*, ĕpistŏla, *f*
lettering, *nn*, littĕrae, *f.pl*
letters (learning), littĕrae, *f. pl*
lettuce, lactūca, *f*
level, *adj*, plānus; (— place), *nn*,
plānĭtĭes, *f*
level, *v.t*, aequo (1);(— to the ground),
sterno (3)
lever, vectis, *m*
levity, lĕvĭtas, *f*
levy, *nn*, dēlectus, *m*
levy, *v.t*, (troops), scrībo (3); (taxes,
etc.), impĕro (1), ĕxĭgo (3)
lewd, incestus, impŭdīcus
lewdness, incestum, *n*
liable, obnoxĭus
liar, hŏmo mendax
libellous, fāmōsus
liberal, lībĕrālis, largus
liberality, lībĕrālĭtas, *f*, largĭtas, *f*
liberate, *v.t*, lībĕro (1)
liberation, lībĕrātĭo, *f*
liberty, lībertas, *f*
librarian, bĭblĭŏthēcārĭus, *m*
library, bĭblĭŏthēca, *f*
licence, lĭcentĭa, *f*; (permission),
pŏtestas, *f*
licentious, dissŏlūtus
lick, *v.t*, lambo (3)
lid, ŏpercŭlum, *n*
lie, *nn*, mendācĭum, *n*
lie, *v.i*, (tell a —), mentĭor (4 *dep*)
lie, *v.i*, iăcĕo (2); (rest), cŭbo (1); (—
ill), iăcĕo (2); (— in wait), insĭdĭor
(1 *dep*)

lieutenant, lēgātus, *m*
life, vīta, *f*, ănĭma, *f*; (vivacity) vĭgor,
m; (— blood), sanguis, *m*
lifeless, exănĭmis, exsanguis
lifelike, *use* sĭmĭlis (similar)
lifetime, aetas, *f*
lift, *v.t*, tollo (3)
ligament, lĭgāmentum, *n*
light, *nn*, lux, *f*, lūmen, *n*; (to bring
to —), in mĕdĭum prōfĕro (*irreg*)
light, *adj* (not dark), illustris; (in
weight), lĕvis; (— armed), expĕdītus; (trivial, of opinions, etc.),
lĕvis
light, *v.t*, (illuminate), illustro (1);
(kindle), accendo (3)
lighten, *v.t*, (burden, etc.), lĕvo (1);
v.i, (of lightning), fulgĕo (2)
lighthouse, phărus, *f*
lightly, *adv*, lĕvĭter
lightning, fulmen, *n*
like, *v.t*, ămo (1)
like, *adj*, sĭmĭlis (*with genit. or dat*),
par (*with dat*)
like, *adv*, sĭmĭlĭter; (just as), sīcut
likelihood, sĭmĭlĭtūdo, (*f*) vĕri
likely, sĭmĭlis vĕri; *often use future
participle, e.g.* likely to come,
venturus
liken, *v.t*, compăro (1)
likeness, sĭmĭlĭtūdo, *f*
likewise, *adv*, ĭtem
liking, *nn*, ămor, *m*, lĭbīdo, *f*
lily, lĭlĭum, *n*
limb, membrum, *n*, artus, *m. p*
lime, calx, *f*; (tree), tīlĭa, *f*
limit, *nn*, fĭnis, *m*, termĭnus, *m*
limit, *v.t*, fīnĭo (4)
limitation, fīnis, *m*
limited (small), parvus
limitless, infīnītus
limp, *adj*, (slack), rĕmissus
limp, *v.i*, claudĭco (1)
limping, *adj*, claudus
limpid, limpĭdus
linden-tree, tīlĭa, *f*
line, līnĕa, *f*; (boundary —), fīnis, *m*;
(of poetry), versus, *m*; (of battle),
ăcĭes, *f*; (front —), prīma ăcĭes, *f*;
(second —), prīncĭpes, *m.pl*; (third
—), trĭārĭi, *m.pl*; (— of march),
agmen, *n*
line, *v.t*, (put in —), instrŭo (3)
lineage, stirps, *f*, gĕnus, *n*
linen, *nn*, lintĕum, *n*; *adj*, lintĕus
linger, *v.i*, mŏror (1 *dep*); cunctor
(1 *dep*)
lingering, *nn*, mŏra, *f*
link, *nn*, (of chain), ănŭlus, *m*
link, *v.t*, coniungo (3)

For List of Abbreviations used, turn to pages 3, 4

lint, līnāmentum, *n*

lintel, līmen sŭpĕrum, *n*

lion, lĕo, *m*; (lioness), lĕaena,,

lip, lābrum, *n*

liquefy, *v.t*, līquĕfăcĭo (3)

liquid, *nn*, līquor, *m*

liquid, *adj*, līquĭdus

liquidate, *v.t*, solvo (3)

liquor, līquor, *m*

lisping, *adj*, blaesus

list, tăbŭla, *f*

listen (to), *v.t*, audĭo (4)

listener, auscultātor, *m*

listless, languĭdus

listlessness, languor, *m*

literal, *use*, prŏprĭus (its own)

literally, *adv. phr*, ad verbum

literary (person), littĕrātus

literature, littĕrae, *f. pl*

lithe, flexĭbĭlis, ăgĭlis

litigation, līs, *f*

litter (of straw, etc.), strāmentum, *n*; (sedan), lectīca, *f*; (of young), fētus, *m*

little, *adj*, parvus, exĭgŭus; (for a —while), *adv*, părumper, paulisper

little, *adv*, paulum

little, *nn*, paulum, *n*, nonnĭhil, *n*; (too little), părum, *n*; *with comparatives*, paulo; *e.g.* a little bigger, paulo māior

littleness, exĭgŭĭtas, *f*

live, *v.i*, vīvo (3); (— in or at), hăbĭto (1), incŏlo (3); (— on), vescor (3 *dep*) (with abl); (— one's life, etc.), vītam ăgo (3)

live, *adj*, vīvus

livelihood, victus, *m*

liveliness, ălăcrĭtas, *f*

lively, *adj*, ălăcer

liver, iĕcur, *n*

livery, vestītus, *m*

livid, līvĭdus

living, *adj*, vīvus

lizard, lăcerta, *f*

load, ŏnus, *n*

load, *v.t*, ŏnĕro (1)

loaded, ŏnustus

loaf, pānis, *m*

loam, lŭtum, *n*

loan, mūtŭum, *n, or use adj*, mūtuus (borrowed, lent)

loathe, *v.t*, ōdi (*defect*)

loathing, *nn*, ŏdĭum, *n*

loathsome, tēter

lobby, vestĭbŭlum, *n*

local, *use genit. of* lŏcus (place)

locality, lŏcus, *m*

lock (bolt), claustra, *n.pl*; (hair), crīnis, *m*

lock, *v.t*, obsĕro (1)

locker, capsa, *f*, armārĭum, *n*

locust, lŏcusta, *f*

lodge, *v.i*, dēversor (1 *dep*); (stick fast), adhaerĕo (2) fixus; *v.t* (accommodate temporarily), excĭpĭo (3)

lodger, inquĭlīnus, *m*

lodgings, dēversōrĭum, *n*

loft, cēnācŭlum, *n*

loftiness, altĭtūdo, *f*

lofty, celsus, altus

log, tignum, *n*

logic, dĭălectĭca, *f*

logical, dĭălectĭcus

loin, lumbus, *m*

loiter, *v.i*, cesso (1); cunctor (1 *dep*)

loiterer, cessātor, *m*

loneliness, sōlĭtūdo, *f*

lonely, *adj*, sōlus

long, *adj*, longus (*with acc. of extent of length*), *e.g.* three feet long, longus tres pĕdes; (a — way), *adv*, prŏcul, longē; (of time), dĭūtĭnus, dĭūturnus; (how —?), quam dĭū? (for a -time), *adv*, dĭū

long, *adv*, (time), dĭū

long for, *v.t*, dēsīdĕro (1), cŭpĭo (3)

longevity, vīvācĭtas, *f*

longing, *nn*, dēsīdĕrĭum, *n*

long-suffering, *adj*, pătĭens

look at, *v.t*, aspĭcĭo (3); (— back), rĕspĭcĭo (3); (— down (upon)), dēspĭcĭo (3); (— for), quaero (3); (— round), circumspĭcĭo (3); *v.i* (— towards), specto (1); (seem), vĭdĕor (2 *pass*)

look, *nn*, aspectus, *m*; (appearance), spĕcĭes, *f*; (expression), vultus, *m*

looking-glass, spĕcŭlum, *n*

loom, tēla, *f*

loop (winding), flexus, *m*

loop-hole, fĕnestra, *f*

loose, *adj*, laxus; (at liberty), sŏlūtus; (hair), passus, prōmissus; (dissolute), dissŏlūtus

loose, *v.t*, laxo (1), solvo (3)

loosely, *adv*, sŏlūtē

loot, *nn*, praeda, *f*

loot, *v.t*, praedor (1 *dep*)

lop off, *v.t*, ampŭto (1)

loquacious, lŏquax

loquacity, lŏquācĭtas, *f*

lord, dŏmĭnus, *m*

lordly, *adv*, rēgālis, sŭperbus

lordship (supreme power), impĕrĭum, *n*

lore, doctrīna, f

lose, v.t. āmitto (3), perdo (3); (— heart), ănĭmo dēfĭcĭo (3)

loss (act of losing), āmissĭo, f; (the loss itself), damnum, n, dētrĭmentum, n; (to be at a —), v.i, haerĕo (2)

lost (adj) āmissus, perdĭtus

lot (chance), sors, f; (to draw —s), sortĭor (4 dep); (much), multum, n

loth (unwilling), invītus

lottery, sortĭtĭo, f

loud, clārus, magnus

loudness, magnĭtūdo, f

lounge, v.i, (recline), rĕcŭbo (1)

louse, pēdĭcŭlus, m

lousy, pēdĭcŭlōsus

lout, hŏmo agrestis

love, nn, ămor, m

love, v.t, ămo (1), dīlĭgo (3)

loveliness, vĕnustas, f

lovely, vĕnustus

lover, ămātor, m, ămans, c

loving, adj, ămans

low, hŭmĭlis; (sounds), grăvis; (— born), hŭmĭli lŏco nātus; (price), vilis; (conduct, etc.), sordĭdus; (in spirits), adv. phr, ănĭmo dēmisso

low, v.i, mūgĭo (4)

lower, comp. adj, infĕrĭor

lower, v.t, dēmitto (3); (— oneself), sē ăbĭcĕre (3 reflex)

lowering, mĭnax

lowest, infĭmus

lowing, mūgītus, m

lowlands, lŏca, plāna, n.pl

lowness, lowliness, hŭmĭlĭtas, f

lowly, hŭmĭlis, obscūrus

loyal, fĭdēlis

loyalty, fĭdes, f

lozenge, pastillus, m

lubricate, v.t, ungo (3)

lucid, lūcĭdus

lucidity, perspĭcŭĭtas, f

luck, fortūna, f, fors, f; (good —), fēlīcĭtas, f; (bad —), infēlīcĭtas,

luckily, adv, fēlīcĭter

luckless, infēlix

lucky, fēlix, fortūnātus

lucrative, quaestŭōsus

ludicrous, rĭdĭcŭlus

lug, v.t, trăho (3)

luggage, impĕdīmenta, n.pl

lugubrious, lūgŭbris

lukewarm, tĕpĭdus

lull, v.t, sēdo (1); v.i, (of wind), sēdor (1 pass)

lull, nn, use vb. intermitto (3)

lumber, scrūta, n.pl

luminary, lūmen, n

luminous, illustris, lūcĭdus

lump, massa, f

lunacy, insānĭa, f, ălĭēnātĭo, f

lunar, lūnāris

lunatic, hŏmo insānus

lunch, nn, prandĭum, n

lunch, v.i, prandĕo (2)

lung, pulmo, m

lurch, v.i, ăgĭtor (1 pass) (leave in the —), rĕlinquo (3)

lure, nn, illex, c, illĕcĕbrae, f. pl

lure, v.t, allĭcĭo (3)

lurid, lūrĭdus

lurk, v.i, lătĕo (2)

lurking in wait, use insĭdĭor (1 dep) (lie in ambush)

luscious, dulcis

lust, nn, lĭbīdo, f

lust after, v.t, concŭpisco (3)

lustful, lĭbĭdĭnōsus

lustiness, vĭgor, m

lustre, splendor, m

lusty, vălĭdus

lute, cĭthăra, f

luxuriance, luxŭrĭa, f

luxuriant, luxŭrĭōsus

luxurious, luxŭrĭōsus, lautus

luxury, luxus, m, luxŭrĭa, f

lying, adj, (telling lies), mendax

lynx, lynx, c

lyre, cĭthăra, f, fĭdes, f, pl

lyrical, lўrĭcus

M

mace-bearer, lictor, m

macerate, v.t, măcĕro (1)

machination, dŏlus, m

machine, māchĭna, f

machinery, māchĭnātĭo, f

mackerel, scomber, m

mad, insānus, vēcors, fŭrĭōsus; (to be —), v.i, fŭro (3)

madden, v.t, mentem ălĭēno (1) (with dat); (excite), accendo (3)

maddening, adj, fŭrĭōsus

madman, hŏmo vēcors

madness, insānĭa, f

magazine, horrĕum, n; (arsenal), armāmentārĭum, n

maggot, vermĭcŭlus, m

magic, adj, măgĭcus

magic, nn, ars măgĭca, f

magician, măgus, m

magistracy, măgistrātus, m

magistrate, măgistrātus, m

magnanimity, magnănĭmĭtas, f

magnanimous, magnănĭmus

magnet, lăpis magnes, m

magnetic, magnēticus

magnificence, magnĭfĭcentĭa, f

magnificent, magnĭfĭcus, splendĭdus

magnify, v.t, amplĭfĭco (1), exaggĕro (1)

magnitude, magnĭtūdo, f

magpie, pīca, f

maid, maiden, virgo, f; (servant), ancilla, f

maiden, adj, virgĭnālis

mail (letters), littĕrae, f. pl, ĕpistŏlae, f. pl; (armour), lōrīca, f

maim, v.t, mŭtĭlo (1)

main, adj, prīmus, praecĭpŭus

mainland, contĭnens terra, f

maintain, v.t, servo (1), sustĭnĕo (2); (with food, etc.), ălo (3); (by argument), affirmo (1)

maintenance, use vb. servo (1) (to maintain)

majestic, augustus

majesty, māiestas, f

major, nn, (officer), praefectus, m

major, adj, māior

majority, māior pars, f

make, v.t, făcĭo (3), effĭcĭo (3), fingo (3), reddo (3); (compel), cōgo (3); (appoint), crĕo (1); (— for, seek), pĕto (3); (— haste), v.i, festīno (1), accĕlĕro (1); (—good), v.t, rĕpăro (1), sarcĭo (1); (— ready), praepăro (1); (— up, a total, etc.), explĕo (2); (— use of), ūtor (3 dep) (with abl)

maker, făbrĭcător, m

maladministration, măla admĭnistrātĭo, f

malady, morbus, m

malcontent, cŭpĭdus nŏvārum rērum (eager for innovations)

male, adj, mascŭlus, mās

male, nn, mās, m

malediction, dīrae, f.pl, (curses)

malefactor, hŏmo mălĕfĭcus, nŏcens

malevolence, mălĕvŏlentĭa, f

malevolent, mălĕvŏlus

malice, mălĕvŏlentĭa, f; (envy), invĭdĭa, f

malicious, mălĕvŏlus

malignant, mălĕvŏlus

maligner, obtrectător, m

malignity, mălĕvŏlentĭa, f

malleable, ductĭlis

mallet, mallĕus, m

maltreat, v.t, vĕxo (1)

maltreatment, vexātĭo, f

man (human being), hŏmo, c; (opp. to woman, child), vĭr, m; (mankind), hŏmĭnes, c.pl; (chess, etc.), latruncŭlus, m; (fighting —), mīles, c

man, v.t, (ships, etc.), complĕo (2)

man-of-war(ship), nāvis longa, f

manacle, nn, mănĭcae, f.pl, vincŭla n.pl

manage, v.t, admĭnistro (1), cūro (1), gĕro (3)

manageable, tractābĭlis, hăbĭlis

management, cūra, f, admĭnistrātĭo, f

manager, prōcūrător, m, admĭnistrātor, m

mandate, impĕrātum, n, mandātum, n

mane (of horse), iŭba, f

manful, vĭrīlis

manger, praesēpe, n

mangle, v.t, lăcĕro (1), lănĭo (1)

mangled, truncus

mangy, scăber

manhood, pūbertas, f, tŏga vĭrīlis, f (manly dress)

mania, insānĭa, f

maniac, hŏmo vēcors, āmens

manifest, v.t, ostendo (3), ăpĕrĭo (4)

manifest, adj, mănĭfestus, ăpertus

manifestation, ostentātĭo, f, or use vbs. above

manifold, multĭplex

maniple (of a legion), mănĭpŭlus, m

manipulate, v.t, tracto (1)

mankind, hŏmĭnes, c.pl

manliness, virtus, f

manly, vĭrīlis

manner (way), mŏdus, m, rătĭo, f; (custom), mos, m; (type), gĕnus, n; (good manners), dĕcōrum, n

mannerism, gestus prŏprĭus

manoeuvre (military), dēcursus, m; (trick), dŏlus, m

manoeuvre, v.i, dēcurro (3)

manor, praedĭum, n

manservant, servus, m

mansion, dŏmus magna, f

manslaughter, hŏmĭcidĭum, n

mantle, palla, f, lăcerna, f

manual, adj, use mănus (hand)

manual, nn, (book), lĭbellus, m

manufacture, nn, făbrĭca, f

manufacture, v.t, făbrĭcor (1 dep)

manufacturer, făbrĭcător, m

manumission, mănŭmissĭo, f

manure, stercus, n

manuscript, lĭber, m

many, adj, multi (pl); (very —), plūrĭmi; (a good —), plērīque, complūres; (as — as), tŏt ... quŏt; (how —?), quŏt?; (so —), tŏt; (— times), adv, saepĕ

map, tābŭla, f

map (to — out), v.t, dēsigno (1)

maple, ăcer, n; adj, ăcernus

mar, v.t, dēformo (1)

marauder, praedător, m

marble, marmor, *n*; *adj*, marmŏrĕus
March, Martĭus (mensis)
march, *nn*, ĭter, *n*; (forced —),
  magnum ĭter; (on the —), *adv.*
  phr, in ĭtĭnĕre
march, *v.i*, ĭter făcĭo (3); (— quickly),
  contendo (3); (advance), prōgrĕdĭor (3 *dep*)
mare, ĕqua, *f*
margin, margo, *m*,*f*
marine, *nn*, mīles classĭcus, *m*
marine, *adj*, mărīnus
mariner, nauta, *m*
maritime, mărītĭmus
mark, nŏta, *f*, signum, *n*, vestīgĭum,
  n; (characteristic), *use genit. case of*
  nn. with esse; *e.g.* it is the — of a
  wise man, est săpĭentis. . . .
mark, *v.t*, nŏto (1); (indicate), dēsigno
  (1); (notice, observe), ănĭmădverto
  (3)
market, fŏrum, *n*, măcellum, *n*;
  (cattle —), fŏrum bŏărĭum, *n*
market, *v.t*, nundĭnor (1 *dep*)
market-day, nundĭnae, *f.pl*, (ninth
  day)
marketing, *nn*, *use vb.* vendo (3) (sell)
market-place, fŏrum, *n*
marriage, conĭŭgĭum, *n*, connūbĭum,
  n, mātrĭmōnĭum, *n*; (— feast),
  nuptĭae, *f.pl*; (— contract), pactĭo
  nuptĭālis, *f*
marriageable, nūbĭlis
marrow, mĕdulla, *f*
marry, *v.t*, (— a woman), dūco (3);
  (— a man), nūbo (3) (*with dat*)
marsh, pălus, *f*
marshal, appārĭtor, *m*
marshal, *v.t*, (troops, etc.), dispōno (3)
marshy, păluster
martial, bellĭcōsus; (court —),
  castrense iūdĭcĭum, *n*
martyr, martyr, *c*
martyrdom, martyrĭum, *n*
marvel (miracle, etc.), mīrăcŭlum, *n*
marvel at, *v.t*, mīror (1 *dep*)
marvellous, mīrus, mīrābĭlis
masculine, vĭrīlis
mash, *nn*, farrāgo, *f*
mash, *v.t*, contundo (3)
mask, *nn*, persōna, *f*; (disguise),
  intĕgŭmentum, *n*
mask, *v.t*, (oneself), persōnam indŭo
  (3); (disguise), dissĭmŭlo (1)
mason, structor, *m*
masonry, structūra, *f*
mass, mōles, *f*; (of people), multĭtūdo,
  f
mass, *v.t*, cŭmŭlo (1), ăcervo (1)
massacre, *nn*, caedes, *f*

massacre, *v.t*, trŭcīdo (1), caedo (3)
massive, sŏlĭdus; (huge), ingens
mast, mālus, *m*
master, dŏmĭnus, *m*; (— of the household), păterfămĭlĭas, *m*; (school —),
  măgister, *m*; (skilled in . . .), *use*
  adj. pĕrītus
master, *v.t*, (subdue), dŏmo (1);
  (knowledge, etc.), bĕne scĭo (4),
  disco (3)
masterful, impĕrĭōsus
masterly, *adj*, bŏnus; (plan, etc.),
  callĭdus
masterpiece, ŏpus summā laude
  dignum (work worthy of the highest
  praise)
mastery (rule), dŏmĭnātus, *m*
masticate, *v.t*, mandūco (1)
mastiff, cănis Mŏlossus (Molossian
  hound)
mat, stŏrĕa, *f*
mat, *v.t*, implĭco (1)
match (contest), certāmen, *n*; (equal),
  adj, pār; (marriage —), nuptĭae,
  f.pl
match, *v.t*, (equal), aequo (1)
matchless, ēgrĕgĭus
matching, *adj*, (equal) pār
mate, sŏcĭus, *m*; (— in marriage),
  conĭunx, *m*,*f*.
mate, *v.i*, conĭungor (3 *pass*)
material, *nn*, mātĕrĭa, *f*
material, *adj*, corpŏrĕus
materially, *adv*, (much), multum
maternal, maternus
maternity, māter, *f*, (mother)
mathematician, măthēmătĭcus, *m*
mathematics, măthēmătĭca, *f*
matter (substance), corpus, *n*, mātĕrĭa,
  f; (affair), res, *f*; (what is the — ?),
  quid est?; (it matters, it is important), rēfert (*v. impers*)
mattress, culcĭta, *f*
mature, *adj*, mātūrus, ădultus
mature, *v.t*, mātūro (1); *v.i*, mātūresco
  (3)
maturity, mātūrĭtas, *f*
maudlin, ĭneptus
maul, *v.t*, mulco (1), lănĭo (1)
maw, inglŭvĭes, *f*
maxim, praeceptum, *n*
maximum, *use adj*, maxĭmus (bigges
May, Māius (mensis)
may, *v. auxiliary*, (having permission
  to), lĭcet (2 *impers. with dat. of person*
  allowed), *e.g.* you may go, lĭcet tĭbĭ
  īre; (having ability to), possum
  (*irreg*); *often expressed by sub-*
  junctive mood of verb
maybe (perhaps), *adv*, fortassĕ

For List of Abbreviations used, turn to pages 3, 4

may-day, Kălendae Māiae (**first day of May**)

mayor, praefectus, *m*

maze, *nn*, lăbўrinthus, *m*

meadow, prātum, *n*

meagre, măcer, iēiūnus

meagreness, iēiūnĭtas, *f*

meal (flour), fārīna, *f*; (food), cĭbus, *m*

mean, *nn*, mŏdus, *m*

mean, *adj*, (middle, average), mĕdĭus; (of low rank), hŭmĭlis; (miserly), sordĭdus

mean, *v.t*, signĭfĭco (1); (intend), in ănĭmo hăbĕo (2)

meander, *v.i*, (of a river), sĭnŭōso cursu flŭo (3) (**flow on a winding course**)

meaning, *nn*, signĭfĭcātĭo, *f*

meanness, hŭmĭlĭtas, *f*; (of disposition), sordes, *f. pl*

means (method), mŏdus, *m*; (opportunity), făcultas, *f*; (resources), ŏpes, *f. pl*; (by no —), *adv*, haudquāquam, nullo mŏdo

meantime, meanwhile (in the —), *adv*, intĕrĕā, intĕrim

measure, mensūra, *f*, mŏdus, *m*; (plan), consĭlĭum, *n*; (music), mŏdi, *m, pl*

measure, *v.t*, mētĭor (4 *dep*)

measureless, immensus

meat, căro, *f*

mechanic, făber, *m*, ŏpĭfex, *c*

mechanical, māchĭnālis

mechanism, māchĭnātĭo, *f*

medal, medallion, phălĕrae, ārum, *f. pl*

meddle, *v.i*, sē interpōnĕre (3 *reflex*)

mediate, *v.i*, sē interpōnĕre (3 *reflex*) intervĕnĭo (4)

mediator, dēprĕcātor, *m*

medical, mĕdĭcus

medicine (art of —), ars mĕdĭcīna, *f*; (the remedy itself), mĕdĭcāmentum, *n*

mediocre, mĕdĭŏcris

mediocrity, mĕdĭŏcrĭtas, *f*

meditate, *v.t*, cōgĭto (1)

Mediterranean Sea, măre nostrum, *n*, (**our sea**)

medium, *use adj*, mĕdĭus (**middle**); (through the — of) per

medley, farrāgo, *f*

meek, mītis

meekness, ănĭmus summissus, *m*

meet, *v.t*, obvĭam fīo (*irreg*) (*with dat*); (go to —, encounter), obvĭam ĕo (*irreg*) (*with dat*); *v.i*, convĕnĭo (4); concurro (3)

meeting, *nn*, conventus, *m*

melancholy, *nn*, tristĭtĭa, *f*

melancholy, *adj*, tristis

mellow, mītis

mellow, *v.i*, mātūresco (3)

melodious, cănōrus

melody, mĕlos, *n*

melon, mēlo, *m*

melt, *v.t*, lĭquĕfăcĭo (3); (people, etc.), mŏvĕo (2); *v.i*, lĭquesco (3)

member (of a society), sŏcĭus, *m*; (of the body), membrum, *n*

membrane, membrāna, *f*

memoirs, commentārĭi, *m. pl*

memorable, mĕmŏrābĭlis

memorandum, lĭbellus mĕmŏrĭālis

memorial, mŏnŭmentum, *n*

memory, mĕmŏrĭa, *f*

menace mĭnae, *f. pl*

menace, *v.t* mĭnor (1 *dep*)

menacing, *adj*, mĭnax

mend, *v.t*, rĕfĭcĭo (3), sarcĭo (4); *v.i*, (in health), mĕlĭor fīo (*irreg*) (**get better**)

mendacious, mendax

mendicant, mendĭcus, *m*

menial, *adj*, servīlis

mensuration, rătĭo, (*f*) mētĭendi; (system of measuring)

mental, *use genitive of* mens, *or* ănĭmus (**mind**)

mention, *nn*, mentĭo, *f*

mention, *v.t*, mĕmŏro (1), dīco (3)

mercantile, mercātōrum, (**of merchants**)

mercenary, *adj*, mercēnārĭus

merchandise, merx, *f*

merchant, mercātor, *m*

merchant-ship, nāvis ŏnĕrārĭa, *f*

merciful, mĭsĕrĭcors

merciless, crūdēlis, inclēmens

mercury (quick silver), argentum vīvum, *n*; (god), Mercŭrĭus

mercy, mĭsĕrĭcordĭa, *f*

mere, *adj*, sōlus, *or use emphatic pron*, ipse

merely, *adv*, tantummŏdo

merge, *v.i*, miscĕor (2 *pass*)

meridian, circŭlus mĕrĭdĭānus, *m*

meridian, *adj*, mĕrĭdĭānus

merit, *nn*, mĕrĭtum, *n*

merit, *v.t*, mĕrĕor (2 *dep*)

meritorious, dignus laude (**worthy of praise**)

merriment, hĭlărĭtas, *f*

merry, hĭlăris

mesh, măcŭla, *f*

mess (confused state), turba, *f*; (dirt), squālor, *m*

message, nuntĭus, *m*

messenger, nuntĭus, *m*

metal, mĕtallum, *n*

metallic, mĕtallĭcus

metamorphosis, *use vb.* transformo (1) (to change in shape)

metaphor, translātĭo, *f*

metaphorical, translātus

meteor, fax, *f*

method, rătĭo, *f*

methodically, ex ordĭne, *or use adv phr.* rătĭōne et vĭā (by reckoning and method)

metre, nŭmĕrus, *m*

metrical, mĕtrĭcus

metropolis, căpŭt, *n*

mettle, fĕrōcĭtas, *f*

mettlesome, ănĭmōsus, fĕrox

mew, *v.i.* (cat), quĕror (3 *dep*)

mica, phengītes, *m*

mid, *adj.* mĕdĭus

midday, *nn.* mĕrīdĭes, *m*

midday, *adj.* mĕrīdĭānus

middle, *adj.* mĕdĭus

middle, *nn. use* mĕdĭus *in agreement with noun, e.g.* the middle of the river, mĕdĭus flŭvĭus

middling, *adj.* mĕdĭōcris

midnight, mĕdĭa nox, *f*

midst, *nn. use adj.* mĕdĭus

midsummer, mĕdĭa aestas, *f*

midwife, obstĕtrix, *f*

might (power), vīs, *f*

mighty, fortis, vălĭdus, magnus

migrate, *v.t.* ăbĕo (4)

migratory bird, advĕna ăvis, *f*

mild, mītis, clēmens, lēvis

mildew, rōbīgo, *f*

mildness, lēnĭtas, *f*,

mile, mille passus (*or* passŭum) (a thousand paces)

milestone, mīlĭārĭum, *n*

military, *adj.* mīlĭtāris; (— service), stĭpendĭa, *n.pl.*

militate against, *v.t.* făcĭo (3) contrā (*with acc*)

milk, lac, *n*

milk, *v.t.* mulgĕo (2)

milky, lactĕus

mill, mŏla, *f*, pistrīnum, *n*

miller, mŏlĭtor, *m*

million, dĕcĭes centēna mīlĭa

mill-stone, mŏla, *f*

mimic, *v.t.* ĭmĭtor (1 *dep*)

mince, *v.t.* concīdo (3)

mincemeat, mĭnūtal, *n*

mind, ănĭmus, *m*, mens, *f*; (intellect), ingĕnĭum, *n*; (to make up one's —) constĭtŭo (3)

mind, *v.t.* (I — my own business), nĕgōtĭum mĕum ăgo (3)

mindful, mĕmor (*with genit*)

mine, *adj.* mĕus

mine, *nn.* mĕtallum, *n*, cŭnĭcŭlus, *m*

mine, *v.i.* fŏdĭo (3)

miner, fŏdĭens, *m*

mineral, *nn.* mĕtallum, *n*

mineral, *adj.* mĕtallĭcus

mingle, *v.i.* sē miscēre (2 *reflex*)

miniature, *nn.* parva tăbella, *f*

minimum, *adj.* mĭnĭmus (smallest)

minister mĭnister, *m*, admĭnister, *m*

ministry (office), mĭnĭstĕrĭum, *n*

minor, *nn.* pūpillus, *m*

minority, mĭnor pars, *f*

minstrel, tībĭcen văgus (wandering —)

mint (plant), menta, *f*; (coinage), mŏnēta, *f*

mint, *v.t.* cūdo (3)

minute, *adj.* exĭgŭus, mĭnūtus

minute, *nn.* (of time), mōmentum, (*n*) tempŏris

miracle, mīrācŭlum, *n*

miraculous, mīrus

mire, lūtum, *n*

mirror, spĕcŭlum, *n*

mirth, hĭlărĭtas, *f*

mirthful, hĭlăris

misadventure, cāsus, *m*

misanthropy, *use phr.* ŏdĭum, (*n*) ergā hŏmĭnes (hatred towards mankind)

misapply, *v.t.* ăbūtor (3 *dep with abl*)

misbehave, *v.i.* mălĕ sē gĕrĕre (3 *reflex*)

miscalculate, *v.i.* fallor (3 *pass*), erro (1)

miscalculation, error, *m*

miscarriage (childbirth), ăbortus, *m*; (— of justice) error, (*m*) iūdĭcum

miscarry, *v.i.* (child), ăbortum făcĭo (3); (fail) frustrā *or* irrĭtum ēvĕnĭo (4)

miscellaneous, vărĭus

mischief (injury, wrong) mălĕfĭcĭum, *n*

mischievous, mălĕfĭcus; (playful), lascīvus

misconduct, *nn.* dēlictum, *n*

miscreant, hŏmŏ scĕlestus

misdeed, dēlictum, *n*

misdemeanour, dēlictum, *n*, peccātum, *n*

miser, hŏmŏ ăvārus

miserable, mĭser, infēlix

miserliness, ăvārĭtĭa, *f*

miserly, *adj.* ăvārus, sordĭdus

misery, mĭsĕrĭa, *f*, angor, *m*

misfortune, rēs adversae, *f*, *pl*

misgiving, praesāgĭum, *n*

misgovern, *v.t.* mălĕ rĕgo (3)

misguided (deceived), dēceptus

misinterpret, *v.t*, mălĕ interprĕtor (1 *dep*)

misjudge, *v.t*, mălĕ iūdĭco (1)

mislay, *v.t*, āmitto (3)

mislead, *v.t*, dēcĭpĭo (3)

misplace, *v.t*, ălĭēno lŏco pōno (3) (put in an unsuitable place)

misprint, *nn*, mendum, *n*

misrepresent, *v.t*, verto (3); (disparage), obtrecto (1)

misrule, *v.t*, mălĕ rĕgo (3)

miss, *v.i*, (fail to hit or meet), ăberro (1), frustrā mittor (3 *pass*); *v.t*, (want), dēsīdĕro (1)

misshapen, dēformis

missile, tēlum, *n*

mission (embassy), lēgātĭo, *f*; (task), ŏpus, *n*

misspend, *v.t*, perdo (3)

mist, nĕbŭla, *f*

mistake, error, *m*; (make a —), *v.i*, erro (1)

mistake, *v.t*, (for someone else), crēdĕre ălĭum esse

mistaken, falsus; (to be —), *v.i*, erro (1)

mistletoe, viscum, *n*

mistress (of the house, etc.), dŏmĭna, *f*; (sweetheart), pŭella, *f*, concŭbīna, *f*

mistrust, *v.t*, diffīdo (3 *semi-dep. with dat*)

misty, nĕbŭlōsus

misunderstand, *v.t*, haud rectē, *or* mălĕ, intellĕgo (3)

misunderstanding, error, *m*

misuse, *v.t*, ăbūtor (3 *dep. with abl*)

mitigate, *v.t*, mītĭgo (1), lēnĭo (4)

mitigation, mītĭgātĭo, *f*

mittens, mănĭcae, *f. pl*

mix, *v.t*, miscĕo (2); (— up together), confundo (3); *v.i*, miscĕor (2 *pass*)

mixed, *adj*, mixtus; (indiscriminate), prōmiscŭus

mixture, mixtūra, *f*

moan, *nn*, gĕmĭtus, *m*

moan, *v.i*, gĕmo (3)

moat, fossa, *f*

mob, turba, *f*, vulgus, *n*

mobile, mōbĭlis

mock, *v.t*, illūdo (3) (*with dat*); dērīdĕo (2)

mockery, irrīsus, *m*, lūdĭbrĭum, *n*

mode, mŏdus, *m*, rătĭo, *f*

model, exemplum, *n*, exemplar, *n*

model, *v.t*, fingo (3)

moderate, mŏdĕrātus, mŏdĭcus

moderate, *v.t*, tempĕro (1)

moderation, mŏdus, *m*, mŏdĕrātĭo, *f*

modern, rĕcens, nŏvus

modest, vĕrēcundus

modesty, vĕrēcundĭa, *f*, pŭdor, *m*

modify, *v.t*, immūto (1)

modulate, *v.t*, flecto (3)

moist, hūmĭdus

moisten, *v.t*, hūmecto (1)

moisture, hūmor, *m*

molar, dens gĕnŭīnus

mole (animal), talpa, *f*; (dam, etc.), mōles, *f*; (on the body), naevus, *m*

molest, *v.t*, vexo (1), sollĭcĭto (1)

mollify, *v.t*, mollĭo (4)

molten, lĭquĕfactus

moment, punctum, (*n*) tempŏris; (in a —), *adv*, stătim; (importance), mōmentum, *n*

momentary, brĕvis

momentous, magni mōmenti (of great importance)

momentum, impĕtus, *m*

monarch, rex, *m*

monarchy, regnum, *n*

monastery, mŏnastērĭum, *n*

money, pēcūnĭa, *f*; (coin), nummus, *m*; (profit), quaestus, *m*

money-bag, fiscus, *m*

money-lender, faenĕrātor, *m*

money-making, quaestus, *m*

moneyed, pēcūnĭōsus

mongrel, *nn*, hibrĭda, *c*

monkey, sīmĭa, *f*

monopolize, *v.i*, use *phr. with* sōlus (alone), *and* hăbĕo (2)

monopoly, mŏnŏpōlĭum, *n*

monotonous, use *phr. with* mŏlestus (laboured), *or* sĭmĭlis (similar)

monster, monstrum, *n*

monstrous (huge), immānis; (shocking), infandus

month, mensis, *m*

monthly, *adj*, menstrŭus

monument, mŏnŭmentum, *n*

mood, affectĭo, (*f*) ănĭmi

moody, mōrōsus

moon, lūna, *f*

moonlight, lūmen, (*n*) lūnae; (by —), ad lūnam

moonlit, *adj*, illustris lūnā (lighted up by the moon)

moor, lŏca dēserta, *n.pl*, (a lonely place)

moor, *v.t*, (ship, etc.), rĕlĭgo (1)

moorhen, fŭlĭca, *f*

moot (it is a — point), nondum convēnit . . . (it is not yet decided . . .)

mop, *nn*, pēnĭcŭlus, *m*

mop, *v.t*, dētergĕo (2)

moral, *adj*, mōrālis; (of good character), hŏnestus

moral, *nn*, (of a story), use *phr. with*

signĭfĭco (1) (to indicate), *e.g.* haec
fābŭla signĭfĭcat ... (this story
indicates ...)

morale, ănĭmus, *m*

morals, morality, mōres, *m. pl*

moralize, *v.i,* dē mōrĭbus dissĕro (3)
(discuss conduct)

morbid, aeger, aegrōtus

more, *nn,* plus, *n, (with genit), e.g.*
more corn, plus frūmentī; *(adv.
before adjs. or advs) use comparative
of adj. or adv, e.g.* more quickly,
cĕlērĭus; *otherwise use* măgis (to a
higher degree) *or* pŏtĭus; (in
addition), amplĭus

moreover, *adv,* praetĕrĕā

moribund, mŏrĭbundus

morning, *nn,* tempus mātūtĭnum, *n;*
(in the —), *adv,* māne

morning, *adj,* mātūtĭnus

morose, tristis

morrow (following day), postĕrus
dĭes, *m*

morsel, offa, *f*

mortal, *adj,* mortālis; (causing death),
mortĭfer

mortality, mortālĭtas, *f*

mortar, mortārĭum, *n*

mortgage, pignus, *n*

mortgage, *v.t,* oblĭgo (1)

mortification, offensĭo, *f*

mortify, *v.t,* (vex) offendo (3)

mosaic, *adj,* tessellātus

mosquito, cŭlex, *m*

moss, muscus, *m*

mossy, muscōsus

most, *adj,* plūrĭmus *or* plūrĭmum, *n,*
with genit, of noun, e.g. most importance, plūrĭmum grăvĭtātis; (for
the — part), *adv,* plērumque

most, *adv, with adjs. and advs. use
superlative; e.g.* most quickly,
cĕlerrĭmē; *with vbs,* maxĭmē

mostly (usually), *adv,* plērumque

moth, blatta, *f*

mother, māter, *f;* (-in-law), socrus, *f*

motherly, *adj,* māternus

motion (movement), mōtus, *m;* (proposal), rŏgātĭo, *f*

motion, *v.t,* gestu indĭco (1) (indicate
by a gesture)

motionless, immōtus

motive, causa, *f*

mottled, măcŭlōsus

motto, sententĭa, *f*

mould (soil), sŏlum, *n;* (shape),
forma, *f*

mould, *v.i,* formo (1)

mouldiness, sĭtus, *m*

mouldy, mūcĭdus

moult, *v.i,* plūmas exŭo (3) (lay down
feathers)

mound, tŭmŭlus, *m*

mount, *v.t* (horse, ship, etc.), conscendo (3); *otherwise,* scando (3)

mounted (on horseback), *adj,* ĕquo
vectus

mountain, mons, *m,* iŭgum, *n*

mountaineer, hŏmŏ montānus

mountainous, montŭōsus

mourn, *v.t. and v.i,* lūgĕo (2)

mournful luctŭōsus; (of sounds, etc.),
lūgŭbris

mourning, luctus, *m,* maeror, *m*

mouse, mūs, *c*

mouse-trap, muscĭpŭlum, *n*

mouth, ōs, *n;* (of river), ostĭum, *n*

mouthful, bucca, *f,* (filled out cheek)

mouth-piece interpres, *c,* ōrātor, *m*

movable, mōbĭlis

move, *v.t,* mŏvĕo (2); *v.i,* sē mŏvēre
(2 *reflex*)

movement, mōtus, *m*

moving, *adj,* (of pity, etc.), mĭsĕrābĭlis

mow, *v.t,* sĕco (1)

much, *adj,* multus; (too —), nĭmĭus

much, *adv,* multum; *with comparative
adj. or adv,* multo, *e.g.* much bigger,
multo māior

muck, stercus, *n*

mucous, *adj,* mūcōsus

mud, muddiness, lŭtum, *n*

muddle, *v.t,* confundo (3)

muddle, *nn,* turba, *f*

muddy, lŭtĕus

muffle, *v.t,* obvolvo (3)

mug, pōcŭlum, *n*

muggy, ūmĭdus

mulberry (tree), mōrus, *f;* (fruit),
mōrum, *n*

mule, mūlus, *m*

mullet, mullus, *m*

multifarious, vărĭus

multiplication, multĭplĭcātĭo, *f*

multiply, *v.t,* multĭplĭco (1)

multitude, multĭtūdo, *f*

multitudinous, plūrĭmus, crēber

mumble, *v.i. and v.t,* murmŭro (1)

munch, *v.t,* mandūco (1)

mundane, *use genit. of* mundus (world)

municipal, mūnĭcĭpālis

municipality, mūnĭcĭpĭum, *n*

munificence, mūnĭfĭcentĭa, *f*

munificent, mūnĭfĭcus

munition, appārātus (*m*) belli (war-
equipment), arma, *n.pl*

murder, *nn,* caedes, *f*

murder, *v.t,* nĕco (1), interfĭcĭo (3)

murderer, hŏmĭcīda, *c,* sīcārĭus, *m*

murky, cālĭgĭnōsus

For List of Abbreviations used, turn to pages 3, 4

murmur, *nn*, murmur, *n*,

murmur, *v.i*, murmŭro (1)

muscle, tŏrus, *m*, lăcertus, *m*

muscular, lăcertōsus

muse, *nn*, mūsa, *f*

muse, *v.i*, mĕdĭtor (1 *dep*)

museum, mūsēum, *n*

mushroom, fungus, *m*

music, mūsĭca, *f*, cantus, *m*

musical, mūsĭcus; (person), stŭdĭōsus mūsĭcōrum (keen on music)

musician, mūsĭcus, *m*

muslin, byssus, *f*

must, *v.i*, (obligation), *use gerundive:* e.g. Carthage must be destroyed, Carthāgo dēlenda est; (duty), ŏportet (2 *impers*) with acc. of person and infinitive, e.g. we must go, nōs ŏportet īre

mustard, sĭnāpi, *n*

muster, *nn*, dēlectus, *m*

muster, *v.t*, convŏco (1), rēcensĕo (2); *v.i*, convĕnĭo (4)

musty, mūcĭdus

mutable, mūtābĭlis

mute, *adj*, mūtus, tăcĭtus

mutilate, *v.t*, mŭtĭlo (1), trunco (1)

mutilated, mŭtĭlus, truncātus

mutiny, sĕdĭtĭo, *f*

mutiny, *v.i*, sĕdĭtĭōnem făcĭo (3)

mutter, *v.i. and v.t*, musso (1)

muttering, *nn*, murmur *n*

mutton, ŏvilla căro, *f*, (sheep's flesh)

mutual, mūtŭus

muzzle (for the mouth), fiscella, *f*

my, mĕus

myriad (10,000), dĕcem mīlĭa (*with genit*)

myrrh, murra, *f*

myrtle, myrtus, *f*

myself (*emphatic*), ipse; (*reflexive*) mē

mysterious, occultus

mystery, rēs abdĭta, *f*; (religious, etc.), mystērĭa, *n.pl*

mystic, mystĭcus

mystification, ambāges, *f*, *pl*

mystify, *use adv. phr*, per ambāges (in an obscure way)

myth, fābŭla, *f*

mythology, fābŭlae, *f*, *pl*

N

nab, *v.t*, (catch), apprĕhendo (3)

nag, *nn*, căballus, *m*

nag, *v.t*, incrĕpĭto (1), obiurgo (1)

nail (finger, toe), unguis, *m*; (of metal), clāvus, *m*

nail, *v.t*, clāvīs affīgo (3) (fix on with nails)

naive, simplex

naked, nūdus

nakedness, *use adj*, nūdus (naked)

name, nōmen, *n*; (personal —, equivalent to our Christian name), praenōmen, *n*; (— of a class of things), vŏcābŭlum, *n*; (reputation), existĭmātĭo, *f*

name, *v.t*, nōmĭno (1), appello (1)

nameless, nōmĭnis expers (without a name)

namely (I mean to say), dīco (3)

namesake, *use phr*, cui est ĭdem nōmen (who has the same name)

nap, *v.i*, (sleep), paulisper dormĭo (4)

napkin, mappa, *f*

narcissus, narcissus, *m*

narcotic, mĕdĭcāmentum somnĭfĕrum, *n*, (sleep-bringing drug)

narrate, narro (1)

narrative, narrātĭo, *f*; *adj*, *use vb*, narro (1) (narrate)

narrator, narrātor, *m*

narrow, angustus

narrow, *v.t*, cŏarto (1); *v.i*, sē cŏartāre (1 *reflex*)

narrowly (nearly, scarcely), *adj*, vix

narrow-minded, anĭmi angusti (of narrow mind)

narrowness, angustĭae, *f*, *pl*

nasal, nārĭum (of the nose)

nastiness, foedĭtas, *f*

nasty, foedus

natal, nātālis

nation, gens, *f*

national, dŏmestĭcus *or use genit. of* gens

nationality, pŏpŭlus, *m*, cīvĭtas, *f*

native, *adj*, indĭgĕna; (— land), pătrĭa, *f*

native, *nn*, indĭgĕna, *c*

nativity (birth), gĕnus, *n*, ortus, *m*

natural, nātūrālis; (inborn), nātīvus, innātus; (genuine), sincērus

naturalize, *v.t*, cīvĭtātem do (1) (*with dat*) (grant citizenship)

naturally, sĕcundum nātūram (according to nature)

nature, nātūra, *f*; (character of persons), ingĕnĭum, *n*

naught, nĭhil, *n*

naughty, imprŏbus, lascīvus

nausea, nausĕa, *f*

nauseate, *v.t*, fastīdĭo (4)

nautical, nāvālis, nautĭcus

navel, umbĭlĭcus, *m*

navigable, nāvĭgābĭlis

navigate, v.i, nāvĭgo (1)
navigation, nāvĭgātĭo, f
navy, classis, f
nay (no), nōn
neap-tide, mĭnĭmus aestus, m
near, adv, prŏpē, iuxtā
near, prep, adv, prŏpē
nearly, adv, prŏpē, fermē
nearness, prŏpinquĭtas, f, vīcīnĭtas, f
neat, nĭtĭdus, mundus
neatly, adv, mundē
neatness, mundĭtĭa, f
nebulous, nēbŭlōsus
necessarily, adv, nĕcessārĭo
necessary, nĕcessārĭus, nĕcesse
necessitate, v.t, (compel), cōgo (3)
necessity (inevitableness), nĕcessĭtas,
    f; (something indispensable), rēs
    nĕcessārĭa, f
neck, collum, n, cervix, f
necklace, mŏnīle, n
need, nn, ŏpus, n, (with abl. of thing
    needed or infinitive); (lack), ĭnōpĭa, f
need, v.t, ĕgĕo (2) (with abl)
needful, nĕcessārĭus, or use nn, ŏpus,
    n, (necessity)
needle, ăcus, f
needless, nōn nĕcessārĭus
needy, ĕgens
nefarious, nĕfārĭus
negation, nĕgātĭo, f
negative, adj, use nōn (not), or nĕgo
    (1) (to deny)
neglect, v.t, neglĕgo (3), praetermitto
    (3)
neglect, nn, neglĕgentĭa, f
negligent, neglĕgens
negotiate, v.t, ăgo (3) dē (with abl. of
    thing) cum (with abl. of person)
negotiation, use vb, ăgo (3), (to
    negotiate)
negress, Aethĭŏpissa, f
negro, Aethĭops, m
neigh, v.i, hinnĭo (4)
neigh, neighing, hinnītus, m
neighbour, vīcīnus, m; (of nations),
    adj, finĭtĭmus
neither, pron, neuter
neither, conj, nĕque, nĕc; neither . . .
    nor, neque . . . neque, or nec . . . nec
nephew, fīlĭus, (m) frātris (or sŏrōris)
nerve, nervi, m. pl
nervous (afraid), tĭmĭdus
nervousness, tĭmĭdĭtas, f, formīdo, f
nest, nīdus, m
nestle, v.i, haerĕo (2), ĭacĕo (2)
nestlings, nīdi, m, pl
net, rētĕ, n
net, v.t, plăgīs căpĭo (3) (catch with a
    net)

nettle, urtīca, f
net-work, rētĭcŭlum, n
neuter, neuter
neutral, mĕdĭus; (to be or remain —),
    neutri parti făvĕo (2) (to favour
    neither side)
neutralize, v.t, aequo (1), compenso (1)
never, adv, numquam
nevertheless, nĭhĭlōmĭnus, tămen
new, nŏvus; (fresh), rĕcens
new-comer, advĕna, c
newly, adv, nūper, mŏdo
newness, nŏvĭtas, f
news, nuntĭus, m
newspaper, acta dĭurna, n.pl
newt, lăcertus, m
next, adj, proxĭmus; (on the — day),
    adv, postrīdĭē
next, adv, (of time), dĕinceps, dĕinde;
    (of place), iuxtā, proxĭmē
nibble, v.t, rōdo (3)
nice (pleasant), dulcis; (particular),
    fastīdĭōsus; (precise), subtīlis
nicety (subtlety), subtīlĭtas, f
niche, aedĭcŭla, f
in the nick of time, in ipso artĭcŭlo
    tempŏris
nickname, agnōmen, n, (an additional
    name)
niece, fīlĭa, (f) frātris (or sŏrōris)
niggardly, ăvārus, parcus
night, nox, f; (by, at —), adv,
    noctu, nocte; (at mid —), mĕdĭā
    nocte; (at the fall of —), primis
    tĕnĕbris
nightingale, luscĭnĭa, f
nimble, ăgĭlis
nine, nŏvem; (— times), adv, nŏvĭens;
    (— each), nŏvēni; (— hundred),
    nongenti
nineteen, undēvīginti
ninety, nōnāginta
ninth, nōnus
nip, v.t, vellĭco (1); (with frost), ūro (3)
nipple, păpilla, f
no, adj, nullus, nĭhil (foll. by genit)
no, adv, nōn, mĭnĭmē; (to say —), v.i,
    nĕgo (1)
nobility, (of birth), nōbĭlĭtas, f;
    (people of noble birth), nōbĭles,
    m. pl
noble (of birth), nōbĭlis; (of birth or
    character), gĕnĕrōsus
nobody, nēmo, m, f
nocturnal, nocturnus
nod, v.i, nūto (1); (assent), annŭo (3)
nod, nn, nūtus, m
noise, strĕpĭtus, m, sŏnĭtus, m; (of
    shouting), clāmor, m; (to make a
    —), v.i, strĕpo (3)

noiseless, tăcĭtus

noisily, *adv*, cum strĕpĭtu

noisy, *use a phr. with* strĕpo (**to make a noise**)

nomadic, văgus

nominal, *use* nōmen (**name**)

nominally, *adv*, nōmĭne

nominate, *v.t*, nōmĭno (1)

nomination, nōmĭnātĭo, *f*

nominee, *use vb.* nōmĭno, (name)

nonchalant, aequo ănĭmo (**with unruffled mind**)

nondescript, nōn insignis

none, nullus

nonentity, nĭhil, *n*

nonsense, nūgae, *f. pl*, Ĭneptĭae, *f. pl*

nonsensical, Ĭneptus, absurdus

nook, angŭlus, *m*

noon, mĕrīdĭes, *m*; (at —), *adv*, mĕrīdĭe; *adj*, mĕrĭdĭanus

noose, lăquĕus, *m*

nor, *conj*, nĕc, nĕque

normal (**usual**), ūsĭtātus

north, *nn*, septentrĭōnes, *m. pl*

north, northern, northerly, *adj*, septentrĭōnālis

north-east wind, ăquĭlo, *m*

north-pole, arctos, *f*

northwards, versus ad septentrĭōnes

north wind, ăquĭlo, *m*

nose, nāsus, *m*, nāres, *f. pl* (**nostrils**)

not, nōn, haud; (— at all), *adv*, haudquăquam; (not even . . .), nē . . . quĭdem; (and not), nĕc, nĕque; (in commands), e.g. do not go, nōli ire

notable, insignis, mĕmŏrābĭlis

notary, scrība, *m*

notch, *nn*, incīsūra, *f*

notch, *v.t*, incīdo (3)

note (explanatory, etc.), adnŏtātĭo, *f*; (mark), nŏta, *f*; (letter), littĕrae, *f. pl*

note, *v.t*, (notice), ănĭmadverto (3); (jot down), ēnŏto (1)

note-book, commentārĭi, *m. pl*

noted (**well-known**), insignis

nothing, nĭhil, *n*; (good for —), nēquam

nothingness, nĭhĭlum, *n*

notice, *v.t*, ănĭmadverto (3)

notice, *nn*, (act of noticing), ănĭmadversĭo, *f*; (written —), prōscriptĭo, *f*

noticeable, insignis

notification, dēnuntĭātĭo, *f*

notify, *v.t*, dēnuntĭo (1)

notion, nōtĭo, *f*

notoriety, infāmĭa, *f*

notorious, nōtus, fāmōsus

notwithstanding, *adv*, nĭhĭlōmĭnus, tămen

nought, nĭhil

noun, nōmen, *n*, (name)

nourish, *v.t*, ălo (3)

nourishment, ălĭmentum, *n*

novel, *nn*, (story), fābŭla, *f*

novel, *adj*, (new), nŏvus

novelist, fābŭlārum scriptor, *m*, (writer of stories)

novelty (strangeness), nŏvĭtas, *f*

November, Nŏvember (mensis)

novice, tīro, *m*

now (at the present time), *adv*, nunc; (at the time of the action), iam; (just —), mŏdŏ; (now . . . now), mŏdŏ . . . mŏdŏ; (— and then), ălĭquandŏ

nowadays, *adv*, nunc

nowhere, *adv*, nusquam

noxious, nŏcens

nozzle, nāsus, *m*

nude, nūdus

nudge, *v.t*, fŏdĭco (1)

nuisance, incŏmmŏdum, *n*, *or use adj*, mŏlestus (**troublesome**)

null, irrĭtus, vānus

nullify, *v.t*, irrĭtum făcĭo (3)

numb, torpens; (to be —), *v.i*, torpĕo (2)

numb, *v.t*, torpĕfăcĭo (3)

number, *nn*, nŭmĕrus, *m*; (what —, how many?), quot?; (a large —), multĭtūdo, *f*

number, *v.t*, nŭmĕro (1)

numbering (in number), ad (*with acc*)

numberless, innŭmĕrābĭlis

numbness, torpor, *m*

numerically, *adv*, nŭmĕro

numerous, plūrĭmi, crēber

nun, mŏnăcha, *f*

nuptial, nuptĭālis, iŭgālis

nuptials, nuptĭae, *f. pl*

nurse, nūtrix, *f*

nurse, *v.t*, (the sick), cūro (1); (cherish), fŏvĕo (2)

nursery (for plants), sēmĭnārĭum, *n*

nurture, ēdŭcātĭo, *f*

nut, nut-tree, nux, *f*

nutriment, ălĭmentum, *n*

nutrition, ălĭmentum, *n*

nutritious, vălens

nutshell, pŭtāmen, *n*

nymph, nympha, *f*

O

o! oh! o! oh!; (Oh that . . .) ŭtĭnam . . .

oak, quercus, *f*; (holm —), īlex, *f*; (oak-wood), rōbur, *n* oak, oaken, *adj*, quernus

oakum, stuppa, *f*

oar, rēmus, *m*

oarsmen, rēmīges, *m. pl*

oats, ăvēna, *f*

oath, iusiūrandum, *n*; (to take an —), *v.i.*, iusiūrandum accĭpĭo (3); (military —), săcrāmentum, *n*

oatmeal, fărīna ăvēnācĕa, *f*

obdurate, obstĭnātus, dūrus

obedience, ŏbēdĭentĭa, *f*; *or use vb*, pārĕo (2) (to obey, *with dat*)

obeisance (to make an —), ădōro (1) (reverence)

obelisk, ŏbĕlĭscus, *m*

obese, ŏbēsus

obey, *v.i. and v.t*, pārĕo (2) (*with dat*), ŏbēdĭo (4) (*with dat*)

object, *nn*, (thing), rēs, *f*; (aim), consĭlĭum, *n*. finĭs, *m*; (to be an — of hatred), ŏdĭo esse (*irreg*)

object, *v.t*, rĕcūso (1), nōlo (*irreg*)

objection, *use vb*, rĕcūso (1) (object to)

objectionable, ingrātus, *m*

objective *nn*, quod petĭtur (that is sought)

obligation (moral), offĭcĭum, *n*; (legal), oblĭgātĭo, *f*; (religious —), conscientiousness), rĕlĭgĭo, *f*; (to put someone under an —), *v.t*, obstringo (3); (to be under an —), *v.i*, dēbĕo (2)

obligatory (it is —), ŏportet (2 *impers*) *or use gerundive of vb*

oblige, *v.t*, obstringo (3); (compel), cōgo (3)

obliging, cōmis

oblique (slanting), oblīquus

obliterate, *v.t*, dēlĕo (2)

oblivion, oblīvĭo, *f*

oblivious, immĕmor

oblong, *adj*, oblongus

obloquy, vĭtŭpĕrātĭo, *f*

obnoxious, invīsus, noxĭus

obscene, obscēnus

obscenity, obscēnĭtas, *f*

obscure, obscūrus, caecus, rĕcondĭtus; (of birth, etc.), hŭmĭlis

obscure, *v.t*, obscūro (1)

obscurity, obscūrĭtas, *f*

obsequies, exsĕquĭae, *f. pl*

obsequious, obsĕquens, offĭcĭōsus

observance, observantĭa, *f*, conservātĭo *f*; (practice), rītus, *m*

observant, attentus, dĭlĭgens

observation, observātĭo, *f*; (attention), ănĭmadversĭo, *f*; (remark), dictum, *n*

observatory, spĕcŭla, *f*

observe, *v.t*, observo (1); (remark), dīco (3); (maintain), conservo (1)

observer, spectātor, *m*

obsolete, obsŏlētus; (to become —), *v.i*, obsŏlesco (3), sĕnesco (3)

obstacle, impĕdīmentum, *n*

obstinacy, pertĭnācĭa, *f*

obstinate, pertĭnax

obstreperous, (noisy), vŏcĭfĕrans

obstruct, *v.t*, obstrŭo (3), obsto (1) (*with dat*)

obstruction, impĕdīmentum, *n*

obtain, *v.t*, ădĭpiscor (3 *dep*), nanciscor (3 *dep*), consĕquor (3 *dep*), (— possession of), pŏtĭor (4 *dep. with abl*)

obtrude, *v.t*, inculco (1)

obtrusive, mŏlestus

obtuse, hēbes

obviate, *v.t*, (meet), obvĭam ĕo (4 *irreg*) (*with dat*)

obvious, ăpertus, mănĭfestus

occasion (opportunity), occāsĭo, *f*; (cause), causa, *f*; (on that —), illo tempŏre

occasion, *v.t* mŏvĕo (2), fĕro (*irreg*)

occasionally, *adv*, interdum, rāro

occult, occultus, arcānus

occupancy, possessĭo, *f*

occupant, possessor, *m*

occupation (act of —), *use vb*, occŭpo (1); (employment), quaestus, *m*; nĕgōtĭum, *n*

occupy, *v.t*, occŭpo (1), obtĭnĕo (2); (to be occupied with something), *v.i*, tĕnĕor (2 *pass*)

occur, *v.i*. (take place), accĭdo (3); (come into the mind), in mentem vēnĭo (4), sŭbĕo (4) (*with dat*)

occurrence, rēs, *f*

ocean, ōcĕănus, *m*

ochre, ōchra, *f*

octagon, octōgōnum, *n*

October, Octōber (mensis)

oculist, ŏcŭlārĭus mĕdĭcus, *m*

odd (numbers, etc.), impar; (strange), nŏvus

odds (to be at — with), *v.i*, dissĭdĕo (2) ab (*with abl*)

odious, ŏdĭōsus, invīsus

odium, invĭdĭa, *f*, ŏdĭum, *n*

odorous, ŏdōrātus

odour, ŏdor, *m*

of, *usually the genit. of the noun, e.g.* the head of the boy, căput pŭĕri; (made —), ex (*with abl*); (about, concerning), dē (*with abl*)

off, *adv*, *often expressed by prefix ab-with vb, e.g.* to cut off, abscĭdo (3); (far —), *adv*, prŏcul; (a little way —), *prep and adv*, prŏpe

offal (waste), quisquĭlĭae, *f. pl*

For List of Abbreviations used, turn to pages 3, 4

offence, offensĭo, *f*; (crime, etc.), dēlictum, *n*; (to take — at), aegrē fĕro (*irreg.*)

offend, *v.t.* offendo (3), laedo (3); (to be offended), aegrē fĕro (*irreg*) (tolerate with displeasure)

offensive, *adj,* ŏdĭōsus, grăvis

offensive, *nn,* (military), *use phr,* bellum infĕro (*irreg*) (to inflict war)

offer, *nn,* condĭcĭo, *f*

offer, *v.t.* offĕro (*irreg*); (stretch out), porrĭgo (3); (give), do (1)

offering (gift), dōnum, *n*

office (political power), măgistrātus, *m*; (duty), officĭum, *n*; (place of business), fŏrum, *n*

officer (military), praefectus, *m*

official, *nn,* măgistrātus, *m,* mĭnister, *m*

official, *adj,* (state), pūblĭcus

officiate, *v.i,* (perform), fungor (3 *dep*)

officious, mŏlestus

offing, (in the —), *use* longē (far off), *or* prŏpē (near), *acc. to sense*

offshoot, surcŭlus, *m*

offspring, prŏgĕnĭes, *f* lībĕri, *m, pl*

often, *adv,* saepĕ; (how —?), quŏtĭes?; (so —), *adv,* tŏtĭes

ogle, *v.t,* ŏcŭlis līmis intŭĕor (2 *dep*) (look at with sidelong glances)

oil, ŏlĕum, *n*

oily, ŏlĕăcĕus

ointment, unguentum, *n*

old, vĕtus; (of persons), sĕnex; (so many years —, of persons), nātus (*with acc. of extent of time*), *e.g.* three years old, tres annos nātus; (— age), sĕnectus, *f*; (— man), sĕnex, *m*; (— woman), ănus, *f*

olden, priscus

oldness, vĕtustas, *f*

oligarchy, dŏmĭnātĭo, (*f*) paucŏrum (rule of a few)

olive (tree), ŏlĕa, *f*

Olympic, *adj,* Ŏlympĭcus; (— Games), Ŏlympĭa, *n.pl*

omelet, lăgănum, *n*

omen, ōmen, *n*

ominous, infaustus

omission, praetermissĭo, *f*

omit, *v.t,* ŏmitto (3); praetermitto (3)

omnipotent, omnĭpŏtens

on, *prep,* in (*with abl*); (in the direction of, *e.g.* on the right), ā, āb (*with abl*); (— everyside), *adv,* undĭque; (of time), *abl case, e.g.* on the Ides of March, Īdĭbus Martĭis; (about a subject), dē (*with abl*)

once, *num. adv,* sĕmel; (— upon a time), ōlim, ălĭquandŏ; (at —, immediately), stătim; (at the same time), sĭmul

one, *num. adj,* ūnus; (in —s, singly), *adv,* singillātim, *adj,* singŭli; (at — time), *adv,* ălĭquandŏ; (one ... another), ălĭus ... ălĭus; (one ... the other), alter ... alter; (a certain), quĭdam; (indefinite), *use* 2*nd pers sing. of the vb*

onerous, grăvis

oneself (*emphatic*) ipsĕ; (*reflexive*), sē

one-sided, ĭnaequālis

onion, caepa, *f*

onlooker, circumstans, *m*

only, *adj,* ūnus, sōlus, ūnĭcus

only, *adv,* sōlum, tantum, mŏdŏ; (not only . . .), non mŏdŏ . . .

onset, impĕtus, *m*

onwards, *adv,* porro, *often use compound vb. with* pro, *e.g.* prŏcēdĕre (3) (to go onwards)

ooze, *nn,* ūlĭgo, *f*

ooze, *v.i,* māno (1)

oozy, ūlĭgĭnōsus

opal, ŏpălus, *m*

opaque, caecus

open, *v.t,* ăpĕrĭo (4), pătĕfăcĭo (3), pando (3); (inaugurate), consĕcro (1); *v.i,* sē ăpĕrĭre (4 *reflex*); (gape open), hisco (3)

open, *adj,* ăpertus; (wide —), pătens, hĭans; (to lie, stand or be —), pătĕo (2); (— handed), *adj,* lībĕrālis

opening (dedication), consĕcrātĭo, *f*; (hole), fŏrāmen, *n*; (opportunity), occāsĭo, *f*

openly, *adv,* pălam

operate, *v.t,* (set in motion), mŏvĕo (2); *v.i,* (in war), rem gĕro (3)

operation (task), ŏpus, *n*; (military —), rēs bellĭca, *f*; (naval —), rēs mărītĭma, *f*

operative, *adj,* efficax

opiate, mĕdĭcāmentum somnĭfĕrum, *n,* (sleep-bringing drug)

opinion, sententĭa, *f,* ŏpīnĭo, *f,* existĭmātĭo, *f*

opium, ŏpĭum, *n*

opponent, adversārĭus, *m*

opportune, opportūnus

opportunity, occāsĭo, *f,* cōpĭa, *f,* făcultas, *f*

oppose, *v.t,* oppōno (3); (resist), rĕsisto (3 *with dat*), adversor (1 *dep*)

opposite, *adj,* adversus, contrārĭus, dīversus

opposite (to), *prep*, contrā (*with acc*)

opposition (from people), *use partic*, adversans *or* rĕsistens; (from a party), *use* factĭo, *f*, (party)

oppress, *v.t*, opprĭmo (3)

oppression (tyranny), iniūrĭa, *f*

oppressive, grăvis, mŏlestus

oppressor, týrannus, *m*

opprobrious, turpis

optical, *adj*, *use genit. case of* ŏcŭlus, *m*, (eye)

option, optĭo, *f*

opulence, ŏpŭlentĭa, *f*, ŏpes, *f*, *pl*

opulent, dīves, lŏcŭples

or, aut, vel; (either . . . or), aut . . . aut, vel . . . vel; (whether . . . or) (*questions*), ŭtrum . . . an; (or not) (*direct questions*), annon, (*indirect questions*), necne

oracle, ōrācŭlum, *n*

oral, *use* vox (voice)

oration, ōrātĭo, *f*

orator, ōrātor, *m*

oratory, ars ōrātŏrĭa, *f*

orb, orbit, orbis, *m*

orchard, pōmārĭum, *n*

orchid, orchis, *f*

ordain, *v.t*, ēdīco (3), stătŭo (3)

ordeal, discrīmen, *n*

order, *nn*, (arrangement), ordo, *m*; (in —), *adv*, ordĭne; (command, direction), iussum, *n*; (class, rank), ordo, *m*; (in — to), ut

order, *v.t*, (command), iŭbĕo (2); (arrange), dispōno (3)

orderly, *adj*, (behaviour), mŏdestus; (arrangement), ordĭnātus dispŏsĭtus

orderly, *nn*, stător, *m*

ordinary, ūsĭtātus, mĕdĭŏcris

ordnance, tormenta, *n.pl*

ore, aes, *n*

organ (of the body), membrum, *n*

organization, dispŏsĭtĭo, *f*

organize, *v.t*, ordĭno (1)

orgies, orgĭa, *n.pl*; (revelry), cōmissātĭo, *f*

orient, ōrĭens, *m*

oriental, *use genit. of* ŏrĭens (orient)

orifice, fŏrāmen, *n*, os, *n*

origin, ŏrīgo, *f*, princĭpĭum, *n*

original, princĭpālis, antīquus, (one's own), prŏprĭus

originally, *adv*, princĭpĭo, ĭnĭtĭo

originate, *v.i*, ŏrĭor (4 *dep*)

originator, auctor, *m*

ornament, *nn*, ornāmentum, *n*

ornament, *v.t*, orno (1)

ornate, *adj*, ornātus, pictus

orphan, orbus, *m*

oscillate, *v.i*, quătĭor (3 *pass*)

oscillation, *nse vb*. quătĭor (*above*) (3 *pass*)

osier, *nn*, vīmen, *n*

osier, *adj*, vīmĭnĕus

osprey, ossĭfrăgus, *m*

ostensible, *use adv. below*

ostensibly, *adv*, per spĕcĭem

ostentation, ostentātĭo, *f*

ostentatious, glōrĭōsus

ostler, ăgāso, *m*

ostracise, *v.t*, vīto (1) (avoid)

ostrich, strūthĭŏcămēlus, *m*

other, *adj*, ălĭus; (the — of two), alter; (the others, the rest), cētĕri

others, *adj*, (belonging to —), ălĭēnus

otherwise, *adv*, (differently), ălĭter; (in other respects also), ălĭŏqui

otter, lūtra, *f*

ought, *v.auxil*, dēbĕo (2), ŏportet (2 *impers*, *with acc. of person*), *e.g*. I ought, ŏportet mē

ounce, uncĭa, *f*

our, ours, noster

ourselves (*in apposition to subject*), ipsi; (*reflexive*), nos

out, *adv*, (being out), fŏris; (going out), fŏras

out of, *prep*, ē, ex, dē (*with abl*); extrā (*with acc*); (on account of), propter (*with acc*)

outbid, *v.t*, *use phr*, plūs offĕro quam . . . (offer more than . . .)

outbreak, *use vb*. ŏrĭor (4 *dep*) (to arise); (beginning), ĭnĭtĭum, *n*

outcast, prŏfŭgus, *m*

outcome (result), exĭtus, *m*

outcry, clāmor, *m*

outdo, *v.t*, sŭpĕro (1)

outdoors, *adv*, fŏras

outer, *adj*, extĕrĭor

outfit (equipment), appărātus, *m*

outflank, *v.i*, circŭmĕo (4)

outgrow, *v.t*, *use phr*, magnĭtūdĭne sŭpĕro (1) (surpass in size)

outhouse, tŭgŭrĭum, *n*

outlast, *v.t*, dĭŭturnĭtāte sŭpĕro (surpass in duration)

outlaw, *nn*, prōscriptus, *m*

outlaw, *v.t*, prōscrībo (3)

outlay, *nn*, sumptus, *m*

outlet, exĭtus, *m*

outline, fīnis, *m*, ădumbrātĭo, *f*

outlive, *v.i*, sŭperstĕs sum (*irreg*) (to be a survivor)

outlook (future), fŭtūra, *n.pl*

outnumber, *v.t*, plūres nŭmĕro esse quam . . . (to be more in number than . . .)

outpost, stătĭo, *f*

outrage, *nn*, iniūrĭa, *f*

outrage, v.t, vĭŏlo (1)
outrageous, indignus
outright, adv, prorsus; (immediately), stătim
outset, inĭtĭum, n
outside, nn, extĕrna pars, f; (on the —), adv, extrinsĕcus; (appearance), spĕcĭes, f, frons, f
outside, adj, externus
outside, adv, extrā
outside of, prep, extrā (with acc)
outskirts, use adj. sŭburbānus (near the city)
outspoken (frank), līber
outstretched, porrectus
outstrip, v.t, sŭpĕro (1)
outward, adj, externus
outwardly, adv, extrā
outweigh, v.t, grăvĭtāte sŭpĕro (1) (surpass in weight)
outwit, v.t, dēcĭpĭo (3)
oval, adj, ōvātus
oven, furnus, m
over, prep, (above, across, more than), sŭper (with acc)
over, adv, (above), sŭper, suprā; (left —), adj, rĕlīquus; (it is —, all up with), actum est; (— and — again), adv, ĭdentĭdem
overawe, v.t, percello (3)
overbearing, sŭperbus
overboard, adv, ex nāvi
overcast (sky), nūbĭlus
overcoat, lăcerna, f
overcome, v.t, vinco (3), sŭpĕro (1)
overdone, use adv, nĭmis (too much)
overdue, use adv, dĭūtĭus (too long), and diffĕro (irreg), (to put off)
overflow, v.i, effundor (3 pass); v.t, ĭnundo (1)
overgrown, obsĭtus
overhang, v.i, immĭnĕo (2), impendĕo (2) (both with dat)
overhanging, impendens
overhasty, praeceps
overhaul, v.t, (repair), rĕsarcĭo (4)
overhead, adv, insŭper
overhear, v.t, excĭpĭo (3)
overjoyed, laetĭtĭā ēlātus (elated with joy)
overland, adv, terrā, per terram
overlap, v.t, (overtake), sŭpervĕnĭo (4)
overlay, v.t, indūco (3)
overload, v.t, grăvo (1)
overlook, v.t, prōspĭcĭo (3); (forgive), ignosco (3) (with dat); (neglect), praetermitto (3)
overmuch, adv, nĭmis
overpower, v.t, opprĭmo (3)

overrate, v.t, plūris aestĭmo (1) (value too highly)
override, v.t, praeverto (3)
overrule, v.t, vinco (3)
overrun, v.t, pervăgor (1 dep)
oversee, v.t, cūro (1), inspĭcĭo (3)
overseer, cūrātor, m
overshadow, v.t, offĭcĭo (3) (with dat)
oversight (omission), error, m, neglĕgentĭa, f, or use vb, praetermitto (3) (overlook)
overspread, v.t, obdūco (3)
overt, ăpertus, plānus
overtake, v.t, consĕquor (3 dep)
overtax (strength, etc.), v.t, nĭmis ūtor (3 dep) (with abl)
overthrow, nn, rŭīna, f
overthrow, v.t, ēverto (3), opprĭmo (3)
overtop, v.t, sŭpĕro (1)
overture (to make —s), use vb. instĭtŭo (3) (to begin)
overweening, sŭperbus
overwhelm, v.t, opprĭmo (3), obrŭo (3)
overwork, v.i, nĭmis lăbōro (1)
overwrought (exhausted), confectus
owe, v.t, dēbĕo (2)
owing to, prep, (on account of), propter, ob (both with acc)
owl, būbo, m, strix, f
own, adj, prŏprĭus; (often expressed by possessive pron, e.g. my own, mĕus
own, v.t, (possess), tĕnĕo (2), possĭdĕo (2); (confess), fătĕor (2 dep)
owner, possessor m, dŏmĭnus, m
ox, bōs, c
oxherd, armentārĭus, m
oyster, ostrĕa, f

P

pace, nn, passus, m
pace (step), spătĭor (1 dep), grădĭor (3 dep)
pacific, pācĭfĭcus
pacification, pācĭfĭcātĭo, f
pacify, v.t, plāco (1), sēdo (1)
pack (bundle), sarcĭna, f; (— of people), turba, f
pack, v.t, (gather together), collĭgo(3); (— close together), stĭpo (1)
package, sarcĭna, f
packet, fascĭcŭlus, m
pack-horse, iūmentum, n
pact, pactum, n, foedus, n
padding, nn, fartūra, f
paddle, nn, (oar), rēmus, m
paddle, v.t, rēmĭgo (1), (to row)
paddock, saeptum, n

padlock, sĕra, f
pagan, păgānus
page (book), păgĭna, f; (boy), pŭer, m
pageant, spectăcŭlum, n, pompa, f
pageantry, spĕcĭes, (f) atque pompa, f (display and public procession)
pail, sītŭla, f
pain, dŏlor, m; (to be in —), v.i, dŏlĕo (2)
pain, v.t, dŏlōre affĭcĭo (3) (inflict pain)
painful, ăcerbus
painless, use adv. phr, sĭne dŏlōre (without pain)
pains (endeavour), ŏpĕra, f; (to take — over), ŏpĕram do (1) (with dat)
painstaking, ŏpĕrōsus
paint, v.t, pingo (3); (colour), fūco (1)
paint, nn, pigmentum, n
paint-brush, pēnĭcullus, m
painter, pictor, m
painting, pictūra, f
pair, pār, m
pair, v.t, iungo (3); v.i, iungor (3 pass)
palace, rēgĭa, f
palatable, iūcundus
palate, pălātum, n
palatial, rēgĭus
pale, adj, pallĭdus; (to be —), v.i, pallĕo (2); (to become —), v.i, pallesco (3)
pale, nn, (stake), pālus, m
paleness, pallor, m
palisade, vallum, n
pall, nn, pallĭum, n
pall, v.i, (it —s), taedet (2 impers)
pallet lectŭlus, m
palliate, v.t, extĕnŭo (1)
palliation, use vb, extĕnŭo (1) (palliate)
palliative, lēnĭmentum, n
pallid, adj pallĭdus
pallor, pallor, m
palm (of hand, tree), palma, f
palm (to — off), v.t, suppōno (3)
palpable (obvious), mănĭfestus
palpitate, v.t, palpĭto (1)
palpitation, palpĭtātĭo, f
palsy, părălўsis, f
paltry, vīlis
pamper, v.t, nĭmĭum indulgĕo (2) (with dat) (to be too kind to . . .)
pamphlet, lĭbellus, m
pamphleteer, scriptor, (m) lĭbellorum
pan, pătĭna, f; (frying —), sartāgo, f
panacea, pănăcĕa, f
pancake, lăgănum, n
pander, v.i, lēnōcĭnor (1 dep)
panegyric, laudātĭo, f
panel (of door, etc.), tympănum, n
panelled, lăquĕātus

pang, dŏlor, m
panic, păvor, m
panic-stricken, păvĭdus
pannier, clītellae, f, pl
panorama, prōspectus, m
pant, v.i, ănhēlo (1)
panther, panthēra, f
panting, nn, ănhēlĭtus, m
pantomime, mīmus, m
pantry, cella pēnārĭa, f
pap (nipple), păpilla, f
paper, charta, f; (sheet of —), schĕda, f; (newspaper), acta dĭurna, n.pl
papyrus, păpўrus, m, f
par (on a — with), adj, pār
parable, părăbŏla, f
parade (military), dēcursus, m; (show), appārātus, m, pompa, f
parade, v.i, (of troops), dēcurro (3); v.t (display), ostento (1)
paradise, Ēlўsĭum, ĭi, n
paragon, spĕcĭmen, n
paragraph, căput, n
parallel, adj, părallēlus; (like), sĭmĭlis
paralyse, v.t, dēbĭlĭto (1)
paralysed, dēbĭlis
paralysis, părălўsis, f, dēbĭlĭtas, f
paramount summus
paramour ădulter, m, ămātor, m
parapet, lōrīca, f, mūnītĭo, f
paraphernalia, appārātus, m
parasite, assecla, c
parasol, umbella, f
parcel, fascĭcŭlus, m
parcel out, v.t, partĭor (4 dep)
parch, v.t, torrĕo (2)
parched (dry), ārĭdus; (scorched), torrĭdus
parchment, membrāna, f
pardon, nn, vĕnĭa, f
pardon, v.t, ignosco (3) (with dat)
pardonable, use phr, cui ignoscendum est (who should be pardoned)
pare, v.t, (circum)sĕco (1) (cut around))
parent, părens, m, f
parentage, gĕnus, n
parental, pătrĭus, or use genit pl, părentum (of parents)
parenthesis, interpŏsĭtĭo, f
parish, păroecĭa, f
park, horti, m. pl
parley, collŏquĭum, n
parley, v.i, collŏquor (3 dep)
parliament, sĕnātus, m
parliamentary, use genit. case of sĕnātus
parlour, conclāve, n

For List of Abbreviations used, turn to pages 3, 4

parody, versus rĭdĭcŭli, *m, pl*

parole, fĭdes, *f* **(promise)**

paroxysm, *use* accessus, *m,* **(approach)**

parricide (person), parrĭcīda, *c;* **(act),** parrĭcīdĭum, *n*

parrot, psittăcus, *m*

parry, *v.t.* prōpulso (1)

parse, *v.t. use phr,* verba sĭngŭlātim percĭpĭo **(understand the words one by one)**

parsimonious, parcus

parsimony, parsĭmōnĭa, *f*

parsley, ăpĭum, *n*

parson (priest), săcerdos, *c*

part, pars, *f;* **(in a play),** persōna, *f,* partes, *f, pl;* **(side, faction),** partes, *f, pl;* **(duty),** offĭcĭum, *n;* **(region),** lŏca, *n.pl;* **(from all —s),** *adv,* undīque; **(for the most —),** *adv,* plērumque; **(to take — in),** intersum *(irreg) (with dat)*

part, *v.t.* dīvĭdo (3), sēpăro (1); *v.i.* discēdo (3)

partake of, *v.t.* partĭceps sum *(irreg) (with genit);* **(food),** gusto (1)

partaker, partĭceps, *adj*

partial (affecting only a part), *use adv. phr,* ex ălĭquā parte; **(unfair),** inīquus

partiality, stŭdĭum, *n*

participate, *v.i.* partĭceps sum *(irreg) (with genit)*

participation, sŏcĭĕtas, *f*

particle, partĭcŭla, *f*

particular (characteristic), prŏprĭus; **(special),** sĭngŭlāris; **(exacting),** dēlĭcātus

particularly (especially), *adv,* praecĭpŭē

parting, *nn,* dīgressus, *m*

partisan, fautor, *m*

partition (act of —), partītĭo, *f;* **(wall),** părĭes, *m*

partly, *adv,* partim

partner, sŏcĭus, *m* (sŏcĭa, *f*)

partnership, sŏcĭĕtas, *f*

partridge, perdix, *c*

party (political, etc.), factĭo, *f;* **(of soldiers),** mănus, *f;* **(for pleasure),** convīvĭum, *n*

pasha, sătrăpes, *m*

pass, *nn* **(mountain),** angustĭae, *f. pl*

pass, *v.t.* **(go beyond),** praetergrĕdĭor (3 *dep*); **(surpass),** excēdo (3); **(— on, — down),** trādo (3); **(of time),** ăgo (3), tĕro (3); **(— over, omit),** praetĕrĕo (4); **(— a law),**

sancĭo (4); **(approve),** prŏbo (1); *v.i,* praetĕrĕo (4); **(of time),** transĕo (4); **(give satisfaction),** sătisfăcĭo (3); **(— over, cross over),** transĕo (4); **(come to —, happen),** fĭo *(irreg)*

passable (road, etc.), pervĭus

passage (crossing), transĭtus, *m,* trāiectĭo, *f;* **(route, way),** ĭter, *n,* vĭa, *f;* **(in a book),** lŏcus, *m*

passenger, vector, *m*

passion, mōtus, *(m)* ănĭmi **(impulse of the mind); (love),** ămor, *m*

passionate, fervĭdus, ardens, īrācundus

passive, pătĭens

passivity, pătĭentĭa, *f*

passport, dĭplōma, *n*

password, tessĕra, *f*

past, *adj,* praetĕrĭtus; **(just —),** proxĭmus

past, *nn,* praetĕrĭtum tempus, *n*

past, *prep,* praeter *(with acc);* **(on the far side of),** ultrā *(with acc)*

past, *adv, use compound vb. with* praeter, *e.g.* praetĕrĕo (4) **(go past)**

paste, fărīna, *f*

paste, *v.t.* glūtĭno (1)

pastime, oblectāmentum, *n*

pastor, pastor, *m*

pastoral pastōrālis

pastry, crustum, *n*

pastry-cook, crustŭlārĭus, *m*

pasture, pascŭum, *n*

pasture, *v.t.* pasco (3)

pat, *v.t.* **(caress),** permulcĕo (2)

patch, *nn,* pannus, *m*

patch, *v.t.* sarcĭo (4)

patent, *adj,* ăpertus

paternal, păternus

path, sēmĭta, *f,* vĭa, *f*

pathetic, mĭsĕrandus

pathless, invĭus

pathos, *f;* affectĭo, *(f)* ănĭmi

pathway, sēmĭta, *f*

patience, pătĭentĭa, *f*

patient, *adj,* pătĭens

patient, *nn, use* aeger **(ill)**

patiently, *adv,* pătĭenter

patrician, *nn. and adj,* pătrĭcĭus

patrimony, pătrĭmōnĭum, *n*

patriot, *use phr,* qui pătrĭam ămat **(who loves his country)**

patriotic, ămans pătrĭae

patriotism, ămor *(m)* pătrĭae

patrol, *nn, use* custōdes, *m. pl,* **(guards)**

patrol, *v.t,* circŭmĕo (4)

patron, pătrōnus, *m*
patronage, pătrōcĭnĭum, *n*
patronize, *v.t.* făvĕo (2) (*with dat*)
patter, *nn*, crĕpĭtus, *m*
patter, *v.i.* crĕpo (1)
pattern, exemplum, *n*, exemplar, *n*
paucity, paucĭtas, *f*
pauper, pauper *c*, ĕgens (needy)
pause, *nn*, mŏra, *f*
pause, *v.i.* intermitto (3)
pave, *v.t.* sterno (3)
pavement, pāvīmentum, *n*
pavilion, *use* praetōrĭum, *n*, (general's tent), *or* tăbernācŭlum, *n*, (tent)
paw, *nn*, pes, *m*
paw, *v.t.* pĕdĭbus calco (1) (tread with the feet)
pawn (chess), lătruncŭlus, *m*; (security), pignus, *n*
pawn, *v.t.* pignĕro (1)
pay, *nn*, stĭpendĭum, *n*
pay, *v.t.* solvo (3), pendo (3), nŭmĕro (1); *v.i* (— attention), ŏpĕram do (1); (— the penalty), poenas do (1)
pay-master (in army), trĭbūnus aerārĭus, *m*
payment, sŏlūtĭo, *f*
pea, pīsum, *n*, cĭcer, *n*
peace, pax, *f*, ōtĭum, *n*
peaceable, plăcĭdus
peaceful, plăcĭdus, pācātus
peacefulness, tranquillĭtas, *f*
peace-offering, plăcŭlum, *n*
peacock, pāvo, *m*
peak, ăpex, *m*; (mountain), căcūmen, *n*
peal (thunder), frăgor, *m*; *otherwise use* sŏnus, *m*, (sound)
peal, *v.i.* sŏno (1)
pear, pȳrum, *n*; (— tree), pȳrus, *f*
pearl, margărīta, *f*
peasant, rustĭcus, *m*, ăgrestis, *m*
peasantry, ăgrestes, *m. pl*
pebble, lăpillus, *m*
peck (measure), mŏdĭus, *m*
peck, *v.t.* vellĭco (1)
peculation, pĕcūlātus, *m*
peculiar (to one person, etc.), prŏprĭus; (remarkable), singŭlāris
peculiarity, prŏprĭĕtas, *f*
pecuniary, pĕcūnĭārĭus
pedagogue, măgister, *m*
pedant, hŏmo ĭneptus
pedantic (affected — of style, etc.), pūtĭdus
peddle, *v.t.* vendĭto (1)
pedestal, băsis, *f*
pedestrian, *nn*, pĕdes, *m*
pedestrian, *adj*, pĕdester

pedigree, stemma, *n*
pedlar, instĭtor, *m*
peel, *nn*, cŭtis, *f*
peel, *v.i.* cŭtem rĕsĕco (1)
peep, *nn*, aspectus, *m*
peep at, *v.t.* inspicio (3); *v.i*, sē prōferre (*irreg*)
peer (equal), par, *m*
peer at, *v.t.* rīmor (1 *dep*)
peerless, ūnĭcus
peevish, stŏmăchōsus
peevishness, stŏmăchus, *m*
peg, clāvus, *m*
pelt, *v.t. use* intorquĕo (2) (hurl at); *v.i*, (of rain, etc.), *use* plŭit (it rains)
pen, călămus, *m*; (for cattle), saeptum, *n*
pen, *v.t.* (write), scrībo (3)
penal, poenālis
penalty, poena, *f*, damnum, *n*; (to pay the —), poenas do (1)
penance (do —), *use vb.* expĭo (1) (to make amends)
pencil, pĕnĭcillum, *n*
pending, *prep*, inter, per (*with acc*)
pendulous, pendŭlus
penetrate, *v.i.* *and v.t.* pĕnĕtro (1) pervādo (3)
penetrating, *adj*, ăcūtus, ācer (mentally), săgax
penetration, ăcūmen, *n*
peninsula, paeninsŭla, *f*
penitence, paenĭtentĭa, *f*
penitent, *use vb*, paenĭtet (2 *impers*) (*with acc. of person*), *e.g.* I am penitent, mē paenĭtet
pennant, vexillum, *n*
penny, as, *m*
pension, annŭa, *n.pl*
pensive, multa pŭtans (thinking many things)
penthouse, vĭnĕa, *f*
penultimate, paenultĭmus
penurious, parcus
penury, ĕgestas, *f*, ĭnŏpĭa, *f*
people (community), pŏpŭlus, *m*; (persons), hŏmĭnes, *c. pl*; (the common —), plebs, *f*, vulgus, *n*
people, *v.t.* frĕquento (1); (inhabit), incŏlo (3)
pepper, pĭper, *n*
perambulate, *v.t.* pĕrambŭlo (1)
perceive, *v.t.* sentĭo (4), percĭpĭo (3), ănĭmadverto (3), intellĕgo (3)
percentage, pars, *f*
perception, perspĭcācĭtas, *f*, *or use adj*, perspĭcax (sharp-sighted)
perceptive, perspĭcax
perch, *nn*, pertĭca, *f*; (fish), perca, *f*
perch, *v.i.* insīdo (3)

perchance, *adv*, fortĕ
percolate, *v.i*, permāno (1)
percussion, ictus, *m*
perdition, exĭtĭum, *n*
peremptory, *use vb.* obstringo (3) (to put under obligation)
perennial, pĕrennis
perfect, perfectus, absŏlūtus
perfect, *v.t*, perfĭcĭo (3), absolvo (3)
perfection, perfectĭo, *f*, absŏlūtĭo, *f*
perfidious, perfĭdus
perfidy, perfĭdĭa, *f*
perforate, *v.t*, perfŏro (1)
perform, *v.t*, fungor (3 *dep. with abl*); perăgo (3), praesto (1), exsĕquor (3 *dep*)
performance, functĭo, *f*
performer, actor, *m*
perfume, ŏdor, *m*
perfume, *v.t*, ŏdōro (1)
perfunctory, neglĕgens
perhaps, *adv*, fortĕ, fortassĕ, forsĭtan
peril, pĕrĭcŭlum, *n*
perilous, pĕrĭcŭlōsus
period, spătĭum, *n*
periodical, *adj*, stătus
perish, *v.i*, pĕrĕo (4)
perishable, frăgĭlis
perjure, *v.t*, pĕrĭūro (1)
perjured, pĕrĭūrus
perjury, pĕrĭūrĭum, *n*
permanence, stăbĭlĭtas, *f*
permanent, stăbĭlis
permanently, *adv*, perpĕtŭo
permeate, *v.i*, permāno (1)
permissible (it is —), lĭcet (2 *impers*)
permission (to give —), permitto (3) (*with dat*); (without your —), tĕ invīto
permit, *v.t*, sĭno (3), permitto (3)
pernicious, pernĭcĭōsus
perpendicular, *adj*, dīrectus
perpetrate, *v.t*, admitto (3)
perpetual, sempĭternus
perpetuate, *v.t*, contĭnŭo (1)
perplex, *v.t*, distrăho (3), sollĭcĭto (1)
perplexed, dŭbĭus
perquisite, pĕcūlĭum, *n*
persecute, *v.t*, insector (1 *dep*)
persecution, insectātĭo, *f*
persecutor, insectātor, *m*
perseverance, persĕvērantĭa, *f*
persevere, *v.i*, persĕvēro (1)
persist, *v.i*, persto (1)
persistence pertĭnācĭa, *f*
person, hŏmo, *c*; (body), corpus, *n*; (in person), *use pron*, ipse (self)
personal (opp. to public), prīvātus
personality, ingĕnĭum, *n*
perspicacious, perspĭcax

perspicacity, perspĭcācĭtas, *f*
perspiration, sūdor, *m*
perspire, *v.i*, sūdo (1)
persuade, *v.t*, persuādĕo (2) (*with dat of person*)
persuasion, persuāsĭo, *f*
persuasive, suāvĭlŏquens
pert, prŏcax
pertain, *v.i*, attĭnĕo (2)
pertinacious, pertĭnax
pertinacity, pertĭnācĭa, *f*
perturb, *v.t*, turbo (1)
perusal, perlectĭo, *f*
peruse, *v.t*, perlĕgo (3)
pervade, *v.i*, permāno (1), perfundo (3)
perverse, perversus
perversion, dēprāvātĭo, *f*
pervert, *v.t*, dēprāvo (1)
pervious, pervĭus
pest, pestis, *f*
pester, *v.t*, sollĭcĭto (1)
pestilence, pestĭlentĭa, *f*
pestilential, pestĭlens
pestle, pistillum, *n*
pet, *nn*, dēlĭcĭae, *f. pl*
pet, *v.t*, in dēlĭcĭis hăbĕo (2) (regard among one's favourites), indulgĕo (2)
petition, *use vb.* pĕto (3) (seek)
petition, *v.t*, rŏgo (1)
petitioners, pĕtentes, *c.pl*
petrify, *v.t*, (with fear, etc.), terrōrem inĭcĭo (3), (*with dat*)
pettifogging, vĭlis
petty, mĭnūtus
petulance, pĕtŭlantĭa, *f*
petulant, pĕtŭlans
phantom, sĭmŭlācrum, *n*, ĭmāgo, *f*
phases (alternations), vĭces, *f. pl*
pheasant, āles, (c) Phāsĭdis (bird of Phasis)
phenomenon, rēs, *f*; (remarkable occurrence), rēs mīrābĭlis
phial, lăguncŭla, *f*
philanthropic, hūmānus
philanthropy, hūmānĭtas, *f*
philologist, phĭlŏlŏgus, *m*
philology, phĭlŏlŏgĭa, *f*
philosopher, phĭlŏsŏphus, *m*
philosophical, phĭlŏsŏphus
philosophy, phĭlŏsŏphĭa, *f*
philtre, phĭltrum, *n*
phlegm, pītŭīta, *f*; (of temperament), aequus ănĭmus, *m*
phoenix, phoenix, *m*
phrase, *nn*, lŏcŭtĭo, *f*
phraseology, *use* verba, *n.pl*, (words)
phthisis, phthĭsis, *f*
physic, mĕdĭcāmentum, *n*

physical (relating to the body), *use*
nn, corpus, n, (body); (natural),
use nătūra, f, (nature)

physician, mĕdĭcus, m

physics, phŷsĭca, n.pl

physiology, phŷsĭŏlŏgĭa, f

pick (axe), dŏlābra, f; (choice), *use*
adj, dēlectus (chosen)

pick, v.t, (pluck), lĕgo (3), carpo (3);
(choose), ēlĭgo (3); (— up, seize),
răpĭo (3)

picked (chosen), dēlectus

picket, stătĭo, f

pickle, mūrĭa, f

pickle, v.t, condĭo (4)

pickpocket, fūr, c

picnic, *use phr*, fŏrīs ĕpŭlor (1 dep) (to
eat out of doors)

picture, tăbŭla, f

picture, v.t, expingo (3)

picturesque, ămoenus

pie, crustum, n

piebald, bĭcŏlor

piece (part), pars, f; (of food), frustrum, n; (to pull or tear to —s),
discerpo (3), dīvello (3); (to fall to
—s), dīlābor (3 pass)

piecemeal, adv, membrātim

piece together, v.t, compōno (3)

pier, mōles, f

pierce, v.t, perfŏdĭo (3)

piercing, adj, ăcūtus

piety, pĭĕtas, f

pig, porcus, m, sūs, c

pigeon, cŏlumba, f

pigheaded, obstĭnātus, diffĭcĭlis

pigsty, hăra, f

pike, hasta, f

pile (heap), ăcervus, m; (building),
mōles, f; (supporting timber),
sublĭca, f

pile, v.t, ăcervo (1), congĕro (3)

pilfer, v.t, surrĭpĭo (3)

pilfering, nn, furtum, n

pilgrim, pĕrĕgrīnător, m

pilgrimage, pĕrĕgrīnātĭo, f

pill, pĭlŭla, f

pillage, nn, răpīna, f, dīreptĭo, f

pillage, v.t, praedor (1 dep), dīrĭpĭo
(3)

pillar, cŏlumna, f

pillory, vincŭla, n.pl

pillow, pulvīnus, m

pillow, v.t, suffulcĭo (4)

pilot, gŭbernător, m

pilot, v.t, gŭberno (1)

pimp, lēno, m

pimple, pustŭla, f

pin, ăcus, f

pin, v.t, ăcu fīgo (3) (fix with a pin)

pincers, forceps, m, f

pinch, nn, (bite), morsus, m

pinch, v.t, ūro (3), vellĭco (1);
(squeeze), cŏarto (1)

pine, nn, pīnus, f; adj, pīnĕus

pine, v.i, tābesco (3); v.t, (—for), dēsīdĕro (1)

pinion (nail), clāvus, m; (bond),
vincŭla, n.pl

pinion, v.t, rĕvincĭo (4)

pink, rŭbor, m

pinnace, lembus, m

pinnacle, fastīgĭum, n

pint, sextārĭus, m

pioneer, explŏrător, m

pious, pĭus

pip (seed), sēmen, n, grānum, n

pipe, cănālis, m; (musical), fistŭla, f

pipe, v.i, căno (3)

piper, tībīcen, m

piquant, ăcerbus

pique, nn, offensĭo, f

pique, v.t, laedo (3)

piracy, lătrōcĭnĭum, n

pirate, praedo, m, pīrāta, m

pit, fŏvĕa, f; (arm —), āla, f; (theatre),
căvĕa, f

pit (— one's wits, etc.), *use* ūtor (3
dep) (to use)

pitch, nn, pix, f; (in music), sŏnus, m

pitch, v.t, (camp, tent, etc.), pōno (3);
(throw), cōnĭcĭo (3); (ships), *use*
ăgĭtor (1 pass) (to be tossed about)

pitcher, urcĕus, m

pitchfork, furca, f

piteous, pĭtĭable, mĭsĕrābĭlis

pitfall, fŏvĕa, f

pith, mĕdulla, f

pitiful mĭser, mĭsĕrĭcors

pitifulness, mĭsĕrĭa, f

pitiless, immĭsĕrĭcors

pittance (small pay) tips, f

pity, v.t, mĭsĕret (2 impers) (with acc.
of subject and genit. of object, e.g. **I**
pity you; mē mĭsĕret tŭi

pity, nn, mĭsĕrĭcordĭa, f

pivot, cardo, m

placard, inscriptum, n

placate, v.t, plāco (1)

place, lŏcus, m; (in this —), adv, hīc;
(in that —), illīc, ĭbĭ; (in what —)
ŭbĭ?; (in the same —), ĭbīdem; (to
this —) hūc; (to that —), illūc;
(to the same —), ĕōdem; (to what
—?), quō; (from this —), hinc;
(from that —), inde; (from the
same—), indĭdem; (from what—?),
unde?; (in the first —), prīmum;
(to take —, happen), v.i, accĭdo (3)

place, v.t, pōno (3), lŏco (1); (— in

For List of Abbreviations used, turn to pages 3, 4

command), praefĭcĭo (3); (— upon), impōno (3)

placid, plăcĭdus, tranquillus

plague, *nn*, pestĭlentĭa, *f*, pestis, *f*

plague, *v.t*, (trouble), sollĭcĭto (1)

plain, *nn*, campus, *m*, plānĭtĭes, *f*

plain, *adj*, (clear), clārus, plānus; (unadorned), subtĭlis, simplex; (frank, candid), sincērus

plainness, perspĭcŭĭtas, *f*, simplĭcĭtas, *f*, sincērĭtas, *f*

plaintiff, pĕtītor, *m*

plaintive, *adj*, mĭsĕrābĭlis

plait, *v.t*, intexo (3)

plan, *nn*, consĭlĭum, *n*; (drawing), dēscriptĭo, *f*; (to make a —), consĭlĭum căpĭo (3)

plan, *v.i*, (intend), in ănĭmo hăbĕo (2); *v.t*, (design), dēscrībo (3)

plane, *nn*, (tool), runcīna, *f*; (tree), plătănus, *f*

plane, *v.t* runcĭno (1)

planet, sīdus, (*n*) errans (moving constellation)

plank, tăbŭla, *f*

plant, *nn*, herba, *f*

plant (seeds, etc.), sĕro (3); (otherwise), pōno (3), stătŭo (3)

plantation, plantārĭum, *n*, arbustum, *n*

planter, sător, *m*

planting, *nn*, sătus, *m*

plaster, *nn*, tectōrĭum, *n*; (medical), emplastrum, *n*

plaster, *v.t*, gypso (1)

plasterer, tector, *m*

plate (dish), cătillus, *m*; (thin layer of metal), lāmĭna, *f*; (silver, gold), argentum, *n*

plate, *v.t*, indūco (3)

platform, suggestus, *m*

Platonic, Plătōnĭcus

platoon, dĕcŭrĭa, *f*

plausible, spĕcĭōsus

play, *nn*, lūdus, *m*, lūsus, *m*; (theatre), fābŭla, *f*; (scope), campus, *m*

play, *v.i*, lūdo (3) (*with abl. of game played*); (musical), căno (3); (a part in a play), partes ăgo (3); (a trick), lūdĭfĭco (1)

player (stage), histrĭo, *m*; (flute —), tībĭcen, *m*; (strings —), fĭdĭcen, *m*; (lute, guitar —), cĭthărista, *m*

playful (frolicsome), lascīvus

playfulness, lascīvĭa, *f*

playground, ārĕa, *f*

playwright, fābŭlārum scriptor, *m*

plea (asking), obsĕcrātĭo, *f*; (excuse), excūsātĭo, *f*

plead, *v.t*, ōro (1), ăgo (3); (as an excuse), excūso (1); (beg earnestly), obsĕcro (1); (law), dīco (3)

pleader (in law), ōrātor, *m*

pleasing, pleasant, iūcundus

pleasantness, iūcundĭtas, *f*

please, *v.t*, plăcĕo (2) (*with dat*); (if you —), si vis

pleasurable, iūcundus

pleasure, vŏluptas, *f*; (will), arbĭtrĭum, *n*; (— gardens), horti, *m. pl*

plebian, plēbēĭus

pledge, *nn*, pignus, *n*; (to make a —, promise), sē obstringĕre (3 *reflex*)

pledge, *v.t*, oblĭgo (1), prōmitto (3)

plenipotentiary, lēgātus, *m*

plenitude, plēnĭtūdo, *f*

plentiful, largus, cōpĭōsus

plenty, cōpĭa, *f*; (enough), sătis (*with genit*)

pleurisy, pleurītis, *f*

pliable, flexĭbĭlis, lentus

plight, angustĭae, *f. pl* (difficulties)

plight, *v.t*, spondĕo (2), oblĭgo (1)

plinth, plinthus, *m*, *f*

plod, *v.i*, lentē prōcēdo (3)

plot (of ground), ăgellus, *m*; (conspiracy), conĭūrātĭo, *f*; (story), argūmentum, *n*

plot, *v.i*, conĭūro (1)

plough, *nn*, ărātrum, *n*; (— share), vōmer, *m*

plough, *v.t*, ăro (1)

ploughman, ărātor, *m*, bŭbulcus, *m*

pluck, *nn*, fortĭtūdo, *f*, ănĭmus, *m*

pluck, *v.t*, carpo (3); (— up courage), ănĭmum rĕvŏco (1)

plug, *nn*, obtūrāmentum, *n*

plum, prūnum, *n*

plum-tree, prūnus, *f*

plumage, plūmae, *f*, *pl*

plume, penna, *f*

plumb-line, līnĕa, *f*

plump, pinguis

plumpness, nĭtor, *m*, pinguĭtūdo, *f*

plunder, *nn*, praeda, *f*; (act of plundering), răpīna, *f*, dīreptĭo, *f*

plunder, *v.t*, praedor (1 *dep*), dīrĭpĭo (3)

plunderer, praedātor, *m*

plunge, *v.i*, sē mergĕre (3 *reflex*); *v.t*, mergo (3)

plural, *adj*, plūrālis

plurality, multĭtūdo, *f*

ply, *v.t*, exercĕo (2)

poach, *v.t*, *use* răpĭo (3), (to seize); (cook), cŏquo (3)

poacher, fur, *c*, raptor *m*.

pocket, sĭnus, *m*

pocket, *v.t.* (money), āverto (3)

pocket-book, pŭgillāres, *m, pl*

pocket-money, pĕcūlĭum, *n*

pod, sīlĭqua, *f*

poem, pŏēma, *n*, carmen, *n*

poet, pŏēta, *m*

poetical, pŏētĭcus

poetry, pŏēsis, *f*, carmĭna, *n.pl*

poignant, ăcerbus

point, ăcūmen, *n*; (of a sword), mūcro, *m*; (spear), cuspis, *f*; (place), lŏcus, *m*; (issue), res, *f*; (on the — of), *use fut. participle of vb, e.g.* on the point of coming; ventūrus

point, *v.t* (make pointed), praeăcŭo (3); (direct), dīrĭgo (3)

point out *or* at, *v.t.*, monstro (1)

pointed, praeăcūtus; (witty) salsus

pointer, index, *m, f*

pointless, insulsus

poison, vĕnēnum, *n*, vīrus, *n*

poison, *v.t.*, vĕnēno nĕco (1) (kill by poison)

poisoning, *nn*, vĕnēfĭcĭum, *n*

poisonous, vĕnēnātus

poke, *v.t.*, fŏdĭco (1)

polar, septentrĭōnālis

pole (rod, staff), contus, *m*, longŭrĭus, *m*; (earth), pŏlus, *m*

polemics, contrōversĭae, *f. pl*

police (men), vĭgĭles, *m, pl*

policy, rătĭo, *f*

polish, *nn*, (brightness), nĭtor, *m*

polish, *v.t*, pŏlĭo (4)

polished, pŏlītus

polite, cōmis, urbānus

politeness, cōmĭtas, *f*, urbānĭtas, *f*

politic, *adj*, prūdens

political, cīvĭlis, pūblĭcus

politician, qui rēïpūblĭcae stŭdet (who pursues state affairs)

politics, rēs pūblĭca, *f*

poll (vote), suffrāgĭum, *n*

pollute, *v.t.*, inquĭno (1)

pollution, collŭvĭo, *f*

polytheism, *use phr*, crēdĕre multos esse dĕos (believe that there are many gods)

pomade, căpillāre, *n*

pomegranate, mālum grānātum, *n*

pommel, *v.t*, verbĕro (1)

pomp, appārātus, *m*

pompous, magnĭfĭcus

pompousness, magnĭfĭcentĭa, *f*

pond, stagnum, *n*; (fish —), piscīna, *f*

ponder, *v.t.*, rĕpŭto (1)

ponderous, grăvis

poniard, pŭgĭo, *m*

pontiff, pontĭfex, *m*

pontoon, pons, *m*

pony, mannus, *m*

pool, lăcūna, *f*

poop, puppis, *f*

poor, pauper, ĭnops; (worthless), vīlis; (wretched), mĭser

poorly, *adj*, (sick, ill), aeger

poorly, *adv*, tĕnŭiter, mălĕ

pop, *v.i*, crĕpo (1)

pope, Pontĭfex Maxĭmus, *m*

poplar, pŏpŭlus, *f*

poppy, păpāver, *n*

populace, vulgus, *n*, plebs, *f*

popular, grātĭōsus; (of the people), pŏpūlāris

popularity, făvor, (*m*) pŏpŭli (good-will of the people)

population, cīves, *c. pl*

populous, frēquens

porch, vestĭbŭlum, *n*

porcupine, hystrix, *f*

pore, fŏrāmen, *n*

pore over, *v.i*, ănĭmum intendo (3) (direct the mind)

pork, porcīna, *f*

porker, porcus, *m*

porous, rārus

porpoise, porcŭlus mărīnus, *m*

porridge, puls, *f*

port, portus, *m*

portable, quod portāri pŏtest (that can be carried)

portal, porta, *f*, iānŭa, *f*

portcullis, cătăracta, *f*

portend, *v.t*, portendo (3)

portent, portentum, *n*

portentous, monstrŭōsus

porter (doorkeeper), iānĭtor, *m*; (baggage carrier), bāĭŭlus, *m*

portfolio, lĭbellus, *m*

portico, portĭcus, *f*

portion, pars, *f*

portion out, *v.t*, partĭor (4 *dep*)

portrait, ĭmāgo, *f*

portray, *v.t*, dēpingo (3)

pose, *nn*, stătus, *m*

position, lŏcus, *m*; (site), sĭtus, *m*

positive, certus

possess, *v.t*, hăbĕo (2), possĭdĕo (2)

possession, possessĭo, *f*; (to take — of), pŏtĭor (4 *dep. with abl*); (property), *often use possessive pron. e.g.* mĕa (my —s), *or* bŏna *n.pl*

possessor, possessor, *m*, dŏmĭnus, *m*

possibility, *use phr. with* posse; (to be possible)

possible, *use vb*, posse (*irreg*) (to be possible); (as . . . as possible), *use* quam *with superlative, e.g.* as large as possible, quam maxĭmus; (as soon as —), quam prīmum

post, cippus, *m*, pālus, *m*; (military), stătĭo, *f*, lŏcus, *m*; (letter), tăbellārĭi pūblĭci, *m. pl* (state couriers)

post, *v.t*, (in position), lŏco (1); (letter), tăbellārĭo do (1) (give to a courier)

posterior, *nn*, nătes, *f. pl*

posterity, postĕri, *m. pl*

postern, postīcum, *n*

posthumous, *use phr*, post mortem (*with genit*) (after the death of . . .)

postman, tăbellārĭus, *m*

postpone, *v.t*, diffĕro (*irreg*)

postscript, verba subiecta, *n.pl*, (words appended)

posture, stătus, *m*

pot, olla, *f*

potent, pŏtens, effĭcax

potentate, tyrannus, *m*

potion, pōtĭo, *f*

potsherd, testa, *f*

potter, figŭlus, *m*

pottery (articles), fictĭlĭa, *n.pl*

pouch, saccŭlus, *m*

poultice, mălagma, *n*

poultry, ăves cŏhortāles, *f. pl*

pounce upon, *v.t*, invŏlo (1)

pound, *nn*, (weight), libra, *f*

pound, *v.t*, tundo (3), tĕro (3)

pour, *v.t*, fundo (3); *v.i*, fundor (3 *pass*)

pouring, *adj*, effūsus

pout, *v.i*, lăbellum extendo (3) (stretch a lip)

poverty, paupertas, *f*, ĕgestas, *f*, ĭnŏpĭa, *f*; (— stricken), *adj*, ĭnops

powder, *nn*, pulvis, *m*

power, vires, *f. pl*; (dominion), pŏtestas, *f*; (authority), ius, *n*, impĕrĭum, *n*; (unconstitutional —), pŏtentĭa, *f*

powerful, pŏtens; (of body), vălĭdus

powerless, invălĭdus; (to be —), *v.i*, mĭnĭmum posse (*irreg*)

practicable, *use phr*, quod fĭĕri pŏtest (that can be done)

practical (person), făbrĭcae pĕrītus (skilled in practical work)

practically (almost), *adv.*, paene

practice, ūsus, *m*; (custom), mos, *m*, consuētŭdo, *f*

practise, *v.t*, exercĕo (2), factĭto (1)

practitioner (medical), mĕdĭcus, *m*

praetor, praetor, *m*

praetorship, praetūra, *f*

praise, *nn*, laus, *f*

praise, *v.t*, laudo (1)

praiseworthy, laudăbĭlis

prance, *v.i*, exsulto (1)

prank, *use* lūdĭfĭcor (1 *dep*) (to make fun of)

prattle, *v.i*, garrĭo (4)

pray, *v.i. and v.t*, ōro (1), prĕcor (1 *dep*)

prayer, prĕces, *f. pl*

preach, *v.t*, contĭōnor (1 *dep*)

preamble, exordĭum, *n*

precarious, incertus

precaution (to take —s (against)), *v.i. and v.t*, praecăvĕo (2)

precede, *v.t*, antĕcēdo (3), antĕĕo (4)

precedence (to give —), *use vb*, cēdo (3); (to take —), prĭor esse (*irreg*)

precedent, exemplum, *n*

preceding, *adj*, prĭor, proxĭmus

precept, praeceptum, *n*

precious (of great price), magni prĕtĭi; (dear), dīlectus

precipice, lŏcus praeceps, *m*

precipitate, *adj*, praeceps

precipitate, *v.t*, praecĭpĭto (1)

precipitous, praeceps

precise, subtīlis

precision, subtīlĭtas, *f*

preclude, *v.t*, prŏhĭbĕo (2)

precocious, praecox

preconceived, praeiūdĭcātus

precursor, praenuntĭus, *m*

predatory, praedātōrĭus

predecessor (my —), *use phr*, qui ante me . . . (who before me . . .)

predicament, angustĭae, *f. pl*

predict, *v.t*, praedīco (3)

prediction, praedictĭo, *f*

predilection, stŭdĭum, *n*

predisposed, inclīnātus

predominant, pŏtens

predominate, *v.i*, *use phr*, qui in pŏtentĭā sunt (who are in authority)

preeminent, praestans

preface, praefātĭo, *f*

preface, *v.t*, praefor (1 *dep*)

prefer, *v.t*, *with infinitive*, mālo (*irreg*); (put one thing before another), antĕpōno (3); (— a charge), dēfĕro (*irreg*)

preferable, pŏtĭor

preference, (desire), vŏluntas, *f*; (in —), *adv*, pŏtĭus

preferment, hŏnor, *m*

pregnant, praegnans, grăvĭda

prejudge, *v.t*, praeiūdĭco (1)

prejudice, praeiūdĭcāta ŏpīnĭo, *f*

prejudice, *v.t*, (impair), immĭnŭo (3)

prejudicial, noxĭus; (to be — to), obsum (*irreg*) (*with dat*)

prelate, săcerdos, *c*

preliminary, *use compound word with* prae, *e.g.* to make a — announcement, praenuntĭo (1) prelude, prŏoemĭum, n

premature, immātūrus

premeditate, v.t, praemĕdĭtor (1 dep)

premeditation, praemĕdĭtātĭo, f

premier, princeps, m

premise, prŏpŏsĭtĭo, m

premises (buildings), aedĭfĭcĭa, n.pl

premium, praemĭum, n

premonition, mŏnĭtĭo, f

preoccupy (to be — with), stŭdĕo (2) (with dat)

preparation, compărātĭo, f, appārātus, m; (to make —s), compăro (1)

prepare, v.t, păro (1), compăro (1)

prepossess, v.t, commendo (1)

prepossessing, adj, suāvis, blandus

preposterous, praepostĕrus

prerogative, iūs, n

presage, praesāgĭum, n

presage, v.t, portendo (3)

prescribe, v.t, praescrībo (3)

presence, praesentĭa, f; (in the — of), prep, cōram (with abl)

present, nn (gift), dōnum, n; (time), praesentĭa, n.pl

present, adj, praesens; (to be —), v.i, adsum (irreg)

present, v.t, offĕro (irreg); (give), dōno (1) (with acc. of person and abl. of gift)

presentation, dōnātĭo, f

presentiment, augŭrĭum, n

presently, adv, (soon), mox

preservation, conservātĭo, f

preserve, v.t, servo (1)

preserver, servātor, m

preside, v.i, praesĭdĕo (with dat)

presidency, praefectūra, f

president, praefectus, m

press, nn, (machine), prēlum, n

press, v.t, prĕmo (3); (urge), urgĕo (2)

pressure, nīsus, m

prestige, fāma, f, ŏpīnĭo, f

presume, v.t, (assume), crēdo (3); (dare), v.i, audĕo (2)

presumption (conjecture), coniectūra, f; (conceitedness), arrŏgantĭa, f

presumptuous, arrŏgans

pretence, sĭmŭlātĭo, f; (under — of), per sĭmŭlātĭōnem

pretend, v.t, sĭmŭlo (1)

pretended, adj, sĭmŭlātus

pretender (claimant), use vb, pĕto (3) (aspire to)

pretension postŭlātĭo, f

pretext, spĕcĭes, f; (on the — of), use vb. sĭmŭlo (1) (to pretend)

prettily, adv, bellē, vĕnustē

prettiness, concinnĭtas, f, vĕnustas, f

pretty, adj, pulcher

pretty, adv, sătis (enough)

prevail, v.i, obtĭnĕo (2), sŭpĕrĭor esse (irreg); (to — upon), v.t, persuādĕo (2) (with dat)

prevalent, vulgātus

prevaricate, v.t, tergĭversor (1 dep)

prevent, v.t, prŏhĭbĕo (2)

prevention, use vb, prŏhĭbĕo (prevent)

previous, prŏxĭmus

previously, adv, antĕā

prey, nn, praeda, f

prey, v.t, praedor (1 dep)

price, nn, prĕtĭum, n; (— of corn), annōna, f

price, v.t, prĕtĭum constĭtŭo (3) (fix the price)

priceless, inaestĭmābĭlis

prick, nn, punctum, n

prick, v.t, pungo (3); (spur), stĭmŭlo (1)

prickly, adj, ăcŭlĕātus

pride, sŭperbĭa, f; (honourable —), spīrĭtus, m

priest, săcerdos, c

priesthood, săcerdōtĭum, n

prim, mōrōsĭor

primarily, adv, princĭpĭo

primary, prīmus

prime, nn, (of life, etc.), use vb, flōrĕo (2) (flourish); (best part), flōs, m

prime, adj, ēgrĕgĭus

primeval, prīmĭgĕnĭus

primitive, prīmĭgĕnĭus

prince (king), rēgŭlus, m; (king's son), fīlĭus, (m) rēgis

princess (king's daughter), fīlĭa, (f) rēgis

principal, adj, princĭpālis, praecĭpŭus

principal, nn, măgister, m

principality, regnum, n

principle, princĭpĭum, n; (element), ĕlĕmentum, n, prīmordĭa, n.pl; (rule, maxim), praeceptum, n

print, nn, (mark), nŏta, f

print, v.t, imprĭmo (3)

prior, adj, prĭor

priority, use adj, prĭor

prism, prisma, n

prison, carcer, m

prisoner, captīvus, m

privacy, sōlĭtūdo, f

private, prīvātus, sēcrētus

private soldier, mīles grĕgārĭus, m

privately, adv, prīvātim, clam

privation, ĭnŏpĭa, f

privet, lĭgustrum, n

privilege, iūs, n

privy, adj, (acquainted with), conscĭus; (secret), prīvātus

For List of Abbreviations used, turn to pages 3, 4

privy, *nn*, fŏrĭca, *f*
privy-council, consĭlĭum, *n*
privy-purse, fiscus, *m*
prize, praemĭum, *n*; (**booty**), praeda, *f*
prize, *v.t*, (**value**), magni aestĭmo (1)
probability, sĭmĭlĭtūdo, (*f*) vēri
probable, sĭmĭlis vēri
probation, prŏbātĭo, *f*
probe, *v.t*, tento (1)
problem, quaestĭo, *f*
problematical (**doubtful**), dŭbĭus
procedure, rătĭo, *f*
proceed, *v.i*, (**move on**), pergo (3); (**originate**) prŏfĭciscor (3 *dep*); (**take legal action against**) lĭtem intendo (3) (*with dat*)
proceedings (**legal**), actĭo, *f*; (**doings**), acta, *n.pl*
proceeds, fructus, *m*
process, rătĭo, *f*; (**in the — of time**), *adv, use phr*, tempŏre praetĕrĕunte (**with time going by**)
procession, pompa, *f*
proclaim, *v.t*, praedĭco (1), prōnuntĭo (1)
proclamation, prōnuntĭātĭo, *f*, ēdictum, *n*
proconsul, prōconsul, *m*
procrastinate, *v.t*, diffĕro (*irreg*)
procrastination, tardĭtas, *f*, mŏra, *f*
procreate, *v.t*, prŏcreo (1)
procreation, prŏcrēātĭo, *f*, partus, *m*
procure, *v.t*, compăro (1)
procurer, lēno, *m*
prodigal, *adj*, prŏdĭgus
prodigality, effūsĭo, *f*
prodigious, immānis
prodigy, prŏdĭgĭum, *n*
produce, *nn*, fructus, *m*
produce, *v.t*, (**into view**) prōfĕro (*irreg*); (**create**), părĭo (3); (**— an effect**), mŏvĕo (2)
product, production, ŏpus, *n*
productive, fĕrax
profanation, vĭŏlātĭo, *f*
profane, impĭus, prŏfānus
profane, *v.t*, vĭŏlo (1)
profanity, impĭĕtas, *f*
profess, *v.t*, prŏfĭtĕor (2 *dep*)
profession (**occupation**), mūnus, *n*, offĭcĭum, *n*; (**avowal**), prŏfessĭo, *f*
professor, prŏfessor, *m*
proffer, *v.t*, pollĭcĕor (2 *dep*)
proficient (**skilled**), pĕrītus
profile, oblīqua făcĭes, *f*
profit, *nn*, ēmŏlŭmentum, *n*, lŭcrum, *n*, quaestus, *m*

profit, *v.t*, (**benefit**), prōsum (*irreg. with dat*)
profitable, fructŭōsus
profitless, ĭnūtĭlis
profligacy, nēquĭtĭa, *f*
profligate, perdĭtus
profound, altus
profuse, effūsus
profusion, effūsĭo, *f*
progeny, prōgĕnĭes, *f*
prognostic, signum, *n*
programme, lĭbellus, *m*
progress (**improvement**, etc.), prōgressus, *m*; (**to make —**), prŏfĭcĭo (3), prōgrĕdĭor (3 *dep*)
progress, *v.i*, prōgrĕdĭor (3 *dep*)
prohibit, *v.t*, vĕto (1)
prohibition, interdictum, *n*
project, *nn*, (**plan**), consĭlĭum, *n*
project, *v.t*, prōĭcĭo (3); *v.i*, ēmĭnĕo (2)
projectile, tēlum *n*,
projecting, ēmĭnens
proletariat, vulgus, *n*
prolific, fēcundus
prolix, verbōsus
prologue, prŏlŏgus, *m*
prolong, *v.t*, prōdūco (3); (**— a command**), prōrŏgo (1)
prolongation, prŏpāgātĭo, *f*
promenade, ambŭlātĭo, *f*
prominence, ēmĭnentĭa, *f*
prominent, ēmĭnens; (**person**), praeclārus
promiscuous, prōmiscŭus
promise, *nn*, prōmissum, *n*, fĭdes, *f*
promise, *v.i*, prōmitto (3), pollĭcĕor (2 *dep*)
promising, *adj*, *use adv. phr*, bŏnā spe (**of good hope**)
promissory note, chīrŏgrăphum, *n*
promontory, prōmontōrĭum, *n*
promote, *v.t*, prōmŏvĕo (2); (**favour, assist**), iŭvo (1), prōsum (*irreg*) (*with dat*)
promoter, auctor, *m*
promotion (**act of —**), *use vb*. prōmŏvĕo (2); (**honour**), hŏnor, *m*
prompt, *adj*, promptus
prompt, *v.t*, (**assist in speaking**), sŭbĭcĭo (3) (*with dat. of person*); (**incite**), incĭto (1)
promptitude, promptness, cĕlĕrĭtas, *f*
promulgate, *v.t*, prōmulgo (1)
prone, prōnus; (**inclined to**), prōpensus
prong, dens, *m*
pronoun, prōnōmen, *n*
pronounce, *v.t*, prōnuntĭo (1)

pronunciation, appellātĭo, f
proof, argūmentum, n, dŏcūmentum n, prŏbātĭo, f
prop, nn, admĭnĭcŭlum, n
prop, v.t, fulcĭo (4)
propagate, v.t, prŏpāgo (1)
propel, v.t, prŏpello (3)
propensity, ănĭmus inclīnātus, m
proper, dĕcōrus, vērus, aptus
properly, adv, (correctly), rectē
property (possessions), bŏna, n.pl, rēs, f; (characteristic quality), prŏprĭĕtas, f
prophecy, praedictĭo, f, praedictum, n
prophesy, v.t, praedīco (3), vātĭcĭnor (1 dep)
prophet, vātes, c
prophetic, dīvīnus
propitiate, v.t, plāco (1)
propitious, prŏpĭtĭus, praesens
proportion, portĭo, f; (in —), prō portĭōne
proportional, use adv. phr, prō por-tĭōne
proposal, condĭcĭo, f
propose, v.t, fĕro (irreg), rŏgo (1)
proposer, lātor, m
proposition, condĭcĭo, f
proprietor, dŏmĭnus, m
propriety (decorum), dĕcōrum, n
prorogation, prŏrŏgātĭo, f
prosaic (flat), iēiūnus
proscribe, v.t, prōscrībo (3)
proscription, prōscriptĭo, f
prose, ōrātĭo sŏlūta, f
prosecute, v.t, (carry through), ex-sĕquor (3 dep); (take legal proceed-ings), lītem intendo (3)
prosecution, exsĕcūtĭo, f; (legal), accūsātĭo, f
prosecutor, accūsātor, m
prospect (anticipation), spes fŭtūra, f; (view), prospectus, m
prospective, fŭtūrus
prosper, v.i, flōrĕo (2)
prosperity, res sĕcundae, f. pl
prosperous, sĕcundus
prostitute, nn, mĕrĕtrix, f
prostitute, v.t, vulgo (1)
prostitution, mĕrĕtrīcĭus quaestus, m
prostrate (in spirit, etc.), fractus; (lying on the back), sŭpīnus; (lying on the face), prōnus
prostrate, v.t, sterno (3), dēĭcĭo (3)
protect, v.t, tĕgo (3), tŭĕor (2 dep), dēfendo (3)
protection, tūtēla, f, praesĭdĭum, n
protector, dēfensor, m

protest against, v.t, intercēdo (3)
prototype, exemplar, n
protract, v.t, dūco (3)
protrude, v.t, prōtrūdo (3); v.i, ēmĭnĕo (2)
protuberance, tūber, n
proud, sŭperbus
prove, v.t, prŏbo (1); (to — oneself) sē praestāre (1 reflex); (test), pērĭclītor (1 dep); v.i, (turn out—of things), fīo (irreg), ēvĕnĭo (4)
proverb, prŏverbĭum, n
proverbial, use nn, prŏverbĭum, n, (proverb)
provide, v.t, (supply), păro (1), praebĕo (2); v.i, (make provision for), prōvĭdĕo (2); (— against), căvĕo (2) ne (with vb. in sub-junctive)
provided that, conj, dum, dummŏdo
providence, prōvĭdentĭa, f
provident, prōvĭdus
province, prōvĭncĭa, f
provincial, prōvĭncĭālis
provision (to make —), prōvĭdĕo (2)
provisional, use adv. phr, ad tempus (for the time being)
provisions, cĭbus, m
provocation, use, vb, irrīto (1) (to provoke)
provoke, v.t, irrīto (1); (stir up), incīto (1)
prow, prōra, f
prowess, virtus, f
prowl, v.i, văgor (1 dep)
proximity, prŏpinquĭtas, f
proxy, prōcūrātor, m
prudence, prūdentĭa, f
prudent, prūdens
prune, nn, prūnum, n, (plum)
prune, v.t, ampŭto (1)
prurient, lĭbīdĭnōsus
pry, v.t, rīmor (1 dep)
psalm, carmen, n
psychological, use genit. of mens, (mind)
puberty, pūbertas, f
public, adj, pūblĭcus; (of the state), use nn, respublĭca, f, (state), or pŏpŭlus, m, (people)
public, nn, hŏmĭnes, c. pl
publican (innkeeper), caupo, m
publication, use ēdo (3), (publish)
publicity, cĕlēbrĭtas, f
publicly, adv, pălam
publish, v.t, effĕro (irreg), prōfĕro (irreg); (book), ēdo (3)
pucker, v.t, corrūgo (1)
puddle, lăcūna, f
puerile (silly), ĭneptus

puff, *v.i*, (pant), ănhēlo (1); *v.t*, (inflate), inflo (1); (**puffed up**), inflātus

pugilist, pŭgil, *m*

pull, *v.t*, trăho (3); (**— down, demolish**), dēstrŭo (3)

pulley, trochlĕa, *f*

pulp, cāro, *f*

pulpit, suggestus, *m*

pulsate, *v.i*, palpĭto (1)

pulse, vēnae, *f. pl*. (veins)

pulverize, *v.t*, in pulvĕrem contĕro (3) (**pound into dust**)

pumice, pūmex, *m*

pump, *nn*, antlĭa, *f*

pump, *v.t*, haurĭo (4)

pumpkin, pēpo, *m*

pun, făcētĭae, *f. pl*

punch, ictus, *m*, pugnus, *m*

punch, *v.t*, percŭtĭo (3)

punctilious, mōrōsus

punctual, punctuality, *use adv. phr*, ad tempus (**at the right time**)

punctuate, *v.t*, distinguo (3)

punctuation, interpunctĭo, *f*

puncture, *nn*, punctum, *n*

puncture, *v.t*, pungo (3)

pungency, morsus, *m*, ăcerbĭtas, *f*

pungent, ācer

punish, *v.t*, pūnĭo (4), ănĭmadverto (3) in (*with acc*), poenas sūmo (3); (**to be —ed**), poenas do (1)

punishment, poena, *f*, supplĭcĭum, *n*; (**to undergo —**), poenam sŭbĕo (4)

punitive; *use vb*, pūnĭo (punish)

puny, pŭsillus

pup, puppy, cătŭlus, *m*

pupil (scholar), discĭpŭlus, *m*; (**of the eye**), pūpilla, *f*

puppet, pūpa, *f*

purchase, *nn*, emptĭo, *f*

purchase, *v.t*, ĕmo (3)

pure, pūrus, mĕrus; (**morally**), intĕger

purgative, *use phr. with* mĕdĭcāmentum, *n*, (**medicine**)

purge, *nn*, *use vb*, purgo (1)

purge, *v.t*, purgo (1)

purification, purgātĭo, *f*

purify, *v.t*, purgo (1), lustro (1)

purity, castĭtas, *f*, intĕgrĭtas, *f*

purloin, *v.t*, surrĭpĭo (3)

purple, *nn*, purpŭra, *f*

purple, *adj*, purpŭrĕus

purport, *nn*, (**meaning**), signĭfĭcātĭo, *f*

purport, *v.t*, (**mean**), signĭfĭco (1)

purpose, *nn*, prŏpŏsĭtum, *n*, consĭlĭum, *n*; (**for the — of doing something**), ĕo consĭlĭo ut (*with vb in subjunctive*); (**on —**), *adv*, consulto; (**to no —, in vain**), *adv*, frustrā; (**for what —?**), quārē

purpose, *v.t*, (intend), in ănĭmo hăbĕo (2)

purr, *v.i*, murmŭro (1)

purse, saccŭlus, *m*

in pursuance of, ex (*with abl*)

pursue, *v.t*, sĕquor (3 *dep*)

pursuit (chase), *use vb*, sĕquor (**to pursue**); (**desire for**), stŭdĭum, *n*

purvey, *v.t*, obsōno (1)

purveyor, obsōnātor, *m*

pus, pūs, *n*

push, pushing, *nn*, impulsus, *m*, impĕtus, *m*

push, *v.t*, pello (3), trūdo (3); (**— back**), rĕpello (3); (**— forward**), prōmŏvĕo (2)

pushing, *adj*, mŏlestus

pusillanimity, ănĭmus hŭmĭlis, *m*

pusillanimous, hŭmĭlis

pustule, pustŭla, *f*

put, *v.t*, (**place**), pōno (3), do (1), impōno (3); (**— aside**), sēpōno (3); (**— away**), abdo (3), condo (3); (**— back**), rĕpōno (3); (**— down**), dēpōno (3); (**suppress**), exstinguo (3); (**— forward**), praepōno (3), prōfĕro (*irreg*); (**— in**), immitto (3); (**— into land, port, etc.**), *v.i*, portum căpĭo (3); (**— off**), *v.t*, pōno (3); (**delay**), diffĕro (*irreg*); (**— on**), impōno (3); (**—clothes**), indŭo (3); (**— out**), ēĭcĭo (3); (**quench**), exstinguo (3); (**— to, drive to**), impello (3); (**— together**), collĭgo (3), confĕro (*irreg*); (**— under**), sŭbĭcĭo (3); (**— up, erect**), stătŭo (3); (**offer**), prōpōno (3); (**put up with, bear**), fĕro (*irreg*); (**— upon**), impōno (3); (**— to flight**) fŭgo (1)

putrefy, *v.i*, pŭtesco (3)

putrid, pŭtrĭdus

putty, glūten, *m or n*

puzzle, *nn*, (**riddle**), nōdus, *m*; (**difficulty**), diffĭcultas, *f*, angustĭae, *f*, *pl*

puzzling, *adj*, perplexus; (**in a — way**), *adv. phr*, per ambāges

pygmy, nānus, *m*

pyramid, pȳrămis, *f*

pyre, rŏgus, *m*

Pyrenees, Montes Pȳrēnaeī, *m. pl*

python, pȳthon, *m*

Q

quack, *nn*, (**medicine**), pharmăcŏpōla, *m*

quadrangle, ārĕa, *f*

quadrant, quădrans, *m*

quadrilateral, quădrĭlătĕrus

quadruped, quădrŭpes

quadruple, *adj*, quădruplex

quaff, *v.t*, haurĭo (4)

quagmire, pălus, *f*

quail, *nn*, cŏturnix, *f*

quail, *v.i*, trēpĭdo (1)

quaint, nŏvus

quake, *nn*, trēmor, *m*

quake, *v.i*, trĕmo (3)

qualification, iŭs, *n*; (condition), condĭcĭo, *f*

qualified (suitable), aptus, ĭdōnĕus

qualify, *v.t*, (fit someone for something),
aptum reddo (3); (restrict), circum-
scrĭbo (3), mītĭgo (1)

quality, nātūra, *f*

qualm (doubt), dŭbĭtātĭo, *f*

quantity, nŭmĕrus, *m*, magnĭtūdo, *f*;
(a certain —), ălĭquantum, *n* (*nn*);
(a large —) cōpĭa, *f*, multum, *n*;
(what —?), *use adj*, quantus (how
great)

quarrel, iurgĭum, *n*, rixa, *f*

quarrel, *v.i*, iurgo (1), rixor (1 *dep*)

quarrelsome, lītĭgĭōsus

quarry (stone), lăpĭcīdĭnae, *f. pl*;
(prey), praeda, *f*

quarry, *v.t*, caedo (3)

quart (measure), dŭo sextārĭi, *m. pl*

quarter, quarta pars, *f*, quădrans, *m*;
(district), rēgĭo, *f*; (surrender),
dēdĭtĭo, *f*

quarter, *v.t*, quădrĭfārĭam dīvĭdo (3),
(divide into four parts)

quarter-deck, puppis, *f*

quartermaster, quaestor mīlĭtāris, *m*

quarterly, *adj*, trĭmestris

quarters (lodging), hospĭtĭum, *n*; (at
close —), *adv*, commĭnus; (to come
to close —), signa confĕro (*irreg*)

quash, *v.t*, opprĭmo (3); (sentence,
verdict), rēscindo (3)

quaver, *v.i*, trēpĭdo (1)

quay, crēpīdo, *f*

queen, rēgīna, *f*

queer, rīdĭcŭlus

queerness, insŏlentĭa, *f*

quell, *v.t*, opprĭmo (3)

quench, *v.t*, exstinguo (3)

quenchless, inexstinctus

querulous, quĕrŭlus

query, quaestĭo, *f*

query, *v.t*, quaero (3)

quest, inquīsītĭo, *f*

question, *nn*, rŏgātĭo, *f*, interrŏgātum,
n, quaestĭo, *f*; *or use vb*, rŏgo (1) (to
ask —); (doubt), dŭbĭum, *n*

question, *v.t*, rŏgo (1), quaero (3);
(doubt), dŭbĭto (1)

questionable, incertus

questioner, interrŏgātor, *m*

quibble, *nn*, captĭo, *f*

quibble, *v.i*, căvillor (1 *dep*)

quick, *adj*, cĕler; (sprightly), ăgĭlis;
(— witted), săgax

quickly, *adv*, cĕlĕrĭter, cĭto

quicken, *v.t*, accĕlĕro (1), stĭmŭlo (1);
v.i, (move quicker), sē incĭtāre (1
reflex)

quickness, vēlōcĭtas, *f*; (— of wit),
săgācĭtas, *f*

quicksilver, argentum vīvum, *n*

quick-tempered, īrācundus

quiescent, quĭescens

quiet, *nn*, quĭes, *f*

quiet, *adj*, quĭētus, tranquillus

quiet, quieten, *v.t*, sēdo (1)

quietly, *adv*, quĭētē, tranquillē

quill, penna, *f*; (for writing), *use* stĭlus,
m, (pen)

quilt, *nn*, strāgŭlum, *n*

quinquennial, quinquennālis

quinsy, angīna, *f*

quintessence, vīs, *f*, flōs, *m*

quip, *nn*, rēsponsum (salsum) ((witty)
reply)

quirk, căvillātĭo, *f*

quit, *v.t*, rĕlinquo (3)

quite, *adv*, admŏdum, prorsus; (—
enough), sătis

quiver, *nn*, phărĕtra, *f*

quiver, *v.i*, trĕmo (3)

quoit, discus, *m*

quota, răta pars, *f*

quotation, prōlātĭo, *f*

quote, *v.t*, prōfĕro (*irreg*)

quotidian, cottīdĭānus

R

rabbit, cŭnĭcŭlus, *m*

rabble, turba, *f*

rabid, răbĭdus

race (family), gĕnus, *n*, prōgĕnĭes, *f*;
(running), cursus, *m*, certāmen, *n*

race, *v.i*, cursu certo (1) (contend by
running)

race-course, stădĭum, *n*, currĭcŭlum,
n

race-horse, ĕquus cursor, *m*

rack (for torture), ĕquŭlĕus, *m*

rack, *v.t*, (torture), torquĕo (2)

racket (bat), rētĭcŭlum, *n*; (noise),
strĕpĭtus, *m*

racy (smart), salsus

radiance, fulgor, *m*

radiant, clārus, fulgens

radiate, *v.i*, fulgĕo (2)

radiation, rădĭātĭo, *f*

For List of Abbreviations used, turn to pages 3, 4

radical (fundamental), tŏtus; (original), innātus; (keen on change), cŭpĭdus rērum nŏvārum

radically, *adv*, pĕnĭtus, fundĭtus

radish, rādix

radius, rādĭus, *m*

raffle, ālĕa, *f*

raft, rătis, *f*

rafter, cantērĭus, *m*

rag, pannus, *m*

rage, fŭror, *m*

rage, *v.i*, fŭro (3)

ragged, pannōsus

raging, *adj*, fŭrens

raid, incursĭo, *f*; (to make a —), invādo (3) in (*with acc.*)

rail, longŭrĭus, *m*

rail at (abuse), mălĕdīco (3) (*with dat.*)

railing, cancelli, *m. pl*

raillery, căvillātĭo, *f*

raiment, vestīmenta, *n.pl*

rain, *nn*, plŭvĭa, *f*, imber, *m*

rain, *v.i*, (it rains), plŭit (3 *impers.*)

rainbow, arcus, *m*

rainy, plŭvĭus

raise, *v.t*, (lift), tollo (3); (forces), compăro (1); (rouse), ērĭgo (3); (—a seige), obsĭdĭōnem solvo (3)

raisin, ăcĭnus passus, *m*, (dried berry)

rake, *nn*, (tool), rastellus, *m*; (person), nĕpos, *c*

rake, *v.t*, rādo (3)

rally, *v.t*, (troops), mīlĭtes in ordĭnes rĕvŏco (1), (call back the soldiers to their ranks); *v.i*, se collĭgĕre (3 *reflex.*)

ram (or battering —), ărĭes *m*; (beak of a ship), rostrum, *n*

ram, *v.t*, fistūco (1); (ship) rostro laedo (3)

ramble, *v.i*, erro (1)

rambler, erro, *m*

rammer, fistūca, *f*

rampart, agger, *m*, vallum, *n*

rancid, rancĭdus

rancorous, infestus

rancour, ŏdĭum, *n*

random, *adj*, fortŭĭtus; (at —), *adv*, fortŭīto

range, ordo, *m*; (— of mountains), iŭga, *n.pl*; (of a missile), iactus, *m*; (scope), campus, *m*

rank, *nn*, ordo, *m*

rank, *v.i*, sē hăbēre (2 *reflex.*)

rank, *adj*, (smell, etc.), fētĭdus

rankle, *v.t*, exulcĕro (1), mordĕo (2)

ransack, *v.t*, dīrĭpĭo (3)

ransom, *nn*, rĕdemptĭo, *f*; (— money), prētĭum, *n*

ransom, *v't*, rĕdĭmo (3)

rant, *v.t*, dēclāmo (1)

ranting, *nn*, sermo tŭmĭdus, *m*, (bombastic speech)

rap, *nn*, pulsātĭo, *f*

rap, *v.t*, pulso (1)

rapacious, răpax

rapacity, răpācĭtas, *f*

rape, *nn*, raptus, *m*

rapid, răpĭdus, cĕler

rapidity, cĕlĕrĭtas, *f*

rapier, glădĭus, *m*

rapine, răpīna, *f*

rapture, laetĭtĭa, *f*

rapturous, laetus

rare, rārus

rarefy, *v.t*, extĕnŭo (1)

rareness, rarity, rārĭtas, *f*

rascal, scĕlestus, *m*

rascality, scĕlĕra, *n.pl*

rase (to the ground), *v.t*, sŏlo aequo (1)

rash, *adj*, tĕmĕrārĭus

rash, *nn*, ēruptĭo, *f*

rashness, tĕmĕrĭtas, *f*

rasp, *nn*, (file), scŏbĭna, *f*

rasp, *v.t*, rādo (3)

rat, mŭs, *c*

rate (price), prĕtĭum, *n*; (tax), vectīgal, *n*; (speed), cĕlĕrĭtas, *f*; (at any —), *adv*, ŭtĭque

rate, *v.t*, (value), aestĭmo (1); (chide), incrĕpo (1); (tax), eensĕo (2)

rather, *adv*, (preferably), pŏtĭus; (somewhat), ălĭquantum; (a little), *with comparatives, e.g.* rather (more quickly), paulo (cĕlĕrĭus)

ratification, sanctĭo, *f*

ratify, *v.t*, rătum făcĭo (3)

ratio, portĭo, *f*

ration, *nn*, dēmensum, *n*, cĭbārĭa, *n.pl*

rational (a — being), partĭceps rătĭonis (participant in reason)

rationally, *adv*, rătĭōne

rattle, *nn*, crĕpĭtus, *m*; (toy), crĕpĭtācŭlum, *n*

rattle, *v.i*, crĕpo (1)

ravage, *v.t*, pŏpŭlor (1 *dep.*)

ravaging, *nn*, pŏpŭlātĭo, *f*

rave, *v.i*, fŭro (3)

raven, corvus, *m*

ravening, ravenous, răpax

ravine, fauces, *f.pl*

raving, *adj*, fŭrens, insānus

raving, *nn*, fŭror, *m*

ravish, *v.t*, răpĭo (3), stŭpro (1)

ravishing, suāvis

raw, crŭdus; **(inexperienced, un-worked),** rŭdis

ray, rădĭus, *m*

razor, nŏvācŭla, *f*

reach, *nn,* **(range),** iactus, *m*; **(space),** spătĭum, *n*

reach, *v.i,* **(extend),** pertĭnĕo (2), attingo (3); *v.t,* **(come to),** pervĕnĭo (4) ad (*with acc.*)

react, *v.t,* **(be influenced),** affĭcĭor (3 *pass.*)

reaction (of feeling, *use vb,* commŏvĕo (2) **(to make an impression on)**

read, *v.t,* lĕgo (3); (**— aloud),** rĕcĭto (1)

readable, făcĭlis lectu

reader, lector, *m*

readily, *adv,* **(willingly),** lĭbenter

readiness (preparedness), *use adj,* părātus **(ready); (willingness),** ănĭmus lĭbens, *m*

reading, *nn,* lectĭo, *f,* rĕcĭtātĭo, *f*

reading-room, bĭblĭŏthēca, *f*

ready, părātus, promptus; **(to be —),** părātus, praesto esse (*irreg.*); **(to make, get —),** păro (1)

real, *adj,* vērus

realism, vērĭtas, *f*

reality, rēs, *f*

realization (getting to know), cognĭtĭo, *f*; **(completion),** confectĭo, *f*

realise, *v.t,* intellĕgo (3); **(a project),** perfĭcĭo 3), perdūco (3)

really, *adv,* rēvērā; **(is it so?),** ĭtăne est?

realm, regnum, *n*

reap, *v.t,* mĕto (3); **(gain),** compăro (1)

reaper, messor, *m*

reaping-hook, falx, *f*

reappear, *v.i,* rĕdĕo (irreg.)

rear, *nn,* **(of a marching column),** agmen nŏvissĭmum, *n*; **(of an army),** ăcĭes nŏvissĭma, *f*; **(in the —),** *adv,* ā tergo

rear, *v.t,* **(bring up),** ēdūco (1), ălo (3); *v.i,* **(of horses),** sē ērĭgĕre (3 *reflex.*)

reason (faculty of thinking), mens, *f*; **(cause),** causa, *f*; **(for this —),** *adv,* ĭdĕo, idcirco; **(for what —, why?),** cur, quārē; **(without —, heedlessly),** *adv,* tĕmĕrē

reason, *v.t,* rătĭōcĭnor (1 *dep.*); **(— with),** dissĕro (3), cum (*with abl.*)

reasonable (fair), aequus, iustus; **(in size),** mŏdĭcus

reasonableness (fairness), aequĭtas, *f*

reasoning, *nn,* rătĭo, *f*

reassemble, *v.t,* cōgo (3), in ūnum lŏcum collĭgo (3), **(collect into one place);** *v.i,* rĕdĕo (4)

reassert, *v.t,* rēstĭtŭo (3)

reassure, *v.t,* confirmo (1)

rebel, *nn,* sĕdĭtĭōsus, *m*

rebel, *v.i,* rĕbello (1), dēfĭcĭo (3)

rebellion, sĕdĭtĭo, *f*

rebellious, sĕdĭtĭōsus

rebound, *v.i,* rĕsĭlĭo (4)

rebuff, *v.t,* rĕpello (3)

rebuff, *nn,* rĕpulsa, *f*

rebuke, *nn,* rĕprĕhensĭo, *f*

rebuke, *v.t,* rĕprĕhendo (3)

recall, *nn,* rĕvŏcātĭo, *f*

recall, *v.t,* rĕvŏco (1); **(— to mind),** rĕpĕto (3)

recapitulate, *v.t,* ēnŭmĕro (1)

recapitulation, ēnŭmĕrātĭo, *f*

recapture, *v.t,* rĕcĭpĭo (3)

recede, *v.i,* rĕcēdo (3)

receipt (act of receiving), acceptĭo, *f*; **(document),** ăpŏcha, *f*

receipts (proceeds), rĕdĭtus, *m*

receive, *v.t,* accĭpĭo (3), excĭpĭo (3)

receiver (of stolen goods), rĕceptor, *m*

recent, rĕcens

recently, *adv,* nūper

receptacle, rĕceptācŭlum, *n*

reception, ădĭtus, *m*

receptive, dŏcĭlis

recess, rĕcessus, *m*; **(holidays),** fērĭae, *f. pl*

reciprocal, mūtŭus

reciprocate, *v.t,* rĕfĕro (*irreg.*)

recital, narrātĭo, *f*

recite, *v.t,* rĕcĭto (1), prōnuntĭo (1)

reckless, tĕmĕrārĭus

recklessness, tĕmĕrĭtas, *f*

reckon, *v.t,* **(count),** nŭmĕro (1); **(— on, rely on),** confīdo (3) (*with dat.*); **(consider),** dūco (3)

reckoning, rātĭo, *f*

reclaim, *v.t,* rĕpĕto (3)

recline, *v.i,* rĕcŭbo (1)

recluse, hŏmo sōlĭtārĭus

recognizable, *use phr,* quod agnosci pŏtest **(that can be recognized)**

recognize, *v.t,* agnosco (3), cognosco (3); **(acknowledge),** confĭtĕor (2 *dep.*)

recognition, cognĭtĭo, *f*

recoil, *v.i,* rĕsĭlĭo (4)

recollect, *v.t,* rĕmĭnĭscor (3 *dep. with genit*)

recollection, mĕmŏrĭa, *f*

recommence, *v.t,* rĕdintĕgro (1)

recommend, *v.t,* commendo (1)

recommendation, commendātĭo, *f*

recompense, *v.t,* rĕmūnĕror (1 *dep*)

reconcile, *v.t,* rĕconcĭlĭo (1)

reconciliation, rĕconcĭlĭātĭo, *f*

reconnoitre, *v.t,* explōro (1)

reconsider, *v.t,* rĕpŭto (1)

record, *v.t.* in tăbŭlas rĕfĕro (*irreg*)

records, tăbŭlae, *f. pl,* fasti, *m. pl*

recount, *v.t.* (expound), ēnarro (1)

recourse (to have — to), *v.i,* confŭgĭo (3) ad (*with acc*)

recover, *v.t.* rĕcŭpĕro (1), rĕcĭpĭo (3); *v.i,* (from illness, etc.), rĕvălesco (3), rĕfĭcĭor (3 *pass*), sē collĭgĕre (3 *reflex*)

recovery, rĕcŭpĕrātĭo, *f;* (from illness), sălus, *f*

recreate, *v.t.* rĕcrĕo (1)

recreation, rĕmissĭo, *f*

recruit, *nn,* tĭro, *m*

recruit, *v.t.* (enrol), conscrībo (3)

recruiting, *nn,* dēlectus, *m*

rectify, *v.t.* corrĭgo (3)

rectitude, prŏbĭtas, *f*

recumbent, rĕcŭbans

recur, *v.i,* rĕdĕo (4)

red, rŭber, rŭfus; (redhanded), *adj,* mănĭfestus

redden, *v.t.* rŭbĕfăcĭo (3); *v.i,* rŭbesco (3)

redeem, *v.t.* rĕdĭmo (3)

redeemer, lĭbĕrātor, *m*

redemption, rĕdemptĭo, *f*

red-lead, mĭnĭum, *n*

redness, rŭbor, *m*

redouble, *v.t.* ingĕmĭno (1)

redound, rĕdundo (1)

redress, *v.t.* rĕstĭtŭo (3)

reduce, *v.t.* rĕdĭgo (3)

reduction, dēmĭnūtĭo, *f;* (taking by storm), expugnātĭo, *f*

redundancy, rĕdundantĭa, *f*

redundant, sŭpervăcŭus

re-echo, *v.i,* rĕsŏno (1)

reed, ărundo, *f*

reef, saxa, *n.pl*

reek, *v.i,* fūmo (1)

reel, *v.i,* (totter), văcillo (1)

re-elect, *v.t.* rĕcrĕo (1)

re-establish, *v.t.* rĕstĭtŭo (3)

refectory, cēnācŭlum, *n*

refer, *v.t.* rĕfĕro *or* dēfĕro (*irreg*) ad (*with acc*); (to — to), perstringo (3), specto (1) ad (*with acc*)

referee, arbĭter, *m*

reference, rătĭo, *f*

refill, *v.t.* rĕplĕo (2)

refine, *v.t.* (polish), expŏlĭo (4)

refined, pŏlītus, hūmānus

refinement, hūmānĭtas, *f*

refinery, offĭcīna, *f*

reflect, *v.t.* rĕpercŭtĭo (3), reddo (3); *v.i,* (ponder), rĕpŭto (1) (ănĭmo) (in the mind)

reflection (image), ĭmāgo, *f;* (thought), cōgĭtātĭo, *f*

reform, ēmendātĭo, *f*

reform, *v.t.* rĕstĭtŭo (3); (correct), corrĭgo (3); *v.i,* sē corrĭgĕre (3 *reflex*)

reformer, ēmendātor, *m*

refract, *v.t.* infringo (3)

refractory, contŭmax

refrain from, *v.i,* sē contĭnēre (2 *reflex*) ab (*with abl*)

refresh, *v.t.* rĕcrĕo (1), rĕfĭcĭo (3)

refreshment (food), cĭbus, *m*

refuge, perfŭgĭum, *n;* (to take —), *v.i,* confŭgĭo (3) ad (*with acc*)

refugee, *adj,* prŏfŭgus

refulgent, splendĭdus

refund, *v.t.* reddo (3)

refusal, rĕcūsātĭo, *f*

refuse, *nn,* purgāmentum, *n*

refuse, *v.t.* rĕcūso (1); (to — to do) nōlo (*irreg*) (*with infin*); (say no), nĕgo (1)

refute, *v.t.* rĕfello (3)

regain, *v.t.* rĕcĭpĭo (3)

regal, rēgālis

regale, *v.t.* excĭpĭo (3)

regalia, insignĭa, *n.pl*

regard, *nn,* (esteem), stŭdĭum, *n,* hŏnor, *m;* (consideration), rĕspectus, *m*

regard, *v.t.* (look at), intŭĕor (2 *dep*); (consider), hăbĕo (2); (esteem), aestĭmo (1)

regardless, neglĕgens

regency, interregnum, *n*

regent, interrex, *m*

regicide, caedes, (*f*) rēgis (killing of a king)

regiment, lĕgĭo, *f*

region, rĕgĭo, *f,* tractus, *m*

register, tăbŭlae, *f.pl*

register, *v.t.* perscrībo (3)

registrar, tăbŭlārĭus, *m*

regret, *nn,* dŏlor, *m*

regret, *v.t.* (repent of), *use* paenĭtet (2 *impers*) (*with acc. of subject*), *e.g.* I repent of, mē paenĭtet (*with genit*)

regular (correctly arranged), ordĭnātus, compŏsĭtus; (customary), sollemnis

regularity, ordo, *m*

regularly, *adv,* (in order), ordĭne; (customarily), sollemnĭter

regulate, *v.t.* ordĭno (1)

regulation (order), iussum, *n;* (rule), praeceptum, *n*

rehabilitate, *v.t.* rĕstĭtŭo (3)

rehearsal (practice), exercĭtātĭo, *f*

rehearse, *v.t.* (premeditate), praemĕdĭtor (1 *dep*)

reign, *nn,* regnum, *n*

reign, *v.i,* regno (1)

reimburse, v.t, rĕpendo (3)

rein, nn, hăbēna, f

rein, v.t, (curb), frēno (1)

reinforce, v.t, confirmo (1)

reinforcement (help), auxĭlĭum, n

reinstate, v.t, rĕstĭtŭo (3)

reiterate, v.t, ĭtĕro (1)

reject, v.t, rēĭcĭo (3)

rejection, rēĭectĭo, f

rejoice, v.i, gaudĕo (2)

rejoicing, nn, laetĭtĭa, f

rejoin, v.i, rĕdĕo (4)

relapse, v.i, rĕcĭdo (3)

relate, v.t, (tell), narro (1), expōno (3); v.i, pertĭnĕo (2)

related (by birth), cognātus; (by marriage), affīnis; (by blood), consanguĭnĕus; (near), prŏpinquus

relation (relative), cognātus m, affīnis m; (connection), rătĭo, f

relationship, cognātĭo, f, affīnĭtas, f

relative, nn, cognātus, m, affīnis, m

relative, adj, compărātus (compared)

relax, v.t, rĕmitto (3); v.i, rĕlanguesco (3)

relaxation, rĕmissĭo, f

relay, v.t, (send), mitto (3)

relays of horses, ĕqui dispŏsĭti, m.pl (horses methodically arranged)

release, nn, lĭbĕrātĭo f

release, v.t, exsolvo (3) lĭbĕro (1)

relent, v.t, rĕmitto (3)

relentless, immĭsĕrĭcors

relevant, use vb, pertĭnĕo (2) (to concern)

reliance, fĭdūcĭa, f

relic, rĕlĭquĭae, f, pl

relief (alleviation), lĕvātĭo, f; (help), auxĭlĭum, n

relieve, v.t, lĕvo (1), rĕmitto (3); (help), subvĕnĭo (4) (with dat); (of command, etc.), succēdo (3) (followed by in with acc. or by dat)

religion, rĕlĭgĭo, f, săcra, n.pl

religious, rĕlĭgĭōsus, pĭus

relinquish, v.t, rĕlinquo (3)

relish, nn, stŭdĭum, n, săpor, m

relish, v.t, frŭor (3 dep. with abl)

reluctance, use adj, invītus (unwilling)

reluctant, invītus

rely on, v.t, confīdo (3) (with dat. of person or abl. of thing)

relying on, adj, frētus (with abl)

remain, v.i, mănĕo (2); (be left over), sŭpersum (irreg)

remainder, rĕlĭquum, n

remaining, adj, rĕlĭquus

remains, rĕlĭquĭae, f, pl

remand, v.t, amplĭo (1)

remark, nn, dictum, n

remark, v.t, (say), dīco (3); (observe), observo (1)

remarkable, insignis

remedy, rĕmĕdĭum, n, mĕdĭcāmentum, n

remedy, v.t, sāno (1); (correct), corrĭgo (3)

remember, v.i, mĕmĭni (v.defect. with genit), rĕcordor (1 dep. with acc)

remembrance, rĕcordātĭo, f, mĕmŏrĭa, f

remind, v.t, mŏnĕo (2)

reminiscence, rĕcordātĭo, f

remiss, neglĕgens

remission (forgiveness), vĕnĭa, f; (release), sŏlūtĭo, f

remit, v.t, rĕmitto (3)

remittance, pĕcūnĭa, f

remnant, rĕlĭquĭae, f. pl

remonstrate, v.i, rĕclāmo (1) (with dat)

remorse, conscĭentĭa, f

remorseless, immĭsĕrĭcors, dūrus

remote, rĕmōtus

remoteness, longinquĭtas, f

removal (driving away), āmōtĭo, f; (sending away), rĕlēgātĭo, f; (— by force), raptus, m

remove, v.t, rĕmŏvĕo (2); (send away), rĕlēgo (1); v.i, migro (1)

remunerate, v.t, rĕmūnĕror (1 dep)

remuneration, rĕmūnĕrātĭo, f

rend, v.t, scindo (3)

render, v.t, reddo (3)

rendezvous (to fix a —), lŏcum (et dĭem) constĭtŭo (3), (place and day)

rending (severing), discĭdĭum, n

renegade (deserter), transfŭga, c

renew, v.t, rĕnŏvo (1), rĕdintĕgro (1)

renewal, rĕnŏvātĭo, f

renounce, v.t, rĕnuntĭo (1), rĕmitto (3)

renovate, v.t, rĕnŏvo (1)

renovation, rĕstĭtŭtĭo, f

renown, fāma, f, glōrĭa, f

renowned, clārus

rent, nn, scissūra, f; (of houses, etc.), merces, f

rent, v.t, (let), lŏco (1); (hire), condūco (3)

renunciation, rĕpŭdĭātĭo, f

repair, v.t, rĕfĭcĭo (3), sarcĭo (4)

repaired, sartus

reparation, sătisfactĭo, f

repast, cĭbus, m

repay, v.t, (grātĭam) rĕfĕro (irreg)

repayment, sŏlūtĭo, f

repeal, nn, abrŏgātĭo, f

repeal, v.t, abrŏgo (1), rēscindo (3)

repeat, v.t, ĭtĕro (1), reddo (3)

For List of Abbreviations used, turn to pages 3, 4

repeatedly, *adv*, ĭdentĭdem
repel, *v.t*, rĕpello (3)
repent, *v.i*, paenĭtet (2 *impers*) (*with acc. of person and genit. of cause*), *e.g.* **I repent of this deed**, mē paenĭtet huius facti
repentance, paenĭtentĭa, *f*
repentant, paenĭtens
repetition, ĭtĕrātĭo, *f*
replace, *v.t*, rĕpōno (3); **(substitute)**, substĭtŭo (3)
replenish, *v.t*, rĕplĕo (2)
replete, rĕplētus
reply, *nn*, rēsponsum, *n*
reply, *v.i*, rēspondĕo (2)
report, *nn*, nuntĭus, *m*; **(rumour)**, fāma, *f*; **(bang)**, crĕpĭtus, *m*
report, *v.t*, rĕfĕro (*irreg*), nuntĭo (1)
repose, *nn*, quĭes, *f*
repose, *v.i*, **(rest)**, quĭesco (3)
repository, rĕceptācŭlum, *n*
reprehend, *v.t*, rĕprĕhendo (3)
reprehensible, culpandus
represent, *v.t*, exprĭmo (3), fingo (3); **(take the place of)**, persōnam gĕro (3)
representation, ĭmāgo, *f*
representative (deputy), prōcūrātor, *m*
repress, *v.t*, cŏhĭbĕo (2)
reprieve, *nn*, **(respite)**, mŏra, *f*
reprieve, *v.t*, **(put off)**, diffĕro (*irreg*)
reprimand, *nn*, rĕprĕhensĭo, *f*
reprimand, *v.t*, rĕprĕhendo (3)
reprisal, *use* poena, *f*, **(punishment)**
reproach, *nn*, exprŏbrātĭo, *f*, opprŏbrĭum, *n*
reproach, *v.t*, exprŏbro (1), ŏbĭcĭo (3) (*both with acc. of thing and dat. of person*)
reproachful, obiurgātōrĭus
reprobate, *nn*, perdĭtus, *m*, nĕbŭlo, *m*
reproduce, *v.t*, rĕcrĕo (1)
reproof, rĕprĕhensĭo, *f*, obiurgātĭo, *f*, vĭtŭpĕrātĭo, *f*
reprove, *v.t*, rĕprĕhendo (3), obiurgo (1), vĭtŭpĕro (1)
reptile, serpens, *f*
republic, respublĭca, *f*
republican, *adj*, pŏpŭlārĭs
repudiate, *v.t*, rĕpŭdĭo (1)
repudiation, rĕpŭdĭātĭo, *f*
repugnance, ŏdĭum, *n*
repugnant, āversus; **(it is — to me, I hate it)**, *use phr*, ŏdĭo esse **(to be hateful)**, *with dat. of person*
repulse, *v.t*, rĕpello (3)
repulsive, foedus, ŏdĭōsus
reputable, hŏnestus

reputation, repute, fāma, *f*; **(good —)**, existĭmātĭo, *f*; **(bad —)**, infāmĭa, *f*
request, *nn*, rŏgātĭo, *f*
request, *v.t*, rŏgo (1), prĕcor (1 *dep*)
require, *v.t*, **(demand)**, postŭlo (1); **(need)**, ĕgĕo (2) (*with abl*)
requirement (demand), postŭlātĭo, *f*; *or use adj*, nĕcessārĭus
requisite, *adj*, nĕcessārĭus
requisition, postŭlātĭo, *f*
requite, *v.t*, rĕpōno (3)
rescind, *v.t*, rĕscindo (3)
rescue, *v.t*, ērĭpĭo (3)
rescue, *nn*, lĭbĕrātĭo, *f*
research, investĭgātĭo, *f*
resemblance, sĭmĭlĭtūdo, *f*
resemble, *v.t*, rĕfĕro (*irreg*), sĭmĭlis esse (*irreg*) (*with genit. or dat*)
resembling, *adj*, sĭmĭlis
resent, *v.t*, aegrĕ fĕro (*irreg*) **(tolerate with displeasure)**
resentful, īrācundus
resentment, īra, *f*
reservation (restriction), exceptĭo, *f*
reserve, *nn*, **(military)**, subsĭdĭum, *n*; **(of disposition)**, grăvĭtas, *f*
reserve, *v.t*, servo (1); **(put aside)**, sēpōno (3)
reserved (of disposition), grăvis
reservoir, lăcus, *m*
reside, *v.i*, hăbĭto (1)
residence, sēdes, *f. pl*, dŏmĭcĭlĭum, *n*
resident, incŏla, *c*
resign, *v.i, and v.t*, concēdo (3); **(to — oneself to)**, sē committĕre (3 *reflex. with* in *and* acc)
resignation (of office, etc.), abdĭcātĭo, *f*; **(of mind)** aequus ănĭmus, *m*
resin, rēsīna, *f*
resist, *v.t*, rĕsisto (3) (*with dat*)
resistance, rĕpugnantĭa, *f*, *or use vb*, rĕsisto (3) **(to resist)**
resolute, firmus, fortis
resolution, obstĭnātĭo, *f*, constantĭa, *f*; **(decision)**, *use vb*, plăcet **(it is resolved)**
resolve, *v.t*, **(determine)**, stătŭo (3); **(solve)**, dissolvo (3)
resort to, *v.t* **(a place)**, cĕlĕbro (1); **(have recourse to)**, confŭgĭo (3) ad (*with acc*)
resort, *nn*, **(plan)**, consĭlĭum, *n*; **(last —)**, extrēma, *n.pl*
resound, *v.i*, rĕsŏno (1)
resource (help), auxĭlĭum, *n*; **(wealth, means)**, ŏpes, *f. pl*
respect, *nn*, **(esteem)**, observantĭa, *f*; **(in all —s)**, omnĭbus partĭbus; **(in**

— of), *use abl. case, e.g.* **stronger in respect of number**, sŭpĕrĭor nŭmĕro

respect, *v.t.* (esteem), observo (1); (reverence), suspĭcĭo (3)

respectability, hŏnestas, *f*

respectable, hŏnestus

respectful, observans

respecting, *prep*, dē (*with abl*)

respective, *use* quisque (**each**) *with* sŭus (**his own**)

respiration, respīrātĭo, *f*

respite (delay), mŏra, *f*

resplendent, splendĭdus

respond, *v.i*, respondĕo (2)

response, rēsponsum, *n*

responsibility (duty, function), offĭcĭum, *n*; *or use imp. vb*, ŏportet (it behoves)

responsible, (to be — for), praesto (1)

rest, *nn*, (repose), quĭes, *f*, ōtĭum, *n*; (remainder), *use adj*, rĕlĭquus, *e.g.* the — of one's life, rĕlĭqua vīta, *f*

rest, *v.i*, quĭesco (3); (— on, depend on), nītor (3 *dep*)

resting-place, cŭbīle, *n*

restitution (to make —), *v.t*, rēstĭtŭo (3)

restive, *use phr*, qui nōn făcĭle dŏmāri pŏtest (that cannot easily be subdued)

restless, inquĭētus

restlessness, inquĭes, *f*

restoration, rēstĭtūtĭo, *f*

restore, *v.t*, rēstĭtŭo (3)

restrain, *v.t*, cŏercĕo (2), rĕprĭmo (3), cŏhĭbĕo (2)

restraint, mŏdĕrātĭo, *f*

restrict, *v.t*, circumscrībo (3)

restriction (bound), mŏdus, *m*

result, *nn*, ēventus, *m*

result, *v.i*, ēvĕnĭo (4)

resume, *v.t*, rĕpĕto (3)

resurrection, rēsurrectĭo, *f*

resuscitate, *v.t*, rĕsuscĭto (1)

retail, *v.t*, dīvendo (3)

retailer, caupo, *m*

retain, *v.t*, rĕtĭnĕo (2)

retainer, sătelles, *c*; (*pl*) soldūrĭi, *m. pl*

retake, *v.t*, rĕcĭpĭo (3)

retaliate, *v.t*, ulciscor (3 *dep*)

retaliation, ultĭo, *f*

retard, *v.t*, mŏror (1 *dep*)

reticent, tăcĭturnus

retinue (companions), cŏmĭtes, *c.pl*

retire, *v.i*, (go away), rĕcēdo (3), ăbĕo (4); (from a post, etc.), dēcēdo (3); (retreat), sē rĕcĭpĕre (3 *reflex*)

retired, rĕmōtus

retirement (act of —), rĕcessus, *m*; (leisure), ōtĭum, *n*

retiring, *adj*, vĕrēcundus

retort, *v.t*, rĕfĕro (*irreg*)

retrace, *v.t*, rĕpĕto (3)

retract, *v.t*, rĕnuntĭo (1)

retreat, *nn*, rĕceptus, *m*; (place of refuge), rĕfŭgĭum, *n*

retreat, *v.i*, sē rĕcĭpĕre (3 *reflex*)

retrench, *v.t*, mĭnŭo (3)

retribution, poena, *f*

retrieve, *v.t*, rĕcŭpĕro (1)

retrograde, *adj, use comp. adj*, pēior (worse)

retrogression, rĕgressus, *m*

retrospect, *use vb*, rĕspĭcĭo (3) (to look back)

return, *nn*, (coming back), rĕdĭtus, *m*; (giving back), rēstĭtūtĭo, *f*; (profit), quaestus, *m*

return, *v.t*, (give back), reddo (3), rĕfĕro (*irreg*); *v.i*, (go back), rĕdĕo (4)

reunite, *v.t*, rĕconcĭlĭo (1)

reveal, *v.t*, pătĕfăcĭo (3)

revel, *nn*, cōmissātĭo, *f*

revel, *v.i*, cōmissor (1 *dep*)

revelation, pătĕfactĭo, *f*

revenge, *nn*, ultĭo, *f*

revenge oneself on, *v.t*, ulciscor (3 *dep*)

revengeful, cŭpĭdus ulciscendi (keen on revenge)

revenue, vectīgal, *n*

reverberate, *v.i*, rĕsŏno (1)

revere, **reverence**, *v.t*, vĕnĕror (1 *dep*)

reverence, vĕnĕrātĭo, *f*

revered, vĕnĕrābĭlis

reverend, vĕnĕrābĭlis

reverent, rĕvĕrens

reverse (contrary), *adj*, contrārĭus (opposite); (defeat), clādes,

reverse, *v.t*, inverto (3)

revert, *v.i*, rĕdĕo (4)

review, *nn*, rĕcognĭtĭo, *f*, rĕcensĭo, *f*

review, *v.t*, rĕcensĕo (2)

revile, *v.t*, mălĕdīco (3) (*with dat*)

reviling, *nn*, mălĕdictĭo, *f*

revise, *v.t*, ēmendo (1)

revision, ēmendātĭo, *f*

revisit, *v.t*, rĕvīso (3)

revival, rĕnŏvātĭo, *f*

revive, *v.t*, rĕcrĕo (1), excĭto (1); *v.i*, rĕvīvisco (3)

revocable, rĕvŏcābĭlis

revoke, *v.t*, abrŏgo (1)

revolt, *nn*, dēfectĭo, *f*, sēdĭtĭo, *f*

revolt, *v.i*, dēfĭcĭo (3)

revolting, *adj*, (disgusting), foedus

revolution (turning round), conversĭo, *f*; (political), nŏvae res, *f. pl*

revolutionize, *v.t*, nŏvo (1)

revolutionary, sēdĭtĭōsus

revolve, *v.i*, sē volvēre (3 *reflex*)
reward, *nn*, praemĭum, *n*
reward, *v.t*, rēmŭnĕror (1 *dep*)
rewrite, *v.t*, rēscrībo (3)
rhetoric, rhētŏrĭca, *f*
rhetorical, rhētŏrĭcus
Rhine, Rhēnus, *m*
rhinoceros, rhĭnŏcĕros, *m*
rhubarb, rādix Pontĭca, *f* (Black Sea root)
rhyme (verse), versus, *m*
rhythm, nŭmĕrus, *m*
rhythmical, nŭmĕrōsus
rib, costa, *f*
ribald, obscēnus
ribbon, taenĭa, *f*
rice, ŏrȳza, *f*
rich, dīves, lŏcŭples; (**fertile**), pinguis
riches, dīvĭtĭae, *f. pl*
richness, ūbertas, *f*
rick (heap), ăcervus, *m*
rid, *v.t* lībĕro (1); (**to get — of**), dēpōno (3), dēpello (3)
riddle, aenigma, *n*; (**in —s**), per ambāges
riddle, *v.t*, (**sift**), cerno (3); (**— with holes**), confŏdĭo (3)
ride, *v.i*, vĕhor (3 *dep*); (**— at anchor**), consisto (3)
rider (horseman), ĕquĕs, *m*
ridge (mountain —), iŭgum, *n*
ridicule, *nn*, rīdĭcŭlum, *n*
ridicule, *v.t*, irrīdĕo (2)
ridiculous, rīdĭcŭlus
riding, *nn*, ĕquĭtātĭo, *f*
rife, frĕquens, crēber
rifle, *v.t*, praedor (1 *dep.*)
rift, rīma, *f*
rig, *v.t*, armo (1)
rigging, armāmentum, *n.pl*
right, *adj*, (**direction**), dexter; (**true**), rectus, vērus; (**correct**), rectus; (**fit**), ĭdōnĕus; (**—hand**), dextra (manus)
right, *nn*, (**moral**), fas, *n*; (**legal**), iŭs, *n*
rightly, *adv*, rectē, vērē
right, *v.t*, rēstĭtŭo (3)
righteous, iustus
righteousness, prŏbĭtas, *f*
rightful, iustus
rigid, rĭgĭdus, dūrus
rigorous, dūrus
rigour, dūrĭtĭa, *f*
rill, rīvŭlus, *m*
rim, ōra, *f*, lābrum, *n*
rime, prŭīna, *f*
rind, crusta, *f*
ring (finger, etc.), ānŭlus, *m*; (**circle**), orbis, *m*

ring, *v.i*, tinnĭo (4); (**surround**) circŭmĕo (4)
ringing, *nn*, tinnītus, *m*
ringing, *adj*, tinnŭlus
ringleader, auctor, *m*
ringlet, cincinnus, *m*
rinse, *v.t*, collŭo (3)
riot, turba, *f*, tŭmultus, *m*; (**to make a —**), tŭmultum făcĭo (3)
riotous, turbŭlentus; (**extravagent**), luxŭrĭōsus
rip, *v.t*, scindo (3)
ripe, mātūrus
ripen, *v.i*, mātūresco (3); *v.t*, mātūro (1)
ripeness, mātūrĭtas, *f*
ripple, *v.i*, (**tremble**), trĕpĭdo (1)
rise, *nn*, (**of sun, etc.**, *or* **origin**), ortus, *m*,
rise, *v.i*, surgo (3); (**of sun, etc.**), ŏrĭor (4 *dep*); (**in rank**), cresco (3); (**in rebellion**), consurgo (3)
rising, *nn*, ortus, *m*; (**in rebellion**), mōtus, *m*
rising (ground), *nn*, clīvus, *m*
risk, *nn*, pĕrīcŭlum, *n*
risk, *v.t*, pĕrīclĭtor (1 *dep*)
ritual, rītus, *m*
rival, *nn*, aemŭlus, *m*, rīvālis, *c*
rival, *v.t*, aemŭlor (1 *dep*)
rivalry, aemŭlātĭo, *f*
river, *nn*, flūmen, *n*, flŭvĭus, *m*
river-bank, rīpa, *f*
river-bed, alvĕus, *m*
rivet, clāvus, *m*
rivulet, rīvŭlus, *m*
road, vĭa, *f*, ĭter, *n*; (**to make a —**), vĭam mūnĭo (4)
road-making, mūnĭtĭo, (*f*) vĭārum
roadstead (for ships), stătĭo, *f*
roam, *v.i*, văgor (1 *dep*), erro (1)
roaming, *adj*, văgus
roar, *nn*, frĕmĭtus, *m*
roar, *v.i*, frĕmo (3)
roast, *v.t*, torrĕo (2)
roasted, assus
rob, *v.t*, spŏlĭo (1) (*with acc. of person robbed, abl. of thing taken*)
robber, lătro, *m*
robbery, lătrōcĭnĭum, *n*
robe, vestis, *f*, vestīmentum, *n*; (**woman's —**), stŏla, *f*; (**— of state**), trăbĕa, *f*; (**— of kings**), purpŭra, *f*
robe, *v.t*, vestĭo (4), indŭo (3)
robust, rōbustus
rock, rūpes, *f*
rock, *v.t*, ăgĭto (1)
rocky, scŏpŭlōsus
rod, virga, *f*; (**fishing —**), ărundo, *f*
roe, căprĕa, *f*; (**of fish**), ōva, *n.pl* (**eggs**)

rogue, scĕlestus, *m*
roguery, nēquĭtĭa, *f*
roll,   *nn*,   (something rolled up),
  vŏlūmen, *n*; (names), album, *n*
roll, *v.t*, volvo (3); *v.i*, volvor (3 *pass*)
roller, cўlindrus, *m*
rolling, *adj*, vŏlūbĭlis
Roman, Rōmānus
romance (story), fābŭla, *f*
romance, *v.i*, fābŭlor (1 *dep*)
romantic (fabulous), commentīcĭus
Rome, Rōma, *f*
romp, *v.i*, lūdo (3)
romp, *nn*, lūsus, *m*
roof, *v.t*, tēgo (3)
roof, *nn*, tectum, *n*
rook (raven), corvus, *m*
room, conclāve, *n*; (space), spătĭum,
  n; (bed —), cŭbĭcŭlum, *n*; (dining
  —), trĭclīnĭum, *n*
roomy, căpax
roost, *nn*, pertīca, *f*
root, rādix, *f*; (to strike —s, become
  rooted), rādīces ăgo (3); (—ed to
  the spot), dēfixus
rope, fūnis, *m*, restis, *f*, rŭdens, *m*
rosary (garden), rŏsārĭum, *n*
rose, rŏsa, *f*
rosemary, ros mărīnus, *m*
rostrum, rostra, *n.pl*
rosy, rŏsĕus
rot, *nn*, tābes, *f*
rot, *v.i*, pūtesco (3)
rotate, *v.i*, sē volvĕre (3 *reflex*)
rotation, turbo, *m*
rotten, pŭtrĭdus
rotundity, rŏtundĭtas, *f*
rouge, *nn*, fūcus, *m*
rouge, *v.t*, fūco (1)
rough, asper; (weather), ătrox; (of
  sea), turbĭdus; (of manner), incultus
roughness, aspĕrĭtas, *f*
round, *adj*, rŏtundus
round, *adv*, circum
round, *prep*, circum (*with acc*)
round, *v.t*, (to make —), rŏtundo (1),
  curvo (1); (to — off), conclūdo (3);
  v.i, (to go —), circumăgor (3 *pass*)
roundabout, *adj*, dēvĭus
rouse, *v.t*, excĭto (1)
rout, *nn*, (flight, defeat), fŭga, *f*
rout, *v.t*, fŭgo (1)
route, ĭter, *n*
routine, ūsus, *m*
rove, *v.i*, văgor (1 *dep*)
roving, *nn*, văgātĭo, *f*
row, (line), ordo, *m*; (quarrel), rixa, *f*;
  (noise), strĕpĭtus, *m*
row, *v.i*, rēmĭgo (1)

rowing, *nn*, rēmĭgĭum, *n*
royal, rēgĭus
royalty, regnum, *n*
rub, *v.t*, tēro (3), frĭco (1); (— out),
  dēlĕo (2)
rubbish, quisquĭlĭae, *f. pl*
rubicund, rŭbĭcundus
ruby, *nn*, carbuncŭlus, *m*
ruby, *adj*, purpŭrĕus
rudder, gŭbernācŭlum, *n*
ruddy, rŭbĭcundus
rude (person), asper, ĭnurbānus
rudeness, ĭnhūmānĭtas, *f*
rudimentary, incŏhātus (incomplete)
rudiments, ĕlĕmenta, *n.pl*
rue, *nn*, rūta, *f*
rueful, maestus
ruff, torquis, *m. or f*
ruffian, perdĭtus, *m*, lătro, *m*
ruffianly, *adj*, scĕlestus
ruffle, *v.t*, ăgĭto (1)
rug, strāgŭlum, *n*
rugged, asper
ruin, exĭtĭum, *n*, rŭīna, *f*; (building),
  părĭĕtĭnae, *f. pl*
ruin, *v.t*, perdo (3)
ruinous, exĭtĭōsus, damnōsus
rule, *nn*, (law), lex, *f*; (precept),
  praeceptum, *n*; (pattern), norma,
  f; (for measuring), rēgŭla, *f*;
  (government), impĕrĭum, *n*
rule, *v.t*, rēgo (3); *v.i*, regno (1)
ruler (person), dŏmĭnus, *m*; (measurement), rēgŭla, *f*
rumble, *nn*, murmur, *n*
rumble, *v.i*, murmŭro (1), mūgĭo (4)
ruminate, *v.t*, cōgĭto (1)
rummage, *v.t*, rīmor (1 *dep*)
rumour, *nn*, rūmor, *m*, fāma, *f*
rump, clūnes, *f. pl*
rumple, *v.t*, corrūgo (1)
run, *v.i*, curro (3); (— about), hūc
  illūc curro (3); (— after), persĕquor
  (3 *dep*); (— away), fŭgio (3); (—
  aground), impingor (3 *pass*), inflĭgor
  (3 pass); (— back), rĕcurro (3); (—
  down), dē curro (3); (— forward),
  prōcurro (3); (— into), incurro (3);
  (— out), excurro (3); (— over, with
  vehicle etc.), obtĕro (3); (—
  through), percurro (3)
runaway, *adj*, fŭgĭtīvus
runner, cursor, *m*
running, *nn*, cursus, *m*
running, *adj*, (water), vīvus
rupture (disease), hernĭa, *f*
rupture, *v.t*, rumpo (3)
rural, rustĭcus
rush, *nn*, (plant), iuncus, *m*; (rushing,
  running), impĕtus, *m*

For List of Abbreviations used, turn to pages 3, 4

rush, *v.i*, rŭo (3); (— forward), sē prōrĭpĕre (3 *reflex*); (— into), irrŭo (3); (— out), sē effundĕre (3 reflex)

rusk, crustum, *n*

russet, rūfus

rust, *nn*, rōbīgo, *f*

rustic, *adj*, rustĭcus

rusticate, *v.i*, rustĭcor (1 *dep*); *v.t*, rēlēgo (1)

rusticity, rustĭcĭtas, *f*

rustle, *v.i*, crēpo (1)

rustle, rustling, *nn*, sŭsurrus, *m*

rusty, rōbīgĭnōsus

rut, orbĭta, *f*

ruthless, immītis, sēvērus

rye, sēcāle, *n*

S

Sabbath, sabbăta, *n.pl*

sable, *adj*, (black), āter

sabre, glădĭus, *m*

sack (bag), saccus, *m*; (pillage), dīreptĭo, *f*

sack, *v.t*, (pillage), dīrĭpĭo (3)

sackcloth, saccus, *m*

sacrament, săcrāmentum, *n*

sacred, săcer, sanctus

sacredness, sanctĭtas, *f*

sacrifice, săcrĭfĭcĭum, *n*; (the victim), hostĭa, *f*

sacrifice, *v.i*, săcrĭfĭco (1); *v.t*, immŏlo (1)

sacrificial, săcrĭfĭcus

sacrilege, săcrĭlĕgĭum, *n*; *or use vb*, dīrĭpĭo (3) (to plunder)

sad, tristis

sadden, *v.t*, tristĭtĭā affĭcĭo (3) (affect with sadness)

saddle, *nn*, ĕphippĭum, *n*

saddle, *v.t*, sterno (3); (impose), impōno (3)

sadness, tristĭtĭa, *f*

safe (free from danger), tūtus; (having escaped from danger), incŏlŭmis

safe-conduct, fĭdes, *f*

safeguard (act of —), cautĭo, *f*; (defence), prōpugnācŭlum, *n*

safely, *adv*, tūtŏ

safety, sălus, *f*

saffron, *nn*, crŏcus, *m*

saffron, *adj*, crŏcĕus

sagacious, prūdens, săgax

sagacity, prūdentĭa, *f*, săgācĭtas, *f*

sage (wise man), săpĭens, *m*; (plant), salvĭa, *f*

sail, *nn*, vēlum, *n*; (to set —), vēla do (1)

sail, *v.i*, nāvĭgo (1), vēhor (3 *pass*); (to go by means of sails), vēla făcĭo (3)

sailing, *nn*, nāvĭgātĭo, *f*

sailor, nauta, *m*

saint, sanctus, *m*

saintly, sanctus

sake (for the — of), *prep*, causā (*with genit*); (on behalf of), prō (*with abl*), ŏb, propter (*with acc*)

salad, ăcētārĭa, *n.pl*

salary, merces, *f*

sale, vendĭtĭo, *f*; (auction), hasta,*f*

salient, *adj*, prīmus (first)

saline, salsus

saliva, sălīva, *f*

sallow, pallĭdus

sally, *nn*, ēruptĭo, *f*

sally, *v.i*, ēruptĭōnem făcĭo (3)

salmon, salmo, *m*

saloon, ātrĭum, *n*

salt, *nn*, sal, *m*

salt, *adj*, salsus

salt, *v.t*, săle condĭo (4) (season with salt)

salt-cellar, sălīnum, *n*

salt-mines, sălīnae, *f. pl*

salubrious, sălūbris

salutary, sălūtāris; (useful), ūtĭlis

salutation, sălūtātĭo, *f*

salute, *v.t*, sălūto (1)

salvation, sălus, *f*

salve, unguentum, *n*

salver, scŭtella, *f*, pătella, *f*

same, *prep*, ĭdem; (the same as), ĭdem qui, ĭdem atque; (in the — place), *adv*, ĭbĭdem (at the — time), sĭmŭl; (fixed, constant), constans

sample, exemplum, *n*

sanctification, sanctĭfĭcātĭo, *f*

sanctify, *v.t*, consĕcro (1)

sanction, auctōrĭtas, *f*; (penalty) poena, *f*

sanction, *v.t*, rătum făcĭo (3)

sanctity, sanctĭtas, *f*

sanctuary, fānum, *n*, templum, *n*: (refuge), rēfŭgĭum, *n*

sand, hărēna, *f*

sandal, sŏlĕa, *f*

sandstone, tōfus, *m*

sandy, hărēnōsus

sane, sānus

sanguinary, crŭentus, sanguĭnārĭus

sanguine, *use* spēs, *f*, (hope)

sanity, mens sāna, *f*

sap, *nn*, sūcus, *m*

sap, *v.t*, subrŭo (3)

sapient, *adj*, săpĭens

sapless, ārĭdus

sapling, arbor nŏvella,

sappers (military), mūnītōres, *m. pl*

sapphire, sapphīrus, *f*

sarcasm, căvillātĭo, *f*, (scoffing)

sarcastic, ăcerbus

sarcophagus, sarcŏphăgus, *m*

sash, cingŭlum, *n*

satanic, nĕfandus

satchel, lŏcŭlus, *m*

satellite (star), stella, *f*; (attendant), sătelles, *c*

satiate, *v.t*, sătĭo (1)

satiety, sătĭĕtas, *f*

satire, sătŭra, *f*

satirical (bitter), ăcerbus

satirize, *v.t*, perstringo (3)

satirist; scriptor sătĭrĭcus, *m*

satisfaction (inner), vŏluptas, *f*; (compensation, punishment), poena, *f*

satisfactorily, *adv*, ex sententĭā

satisfactory, ĭdŏnĕus, *or* sătis (enough)

satisfied, contentus

satisfy, *v.t*, (a need), explĕo (2), (*with dat*); (convince), persuădĕo (2)

satrap, sătrăpes, *m*

saturate, *v.t*, sătŭro (1)

satyr, sătўrus, *m*

sauce, condĭmentum, *n*

saucepan, cācăbus, *m*, cortīna, .

saucer, pătella, *f*

saucy, pĕtŭlans

saunter, *v.i*, văgor (1 *dep*)

sausage, farcīmen, *n*

savage, *adj*, fĕrus, ătrox, effĕrātus

savageness, savagery fĕrĭtas, *f*, saevĭtĭa, *f*

save, *v.t*, servo (1); (defend), tŭĕor (2 *dep*); (lay by), rĕservo (1)

save, *prep*, praeter (*with acc*)

saving, *nn*, conservātĭo, *f*

savings, pĕcūlĭum, *n*

saviour, servātŏr, *m*

savour, *nn*, săpor, *m*

savour, *v.t*, săpĭo (3)

savoury, *adj*, condītus

saw serra, *f*

saw, *v.t*, serrā sĕco (1) (cut with a saw)

sawdust, scŏbis, *f*

say, *v.t*, dīco (3), lŏquor (3 *dep*); (to — that something will *not* . . .), *use* nĕgo (1) (to deny); (it is said), fertur

saying, *nn*, dictum, *n*

scab, crusta, *f*

scabbard, văgīna, *f*

scabby, scăber

scaffold (frame), māchĭna, *f*; (execution), supplĭcĭum, *n*

scald, *nn*, ădusta, *n.pl*

scale (pair of —s), lībra, *f*; (of fish), squāma, *f*; (gradation), grădus, *m*

scale, *v.t*, (climb with ladders), scālis ascendo (3)

scaling-ladders, scălae, *f. pl*

scallop, pecten, *m*

scalp, cŭtis, *f*, (skin)

scalpel, scalpellum, *n*

scamp, scĕlestus, *m*

scamper, *v.i*, fŭgĭo (3)

scan, *v.t*, contemplor (1 *dep*)

scandal, opprŏbrĭum, *n*; (disparagement) obtrectātĭo, *f*

scandalous, infāmis

scanty, exĭgŭus

scantiness, exĭgŭĭtas, *f*

scapegrace, nēbŭlo, *m*

scar, cĭcātrix, *f*

scarce, rārus

scarcely, *adv*, vix, aegrē

scarcity, (of supplies, etc.), ĭnŏpĭa, *f*

scare, *v.t*, terrĕo (2)

scarecrow, formīdo, *f*

scarf, chlămys, *f*

scarlet, *nn*, coccum, *n*

scarlet, *adj*, coccĭnĕus

scathing, ăcerbus

scatter, *v.t*, spargo (3); *v.i*, sē spargĕre (3 *reflex*)

scene (of play), scēna, *f*; (spectacle), spectăcŭlum, *n*

scenery (natural —), *use* rĕgĭo, *f*, (region)

scent (sense of smell), ŏdŏrātus, *m*; (the smell itself), ŏdor, *m*

scent, *v.t*, (discern by smell), ŏdŏror (1 *dep*);

scented, ŏdŏrātus

sceptical, dŭbĭtans

sceptre, sceptrum, *n*

schedule, tăbŭla, *f*

scheme, *nn*, consĭlĭum, *n*

scheme, *v.t*, consĭlĭum căpĭo (3) (make a plan)

scholar (pupil), discĭpŭlus, *m*; (learned man), doctus, *m*

scholarly, doctus

scholarship, littĕrae, *f. pl*

school, lūdus, *m*, schŏla, *f*

school, *v.t*, ērŭdĭo (4)

school-master, măgister, *m*

school-mistress, măgistra, *f*

schooner, phăsēlus, *m*

sciatica, ischĭas, *f*

science, scĭentĭa, *f*, discĭplīna, *f*, rătĭo, *f*

scientific, *use genit. of nouns above*

scimitar, ăcĭnăces, *m*

scintillate, *v.i*, scintillo (1)

scion, prōles, *f*

scissors, forfĭces, *f. pl*

scoff at, *v.t*, irrīděo (2)

scoffer, irrīsor, *m*

scoffing, *nn*, irrīsĭo, *f*

scold, *v.t*, obiurgo (1), incrĕpo (1)

scoop out, *v.t*, căvo (1)

scoop, *nn*, trulla, *f*

scope (room), campus, *m*

scorch, *v.t*, ambūro (3)

scorched, torrĭdus

scorching, torrĭdus

score (total), summa, *f*; (account, reckoning), rătĭo, *f*; (mark), nŏta, *f*

score, *v.t*, (note, mark), nŏto (1); (— a victory), victōrĭam rĕporto (1)

scorn, *nn*, contemptus, *m*

scorn, *v.t*, sperno (3), contemno (3)

scornful, sŭperbus

scorpion, scorpĭo, *m*

scoundrel, nēbŭlo, *m*

scour, *v.t*, (clean), tergĕo (2); (run over) percurro (3)

scourge, *nn*, (whip), flăgellum, *n*; (pest), pestis, *f*, pernĭcĭes, *f*

scourge, *v.t*, verbĕro (1)

scourging, *nn*, verbĕra, *n.pl*

scout, explōrātor, *m*

scout, *v.t*, (spy out), spĕcŭlor (1 *dep*)

scowl, *nn*, frontis contractĭo, *f*

scowl, *v.i*, frontem contrăho (3), (contract the brow)

scramble for, *v.t*, *use phr*, inter sē certāre (**struggle among themselves**)

scrap, frustrum, *n*

scrape, *v.t*, rādo (3)

scraper, strĭgĭlis, *f*

scratch, *v.t*, rādo (3), scalpo (3)

scream, *nn*, vōcĭfĕrātĭo, *f*

scream, *v.i*, vōcĭfĕror (1 *dep*)

screech-owl, ŭlŭla, *f*

screen, tĕgĭmen, *n*

screen, *v.t*, tēgo (3)

screw, *nn*, clāvus, *m*

scribble, *v.t*, scrībo (3)

scribe, scrība, *m*

Scripture, Scrīptūra, *f*

scroll, vŏlūmen, *n*

scrub, *v.t*, tergĕo (2)

scruple (religious, etc.), rĕlĭgĭo, *f*

scrupulous, rĕlĭgĭōsus, dĭlĭgens

scrutinize, *v.t*, scrūtor (1 *dep*)

scrutiny, scrūtātĭo, *f*

scuffle, *nn*, rixa, *f*

scull (oar), rēmus, *m*; (*v.i*, rēmĭgo (1)

sculptor, sculptor, *m*

sculpture (art of —), sculptūra, *f*; (the work itself), ŏpus, *n*

scum, spūma, *f*

scurf, furfur, *m*

scurrility, prŏcācĭtas, *f*

scurrilous, scurrīlis, prŏcax

scurvy, foedus

scuttle, *v.t*, (a ship), *use phr*, nāvem ultro dēprīmo (3) (**sink the ship of their own accord**)

scythe, falx, *f*

sea, măre, *n*, (to be at —), nāvĭgo (1)

sea, *adj*, mărĭtĭmus, mărīnus

sea-coast, ōra mărĭtĭma, *f*

sea-faring, *adj*, mărĭtĭmus

sea-fight, pugna nāvālis, *f*

sea-gull, lărus, *m*

seal, *nn*, (of letter), signum, *n*; (animal), phōca, *f*

seal, *v.t*, (letter), signo (1); (close up), comprĭmo (3)

sealing-wax, cēra, *f*

seam, sūtūra, *f*

seaman, nauta, *m*

sear, *v.t*, ădūro (3)

search for, *v.t*, quaero (3); (explore), rīmor (1 dep)

search, *nn*, investīgātĭo, *f*

seasick, *adj*, nausĕăbundus; (to be —), *v.i*, nauséo (1)

seasickness, nausĕa, *f*

season, tempus, *n*, tempestas, *f*; (right time), tempus, *n*

season, *v.t*, condĭo (4)

seasonable, tempestīvus

seasoned (flavoured), condītus; (hardened), dūrātus

seasoning, *nn*, condīmentum, *n*

seat, sēdes, *f*, sĕdĭle, *n*, sella, *f*; (home), dŏmĭcĭlĭum, *n*: *v.t*, collŏco (1)

sea-weed, alga, *f*

secede, *v.i*, dēcēdo (3)

secession, dēfectĭo, *f*

secluded, sēcrētus

seclusion, sōlĭtūdo, *f*

second, *adj*, sĕcundus; (— of two), alter; (for the — time), *adv*, ĭtĕrum; (—ly), *adv*, de inde

second, *nn*, (time), mōmentum, *n*

second, *v.t*, adiŭvo (1)

secondary, infĕrĭor

second-hand, ūsu trītus (worn with usage)

secrecy, sēcrētum, *n*

secret, arcāna, *n.pl*

secret, *adj*, occultus, arcānus; (hidden), clandestīnus; (to keep something —), *v.t*, cēlo (1)

secretary, scrība, *m*

secrete, *v.t*, cēlo (1), abdo (3)

secretly, *adv*, clam

sect, secta, *f*

section, pars, *f*

secular (not sacred), prŏfānus

secure, *v.t*, mūnĭo (4), firmo (1), lĭgo (1) (tie up)

secure, *adj*, tūtus

security, sălus, *f*; (guarantee), pĭgnus, *n*; (to give —), căvĕo (2)

sedate, grăvis

sedative, mĕdĭcāmentum sŏpōrĭfĕrum

sedentary, sĕdentārĭus

sedge, ulva, *f*

sediment, faex, *f*

sedition, sēdĭtĭo, *f*

seditious, sēdĭtĭōsus

seduce, *v.t*, tento (1), sollĭcĭto (1)

seducer, corruptor, *m*

seduction, corruptēla, *f*

sedulous, assĭdŭus

see, *v.t*, vĭdĕo (2), cerno (3), aspĭcĭo (3); (to — to it that . .), cūro (1) ad (*with gerund phr*); (understand), intellĕgo (3)

seed, sēmen, *n* (literal and metaphorical)

seedling, arbor nŏvella, *f*

seedy, grānōsus

seeing that, *conj*, cum

seek, *v.t*, quaero (3), pĕto (3), affecto (1)

seem, *v.i*, vĭdĕor (2 *pass.*)

seeming, *nn*, spĕcĭes, *f*

seemly, *adj*, dĕcōrus, (it is —), dĕcet (2 *impers*)

seer, vātes, *c*

seethe, *v.i*, fervĕo (2)

segment, segmentum, *n*

segregate, *v.t*, sēcerno (3)

seize, *v.t*, răpĭo (3), corrĭpĭo (3), prendo (3), occŭpo (1); (of illness, passion, etc.), afficĭo (3)

seizure, comprĕhensĭo, *f*

seldom, *adv*, rārō

select, *v.t*, lĕgo (3)

select, *adj*, lectus

selection, dēlectus, *m*

self, *pron*, (emphatic), ipse; (reflexive), sē

self-confident, confīdens

self-satisfied, contentus

selfish, selfishness, (to be —), sē ămāre (1 *reflex*)

sell, *v.t*, vendo (3)

seller, vendĭtor, *m*

semblance, ĭmāgo, *f*

semicircle, hēmĭcyclĭum, *n*

senate, sĕnātus, *m*

senate-house, cūrĭa, *f*

senator, sĕnātor, *m*

send, *v.t*, mitto (3); (— away), dīmitto (3); (— back), rĕmitto (3); (— for), arcesso (3); (— forward), praemitto (3); (— in), immitto (3)

senile, sĕnīlis

senior, (in age) nātu maior

sensation (feeling), sensus, *m*; mōtus (*m*) ănĭmi (impulse)

sensational, nŏtābĭlis

sense (feeling), sensus, *m*; (understanding), prūdentĭa, *f*; (meaning), sententĭa, *f*

senseless (unconscious), *use adv. phr*, sensu ablāto (with feeling withdrawn); (stupid), sōcors

sensible, prūdens

sensitive, sensĭlis

sensitiveness, mollĭtĭa,

sensual, lĭbīdĭnōsus

sensuality, lĭbīdo, *f*

sentence (criminal), iūdĭcĭum, *n*; (writing, etc.), sententĭa, *f*

sentence, *v.t*, damno (1)

sententious, sententĭōsus

sentiment (feeling), sensus, *m*; (opinion), ŏpīnĭo, *f*

sentimental, mollis

sentimentality, mollĭtĭa, *f*

sentinel, vĭgil, *m*; (to be on — duty), in stătĭōne esse (*irreg*)

separable, dīvĭdŭus

separate, *v.t*, sēpăro (1), dīvĭdo(3), sēiungo (3), sēcerno (3)

separate, *adj*, sēpărātus, sēcrētus

separately, *adv*, sēpărātim

separation, sēpărātĭo, *f*

September, September (mensis)

sepulchre, sĕpulcrum, *n*

sequel (outcome), exĭtus, *m*

sequence, ordo, *m*

serene, tranquillus

serf, servus, *m*

series, sĕrĭes, *f*

serious, grăvis

seriousness, grăvĭtas,

sermon, ōrātĭo, *f*

serpent, serpens, *f*

serried, confertus

servant, mĭnister, *m*, fămŭlus, *m*, servus, *m*

serve, *v.t*, servĭo (4), (*with dat*); (at table, etc.), mĭnistro (1); (in the army), stĭpendĭa mĕrĕor (2 *dep*); (to — as), esse (*irreg*) (*with prō and abl*)

service, mĭnistĕrĭum, *n*, ŏpĕra, (military), mĭlĭtĭa, *f*

serviceable, ūtĭlis

servile, servīlis

servitude, servĭtus, *f*

session (assembly), conventus, *m*

set, *nn*, (of people), glŏbus, *m*

set, *adj*, stătus

set, *v.t*, (place), stătŭo (3), pōno (3); *v.i*, (of the sun), occĭdo (3); (— about, begin), incĭpĭo (3); (— aside), *v.t*, sēpōno (3); (— down in writing), nōto (1); (— free), lībĕro (1); (set off or out), *v.i*, prŏfĭciscor (3 *dep*); (— up), *v.t*, stătŭo (3)

settee, lectŭlus, *m*

setting (of sun), occāsus, *m*

settle, *v.t*, constĭtŭo (3); (a dispute), compōno (3); (debt), solvo (3); *v.i* (in a home, etc.), consīdo (3)

settled, certus

settlement (colony), cŏlōnĭa, *f*; (— of an affair), compŏsĭtĭo, *f*

settler, cŏlōnus, *m*

seven, septem; (— hundred), septin-genti; (— times), *adv*, septĭes

seventeen, septendĕcim

seventeenth, septĭmus dĕcĭmus

seventh, septĭmus

seventieth, septŭāgēsĭmus

seventy, septŭāginta

sever, *v.t*, sēpăro (1); sēiungo (3)

several, complūres, ălĭquot

severe, sĕvērus, dūrus

severity, sĕvērĭtas, *f*, ăcerbĭtas, *f*

sew, *v.t*, sŭo (3)

sewer (drain), clŏāca, *f*

sex, sexus, *m*

sexagenarian, sexāgēnărĭus, *m*

sexual, *use nn*. sexus, *m*, (sex)

shabbiness, sordes, *f. pl*

shabby, sordĭdus

shackle, *v.t*, vincŭlis constringo (3) (bind with chains)

shackle(s), *nn*, vincŭla, *n.pl*

shade, *nn*, umbra, *f*; (the —s of the dead), mānes, *m. pl*

shade, *v.t*, ŏpāco (1)

shadow, umbra, *f*

shadowy, ŏpācus, ĭnānis

shady, ŏpācus

shaft (of a weapon), hastīle, *n*; (an arrow), săgitta, *f*; (of a mine), pŭtĕus, *m*

shaggy, hirtus, hirsūtus

shake, *v.t*, quătĭo (3), ăgĭto (1) lăbĕfăcĭo (3); *v.i*, trĕmo (3), trĕpĭdo (1); (— hands), dextras iungo (3) (join right hands)

shaking, *nn*, quassātĭo, *f*

shallow, *adj*, (sea), vădōsus, brĕvis

shallows, *nn*, văda, *n.pl*

sham, *adj*, sĭmŭlātus

sham, *nn*, sĭmŭlātĭo, *f* (pretence)

sham, *v.t*, sĭmŭlo (1)

shambles, *use* turba, *f*

shame, *nn*, (feeling), pŭdor, *m*; (disgrace), dēdĕcus, *n*

shame, *v.t*, rŭbōrem incŭtĭo (3) (*with dat*)

shamefaced, vĕrēcundus

shameful, turpis

shamefulness, turpĭtūdo, *f*

shameless, impŭdens

shamelessness, impŭdentĭa, *f*

shamrock, trĭfŏlĭum, *n*

shank, crus, *n*

shape, *nn*, forma, *f*

shape, *v.t*, formo (1)

shapeless, informis

shapely, formōsus

share (part), pars, *f*; (plough —), vōmer, *m*

share, *v.t*, partĭor (4 *dep*)

sharer, partĭceps, *c*

shark, pistrix, *f*

sharp, ăcūtus, ācer

sharp-sighted, perspĭcax

sharp-witted, ăcūtus

sharpen, *v.t*, ăcŭo (3)

sharply, *adv*, ăcūte, ācrĭter

sharpness (of tongue), aspĕrĭtas, *f*; (mental), ăcūmen, *n*

shatter, *v.t*, frango (3)

shave, *v.t*, rādo (3)

shawl, ămĭcŭlum, *n*

she, *pron*, illa, ĕa, haec, ista

sheaf, mănĭpŭlus, *m*

shear, *v.t*, tondĕo (2)

shearing, *nn*, tonsūra, *f*

shears, forfex, *f*

sheath, vāgĭna, *f*

sheathe, *v.t*, in vāgĭnam rĕcondo (3) (put back into the sheath)

shed, *nn*, tĭgŭrĭum, *n*

shed, *v.t*, fundo (3)

sheen, fulgor, *m*

sheep, ŏvis, *f*

sheep-fold, saeptum, *n*

sheep-skin, pellis ŏvilla, *f*

sheepish, sōcors, *or use adv. phr*, dēmisso vultu (with downcast face)

sheer (steep), abruptus; (pure, abso-lute), mērus

sheet (cloth), lintĕum, *n*; (paper), schĕda, *f*; (— of a sail), pes, *m*

shelf, plŭtĕus, *m*

shell, concha, *f*, crusta, *f*

shell-fish, conchȳlĭum, *n*

shelter, *nn*, perfŭgĭum, *n*, tectum, *n*

shelter, *v.t*, tĕgo (3); *v.i, use phr,* ad perfŭgĭum sē conferre (*irreg*) (**betake oneself to shelter**)

shelving, *adj*, dēclīvis

shepherd, pastor, *m*

shield, *nn*, scūtum, *n*

shield, *v.t*, tĕgo (3), dēfendo (3)

shift (change), vĭcissĭtūdo, *F.*

shift, *v.t*, mūto (1); *v.i*, mūtor (1 *pass*)

shifty, versūtus

shin, crūs, *n*

shine, *v.i*, lūcĕo (2), fulgĕo (2)

ship, *nn*, nāvis, *f*; (war —), nāvis longa, *f*; (transport —), nāvis ŏnĕrārĭa, *f*

ship, *v.t*, (**put on board**), in nāvem impōno (3); (transport), nāve transporto (1)

ship-owner, nāvĭcŭlārĭus, *m*

shipping, nāvĭgĭa, *n.pl*

shipwreck, naufrăgĭum, *n*

shipwrecked, naufrăgus

shirt, sŭbūcŭla, *f*

shiver, *v.i*, horrĕo (2)

shivering, *nn*, horror, *m*

shoal (**water**), vădum, *n*; (**fish**), exāmen, *n*

shock, offensĭo, *f*, ictus, m; (**of battle**), concursus, *m*

shock, *v.t*, offendo (3), percŭtĭo (3)

shocking, *adj*, ătrox

shoe, *nn*, calcĕus, *m*

shoe, *v.t*, calcĕo (1)

shoe-maker, sūtor, *m*

shoot, *nn*, (**sprout**), surcŭlus, *m*

shoot, *v.t*, (**a missile**), mitto (3); *v.i*, (— along, across), vŏlo (1)

shooting-star, fax caelestis, *f*

shop, tăberna, *f*

shop-keeper, tăbernārĭus, *m* (*pl. only*)

shore, lĭtus, *n*, ōra, *f*

shore-up, *v.t*, fulcĭo (4)

short, brĕvis, ĕxĭgŭus; (— cut), vĭa compendĭārĭa, *f*; (in —), *adv*, dēnīque

shortage, ĭnŏpĭa, *f* (lack)

shortcoming, dēlictum, *n*

shorten, *v.t*, contrăho (3)

shortly, *adv*, (of time), brĕvi; (briefly), brĕvĭter

shortness, brĕvĭtas, *f*

shot (firing), ictus, *m*

shoulder, hŭmĕrus, *m*; (— blade), scăpŭlae, *f. pl*

shoulder, *v.t*, fĕro (*irreg*) (**to bear**)

shout, *nn*, clāmor, *m*

shout, *v.i*, clāmo (1)

shove, *v.t*, trūdo (3)

shovel, pāla, *f*

show, *nn*, (**appearance**), spĕcĭes, *f*; (**spectacle**), spectācŭlum, *n*; (**procession**, etc.), pompa, *f*

show, *v.t*, monstro (1), praebĕo (2), ostendo (3); (— off), *v.t*, ostento (1); *v.i*, sē ostentare (1 *reflex*)

shower, imber, *m*

shower, *v.t*, fundo (3)

showery, plŭvĭus

showy, spĕcĭōsus

shred, pannus, *m*

shrew, fēmĭna prŏcax

shrewd, ăcūtus, săgax

shrewdness, săgācĭtas, *f*

shriek, *nn*, ŭlŭlātus, *m.*

shriek, *v.i*, ŭlŭlo (1)

shrill, ăcūtus, ācer

shrine, dēlūbrum, *n*

shrink, *v.t*, contrăho (3); *v.i*, (—from), ăbhorrĕo (2)

shrinking, *nn*, contractĭo, *f*

shrivel, *v.t*, corrūgo (1) (**walk slowly**)

shrivelled, rūgōsus

shroud, *use* lintĕum, *n*, (**cloth**)

shroud, *v.t*, involvo (3)

shrub, frŭtex, *m*

shrubbery, frŭtĭcētum

shudder, *v.i*, horrĕo (2)

shudder, *nn*, horror, *m*

shuffle, *v.t*, miscĕo (2); *v.i*, *use phr,* lentē ambŭlo (1) (**walk slowly**)

shun, *v.t*, fŭgĭo (3), vīto (1)

shut, *v.t*, claudo (3); (— in or up), inclūdo (3); (— out), exclūdo (3)

shutters, fŏrĭcŭlae, *f. pl*

shuttle, rādĭus, *m*

shy, vĕrēcundus

shy, *v.i*, (**of horses**), consternor (1 *pass*)

shyness, vĕrēcundĭa, *f*

sick, aeger; (to be —), *v.i*, aegrōto (1); (**vomit**), *v.i, and v.t*, vŏmo (3)

sicken, *v.t*, fastīdĭum mŏvĕo (2); *v.i*, aeger fīo (*irreg*)

sickle, falx, *f*

sickly, infirmus

sickness morbus, *m*

side (**of the body**), lătus, *n*; (**part, region**), pars, *f*; (**party, faction**), pars, *f*; (**from (or on) all —s**), *adv*, undīque; (**on both —s**), ŭtrimque; (**on this —**), hinc; (**on that —**), illinc; (**on this — of**), *prep*, citra (*with acc*); (**on that — of**), ŭltra

side, *adj*, (**sidelong**), oblīquus

sideboard, ăbăcus, *m*

sideways, *adv*, oblīquē

siege, *nn*, obsĭdĭo, *f*

siege-works, ŏpĕra, *n.pl*

sieve, crībrum, *n*

sift, *v.t*, crībro (1); (— evidence, etc.), scrūtor (1 *dep*)

sigh, *nn*, suspīrĭum, *n*

sigh, *v.i*, suspīro (1)

sight (sense or act), vīsus, *m*; (view), conspectus, *m*; (spectacle), spectācŭlum, *n*

sight, *v.t*, conspĭcor (1 *dep*)

sightly, formōsus, vĕnustus

sign, *nn*, signum, *n*; (mark), nŏta, *f*; (trace, footprint), vestigĭum, *n*; (portent), portentum, *n*

sign, *v.t*, subscrībo (3); (give a —), *v.i*, signum do (1)

signal, signum, *n*

signal, *v.i*, signum do (1)

signature, nōmen, *n*

signet, signum, *n*

significance, signĭfĭcātĭo, *f*

significant, signĭfĭcans

signify, *v.t*, signĭfĭco (1)

silence, sĭlentĭum, *n*

silent, tăcĭtus, (to be —), *v.i*, tăcĕo (2), sĭlĕo (2)

silk, *nn*, bombyx, *m*

silk, silken, *adj*, sērĭcus

silk-worm, bombyx, *m*

silky, mollis

sill, līmen, *n*

silliness, stultĭtĭa, *f*

silly, stultus

silt, *nn*, līmus, *m*, sentīna, *f*

silver, *nn*, argentum, *n*

silver, *adj*, argentĕus

silver-mine, argentārĭum metallum

similar, sĭmĭlis (*with genit. or dat*)

similarity, sĭmĭlĭtūdo, *f*

similarly, *adv*, sĭmĭlĭter

simmer, *v.i*, lentē fervĕo (3) (boil slowly)

simper, *v.i*, subrīdĕo (2)

simple, simplex; (weak-minded), ĭneptus

simpleton, stultus, *m*

simplicity, simplĭcĭtas, *f*

simplify, *v.t*, făcĭlem reddo (3)

simulation, sĭmŭlātĭo, *f*

simultaneous, *use adv*, sĭmul (at the same time)

sin, *nn*, peccātum, *n*

sin, *v.i*, pecco (1)

since, *conj*, cum (*foll. by vb. in subjunctive*); (temporal) postquam

since, *adv*, ăbhinc

since, *prep*, ē, ex, ā, ăb (*with ăbl*)

sincere, sincērus, simplex

sincerity, sincērĭtas, *f*, simplĭcĭtas, *f*

sinew, nervus, *m*

sinful, impĭus

sinfulness, impĭĕtas, *f*

sing, *v.i. and v.t*, căno (3)

singe, *v.t*, ădūro (3)

singer, cantātor, *m*

singing, *nn*, cantus, *m*

single, *adj*, (one, sole), ūnus, sōlus; (unmarried), caelebs

single out, *v.t*, ēlĭgo (3)

singly, *adv*, singŭlātim

singular, (one), singŭlāris; (strange), nŏvus

singularly, *adv*, ūnĭcē

sinister, sĭnister

sink, *v.t*, mergo (3); *v.i*, sīdo (3), consīdo (3)

sinner, peccātor, *m*

sinuous, sĭnŭōsus

sip, *v.t*, dēgusto (1), lībo (1)

sir (respectful address), bŏne vir

sire, păter, *m*

siren, sīrēn, *f*

sister, sŏror, *f*

sit, *v.i*, sĕdĕo (2); (— down), consīdo (3); (— up, stay awake), vĭgĭlo (1)

site, sĭtus, *m*

sitting, *nn*, sessĭo, *f*

situated, sĭtus

situation sĭtus, *m*

six, sex; (— each), sēni; (— times), *adv*, sexĭens

sixteen, sēdĕcim

sixteenth, sextus dĕcĭmus

sixth, sextus

sixtieth, sexāgēsĭmus

sixty, sexāgĭnta

size, magnĭtūdo, *f*; (of great —), *adj*, magnus; (of small —), parvus; (of what —?), quantus?

skeleton, ossa, *n.pl*, (bones)

sketch, *nn*, ădumbrātĭo, *f*

sketch, *v.t*, ădumbro (1)

skewer, vĕrūcŭlum, *n*

skiff, scăpha, *f*

skilful, skilled, pĕrītus

skilfulness, skill, pĕrītĭa, *f*

skim, *v.t*, (— off), dēspūmo (1); (— over), percurro (3)

skin, cŭtis, *f*, pellis, *f*

skin, *v.t*, pellem dīrĭpĭo (3) (tear away the skin)

skip, *v.i*, exsulto (1); (— over), *v.i. and v.t*, praetĕrĕo (4)

skipper, nauarchus, *m*

skirmish, *nn*, lĕve certāmen, *n*

skirmish, *v.i*, parvŭlis proelĭis contendo (3) (fight in small engagements)

skirmisher, vēlĕs, *m*

skirt, *nn*, limbus, *m*

skirt, *v.t*, (scrape past), rādo (3)

skittish, lascīvus

skulk, *v.i*, lătĕo (2)
skull, calvārĭa, *f*
sky, caelum, *n*
sky-blue, caerŭlĕus
sky-lark, ălauda, *f*
slab (of stone), ăbăcus, *m*
slack, rĕmissus
slacken, *v.t*, rĕmitto (3); *v.i*, rĕmittor
(3 *pass*)
slackness, rĕmissĭo, *f*; (idleness),
pĭgrĭtĭa, *f*
slake (thirst), *v.t*, (sĭtim) exstinguo
(3)
slander, *nn*, călumnĭa, *f*
slander, *v.t*, călumnĭor (1 *dep*)
slanderer, obtrectātor, *m*
slanderous, fāmōsus
slanting, *adj*, oblīquus
slap, *nn*, ălăpa, *f*
slap, *v.t*, fĕrĭo (4)
slash, *nn*, (blow), ictus, *m*
slash, *v.t*, caedo (3)
slate (roofing), tēgŭlae, *f. pl.*
slate, *v.t*, rĕprĕhendo (3)
slaughter, *nn*, caedes, *f*, strāges, *f*
slaughter, *v.t*, caedo (3)
slaughter-house, *use* lānĭēna, *f* (butcher's stall)
slave, servus, *m*
slave-dealer, vēnālĭcĭus, *m*
slavery, servĭtus, *f*
slave-trade, vēnālĭcĭum, *n*
slavish, servīlis
slay, *v.t*, interfĭcĭo (3)
slayer, interfector, *m*
slaying, *nn*, trŭcīdātĭo, *f*
sledge, trăhĕa, *f*
sleek, nĭtĭdus
sleep, *nn*, somnus, *m*
sleep, *v.i*, dormĭo (4), quĭesco (3);
(to go to —), obdormisco (3)
sleepless, insomnis
sleeplessness, insomnĭa, *f*
sleepy, somnĭcŭlōsus
sleeve, mănĭcae, *f. pl*
sleigh, trăhĕa, *f*
sleight-of-hand, praestīgĭae, *f. pl*
slender, grăcĭlis
slenderness, grăcĭlĭtas, *f*
slice, segmentum, *n*, frustum, *n*
slice, *v.t*, concīdo (3)
slide, *v.i*, lābor (3 *dep*)
slight, *adj*, lĕvis, exĭgŭus
slight, *v.t*, neglĕgo (3)
slim, grăcĭlis
slime, līmus, *m*
slimy, līmōsus
sling, *nn*, (for throwing), funda, *f*;
(bandage), mĭtella, *f*
sling, *v.t*, mitto (3)

slinger, fundĭtor, *m*
slip, *v.i*, lābor (3 *dep*); (— away), sē
subdūcĕre (3 *reflex*); (— out from),
ēlābor (3 *dep*)
slip, *nn*, lapsus, *m*; (mistake), error, *m*
slipper, sŏlĕa, *f*
slippery, lūbrĭcus
slipshod, neglĕgens
slit, *nn*, scissūra, *f*
slit, *v.t*, incīdo (3)
sloop, nāvis longa, *f*
slope, *nn*, clīvus, *m*
slope, *v.i*, sē dēmittĕre (3 *reflex*),
vergo (3)
sloping, *adj*, (down), dēclīvis; (up),
acclivis
sloth, segnĭtĭa, *f*, ignāvĭa, *f*
slothful, segnis
slough (mire), pălus, *f*
slovenliness, cultus neglectus (neglected dress)
slow, tardus, lentus
slowly, *adv*, tardē, lentē
slowness, tardĭtas, *f*
slug, līmax, *f*
sluggish, pĭger, segnis
sluggishness, pigrĭtĭa, *f*
sluice, ductus, (*m*) ăquārum (bringing
of water)
slumber, *nn*, somnus, *m*
slumber, *v.i*, dormĭo (4)
slur, *nn*, măcŭla, *f*
sly, astūtus, callĭdus
smack, *nn*, (blow), ălăpa, *f*; (taste),
săpor, *m*
smack, *v.t*, (slap), verbĕro (1)
small, parvus, exĭgŭus
smallness, exĭgŭĭtas, *f*
smart, *adj*, ācer; (clothes, etc.),
nĭtĭdus; (witty), făcētus
smart, *nn*, dŏlor, *m*
smart, *v.i*, dŏlĕo (2), ūror (3 *pass*)
smartness (alertness), ălăcrĭtas, *f*
smash, *nn*, fractūra, *f*
smash, *v.t*, confringo (3)
smattering, lĕvis cognĭtĭo, *f*, (slight
knowledge)
smear, *v.t*, līno (3)
smell, *nn*, (sense of —), ŏdōrātus, *m*;
(scent), ŏdor, *m*
smell, *v.t*, olfăcĭo (3); *v.i*, ŏlĕo (2)
smelt, *v.t*, cŏquo (3)
smile, *nn*, rīsus, *m*
smile, *v.i*, subrīdĕo (2)
smirk, *nn*, rīsus, *m*
smite, *v.t*, fĕrĭo (4)
smith, făber, *m*
smithy, făbrĭca, *f*
smock, indūsĭum, *n*
smoke, *nn*, fūmus, *m*

For List of Abbreviations used, turn to pages 3, 4

smoke, *v.i*, fūmo (1)
smoky, fūmōsus
smooth, lēvis, (of the sea), plăcĭdus; (of temper), aequus
smooth, *v.t*, lēvo (1)
smoothness, lēvĭtas, *f*, lēnĭtas, *f*
smother, *v.t*, suffōco (1), opprĭmo (3)
smoulder, *v.i*, fūmo (1)
smudge, *nn*, lābes, *f*
smuggle, *v.t*, furtim importo (1) (bring in secretly)
snack, cēnŭla, *f*
snail, cochlĕa, *f*
snake, anguis, *m*, *f*
snaky, vīpĕrĕus
snap, *v.t*, rumpo (3); (— the fingers), *v.i*, concrĕpo (1); (— up), *v.t*, corrĭpĭo (3)
snare, lăquĕus, *m*
snarl, *nn*, gannītus, *m*
snarl, *v.i*, gannĭo (4)
snatch, *v.t*, răpĭo (3)
sneak, *v.i* corrĕpo (3)
sneer, *nn*, obtrectātĭo, *f*
sneer at, *v.t*, dērīdĕo (2)
sneeze, *v.i*, sternŭo (3)
sneezing, sternūmentum, *n*
sniff at (smell at), *v.t*, ŏdōror (1 *dep*)
snip, *v.t*, (cut off), ampŭto (1)
snob, nŏvus hŏmo (upstart)
snore, *v.i*, sterto (3)
snore, snoring, *nn*, rhonchus, *m*
snort, *v.i*, frĕmo (3)
snorting, *nn*, frĕmĭtus, *m*
snout, rostrum, *n*
snow, *nn*, nix, *f*
snow (it —s), ningit (*v. impers*)
snowy, nĭvĕus
snub, *v.t*, rĕprĕhendo (3)
snub-nosed, sīlus
snuff, *v.t*, (extinguish), exstinguo (3)
snug, commŏdus
so, *adv*, (in such a way), sīc, ĭtă; (to such an extent), ădĕo; (*with adj and adv*) tam, *e.g.* so quickly, tam cĕlĕrĭter; (*with a purpose or consecutive clause*, so that . . .) ut; (— big, — great), tāntus; (— many), tot; (— much), tantum; (— often), tŏtĭes
soak, *v.t*, mădĕfăcĭo (3)
soaking, mădens; (of rain), largus
soap, *nn*, săpo, *m*
soar, *v.i*, sublīme fĕror (*irreg pass*) (be borne aloft)
sob, *nn*, singultus, *m*
sob, *v.i*, singulto (1)
sober, sōbrĭus

sobriety, sōbrĭĕtas, *f*, mŏdĕrātĭo, *f*
sociability, făcĭlĭtas, *f*
sociable, făcĭlis
social, commūnis
society (in general), sŏcĭĕtas, *f*; (companionship), sŏdālĭtas, *f*
sock, tībĭāle, *n*
sod, caespes, *m*
soda, nĭtrum, *n*
sodden, mădĭdus
sofa, lectŭlus, *m*
soft, mollis
soften, *v.t*, mollĭo (4); *v.i*, mollĭor (4 *pass*)
softness, mollĭtĭa, *f*
soil, sŏlum, *n*
soil, *v.t*, inquĭno (1)
sojourn, *nn*, commŏrātĭo, *f*
sojourn, *v.i*, commŏror (1 *dep*)
solace, *nn*, sōlātĭum, *n*
solace, *v.t*, consōlor (1 *dep*)
solar, *use genit. case of* sōl, *m*, (sun)
solder, *nn*, ferrūmen, *n*
solder, *v.t*, ferrūmĭno (1)
soldier, mīles, *c*; (foot —), pĕdes, *m*; (cavalry —), ĕques, *m*; *v.i*, (serve as a —), stĭpendĭa mĕrĕor (2 *dep*)
soldierly, *adj*, mīlĭtāris
sole, *adj*, sōlus
sole, *nn*, sōlum, *n*; (fish), sŏlĕa, *f*
solely, *adv*, sōlum
solemn (serious), grăvis; (festivals, etc.), sollemnis
solemnity, grăvĭtas, *f*; (religious —), sollemne, *n*.
solemnize, *v.t*, cĕlĕbro (1)
solicit, *v.t*, pĕto (3), obsĕcro (1), sollĭcĭto (1)
solicitation, flāgĭtātĭo, *f*
solicitor, advŏcātus, *m*
solicitude, anxĭĕtas, *f*
solid, *adj* sōlĭdus
solid, *nn*, sōlĭdum, *n*
solidity, sōlĭdĭtas, *f*
soliloquize, *v.i*, sēcum lŏquor (3 *dep*) (speak with oneself)
solitary, sōlus, sōlĭtārĭus; (places), dēsertus
solitude, sōlĭtūdo, *f*
solstice (summer —), solstĭtĭum, *n*; (winter —), brūma, *f*
solution, *use vb.* solvo (3) (to solve), *or nn*, explĭcātĭo, *f*
solve, *v.t*, explĭco (1)
solvent (to be —), solvendo esse (*irreg*)
sombre, obscūrus
some, *adj*, ălĭquis, nonnullus; (a certain), quĭdam

somebody, someone, *pron*, ălĭquis, nonnullus; (a certain one), quĭdam; (— or other), nescĭo quis; (some ... others), ălĭi ... ălĭi

somehow, *adv*, nescĭŏ quŏmŏdŏ

something, *pron*, ălĭquid

sometime, *adv*, ălĭquandŏ

sometimes *adv*, ălĭquandŏ, intĕrdum; (occasionally), sŭbĭnde; (sometimes ... sometimes ...), mŏdŏ ... mŏdŏ ...

somewhat, *adv*, ălĭquantum

somewhere, *adv*, ălĭcŭbĭ; (to —), ălĭquo

somnolent, sēmĭsomnus

son, fīlĭus, *m*; (— in-law), gĕner, *m*

song, carmen, *n*

sonorous, sŏnōrus,

soon, *adv*, mox; (as — as), sĭmul ac, sĭmŭl atque, cum prīmum; (as— as possible), quam prīmum

sooner (earlier), mātūrĭus; (rather), pŏtĭus

soot, fūlīgo, *f*

soothe, *v.t*, mulcĕo (2), lēnĭo (4)

soothing, *adj*, lēnis

soothsayer, auspex, *c*, hăruspex, *m*

sooty, fūlĭgĭnōsus

sop, offa, *f*

sophist, sŏphistes, *m*

soporific, sŏpōrĭfer

sorcerer, vĕnēfĭcus, *m*

sorcery, vĕnēfĭcĭa, *n.pl*

sordid, sordĭdus

sore, ăcerbus

sore, *nn*, ulcus, *n*

sorrel, lăpăthus, *f*

sorrow, *nn*, dŏlor, *m*, maeror, *m*

sorrow, *v.i*, dŏlĕo (2)

sorrowful, maestus, tristis

sorry (to be —), mĭsĕret (2 *impers*) (*with acc. of subject and genit. of object*), *e.g*. I am sorry for you, me mĭsĕret tŭi

sort, gĕnus, *n*; (what — of?), quālis?

sort, *v.t*, dĭgĕro (3)

sot, pōtātor, *m*

soul, ănĭma, *f*, ănĭmus, *m*, spīrĭtus, *m*

sound, *nn*, sŏnus, *m*, sŏnĭtus, *m*

sound, *adj*, sānus; (of sleep), artus; (of arguments), firmus

sound, *v.i*, sŏno (1); *v.t*, inflo (1); (— the trumpet), būcĭnam inflo (1), căno (3)

soundness, sānĭtas, *f*, intĕgrĭtas, *f*

soup, iūs, *n*

sour, ăcerbus, ācer, ămārus

source, fons, *m*, căput, *n*

sourness, ăcerbĭtas, *f*

south, *nn*, mĕrīdĭes, *m*

south, southern, *adj*, mĕrīdĭānus

southwards, *adv. phr*, in mĕrīdĭem

sovereign, *nn*, princeps, *m*, rex, *m* tўrannus, *m*

sovereign (independent), *adj*, *use phr* sŭi iūris (of one's own authority)

sovereignty, impĕrĭum, *n*

sow, *nn*, sūs, *f*

sow, *v.t*, sĕro (3)

sower, sător, *m*

space, spătĭum, *n*; (— of time), spătĭum, (*n*) tempŏris

spacious, amplus

spaciousness, amplĭtūdo, *f*

spade, pāla, *f*

span palmus, *m*

span, *v.t*, (river, etc.), *use vb*, iungo (3) (join)

spangled, distinctus

Spanish, Hispānus

spar (of timber), asser, *m*

spare, *adj*, exīlis (thin)

spare, *v.t*, parco (3) (*with dat*)

sparing, *adj*, (frugal), parcus

spark, *nn*, scintilla, *f*

sparkle, *v.i*, scintillo (1)

sparkling, *adj*, scintillans

sparrow, passer, *m*

sparse, rārus

spasm, spasmus, *m*

spatter, *v.t*, aspergo (3)

spawn, *nn*, ōva, *n.pl*

spawn, *v.i*, ōva gigno (3) (produce eggs)

speak, *v.t*, lŏquor (3 *dep*), dīco (3); (— out), ēlŏquor (3 *dep*); (— to), allŏquor (3 *dep*)

speaker, ōrātor, *m*

spear, hasta, *f*

special (one in particular), pĕcūlĭāris; (one's own), prŏprĭus; (outstanding), praecĭpŭus

speciality, *use adj*, prŏprĭus (one's own)

specially, *adv*, praecĭpŭē, praesertim

species, gĕnus, *n*

specific, dĭsertus; *or use emphatic pron*, ipse

specify, *v.t*, ēnŭmĕro (1)

specimen, exemplum, *n*

specious, prŏbābĭlis

speck, măcŭla, *f*

spectacle, spectācŭlum, *n*

spectator, spectātor, *m*

spectre, ĭmāgo, *f*

spectrum, spectrum, *n*

speculate, *v.i*, cōgĭto (1); (guess), cōnĭcĭo (3)

speculation, cōgĭtātĭo, *f*; (guess), cōniectūra, *f*

speech, ōrātĭo, f
speechless (literally so), mūtus; (struck with fear, etc.), stŭpĕfactus
speed, cĕlĕrĭtas, f
speed, v.t, mātūro (1); v.i, festīno (1)
speedy, cĕler, cĭtus
spell (charm), carmen, n
spell, v.t, use phr. with littĕra, f, (letter)
spellbound, obstŭpĕfactus
spend, v.t, (money), impendo (3), insūmo (3); (time), ăgo (3)
spendthrift, nĕpos, m, f
spew, v.t, vŏmo (3)
sphere, glŏbus, m; (— of responsibility, etc.), prōvincĭa, f
spherical, glŏbōsus
sphinx, sphinx, f
spice, condĭmentum, n
spice, v.t, condĭo (4)
spicy, condītus
spider, ărănĕa, f
spider's web, ărănĕa, f
spike, clāvus, m
spill, v.t, effundo (3)
spin, v.t, (thread, etc.), nĕo (2); (turn rapidly), verso (1); v.i, versor (1 pass)
spinster, virgo, f
spiral, nn, cochlĕa, f
spiral, adj, invŏlūtus
spire, turris, f
spirit (breath of life), ănĭma, f; (mind, soul), ănĭmus, m; (disposition), ingĕnĭum, n; (character), mōres, m. pl; (courage), ănĭmus, m; (departed —), mānes, m. pl
spirited, ănĭmōsus
spiritual (of the mind), use ănĭmus, m
spit, nn, (for roasting), vĕru, n
spit, v.t, spŭo (3)
spite, mălĕvŏlentĭa, f; (in — of), often use abl. phr. with obstans (standing in the way)
spiteful, mălignus
spittle, spūtum, n
splash, v.t, aspergo (3)
spleen, lĭen, m; (vexation), stŏmăchus, m
splendid, splendĭdus
splendour, splendor, m
splint, fĕrŭlae, f. pl
splinter, fragmentum, n
split, v.t, findo (3); v.i, findor (3 pass)
split, nn, fissūra, f
splutter, v.i, balbŭtĭo (4)
spoil, nn, praeda, f, spŏlĭa, n.pl
spoil, v.t, corrumpo (3), vĭtĭo (1)
spokesman, ōrātor, m
sponge, nn, spongĭa, f

spongy, spongĭōsus
sponsor auctor, c
spontaneous, use adv. phr, sŭā (mĕā) sponte (of his (my) own accord)
spoon, coclĕar, n
sporadic, rārus
sport, nn, lūdus, m, lūsus, m; (ridicule), lūdĭbrĭum, n
sport, v.i, lūdo (3)
sportive (playful), lascīvus
sportsman, vēnātor, m
spot, nn, (stain), măcŭla, f; (place), lŏcus, m
spot, v.t, (look at), aspĭcĭo (3); (stain), măcŭlo (1)
spotless (of character, etc.), intĕger, pūrus
spotted, măcŭlōsus
spouse, conĭunx, c
spout, nn, ōs, n
spout, v.i, ēmĭco (1); v.t, (pour out), effundo (3)
sprain, v.t, intorquĕo (2)
sprawl, v.i, fundor (3 pass)
spray, nn, aspergo, f
spread, v.t, extendo (3), pando (3), diffundo (3); (— about, publish), diffĕro (irreg) dīvulgo (1); v.i, diffundor (3 pass), incrēbresco (3)
sprightly, ălăcer
spring, nn, (season), vēr, n; (leap), saltus, m; (fountain), fons, m
spring, adj, vernus
spring, v.i, (leap), sălĭo (4); (— from), proceed from), ŏrĭor (4 dep) (— upon, assault), ădŏrĭor (4 dep)
sprinkle, v.t, spargo (3)
sprout, nn, surcŭlus, m
sprout, v.i, pullŭlo (1)
spruce, adj, nĭtĭdus
spruce, nn, (fir), pīnus, f
spur, nn, calcar, n
spur, v.t, concĭto (1)
spurious, ădultĕrīnus
spurn, v.t, aspernor (1 dep)
spurt, v.i, ēmĭco (1)
spy, nn, explŏrātor, m, dēlātor, m
spy, v.t, spĕcŭlor (1 dep)
squabble, nn, rixa, f
squabble, v.i, rixor (1 dep)
squadron (of cavalry), turma, f; (of ships), classis, f
squalid, sordĭdus
squall (storm), prŏcella, f
squall, v.i, (cry), vāgĭo (4)
squalor, sordes, f. pl
squander, effundo (3)
squanderer, nĕpos, m, f
square, adj, quădrātus; nn, quădrātum, n

square, *v.t*, quădro (1); (accounts, etc.), subdūco (3), constĭtŭo (3)
squash, *v.t*, contĕro (3)
squat, *v.i*, subsīdo (3)
squat, *adj*, (of figure), brĕvis
squeak, *nn*, strīdor, *m*
squeak, *v.i*, strīdĕo (2)
squeamish, fastīdiōsus
squeeze, *v.t*, prĕmo (3)
squint, *v.i*, străbo esse (*irreg*)
squirrel, sciūrus, *m*
squirt, *v.t*, ēĭcĭo (3); *v.i*, ēmĭco (1)
stab, *v.t*, fŏdĭo (3)
stab, *nn*, ictus, *m*
stability, stăbĭlĭtas, *f*
stable, *adj*, stăbĭlis
stable, *nn*, stăbŭlum, *n*
stack, *nn*, ăcervus, *m*
stack, *v.t*, cŏăcervo (1)
staff, băcŭlum, *n*; (advisers), consĭlĭārĭi, *m. pl*
stag, cervus, *m*
stage (theatre), proscaenĭum, *n*; (step), grădus, *m*
stagger, *v.i*, văcillo (1); *v.t*, concŭtĭo (3), commŏvĕo (2)
stagnant, stagnans
stagnate, *v.i*, stagno (1)
staid, grăvis
stain, *nn*, măcŭla, *f.*
stain, *v.t*, măcŭlo (1)
stainless, pūrus, intĕger
stairs, scălae, *f. pl*
stake (post, etc), pālus, *m*, sŭdis, *f*, stĭpes, *m*; (pledge, wager), pignus, *n*
stake, *v.t*, (wager), dēpōno (3)
stale, vĕtus
stalk, stirps, *f*
stalk, *v.i*, incēdo (3); (game, etc), *use phr*, cautē sĕquor (3 *dep*) (follow cautiously)
stall (cattle), stăbŭlum, *n*; (shop, etc.), tăberna, *f*
stallion, admissărĭus, *m*
stalwart, *adj*, fortis
stamina, vīres, *f. pl*
stammer, *nn*, haesĭtantĭa (*f*) linguae (hesitation of speech)
stammer, *v.i*, balbūtĭo (4)
stamp (mark), nŏta, *f*; (with a ring, etc.), signum, *n*
stamp, *v.t*, (mark), signo (1); (— with the foot), supplōdo (3)
stand, *nn* (halt), mŏra, *f*; (to make a —) consisto (3) rēsisto (3), (*with dat.*); (platform), suggestus, *m*; (stall), mensa, *f*
stand, *v.i*, sto (1), consisto (3); (— back), rĕcēdo (3), (— by, help), adsum (*irreg with dat*); (— for,

seek a position), *v.t*, pĕto (3); (endure), pătĭor (3 *dep*); (— out, project) exsto (1); (— up), surgo (3)
standard, signum, *n*; (of the legion), ăquĭla, *f*; (measure), norma, *f*; (— bearer), signĭfer, *m*
standing, *nn*, (position), stătus, *m*
staple products, merces, *f*, *pl*
star, stella, *f*, sīdus, *n*
starboard, *use adj*, dexter (right)
starch, *nn*, ămўlum, *n*
stare, *nn*, obtūtus, *m*
stare, *v.t*, (— at), intŭĕor (2 *dep*)
stark (stiff), rĭgĭdus; (— naked), nūdus; (—mad) āmens
starling, sturnus, *m*
start, *nn*, (movement), trĕmor, *m*; (beginning), ĭnĭtĭum, *n*; (setting out), prŏfectĭo, *f*; (starting point), carcĕres, *m. pl*
start, *v.i*, (make a sudden movement), trĕmo (3), horrĕo (2); (— out), prŏfīciscor (3 *dep*); *v.t* (establish), instĭtŭo (3)
startle, *v.t*, terrĕo (2)
startling, *adj*, terrĭbĭlis
starvation, fămes, *f*
starve, *v.t*, făme nĕco (1) (kill by starvation); *v.i*, făme nĕcor (1 *pass*)
state (condition), stătus, *m*, condĭcĭo, *f*; (the —), respublĭca, *f*, cīvĭtas, *f*
state, *v.t*, prŏfĭtĕor (2 *dep*)
stately, magnĭfĭcus, cĕlĕber
statement, dictum, *n*
statesman, *use phr. with* respublĭca (state), *and* admĭnistro · (1), (to manage)
station (standing), stătus, *m*; (occupied place), stătĭo, *f*
station, *v.t*, lŏco (1)
stationary, *adj*, immōtus
stationer, bĭblĭŏpōla, *m*
statistics, census, *m*
statue, stătŭa, *f*
stature, stătūra, *f*
status, stătus, *m*
statute, lex, *f*
staunch, *adj*, fīrmus
stave off, *v.t*, arcĕo (2)
stay, *nn*, (prop), fīrmāmentum, *n*; (rest, etc), mansĭo, *f*, commŏrātĭo, *f*
stay, *v.i*, mănĕo (2), mŏror (1 *dep*); *v.t*, (obstruct, stop), mŏror (1 *dep*)
steadfast, fīrmus, stăbĭlis
steady, fīrmus, stăbĭlis
steadfastness, stăbĭlĭtas, *f*
steadiness, stăbĭlĭtas, *f*
steak, offa, *f*

For List of Abbreviations used, turn to pages 3, 4

steal, *v.t*, fūror (1 *dep*); *v.i*, (— upon), surrēpo (3)(*with dat*)

stealing, *nn*, (theft), furtum, *n*

stealth, (by —), (*adv*) furtim

stealthy, furtīvus

steam, văpor, *m*

steam, *v.i*, exhālo (1)

steed, ĕquus, *m*

steel, chălybs, *m*; (iron, sword, etc.), ferrum, *n*

steel, *v.t*, (strengthen), confirmo (1)

steep, praeruptus

steep, *v.t*, (soak), mădĕfăcĭo (3)

steeple, turris, *f*

steer, *nn*, iŭvencus, *m*

steer, *v.t*, gŭberno (1)

steersman, gŭbernātor, *m*

stem, stirps, *f*, (— *literal and metaphorical*)

stem, *v.t*, (check), sisto (3), rĕsisto (3) (*with dat*)

stench, fētor, *m*

step, *nn*, grădus, *m*, passus, *m*; (foot —), vestīgĭum, *n*; (— by —), pĕdētentim; (steps, stairs), scālae, *f.pl*

step, *v.i*, grădĭor (3 *dep*); (— forward); prōgrĕdĭor (3 *dep*)

step-brother (father's side), fīlĭus vītrīcī; (mother's side), fīlĭus nŏvercae; (— daughter), prīvigna, *f*; (— father) vītrīcus, *m*; (— mother), nŏverca, *f*; (— sister), fīlĭa vītrīcī *or* nŏvercae; (— son), prīvignus, *m*

sterile, stĕrĭlis

sterility, stĕrĭlĭtas, *f*

sterling, *adj*, (genuine), vērus

stern, *nn*, puppis, *f*

stern, *adj*, dūrus

sternness, sĕvērĭtas, *f*

stew, *v.t*, cŏquo (3)

steward, vīlĭcus, *m*

stick, *nn*, băcŭlum, *n*

stick, *v.t*, (fix), fīgo (3); *v.i*, haerĕo (2)

sticky, *adj*, tēnax

stiff, rĭgĭdus; (to be —), *v.i*, rĭgĕo (2)

stiffen, *v.i*, rĭgĕo (2); *v.t*, rĭgĭdum făcĭo (3)

stiffness, rĭgor, *m*

stifle, *v.t*, suffōco (1); (suppress), opprĭmo (3)

stigma, stigma, *n*

stigmatize, *v.t*, nŏto (1)

still, *adj*, immōtus, tranquillus

still, *adv*, (nevertheless), tămen; (up to this time), ădhuc; (even), ĕtĭam

still, *v.t*, sēdo (1)

stillness, quĭes, *f*

stilts, grallae, *f. pl*

stimulant (incentive), stĭmŭlus, *m*

stimulus (incentive), stĭmŭlus, *m*

stimulate, *v.t*, stĭmŭlo (1)

sting, *nn*, ăcŭlĕus, *m*

sting, *v.t*, pungo (3)

stinging, *adj*, mordax

stingy, sordĭdus

stink, *nn*, fētor, *m*

stink, *v.i*, fētĕo (2)

stipend, merces, *f*

stipulate, *v.i*, stĭpŭlor (1 *dep*)

stir, *nn*, mōtus, *m*

stir, *v.t*, mŏvĕo (2); *v.i*, mŏvĕor (2 *pass*)

stitch, *v.t*, sŭo (3)

stock (of tree, family, etc.), stirps, *f*; (amount), vis, *f*

stock, *v.t*, complĕo (2)

stockbroker, argentārĭus, *m*

stocking, tībĭāle, *n*

stoic, *nn. and adj*, stōĭcus

stoical, dūrus

stoicism, rătĭo Stōĭca, *f*

stolen, furtīvus

stomach, stŏmăchus, *m*

stomach, *v.t*, (put up with), perfĕro (*irreg*)

stone, lăpis, *m*; (precious —), gemma, *f*; (fruit —), nŭclĕus, *m*

stone, *adj*, lăpĭdĕus

stone, *v.t*, (— to death), lăpĭdĭbus cŏōpĕrĭo (4) (overwhelm with stones)

stone-quarry, lăpĭcīdīnae, *f. pl*

stony, lăpĭdōsus; (of heart), asper

stool, scăbellum, *n*

stoop, *v.i*, sē dēmittĕre (3 *reflex*); (condescend), dēscendo (3)

stop, *nn*, intermissĭo, *f*

stop, *v.t*, sisto (3); (— up a hole, etc.), obtūro (1); *v.i*, (pause), sisto (3); (desist), dēsĭno (3); (remain), mănĕo (2)

stoppage (hindrance), impĕdīmentum, *n*

stopper, obtūrāmentum, *n*

store (supply), cōpĭa, *f*; (place), rĕceptācŭlum, *n*

store, *v.t*, condo (3)

storey, tăbŭlātum, *n*

stork, cĭcōnĭa, *f*

storm, *nn*, tempestas, *f*

storm, *v.t*, (attack), expugno (1)

storming, *nn*, expugnātĭo, *f*

stormy (weather), turbĭdus

story, fābŭla, *f*

story-teller, narrātor, *m*

stout, (fat), pinguis; (strong), vălĭdus;
(— hearted), fortis

stove, fŏcus, *m*

stow, *v.t*, rēpōno (3)

straddle, *v.i*, vārĭco (1)

straggle, *v.i*, văgor (1 *dep*)

straight, *adj*, rectus

straight, *adv*, rectā

straight away, *adv*, stătim

straighten, *v.t*, corrĭgo (3)

straightforward, simplex

strain, *nn*, contentĭo, *f*

strain, *v.t*, (stretch), tendo (3); (liquids,
etc.), cōlo (3); *v.i*, (strive), nītor (3
dep)

strait, *adj*, angustus

strait, *nn*, (a narrow place or a
difficulty), angustĭae, *f. pl* (sea) frē-
tum *n*.

strand (shore), lītus, *n*

stranded, rĕlictus

strange, insŏlĭtus, nŏvus

strangeness, insŏlentĭa, *f*

stranger, hospes, *m*

strangle, *v.t*, strangŭlo (1)

strap, *nn*, lōrum, *n*

stratagem, dŏlus, *m*

strategist, *use phr. with* pĕrītus
(skilled in), *with phr. below*

strategy, ars, (*f*) bellandi (the art of
making war)

straw, strāmentum, *n*

strawberry, frāgum, *n*

stray, *v.i*, erro (1)

stray, *adj*, errābundus

streak, *nn*, līnĕa, *f*

streak, *v.t*, līnĕis vărĭo (1), (varie-
gate with streaks)

streaky, virgātus

stream, *nn*, flūmen, *n*

stream, *v.i*, effundor (3 *pass*)

street, vĭa, *f*

strength, vīres, *f. pl*, rōbur, *n*

strengthen, *v.t*, firmo (1)

strenuous, impĭger

stress (importance), mōmentum, *n*

stretch, *nn*, (extent), spătĭum, *n*

stretch, *v.t*, tendo (3); (— out),
extendo (3); *v.i*, sē tendĕre (3 *reflex*)

stretcher, lectĭca, *f*

strew, *v.t*, sterno (3)

strict (severe), dūrus; (careful),
dīlĭgens

strictness, sĕvērĭtas, *f*

stricture, rĕprĕhensĭo, *f*

stride, *nn*, passus, *m*

strife, certāmen, *n*, discordĭa, *f*

strike, *v.t*, fērĭo (4), percŭtĭo (3),
pulso (1); (— the mind, occur to),
subvĕnĭo (4)

striking, *adj*, insignis

string, līnĕa, *f*; (of bow or instrument),
nervus, *m*

stringent, sĕvērus

strip, *v.t*, spŏlĭo (1), nūdo (1)

strip, *nn*, (flap, edge), lăcĭnĭa, *f*

stripe, līmes, *m*; (blow), verber, *n*

stripling, ădŏlescentŭlus, *m*

strive, *v.i*, nītor (3 *dep*), contendo (3)

striving, *nn*, contentĭo, *f*

stroke, *nn*, verber, *n*, ictus, *m*; (line),
līnĕa, *f*

stroke, *v.t*, mulcĕo (2)

stroll, *nn*, ambŭlātĭo, *f*

stroll, *v.i*, ambŭlo (1)

strong, vălĭdus, firmus; (powerful),
fortis; (to be —), *v.i*, vălĕo (2)

stronghold, arx, *f*

structure (building), aedĭfĭcĭum, *n*

struggle, *nn*, certāmen, *n*

struggle, *v.i*, luctor (1 *dep*), nītor (3
dep)

strumpet, mĕrētrix, *f*

strut, *v.i*, incēdo (3)

stubble, stĭpŭla, *f*

stubborn, pertĭnax

stucco, tectōrĭum, *n*

stud, clāvus, *m*; (horses), ĕquārĭa, *f*

stud, *v.t*, insĕro (3)

student, *use adj*, stŭdĭōsus (devoted
to), *with a suitable noun*

studied, mĕdĭtātus

studious, stŭdĭōsus

study, *nn*, stŭdĭum, *n*; (room,
library), bĭblĭŏthēca, *f*

study, *v.t*, stŭdĕo (2) (*with dat*)

stuff (material), mātĕrĭa, *f*; (woven-),
textĭle, *n*

stuff, *v.t*, farcĭo (4)

stuffing, *nn*, fartum, *n*

stumble, *nn*, (fall), lapsus, *m*

stumble, *v.i*, offendo (3)

stumbling-block, impĕdīmentum, *n*.

stump (post), stĭpes, *m*

stun, *v.t*, obstŭpĕfăcĭo (3)

stupefaction, stŭpor, *m*

stupefy, *v.t*, obstŭpĕfăcĭo (3)

stupendous, mīrābĭlis

stupid, stŏlĭdus, stultus

stupidity, stultĭtĭa, *f*

stupor, stŭpor, *m*

sturdiness, firmĭtas, *f*

sturdy, firmus, vălĭdus

sturgeon, ăcĭpenser, *m*

stutter, *v.i*, balbūtĭo (4)

sty, hăra, *f*; (in the eye), hordĕŏlus, *m*

style, gĕnus, *n*

style, *v.t* (name), appello (1)

stylish, spĕcĭōsus

suave, suāvis

subaltern, subcentŭrĭo, *m*
subdivide, *v.t*, dīvĭdo (3)
subdue, *v.t*, sŭbĭcĭo (3)
subject, *adj*, subiectus
subject, *nn*, (of a state, etc), cīvis, *c*; (matter), rēs, *f*
subject, *v.t*, sŭbĭcĭo (3)
subjection (slavery), servĭtus, *f*
subjoin, *v.t*, subiungo (3)
subjugate, *v.t*, sŭbĭgo (3)
sublime, ēlātus
sublimity, ēlātĭo, *f*
submerge, *v.t*, submergo (3)
submission (compliance), obsĕquĭum, *n*
submissive, ŏbēdĭens
submit, *v.t*, sŭbĭcĭo (3); (present), rĕfĕro (*irreg*); *v.i*, cēdo (3)
subordinate, *adj*, subiectus
subordination (obedience), obsĕquĭum, *n*
subscribe, *v.t*, (give money, etc.), confĕro (*irreg*); (signature), subscrībo (3)
subscription (of money, etc.), collātĭo, *f*
subsequent, sĕquens
subsequently, *adv*, postĕā
subservient, obsĕquens
subside, *v.i*, rēsīdo (3)
subsidize, *v.t*, pĕcūnĭam suppĕdĭto (1), (furnish with money)
subsidy, subsĭdĭum, *n*
subsist, *v.i*, consto (1)
subsistence, victus, *m*
substance (essence), nātūra, *f*; (being), rēs, *f*; (goods), bŏna, *n.pl*
substantial (real), vērus; (important), grăvis
substitute, *nn*, vĭcārĭus, *m*
substitute, *v.t*, suppōno (3)
subterfuge, lătĕbra, *f*
subterranean, subterrānĕus
subtle (crafty), astūtus; (refined), subtīlis
subtlety (craftiness), astūtĭa, *f*; (fineness), subtīlĭtas, *f*
subtract, *v.t*, dēdūco (3)
subtraction, dētractĭo, *f*
suburb, sŭburbĭum, *n*
suburban, sŭburbānus
subvert, *v.t*, ēverto (3)
succeed, *v.t*, (in, do well), bĕnĕ effĭcĭo (3); (of things), *v.i*, prospĕrē ēvĕnĭo (4); *v.t*, (follow), sĕquor (3 *dep*); (to an office), succēdo (3)
success, res sĕcundae, *f.pl*
successful (persons), fēlix; (things), prospĕrus
succession (to an office, etc.), successĭo, *f*; (series), contĭnŭātĭo, *f*

successive, contĭnŭus
successor, successor, *m*
succinct, brĕvis
succour, *nn*, auxĭlĭum, *n*
succour, *v.t*, succurro (3) (*with dat*)
succulent, sūcōsus
succumb, *v.i*, cēdo (3)
such, *adj*, tālis, hūius mŏdi (of this kind)
suck, *v.t*, sūgo (3)
sucker, planta, *f*
suckle, *v.t*, ūbĕra do (1) (*with dat*)
suction, suctus, *m*
sudden, sŭbĭtus
suddenly, *adv*, sŭbĭto, rĕpentē
sue, *v.t*, (in law), in ius vŏco (1); (— for, beg for), rŏgo (1)
suet, sēbum, *n*
suffer, *v.t*, pătĭor (3 *dep*); fĕro (*irreg*); (permit), permitto (3) (*with dat*); *v.i*, afficĭor (3 pass)
sufferance, pătĭentĭa, *f*
sufferer (of illness), aeger, *m*
suffering, *nn*, dŏlor, *m*
suffice, *v.i*, sătis esse (*irreg*)
sufficiency, *use adv*, sătis (enough)
sufficient, *use* sătis, *adv*, (with genit. of noun)
suffocate, *v.t*, suffōco (1)
suffrage, suffrāgĭum, *n*
sugar, sacchăron, *n*
suggest, *v.t*, sŭbĭcĭo (3) (*with acc. of thing and dat. of person*)
suggestion, admŏnĭtus, *m*
suicide, mors vŏluntārĭa, *f*; (to commit —), sĭbĭ mortem conscisco (3) (inflict death upon oneself)
suit (law —), lis, *f*; (clothes), vestīmenta, *n.pl*
suit, *v.i*, convĕnĭo (4); *or use impers. vb*, dĕcet (it —s)
suitable, aptus, ĭdōnĕus
suite (retinue), cŏmĭtes, *c, pl*
suitor, prŏcus, *m*
sulky, mōrōsus
sullen, torvus
sully, *v.t*, inquĭno (1)
sulphur, sulfur, *n*
sultry, aestŭōsus
sum (total), summa, *f*; (— of money), pĕcūnĭa, *f*
sum up, *v.t*, compŭto (1); (speak briefly), summātim dīco (3)
summarily, *adv*, (immediately), sĭne mŏrā
summary, *nn*, ĕpĭtŏme, *f*
summary, *adj*, (hasty), sŭbĭtus
summer, *nn*, aestas, *f*; *adj*, aestīvus
summit, căcūmen, *n, or use adj*, summus (top of)

summon, *v.t*, accesso (3)
summon up, *v.t*, excĭto (1)
summons, vŏcātĭo, *f*, accītu (*abl. case only:* at the — of)
sumptuous, sumptŭōsus
sumptuousness, appărātus, *m*
sun, sōl, *m*
sun, *v.i*, (— oneself), ăprīcor (1 *dep*)
sunbeam, rădĭus, (*m*) sōlis
sunburnt, ădustus
sundial, sōlārĭum, *n*
sunny, aprīcus
sunrise, ortus, (*m*) sōlis
sunset, occāsus, (*m*) sōlis
sunshine, sōl, *m*
sup, *v.i*, cēno (1)
superabound, *v.i*, sŭpersum (*irreg*)
superb, magnĭfĭcus
supercilious, sŭperbus
superficial, lĕvis
superfluous, sŭpervăcănĕus
superhuman, dīvīnus
superintend, *v.t*, prōcūro (1)
superintendent, cūrātor, *m*, prae-fectus, *m*
superior, sŭpĕrĭor; (to be —), *v.i*, sŭpĕro (1)
superiority, *use adj*, sŭpĕrĭor
superlative, exĭmĭus
supernatural, dīvīnus
supernumerary, ascriptīvus
superscription, tĭtŭlus, *m*
supersede, *v.t*, succēdo (3) (*with dat*)
superstition, sŭperstĭtĭo, *f*
superstitious, sŭperstĭtĭōsus
supervise, *v.t*, prōcūro (1)
supper, cēna, *f*
supplant, *v.t*. (surpass), praeverto (3)
supple, flexĭbĭlis
supplement, supplēmentum, *n*
suppliant, supplex, *c*
supplication, obsĕcrātĭo, *f*
supply, *nn*, cōpĭa, *f*; (supplies, esp. military), commĕātus, *m*
supply, *v.t*, suppĕdĭto (1); afféro(*irreg*)
support, *nn*, (bearing), firmāmen-tum, *n*; (military), subsĭdĭa, *n.pl*; (sustenance), ălĭmentum, *n*
support, *v.t*, sustĭnĕo (2); (aid), adiŭvo (1); (nourish), ălo (3)
supportable, tŏlĕrābĭlis
supporter, adiŭtor, *m*
suppose, *v.t*, pŭto (1), ŏpīnor (1 *pass*)
supposition, ŏpīnĭo, *f*
suppress, *v.t*, opprĭmo (3)
suppurate, *v.i*, suppūro (1)
supremacy, impĕrĭum, *n*
supreme, sŭprēmus
sure, certus; (reliable), fĭdēlis; (I am —), compertum hăbĕo (2)

surely, *adv*, prŏfecto; (no doubt), nīmīrum; (*in questions; if an affirmative answer is expected*) nonne; (*if a negative answer*), num
surety, vas, *m*, sponsor, *m*
surf, fluctus, *m*
surface, sŭperfĭcĭes, *f*
surge, *v.i*, surgo (3)
surgeon, chīrurgus, *m*
surgery, chīrurgĭa, *f*
surly, mōrōsus
surmise, *nn*, coniectūra, *f*
surmise, *v.t*, suspĭcor (1 *dep*)
surmount, *v.t*, sŭpĕro (1)
surname, cognōmen, *n*
surpass, *v.t*, sŭpĕro (1)
surplus, rĕlĭquum, *n*
surprise, *nn*, mīrātĭo, *f*
surprise, *v.t*, admīrātĭōnem mŏvĕo (2) (*with dat*); (to attack), ădŏrĭor (4 *dep*)
surrender, *nn*, dēdĭtĭo, *f*
surrender, *v.t*, dēdo (3), trādo (3); *v.i*, sē dēdĕre (3 *reflex*)
surround, *v.t*, cingo (3), circumdo (1)
survey, *v.t*, contemplor (1 *dep*); (land), mētĭor (4 *dep*)
surveyor, fīnĭtor, *m*
survive, *v.i*, sŭpersum (*irreg*)
survivor, sŭperstes, *m*, *f*
susceptibility, mollĭtĭa, *f*
susceptible, mollis
suspect, *v.t*, suspĭcor (1 *dep*)
suspend, *v.t*, suspendo (3); (inter-rupt), intermitto (3); (— from office), dēmŏvĕo (2)
suspense, dŭbĭtātĭo, *f*
suspension (interruption), intermissĭo, *f*
suspicion, suspĭcĭo, *f*
suspicious, suspĭcĭōsus
sustain, *v.t*, sustĭnĕo (2)
sustenance, ălĭmentum, *n*
swaddling-clothes, incūnābŭla, *n.pl*
swagger, *v.i*, sē iactāre (1 *reflex*)
swallow, *nn*, hĭrundo, *f*
swallow, *v.t*, gluttĭo (4), sorbĕo (2)
swamp, *nn*, pălus, *f*
swamp, *v.t*, opprĭmo (3)
swampy, pălūdōsus
swan, cycnus, *m*
swarm (people), turba, *f*; (bees), exāmen, *n*
swarm, *v.i*, glŏmĕror (1 *pass*)
swarthy, fuscus
swathe, *v.t*, collĭgo (1)
sway, *nn*, impĕrĭum, *n*
sway, *v.t*, (rule), rĕgo (3); *v.i* (— to and fro), văcillo (1)

For List of Abbreviations used, turn to pages 3, 4

swear, *v.i*, iūro (1); (— allegiance to), iūro in nōmen (*with genit. of person*)

sweat, *nn*, sūdor, *m*

sweat, *v.i*, sūdo (1)

sweep, *v.t*, verro (3)

sweet, dulcis

sweeten, *v.t*, dulcem reddo (3) (**make sweet**)

sweetheart, dēlīcĭae, *f. pl*

sweetness, dulcĭtūdo, *f*

swell, *nn*, (wave), fluctus, *m*

swell, *v.i*, tŭmĕo (2); *v.t*, augĕo (2)

swelling, tŭmor, *m*

swerve, *v.i*, dēclīno (1)

swift, *adj*, cĕler

swiftness, cĕlĕrĭtas, *f*

swill, *v.t*, (drink), pōto (1)

swim, *v.i*, nāto (1)

swimmer, nătātor, *m*

swimming, *nn*, nătātĭo, *f*

swindle, *nn*, fraus, *f*

swindle, *v.t*, fraudo (1)

swindler, fraudātor, *m*

swine, sūs, *m, f*

swineherd, sŭbulcus, *m*

swing, *nn*, oscillātĭo, *f*

swing, *v.t*, ăgĭto (1); *v.i*, pendĕo (2)

switch, (cane), virga, *f*

switch, *v.t*, mūto (1)

swollen, tŭmĭdus

swoon, *v.i*, *use phr*, ănĭmus rĕlinquit . . . (**sensibility leaves . . .**)

swoop, *nn*, *use vb*. advŏlo (1)

swoop on, *v.i*, advŏlo (1)

sword, glădĭus, *m*

sword-edge, ăcĭes, *f*

swordfish, xĭphĭas, *m*

sworn (treaty, etc.), confirmātus iūrĕiūrando (**confirmed by swearing**)

sycamore, sȳcămōrus, *f*

sycophant, sȳcŏphanta, *m*

syllable, syllăba, *f*

symbol, signum, *n*

symmetrical, congrŭens

symmetry, convĕnĭentĭa, *f*

sympathetic, mĭsĕrĭcors

sympathize, *v.t*, consentĭo (4)

sympathy, consensus, *m*

symphony, symphōnĭa, *f*

symptom, signum, *n*

synagogue, sŏnăgōga, *f*

syndicate, sŏcĭĕtas, *f*

synonym, verbum ĭdem signĭfĭcans (**word expressing the same thing**)

synopsis, ĕpĭtŏma, *f*

syntax, syntaxis, *f*

syringe, sīpho, *m*

syringe, *v.t*, aspergo (3) (**sprinkle**)

system, formŭla, *f*, rătĭo, *f*

systematic, ordĭnātus

T

table, mensa, *f*, tăbŭla, *f*; (**list**), index, *m*

tablecloth, mantēle, *n*

tablet, tăbŭla, *f*

tacit, tăcĭtus

taciturn, tăcĭturnus

tack, clāvŭlus, *m*

tack, *v.t*, (**fix**), fīgo (3); *v.i*,(ships), rēcīprŏcor (1 *pass*)

tackle (fittings), armāmenta, *n.pl*

tact, dextĕrĭtas, *f*, urbānĭtas, *f*

tactician, pĕrītus, (*m*) rēi mīlĭtāris

tactics (military), rătĭo, (*f*) bellandi (**method of making war**)

tadpole, rānuncŭlus, *m*

tag, *v.t*, *use* fīgo (3) (**fix**)

tail, cauda, *f*

tailor, vestītor, *m*

taint, *nn*, contāgĭo, *f*

taint, *v.t*, inficĭo (3)

take, *v.t*, căpĭo (3); (**grasp**), prĕhendo (3); (**receive**), accĭpĭo (3); (**seize**), răpĭo (3); (**take possession of**), occŭpo (1); (— **by storm**), expugno (1); (— **away**), aufĕro (*irreg*) ădĭmo (3); (— **in**), excĭpĭo (3); (— **off**), dēmo (3); (— **on**), suscĭpĭo (3); (— **up**), sūmo (3)

taking (**capture of a city**), expugnātĭo, *f*

tale, fābŭla, *f*

talent (**ability**), ingĕnĭum, *n*; (**money**), tălentum, *n*

talk, *nn*, sermo, *m*

talk, *v.i*, lŏquor (3 *dep*)

talkative, lŏquax

tall, prōcērus

tallness, prōcērĭtas, *f*

tallow, sēbum, *n*

tally, *v.i*, convĕnĭo (4)

talon, unguis, *m*

tamable, dŏmābĭlis

tame, *v.t*, dŏmo (1), mansŭĕfăcĭo (3)

tame, *adj*, mansŭĕfactus, dŏmĭtus

tameness, mansŭĕtūdo, *f*

tamer, dŏmĭtor, *m*

tamper with, *v.t*, tempto (1)

tan, *v.t*, (leather, etc.), confĭcĭo (3)

tangent, *use* līnĕa, *f*, (**line**)

tangible, tractābĭlis

tangle, *nn*, implĭcātĭo, *f*

tangle, *v.t*, implĭco (1)

tank, lăcus, *m*

tanner, cŏrĭārĭus, *m*

tantalize, *v.t*, (torment), fătīgo (1)

tap, *nn*, (blow), ictus, *m*

tap, *v.t*, (hit), fĕrĭo (4), pulso (1); *with*
lĕvĭter (lightly)

tape, taenĭa, *f*

taper, cērĕus, *m*

taper, *v.i*, fastīgor (1 *pass*)

tapestry, *use* vēlum, *n*, (curtain)

tar, pix līquĭda, *f*

tardiness, tardĭtas, *f*

tardy, tardus

tare, lōlĭum, *n*

target, scōpus, *m*

tarnish, *v.i*, hēbesco (3); *v.t*, inquĭno
(1)

tarry, *v.i*, mŏror (1 *dep*)

tart, *nn*, crustŭlum, *n*

tart, *adj*, ăcĭdus

task, ŏpus, *n*

taste, *nn*, (sense of —), gustātus, *m*;
(flavour), săpor, *m*; (judgement),
iudĭcĭum, *n*

taste, *v.t*, gusto (1); *v.i* (have a
flavour), săpĭo (3)

tasteful (elegant), ēlĕgans

tasteless, insulsus

tasty, săpĭdus

tattered, pannōsus

tatters, pannus, *m*

tattle, *v.i*, garrĭo (4)

taunt, *nn*, convĭcĭum, *n*

taunt, *v.t*, ŏbĭcĭo (3) (*dat. of person and
acc. of thing*)

taunting, *adj*, contŭmēlĭōsus

tavern, caupōna, *f*

tavern-keeper, caupo, *m*

tawdry, fūcōsus

tawny, fulvus

tax, *nn*, vectīgal, *n*

tax, *v.t*, (impose —), vectīgal impōno
(3) (*with dat*)

taxable, vectīgālis

tax-collector, exactor, *m*, pūblĭcānus,
m

teach, *v.t*, dŏcĕo (2) (*with acc. of person
and acc. of thing*)

teacher, doctor, *m*, măgister, *m*

teaching, *nn*, doctrīna, *f*

team (— of horses), iŭgum, *n*

tear, *nn*, lăcrĭma, *f*; (to shed —s),
lăcrĭmas fundo (3); (rent), scissūra, *f*

tear, *v.t*, scindo (3); (— away),
abscindo (3); (— down, open),
rescindo (3); (— up, in pieces),
distrăho (3)

tearful, flēbĭlis

tease, *v.t*, obtundo (3)

teat, mamma, *f*

technical, *use phr*, prŏprĭus artis
(particular to a skill)

tedious, lentus

teem with, *v.i*, scătĕo (2)

teethe, *v.i*, dentĭo (4)

teething, *nn*, dentītĭo, *f*

tell, *v.t*, (give information), dīco (3);
narro (1) (*with acc. of thing said and
dat. of person told*), certĭōrem făcĭo
(3) (*acc. of person told, foll. by* dē
with abl. of thing said); (order),
iŭbĕo (2)

teller (counter), nŭmĕrātor, *m*

temerity, tĕmĕrĭtas, *f*

temper (of mind), ănĭmus, *m*; (bad —),
īrācundĭa, *f*

temper, *v.t*, tempĕro (1)

temperament, nātūra, *f*, ingĕnĭum,
n

temperance, tempĕrantĭa, *f*

temperate, tempĕrātus

temperate climate, tĕmpĕrĭes, *f*

temperateness, mŏdĕrātĭo, *f*

tempest, tempestas, *f*

tempestuous, prŏcellōsus

temple, templum, *n*, aedes, *f*; (of the
head), tempus, *n*

temporal, hūmānus

temporary, *use adv. phr*, ad tempŭs
(for the time being)

tempt, *v.t*, tento (1)

temptation (allurement), illĕcĕbra, *f*

tempter, tentātor, *m*

tempting, *adj*, illĕcĕbrōsus

ten, dĕcem; (— each), dēni; (—
times), *adv*, dĕcĭes

tenacious, tĕnax

tenacity, tĕnācĭtas, *f*

tenant, inquĭlīnus, *m*

tend, *v.t*, (care for), cŏlo (3); *v.i*, (go,
direct oneself), tendo (3); (incline
to), inclīno (1); (be accustomed),
consŭesco (3)

tendency, inclīnātĭo, *f*

tender, *adj*, tĕner, mollis

tender, *v.t*, (offer), dēfĕro (*irreg*)

tenderness, mollĭtĭa, *f*, indulgentĭa, *f*

tenement, conductum, *n*

tenour (course), tĕnor, *m*, cursus, *m*

tense, *adj*, tentus, intentus

tense, *nn*, tempus, *n*

tension, intentĭo, *f*

tent, tăbernācŭlum, *n*; (general's —),
praetōrĭum, *n*

tentacle, cornĭcŭlum, *n*

tenth, dĕcĭmus

tepid, ēgĕlĭdus, tĕpĭdus; (to be —),
v.i, tĕpĕo (2)

term (period of time), spătĭum, *n*; (limit), fīnis, *m*; (word), verbum, *n*; (condition), condĭcĭo, *f*

term, *v.t,* vŏco (1)

terminate, *v.t,* termĭno (1)

termination, fīnis, *m*

terrace, sōlārĭum, *n*

terrestrial, terrestris

terrible, terrĭbĭlis

terrify, *v.t,* terrĕo (2)

territory, fīnes, *m. pl,* ăger, *m*

terror, terror, *m,* păvor, *m*

terse, brĕvis

terseness, brĕvĭtas, *f*

test, *nn,* expĕrīmentum, *n*

test, *v.t,* expĕrĭor (4 *dep*)

testament, testāmentum, *n*

testator, testātor, *m*

testify, *v.t,* testĭfĭcor (1 *dep*)

testimony, testĭmōnĭum, *n*

testy, stŏmăchōsus

text, scriptum, *n*

textile, textĭle, *n*

texture, textus, *m*

than, *conj,* quam

thank, *v.t,* grātĭas ăgo (3) (*with dat. of person*)

thankfulness, grātus ănĭmus, *m*

thankless, ingrātus

thanks, grātĭae, *f. pl*

thanksgiving, actĭo, (*f*) grātĭārum

that, *demonstrative pron,* ille, is, iste

that, *relative pron,* qui, quae, quad

that, *conj,* (*with purpose or consecutive clauses*) ut (ne *if negative*); (*after vbs introducing statements*) no separate word, but rendered by the expression itself: e.g. he said that the king was coming, rēgem vĕnīre dixit

thatch, strāmentum, *n*

thaw, *v.t,* solvo (3); *v.i,* sē rĕsolvĕre (3 *reflex*)

the, *no equivalent in Latin*

theatre, thĕātrum, *n*

theatrical, thĕātrālis

theft, furtum, *n*

their, *reflexive,* sŭus; *otherwise* ĕōrum, (*f,* ĕārum)

them, *use appropriate case of pron,* is, ille, iste

theme, prŏpŏsĭtĭo, *f*

themselves, *reflexive pron,* sē; (emphatic), ipsi, ae, a

then, *adv. of* (time), tum (therefore), ĭgĭtur

thence, *adv,* inde, illinc

theologian, thĕŏlŏgus, *m*

theology, thĕŏlŏgĭa, *f*

theorem, thĕōrēma, *n*

theoretical, rătĭōnālis

theory, rătĭo, *f*

there (in *or* at that place), ĭbĭ; (to that place), ĕō; (— is), est; (— are), sunt (*from* esse)

thereabouts, *adv,* circā

thereafter, *adv,* dĕinde

therefore, *adv,* ĭgĭtur, ergo

thereupon, *adv,* sŭbinde

thesis, prŏpŏsĭtum, *n*

they, *as subject of vb. usually not rendered; otherwise use* ĭi, illi, isti.

thick, crassus, densus, confertus

thicken, *v.t,* denso (1); *v.i,* concresco (3)

thicket, dūmētum, *n*

thick-headed, crassus

thickness, crassĭtūdo, *f*

thick-set (of body), compactus

thick-skinned, (indifferent), neglĕgens

thief, fur, *c*

thieve, *v.t,* fūror (1 *dep*)

thieving, *nn,* (theft), furtum, *n*

thigh, fĕmur, *n*

thin, tĕnŭis, grăcĭlis

thin, *v.t,* tĕnŭo (1)

thing, rēs, *f*

think, *v.t,* cōgĭto (1); (believe, suppose), crēdo (3), arbĭtror (1 *dep*), pŭto (1), existĭmo (1)

thinker, phĭlŏsŏphus, *m*

thinness, tĕnŭĭtas, *f*

third, *adj,* tertĭus; (a — part), tertĭa pars, *f*; (thirdly), *adv,* tertĭo

thirst, *v.i,* sĭtĭo (4)

thirst, *nn,* sĭtis, *f*

thirsty, sĭtĭens

thirteen, trĕdĕcim

thirteenth, tertĭus dĕcĭmus

thirtieth, trĭgēsĭmus

thirty, trĭginta

this, *demonstrative pron,* hĭc, haec, hōc

thistle, cardŭus, *m*

thither, *adv,* ĕō, illūc; (hither and —), hūc atque illūc

thong, lōrum, *n*

thorn, sentis, *m,* spīna, *f*

thorn-bush, vĕpres, *m*

thorny, spīnōsus

thorough, perfectus; (exact), subtīlis

thoroughbred, gĕnĕrōsus

thoroughfare, pervĭum, *n*

those, *demonstrative pron,* illi

though, *conj,* etsi

thought (act or faculty of thinking), cōgĭtātĭo, *f*; (opinion), cōgĭtātum, *n*; (plan, intention), consĭlĭum, *n*

thoughtful (careful), prŏvĭdus; (deep in thought), multa pŭtans thoughtfulness, cūra, f, cōgĭtātĭo, f

thoughtless, tĕmĕrārĭus, inconsultus

thoughtlessness, nĕglegentĭa, f, tĕmĕrĭtas, f

thousand, mille (*indeclinable adj*); in pl, mīlĭa (*n.pl, nn*)

thrash, *v.t.* tundo (3); (**corn**), tĕro (3)

thrashing, *nn*, trītūra, f; (**chastisement**), verbĕrātĭo, f

thrashing-floor, ārĕa, f

thread, fīlum, n

thread, *v.t*, (**— one's way**), sē insĭnŭāre (1 *reflex*)

threadbare, obsŏlētus

threat, mĭnae, f. pl

threaten, *v.t.* mĭnor (1 *dep*) (*with acc. of thing and dat. of person*); *v.i,* (**impend**), immĭnĕo (2)

threatening, *adj*, mĭnax

three, tres; (**— each**), terni; (**— times**), *adv,* ter

threefold (**triple**), trĭplex

threehundred, trēcenti

threehundredth, trēcentēsĭmus

thresh, *v.t.* tĕro (3)

threshold, līmen, n

thrice, *adj,* ter

thrift, frūgālĭtas, f

thrifty, parcus

thrill, *v.t,* use afficĭo (3) (**affect**)

thrill (**of pleasure**), hĭlărĭtas, f; (**a shock**), stringor, m

thrilling, *adj,* use *vb,* afficĭo (3) (**to affect**)

thrive, *v.i,* vĭgĕo (2)

throat, fauces, f. pl

throb, *v.i,* palpĭto (1)

throbbing, *nn*, palpĭtātĭo, f

throne, sŏlĭum, n; (**regal, imperial power**), regnum, n

throng, *nn*, multĭtūdo, f

throng, *v.t,* cĕlĕbro (1)

throttle, *v.t,* strangŭlo (1)

through, *prep*, per (*with acc*); (**on account of**), propter (*with acc*)

through, *adv, often expressed by a compound vb, with per: e.g. perfĕro (carry through)*

throughout, *prep*, per; *adv,* pĕnĭtus (**entirely, wholly**)

throw, *nn*, iactus, m

throw, *v.t,* iăcĭo (3), cōnĭcĭo (3) (**— away**), ăbĭcĭo (3); (**— back**), rēĭcĭo (3); (**— down**), dēĭcĭo (3); (**— oneself at the feet of**), se prōĭcĕre ad pĕdes (*with genit. of person*); (**— out**), ēĭcĭo (3)

thrush, turdus, m

thrust, *nn*, pĕtītĭo, f

thrust, *v.t*, trūdo (3); (**— forward**), prōtrūdo (3)

thumb, pollex, m

thump, *nn,* cŏlăphus, m

thump, *v.t*, tundo (3)

thunder, *nn*, tŏnĭtrus, m; (**— bolt**), fulmen, n

thunder, *v.i,* tŏno (1)

thunderstruck, attŏnĭtus

thus, *adv,* ĭta, sīc

thwart, *nn*, (**seat**), transtrum, n

thwart, *v.t,* obsto (1) (*with dat. of person*), impĕdĭo (4)

tiara, tĭāra, f

ticket, tessĕra, f

tickle, *v.t,* tītillo (1)

tickling, *nn*, tītillātĭo, f

ticklish, lūbrĭcus

tide, aestus, m

tidiness, mundĭtĭa, f

tidings, nuntĭus, m

tidy, mundus

tie, *nn*, vincŭlum, n

tie, *v.t*, lĭgo (1), nōdo (1)

tier, ordo, m

tiger, tigris, c

tight, strictus

tighten, *v.t*, stringo (3)

tile, tēgŭla, f

till, *prep*, usque ad (*with acc*)

till, *conj*, dum, dōnĕc

till, *nn*, arca, f

till, *v.t*, cŏlo (3)

tillage, tillage, *nn*, cultus, m

tiller (**boat**), clāvus, (m) gŭbernācŭli (**handle of the rudder**)

tilt, *v.t,* (**bend**), dēclīno (1)

timber, mātĕrĭa, f

time, tempus, n; (**period, space of —**), intervallum, n, spătĭum, n; (**generation, age**), aetas, f; (**— of day**), hōra, f; (**at the right —**), *adv. phr*, ad tempus; (**at —s**), *adv,* interdum; (**once upon a —**), *adv,* ōlim; (**at the same —**), *adv,* sĭmŭl; (**at that —**), *adv,* tum

timely, *adj,* opportūnus

timid, tĭmĭdus

timidity, tĭmĭdĭtas, f

tin, plumbum album, n

tincture, cŏlor, m

tinder, fōmes, m

tinge, *v.t,* tingo (3)

tingle, *v.i,* prūrĭo (4)

tinker, făber, m, (**artificer**)

tinkle, *v.i,* tinnĭo (4)

tiny, exĭgŭus, parvŭlus

tip, căcūmen, n

tip, *v.t*, (**put a point on**), praefīgo (3); (**tip over**), verto (3)

For List of Abbreviations used, turn to pages 3, 4

tire, *v.t*, fătīgo (1); *v.i*, dēfătīgor (1 *dep*)

tired, fessus

tiresome, mŏlestus

tissue, textus, *m*

tit-bits, cūpēdĭa, *n.pl*

tithe, dĕcŭma, *f*

title, tĭtŭlus, *m*

titled (of nobility), nōbĭlis

titter, *nn*, rīsus, *m*

to, *prep*, (motion towards a place, and expressions of time), ad (*with acc*); (*sometimes, e.g. names of towns, acc. of nn. alone*); often dat. case can be used, *e.g. indirect object after vb.* to give; (*before a clause expressing purpose*), ut; (*sometimes indicates the infinitive of a vb*), *e.g.* to love, ămāre

toad, būfo, *m*

toast, *v.t*, torrĕo (2); (a person's health), prŏpīno (1) (*with dat. of person*)

today, *adv*, hŏdĭē

toe, dĭgĭtus, *m*

together, *adv*, sĭmŭl, ūnā

toil, *nn*, lăbor, *m*

toil, *v.i*, lăbōro (1)

toilet (care of person, etc.), cultus, *m*

token, signum, *n*

tolerable, tŏlĕrābĭlis

tolerance, tŏlĕrantĭa, *f*

tolerate, *v.t*, tŏlĕro (1)

toll, *nn*, vectīgal, *n*

tomb, sĕpulcrum, *n*, tŭmŭlus, *m*

tombstone, lăpis, *m*

tomorrow, *adv*, crās

tomorrow, *nn*, crastīnus dĭes, *m*

tone, sŏnus, *m*

tongs, forceps, *m*

tongue, lingua, *f*

tonight, *adv*, hŏdĭē nocte

tonsils, tonsillae, *f. pl*

too (also), ĕtĭam; (— little), părum; (— much), nĭmis; *comparative adj. or adv. can be used, e.g.* too far, longĭus

tool, instrūmentum, *n*

tooth, dens, *m*

toothache, dŏlor (*m*) dentĭum

toothed, dentātus

toothless, ēdentŭlus

toothpick, dentiscalpĭum, *n*

top, *use adj*, summus *in agreement with nn, e.g.* the top of the rock, summum saxum, *n*; (summit), căcūmen, *n*

top, *v.t*, sŭpĕro (1)

topic, rēs, *f*

topmost, summus

topography, *use phr*, nătūra (*f*) lŏci (nature of the land)

torch, fax, *f*

torment, *nn*, crŭcĭātus, *m*

torment, *v.t*, crŭcĭo (1)

tornado, turbo, *m*

torpid, torpens, pĭger

torpor, torpor, *m*

torrent, torrens, *m*

tortoise, testūdo, *f*

tortuous, sĭnŭōsus

torture, *nn*, crŭcĭātus, *m*

torture, *v.t*, crŭcĭo (1)

torturer, carnĭfex, *m*

toss, *nn*, iactus, *m*

toss, *v.t*, iacto (1)

total, *nn*, summa, *f*

total, *adj*, tōtus

totally, *adv*, omnīno

totter, *v.i*, lābo (1)

touch, *nn*, tactus, *m*; (contact), contāgĭo, *f*

touch, *v.t*, tango (3), attingo (3); (move), mŏvĕo (2)

touchy, stŏmăchōsus

tough, *adj*, lentus

toughness, dūrĭtĭa, *f*

tour, pĕrĕgrīnātĭo, *f*, ĭter, *n*

tourist, pĕrĕgrīnātor, *m*

tournament, *use* certāmen, *n*, (contest)

tow, *v.t*, trăho (3)

tow, *nn*, (hemp), stuppa, *f*

towards, *prep*, (of direction, position) ad (*with acc*); (of time), sub (*with acc*); (emotions), ergā, in (*with acc*); (with names of towns), versus (*placed after the noun*)

towel, mantēle, *n*

tower, *nn*, turris, *f*

tower, *v.i*, exsto (1)

town, urbs, *f*, oppĭdum, *n*

townsman, oppĭdānus, *m*

toy (child's rattle), crĕpundĭa, *n.pl*

toy with, *v.i*, illūdo (3)

trace, *nn*, vestīgĭum, *n*, signum, *n*

trace, *v.t*, sĕquendo invĕnĭo (4) (find by following)

track, *nn*, (path), callis, *m*; (footsteps, etc.), vestigĭum, *n*

track, *v.t* (— down), investīgo (1); (pursue), sĕquor (3 *dep*)

trackless, ăvĭus

tract (region), rĕgĭo, *f*; (booklet), lĭbellus, *m*

tractable, dŏcĭlis

trade, mercātūra, *f*; (a particular —), ars, *f*

trade, *v.i*, mercātūram făcĭo (3)

trader, mercātor, *m*

tradition, mĕmŏrĭa, *f*

traditional, *use phr*, trādĭtus ā māĭōrĭbus (handed down from our ancestors)⁴

traffic (trade, etc.), commercĭum, *n*; (streets, etc.), *use phr. with* frĕquento (1) (to crowd)

tragedy, trăgoedĭa, *f*

tragic, trăgĭcus; (unhappy), tristis

trail (path), callis, *m*

train, ordo, *m*; (procession), pompa, *f. pl*; (of a dress), pēnĭcŭlāmentum, *n*

train, *v.t*, instĭtŭo (3), exercĕo (2)

trainer, exercĭtor, *m*

training, *nn*, disciplīna, *f*

traitor, prŏdĭtor, *m*

traitorous, perfĭdus

tramp, *v.i*, ambŭlo (1)

trample on, *v.t*, obtĕro (3)

trance (elation, exaltation), ēlātĭo, *f*

tranquil, tranquillus, plăcĭdus

transact, *v.t*, ăgo (3)

transaction, rēs, *f*, nĕgŏtĭum, *n*

transcend, *v.t*, sŭpĕro (1)

transcribe, *v.t*, transcrībo (3)

transfer, *nn*, (of property), mancĭpĭum, *n*

transfer, *v.t*, transfĕro (*irreg*)

transfix, *v.t*, transfīgo (3)

transform, *v.t*, mūto (1)

transgress, *v.t*, vĭŏlo (1); *v.i*, pecco (1)

transgression (fault), dēlictum, *n*

transit, transĭtus, *m*

transitory, cădūcus

translate, *v.t*, verto (3)

translation (a work), ŏpus translātum, *n*; (act), translātĭo, *f*

translator, interpres, *c*

transmigrate, *v.i*, transmĭgro (1)

transmit, *v.t*, transmitto (3)

transparent, perlūcĭdus

transpire, *v.i*, (get about), vulgor (1 *pass*)

transplant, *v.t*, transfĕro (*irreg*)

transport, *nn*, *use vb. below*; (joy), laetĭtĭa, *f*, exsultātĭo, *f*

transport, *v.t*, transporto (1), trāĭcĭo (3)

trap, *nn*, insĭdĭae, *f. pl*; (for animals), lăquĕus, *m*

trap, *v.t*, *use phr*, illĭcĭo (3) in insĭdĭas (entice into a trap)

trappings, insignĭa, *n.pl*

trash, scrūta, *n.pl*, nūgae, *f. pl*

travel, *nn*, ĭter, *n*

travel, *v.i*, ĭter făcĭo (3)

traveller, vĭātor, *m*

traverse, *v.t*, ŏbĕo (4)

travesty (mockery), lūdĭbrĭum, *n*

tray, fercŭlum, *n*

treacherous, perfĭdus

treachery, perfĭdĭa, *f*, fraus, *f*

tread, *nn*, grădus, *m*

tread, *v.i*, ingrĕdĭor (3 *dep*); *v.t* (— on), calco (1)

treason, māiestas, *f*

treasure, ŏpes *f. pl*; (hoard, treasure-house), thēsaurus, *m*

treasure, *v.t*, (regard highly), magni aestĭmo (1); (store up), rĕcondo (3)

treasurer, praefectus, (*m*) aerārĭi (director of the treasury)

treasury, aerārĭum, *n*

treat, *nn*, dēlectātĭo, *f*

treat, *v.t*, (deal with, behave towards), hăbĕo (2); (medically), cūro (1); (discuss), ăgo (3)

treatise, lĭber, *m*

treatment, tractātĭo, *f*; (cure), cūrātĭo, *f*

treaty, foedus, *n*

treble, *adj*, trĭplex

treble, *v.t*, trĭplĭco (1)

tree, arbor, *f*

trellis, cancelli, *m. pl*

tremble, *v.i*, trĕmo (3)

trembling, *nn*, trĕmor, *m*

tremendous, ingens

tremulous, trĕmŭlus

trench, fossa, *f*

trepidation, trĕpĭdātĭo, *f*

trespass (crime), dēlictum, *n*

trespass, *v.i*, *use phr. with* ingrĕdi (to enter), *and* te (me, *etc*.), invīto (without your (my) permission)

tress (hair), grădus, *m*

trial (legal), iūdĭcĭum, *n*; (experiment), expĕrĭentĭa, *f*

triangle, trĭangŭlum, *n*

triangular, trĭangŭlus

tribe (Roman), trĭbus, *f*; (other), pŏpŭlus, *m*

tribunal, iūdĭcĭum, *n*

tribune, trĭbūnus, *m*

tributary, *adj*, (paying tribute), vectĭgālis

.tributary, *nn*, (river), *use phr*, qui in flūmen inflŭit (which flows into a river)

tribute, trĭbūtum, ·*n*, vectĭgal, *n*

trick, *nn*, dŏlus, *m*, fraus, *f*

trick, *v.t*, dēcĭpĭo (3)

trickery, dŏlus, *m*

trickle, *v.i*, māno (1)

trickster, hŏmo dŏlōsus, fallax

tricky (dangerous), pĕrĭcŭlōsus

trident, trĭdens, *m*

tried (well —), prŏbātus

trifle, *nn*, rēs parva, *f*, nūgae, *f. pl*

trifle, *v.i*, lūdo (3)

trifling, *adj*, lēvis

trim, *adj*, nĭtĭdus

trim, *v.t*, pŭto (1)

trinkets, mundus, *m*

trip, *nn*, (journey), ĭter, *n*

trip, *v.t*, supplanto (1); *v.i* (stumble), offendo (3), lābor (3 dep)

tripe, ŏmāsum, *n*

triple, trĭplex

tripod, trĭpūs, *m*

trite, trītus

triumph (Roman celebration of victory), trĭumphus, *m*; (victory), victōrĭa, *f*

triumph, *v.i, and v.t*, trĭumpho (1)

triumphant, victor

triumvirate, trĭumvĭrātus, *m*

trivial, lēvis, vīlis

troop (band), mănus, *f*; (— of cavalry), turma, *f*; (—s), cōpĭae, *f, pl*

troop, *v.i*, conflŭo (3)

trooper, ĕques, *m*

trophy, trŏpaeum, *n*

trot, *nn*, lentus cursus, *m*

trot, *v.i*, lento cursu ĕo (4); (proceed on a slow course)

trouble, *nn*, (disadvantage), incommŏdum, *n*; (exertion), ŏpĕra, *f*; (commotion), tŭmultus, *m*; (annoyance), mŏlestĭa, *f*

trouble, *v.t*, (disturb), sollĭcĭto (1); (harass), vexo (1); (— oneself about), cūro (1)

troublesome, mŏlestus

trough, alvĕus, *m*

trousers, brācae, *f. pl*

trowel, trulla, *f*

truant, *nn, use phr*, qui consultō ăbest (who is absent deliberately)

truce, indūtĭae, *f. pl*

truck, plaustrum, *m*

truculent (grim), trux

trudge, *v.i, use phr*, aegrē ambŭlo (1) (walk with difficulty)

true, vērus; (faithful), fīdus

truffle, tūber, *n*

truly, *adv*, vērē, prŏfectō

trumpery, scrūta, *n.pl*

trumpet, *nn*, tŭba, *f*, būcĭna, *f*

trumpeter, tŭbĭcen, *m*

truncheon, fustis, *m*

trundle, *v.t*, volvo (3)

trunk, truncus, *m*; (of elephant) prŏboscis, *f*; (box), arca, *f*

truss, fascĭa, *f*

trust, *nn*, fīdes, *f*

trust, *v.t*, confīdo (3 *semi-dep*) (*with dat. of person*), crēdo (3); (commit to), committo (3)

trustworthy, trusty certus, fīdus

truth, vērĭtas, *f*; (true things), vēra, *n.pl*; (in —), *adv*, vēro

truthful, vērax

truthfulness, vērĭtas, *f*

try, *v.i*, (attempt), cōnor (1 *dep*); *v.t*, (put to the test), tento (1); (— in court), iūdĭco (1)

trying, *adj*, mŏlestus

tub, lābrum, *n*

tube, tŭbŭlus, *m*

tuber, tūber, *n*

tubular, tŭbŭlātus

tuck up, *v.t*, succingo (3)

tuft, crīnis, *m*

tug, *v.t*, trăho (3)

tuition, instĭtūtĭo, *f*

tumble, *nn*, cāsus, *m* ·

tumble, *v.i*, cădo (3)

tumbler (beaker), pōcŭlum, *n*

tumour, tŭmor, *m*

tumult, tŭmultus, *m*

tumultuous, tŭmultŭōsus

tun (cask), dōlĭum, *n*

tune (melody), cantus, *m*; (out of —), *adj*, absŏnus

tune, *v.t*, (stringed instrument), tendo (3)

tuneful, cănōrus

tunic, tŭnĭca, *f*

tunnel, cănālis, *m*, cŭnĭcŭlus, *m*

tunny fish, thunnus, *m*

turban, mĭtra, *f*

turbid, turbĭdus

turbot, rhombus, *m*

turbulence, tŭmultus, *m*

turbulent, turbŭlentus

turf, caespes, *m*

turgid, turgĭdus

turmoil, turba, *f*, tŭmultus, *m*

turn (movement), conversĭo, *f*; (bending), flexus, *m*; (change), commūtātĭo, *f*; (by —s, in —), *adv*, invĭcem, per vĭces; (a good —), offĭcĭum, *n*

turn, *v.t*, verto (3); (bend), flecto (3); (— aside), dēflecto (3); *v.i*, sē dēclīnāre (1 *reflex*); (— away), āverto (3); (— the back), *v.i*, tergum verto (3); (change), *v.i*, mūtor (1 *pass*); (— back), *v.i*, rĕvertor (3 *pass*); (— out), *v.t*, ēĭcĭo (3); *v.i*, ēvĕnĭo (4); (— round), *v.t*, circumăgo (3); *v.i*, circumăgor (3 *pass*)

turning, *nn*, flexus, *m*

turnip, rāpum, *n*

turpitude, turpĭtūdo, *f*
turret, turris, *f*
turtle-dove, turtur, *m*
tusk, dens, *m*
tutelage, tūtēla, *f*
tutor, măgister, *m*
twang, *nn*, sŏnĭtus, *m*
twang, *v.i*, sŏno (1)
tweak, *v.t*, vellĭco (1)
tweezers, volsella, *f*
twelfth, dŭŏdĕcĭmus
twelve, dŭŏdĕcim; (— each), duodeni
twentieth, vīcēsĭmus
twenty, vīginti
twice, *adj*, bis
twig, rāmŭlus, *m*
twilight, crĕpuscŭlum, *n*
twin, *nn and adj*, gĕmĭnus
twine, *nn*, līnum, *n*
twine, *v.t*, circumplĭco (1); *v.i*, circumplector (3 *dep*)
twinge, *nn*, dŏlor, *m*
twinkle, *v.i*, mĭco (1)
twirl, *v.t*, verso (1)
twist, *v.t*, torquĕo (2); *v.i*, sē tor-
  quēre (2 *reflex*)
twit, *v.t*, ōbĭcĭo(3) (*acc. of thing and
  dat, of person*)
twitch, *v.t*, vellĭco (1)
twitter, *v.i*, (chirp), pīpĭlo (1)
two, dŭŏ; (— each), bīni
two-fold, dŭplex
two-footed, bĭpes
two hundred, dŭcenti
type (class, sort), gĕnus, *n*; (example),
  exemplar, *n*
typical, *use adj*, ūsĭtātus (familiar)
tyrannical, tўrannĭcus, sŭperbus
tyrannize, *v.i*, dŏmĭnor (1 *dep*)
tyranny, dŏmĭnātĭo, *f*
tyrant, tўrannus, *m*

U

ubiquitous, praesens (present)
udder, ūber, *n*
ugliness, dēformĭtas, *f*
ugly, dēformĭs
ulcer, vŏmĭca, *f*
ulcerate, *v.i*, suppūro (1)
ulceration, ulcĕrātĭo, *f*
ulcerous, ulcĕrōsus
ulterior, ultĕrĭor
ultimate, ultĭmus
ultimatum (to present —) ultĭmam
  condĭcĭōnem ferre (*irreg*)
umbrage (to take — at), *v.t*, aegrē fĕro
  (*irreg*)
umbrella, umbella, *f*
umpire, arbĭter, *m*

un-, *prefix, often* nōn, haud, *can be
  used*
unabashed,   intrĕpĭdus;   (brazen),
  impŭdens
unabated, immĭnūtus
unable, *use vb. phr. with* non posse (to
  be unable)
unacceptable, ingrātus
unaccompanied, incŏmĭtātus
unaccomplished, infectus
unaccountable, inexplĭcābĭlis
unaccustomed, insŏlĭtus
unacquainted, ignārus
unadorned, ĭnornātus
unadulterated, sincērus
unadvisable (foolhardy), audax
unadvised, inconsĭdĕrātus
unaffected (natural), simplex; (untouched), intĕger
unaided, *use adv. phr*, sĭne auxĭlĭo
  (without help)
unalloyed, pūrus
unalterable, immūtābĭlis
unambitious, hŭmĭlis
unanimity, ūnănĭmĭtas, *f*
unanimous, ūnĭversus (all together)
unanimously, *adv*, ūnā vōce
unanswerable, non rĕvincendus
unanswered, *use vb*. rĕspondĕo (2) (to
  answer)
unappeased, implācātus
unapproachable, nōn ădĕundus
unarmed, ĭnermis
unassailable, inexpugnābĭlis
unassailed, intactus
unassuming, mŏdestus
unattainable, *use phr. with vb*. attingo
  (3) (to reach)
unattempted, ĭnexpertus
unauthorized, illĭcĭtus
unavailing, fūtĭlis
unavoidable, ĭnēvĭtābĭlis
unaware, inscĭus
unawares, *adv*, dē imprōvīso
unbar, *v.t*, rĕsĕro (1)
unbearable, intŏlĕrābĭlis
unbecoming, indĕcōrus
unbelieving, incrēdŭlus
unbend, *v.t*, rĕmitto (3)
unbending, rĭgĭdus
unbiassed, intĕger
unbidden, iniussus
unbind, *v.t*, solvo (3)
unblemished, pūrus
unbound, sŏlūtus
unbounded, infinĭtus
unbreakable, *use phr*, quod frangi non
  pŏtest (that cannot be broken)
unbridled, effrēnātus
unbroken, intĕger, perpĕtŭus

For List of Abbreviations used, turn to pages 3, 4

unbuckle, *v.t,* diffībŭlo (1)
unburden, *v.t,* exŏnĕro (1)
unburied, īnhŭmātus
uncared for, neglectus
unceasing, perpĕtŭus
uncertain, incertus, dŭbĭus; (to be —),
  v.i, dŭbĭto (1)
uncertainty, dŭbĭtātĭo, *f*
unchangeable, immūtābĭlis
unchanged, constans; (to remain —),
  v.i, permănĕo (2)
uncharitable, inhūmānus
uncivil, inurbānus
uncivilized, incultus
uncle (father's side), pătrŭus, *m;*
  (mother's side), ăvuncŭlus, *m*
unclean, inquīnātus
unclouded, sĕrēnus
uncoil, *v.t,* ēvolvo (3); *v.i,* se ēvolvĕre
  (3 *reflex*)
uncombed, incomptus
uncomfortable, mŏlestus
uncommon, rārus, insŏlītus
uncompleted, imperfectus
unconcerned, sēcūrus
unconditional, simplex; (to surrender -ly), mănŭ do (1)
uncongenial, ingrātus
unconnected, disiunctus
unconquerable, invictus
unconquered, invictus
unconscious (unaware), inscĭus; (insensible), *use phr,* sensu ablāto (with
  feeling withdrawn)
unconstitutional, non lēgĭtĭmus
uncontaminated, incontāmĭnātus
uncontested, *use phr,* quod in con-
  tentĭōnem non vēnit (that has not
  come into dispute)
uncontrollable, impŏtens
uncontrolled, lĭber
uncooked, incoctus
uncouth, incultus
uncover, *v.t,* dētĕgo (3)
unction, unctĭo, *f*
uncultivated, incultus; (person),
  ăgrestis
uncut (hair), intonsus, prōmissus
undamaged, intĕger
undaunted, fortis
undeceive, *v.t,* errōrem ērĭpĭo (3)
undecided, incertus; (of a battle),
  anceps
undefended, nūdus, indēfensus
undeniable, certus
under, *prep,* sub (*with abl.* to denote
  rest, *and* acc. *to denote motion*);
  infra (*with acc*); (— the leadership

of), *use abl. phr, e.g.* tŭ dūce (—
  your leadership)
underclothes, sŭbūcŭla, *f*
under-current, flŭentum subterlābens,
  n
underestimate, *v.t,* mĭnōris aestĭmo (1)
undergo, *v.t,* sŭbĕo (3), fĕro (*irreg*)
underground, *adj,* subterrānĕus
undergrowth, virgulta, *n.pl*
underhand, *adj,* clandestīnus
underlying (lying hidden), lătens
undermine, *v.t,* subrŭo (3)
undermost, *adj,* infĭmus
underneath, *adv,* infrā
underrate, *v.t,* mĭnōris aestĭmo (1)
understand, *v.t,* intellĕgo (3), comprĕhendo (3)
understanding, *nn,* mens, *f;* (agreement), conventum, *n*
undertake, *v.t,* suscĭpĭo (3); (put in
  hand), incĭpĭo (3)
undertaker, vespillo, *m*
undertaking, *nn,* inceptum, *n*
undervalue, *v.t,* mĭnōris aestĭmo (1)
undeserved, immĕrĭtus
undeserving, indignus
undesirable, *use phr. with* nōn *and*
  cŭpĭo (3) *or* expĕto (3) (to desire)
undetected, tectus
undeveloped, immātūrus
undigested, crūdus
undiminished, immĭnūtus
undisciplined, inexercĭtātus
undisguised, non dissĭmŭlātus
undistinguished, ignōbĭlis
undisturbed, stăbĭlis, immōtus
undo, *v.t,* solvo (3); (render ineffec-
  tual), irrĭtum făcĭo (3)
undone, infectus
undoubted, certus
undoubtedly, *adv,* sīne dŭbĭo
undress, *v.t,* vestem dētrăho (3) (*with
  dat. of person*)
undressed, *adj,* nūdus
undue, nĭmĭus
undulate, *v.i,* fluctŭo (1)
unduly, *adv,* (excessively), nĭmĭum
undying, immortālis
unearth, *v.t,* dētĕgo (3)
unearthly, *adv, use* terrĭbĭlis (frightful)
uneasiness, anxĭĕtas, *f*
uneasy, anxĭus
uneducated, indoctus
unemployed, ōtĭōsus
unending, aeternus, infinītus
unenterprising, iners, inaudax
unequal, impar, inīquus
unequalled, singŭlāris

unequivocal, non dŭbĭus

unerring, certus

uneven, ĭnaequālis; (of ground), ĭnīquus

unevenness, ĭnīquĭtas, f

unexampled, ĭnaudītus, ūnĭcus

unexpected, ĭnŏpīnātus

unexpectedly, adv, ex (or dē) imprōvīso

unexplored, ĭnexplōrātus

unfailing, pĕrennis

unfair, ĭnīquus, iniustus

unfairness, ĭnīquĭtas, f

unfaithful, infĭdēlis, perfĭdus

unfaithfulness, infĭdēlĭtas,

unfamiliar, insŭētus

unfashionable, use phr. with extrā consŭĕtūdĭnem (outside of custom)

unfasten, v.t, solvo (3), rĕfīgo (3)

unfathomable, infīnītus

unfavourable, ĭnīquus; (omen), sĭnister, infēlix

unfeeling, dūrus

unfeigned, sincērus, simplex

unfinished, imperfectus; (task) infectus

unfit, incommŏdus

unfitness, ĭnūtĭlĭtas, f

unfitting, indĕcōrus

unfix, v.t, rĕfīgo (3)

unfold, v.t, explĭco (1)

unforseen, imprōvīsus

unforgiving, implācābĭlis

unforgotten, use phr. with mĕmor, adj, (remembering)

unfortified, immūnītus

unfortunate, infēlix

unfounded (groundless), vānus

unfriendliness, ĭnĭmīcĭtĭa, f

unfriendly, ĭnĭmīcus

unfulfilled, irrĭtus, ĭnānis

unfurl, v.t, pando (3)

ungainly, rŭdis

ungentlemanly, illĭbĕrālis

ungodly, incestus

ungovernable, impŏtens, indŏmĭtus

ungraceful, ĭnēlĕgans

ungrateful, ingrātus

unguarded, incustōdītus; (speech or action), incautus

unhappiness, mĭsĕrĭa, f

unhappy, mĭser, infēlix

unharmed, incŏlŭmis

unhealthiness, vălētūdo, f; (of place, etc.), grăvĭtas, f

unheard (of), ĭnaudītus

unheeded, neglectus

unhesitating, confĭdens

unhindered, expĕdītus

unhoped for, inspērātus

unhorse, v.t, ĕquo dēĭcĭo (3) (throw down from a horse)

unicorn, mŏnŏcĕros, m

uniform, nn, (military —), hăbĭtus mĭlĭtāris, m

uniform, adj, aequābĭlis

unimaginable, use phr, quod mente concĭpi non pŏtest (that cannot be conceived in the mind)

unimpaired, intĕger

unimportant, lĕvis

uninhabitable, ĭnhăbĭtābĭlis

uninhabited, dēsertus

uninitiated, prŏfānus

uninjured, incŏlŭmis

unintelligible, obscūrus

unintentional, non praemĕdĭtātus

uninteresting (flat, insipid), frīgĭdus

uninterrupted, contĭnŭus

uninvited, invŏcātus

union (act of joining), iunctĭo, f; (— of states), cīvĭtātes foedĕrātae, f.pl; (agreement), consensus, m

unique, ūnĭcus

unit (one), ūnus

unite, v.t, coniungo (3), consŏcĭo (1); v.i, sē consŏcĭāre (1 reflex), sē coniungĕre (3 reflex)

united, consŏcĭātus

unity (one), ūnus; (agreement), concordĭa, f

universal, ūnĭversus

universe, mundus, m

university, ăcădēmĭa, f

unjust, iniustus

unjustifiable, use phr, quod excūsāri non pŏtest (that cannot be excused)

unkind, ĭnhūmānus

unkindness, ĭnhūmānĭtas, f

unknowingly, adj. imprūdens

unknown, ignōtus, incognĭtus

unlawful (forbidden), vĕtĭtus

unlearned, indoctus

unless, conj, nĭsi

unlettered, indoctus, illittĕrātus

unlike, dissĭmĭlis (foll. by dat. or genit)

unlikely, non vēri sĭmĭlis (not like the truth)

unlimited, infīnītus

unload, v.t, exŏnĕro (1); (goods, etc.), expōno (3)

unlock, v.t, rĕsĕro (1)

unlooked for, ĭnexpectātus

unloose, v.t, solvo (3)

unlucky, infēlix

unmanageable, impŏtens; (things), ĭnhăbĭlis

unmanly, mollis

unmarried, caelebs

unmask, v.t, (plans, etc.), ăpĕrĭo (4)

unmerciful, immĭsĕrĭcors
unmindful, immĕmor
unmistakable, certus
unmitigated, mĕrus
unmolested, intĕger
unmoved, immōtus
unnatural, monstrŭōsus; (far-fetched), arcessītus
unnavigable, innāvĭgābĭlis
unnecessary, non nĕcessārĭus, sŭpervăcānĕus
unnoticed, *use vb*, lătĕo (2) (to lie hidden)
unnumbered, innŭmĕrābĭlis
unoccupied (at leisure), ōtĭōsus; (of land), ăpertus
unoffending, innŏcens
unopposed (militarily), *use phr*, nullo hoste prŏhĭbente (with no enemy impeding)
unpack, *v.t*, exŏnĕro (1)
unpaid, *use* rĕlĭquus (remaining)
unparalleled, ūnĭcus
unpitied, immĭsĕrābĭlis
unpleasant, iniŭcundus
unpleasantness (trouble), mŏlestĭa, *f*
unpolished, impŏlītus
unpolluted, intactus
unpopular, invĭdĭōsus,
unpopularity, invĭdĭa, *f*
unprecedented, nŏvus
unprejudiced, intĕger
unpremeditated, sŭbĭtus
unprepared, impărātus
unpretentious, hŭmĭlis
unprincipled (good for nothing), nēquam
unproductive, infēcundus
unprofitable, non quaestŭōsus
unprotected, indēfensus
unprovoked, illăcessītus
unpunished, impūnītus
unqualified, nōn aptus; (unlimited), infīnītus
unquestionable, certus
unravel, *v.t*, rĕtexo (3); (a problem, etc.), explĭco (1)
unreasonable, inīquus
unrelenting, ĭnexŏrābĭlis
unremitting, assĭdŭus
unreserved, līber
unrestrained, effrēnātus
unrewarded, ĭnhŏnōrātus
unrighteous, iniustus
unripe, immātūrus
unrivalled, praestantissĭmus
unroll, *v.t*, ēvolvo (3)
unruffled, immōtus
unruly, effrēnātus, impŏtens
unsafe, intūtus

unsatisfactory, nōn aptus
unscrupulous (wicked), mălus
unseal, *v.t*, rĕsigno (1)
unseasonable, intempestīvus
unseemly, indĕcōrus
unseen, invīsus
unselfish (persons), innŏcens; (actions), grātŭĭtus
unselfishness, innŏcentĭa, *f*
unserviceable, ĭnūtĭlis
unsettle, *v.t*, turbo (1)
unsettled, incertus, dŭbĭus
unshaken, immōtus
unshaved, intonsus
unsheath, *v.t*, stringo (3)
unship, *v.t*, expōno (3)
unsightly, foedus
unskilful, impĕrītus
unskilfulness, impĕrītĭa, *f*
unslaked (thirst), nōn explētus
unsociable, diffĭcĭlis
unsophisticated, simplex
unsound (of health or opinions), infirmus; (of mind), insānus
unsoundness, infirmĭtas, *f*, insānĭtas, *f*
unsparing (severe), sĕvērus; (lavish), prōdĭgus; (effort, etc.), non rĕmissus
unspeakable, infandus
unspoiled, intĕger
unstained, pūrus
unsteadiness, mōbĭlĭtas, *f*
unsteady, instăbĭlis, vărĭus
unstring, rĕtendo (3)
unsuccessful, irrĭtus; (person), infaustus
unsuitable, incommŏdus
unsuitableness, incommŏdĭtas, *f*
unsuspected, non suspectus
unsuspecting, incautus
untameable, impŏtens
untamed, indŏmĭtus
untaught, indoctus
unteachable, indŏcĭlis
untenable (position), *use phr*, quod tĕnēri non pŏtest (that cannot be held)
unthankful, ingrātus
unthinking (inconsiderate), inconsīdĕrātus
untie, *v.t*, solvo (3)
until, *conj*, dum, dōnec
until, *prep*, ad, (with acc)
untilled, incultus
untimely, *adj*, immātūrus
untiring, assĭdŭus
untold (numbers), innŭmĕrābĭlis
untouched, intĕger
untried, ĭnexpertus
untroubled, sēcūrus
untrue, falsus
untruth, mendācĭum, *n*

unused (of persons), insŏlĭtus; (things) intĕger

unusual, insŏlĭtus, ĭnŭsĭtātus

unutterable, infandus

unveil, *v.t*, dētĕgo (3)

unwarily, *adv*, incautē

unwarlike, imbellis

unwarrantable, ĭnīquus

unwary, incautus

unwavering, constans

unwearied, indēfessus

unwelcome, ingrātus

unwell, aeger

unwholesome, grăvis

unwieldy, ĭnhăbĭlis

unwilling, invītus; (to be —), *v.i*, nolle (*irreg*)

unwillingly, unwillingness, *use adj*, invītus (**unwilling**)

unwind, *v.t*, rētexo (3), rĕvolvo (3)

unwise, stultus, imprūdens

unworthiness, indignĭtas, *f*

unworthy, indignus, immĕrĭtus

unwrap, *v.t*, explĭco (1)

unyielding, firmus, inflexĭbĭlis

unyoke, *v.t*, disiungo (3)

up, *prep*, (— stream or hill), adversus (*in agreement with noun*); (— to), tĕnus (*with abl*)

up, *adv*, sursum; (— and down), sursum dĕorsum

upbraid, *v.t*, obiurgo (1)

upbraiding, *nn*, exprŏbrātĭo, *f*

uphill, *adv. phr*, adverso colle

uphold, *v.t*, sustĭnĕo (2)

uplift, *v.t*, tollo (3)

upon, *prep*, sŭper (*with acc*); (on), in (*with abl*)

upper, *adj*, sŭpĕrĭor; (to get the — hand), sŭpĕrĭor esse (*irreg*)

uppermost, *adj*, summus

upright, rectus; (of morals), prŏbus

uprightness, prŏbĭtas, *f*

uproar, clāmor, *m*

uproarious, tŭmultŭōsus

uproot, ēvello (3)

upset, *v.t*, ēverto (3)

upset, *adj*, mōtus; (troubled), anxĭus

upshot, exĭtus, *m*

upside down, (to turn —), *use vb.* verto (3) (to overturn) *or* miscĕo (2) (throw into confusion)

upstart, nŏvus hŏmo

upwards, *adv*, sursum; (of number, — of), amplĭus quam

urbane, urbānus

urbanity, urbānĭtas, *f*

urchin, pŭsĭo, *m*

urge, *v.t*, urgĕo (2); (persuade), suādĕo (2) (*with dat. of person*)

urgency, grăvĭtas, *f*

urgent, grăvis

urine, ūrīna, *f*

urn, urna, *f*

us, *obj. pron*, nos

usage, mos, *m*

use, ūsus, *m*; (advantage), commŏdum, *n*

use, *v.t*, ūtor (3 *dep. with abl*)

useful, ūtĭlis

usefulness, ūtĭlĭtas, *f*

useless, ĭnūtĭlis

uselessness, ĭnūtĭlĭtas, *f*

usher in, *v.t*, intrŏdūco (3)

usual, ūsĭtātus, sŏlĭtus

usually, *adv*, plērumque, fĕrē

usurer, fēnĕrātor, *m*

usurious, fēnĕrātŏrĭus

usurp, *v.t*, occŭpo (1); (seize), răpĭo (3)

usury, fēnĕrātĭo, *f*, ūsūra, *f*

utensils, vāsa, *n.pl*

utilize, *v.t*, ūtor (3 *dep. with abl*)

utility, ūtĭlĭtas, *f*

utmost, extrēmus, summus

utter, *adj*, tōtus

utter, *v.t*, dīco (3)

utterance, dictum, *n*

utterly, *adv*, omnīno

V

vacancy, (empty post), lŏcus văcŭus, *m*

vacant, *adj*, văcŭus, ĭnānis

vacate, *v.t*, rĕlinquo (3) (a post), ējūro (1)

vacation, fērĭae, *f.pl*

vacillate, *v.i*, văcillo (1)

vacillation, văcillātĭo, *f*

vacuum, ĭnāne, *n*

vagabond, erro, *m*

vagabond, *adj*, văgus

vagary, lĭbīdo, *f*

vagrant, *adj*, văgus

vague, incertus

vagueness, obscūrĭtas, *f*

vain, vānus; (boastful, etc.), glōrĭōsus; (in —), *adv*, frustrā

vainglorious, glōrĭōsus

vainglory, glōrĭa, *f*

vale, valles, *f*

valet, cŭbĭcŭlārĭus, *m*

valetudinarian, vălētūdĭnārĭus, *m*

valiant, fortis

valid, firmus, vălĭdus

validity, grăvĭtas, *f*

valise, capsa, *f*

valley, valles, *f*

valorous, fortis

For List of Abbreviations used, turn to pages 3, 4

valour, virtus, *f*
valuable, prĕtĭōsus
valuation, aestĭmātĭo, *f*
value, *nn*, prĕtĭum, *n*
value, *v.t.* aestĭmo (1); (— highly), magni dūco (3) (— little), parvi dūco
valueless, vīlis
valve, ĕpistŏmĭum, *n*
van (vanguard), prīmum agmen, *n*
vanish, *v.i.* vānesco (3), dīlābor (3 *dep*)
vanity, vānĭtas, *f*, iactātĭo, *f*
vanquish, *v.t.* vinco (3)
vanquisher, victor, *m*
vantage-point, lŏcus sŭpĕrĭor, *m*
vapid, văpĭdus
vapour, văpor, *m*,
variability, mūtābĭlĭtas, *f*
variable, vărĭus, mūtābĭlis
variance, dissensĭo, *f*; (to be at — with), dissĭdĕo (2) ab (*with abl*)
variation, vărĭĕtas, *f*
varicose, vărĭcōsus; (a — vein), vărix, *c*
variegated, vărĭus
variety, vărĭĕtas, *f*, dīversĭtas, *f*
various, vărĭus, dīversus
varnish, *nn*, ātrāmentum, *n*
vary, *v.i and v.t.* vărĭo (1)
vase, vās, *n*
vassal, clĭens, *m*, *f*
vast, vastus, ingens
vastness, immensĭtas, *f*
vat, cūpa, *f*
vault, fornix, *m*
vault, *v.i.* sălĭo (4)
vaunt, *v.t.* iacto (1); *v.i.* glōrĭor (1 *dep*)
vaunting, *nn*, iactātĭo, *f*
veal, vītŭlīna căro, *f*, (calf's flesh)
veer, *v.i.* sē vertĕre (3 *reflex*)
vegetable, hŏlus, *n*
vehemence, vīs, *f*
vehement, vĕhĕmens, ācer
vehicle, vĕhĭcŭlum, *n*
veil, *v.t.* vēlo (1), tĕgo (3)
veil, *nn*, rīca, *f*; (bridal —), flammĕum, *n*; (disguise), intĕgŭmentum, *n*
vein, vēna, *f*
velocity, vēlōcĭtas, *f*
venal, vēnālis
venality, vēnālĭtas, *f*
vendor, vendĭtor, *m*
veneer, *nn*, *use* cortex, *m*, (bark, shell)
venerable, vĕnĕrābĭlis
venerate, *v.t.* cŏlo (3), vĕnĕror (1 *dep*)
veneration, cultus, *m*
venereal, vĕnĕrĕus

vengeance, ultĭo, *f*; (to take —), ulciscor (3 *dep*)
venial, *use phr*, cui ignosci pŏtest (that can be pardoned)
venison, fĕrīna căro, *f*
venom, vĕnēnum, *n*
venemous, vĕnēnātus
vent, *nn*, spīrāmentum, *n*
vent, *v.t.* (pour out), effundo (3)
ventilate, *v.t.* ventĭlo (1); (discuss, etc.), *use vb*, prōfĕro (*irreg*) (to bring out)
ventilator, spīrāmentum, *n*
ventricle, ventrĭcŭlus, *m*
venture, *nn*, (undertaking), rēs, *f*, inceptum, *n*
venture, *v.t.* pĕrīclĭtor (1 *dep*)
venturous, audax
veracious, vērus
veracity, vērĭtas, *f*
veranda, pŏdĭum, *n*
verb, verbum, *n*
verbal, *nn*, *see adv*, verbally
verbally, per verba (by means of words)
verbatim, *adv*, tŏtĭdem verbis (with the same number of words)
verbose, verbōsus
verdant, vĭrĭdis
verdict (of a person or jury), sententĭa, *f*; (of a court), iūdĭcĭum, *n*
verdigris, aerūgo, *f*
verge, *nn*, ōra, *f*, margo, *c*; (on the — of) *use phr*. minimum abest quin .. (it is very little wanting that . . .)
verge, *v.i.* vergo (3)
verger, appārĭtor, *m*
verification, prŏbātĭo, *f*
verify, *v.t.* prŏbo (1)
veritable, vērus
vermilion, mĭnĭum, *n*
versatile, vărĭus
versatility, ăgĭlĭtas, *f*
verse, versus, *m*
versed in, *adj*, exercĭtātus
versify, *v.i.* versus făcĭo (3)
version, *use vb*, converto (3) (turn)
vertebra, vertĕbra, *f*
vertical, rectus
vertigo, vertīgo, *f*
very, *adj*, *use emphatic pron*, ipse
very, *adv*, *use superlative of adj. or adv*, *e.g.* —beautiful, pulcherrĭmus; —quickly, cĕlerrĭme; *otherwise* maxĭmē, valdē, admŏdum
vessel (receptacle), vās, *n*; (ship), nāvis, *f*
vest, tŭnĭca, *f*

vest, *v.t,* (**invest, impart**), do (1)

vestal virgin, vestālis virgo, *f*

vestibule, vestĭbŭlum, *n*

vestige, vestīgĭum, *n;* (**mark**), nŏta, *f,* indĭcĭum, *n*

vestry, aedĭcŭla, *f*

veteran, *adj,* vĕtĕrānus; (— **soldier**), vĕtĕrānus mīles, *m*

veterinary, vĕtĕrīnārĭus

veto, *nn,* intercessĭo, *f*

veto, *v.i,* intercēdo (3) (*with dat*)

vex, *v.t,* vexo (1), sollĭcĭto (1)

vexation, indignātĭo, *f,* dŏlor, *m*

vexatious, mŏlestus

vial, lăgēna, *f*

viands, cĭbus, *m*

viaticum, vĭātĭcum, *n*

vibrate, *v.i. and v.t,* vĭbro (1)

vibration, ăgĭtātĭo, *f*

vicarious, vĭcārĭus

vice, turpĭtūdo, *f*

viceroy, lēgātus, *m*

vicinity, vīcīnĭtas, *f*

vicious, vĭtĭōsus; (**fierce**), fĕrus

vicissitude, vĭces, *f. pl,* vĭcissĭtūdo, *f*

victim, hostĭa, *f,* victĭma, *f*

victor, victor, *m,* victrix, *f*

victorious, victor

victory, victōrĭa, *f*

victual, *v.t, use phr,* rem frūmentārĭam prōvĭdĕo (2) (**to look after the supply of provisions**)

victuals, cĭbus, *m*

vie with, *v.i,* certo (1) cum (*with abl*)

view, *nn,* aspectus, *m,* conspectus, *m;* (**opinion**), sententĭa, *f*

view, *v.t,* conspĭcĭo (3); (**consider**), *use* sentĭo (4) (**to feel**)

vigil, pervĭgĭlātĭo, *f*

vigilance, vĭgĭlantĭa, *f*

vigilant, vĭgĭlans

vigorous, impĭger

vigour, vīs, *f,* vĭgor, *m*

vile, turpis

vileness, turpĭtūdo, *f*

vilify, *v.t,* infāmo (1), dētrăho (3)

villa, villa, *f*

village, pāgus, *m*

villager, pāgānus, *m*

villain, hŏmo scĕlĕrātus

villainy, prāvĭtas, *f,* scĕlus, *n*

vindicate, *v.t,* vindĭco (1); (**justify**), purgo (1)

vindication, purgātĭo, *f*

vindictive, *use phr,* ăvĭdus inĭūrĭae ulciscendae (**eager to avenge a wrong**)

vine, vītis, *f*

vine-grower, cultor, (*m*) vītis

vinegar, ăcētum, *n*

vineyard, vīnĕa, *f*

vintage, *nn,* vindēmĭa, *f*

vintner, vīnārĭus, *m*

violate, *v.t,* vĭŏlo (1)

violation, vĭŏlātĭo, *f*

violator, vĭŏlātor, *m*

violence, vīs, *f,* vĭŏlentĭa, *f,* impĕtus, *m*

violent, vĭŏlentus, impŏtens

violet, *nn,* vĭŏla, *f*

violet, *adj* (— **colour**), ĭanthĭnus

viper, vīpĕra, *f; adj,* vīpĕrīnus

virago, vīrāgo, *f*

virgin, *nn,* virgo, *f*

virgin, *adj,* virgĭnālis

virginity, virgĭnĭtas, *f*

virile, vīrīlis

virtually, *adv* re ipsā

virtue, virtus, *f,* hŏnestas, *f;* (**by — of**), *use abl. case of noun alone, or use* per (*with acc*)

virtuous, hŏnestus

virulent, ăcerbus

viscous, lentus

visible (noticeable), mănifestus; *or use nn.* conspectus, *m,* (**view**)

vision, visus, *m;* (**phantom, apparition**), ĭmāgo, *f,* spĕcĭes, *f*

visionary, vānus

visit, *nn,* (**call**), sălūtātĭo, *f;* (**stay**), commŏrātĭo, *f*

visit, *v.t* vīso (3)

visitor, sălūtātor, *m,* hospes, *m*

visor, buccŭla, *f*

vista, prospectus, *m*

visual, *use phr. with* ŏcŭlus, *m,* (**eye**)

vital, vītālis; (**important**), grăvis

vitality, vīs, *f,* vīvācĭtas, *f*

vitiate, *v.t,* vĭtĭo (1), corrumpo (3)

vitreous, vītrĕus

vituperation, vĭtŭpĕrātĭo, *f*

vituperate, *v.t,* vĭtŭpĕro (1)

vivacious, ălăcer

vivacity, ălăcrĭtas, *f*

vivid, vīvus

vivify, *v.t,* ănĭmo (1)

vixen, vulpes, *f*

vocabulary, verba, *n.pl*

vocal, vōcālis

vocation, offĭcĭum, *n*

vociferate, *v.i,* clāmo (1)

vociferous, clāmōsus

vociferously, *adv,* magno clāmōre

vogue, mos, *m,* (**custom**)

voice, vox, *f*

voice, *v.t,* dīco (3)

void, *nn,* ĭnāne, *n*

void, *adj,* ĭnānis; (— **of**), văcŭus (*with abl*)

volatile, lĕvis

volcano, mons qui ēructat flammas (a mountain which emits flames)

volition, vŏluntas, f; (of his own —), sŭā sponte

volley (of javelins), tēla missa, n.pl

volubility, vŏlūbĭlĭtas, f

voluble, vŏlūbĭlis

volume (book), lĭber, m; (of noise), magnĭtūdo, f

voluminous, cōpĭōsus

voluntarily, adv, sponte (of one's own accord) with appropriate pron, mĕā, tŭā, sŭā

voluntary, vŏluntārĭus

volunteer, nn, mīles vŏluntārĭus, m

volunteer, v.i, (of soldiers), use phr, ultro nōmen dăre (enlist voluntarily)

voluptuous, vŏluptārĭus

voluptuousness, luxŭrĭa, f

vomit, nn, vŏmĭtĭo, f

vomit, v.i. and v.t, vŏmo (3)

voracious, ĕdax, vŏrax

voracity, ĕdācĭtas, f

vortex, vertex, m

vote, suffrāgĭum, n, sententĭa, f

vote, v.i, suffrāgĭum fĕro (irreg); (to — in favour of), in sententĭam īre (irreg) (with genit)

voter, suffrāgātor, m

voting-tablet (ballot-paper), tăbella, f

vouch for, v.t praesto (1), testor (1 dep), testīfĭcor (1 dep.)

voucher (authority), auctōrĭtas, f

vow, vōtum, n; (promise), fĭdes, f

vow, v.t. prōmitto (3), vŏvĕo (2)

vowel, vōcālis littĕra, f

voyage, nn, nāvĭgātĭo, f

voyage, v.i, nāvĭgo (1)

voyager, pĕrĕgrīnātor, m

vulgar, vulgāris, plēbēius, sordĭdus

vulgarity (of manner, etc.), use phr, mōres sordĭdi, m.pl

vulgarize, v.t, pervulgo (1)

vulnerable, ăpertus

vulture, vultur, m

W

wadding, use lānūgo, f, (woolly down)

wade, v.i, use phr, per văda īre (irreg) (to go through the shallows)

wafer, crustŭlum (pastry)

wait, v.t, fĕro (irreg)

wag, nn, (jester), iŏcŭlātor, m

wag, v.t, quasso (1)

wage (war), v.t, gĕro (3) (bellum)

wager, nn, sponsĭo, f

wager, v.i, sponsĭōnem făcĭo (3)

wages, merces, f

waggish, făcētus

waggon, plaustrum, n

wagtail, mōtācilla, f

wail, wailing, nn, plōrātus, m, flētus, m

wail, v.i, plōro (1) flĕo (2)

waist, mĕdĭum corpus, n

waistcoat, sūbūcŭla, f, (undergarment)

wait, v.i, mănĕo (2); v.t, (to — for), exspecto (1); (serve), fămŭlor (1 dep.); (— in ambush), insĭdĭas făcĭo (3) (with dat)

wait, nn, mŏra, f

waiter, fămŭlus, m

waiting, exspectātĭo, f, mansĭo, f

waive, v.t, rēmitto (3)

wake, v.t, excĭto (1); v.i, expergiscor (3 dep.)

wakeful, vĭgil

wakefulness, vĭgĭlantĭa, f, insomnĭa, f

walk, nn, ambŭlātĭo, f; (gait), incessus, m; (— of life, occupation), quaestus, m

walk, v.i, ambŭlo (1), grădĭor (3 dep.), incēdo (3)

walker, pĕdes, m

walking, nn, ambŭlātĭo, f

wall, mūrus, m; (ramparts), moenĭa, n.pl; (inner —), părĭes, m

wall, v.t, mūnĭo (4) (fortify)

wallet, saccŭlus, m

wallow, v.i, vŏlūtor (1 pass)

walnut (tree and nut), iūglans, f

wan, adj, pallĭdus

wand, virga, f, cādūcĕus, m

wander, v.i, erro (1), văgor (1 dep.)

wanderer, erro, m

wandering, nn, error, m

wane, v.i, dēcresco (3)

want, nn, (lack), ĭnōpĭa, f, pēnūrĭa, f; (longing for), dēsīdĕrĭum, n; (failing), dēfectĭo, f; (in —), adj, ĭnops

want, v.i, (wish), vŏlo (irreg); v.t, (to lack), cărĕo (2), ĕgĕo (2) (with abl); (long for), dēsīdĕro (1); (desire), cŭpĭo (3)

wanting (to be —, to fail), v.i, dēsum (irreg)

wanton, adj, lascīvus, lĭbīdĭnōsus

wantoness, lascīvĭa, f

war, bellum, n; (civil —), bellum cīvīle, n; (in —), adv, bello; (to make — on), bellum infĕro (irreg, with dat); (to declare — on), bellum indīco (3) (with dat); (to wage —), bellum gĕro (3)

warble, v.i, căno (3)

war-cry, clāmor, m

ward, pŭpillus, m, pŭpilla, f; (district), rēgĭo, f

ward off, v.t, arcĕo (2)

warden, cūrātor, m

warder, custos, c

wardrobe, vestiārĭum, n

warehouse, horrĕum, n

wares, merx, f

warfare, mīlĭtĭa, f

warily, adv, cautē

wariness, cautĭo, f

warlike, adj, bellĭcōsus, mīlĭtāris

warm, călĭdus; (to be —), v.i, călĕo (2)

warm, v.t, călĕfăcĭo (3)

warmly (eagerly), adv, vĕhementer

warmth, călor, m

warn, v.t, mŏnĕo (2)

warning, nn, (act of —), mŏnĭtĭo, f; (the warning itself), mŏnĭtum, n

warp, nn, stāmen, n

warp, v.t, (distort, of mind, etc.), dēprāvo (1)

warrant, nn, mandātum, n; (authority), auctōrĭtas, f

warrant, v.t, (guarantee), firmo (1), praesto (1)

warranty, sătisdătĭo, f

warren, lĕpŏrārĭum, n

warrior, mīles, c, bellātor, m

wart, verrūca, f

wary, prōvĭdus, prūdens

wash, v.t, lăvo (1); v.i, lăvor (1 pass)

wash, washing, nn, lăvātĭo, f

wash-basin, ăquālis, c

wasp, vespa, f

waspish, ācerbus

waste, nn, damnum, n; (careless throwing away), effūsĭo, f; (—land), vastĭtas, f

waste, adj, vastus, dēsertus

waste, v.t, consūmo (3), perdo (3); (— time), tempus tĕro (3); v.i, (— away), tābesco (3)

wasteful, prōfūsus

wastefulness, prōfūsĭo, f

watch (a — of the night), vĭgĭlĭa, f; (watching on guard), excŭbĭae, f.pl

watch, v.t, (observe), specto (1); (guard), custōdĭo (4); v.i, (not to sleep), excŭbo (1)

watchful, vĭgĭlans

watchfulness, vĭgĭlantĭa, f

watchman, custos, m

watchword, tessĕra, f

water, ăqua, f; (fresh —), ăqua dulcis, f; (salt —), ăqua salsa, f

water, v.t, rĭgo (1), irrĭgo (1)

water-carrier, ăquārĭus, m

water-closet, lātrīna, f

waterfall, ăqua dēsĭlĭens, f, (water leaping down)

watering-place, ăquātĭo, f; (resort), ăquae, f.pl

water-snake, hydrus, m

waterworks, ăquaeductus, m

watery, ăquātĭcus

wattle, crātis, f

wave, nn, unda, f, fluctus, m

wave, v.i, undo (1), fluctŭo (1); v.t, ăgĭto (1)

waver, v.i, fluctŭo (1) dŭbĭto (1)

wavering, adj, dŭbĭus

wavering, nn, dŭbĭtātĭo, f

wavy (of hair), crispus

wax, nn, cēra, f; adj, cērĕus

wax, v.i, cresco (3)

way, vĭa, f; (journey), ĭter, n; (pathway), sēmĭta, f; (course), cursus, m; (manner), mŏdus, m; (habit), mos, m; (system), rătĭo, f; (in the —), adj, obvĭus; (in this —), adv, ĭta, sīc; (out of the —), adj, āvĭus; (to give or to make —), v.i, cēdo (3); (to get one's own —), vinco (3)

wayfarer, vĭātor, m

waylay, v.t, insĭdĭor (1 dep.) (with dat)

wayward, pertĭnax

we, pron, nos; often expressed by 1st person plural of vb, e.g. we are, sumus

weak, infirmus, dēbĭlis; (overcome), confectus; (of arguments, etc.), lĕvis

weaken, v.t, infirmo (1), dēbĭlĭto (1); v.i, languesco (3), dēfĭcĭo (3)

weak-hearted, pŭsilli ănĭmi (of weak heart)

weakness, infirmĭtas, f, dēbĭlĭtas, f, lēvĭtas, f

weal (the common —), bŏnum pūblĭcum, n; (on skin), vībex, f

wealth, dīvĭtĭae, f.pl, ōpes, f.pl; (large supply), cōpĭa, f

wealthy, dīves, lŏcŭples

wean, v.t, lacte dēpello (3) (remove from the milk)

weapon, tēlum, n; (pl) arma, n.pl

wear, v.t, (rub), tĕro (3); (— out), contĕro (3); (— a garment), gĕro (3); v.i, (last), dūro (1)

weariness, lassĭtūdo, f

wearisome, lăbōrĭōsus

weary, adj, fessus, fătīgātus

weary, v.t, fătīgo (1); v.i, (grow —), dēfătīgor (1 pass)

weasel, mustēla, f

weather, tempestas, f

weather, v.t, (endure, bear), perfĕro (irreg)

weave, v.t, texo (3)

weaver, textor, m

web, tēla, f

wed, v.t, (of the husband), dūco (3); (of the wife), nūbo (3) (with dat)

For List of Abbreviations used, turn to pages 3, 4

wedding, *nn*, nuptĭae, *f.pl*; (— day), dĭes (*m*) nuptĭārum

wedge, *nn*, cŭnĕus, *m*

wedlock, mātrĭmōnĭum, *n*

weed, *nn*, herba ĭnūtĭlis, *f* (harmful plant)

weed, *v.t.* runco (1)

week, *use phr*, spătĭum septem dĭērum (a space of seven days)

weep, *v.i*, lăcrĭmo (1)

weeping, *nn*, flētus, *m*

weeping-willow, sălix, *f*

weevil, curcŭlĭo, *m*

weigh, *v.t*, pendo (3), penso (1); (consider), pondĕro (1); (— down), grăvo (1)

weight, pondus, *n*; (a —), lībrāmentum, *n*; (influence, etc.), *use adj*. grăvis (important)

weightiness, grăvĭtas, *f*

weighty, grăvis

weir (dam), mōles, *f*

welcome, *adj*, grātus, acceptus

welcome, *nn*, sălūtātĭo, *f*

welcome! salve! (*pl*. salvēte!)

welcome, *v.t*, excĭpĭo (3)

weld, *v.t*, ferrūmĭno (1)

welfare, bŏnum, *n*, sălus, *f*

well, *adv*, bĕnĕ; (very —), optĭmē

well, *nn*, pŭtĕus, *m*

well, *adj*, (safe), salvus; (healthy), sānus, vălens; (to be —), *v.i*, vălĕo (2)

well-being, *nn*, sălus, *f*

well-born, nōbĭlis

well-disposed, bĕnĕvŏlus

well-favoured, pulcher

well-known, nōtus

well-wisher, *use adj*, bĕnĕvŏlus (well-disposed)

welter, *v.i*, vŏlūtor (1 *pass*)

wench, pŭella, *f*

west, *nn*, occĭdens, *m*

west, *adj*, occĭdentālis

westward, *adv*, ad occĭdentem (sōlem)

wet, *adj*, hūmĭdus, mădĭdus

wet, *v.i*, mădĕfăcĭo (3)

wether, vervex, *m*

wet-nurse, nūtrix, *f*

whale, bālaena, *f*

wharf, nāvāle, *n*

what, *interrog. pron*, quid? *interrog. adj*, qui, quae, quod; *relative pron*, quod, *pl*, quae; (— for, wherefore, why), quārē; (— sort), quālis?

whatever, *pron*, quodcumque; *adj*, quĭcumque

wheat, trītĭcum, *n*

wheel, rŏta, *f*

wheel, *v.t*, circŭmăgo (3)

wheelbarrow, păbo, *m*

wheeling, *adj*, circumflectens

whelp, *nn*, cătŭlus, *m*

when? *interrog*, quando? (*temporal*), cum (*with vb, in indicative or subjunctive mood*), ŭbĭ (*vb. in indicative*)

whence, *adv*, undĕ

whenever, *adv*, quandōcumque

where? *interrog*, ŭbĭ?; (*relative*), quā; (— from), undĕ; (— to), quō; (anywhere, everywhere), *adv*, ŭbĭque

whereas, *adv*, quŏnĭam

wherever, quācumque

wherefore, *adv*, quārē

whereupon, *use phr*, quo facto (with which having been done)

whet, *v.t*, (sharpen), ăcŭo (3)

whether, *conj*. (*in a single question*), num, nĕ; (*in a double question*, whether ... or), ŭtrum ... an; (*in a conditional sentence*), sīve ... sīve

whetstone, cōs, *f*

whey, sĕrum, *n*

which, *interrog*, quis, quid; (*relative*), qui, quae, quod; (which of two), ŭter

while, *conj*, dum (*often foll. by. vb. in present tense indicative*)

while, *nn*, tempus, *n*, spătĭum, *n*; (for a little —), *adv*, părumper; (in a little —), brĕvi (tempŏre)

while away, *v.t*, fallo (3), tĕro (3)

whim, lĭbīdo, *f*

whimper, *v.i*, vāgĭo (4)

whimsical, rĭdĭcŭlus

whine, *v.i*, vāgĭo (4)

whinny, *v.i*, hinnĭo (4)

whip, *nn*, flăgellum, *n*

whip, *v.t*, verbĕro (1), flăgello (1)

whirl, *v.t*, torquĕo (2); *v.i*, torquĕor (2 *pass*)

whirlpool, *m*, gurges, *m*

whirlwind, turbo, *m*

whirr, *nn*, strīdor, *m*

whirr, *v.i*, strīdĕo (2)

whiskers, *use* barba, *f*, (beard)

whisper, *nn*, sŭsurrus , *m*

whisper, *v.i*, sŭsurro (1)

whispering, *adj*, sŭsurrus

whistle, whistling, *nn*, sībīlus, *m*

whistle, *v.i*, sībīlo (1)

white, *adj*, albus; (shining —), candĭdus

white, *nn*, album, *n*

whiten, *v.t*, dĕalbo (1); *v.i*, albesco (3)

whiteness, candor, *m*

whitewash, *nn*, albārĭum, *n*

white-wash, *v.t*, dēalbo (1)

whither, (*interrog. and relative*), quo

whiz, *v.i*, strīdĕo (2)

whiz, whizzing, *nn*, strīdor, *m*

who, *interrog*, quis? (*relative*), qui, quae

whoever, *pron*, quīcunque

whole, *adj*, tōtus; (untouched), intĕger

whole, *nn*, tōtum, *n*, ūnĭversĭtas, *f, or use adj*, tōtus, *e.g.* the — of the army, tōtus exercĭtus, *m*.

wholesale trader, mercātor, *m*

wholesale trading, mercātūra, *f*

wholesome, sălūbris

wholly, *adv*, omnīno

whoop, *nn*, ŭlŭlātus, *m*

whom, *acc. case of rel. pron*, quem, quam; *pl*, quos, quas

whore, mĕrĕtrix, *f*

whose, *genit. case of rel. pron*, cūius; *pl*, quōrum, quārum

why, *adv*, cur, quārē

wick, ellychnĭum, *n*

wicked, scĕlestus, mălus, imprŏbus

wickedness, scĕlus, *n*, imprŏbĭtas, *f*

wicker, vīmĭnĕus

wide, lātus; (— open), pătens

widen, *v.t*, dīlăto (1); *v.i*, sē dīlătāre (1 *reflex*)

widow, vĭdŭa, *f*

widower, vĭdŭus vir, *m*

widowhood, vĭdŭĭtas, *f*

width, lātĭtūdo, *f*

wield, *v.t*, tracto (1)

wife, uxor, *f*

wig, căpillāmentum, *n*

wild, indŏmĭtus, fĕrus; (uncultivated), incultus; (mad), āmens

wilderness, dēserta lŏca, *n.pl*

wildness, fĕrĭtas, *f*

wile, dŏlus, *m*

wilful, pervĭcax

wilfully, *adv*, pervĭcācĭter; (deliberately), consultō

wilfulness, pervĭcācĭa, *f*

wiliness, callĭdĭtas, *f*

will (desire), vŏluntas, *f*; (purpose), consĭlĭum, *n*; (pleasure), lĭbīdo, *f*; (decision, authority), arbĭtrĭum, *n*; (legal), testāmentum, *n*

will, *v.t*, (bequeath), lēgo (1)

willing, *adj*, lĭbens

willingly, *adv*, lĭbenter

willingness, vŏluntas, *f*

willow, sălix, *f*

wily, callĭdus, văfer

win, *v.i*, vinco (3); *v.t*, consĕquor (3 *dep*), ădĭpiscor (3 *dep*)

wind, ventus, *m*; (breeze), aura, *f*

wind, *v.t*, volvo (3)

winding, *nn*, flexus, *m*

winding, *adj*, flexŭōsus

windlass, sŭcŭla, *f*

window, fĕnestra, *f*

windward, *use phr*, conversus ad ventum (turned towards the wind)

windy, ventōsus

wine, vīnum, *n*

wine-cask, dōlĭum, *n*

wine-cellar, ăpŏthēca, *f*

wine-cup, pōcŭlum, *n*

wine-merchant, vīnārĭus, *m*

wing, āla, *f*; (of army, etc.), cornu, *n*

winged, pennĭger

wink, *nn*, nictātĭo, *f*

wink, *v.i*, nicto (1); (overlook), cōnīvĕo (2)

winner, victor, *m*

winning, *adj*, (of manner), blandus

winnow, *v.t*, ventĭlo (1)

winter, *nn*, hĭems, *f*

winter, *adj*, hĭĕmālis

winter, *v.i*, hĭĕmo (1)

wintry, hĭĕmālis

wipe, *v.t*, tergĕo (2)

wire, fĭlum, *n*, (thread)

wisdom, săpĭentĭa, *f*, prūdentĭa, *f*

wise, *adj*, săpĭens, prūdens

wisely, *adv*, săpĭenter, prūdenter

wish, *nn*, (desire), vŏluntas, *f*; (the wish itself), optātum, *n*; (longing), dēsĭdĕrĭum, *n*

wish, *v.t*, vŏlo (*irreg*), cŭpĭo (3), opto (1); (long for), dēsĭdĕro (1)

wishing, *nn*, optātĭo, *f*

wisp, mănĭpŭlus, *m*

wistful, cŭpĭdus (longing for); (dejected), tristis

wit, ingĕnĭum, *n*; (humour), făcētĭae, *f. pl*; (out of one's — s), *adj*, āmens

witch, sāga, *f*

witchcraft, ars măgĭca, *f*

with, *prep*, cum (*with abl, but when denoting the instrument, use abl. case, alone*; (among, at the house of), ăpud (*with acc*)

withdraw, *v.i*, cēdo (3), sē rĕcĭpĕre (3 *reflex*); *v.t*, dēdūco (3), rĕmŏvĕo (2)

withdrawal, regressus, *m*

wither, *v.i*, languesco (3); *v.t*, (parch), torrĕo (2)

withered, flaccĭdus

withhold, *v.t*, rĕtĭnĕo (2)

within, *adv*, intus

within, *prep*, (time and space), intrā (*with acc*); (time), *use abl. case alone*, *e.g.* within three days, trĭbus dĭēbus

without, *prep*, sĭne (*with abl*); (outside of), extrā (*with acc*); *when* without *is followed by a gerund* (*e.g.* I returned without seeing him) *use a clause introduced by* nĕque, quĭn, ĭta . . . ut: *e.g.* rĕgressus sum, nĕque ĕum vīdi

without, *adv*, extrā

withstand, *v.t*, rĕsisto (3) (*with dat*)

witness, *nn*, (person), testis, *c*; (testimony), testĭmōnĭum, *n*

witness, *v.t*, testor (1 *dep*), testĭfīcor (1 *dep*); (to see), vĭdĕo (2)

witticism, făcĕtĭae, *f. pl*

witty, făcētus; (sharp), salsus

wizard, măgus, *m*

woad, vītrum, *n*

woe, dŏlor, *m*, luctus, *m*

woeful, tristis

wolf, lŭpus, *m*

wolfish (greedy, rapacious), răpax

woman, fēmĭna, *f*, mŭlĭer, *f*; (young —), pŭella, *f*; (old —), ănus, *f*

womanish, womanly, mŭlĭēbris

womb, ŭtĕrus, *m*

wonder, mīrātĭo, *f*; (a marvel), mīrācŭlum, *n*

wonder, *v.i. and v.t*, mīror (1 *dep*)

wonderful, mīrus, mīrābĭlis

wont, wonted, *adj*, sŭētus

wont, *nn*, mos, *m*

woo, *v.t*, pĕto (3), ămo (1)

wood (material), mātĕrĭa, *f*; (forest), silva, *f*

wood-collector, lignātor, *m*

wooded, silvestris

wooden, lignĕus

woodland, silvae, *f. pl*

woodpecker, pīcus, *m*

wooer, prŏcus, *m*

wool, lāna, *f*

woollen, lānĕus

word, verbum, *n*; (promise), fĭdes, *f*; (information), nuntĭus, *m*; send word, *v.t*, nuntĭo (1)

wordy, verbōsus

work, *nn*, ŏpus, *n*; (labour), lăbor, *m*

work, *v.i*, ŏpĕror (1 *dep*)

work, *v.t*, exercĕo (2); (handle, manipulate), tracto (1); (bring about), efficĭo (3)

worker, ŏpĭfex, *c*, ŏpĕrārĭus, *m*

workman, ŏpĭfex, *c*, ŏpĕrārĭus, *m*

workmanship, ars, *f*

workshop, officīna, *f*

world, mundus, *m*, orbis (*m*) terrārum; (people), hŏmĭnes, *c. pl*

worldliness, *use phr*, stŭdĭum rērum prŏfānārum (fondness for common matters)

worm, vermis, *m*

worm-eaten, vermĭnōsus

worm (one's way), *v.i*, sē insĭnŭāre (1 *reflex*)

wormwood, absinthĭum, *n*

worn (— out), *adj*, trītus; (as clothes), gestus

worry, *nn*, anxĭĕtas, *f*

worry, *v.t*, vexo (1); *v.i*, cūrā affĭci (3 *pass*) (to be affected by worry)

worse, *adj*, pēior

worse, *adv*, pēius

worship, *v.t*, vĕnĕror (1 *dep*), cŏlo (3)

worship, *nn*, vĕnĕrātĭo, *f*, cultus, *m*

worshipper, cultor, *m*

worst, *adj*, pessĭmus

worst, *adv*, pessĭmē

worst, *v.t*, vinco (3)

worth, *nn*, (price), prĕtĭum, *n*; (valuation), aestĭmātĭo, *f*; (worthiness), virtus, *f*, dignĭtas, *f*; (— nothing), nĭhĭli; (to be — much), *v.i*, multum vălĕo (2); (*adj*) dignus

worthiness, dignĭtas, *f*

worthless, vīlis

worthy (*with noun*), dignus (*with abl*); (*with phr*) dignus qui (ut) (*with vb. in subjunctive*); (man), prŏbus

wound, *nn*, vulnus, *n*

wound, *v.t*, vulnĕro (1), saucĭo (1)

wounded, vulnĕrātus, saucĭus

wrangle, *v.i*, rixor (1 *dep*)

wrangle, wrangling, *nn*, rixa, *f*

wrap, *v.t*, involvo (3)

wrapper, invŏlūcrum, *n*

wrath, īra, *f*

wrathful, īrātus

wreak vengeance on, *v.t*, ulciscor (3 *dep*)

wreath, *nn*, serta, *n.pl*

wreathe, *v.t*, torquĕo (2)

wreck, *nn*, naufrăgĭum, *n*

wreck, *v.t*, frango (3)

wrecked, naufrăgus

wren, rēgŭlus, *m*

wrench away, wrest, *v.t*, extorquĕo (2)

wrestle, *v.i*, luctor (1 *dep*)

wrestler, luctātor, *m*

wrestling, *nn*, luctātĭo, *f*

wretch, perdĭtus, *m*

wretched, mĭser

wretchedness, mĭsĕrĭa, *f*

wriggle, *v.t*, torquĕor (2 *pass*)

wring, *v.t*, torquĕo (2)

wrinkle, rūga, *f*

wrinkled, rūgōsus

wrist, *use* bracchĭum, *n*, (forearm)

writ (legal —), mandātum, *n*

write, *v.t*, scrībo (3)

writer, scriptor, *m*; (author), auctor, *c*

writhe, *v.i*, torquĕor (2 *pass*)

writing, scriptĭo, *f*; (something written), scriptum, *n*, ŏpus, *n*

wrong, *adj*, falsus; (improper, bad), prāvus; (to be —), *v.i*, erro (1)

wrong, *nn*, nĕfas, *n*, peccātum *n*; (a —), iniūrĭa, *f*

wrongly *adv*, (badly), mălĕ; (in error), falso

wrong, *v.t*, fraudo (1), iniūrĭam infĕro (*irreg*) (*with dat*)

wrongful, iniustus

wroth, īrātus

wrought, confectus

wry, distortus

Y

yacht, cĕlox, *f*

yard (measurement), *often* passus, *m*, (five feet approx.) (court —), ārĕa, *f*

yarn (thread), fīlum, *n*; (story), fābŭla, *f*

yawn, *nn*, oscĭtātĭo, *f*

yawn, *v.i*, oscĭto (1)

year, annus, *m*; (a half —), sēmestre spătĭum, *n*, (space of six months)

yearly, *adj*, (throughout a year), annŭus; (every year), *adv*, quŏtannis

yearn for, *v.t*, dēsīdĕro (1)

yearning, dēsīdĕrĭum, *n*

yeast, fermentum, *n*

yell, clāmor, *m*, ŭlŭlātus, *m*

yell, *v.i*, magnā vōce clāmo (1)

yellow, flāvus

yellowish, subflāvus

yelp, *v.i*, gannĭo (4)

yelping, *nn*, gannītus, *m*

yeoman, cŏlōnus, *m*

yes, *adv*, ĭta

yesterday, *adv*, hĕrī; *nn*, hesternus dĭes, *m*

yet, *adv*, (nevertheless), tămen; (*with comparatives*) ĕtĭam, *e.g.* yet bigger, ĕtĭam māior; (of time; still), ădhuc

yew, taxus, *f*

yield, *v.i*, cēdo (3) (*with dat*); (surrender), sē dēdĕre (3 *reflex*)

yielding, *nn*, concessĭo, *f*

yielding, *adj*, (soft), mollis

yoke, *nn*, iŭgum, *n*

yoke, *v.t*, iungo (3)

yoked, iŭgālis; (— pair), iŭgum, *n*

yolk, vĭtellus, *m*

yonder, *adv*, illic

yore, *adv*, ōlim (once, in time past)

you, *pron*, *often not expressed*, *e.g.* you come, vĕnis; *pl*, vĕnītis; *otherwise use appropriate case of* tu; *pl*, vos

young, *adj*, iŭvĕnis, parvus; (child), infans; (— person), ădŏlescens

young, *nn*, (offspring), partus, *m*

younger, iūnĭor, mĭnor nātu (less in age)

young man, iŭvĕnis, *m*.

youngster, iŭvĕnis, *c*

your, **yours** (*singular*), tŭus; (*of more than one*), vester

yourself (*emphatic*), *use* ipse *in agreement with pron*; (*reflexive*), te; *pl*, vos

youth (time of —), iŭventus, *f*, ădŏlescentĭa, *f*; (young man), ădŏlescens, iŭvĕnis, *c*; (body of young persons), iŭventus, *f*

youthful, iŭvĕnīlis

Z

zeal, stŭdĭum, *n*

zealous, stŭdĭōsus

zenith, *use* summus, *adj*, (top of)

zephyr, Zĕphўrus, *m*, Făvōnĭus, *m*

zero (nothing), nĭhil

zest, ălăcrĭtas, *f*

zodiac, signĭfer orbis, *m*, (sign-bearing orb)

zone, lŏcus, *m*

LIST OF PROPER NAMES

With Classical equivalents

Adriatic, Măre Sŭpĕrum, *n*

Aegean, Măre Aegaeum, *n*

Africa, Afrĭca, ae, *f*

African, *adj*, Afrĭcānus, a, um

Alps, Alpes, ĭum, *f. pl*

Antioch, Antĭŏchĭa, ae, *f*

Anthony, Antōnĭus

Apennines, Mons Āpennīnus, *m*

Ardennes, Ardŭenna, ae, *f*

Athens, Athēnae, ārum, *f. pl*

Athenian, *adj*, Athēnĭensis, e

Aventine, Āventīnus, i, *m*

Babylon, Băbўlōn, ōnis, *f*

Bath, Āquae, (*f. pl*,) Sulis

Belgium, Gallĭa Belgĭca, *f*

The Belgians, Belgae, *m. pl*

Black Sea, Pontus Euxīnus, *m*

Britain, Brĭtannĭa, ae, *f*

British, *adj*, Brĭtannĭcus, a, um

Caerleon, Isca, ae, *f*

Capri, Caprĕae, ārum, *f. pl*

Cyprus, Cўprus, i, *f*

Damascus, Dămascus, i, *f*

Danube (lower part), Hister, tri, *m*; (upper), Dānŭvĭus, ii, *m*

Ebro, Hĭbērus, i, *m*

Egypt, Aegyptus, i, *m*

Egyptian, *adj*., Aegyptĭus

Etna, Aetna, ae, *f*

Europe, Eurōpa, ae, *f*

France, Gallĭa, ae, *f*

Gaul, Gallĭa, ae, *f*

Geneva (Lake —), lacus Lĕmannus, *m*

German, *adj*, Germānus, a, um

Germany, Germānĭa, ae, *f*

Gloucester, Glevum, i, *n*

Greece, Graecĭa, ae, *f*

Greek, *adj*, Graecus, a, um

Helen, Hĕlĕna, ae, *f*

Horace, Hŏrātĭus

Ireland, Hĭbernĭa, *f*

Italy, Itălĭa, ae, *f*

Jerusalem, Hĭĕrŏsŏlўma, ōrum, *n.pl*

Kent, Cantĭum, i, *n*

Lincoln, Lindum, *n*

Loire, Lĭger, ĕris, *m*

London, Londinĭum, i, *n*

Lyons, Lugdūnum, i, *n*

Majorca, Bălīārĭs Māior, *f*

Malta, Mēlĭta, ae, *f*

Marseilles, Massĭlĭa, ae, *f*

Messina, Messāna, ae, *f*

Mediterranean, măre nostrum, *n*

Provence, Prŏvincĭa, ae, *f*

Pyrenees, Pўrēnaei Montes, *m. pl*

Rhine, Rhēnus, i, *m*

Rhodes, Rhŏdos, i, *f*

Rhone, Rhŏdănus, i, *m*

Roman, Rōmānus, a, um,

Rome, Rōma, ae, *f*

Scotland, Călēdŏnĭa, ae, *f*

Severn, Sabrīna, ae, *f*

Sicily, Sĭcĭlĭa, ae, *f*

Spain, Hispānĭa, ae, *f*

St. Albans, Vĕrŭlāmĭum, i, *n*

Syracuse, Sўrăcūsae, ārum, *f. pl*

Thames, Tămĕsis, is, *m*

Tiber, Tĭbĕris, is, *m*

Tuscany, Ětrūrĭa, ae, *f*

Isle of Wight, Vectis, is, *f*

Names of the Winds

North, Bŏrĕas, ae, *m*

North-east, Āquĭlo, ōnis, *m*

East, Eurus, i, *m*

South-east, Vulturnus, i, *m*

South, Auster, tri, *m*, Nŏtus, i, *m*

South-west, Afrĭcus, i, *m*

West, Făvōnĭus, i, *n*

　　　　Zĕphўrus, i, *m*

North-west, Cōrus, i, *m*

CONCISE GRAMMAR
ALPHABET

The Latin alphabet contained twenty-three letters:

A B C D E F G H I K L M N O P Q R S T V X Y Z

Pronunciation

Although there is not complete agreement about the way in which the Romans spoke Latin, this is one method of pronunciation which many people believe to have been used by the Romans.

Vowels

ă (short a) as in "fat"; ā (long a) as in "father".
ĕ (short e) as in "net"; ē (long e) as in "they".
ĭ (short i) as in "pin"; ī (long i) as in "police".
ŏ (short o) as in "not"; ō (long o) as in "note".
ŭ (short u) as "oo" in "wood"; ū (long u) as "oo" in "mood".

Long vowels only are marked in this section. Other vowels are short, unless they are made long by two consonants or *x* immediately following them.

Diphthongs

Two vowels pronounced together to form one sound are called Diphthongs, e.g. ae, au, oe, and are pronounced as follows.

ae, as "ai" in "aisle".
au, as "ow" in "cow".
oe, as "oi" in "oil".

Consonants

These are mostly pronounced as in English, but note:

c is always hard, as in "cat".
g is always hard, as in "get".
i, when it is used as a consonant, is always pronounced as y in "yellow"
    e.g. *iam*, "yam".
s is always pronounced as in "son".
t is always pronounced as in "top".
v is pronounced as "w" in "wall", e.g. *servi*, pronounced "serwee".
th is pronounced as "t" and *ch* as "k".

NOUNS

Latin is a language of "endings", or, as they are sometimes called "inflections". It is usually by the ending of a noun in Latin that we can tell what its relationship is to the other words in the sentence. Nouns which have the same sets of endings are grouped together in what is known as a Declension. There are five of these in Latin, and each one is distinguished by the way in which the nouns belonging to it form their genitive singular case, e.g.

First Declension—*ae*—insul*ae*
Second Declension—*i*—mur*i*
Third Declension—*is*—reg*is*
Fourth Declension—*us*—exercit*us*
Fifth Declension—*ei*—di*ei*

The genitive is one of the six cases which each noun in Latin has. These are:

Nominative: This is used when the noun is the *subject* of the sentence, e.g.
   The sailor loves the queen.
Vocative: This is the case of the person *addressed*, e.g.
   Sailor, where are you going?
Accusative: This is used whenthe noun is the *object* of the sentence, e.g.
   The queen loves *the sailor*.
Genitive: This case denotes *possession*, and translates the English word "of", e.g.
   The dog *of the sailor*, or, *The sailor's* dog.
Dative: This is used when the noun is the *indirect object* of the sentence, and usually translates the English words "to" and "for", e.g.
   He gives money *to the sailor*.
Ablative: This translates the English words "by", "with", "from", "on", and "in".

These cases have different endings when they are used in the singular and in the plural.

First Declension

Most nouns of the First Declension end in "a" and are feminine, e.g *insula*, f . . . an island.

	Singular	Plural
Nom.	insula	insulae
Voc.	insula	insulae
Acc.	insulam	insulās
Gen.	insulae	insulārum
Dat.	insulae	insulīs
Abl.	insulā	insulīs

Second Declension

Some nouns in this declension are masculine, and end in *"us"* or *"er"*, e.g. *mūrus*, m . . . a wall, and *ager*, m . . . a field.

	Singular	Plural		Singular	Plural
Nom.	mūrus	mūrī		ager	agrī
Voc.	mūre	mūrī		ager	agrī
Acc.	mūrum	mūrōs		agrum	agrōs
Gen.	mūrī	mūrōrum		agrī	agrōrum
Dat.	mūrō	mūrīs		agrō	agrīs
Abl.	mūrō	mūrīs		agrō	agrīs

Some nouns in this declension are neuter, and end in *"um"*, e.g. *bellum*, n . . . war.

	Singular	Plural
Nom.	bellum	bella
Voc.	bellum	bella
Acc.	bellum	bella
Gen.	bellī	bellōrum
Dat.	bellō	bellīs
Abl.	bellō	bellīs

Third Declension

In this declension are nouns of all three genders, masculine, feminine, and neuter.

(*a*) Masculine and feminine nouns are usually declined like *rex*, m . . . a king, or *cīvis*, m . . . a citizen.

	Singular	Plural	Singular	Plural
Nom.	rex	rēgēs	cīvis	cīvēs
Voc.	rex	rēgēs	cīvis	cīvēs
Acc.	rēgem	rēgēs	cīvem	cīvēs
Gen.	rēgis	rēgum	cīvis	cīvium
Dat.	rēgī	rēgibus	cīvī	cīvibus
Abl.	rēge	rēgibus	cīve	cīvibus

Parisyllabic nouns (i.e. with the same number of syllables in nominative and genitive singular) e.g. *nāvis* (nom.), *nāvis* (gen.) are declined like *cīvis*, except the following "family" nouns:

> *pater*, m, father   *senex*, m, old man
> *māter*, f, mother   *iuvenis*, m, young man
> *frāter*, m, brother   *canis*, m, dog

These nouns have the same genitive plural ending as *rex*.

Imparisyllabic nouns (i.e. with more syllables in genitive than in the nominative singular case) e.g. *ōrātor* (nom.), *ōrātōris* (gen.) are declined like *rex*, except those which are monosyllabic and whose stem ends in two consonants e.g. *urbs*, *urbis*—city; *mens*, *mentis*—mind.

They have the same genitive plural ending as *cīvis*.

(*b*) Neuter nouns are declined like *mare*, n . . . the sea, or *tempus*, n . . . time.

	Singular	Plural	Singular	Plural
Nom.	mare	maria	tempus	tempora
Voc.	mare	maria	tempus	tempora
Acc.	mare	maria	tempus	tempora
Gen.	maris	marium	temporis	temporum
Dat.	marī	maribus	temporī	temporibus
Abl.	marī	maribus	tempore	temporibus

The nouns whose stems end in *ar*, *al*, *il*, are declined like *mare*, others like *tempus*.

Fourth Declension

In this declension, masculine and feminine nouns end in "*us*", e.g. *exercitus*, m . . . an army, *manus*, f . . . a hand, and neuter nouns in "*u*", e.g. *cornū*, n . . . horn.

	Singular	Plural	Singular	Plural
Nom.	exercitus	exercitūs	cornū	cornua
Voc.	exercitus	exercitūs	cornū	cornua
Acc.	exercitum	exercitūs	cornū	cornua
Gen.	exercitūs	exercituum	cornūs	cornuum
Dat.	exercituī	exercitibus	cornū	cornibus
Abl.	exercitū	exercitibus	cornū	cornibus

Fifth Declension

The nouns in this declension are all declined like *diēs*, m, or f . . . a day, or *rēs*, f . . . a thing.

	Singular	Plural	Singular	Plural
Nom.	diēs	diēs	rēs	rēs
Voc.	diēs	diēs	rēs	rēs
Acc.	diem	diēs	rem	rēs
Gen.	diēī	diērum	reī	rērum
Dat.	diēī	diēbus	reī	rēbus
Abl.	diē	diēbus	rē	rēbus

Irregular Nouns·

A few of the commoner nouns which contain irregularities of inflexion are given below:

domus, f . . . house, home; *vīs*, f . . . force; *bos*, c . . . ox; *Iuppiter*, m . . . Juppiter

	Singular	Plural	Singular	Plural
Nom. Voc.	*domus*	*domūs*	*vīs*	*vīrēs*
Acc.	*domum*	*domūs (domōs)*	*vim*	*vīrēs*
Gen.	*domūs (or domī)*	*domōrum*	—	*vīrium*
Dat.	*domuī (domō)*	*domibus*	—	*vīribus*
Abl.	*domū (domō)*	*domibus*	*vī*	*vīribus*

	Singular	Plural	Singular
Nom. Voc.	*bos*	*bovēs*	*Iuppiter*
Acc.	*bovem*	*bovēs*	*Iovem*
Gen.	*bovis*	*boum*	*Iovis*
Dat.	*bovī*	*bōbus (būbus)*	*Iovī*
Abl.	*bove*	*bōbus (būbus)*	*Iove*

ADJECTIVES

In Latin, adjectives, like nouns, have different "endings", or inflections. If an adjective describes a singular masculine noun it has one set of endings, if it describes a singular feminine noun it has another set. All adjectives must agree with the noun they describe in three respects:

(a) Number, i.e. Singular or Plural
(b) Gender, i.e. Masculine, Feminine or Neuter
(c) Case, whichever case the noun is in.

Therefore each adjective must have three different sets of endings, in singular and plural, in order to be able to agree with masculine, feminine, and neuter nouns.

There are two main classes of adjectives in Latin.

Class I

In this class, adjectives have the endings of First and Second Declension nouns and are declined either like *bonus, -a, -um* . . . good; *asper, aspera, asperum* . . . rough; or *āter, ātra, ātrum* . . . black.

	Singular			Plural		
	MASC.	FEM.	NEUT.	MASC.	FEM.	NEUT.
Nom.	*bonus*	*-a*	*-um*	*bonī*	*-ae*	*-a*
Voc.	*bone*	*-a*	*-um*	*bonī*	*-ae*	*-a*
Acc.	*bonum*	*-am*	*-um*	*bonōs*	*-ās*	*-a*
Gen.	*bonī*	*-ae*	*-ī*	*bonōrum*	*-ārum*	*-ōrum*
Dat.	*bonō*	*-ae*	*-ō*	*bonīs*	*-īs*	*-īs*
Abl.	*bonō*	*-ā*	*-ō*	*bonīs*	*-īs*	*-īs*
Nom. Voc.	*asper*	*aspera*	*asperum*	*asperī*	*-ae*	*-a*
Acc.	*asperum*	*-am*	*-um*	*asperōs*	*-ās*	*-a*
Gen.	*asperī*	*-ae*	*-ī*	*asperōrum*	*-ārum*	*-ōrum*
Dat.	*asperō*	*-ae*	*-ō*	*asperīs*	*-īs*	*-īs*
Abl.	*asperō*	*-ā*	*-ō*	*asperīs*	*-īs*	*-īs*
Nom. Voc.	*āter*	*ātra*	*ātrum*	*ātrī*	*-ae*	*-a*
Acc.	*ātrum*	*-am*	*-um*	*ātrōs*	*-ās*	*-a*
Gen.	*ātrī*	*-ae*	*-ī*	*ātrōrum*	*-ārum*	*-ōrum*
Dat.	*ātrō*	*-ae*	*-ō*	*ātrīs*	*-īs*	*-īs*
Abl.	*ātro*	*-ā*	*-ō*	*ātrīs*	*-īs*	*-īs*

Class II

These adjectives are declined like nouns of the Third Declension. If the nominative ends in *is* (*omnis* ... all), *er* (*ācer* ... keen), *x* (*fēlix* ... happy), *ens* (*ingens* ... huge), they are declined as follows:

	Singular		Plural	
	MASC. AND FEM.	NEUT.	MASC. AND FEM.	NEUT.
Nom. Voc.	*omnis*	*omne*	*omnēs*	*-ia*
Acc.	*omnem*	*-e*	*omnēs*	*-ia*
Gen.	*omnis*	*-is*	*omnium*	*-ium*
Dat.	*omnī*	*-ī*	*omnibus*	*-ibus*
Abl.	*omnī*	*-ī*	*omnibus*	*-ibus*

	MASC.	FEM.	NEUT.	MASC. AND FEM.	NEUT.
Nom. Voc.	*ācer*	*ācris*	*ācre*	*ācrēs*	*-ia*
Acc.	*ācrem*	*-em*	*-e*	*ācrēs*	*-ia*
Gen.	*ācris*	*-is*	*-is*	*ācrium*	*-ium*
Dat.	*ācrī*	*-ī*	*-ī*	*ācribus*	*-ibus*
Abl.	*ācrī*	*-ī*	*-ī*	*ācribus*	*-ibus*

	MASC. AND FEM.	NEUT.	MASC. AND FEM.	NEUT.
Nom. Voc.	*fēlix*	*-ix*	*fēlicēs*	*-ia*
Acc.	*fēlicem*	*-ix*	*fēlicēs*	*-ia*
Gen.	*fēlicis*	*-is*	*fēlicium*	*-ium*
Dat.	*fēlicī*	*-ī*	*fēlicibus*	*-ibus*
Abl.	*fēlicī*	*-ī*	*fēlicibus*	*-ibus*

Nom. Voc.	*ingens*	*-ens*	*ingentēs*	*-ia*
Acc.	*ingentem*	*-ens*	*ingentēs*	*-ia*
Gen.	*ingentis*	*-is*	*ingentium*	*-ium*
Dat.	*ingentī*	*-ī*	*ingentibus*	*-ibus*
Abl.	*ingentī*	*-ī*	*ingentibus*	*-ibus*

Other adjectives of the Class II are declined like *melior* ... better, or *vetus* ... old.

	MASC. AND FEM.	NEUT.	MASC. AND FEM.	NEUT.
Nom. Voc.	*melior*	*-ius*	*meliōrēs*	*-a*
Acc.	*meliōrem*	*-ius*	*meliōrēs*	*-a*
Gen.	*meliōris*	*-is*	*meliōrum*	*-um*
Dat.	*meliōrī*	*-ī*	*meliōribus*	*-ibus*
Abl.	*meliōre*	*-e*	*meliōribus*	*-ibus*

Nom. Voc.	*vetus*	*-us*	*veterēs*	*-a*
Acc.	*veterem*	*-us*	*veterēs*	*-a*
Gen.	*veteris*	*-is*	*veterum*	*-um*
Dat.	*veterī*	*-ī*	*veteribus*	*-ibus*
Abl.	*vetere*	*-e*	*veteribus*	*-ibus*

Adjectives with ... *ius* in the Genitive Singular and ... *i* in the Dative Singular

There is also a class of adjectives which, from the endings of the nominative singular, one would expect to belong to Class I. They are in fact exactly the same in declension as adjectives of Class I, except in the genitive and dative singular. The genitive has the ending-*ius* in all genders, and the dative—*ī*. These adjectives are *sōlus* (alone); *tōtus* (whole); *ūnus* (one); *ullus* (any); *nullus* (not any, no one); *alius* (other, another); *alter* (one of two); *uter?* (which of two?); *neuter* (neither of two).

Singular

	MASC.	FEM.	NEUT.
Nom.	*sōlus*	*-a*	*-um*
Acc.	*sōlum*	*-am*	*-um*
Gen.	*sōlĭus*	*-ĭus*	*-ĭus*
Dat.	*sōlĭ*	*-ĭ*	*-ĭ*
Abl.	*sōlō*	*-ā*	*-ō*

The plural is quite regular, like *bonus*.

COMPARISON OF ADJECTIVES

In English we talk of one thing being "hard", of another being "harder" and of a third thing being "hardest" of all. These are called different "degrees" of the adjective, the first being called the Positive Degree, the second the Comparative Degree, the third the Superlative Degree. In English we usually form the comparative and superlative by adding -er and -est to the adjective, e.g. harder, hardest. In Latin we add *-ior* and *-issimus* to the *stem* of the adjective. (The stem is the genitive singular without its ending). Thus positive *dūrus*—hard, genitive *dūrī*, gives comparative *dūrior*, (harder) and superlative *"dūrissimus"*, (hardest). Comparative adjectives are declined like *melior* (P. 298) and superlative adjectives like *bonus* (P. 297).

Besides "harder", *durior* can mean "too hard", and besides "hardest", *dūrissimus* can mean "very hard".

N.B. Adjectives which end in *-er* form the superlative by doubling the "*r*" and adding *-imus*, e.g.

> *asper—asperrimus, niger—nigerrimus*
> *ācer—ācerrimus, celer—celerrimus*

Six adjectives form the superlative by doubling the "*l*" and adding *-imus*. They are:

facilis, (easy)—*facillimus*	*difficilis*, (difficult)—*difficillimus*
similis, (like)—*simillimus*	*dissimilis*, (unlike)—*dissimillimus*
gracilis, (slender)—*gracillimus*	*humilis*, (low)—*humillimus*

Irregular Comparisons

bonus, good	*melior*, better	*optimus*, best
malus, bad	*pēior*, worse	*pessimus*, worst
magnus, great	*māior*, greater	*maximus*, greatest
parvus, small	*minor*, smaller	*minimus*, smallest
multus, much	*plūs*, more	*plūrimus*, most
senex, old	*nātū māior*, older	*nātū maximus*, oldest
iuvenis, young	*nātū minor*, younger	*nātū minimus*, youngest

When two things are compared after the comparative one may use *quam* (than), and put the two things in the same case, or omit the *quam* and put the second thing in the ablative case:

Illud est durius quam hoc (nom. sing. neut.). That is harder than this.
Illud est hoc (abl. sing. neut.) *durius*. That is harder than this.

VERBS

In Latin, when the subject of a verb is a pronoun, I, you, he, etc., it is represented by the ending or inflection only. Further, different inflections show differences of tense, e.g. Present, I am loving, *am-ō*; Future, I shall love, *am-ābō*. Verbs which have a similar set of endings are classed together into what is known as a Conjugation. There are four of these in Latin. All verbs, except irregular ones, fall into one of these conjugations, according to the termination of their present infinitive. To love, to advise, to rule, to hear, are present infinitives in English. *Am-āre, mon-ēre, reg-ěre, aud-īre* are the corresponding infinitives in Latin. So, verbs with infinitives ending in *-āre* belong to the First Conjugation. Verbs with infinitives ending in *-ēre* belong to the Second Conjugation. Verbs with infinitives ending in *-ěre* belong to the Third Conjugation. Verbs with infinitives ending in *-īre* belong to the Fourth Conjugation.

TABLES OF THE REGULAR VERBS

Active Voice

First Conjugation. Example, *Amō*, I love.
(From Present Stem *Am-*)

INDICATIVE MOOD	SUBJUNCTIVE MOOD
Present	*Present*
Am-ō, I love, I am loving	*Am-em*
Am-ās, you love, you are loving	*Am-ēs*
Am-at, he, she, it loves; he, she, it is loving	*Am-et*
Am-āmus, we love, we are loving	*Am-ēmus*
Am-ātis, you love, you are loving	*Am-ētis*
Am-ant, they love, they are loving	*Am-ent*
Imperfect	*Imperfect*
Am-ābam, I was loving, I used to love	*Am-ārem*
Am-ābās, you were loving, you used to love	*Am-ārēs*
Am-ābat, he, she, it was loving, he, she, it used to love	*Am-āret*
Am-ābāmus, we were loving, we used to love	*Am-ārēmus*
Am-ābātis, you were loving, you used to love	*Am-ārētis*
Am-ābant, they were loving, they used to love	*Am-ārent*

Future

Am-ābō, I shall love	Present Participle
Am-ābis, you will love	*Am-ans*, loving
Am-ābit, he, she, it will love	Present Infinitive
Am-ābimus, we shall love	*Am-āre*, to love
Am-ābitis, you will love	Gerund
Am-ābunt, they will love	*Am-andum-ī*, loving (noun)

IMPERATIVE MOOD

Am-ā, love thou	*Am-āte*, love ye	*Am-ātō*, thou shalt love
Am-ātōte, ye shall love	*Am-ātō*, he shall love	*Am-antō*, they shall love

(From Perfect Stem *Amāv-*)

INDICATIVE MOOD	SUBJUNCTIVE MOOD
Perfect	*Perfect*
Amāv-ī, I loved, I did love, I have loved	*Amāv-erim*
Amāv-istī, you loved, etc.	*Amāv-erīs*
Amāv-it, he, she, it loved, etc.	*Amāv-erit*
Amāv-imus, we loved, etc.	*Amāv-erīmus*
Amāv-istis, you loved, etc.	*Amāv-erītis*
Amāv-ērunt, or *-ěre*, they loved, *etc*	*Amāv-erint*

INDICATIVE MOOD	SUBJUNCTIVE MOOD
Pluperfect	*Pluperfect*

Amāv-eram, I had loved   *Amāv-issem*
Amāv-erās, you had loved   *Amāv-issēs*
Amāv-erat, he, she, it had loved   *Amāv-isset*
Amāv-erāmus, we had loved   *Amāv-issēmus*
Amāv-erātis, you had loved   *Amāv-issētis*
Amāv-erant, they had loved   *Amāv-issent*

Future Perfect

Amāv-erō, I shall have loved   Perfect Infinitive
Amāv-eris, you will have loved   *Amāv-isse*, to have
Amāv-erit, he, she, it will have loved   loved
Amāv-erimus, we shall have loved
Amāv-eritis, you shall have loved
Amāv-erint, they will have loved

(From Supine Stem *Amāt-*)
First Supine, *Amāt-um*   Second Supine, *Amāt-ū*

Future Participle, *Amāt-ūrus, -a, -um*, about to love
Future Infinitive = Future Participle + *esse* = *Amātūrus esse*, to be about
to love.

Second Conjugation. Example, *Moneō*, I warn.
(From Present Stem *Mon-*)

INDICATIVE MOOD		SUBJUNCTIVE MOOD	
Present		*Present*	
Mon-eō	*Mon-ēmus*	*Mon-eam*	*Mon-eāmus*
Mon-ēs	*Mon-ētis*	*Mon-eās*	*Mon-eātis*
Mon-et	*Mon-ent*	*Mon-eat*	*Mon-eant*
Imperfect		*Imperfect*	
Mon-ēbam	*Mon-ēbāmus*	*Mon-ērem*	*Mon-ērēmus*
Mon-ēbās	*Mon-ēbātis*	*Mon-ērēs*	*Mon-ērētis*
Mon-ēbat	*Mon-ēbant*	*Mon-ēret*	*Mon-ērent*
Future			
Mon-ēbō	*Mon-ēbimus*	Present Participle.	*Mon-ens*
Mon-ēbis	*Mon-ēbitis*	Present Infinitive.	*Mon-ēre*
Mon-ēbit	*Mon-ēbunt*	Gerund.	*Mon-endum, -ī.*

IMPERATIVE MOOD

Mon-ē warn thou   *Mon-ēte* warn ye   *Mon-ētō* thou shalt warn
Mon-ētōte ye shall warn   *Mon-ētō* he shall warn   *Mon-ento* they shall warn

(From Perfect Stem *Monu-*)

INDICATIVE MOOD		SUBJUNCTIVE MOOD	
Perfect		*Perfect*	
Monu-ī	*Monu-imus*	*Monu-erim*	*Monu-erīmus*
Monu-istī	*Monu-istis*	*Monu-erīs*	*Monu-erītis*
Monu-it	*Monu-ērunt* or *-ēre*	*Monu-erit*	*Monu-erint*

INDICATIVE MOOD		SUBJUNCTIVE MOOD	
Pluperfect		*Pluperfect*	
Monu-eram	*Monu-erāmus*	*Monu-issem*	*Monu-issēmus*
Monu-erās	*Monu-erātis*	*Monu-issēs*	*Monu-issētis*
Monu-erat	*Monu-erant*	*Monu-isset*	*Monu-issent*

Future Perfect		
Monu-erō	*Monu-erimus*	Perfect Infinitive, *Monu-isse,*
Monu-eris	*Monu-eritis*	
Monu-erit	*Monu-erint*	

(From Supine Stem *Monit-*)

First Supine, *Monit-um* Second Supine, *Monit-ū*

Future Participle, *Monit-ūrus, -a, -um*

Future Infinitive = Future Participle + *esse* = *Monitūrus esse*

Third Conjugation. Example, *Regō*, I rule.
(From Present Stem *Reg-*.)

INDICATIVE MOOD		SUBJUNCTIVE MOOD	
Present		*Present*	
Reg-ō	*Reg-imus*	*Reg-am*	*Reg-āmus*
Reg-is	*Reg-itis*	*Reg-ās*	*Reg-ātis*
Reg-it	*Reg-unt*	*Reg-at*	*Reg-ant*

Imperfect		*Imperfect*	
Reg-ēbam	*Reg-ēbāmus*	*Reg-erem*	*Reg-erēmus*
Reg-ēbās	*Reg-ēbātis*	*Reg-erēs*	*Reg-erētis*
Reg-ēbat	*Reg-ēbant*	*Reg-eret*	*Reg-erent*

Future			
Reg-am	*Reg-ēmus*	Present Participle.	*Reg-ens*
Reg-ēs	*Reg-ētis*	Present Infinitive.	*Reg-ere*
Reg-et	*Reg-ent*	Gerund.	*Reg-endum, -ī*

IMPERATIVE MOOD

Rege, rule thou	*Regite*, rule ye	*Regito*, thou shalt rule
Regitōte, ye shall rule	*Regitō*, he shall rule	*Reguntō*, they shall rule

(From Perfect Stem *Rex-*)

INDICATIVE MOOD		SUBJUNCTIVE MOOD	
Perfect		*Perfect*	
Rex-ī	*Rex-imus*	*Rex-erim*	*Rex-erīmus*
Rex-istī	*Rex-istis*	*Rex-eris*	*Rex-erītis*
Rex-it	*Rex-ērunt* or *-ēre*	*Rex-erit*	*Rex-erint*

Pluperfect		*Pluperfect*	
Rex-eram	*Rex-erāmus*	*Rex-issem*	*Rex-issēmus*
Rex-erās	*Rex-erātis*	*Rex-issēs*	*Rex-issētis*
Rex-erat	*Rex-erant*	*Rex-isset*	*Rex-issent*

Future Perfect		
Rex-erō	*Rex-erimus*	Perfect Infinitive, *Rex-isse*
Rex-eris	*Rex-eritis*	
Rex-erit	*Rex-erint*	

(From Supine Stem *Rect-*)

First Supine, *Rect-um*   Second Supine, *Rect-ū*

Future Participle, *Rect-ūrus, -a, -um*

Future Infinitive = Future Participle + *esse* = *Rectūrus esse*

Fourth Conjugation. Example, *Audiō*, I hear.

(From Present Stem *Aud-*)

INDICATIVE MOOD		SUBJUNCTIVE MOOD	
Present		*Present*	
Aud-iō	*Aud-īmus*	*Aud-iam*	*Aud-iāmus*
Aud-īs	*Aud-ītis*	*Aud-iās*	*Aud-iātis*
Aud-it	*Aud-iunt*	*Aud-iat*	*Aud-iant*
Imperfect		*Imperfect*	
Aud-iēbam	*Aud-iēbāmus*	*Aud-īrem*	*Aud-īrēmus*
Aud-iēbās	*Aud-iēbātis*	*Aud-īrēs*	*Aud-īrētis*
Aud-iēbat	*Aud-iēbant*	*Aud-īret*	*Aud-īrent*

Future

Aud-iam	*Aud-iēmus*	Present Participle.	*Aud-iens*
Aud-iēs	*Aud-iētis*	Present Infinitive.	*Aud-īre*
Aud-iet	*Aud-ient*	Gerund.	*Aud-iendum, -ī*

IMPERATIVE MOOD

Aud-ī, hear thou   *Aud-īte*, hear ye   *Aud-ītō*, thou shalt hear
Aud-ītōte, ye shall hear   *Aud-ītō*, he shall hear *Aud-iuntō*, they shall hear

(From Perfect Stem *Audīv-*)

INDICATIVE MOOD		SUBJUNCTIVE MOOD	
Perfect		*Perfect*	
Audīv-ī	*Audīv-imus*	*Audīv-erim*	*Audīv-erīmus*
Audīv-istī	*Audīv-istis*	*Audīv-erīs*	*Audīv-erītis*
Audīv-it	*Audīv-ērunt* or *-ēre*	*Audīv-erit*	*Audīv-erint*
Pluperfect		*Pluperfect*	
Audīv-eram	*Audīv-erāmus*	*Audīv-issem*	*Audīv-issēmus*
Audīv-erās	*Audīv-erātis*	*Audīv-issēs*	*Audīv-issētis*
Audīv-erat	*Audīv-erant*	*Audīv-isset*	*Audīv-issent*

Future Perfect		
Audīv-erō	*Audīv-erimus*	Perfect Infinitive, *Audīv-isse*
Audīv-eris	*Audīv-eritis*	
Audīv-erit	*Audīv-erint*	

(From Supine Stem *Audīt-*)

First Supine   *Audīt-um*   Second Supine, *Audīt-ū*

Future Participle, *Audīt-ūrus, -a, um*, about to hear

Future Infinitive = Future Participle + *esse* = *Audītūrus esse*

Passive Voice
First Conjugation. *Amor*, I am loved.

(From Present Stem *Am-*)

INDICATIVE MOOD	SUBJUNCTIVE MOOD
Present	*Present*

Am-or, I am being loved

Am-er

Am-āris (-āre), you are being loved

Am-ēris (ēre)

Am-ātur, he is being loved

Am-ētur

Am-āmur, we are being loved

Am-ēmur

Am-āminī, you are being loved

Am-ēminī

Am-antur, they are being loved

Am-entur

Imperfect *Imperfect*

Am-ābar, I was being loved

Am-ārer

Am-ābāris (-ābāre), you were being loved

Am-ārēris (-ārēre)

Am-ābātur, he was being loved

Am-ārētur

Am-ābāmur, we were being loved

Am-ārēmur

Am-ābāminī, you were being loved

Am-ārēminī

Am-ābantur, they were being loved

Am-ārentur

Future

Am-ābor, I shall be loved

Present Participle
—

Am-āberis (-ābere), you will be loved

Present Infinitive

Am-ābitur, he will be loved

Amārī, to be loved

Am-ābimur we shall be loved

Gerundive

Am-ābiminī, you shall be loved

Amandus, -a, -um, fit to

Am-ābuntur, they will be loved

be loved

IMPERATIVE MOOD

Am-āre } be thou loved
Am-ātor }

Am-āminī, be ye loved

Am-ātor, let him be loved

Am-antor, let them be loved

Perfect Tenses

INDICATIVE MOOD	SUBJUNCTIVE MOOD
Perfect	*Perfect*

Amātus, a, um, I have been loved

Amātus, etc., *sim*

Amātus, etc., *es*, you have been loved

Amātus, etc., *sīs*

Amātus, etc., *est*, he has been loved

Amātus, etc., *sit*

Amātī, etc., *sumus*, we have been loved

Amātī, etc., *sīmus*

Amātī, etc., *estis*, you have been loved

Amātī, etc., *sītis*

Amātī, etc., *sunt*, they have been loved

Amātī, etc., *sint*

Pluperfect *Pluperfect*

Amātus eram, I had been loved

Amātus essem

Amātus erās, you had been loved

Amātus essēs

Amātus erat, he had been loved

Amātus esset

Amātī erāmus, we had been loved

Amātī essēmus

Amātī erātis, you had been loved

Amātī essētis

Amātī erant, they had been loved

Amātī essent

Future Perfect

Amātus erō, I shall have been loved

Perfect Infinitive

Amātus eris, you will have been loved

Amātus esse, to have

Amātus erit, he will have been loved

been loved

Amātī erimus, we shall have been loved

Amātī eritis, you will have been loved

Amātī erunt, they will have been loved

(From Supine Stem *Amāt-*)

Past Participle Passive, *Amātus, -a, -um.* Future Infinitive Passive, *Amātum īrī*, to be about to be loved.

Second Conjugation. *Moneor*, I am warned.

(From Present Stem *Mon-*)

INDICATIVE MOOD		SUBJUNCTIVE MOOD	
Present		*Present*	
Mon-eor	Mon-ēmur	Mon-ear	Mon-eāmur
Mon-ēris	Mon-ēminī	Mon-eāris	Mon-eāminī
(or -*ēre*)		(or -*eāre*)	
Mon-ētur	Mon-entur	Mon-eātur	Mon-eantur
Imperfect		*Imperfect*	
Mon-ēbar	Mon-ēbāmur	Mon-ērer	Mon-ērēmur
Mon-ēbāris	Mon-ēbāminī	Mon-ērēris	Mon-ērēminī
(or -*ēbāre*)		(or *ērēre*)	
Mon-ēbātur	Mon-ēbantur	Mon-ērētur	Mon-ērentur
Future			
Mon-ēbor	Mon-ēbimur	Present Participle, —	
Mon-ēberis (or -*ēbere*)	Mon-ēbiminī	Present Infinitive, *Mon-ērī*	
Mon-ēbitur	Mon-ēbuntur	Gerundive, *Mon-endus, -a, -um*	

IMPERATIVE MOOD			
Mon-ēre	Mon-ēminī	Mon-ētor	
		Mon-ētor	Mon-entor

Perfect Tenses

INDICATIVE MOOD		SUBJUNCTIVE MOOD	
Perfect		*Perfect*	
Monitus sum	Monitī sumus	Monitus sim	Monitī sīmus
Monitus es	Monitī estis	Monitus sīs	Monitī sītis
Monitus est	Monitī sunt	Monitus sit	Monitī sint
Pluperfect		*Pluperfect*	
Monitus eram	Monitī erāmus	Monitus essem	Monitī essēmus
Monitus erās	Monitī erātis	Monitus essēs	Monitī essētis
Monitus erat	Monitī erant	Monitus esset	Monitī essent
Future Perfect		Perfect Infinitive, *Monitus esse*	
Monitus erō	Monitī erimus		
Monitus eris	Monitī eritis		
Monitus erit	Monitī erunt		

(From Supine Stem *Monit*)

Past Participle Passive, *Monitus, -a, -um*
Future Infinitive Passive, *Monitum īrī*

Third Conjugation. *Regor*, I am ruled.
(From Present Stem *Reg-*)

INDICATIVE MOOD		SUBJUNCTIVE MOOD	
Present		*Present*	
Reg-or	Reg-imur	Reg-ar	Reg-āmur
Reg-eris (-*ere*)	Reg-iminī	Reg-āris (-*āre*)	Reg-āminī
Reg-itur	Reg-untur	Reg-ātur	Reg-antur

INDICATIVE MOOD		SUBJUNCTIVE MOOD	
Imperfect		*Imperfect*	
Reg-ēbar	*Reg-ēbāmur*	*Reg-erer*	*Reg-erēmur*
Reg-ēbāris	*Reg-ēbāminī*	*Reg-erēris*	*Reg-erēminī*
(*-ēbāre*)		(*-erēre*)	
Reg-ēbātur	*Reg-ēbantur*	*Reg-erētur*	*Reg-erentur*

Future			
Reg-ar	*Reg-ēmur*	Present Participle, —	
Reg-ēris (*-ēre*)	*Reg-ēminī*	Present Infinitive, *Reg-i*	
Reg-ētur	*Reg-entur*	Gerundive, *Reg-endus, -a, -um*	

IMPERATIVE MOOD

Reg-ere	*Reg-iminī*	*Reg-itor*	
		Reg-itor	*Reg-untor*

Perfect Tenses

INDICATIVE MOOD		SUBJUNCTIVE MOOD	
Perfect		*Perfect*	
Rectus sum	*Rectī sumus*	*Rectus sim*	*Rectī sīmus*
Rectus es	*Rectī estis*	*Rectus sīs*	*Rectī sītis*
Rectus est	*Rectī sunt*	*Rectus sit*	*Rectī sint*

Pluperfect		*Pluperfect*	
Rectus eram	*Rectī erāmus*	*Rectus essem*	*Rectī essēmus*
Rectus erās	*Rectī erātis*	*Rectus essēs*	*Rectī essētis*
Rectus erat	*Rectī erant*	*Rectus esset*	*Rectī essent*

Future Perfect		Perfect Infinitive, *Rectus esse*	
Rectus erō	*Rectī erimus*		
Rectus eris	*Rectī eritis*		
Rectus-erit	*Recti erunt*		

(From Supine Stem *Rect-*)

Past Participle Passive, *Rectus, -a, -um*

Future Infinitive Passive, *Rectum īrī.*

Fourth Conjugation. *Audior,* I am heard.

(From Present Stem *Aud-*)

INDICATIVE MOOD		SUBJUNCTIVE MOOD	
Present		*Present*	
Aud-ior	*Aud-īmur*	*Aud-iar*	*Aud-iāmur*
Aud-īris (*-īre*)	*Aud-īminī*	*Aud-iāris*	*Aud-iāminī*
		(*-iāre*)	
Aud-ītur	*Aud-iuntur*	*Aud-iātur*	*Aud-iantur*

Imperfect		*Imperfect*	
Aud-iēbār	*Aud-iēbāmur*	*Aud-īrer*	*Aud-īrēmur*
Aud-iēbāris	*Aud-iēbāminī*	*Aud-īrēris*	*Aud-īrēminī*
(*-iēbāre*)		(*-īrēre*)	
Aud-iēbātur	*Aud-iēbantur*	*Aud-īrētur*	*Aud-īrentur*

Future			
Aud-iar	*Aud-iēmur*	Present Participle, —	
Aud-iēris	*Aud-iēminī*	Present Infinitive, *Aud-īrī*	
(*-iēre*)		Gerundive, *Aud-iendus, -a, -um*	
Aud-iētur	*Aud-ientur*		

IMPERATIVE MOOD

Aud-īre	*Aud-īminī*	*Aud-ītor*	
		Aud-ītor	*·Aud-iuntor*

Perfect Tenses

INDICATIVE MOOD		SUBJUNCTIVE MOOD	
Perfect		*Perfect*	
Audītus sum	*Audītī sumus*	*Audītus sim*	*Audītī sīmus*
Audītus es	*Audītī estis*	*Audītus sīs*	*Audītī sītis*
Audītus est	*Audītī sunt*	*Audītus sit*	*Audītī sint*
Pluperfect		*Pluperfect*	
Audītus eram	*Audītī erāmus*	*Audītus essem*	*Audītī essēmus*
Audītus erās	*Audītī erātis*	*Audītus essēs*	*Audītī essētis*
Audītus erat	*Audītī erant*	*Audītus esset*	*Audītī essent*
Future Perfect			
Audītus erō	*Audītī erimus*	Perfect Infinitive, *Audītus esse*	
Audītus eris	*Audītī eritis*		
Audītus erit	*Audītī erunt*		

(From Supine Stem *Audīt-*)
Past Participle Passive, *Audītus, -a, -um*
Future Infinitive Passive, *Audītum īrī.*

IRREGULAR VERBS

Verb *Sum*, I am

(Tenses from the Present Stems)

INDICATIVE	SUBJUNCTIVE
Present	*Present*
sum, I am	*sim*
es, you are	*sīs*
est, he is	*sit*
sumus, we are	*sīmus*
estis, you are	*sītis*
sunt, they are	*sint*
Imperfect	*Imperfect*
eram, I was	*essem*
erās, you were	*essēs*
erat, he was	*esset*
erāmus, we were	*essēmus*
erātis, you were	*essētis*
erant, they were	*essent*
Future	
erō, I shall be	Present Infinitive
eris, you will be	*Esse*, to be
erit, he will be	
erimus, we shall be	
eritis, you will be	
erunt, they will be	

IMPERATIVE

Es, be (thou)	*Estō*, you shall be
Este, be (ye)	*Estôte*, you shall be
	Estō, he shall be
	Suntō, they shall be

(From Perfect Stem *Fu-*)

INDICATIVE	SUBJUNCTIVE
Perfect	*Perfect*

Fu-ī, I have been or I was	*Fu-erim*
Fu-istī, you have been or you were	*Fu-erīs*
Fu-it, he has been or he was	*Fu-erit*
Fu-imus, we have been or we were	*Fu-erīmus*
Fu-istis, you have been or you were	*Fu-erītis*
Fu-ērunt or *-ēre*, they have been or they were	*Fu-erint*

Pluperfect	*Pluperfect*
Fu-eram, I had been	*Fu-issem*
Fu-erās, you had been	*Fu-issēs*
Fu-erat, he had been	*Fu-isset*
Fu-erāmus, we had been	*Fu-issēmus*
Fu-erātis, you had been	*Fu-issētis*
Fu-erant, they had been	*Fu-issent*

Future Perfect	
Fu-erō, I shall have been	Perfect Infinitive,
Fu-eris, you will have been	*Fu-isse*, to have been
Fu-erit, he will have been	
Fu-erimus, we shall have been	
Fu-eritis, you will have been	
Fu-erint, they will have been	

(From Supine Stem *Fut-*)

First Supine, wanting. Second Supine, wanting
Future Participle, *Futūrus, -a, -um*, about to be
Future Infinitive, *Futūrus esse*, to be about to be

Tables of the commoner irregular verbs are given below:

Possum	*posse*	*potuī*	—	to be able
Volō	*velle*	*voluī*	—	to wish
Nōlō	*nolle*	*nōluī*	—	to be unwilling
Ferō	*ferre*	*tulī*	*lātum*	to bear, bring
Fīō	*fierī*	*factus sum*		to become, be made
Eō	*īre*	*iī*	*itum*	to go

Ferre, (to bear) and *īre*, (to go) have many compounds which are conjugated
like the basic verb given below:

Active
INDICATIVE

	Singular			Plural	
Present					
Pos-sum	*pot-es*	*pot-est*	*pos-sumus*	*pot-estis*	*pos-sunt*
Volō	*vīs*	*vult*	*volumus*	*vultis*	*volunt*
Nōlō	*nōnvīs*	*nōnvult*	*nōlumus*	*nōnvultis*	*nōlunt*
Mālō	*māvīs*	*māvult*	*mālumus*	*māvultis*	*mālunt*
Ferō	*fers*	*fert*	*ferimus*	*fertis*	*ferunt*
Fīō	*fīs*	*fit*	—		*fiunt*
Eō	*īs*	*it*	*īmus*	*ītis*	*eunt*

Imperfect

Pot-eram	-erās	-erat	-erāmus	-erātis	-erant

Volē- Nōlē- Mālē- Ferē- Fiē- Ī- } bam	-bās	-bat	-bāmus	-bātis	-bant

Future

Pot-erō	-eris	-erit	-erimus	-eritis	-erun

Vol- Nōl- Māl- Fer- Fī-ō } am	-ēs	-et	-ēmus	-ētis	-ent
Ib-ō	-is	-it	-imus	-itis	-unt

Perfect, Pluperfect, Future Perfect Tenses are formed regularly from the Perfect Stem.

PARTICIPLE	INFINITIVE	GERUND
	posse	
Vol- Nōl- Māl- Fer- } ens	velle nolle malle ferre	vol- nōl- māl- fer- } endum, -ī
Ī— Gen. *euntis*	fieri ire	e-undum

SUBJUNCTIVE

	Singular			*Plural*	
Present					
Pos-sim	pos-sīs	pos-sit	pos-sīmus	pos-sītis	pos-sint
Vel- Nōl- Māl- } im	-īs	-it	-īmus	-ītis	-int
Fer- Fī- E- } am	-ās	-at	-āmus	-ātis	-ant

	Singular			*Plural*	
Imperfect					
Poss- Vell- Noll- Mall- Ferr- Fier- Ir- } em	-ēs	-et	-ēmus	-ētis	-ent

IMPERATIVE

	Singular		*Plural*	
—	—	—	—	—
Nōl-ī, nōl-ītō	nōl-ītō	nōl-īte, nōl-ītōte	nōl-untō
Fer, fer-tō	fer-tō	fer-te, fer-tōte	fer-untō
Fī	—	fī-te	—
Ī, ī-tō	ī-tō	ī-te, ī-tōte	e-untō

Passive

INDICATIVE

	Singular			*Plura*	
Present					
Fer-or	*fer-ris*	*fer-tur*	*fer-imur*	*fer-iminī*	*fer-untur*
Imperfect					
Fer-ēbar	*fer-ēbāris*	*fer-ēbātur*	*fer-ēbāmur*	*fer-ēbāminī*	*fer-ēbāntur*
Future					
Fer-ar	*Fer-ēris*	*er-ētur*	*fer-ēmur*	*fer-ēminī*	*fer-entur*

SUBJUNCTIVE

Present					
Fer-ar	*fer-āris*	*fer-ātur*	*fer-āmur*	*fer-āminī*	*fer-antur*
Imperfect					
Ferr-er	*ferr-ēris*	*ferrētur*	*ferr-ēmur*	*ferr-ēminī*	*ferr-entur*

IMPERATIVE

Fer-re, fer-tor	*fer-tor*	*fer-iminī*	*fer-untor*

Gerundive: *Fer-endus*   Present Infinitive: *Ferr-ī*

DEPONENT VERBS

Many Latin verbs are passive in form but active in meaning, e.g. *hortor* "I exhort"; *hortātus sum*, "I have exhorted"; *hortārī*, "to exhort". They are conjugated like ordinary passive verbs, but of course they have no passive meanings themselves. *Hortor* means "I exhort". If you want to say in Latin "I am exhorted", you have to use a different verb.

There are, however, two exceptions to the above rule.

1. Most deponent verbs still keep their active voice forms for the present and future participle, future infinitive and gerund, e.g. *morior*, "I die"; *moriens*, "dying"; *moritūrus*, "about to die"; *moritūrus esse*, "to be about to die"; *moriendum* (gerund) "dying".

2. Their gerundives are passive both in form and meaning. E.g. *hortandus*, "fit to be exhorted".

N.B. The past participle is passive in form, but active in meaning, e.g. *veritus*, "having feared".

Here is a list of some of the commoner deponent verbs:

	Present Tense	*Infinitive*	*Perfect Tense*	*Meaning*
1st conjugation	*cōnor*	*cōnārī*	*cōnātus sum*	to try
	hortor	*hortārī*	*hortātus sum*	to exhort
	vēnor	*vēnārī*	*vēnātus sum*	to hunt
2nd conjugation	*vereor*	*verērī*	*veritus sum*	to fear
	polliceor	*pollicērī*	*pollicitus sum*	to promise
3rd conjugation	*patior*	*patī*	*passus sum*	to suffer
	ūtor	*ūtī*	*ūsus sum*	to use
	morior	*morī*	*mortuus sum*	to die
	aggredior	*aggredī*	*agressus sum*	to attack
	prōgredior	*prōgredī*	*prōgressus sum*	to set out
	ingredior	*ingredī*	*ingressus sum*	to enter
	regredior	*regredī*	*regressus sum*	to return
	loquor	*loquī*	*locūtus sum*	to speak
	proficiscor	*proficiscī*	*profectus sum*	to set out
4th conjugation	*partior*	*partīrī*	*partītus sum*	to share
	orior	*orīrī*	*ortus sum*	to rise

IMPERSONAL VERBS

There are certain verbs in Latin which can only be used in the third person singular and in the infinitive. They never have a personal subject but always the pronoun "it"; hence they are called Impersonal Verbs. These verbs have only the third person singular *of each tense*, an infinitive, and a gerund. They may be divided into four types.

(*a*) Verbs which have an accusative of the person and a genitive of the cause:

Present	Perfect	Infinitive	Meaning
Miseret	miseruit	miserēre	it pities
Paenitet	paenituit	paenitēre	it repents
Pudet	puduit	pudēre	it shames
Taedet	taeduit	taedēre	it wearies
Piget	piguit	pigēre	it annoys, vexes

Example:
Pudet me huius facti, I am ashamed of this deed.

(*b*) In this class are two verbs which take a genitive of person, unless a personal pronoun is used, in which case they take the feminine ablative singular of the possessive pronoun. These verbs are *interest* (from *intersum*) and *rēfert* (from *re-fero*), both meaning "it matters", "it is important", "it is in the interests of—".

Example:
Interest civium regem bene regere. It is in the interest of the citizens that the king should rule well.
Quid id refert tua? What does it matter to you?

(*c*) Verbs taking the accusative and infinitive:
Oportet me, it behoves me; I ought
Decet me, it becomes me
Dēdecet me, it does not become me
Iuvat me, it delights me, I delight.

Example:
Oportet me hoc facere, I ought to do this
Oportuit me hoc facere, I ought to have done this.

(*d*) Verbs taking the dative and infinitive:
Licet mihi, it is permitted to me, I may
Accidit tibi, it happens to you
Libet } *eis*, it is pleasing to them, they are pleased.
Placet

Example:
Tibi abesse licet, you may be absent.

DEFECTIVE VERBS

There are a number of verbs in Latin which lack a considerable number of parts. The commonest of them are:

Coepī, I have begun

	Perfect	Fut. Perfect	Pluperfect	Infinitive	Perf. Subj.	Pluperf. Subj
	Coepī	coeperō	coeperam	coepisse	coeperim	coepissem

Ōdī, I hate

Ōdī	ōderō	ōderam	ōdisse	ōderim	ōdissem

Meminī, I remember

Meminī	meminerō	memineram	meminisse	meminerim	meminissem

Nōvī, I have got to know, I know

Nōvī	nōverō	nōveram	nōvisse	nōverim	nōvissem

Inquam, I say

Pres. tense	Inquam,	inquis	inquit	inquimus	inquitis	inquiunt
Imperfect	—	—	inquiēbat	—	—	inquiēbant
Future	—	—	inquiet	—	—	—
Perfect	—	inquistī	inquit	—	—	—

Fārī, to speak

Pres. tense	—	—	fātur	—	—	—
Future	Fābor	—	fābitur	—	—	—

Present Participle, acc. Fantem; Perfect, Fātus.
Gerund, Fandī, fando; Gerundive, Fandus.

Note that *memini* and *odi* are perfect in form, but present in meaning. The tenses which are missing from these verbs can often be supplied by other verbs with the same meaning, e.g. *incipio* (begin) can supply present, future, and imperfect tenses meaning I begin, I shall begin, etc.

PRONOUNS

1. *Personal Pronouns*. Latin has pronouns to translate our English "I" and "you", but they are employed in the nominative cases, only when very emphatic.

	Singular		Plural	
Nom.	ego	I	nōs	we
Acc.	mē	me	nōs	us
Gen.	meī	of me	nostrum, nostri[1]	of us
Dat.	mihī	to, for me	nōbīs	to, for us
Abl.	mē	from me	nōbīs	from us
Nom.	tū	you	vōs	you
Acc.	tē	you	vōs	you
Gen.	tūī	of you	vestrum, vestri[1]	of you
Dat.	tibī	to, for you	vōbīs	to, for you
Abl.	tē	from you	vōbīs	from you

[1] *Nostrum* and *vestrum* are partitive genitives, e.g. *Unus vestrum*, one of you. *Nostri* and *vestri* are objective genitives, e.g. *memor vestri*, mindful of you.

2. *Reflexive Pronouns.* This pronoun is used when the subject of the verb is denoted as acting on itself, e.g. The enemy are slaying themselves. *Hostes se interficiunt.*

Acc. *sē* (or *sēsē*), himself, herself, itself, themselves.
Gen. *suī*, of himself, etc.
Dat. *sibī*, to, for himself, etc.
Abl. *sē* (or *sēsē*), by, with, from himself, etc.

3. *Demonstrative Pronouns.* There are two common demonstrative pronouns in Latin which mean that; *is* and *ille.* They can also mean "he", "she" or "it". *Ille* has a stronger demonstrative force than *is*, meaning "that" (over there, near him). Declined exactly like *ille* is *iste*, meaning "that over there, near you".

	Singular			*Plura*		
	Masc.	Fem.	Neut.	Masc.	Fem.	Neut.
Nom.	*is*	*ea*	*id*	*eī (iī)*	*eae*	*ea*
Acc.	*eum*	*eam*	*id*	*eōs*	*eās*	*ea*
Gen.	*eius*	*eius*	*eius*	*eōrum*	*eārum*	*eōrum*
Dat.	*eī*	*eī*	*eī*	*eīs (iīs)*	*eīs*	*eīs*
Abl.	*eō*	*eā*	*eō*	*eīs*	*eīs*	*eīs*
Nom.	*ille*	*illa*	*illud*	*illī*	*illae*	*illa*
Acc.	*illum*	*illam*	*illud*	*illōs*	*illās*	*illa*
Gen.	*illīus*	*illīus*	*illīus*	*illōrum*	*illārum*	*illōrum*
Dat.	*illī*	*illī*	*illī*	*illīs*	*illīs*	*illīs*
Abl.	*illō*	*illā*	*illō*	*illīs*	*illīs*	*illīs*

The pronoun meaning "this" is *hic, haec, hoc.*

	Masc.	Fem.	Neut.	Masc.	Fem.	Neut.
Nom.	*hĭc*	*haec*	*hōc*	*hī*	*hae*	*haec*
Acc.	*hunc*	*hanc*	*hōc*	*hōs*	*hās*	*haec*
Gen.	*huius*	*huius*	*huius*	*hōrum*	*hārum*	*hōrum*
Dat.	*huic*	*huic*	*huic*	*hīs*	*hīs*	*hīs*
Abl.	*hōc*	*hāc*	*hōc*	*hīs*	*hīs*	*hīs*

The pronoun meaning "the same" is *idem.*

	Singular			*Plural*		
	Masc.	Fem.	Neut.	Masc.	Fem.	Neut.
Nom.	*ĭdem*	*eadem*	*idem*	*eīdem*	*eaedem*	*eadem*
Acc.	*eundem*	*eandem*	*idem*	*eōsdem*	*eāsdem*	*eadem*
Gen.	*eiusdem*	*eiusdem*	*eiusdem*	*eōrundem*	*eārundem*	*eōrundem*
Dat.	*eīdem*	*eīdem*	*eīdem*	*eīsdem*	*eīsdem*	*eīsdem*
				(or *īsdem*)		
Abl.	*eōdem*	*eādem*	*eōdem*	*eīsdem*	*eīsdem*	*eīsdem*

4. *Emphatic Pronoun. Ipse,* a pronoun meaning "— self", simply emphasizes the noun or pronoun to which it refers, e.g. *Puer ipse cantat.* The boy himself sings.

	Singular			*Plural*		
	Masc.	Fem.	Neut.	Masc.	Fem.	Neut.
Nom.	*ipse*	*ipsa*	*ipsum*	*ipsī*	*ipsae*	*ipsa*
Acc.	*ipsum*	*ipsam*	*ipsum*	*ipsōs*	*ipsās*	*ipsa*
Gen.	*ipsīus*	*ipsīus*	*ipsīus*	*ipsōrum*	*ipsārum*	*ipsōrum*
Dat.	*ipsī*	*ipsī*	*ipsī*	*ipsīs*	*ipsīs*	*ipsīs*
Abl.	*ipsō*	*ipsā*	*ipsō*	*ipsīs*	*ipsīs*	*ipsīs*

5. *Relative Pronouns*. The relative pronoun, "who", "which", is *qui, quae, quod*. In Latin this pronoun takes its number (singular or plural) and its gender (masc., fem., or neut.) from the word in the main clause of the sentence to which it refers (its antecedent). But its case is determined by its own clause, i.e. depending on whether it is the subject or object, etc., of the verb. The pronoun is declined as follows.

	Singular			*Plural*		
	Masc.	Fem.	Neut.	Masc.	Fem.	Neut.
Nom.	*quī*	*quae*	*quod*	*quī*	*quae*	*quae*
Acc.	*quem*	*quam*	*quod*	*quōs*	*quās*	*quae*
Gen.	*cuius*	*cuius*	*cuius*	*quōrum*	*quārum*	*quōrum*
Dat.	*cui*	*cui*	*cui*	*quibus*	*quibus*	*quibus*
Abl.	*quō*	*quā*	*quō*	*quibus*	*quibus*	*quibus*

6. *Interrogative Pronoun*. *Quis*, who? what? is declined in all cases except the nominative and accusative in the same way as the relative pronoun.

	Singular		
	Masc.	Fem.	Neut.
Nom.	*quis*	*quis*	*quid*
Acc.	*quem*	*quam*	*quid*

7. *Other Pronouns*. A list of other pronouns in common use is given below:

Masc.	Fem.	Neut.	Meaning
quīdam	*quaedam*	*quoddam*	a certain (person) (thing)
aliquis	*aliqua*	*aliquid*	someone, something
quivīs	*quaevīs*	*quodvīs* ⎫	anyone you like
quilibet	*quaelibet*	*quodlibet* ⎬	
quisque	*quaeque*	*quodque*	each
quīcumque	*quaecumque*	*quodcumque* ⎫	whosoever, whatsoever
quisquis	*quisquis*	*quidquid* ⎬	
quisquam	*quaequam*	*quidquam*	anyone

PREPOSITIONS

In Latin prepositions help the inflections or endings of nouns, adjectives, and pronouns to show the relations between them and other words in a sentence. They are also compounded with verbs, to change the meaning of the original verb, e.g. *eo*, I go; *abeo*, I go away.

The following is a list of the prepositions used with the ablative case:
ā, ab, cum, dē, cōram, palam, ē, ex, sine, tenus, prō, prae
Nearly all other prepositions are used with the accusative case.

The following prepositions take the accusative when "motion towards" is meant, and the ablative when "place where" is meant.

| *in* | in, on, into | *super* | upon, over |
| *sub* | under, up to | *subter* | under |

CONJUNCTIONS

Conjunctions are words which join together words or sentences. The commonest of them are given, with their meanings, and in alphabetical order, below.

after	*postquam* (with verb in indicative)
and	*et, atque, āc, -que* (joined to a word)
and ... lest	*neu, nēve* (with verb in subjunctive)
and ... not	*nec, neque*
although	*quamquam* (with factual concessive clause); *quamvis* (hypothetical)
as	*ut* (with verb in indicative)
as if	*quasi*
as soon as	*cum prīmum, ut prīmum, simul āc (atque)*
because	*quod, quia, quoniam, cum*
before	*antequam, priusquam* (with indicative when purely temporal; subjunctive when there is an additional idea of intention)
both ... and	*et ... et*
but	*sed, autem* (second word)
but ... not	*neque ... vēro*
either ... or	*aut ... aut, vel ... vel*
for	*nam, namque, enim* (second word)
for ... not	*neque ... enim*
however	*tamen, autem*
if	*sī* (with indicative or subjunctive, depending on the type of conditional sentence)
if not	*nisi, sī ... non*
just as if	*tamquam sī* (with verb in subjunctive)
neither	*nec, neque*
neither ... nor	*neque ... neque, nec ... nec*
nevertheless	*tamen*
or	*aut, vel;* (in questions) *an*
questions are introduced by	*ne* (joined to the first word in the sentence)
	nonne (introducing a question expecting the answer "yes")
	num (introducing a question expecting the answer "no")
since	*cum, quoniam*
so (in such a way) ... that	*ita ... ut*
so that (purpose)	*ut*
so that ... never	*ut numquam* (consecutive); *nē umquam* (purpose)
so that ... not	*ut nōn* (consecutive); *nē* (purpose)
so that ... no-one	*ut nēmo* (consecutive); *nē quis* (purpose)
so that ... nowhere	*ut nusquam* (consecutive); *nē usquam* (purpose)
therefore	*itaque, igitur*
until	*dum, dōnec* (with verb in indicative when purely temporal, subjunctive when there is an additional idea of purpose)
when	*cum, ubĭ* (temporal); *quandō* (interrogative)
where	*ubĭ* (relative and interrogative)
whether	*num* (introducing single indirect questions); *ŭtrum* (introducing alternative indirect questions); *sīve, seu* (introducing alternative conditional sentences)
while	*dum* (usually with verb in indicative)
whither	*quō* (relative and interrogative)
why	*cur, quārē*

ADVERBS

In Latin it is easy to make adverbs from adjectives. With adjectives of Class I, simply add -e to the stem of the adjective to form the adverb, e.g. *benignus* (kind), genitive singular, *benigni*, adverb, *benignē* (kindly); *līber* (free), genitive singular, *līberi*, adverb, *līberē* (freely). Note these common exceptions to this rule, *subitus* (sudden), gives *subitō*; *falsus* (false), gives *falsō*; *necessārius* (necessary), gives *necessāriō*.

In adjectives of the second class, add -iter to the stem, e.g. *ferox*, (fierce,) genitive singular, *ferōc-is*, adverb, *ferōciter*. Note that adjectives like *prūdens* (prudent), simply add -er to the stem, *prūdenter*, (prudently).

Common Irregular Adverbs

bene, well
multum, much
magnoperē, greatly

diū, for a long time
saepe, often
tandem, at length

Comparison of Adverbs

The comparative of an adverb is simply the neuter singular of the comparative adjective. The superlative is obtained from the superlative of the adjective by changing the -us ending into -e, e.g.

	Positive	Comparative	Superlative
Adjective	*līber*, free	*līberior*	*līberrimus*
Adverb	*līberē*, freely	*līberius*	*līberrimē*
Adjective	*prūdens*, prudent	*prūdentior*	*prūdentissimus*
Adverb	*prūdenter*, prudently	*prūdentius*	*prūdentissimē*

A few adverbs are compared irregularly:

bene (*bonus*), well	*melius*, better	*optimē*, best
male (*malus*), badly	*pēius*, worse	*pessimē*, worst
multum (*multus*), much	*plūs*, more	*plūrimum*, most
magnoperē (*magnus*), greatly	*magis*, more	*maximē*, most
paulum (*parvus*), little	*minus*, less	*minimē*, least
diū, for a long time	*diūtius*, longer	*diūtissimē*, longest
saepe, often	*saepius*, oftener	*saepissimē*, oftenest

NUMERALS

	CARDINAL	ORDINAL
1	*Ūn-us, -a, -um*, one	*Prīm-us, -a, -um*, first
2	*Du-o, -ae, -o*, two	*Secund-us, -a, -um, (alter)*, second
3	*Trēs, tria*, three	*Terti-us, -a, -um*, third
4	*Quattuor*, four	*Quart-us, -a, -um*, fourth
5	*Quinque*	*Quint-us, -a, -um,*
6	*Sex*	*Sext-us, -a, -um*
7	*Septem*	*Septim-us, -a, -um*
8	*Octō*	*Octāv-us, -a, -um*
9	*Novem*	*Nōn-us, -a, -um*
10	*Decem*	*Decim-us, -a, -um*
11	*Undecim*	*Undecim-us, -a, -um*
12	*Duodecim*	*Duodecim-us, -a, -um*
13	*Trēdecim*	*Tertius decim-us, -a, -um*, etc.
14	*Quattuordecim*	*Quart-us decim-us*, etc.
15	*Quindecim*	*Quint-us decim-us*, etc.
16	*Sēdecim*	*Sext-us decim-us*, etc.

17	*Septendecim*	*Septim-us decim-us*, etc.
18	*Duodēvīgintī*	*Duodēvīcēsim-us*, etc.
19	*Undēvīgint*	*Undēvīcēsim-us*, etc.
20	*Vīgintī*	*Vīcēsim-us*, etc.
30	*Trīgintā*	*Trīcēsim-us*, etc.
40	*Quādrāgintā*	*Quādrāgēsim-us*, etc.
50	*Quinquāgintā*	*Quinquāgēsim-us*, etc.
60	*Sexāgintā*	*Sexāgēsim-us*, etc.
70	*Septuāgintā*	*Septuāgēsim-us*, etc.
80	*Octōgintā*	*Octōgēsim-us*, etc.
90	*Nōnāgintā*	*Nōnāgēsim-us*, etc.
100	*Centum*	*Centēsim-us*, etc.
200	*Ducent-ī, -ae, -a*	*Ducentēsim-us*, etc.
300	*Trecent-ī, -ae, -a*	*Trecentēsim-us*, etc.
400	*Quādringent-ī, -ae, -a*	*Quādringentēsim-us*, etc.
500	*Quingent-ī, -ae, -a*	*Quingentēsimus*
600	*Sescent-ī, -ae, -a*	*Sexcentēsim-us*, etc.
700	*Septingent-ī, -ae, -a*	*Septingentēsim-us*, etc.
800	*Octingent-ī, -ae, -a*	*Octingentēsim-us*, etc.
900	*Nongent-ī, -ae, -a*	*Nongentēsim-us*, etc.
1,000	*Mille* (indeclinable)	*Millēsim-us*, etc.
2,000	*Duo mīlia* (followed by genitive case)	*Bis millēsim-us*, etc.
100,000	*Centum mīlia*	*Centiēs millēsim-us*, etc.
1,000,000	*Deciēs centēna mīlia*	*Deciēs centiēs millēsim-us*, etc.

	DISTRIBUTIVE	NUMERAL ADVERBS
1	*Singul-ī, -ae, -a*, one each	*Semel*, once
2	*Bīn-ī, -ae, -a*, two each	*Bis*, twice
3	*Tern-ī (trīn-ī), -ae, -a*, three each	*Ter*, thrice
4	*Quatern-ī, -ae, -a*, four each	*Quater*, four times
5	*Quīn-ī, -ae, -a*	*Quinquiēs*
6	*Sēn-ī, -ae, -a*	*Sexiēs*
7	*Septēn-ī, -ae, -a*	*Septiēs*
8	*Octōn-ī, -ae, -a*	*Octiēs*
9	*Novēn-ī, -ae, -a*	*Noviēs*
10	*Dēn-ī, -ae, -a*	*Deciēs*
11	*Undēn-ī, -ae, -a*	*Undeciēs*
12	*Duodēn-ī, -ae, -a*	*Duodeciēs*
13	*Tern-ī dēn-ī, -ae, -a*	*Ter deciēs*
14	*Quatern-ī dēn-ī, -ae, -a*	*Quater deciēs*
15	*Quīn-ī dēn-ī, -ae, -a*	*Quinquiēs deciēs*
16	*Sēn-ī dēn-ī, -ae, -a*	*Sexiēs deciēs*
17	*Septēn-ī dēn-ī, -ae, -a*	*Septiēs deciēs*
18	*Duodēvīcēn-ī, -ae, -a*	*Duodēvīciēs*
19	*Undēvīcēn-ī, -ae, -a*	*Undēvīciēs*
20	*Vīcēn-ī, -ae, -a*	*Vīciēs*
30	*Trīcēn-ī, -ae, -a*	*Trīciēs*
40	*Quādrāgēn-ī, -ae, -a*	*Quādrāgiēs*
50	*Quinquāgēn-ī, -ae, -a*	*Quinquāgiēs*
60	*Sexāgēn-ī, -ae, -a*	*Sexāgiēs*
70	*Septuāgēn-ī, -ae, -a*	*Septuāgiēs*
80	*Octōgēn-ī, -ae, -a*	*Octōgiēs*
90	*Nōnāgēn-ī, -ae, -a*	*Nōnāgiēs*
100	*Centēn-ī, -ae, -a*	*Centiēs*
200	*Ducēn-ī, -ae, -a*	*Ducentiēs*
300	*Trecēn-ī, -ae, -a*	*Trecentiēs*
400	*Quādringēn-ī, -ae, -a*	*Quādringentiēs*

500	*Quingēn-ī, -ae, -a*	*Quingentiēs*
600	*Sescēn-ī, -ae, -a*	*Sexcentiēs*
700	*Septingēn-ī, -ae, -a*	*Septingentiēs*
800	*Octingēn-ī, -ae, -a*	*Octingentiēs*
900	*Nōngēn-ī, -ae, -a*	*Nongentiēs*
1,000	*Singula mīlia*	*Mīliēs*
2,000	*Bīna mīlia*	*Bis mīliēs*
100,000	*Centēna mīlia*	*Centiēs mīliēs*
1,000,000	*Deciēs centēna mīlia*	*Deciēs centiēs mīliēs*

Ūnus, duo, and *trēs* are declined as follows. The cardinals from *quattuor* to *centum* are indeclinable. *Ducentī, trecentī,* etc., are declined as the plural of *bonus.*

	Singular			Plural		
	Masc.	Fem.	Neut.	Masc.	Fem.	Neut.
Nom.	*ūnus*	*ūna*	*ūnum*	*ūnī*	*ūnae*	*ūna*
Acc.	*ūnum*	*ūnam*	*ūnum*	*ūnōs*	*ūnās*	*ūna*
Gen.	*ūnīus*	*ūnīus*	*ūnīus*	*ūnōrum*	*ūnārum*	*ūnōrum*
Dat.	*ūnī*	*ūnī*	*ūnī*	*ūnīs*	*ūnīs*	*ūnīs*
Abl.	*ūnō*	*ūnā*	*ūnō*	*ūnīs*	*ūnīs*	*ūnīs*

	Plural			Plural		
	Masc.	Fem.	Neut.	Masc.	Fem.	Neut.
Nom.	*duo*	*duae*	*duo*	*trēs*	*trēs*	*tria*
Acc.	*duōs, (duo)*	*duās*	*duo*	*trēs*	*trēs*	*tria*
Gen.	*duōrum*	*duārum*	*duōrum*	*trium*	*trium*	*trium*
Dat.	*duōbus*	*duābus*	*duōbus*	*tribus*	*tribus*	*tribus*
Abl.	*duōbus*	*duābus*	*duōbus*	*tribus*	*tribus*	*tribus*

ROMAN CALENDAR

There were twelve months in the Roman year. The Latin word for month is *mensis,* m., and the names of the months are given as adjectives, agreeing with *mensis* (understood).

Thus:

Jānuārius	January	*Jūlius* (or *Quintīlis*)	July
Februārius	February	*Augustus* (or *Sextīlis*)	August
Martius	March	*September*	September
Aprīlis	April	*Octōber*	October
Māius	May	*November*	November
Jūnius	June	*December*	December

There were three chief days in each month:

    1st = *Kalendae* (Calends)
    5th = *Nōnae* (Nones)
  13th = *Īdus* (Ides)

but "in March, July, October, May the Nones fall on the 7th day," and the Ides 8 days later, on the 15th.

Dating

(*a*) For one of the chief days, e.g. on the first of January, use the ablative case (point of time) with the name of the month in agreement, *Kalendīs Januariīs*; 13th November, *Idibus Novembribus.*

(b) For the day before one of the chief days, e.g. on the 4th of January; use the word *pridiē* (on the day before) with the chief day and the name of the month in the accusative case, *pridie Nonas Januarias*; 30th September, *pridie Kalendas Octobres*.

(c) For any other day, e.g. 3rd January, reckon backwards from the next chief day, in this case the *Nonae* (5th), but do so "inclusively", counting in the days at both ends. So, for days before the *Nonae*, or the *Idus*, subtract the day you require from the day on which the next chief day falls, and increase by one. For days before the *Kalendae* subtract the day you require from the number of days in the month, and increase by two. Then use the following formula: *ante diem* (ordinal number), *important day* (acc.), *name of month* (acc.).

Examples: 3rd January—*ante diem* tertium *Nonas Januarias*
26th September: *ante diem* sextum *Kalendas Octobres*.

MONEY, WEIGHTS, MEASURES

I. *Roman Money* (1)

Bronze or Copper Coinage
As—originally a bar of bronze, 1 lb in weight, later 2 ounces

Sēmis	one-half *as*
Triens	one-third *as*
Quădrans	one-quarter *as*
Sextans	one-sixth *as*
Uncia	one-twelfth *as*, *as* one ounce.

(2) Silver Coinage

Dēnārius	10 *asses*, later 16
Quīnārius	5 *asses*, later 8
Sestertius	2½ *asses*, later 4; this was the ordinary coin of the Romans, used in the reckoning of even the largest sums. Its symbol was HS.

Sestertium = 1,000 *Sestertii*.

(3) Gold Coinage

Denarius aureus (or simply "*aureus*") was the standard gold coin of the Romans, equivalent in value to 25 silver *denarii*, or 100 *sestertii*.

II. *Weights*

Libra. This was the unit of weight, the Roman pound.
Uncia. The *libra* (pound) was divided into 12 *unciae* (ounces).

III. *Measures*

Length: *Pes.* This was the unit of length, equivalent to our "foot".
        Uncia. This *pes* (foot) was divided into 12 *unciae* (inches).
        Passus. This was equivalent to 5 *pedes* (5 feet).
        Mille Passus (pl. *milia passuum*) was one Roman mile (1,620 yards).

Area: *iugerum*, equivalent to five-eighths of an acre.

Capacity: *coclear* = a "spoonful"
         cyathus = one-twelfth sextarius = 0·08 of a pint
         sextūrius = 0·96 of a pint
         modius = 16 sextarii = 15 pints
         amphora = 48 sextarii = 5 gallons 6 pints.

TIME, PLACE, SPACE

Time

(a) Point of time, or the time *at which* something happens, is expressed in Latin by the ablative case, e.g.

Auctumno folia sunt rubra.
In autumn the leaves are red.

(b) Duration of time, or the time *during which* something happens, is expressed in Latin by the accusative case, e.g.

Viginti annos Poeni cum Romanis bellabant.
During twenty years the Carthaginians waged war with the Romans.

(c) The time *within which* something happens (usually denoted by the word "in" or "within" in the English) is expressed in Latin by the ablative case, e.g.

Tribus mensibus redibit.
He will return *within three months*.

Place

(a) *Motion towards* a place is expressed in Latin by a preposition (*in, ad*) with the accusative case, except where names of towns or small islands, *domus* (house), and *rus* (countryside) are concerned. With these use the accusative case without a preposition, e.g.

Ad villam eo, I go to the country-house.
Romam eo, I go to Rome.

(b) *Motion from* a place is expressed in Latin by a preposition (*a, ab, e, ex*) with the ablative case, except where the names of towns or small islands, *domus* (house) and *rus* (countryside) are concerned. With these use the ablative case without a preposition, e.g.

Ab Africa navigavit, he sailed from Africa.
Rure venit, he comes from the country.

(c) *Place where, Rest in* a place is expressed in Latin by the preposition *in* with the ablative case, except where the names of towns or small islands, *domus* (house) and *rus* (countryside) are concerned. With these use the locative case, which in a singular noun of the First or Second Declension is like the genitive case, e.g. *Romae* (at Rome), *Londinii* (in London), and in all other nouns is like the ablative case, e.g. *Carthagine* (at Carthage), *Athenis* (in Athens).

N.B. at home, *domi*; in the countryside, *ruri*.

Space

Extent of space is expressed in Latin by the accusative case, e.g.

Tria milia passuum progressus est.
He advanced three miles.

Space which is the *amount of difference* between two points is expressed in Latin by the ablative case. (There is usually a comparative adjective in such a phrase.) e.g. This wall is three feet higher than that one. *Altior illo hic murus est tribus pedibus*.

TEACH YOURSELF BOOKS

FRENCH

J. Adams & N. Scarlyn Wilson

No previous knowledge of French is necessary for the reader wishing to learn the language through this book. It has been specially prepared with the beginner and his problems in mind.

Part I of this course consists of an introduction to pronunciation and a series of graded lessons thoroughly covering the groundwork of the French language. Included in each lesson are working exercises and the Key to these is in Part II along with detailed explanatory notes where every effort is made to build up the student's vocabulary as he progresses through the course. An extensive vocabulary and lists of irregular verbs are to be found at the end of the book.

As a result of studying this course, the student should emerge with a sound working knowledge of everyday French.

GERMAN

J. Adams

Intended essentially for the beginner, this complete
course in contemporary German has been specially
designed to enable the student to learn the language as
quickly and effectively as possible.

Both the German alphabet and pronunciation are
thoroughly covered in separate sections while a course
of thirty carefully graded lessons leads the student
through the various points of the grammar. At the same
time the vocabulary is gradually built up in conjunction
with the exercises to be found in each lesson.

Having thoroughly worked his way through this book,
the student should emerge with a sound practical knowledge of written and spoken German.

TEACH YOURSELF BOOKS

RUSSIAN

Michael Frewin

Russian is always thought to be a very difficult language but, in fact, it is not so much difficult as different. Only half the population of the Soviet Union speaks Russian as their mother tongue – the other hundred million learn it as a foreign language and accept this as natural.

This book aims to give a good working knowledge of the language. It consists of twenty lessons, each containing a reading passage, a section to explain new grammatical points, and exercises which practise the new material in many different ways. A key to the exercises is included and, as well as the grammar notes in each lesson, a summary of all the main forms is given in the appendix.

At the end of the book, a selection of reading passages is provided which are all derived from contemporary Soviet sources and are completely unabridged. They are thus a real guide to the progress the student is making and hence a particularly valuable feature of the book.

TEACH YOURSELF BOOKS

SPANISH

N. Scarlyn Wilson

As a language of world importance, Spanish rivals French and German. There are over 115 million speakers of the language in the world, both in South America and Spain, and obviously a knowledge of Spanish is useful — not only to the student but also to the tourist and the businessman.

Because of its phonetic simplicity and the basic regularity of its grammatical forms, Spanish is a relatively easy language to learn. This book takes the reader through a series of graded lessons which have been designed both for use in the classroom and for study at home. Each lesson comes complete with exercises and translation pieces and the aim is that the reader, on working his way through the course, should have a sound command of Spanish.

'Anyone who works through this volume intelligently should be able to read and speak Spanish. No student should fail to obtain this excellent course'
Journal of the Incorporated Association of Assistant Masters

TEACH YOURSELF BOOKS

LATIN

F. Kinchin Smith

Although Latin is one of the so-called 'dead languages', its literature is still very much alive. A knowledge of Latin opens up to the reader the works of such classical writers as Cicero and Virgil.

This book offers a complete course in Latin for beginners. The student is first taken through the basic grammar and vocabulary and then introduced to the more difficult aspects of Latin. Throughout the text are to be found Latin passages for translation as well as useful exercises. Each section is clearly laid out and the aim has been to provide a course which the beginner can work through on his own and which will enable him to translate English into Latin and read Latin with ease.

A practical working course in Latin, invaluable to the beginner and the student, for use both at home and in the classroom.

TEACH YOURSELF BOOKS

ITALIAN

Kathleen Speight

A working knowledge of Italian is not difficult to acquire, and the pronunciation of the language is relatively simple and consistent.

This book offers a complete course in modern conversational Italian for beginners studying at home. Pronunciation, grammar and syntax are fully explained in easy stages illustrated by examples, and a basic grounding in the everyday vocabulary is provided.

TEACH YOURSELF BOOKS

GERMAN GRAMMAR

P. G. Wilson

This grammar is not intended for the beginner but for the student who has already made some progress with German, from working through a course such as *Teach Yourself German*.

The reader will find here a thorough and exhaustive course in German grammar. The book is so arranged that the student can not only work his way through the course and emerge with a detailed knowledge of German grammar, but also use the contents of the book as a handy form of reference in his reading and German studies in general. This book will be particularly useful to those students wishing to revise their grammar, apart from those embarking on an advanced course in German.

'A praiseworthy attempt to clarify in a practical way what is to most a rather forbidding subject'
The Times Educational Supplement

TEACH YOURSELF BOOKS

SPANISH DICTIONARY

Margaret H. Raventós

This book offers an invaluable aid for students, tourists, businessmen and all who wish to become proficient in modern Spanish.

Full Spanish–English and English–Spanish sections, each with some 25,000 entries, provide clear definitions for a wide range of words and phrases in convenient form in addition there are special sections on proper names and abbreviations in each language, and on weights, measures and currency.

'One of the best, if not the best, class dictionaries available'

Higher Education Journal

TEACH YOURSELF BOOKS

FRENCH DICTIONARY

N. Scarlyn Wilson

This dictionary provides the user with a comprehensive vocabulary for working French. With over 35,000 words in both sections, special care has been taken to include current usage including some slang. A complete list of Irregular Verbs, a selection of French Idioms and Phrases, lists of Christian Names and Geographical Places are all included. For the student of French, an extensive and workmanlike dictionary which will prove to be invaluable.

FRENCH GRAMMAR

E. S. Jenkins

This grammar is not intended for the beginner but for the student who has already made some progress with French, from working through a course such as *Teach Yourself French*.

The reader will find here a grammar course which is both thorough and exhaustive. The book is so arranged that the student can not only work his way through the course and emerge with a detailed knowledge of French grammar, but also use the contents of this book as a handy form of reference in his reading and French studies. This book will be particularly useful for those students wishing to revise their grammar, as well as for those embarking on an advanced course in French.

'An excellent book for examination revision if only for the clarity of its layout and the multiplicity of well chosen French examples'

The Times Literary Supplement